O

Italia

Edited by
Colin McIntosh

OXFORD
UNIVERSITY PRESS

OXFORD

UNIVERSITY PRESS

Great Clarendon Street, Oxford OX2 6DP

Oxford University Press is a department of the University of Oxford.
It furthers the University's objective of excellence in research, scholarship,
and education by publishing worldwide in

Oxford New York

Auckland Bangkok Buenos Aires Cape Town Chennai
Dar es Salaam Delhi Hong Kong Istanbul Karachi Kolkata
Kuala Lumpur Madrid Melbourne Mexico City Mumbai Nairobi
São Paulo Shanghai Taipei Tokyo Toronto

Oxford is a registered trade mark of Oxford University Press
in the UK and in certain other countries

Published in the United States
by Oxford University Press Inc., New York

British Library Cataloguing in Publication Data

Data available

Library of Congress Cataloging in Publication Data

Data available

ISBN 0-19-860714-8

10 9 8 7 6 5 4 3 2

Typeset in Swift and Arial
by Latimer Trend & Company Ltd, Plymouth
Printed in Italy by
«La Tipografica Varese S.p.A.» Varese

Contents

Introduction   iv

How to use the dictionary   v

The structure of Italian–English entries   vii

The structure of English–Italian entries   viii

Glossary of grammatical terms   ix

Index of lexical and grammar notes   xii

Guide to Italian pronunciation   xiii

Italian–English dictionary   **1**

Numbers in Italian   122

English–Italian dictionary   **123**

Italian verbs   286

Contributors

Chief Editor
Colin McIntosh

Editors
Francesca Logi
Francesca Moy
Loredana Riu
Paola Tite

Proprietary terms

This dictionary includes some words which are, or are asserted to be, proprietary names or trade marks. Their inclusion does not imply that they have acquired for legal purposes a non-proprietary or general significance, nor is any other judgement implied concerning their legal status. In cases where the editor has some evidence that a word is used as a proprietary name or trade mark, this is indicated by the symbol ®, but no judgement concerning the legal status of such words is made or implied thereby.

Introduction

The Oxford Starter Italian Dictionary represents a major departure from traditional dictionaries on several fronts: it looks different; it provides essential information in a totally new way; the two sides of the dictionary have very distinct functions. In all, the *The Oxford Starter Italian Dictionary* approaches the needs of the English-speaking learner of Italian from a very different angle, making it a uniquely accessible and user-friendly introduction to the Italian language.

It looks different

The dictionary page is uncluttered, with a streamlined typeface providing a consistent structure for the information, both in English and in Italian. Subdivisions are clearly indicated, using bullet points and numbers. The move from one language to another is explicitly indicated with = signs. Points of basic grammar are reinforced using the **!** sign, informal Italian usage is marked with the **✱** symbol, and **✺** indicates words to be used with special care.

It provides information in a new way

Every effort has been made to approach the foreign language from the point of view of the beginner who may be unfamiliar with the conventions of the more traditional bilingual dictionary.

Parts of speech and grammatical terms are given in full, not in abbreviated form, with a glossary providing explanations of all the terms used. Basic grammatical issues and specific points of usage are dealt with in short notes at appropriate points in the text.

Sets of words which behave in a similar way are treated in a consistent manner, and the user is encouraged to cross-refer to different parts of the dictionary, for example to verb tables and usage notes dealing with such concepts as jobs, illnesses, and telling the time.

The language used in examples and sense indicators (or signposts to the correct translation) has been carefully screened to ensure maximum clarity. The word list contains all the material a beginner would need and reflects current American and British English and Italian in clear, lively examples.

The two sides have different functions

Each side of the dictionary is shaped by its specific function. The English–Italian side is longer, providing the user with maximum help in expressing the message in the foreign language in the form of detailed coverage of essential grammar, clear signposts to the correct translation for a particular context, and a wide selection of example material.

The English–Italian side is designed to capitalize on what English speakers already know about their language, hence the more streamlined presentation of English-language information. From irregular verb forms to common idiomatic usage, such as might be encountered in the media, the *The Oxford Starter Italian Dictionary* provides generous coverage of those aspects of Italian which are less easy to decipher for English speakers. Irregular verbs, adjectives, and plurals are all featured in the wordlist, referring the user to the base form where the translations are given.

How to use the dictionary

Every entry in the dictionary tells you whether that particular word is a noun, verb, adjective, or another part of speech. If you need to know what the parts of speech are, look them up in the glossary of grammatical terms on page ix.

If there is more than one part of speech within an entry, numbers are used to separate them. Within each part of speech, different senses are given bullet points (•):

bene
1 *adverb*
= well
stanno bene = they're well
bene! = good!
va bene! = OK!
tutto bene? = is everything OK?
2 *noun, masculine*
i beni = possessions

Italian ▶ 199|
1 *adjective*
= italiano/italiana
2 *noun*
• (*the people*)
the Italians = gli italiani
• (*the language*)
Italian = l'italiano

The English–Italian entries tend to be longer, in order to offer detailed guidance on how to write and speak correctly in Italian, so it is a good idea to scan the whole entry to find the sense which is closest to the one you need.

Each Italian verb entry is marked with a number pointing you to the table of Italian verbs at the back of the dictionary. The number refers to the model verb in the table where you can find the information you need about how to form the tenses.

perdonare *verb* 1
= to forgive

Cross-references are shown by an arrow ▶. These are especially useful for identifying verb forms, which you might not otherwise recognize:

so ▶ sapere

In examples, different words with which a phrase can be used are put in square brackets. This means that it is possible to substitute another word for the alternatives given in the dictionary.

little¹
1 *determiner*
= poco/poca
little [sugar | wine | time] = poco [zucchero | vino | tempo]

Notes giving additional information are designed to help you produce correct Italian in areas where it is all too easy to forget important points of grammar or usage:

uovo *noun, masculine* (*plural* **uova**)
un uovo = an egg
! *Note that* **uova** *is feminine.*

actually *adverb*
! *Note that* **actually** *is not translated by* **attualmente**.
did she actually say that? = ha veramente detto così?
actually, I'm rather tired = veramente sono piuttosto stanco

Boxed usage notes covering certain themes and sets of related words form a very useful feature of this dictionary. Topics covered include dates, the human body, illnesses, and the time of day. In relevant entries, a number refers you to the page with a note on the particular topic:

January *noun* ▶ **155**
  January = gennaio

The structure of Italian–English entries

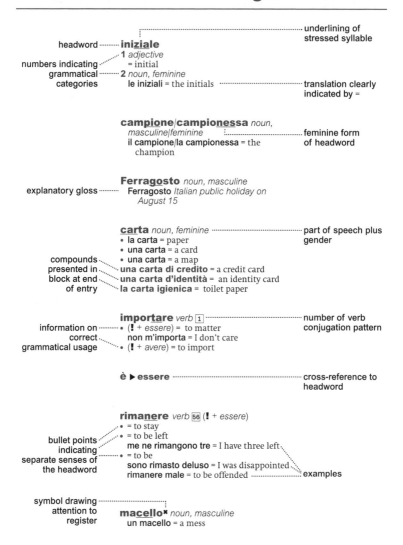

headword ········· **iniziale** — underlining of stressed syllable

numbers indicating grammatical categories
1 *adjective*
= initial
2 *noun, feminine*
le iniziali = the initials — translation clearly indicated by =

campione/**campionessa** *noun, masculine*/*feminine* — feminine form of headword
il campione/la campionessa = the champion

explanatory gloss ········· **Ferragosto** *noun, masculine*
Ferragosto *Italian public holiday on August 15*

carta *noun, feminine* — part of speech plus gender
• **la carta** = paper
• **una carta** = a card
compounds presented in block at end of entry
• **una carta** = a map
una carta di credito = a credit card
una carta d'identità = an identity card
la carta igienica = toilet paper

importare *verb* 1 — number of verb conjugation pattern
information on correct grammatical usage
• (**!** + *essere*) = to matter
non m'importa = I don't care
• (**!** + *avere*) = to import

è ▶ essere — cross-reference to headword

rimanere *verb* 56 (**!** + *essere*)
bullet points indicating separate senses of the headword
• = to stay
• = to be left
me ne rimangono tre = I have three left
• = to be
sono rimasto deluso = I was disappointed
rimanere male = to be offended ········· examples

symbol drawing attention to register
macello* *noun, masculine*
un macello = a mess

The structure of English–Italian entries

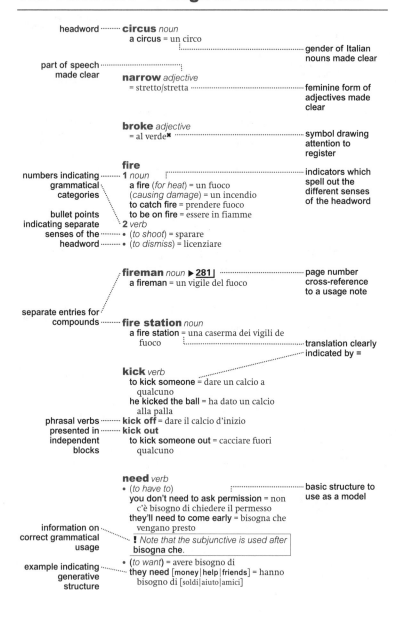

headword .... **circus** *noun*
a circus = un circo
.... gender of Italian nouns made clear

part of speech made clear ....

narrow *adjective*
= stretto/stretta .... feminine form of adjectives made clear

broke *adjective*
= al verde✶ .... symbol drawing attention to register

fire
numbers indicating grammatical categories ....
1 *noun*
a fire (*for heat*) = un fuoco
(*causing damage*) = un incendio
to catch fire = prendere fuoco
to be on fire = essere in fiamme
.... indicators which spell out the different senses of the headword
bullet points indicating separate senses of the headword ....
2 *verb*
• (*to shoot*) = sparare
• (*to dismiss*) = licenziare

fireman *noun* ▶ **281|** .... page number cross-reference to a usage note
a fireman = un vigile del fuoco

separate entries for compounds ....
fire station *noun*
a fire station = una caserma dei vigili de fuoco
.... translation clearly indicated by =

kick *verb*
to kick someone = dare un calcio a qualcuno
he kicked the ball = ha dato un calcio alla palla
phrasal verbs presented in independent blocks ....
kick off = dare il calcio d'inizio
kick out
to kick someone out = cacciare fuori qualcuno

need *verb*
• (*to have to*) .... basic structure to use as a model
you don't need to ask permission = non c'è bisogno di chiedere il permesso
they'll need to come early = bisogna che vengano presto
information on correct grammatical usage ....
! *Note that the subjunctive is used after* bisogna che.
example indicating generative structure ....
• (*to want*) = avere bisogno di
they need [money|help|friends] = hanno bisogno di [soldi|aiuto|amici]

Glossary of grammatical terms

This section explains the basic terms that are used in this dictionary to help you find the information that you need.

Adjective An adjective is used to add extra information to a noun:

> an **honest** politician, a **black** cat, a **heavy** book
> = un politico **onesto**, un gatto **nero**, un libro **pesante**

Note that in English the adjective usually comes before the noun, whereas in Italian it usually comes after.

Sometimes, of course, the adjective is separated from its noun:

> the flowers are **beautiful**
> = i fiori sono **bellissimi**

Adverb An adverb is used to add extra information to a verb, an adjective, or another adverb. In Italian adverbs often end in *-mente*:

> to walk **slowly**, **extremely** delicate, **fairly** often
> = camminare **lentamente**, **estremamente** delicato, **abbastanza** spesso

Agreement There are two types of agreement in Italian which you must be careful about.

The first is the agreement of nouns and adjectives. All nouns in Italian have a gender, and most can also be either singular or plural. Any adjective which describes a noun must 'agree' with it in both gender (masculine or feminine) and number (singular or plural). In other words, the adjective must always be masculine or feminine, singular or plural:

> un ragazz**o** italian**o**, una ragazz**a** italian**a**, ragazz**i** italian**i**, ragazz**e** italian**e**

The other kind of agreement is that between a verb and its subject. You must always ensure that the ending of the verb is the one which matches the subject, whether the subject is expressed or not:

> Renato e Claudio **stanno** bene
> = Renato and Claudio are well
> io e Stefano **abbiamo** litigato
> = Stefano and I had an argument

When *essere* is used as an auxiliary verb, the past participle should agree with the subject:

> Monica si è svegliat**a** presto
> = Monica woke up early

Auxiliary verbs An auxiliary verb is a verb which is combined with another verb to form a new tense. In Italian auxiliary verbs are used to form the perfect tense, along with the past participle. There are two auxiliary verbs in Italian, *avere* and *essere*, and each is used with a particular group of verbs.

The auxiliary verb *essere* is used first of all to form the compound tenses of all reflexive verbs:

> a che ora ti **sei** alzato?
> = what time did you get up?

It is also used to form the compound tenses of a group of verbs, marked (**!** + *essere*) in this dictionary:

> il pullman **è** partito
> = the bus has gone

The auxiliary verb *avere* is used to form the compound tenses of all other verbs:

> **ho** dormito bene
> = I slept well

There is a small group of verbs which can take either *essere* or *avere*, sometimes depending on the meaning, sometimes depending on personal preference. Help is given with these in the dictionary.

Comparative The comparative, as its name indicates, is the form of the adjective or adverb which enables us to compare two or more nouns or pronouns. In English this is usually done by putting *more* before the appropriate adjective or adverb:

> my book is **more** interesting than yours

In Italian the equivalent is *più*:

> il mio libro è **più** interessante del tuo

In English, a few adjectives have an irregular comparative form: *good* (comparative *better*), *bad* (comparative *worse*). Some shorter English adjectives have a special comparative ending in *–er* (for example *bigger, smaller, happier*). In Italian the adjectives which have an irregular comparative form are *buono* (comparative *migliore*) and *cattivo* (comparative *peggiore*), and the adverbs which have an irregular comparative form are *bene* (comparative *meglio*) and *male* (comparative *peggio*). Note that *più buono* rather than *migliore* is used when talking about food.

Conjunction A word used to join words or sentences together:

> David **and** Peter
> = David **e** Peter

> we didn't go to school **because** there was a strike
> = non siamo andati a scuola **perché** c'era uno sciopero

Determiner A determiner is used before a noun in order to identify more precisely what is being referred to. Here are some examples of determiners in English:

> *a car, the car, my car, this car, these cars*

In Italian:

> **un** panino, **il** conto, **le** scarpe

Exclamation An exclamation is a word or phrase expressing a strong feeling, such as annoyance or joy:

> *hi!= ciao!*

Feminine One of the two noun genders. In Italian feminine nouns usually end in -a or -e:

> una donna = *a woman*
> una stazione = *a station*

Occasionally feminine nouns have another ending:

> una radio = *a radio*

Future tense The future tense of a verb refers to something that happens in the future:

> verrò = *I'll come*

Gender You will see when using the Italian-English half of this dictionary that some Italian words are marked *noun, masculine* or *noun, feminine*. Unlike English nouns, every Italian noun has a gender: it is either masculine or feminine. For example the Italian words for 'office', 'tree' and 'roof' are masculine (**un** ufficio, **un** albero, **un** tetto), and the words for 'car', house and 'wing' are feminine (**una** macchina, **una** casa, **un'**ala). It is important to know the gender of an Italian noun because the ending of many words that go with it will depend on whether the noun is masculine or feminine. You may find it helpful to remember genders by learning new words in the form given in this dictionary, i.e. preceded by *un/una*, etc or *il/la*, etc:

> **una** vittima = *a victim*
> **la** sabbia = *sand*

Gerund The gerund is the form of a verb that ends in -ing and in Italian ends in -ando or -endo:

> *it's raining* = sta **piovendo**

Imperative The imperative is the form of the verb that expresses a command, for example *go away!* Italian has two forms, depending on whether the informal *tu* form or the more formal *lei* form is being used:

> stai zitto!
> = *shut up!*
> si accomodi!
> = *take a seat!*

There is also a form of the imperative which is used to influence the behaviour of the group one is part of. In English this is shown by using *let's* before the verb. In Italian the form is identical to the first person plural:

> andiamo a casa
> = *let's go home*

Imperfect tense The imperfect tense of a verb refers to a continuous or habitual action in the past:

> andavo = *I was going, I used to go*

Infinitive The infinitive is the basic form of a verb, and has no indication of person or tense. In English it is often preceded by *to*: *to walk, to run, to receive*. In Italian the infinitive ends in -are, -ere, -ire or -rre. In the dictionary, you will usually find information about a verb by looking up the infinitive form:

> cadere = *to fall*

When an infinitive is immediately followed by another infinitive in Italian, very often the final -e of the first infinitive is dropped. This also happens in some fixed phrases and common expressions:

> poter dormire
> = *to be able to sleep*
> aver fame
> = *to be hungry*

Masculine One of the two noun genders. In Italian masculine nouns usually end in -o or -e:

> un ragazz**o** = *a boy*
> un bicchier**e** = *a glass*

Occasionally masculine nouns have another ending:

> un problem**a** = *a problem*

Noun A noun is a word that names a person, place, or thing:

> *Fellini, granny, Rome, tree*
> = Fellini, nonna, Roma, albero

It can also name things like concepts, emotions, abstract qualities, or actions:

> *health, happiness, intelligence, departure*
> = salute, felicità, intelligenza, partenza

Object The direct object of a sentence is the word or group of words which is immediately affected by the action indicated by the verb. So, in the sentence

> *the dog chewed the bone*

dog is the subject, *chewed* is the verb, and *bone* is the object.

There may also be a second object in the sentence: an indirect object. In general terms the indirect object indicates the person or thing which benefits from the action of the verb upon the direct object. In the sentence

> *John gave the dog a bone*

bone is the direct object and *dog* is the indirect object.

Past historic tense The past historic is an Italian tense that refers to something that happened in the past. It is generally used to talk about events in the fairly distant past, and is more common in writing than speech, especially in the north of Italy:

pagò il conto = *she paid the bill*

Past participle The past participle is the form of a verb that is used to form the perfect tense in Italian:

ha mangiato tutto = *he's eaten everything*

Perfect tense The perfect tense is an Italian tense that refers to something that happened in the past. The perfect is generally used to talk about events in the fairly recent past, or that have had some kind of effect on the present:

ha finito = *he finished, he has finished*

Phrasal verb A phrasal verb is a verb combined with a preposition or an adverb which has a particular meaning. For example, *to run away*, meaning 'to flee', or *to see to something*, meaning 'to ensure that something is done'.

Phrasal verbs are much less common in Italian than English, which means that English phrasal verbs usually have to be translated by a single verb. You therefore need to use your dictionary carefully in order to select the correct translation. If you look up *to run away*, for example, you will see that phrasal verbs are listed after all the other meanings of the word *run*, and in alphabetical order of the following adverb or preposition.

Plural As in English, most nouns in Italian can be singular or plural. Plural nouns are used to refer to more than one example of that object. In Italian, nouns change their ending to show that they are plural. Nouns ending in -*o* or -*e* in the singular usually end in -*i* in the plural, and nouns ending in -*a* in the singular usually end in -*e* in the plural. There are many exceptions to this rule, however, and these are given in the Italian-English part of the dictionary. Unlike in English, adjectives also have plural forms, used whenever the nouns they are describing are plural:

fiori gialli = *yellow flowers*

Preposition A word that stands in front of a noun or pronoun, relating it to the rest of the sentence:

play with me = gioca con me

I did it for you = l'ho fatto per te

Present tense The present tense is the tense of a verb that refers to something that is happening now, or round about now:

leggo = *I read, I am reading*

Pronoun A pronoun is a word that is used instead of a noun to avoid repeating it unnecessarily:

I, you, he, she, it, we, they = io, tu, lui, lei, esso, noi, loro

these = questi, *those* = quelle

mine = il mio, *yours* = il tuo

Reflexive verb A reflexive verb is one whose object is the same as its subject. In English reflexive verbs are indicated by the use of reflexive pronouns such as *myself*, *yourself*, *herself*, etc. The Italian reflexive pronouns are *mi. ti, si, ci* and *vi*. These are sometimes joined on to the verb when it occurs in the infinitive, the imperative, or the gerund:

divertir**si** = *to enjoy **oneself***

guardati! = *look at **yourself**!*

si divertono = *they enjoy **themselves***

Singular Of nouns, etc, referring to just one:

una sedia = *a chair*

Subject The subject of a sentence is the noun or pronoun that generally causes the action of the verb:

l'**autista** ha frenato
= ***the driver*** braked

When the subject is already known or is obvious, it can often be omitted in Italian, and the verb ending does the work of showing what the subject is:

ho perso l'autobus
= ***I** missed the bus*

dicono sempre la stessa cosa
= ***they** always say the same thing*

Subjunctive The subjunctive is a special form of the verb that expresses doubt, unlikelihood or desire:

voglio che tu **venga** = *I want you to come*

Superlative The superlative is the form of the adjective or adverb which is used to express the highest degree. In English the adjective or adverb is usually preceded by *most*. Some English adjectives and adverbs have forms ending in -*est* (*slowest*, *biggest*) and some have irregular superlatives (*best*, *worst*).

In Italian the superlative is usually formed by putting *più* before the adjective or adverb. The definite article *il/la* is always used with superlative adjectives. In Italian the adjectives which have an irregular superlative form are *buono* (*il/la migliore*) and *cattivo* (*il/la peggiore*), and the adverbs which have an irregular superlative form are *bene* (*meglio*) and *male* (*peggio*).

Tense The tense is the particular form of the verb that tells us approximately when the action of the verb takes place. Common tenses in Italian are the present, the perfect, the future, and the imperfect.

Verb A verb is a word or phrase which indicates what is being done or what is happening:

i ragazzi **giocano** a carte = *the boys are playing cards*

la scala si **è rotta** = *the ladder broke*

scrivi il tuo indirizzo qua = **write** *your address here*

It can also tell us about a state of affairs:

era troppo tardi = *it* **was** *too late*

ha quindici anni = *she's fifteen*

il computer non **funziona** = *the computer isn't* **working**

Index of lexical and grammar notes

Lexical notes

Age	125
The human body	137
The clock	146
Colours	147
Countries, cities, and continents	151
Dates, days, and months	155
Forms of address	175
Games and sports	178
Illnesses, aches, and pains	193
Languages and nationalities	199
Length and weight measurements	202
Numbers	122
Quantities	233
Talking about time	267
Useful everyday expressions in Italian	167
Work and jobs	281

English grammar notes

be	133
do	159
get	179
go	180
have	186
little	204
the	263
to	268
you	284

Italian grammar notes

avere	12
dovere	38
essere	42
si	102
volere	120

A guide to Italian pronunciation

Because Italian spelling is very regular, it is usually easy to work out how a word is pronounced from the way it is written. The table below shows the sounds of Italian along with the letters that are used to represent them.

Double consonants in Italian can pose problems for English speakers. Double consonants are pronounced by prolonging the sound; generally speaking, where there is a single written consonant it should be pronounced as single and where there is a double it should be pronounced as double. Any consonant can be single or double, and differentiating between them is important because the meaning of a word can sometimes change according to whether a consonant is single or double. For example *cade* means "he falls" and *cadde* means "he fell"; *sono* means "I am" and *sonno* means "sleep".

One aspect of Italian pronunciation is not represented in the spelling. The stress in a word (the part of the word that is pronounced most forcefully) can fall on any syllable, in a way that is not predictable. If the stress falls on the last syllable of a word it is given a written accent (*città*, *perché*), but otherwise it is a question of learning where the stress falls in each word you learn (generally speaking, the most common pattern is for the penultimate syllable to be stressed: *pizza*, *spaghetti*). In this dictionary the stress is represented by underlining the stressed syllable: *telefono*, *trattoria*.

The table is designed to help English speakers bridge the gap between the sound systems of English and Italian, and to show the relationship betwen written letters and spoken sounds. In most cases the English equivalent is only an approximation to the Italian system, and so cannot take the place of a teacher or a recording.

phonetic symbol	sounds like English	written in Italian as	examples
a	cat, flat	a, à	mare, città
e	hay, tray but **shorter**	e, é	tre, pera, perché
ε	pet, threat	e, è	vento, caffè
i	treat, fleet	i, ì	vino, così
o	horse, course	o	ponte, caro
ɔ	hot, what	o, ò	nove, fuoco, però
u	hoot, flute	u, ù	tutto, tribù
p	as English	p	pasta, gruppo
b	as English	b	birra, babbo
m	as English	m	mela, programma
t	as English	t	tavola, gatto
d	as English	d	dare, freddo
n	as English	n	neve, panna
ɲ	new, onion	gn	bagno, gnocchi
k	as English	c, ch, q	costa, chilo, qua, mucca
g	as English	g, gh	paga, luoghi, leggo

ts	ca*ts*uit, we*ts*uit	z	stazione, pa**zz**o
dz	Le**d** **Z**epellin	z	**z**ero, me**zz**o
tʃ	**ch**in, pa**tch**	c, ci	pa**c**e, fre**cc**e, ba**ci**o, a**cci**uga
dʒ	**j**ab, **g**em	g, gi	**g**ira, **gi**à, o**gg**i, ma**gg**io
f	as English	f	**f**uoco, tele**f**ono, ba**ff**i
v	as English	v	**v**aligia, pio**vv**e
s	as English	s	**s**era, fi**ss**o
z	as English	s	ro**s**a
ʃ	ra**sh**, **sh**oe	sc, sci	pe**sc**e, **sci**occo
r	**r**ed, **r**at	r	**r**osso, bu**rr**o
l	as English	l	pi**l**a, pa**ll**a
ʎ	mi**lli**on	gl, gli	**gl**i, pa**gli**a
j	**y**es, **y**acht	i	pa**i**o, ch**i**uso, p**i**ove
w	**w**e, **w**ater	u	**u**omo, acq**u**a, v**u**ole, g**u**asto

a (sometimes **ad** *before a vowel*)
preposition

> **!** *Note that* a *combines with* il, la, *etc.*
> A + il = al; a + l' = all'; a + lo = allo;
> a + i = ai; a + gli = agli; a + la = alla;
> a + le = alle.

- = to
  vado a Ravenna = I'm going to Ravenna
  l'ho dato a Luca = I gave it to Luca
- = at
  alla stazione = at the station
  alle quattro = at four o'clock
- = in
  a Perugia = in Perugia
- (*indicating distance*)
  a cinquanta chilometri da Torino = 50 km
  from Turin
- (*with the infinitive*)
  comincia a piovere = it's starting to rain
- (*indicating price, rate*)
  dieci euro al chilo = ten euros a kilo
  duecento chilometri all'ora = two
  hundred kilometres an hour

abbaiare *verb* 6
= to bark

abbandonare *verb* 1
= to abandon

abbassare *verb* 1
- = to lower
- (*the radio, TV*) = to turn down

abbastanza *adverb*
- = enough
  abbastanza soldi = enough money
  non è abbastanza caldo = it's not warm
  enough
- = quite, rather
  abbastanza noioso = rather boring
- = quite a lot (of), rather a lot (of)
  abbastanza traffico = quite a lot of traffic

abbia, **abbiamo**, **etc** ▶ **avere**

abbigliamento *noun, masculine*
= clothing

abbonamento *noun, masculine*
- (*for a magazine*)
  un abbonamento = a subscription
- (*for public transport*)
  un abbonamento = a season ticket

abbonarsi *verb* 1 (**!** + *essere*)
- (*to a magazine*)
  = to subscribe
- (*for public transport*) = to take out a
  season ticket

abbondante *adjective*
= plentiful

abbracciare *verb* 2
= to hug

abbraccio *noun, masculine* (*plural*
abbracci)
- **un abbraccio** = a hug
- (*in a letter*)
  un abbraccio, Chiara = lots of love,
  Chiara

abbronzante *adjective*
la crema abbronzante = suntan lotion

abbronzato/abbronzata *adjective*
= tanned

abbronzatura *noun, feminine*
un'abbronzatura = a tan

abile *adjective*
= skil(l)ful

abilità *noun, feminine* (**!** *never changes*)
un'abilità = a skill

abitante *noun, masculine/feminine*
un abitante/un'abitante = an inhabitant

abitare *verb* 1
= to live

abito *noun, masculine*
un abito = a suit
un abito = a dress
gli abiti = clothes

abituale *adjective*
= ususal

abituarsi *verb* 1 (**!** + *essere*)
abituarsi a = to get used to

abituato/abituata *adjective*
abituato a = used to

abitudine *noun, feminine*
un'abitudine = a habit

abolire *verb* 9
= to abolish

aborto *noun, masculine*
un aborto = an abortion

abusare *verb* 1
abusare di = to abuse

abusivo/abusiva *adjective*
= illegal

abuso *noun, masculine*
un abuso = an abuse

accadde, **accaddero**, **etc** ▶
accadere

accademia *noun, feminine*
un'accademia = an academy

accademico/accademica *adjective*
(*plural* **accademici/accademiche**)
= academic

accadere verb 19 (! + essere)
= to happen

accanto
1 adverb
= nearby
qui accanto = near here
2 accanto a preposition
= next to

accappatoio noun, masculine (plural accappatoi)
un accappatoio = a bathrobe

accelerare verb 1
= to accelerate

acceleratore noun, masculine
l'acceleratore = the accelerator

accendere verb 53
• (when it's a fire) = to light
• (when it's a light, TV, etc) = to turn on

accendino noun, masculine
un accendino = a lighter

accennare verb 1
accennare a = to mention

accento noun, masculine
un accento = an accent

accese, **accesero**, etc ▶ accendere

acceso/accesa
1 ▶ accendere
2 adjective
= on

accessorio noun, masculine (plural accessori)
un accessorio = an accessory

accettabile adjective
= acceptable

accettare verb 1
= to accept

acciaio noun, masculine
l'acciaio = steel

accidenti* exclamation
accidenti! = damn!
= wow!

acciuga noun, feminine (plural acciughe)
un'acciuga = an anchovy

accogliente adjective
= cosy, cozy

accoglienza noun, feminine
un'accoglienza = a welcome

accogliere verb 22
= to welcome

accolgo, **accolse**, etc ▶ accogliere

accoltellare verb 1
= to stab

accolto/accolta ▶ accogliere

accomodare verb 1
1 = to fix
2 accomodarsi (! + essere)
accomodarsi = to sit down
si accomodi! = take a seat!

accompagnare verb 1
= to accompany

acconto noun, masculine
un acconto = a deposit

accordo noun, masculine
• un accordo = an agreement
• d'accordo! = OK!
essere d'accordo = to agree
sono d'accordo con te = I agree with you
mettersi d'accordo = to agree
andare d'accordo = to get on well

accorgersi verb 59 (! + essere)
• accorgersi di = to notice
• accorgersi che = to realize that

accorse, **accorto/accorta**, etc ▶ accorgersi

accumulare verb 1
= to accumulate

accurato/accurata adjective
= careful

accusa noun, feminine
un'accusa = an accusation

accusare verb 1
= to accuse

aceto noun, masculine
l'aceto = vinegar

acido/acida
1 adjective
= sour
2 acido noun, masculine
l'acido = acid

acqua noun, feminine
l'acqua = water
l'acqua minerale = mineral water

acquaio noun, masculine (plural acquai)
l'acquaio = the sink

acquario noun, masculine
• (plural acquari)
un acquario = an aquarium
• Acquario
Acquario = Aquarius

acquisire verb 9
= to acquire

acquistare verb 1
= to purchase

acquisto noun, masculine
un acquisto = a purchase
fare acquisti = to go shopping

acuto/acuta adjective
• = sharp
• = acute

---

* in informal situations

ad ▶ a

adattare verb [1]
1 = to adapt
2 **adattarsi** (! + *essere*)
  adattarsi a = to adapt to

adattatore noun, masculine
  un adattatore = an adaptor

adatto/adatta adjective
  = suitable
  adatto a = suitable for

addio exclamation
addio! = goodbye!

addirittura
1 adverb
  = even
  addirittura cinque milioni = as much as
    five million
2 exclamation
  addirittura! = really!

addizione noun, feminine
  l'addizione = addition
  un'addizione = a sum

addormentarsi verb [1] (! + *essere*)
  = to fall asleep

addosso adverb
  = on
  senza niente addosso = without
    anything on
  saltare addosso a qualcuno = to jump on
    someone

adeguato/adeguata adjective
  = suitable

aderente adjective
  = tight

aderire verb [9]
  aderire a = to stick to

adesivo noun, masculine
  un adesivo = a sticker

adesso adverb
  = now

adolescente noun, masculine/feminine
  un adolescente/un'adolescente = a
    teenager

adottare verb [1]
  = to adopt

adulto/adulta noun, masculine/feminine
  un adulto/un'adulta = an adult

aereo noun, masculine
  un aereo = a plane

aeroporto noun, masculine
  un aeroporto = an airport

affamato/affamata adjective
  = hungry

affare noun, masculine
• **gli affari** = business
  per affari = on business
• **un affare** = a deal
• **un affare** = a bargain

affascinante adjective
  = charming

affatto adverb
  = at all
  non mi piace affatto = I don't like it at all
  niente affatto! = not at all!

affermare verb [1]
  = to state

affermazione noun, feminine
  un'affermazione = a statement

afferrare verb [1]
• = to grab
  = to catch
• = to understand

affettare verb [1]
  = to slice

affettato noun, masculine
  gli affettati = cold meat

affetto noun, masculine
  l'affetto = affection

affettuoso/affettuosa adjective
  = affectionate

affezionato/affezionata adjective
  affezionato/affezionata a = fond of

affidabile adjective
  = trustworthy

affinché conjunction
  = so that

affittare verb [1]
• = to rent
• = to rent out

affitto noun, masculine
  l'affitto = the rent

affogare verb [5] (! + *essere* or *avere*)
  = to drown

affollato/affollata adjective
  = crowded

affondare verb [1] (! + *essere* or *avere*)
  = to sink

affrettarsi verb [1] (! + *essere*)
  = to hurry

affrontare verb [1]
  = to face

affumicato/affumicata adjective
  = smoked

afoso/afosa adjective
  = stiflingly hot

africano/africana adjective
  = African

agenda noun, feminine
  un'agenda = a diary

agente noun, masculine/feminine
  un agente/un'agente = an agent

agenzia noun, feminine
  un'agenzia = an agency
  un'agenzia di viaggi = a travel agency

agganciare verb 2
* = to hook
  = to hitch
* (on the telephone) = to hang up

aggiornamento noun, masculine
un aggiornamento = an update
un corso di aggiornamento = a refresher course

aggiornare verb 1
1 = to bring up to date
2 aggiornarsi (! + essere)
aggiornarsi = to keep up to date

aggiornato/aggiornata adjective
= up-to-date

aggiungere verb 48
= to add

aggiunse ▶ aggiungere

aggiunta noun, feminine
un'aggiunta = an addition

aggiunto/aggiunta ▶ aggiungere

aggiustare verb 1
= to fix

aggredire verb 9
= to attack

aggressione noun, feminine
un'aggressione = an attack

aggressivo/aggressiva adjective
= aggressive

agio noun, masculine
non mi sento a mio agio = I don't feel at ease

agire verb 9
= to act

agitare verb 1
1 = to wave
2 agitarsi (! + essere)
agitarsi = to get worked up

agli ▶ a

aglio noun, masculine
l'aglio = garlic

agnello noun, masculine
un agnello = a lamb
l'agnello = lamb

ago noun, masculine (plural aghi)
un ago = a needle

agosto noun, masculine
= August

agricoltura noun, feminine
l'agricoltura = agriculture

agro/agra adjective
= sour

ai ▶ a

aiutare verb 1
= to help

aiuto noun, masculine
l'aiuto = help

al ▶ a

ala noun, feminine (plural ali)
un'ala = a wing

alba noun, feminine
l'alba = dawn

albergo noun, masculine (plural alberghi)
un albergo = a hotel

albero noun, masculine
un albero = a tree

albicocca noun, feminine (plural albicocche)
un'albicocca = an apricot

alcol noun, masculine
l'alcol = alcohol

alcolico/alcolica adjective (plural alcolici/alcoliche)
= alcoholic

alcolizzato/alcolizzata adjective
= alcoholic

alcuni/alcune adjective
= some
= a few

alfabeto noun, masculine
l'alfabeto = the alphabet

alga noun, feminine (plural alghe)
le alghe = seaweed

ali ▶ ala

alimentari noun, masculine (! never changes)
un alimentari = a grocer's

alla ▶ a

allacciare verb 2
= to fasten

allagato/allagata adjective
= flooded

allargare verb 5
1 = to widen
2 allargarsi (! + essere)
allargarsi = to widen
= to stretch

allarme noun, masculine
un allarme = an alarm

alle ▶ a

alleanza noun, feminine
un'alleanza = an alliance

alleato/alleata
1 adjective
= allied
2 noun, masculine/feminine
un alleato/un'alleata = an ally

allegare verb 5
= to enclose

allegria noun, feminine
l'allegria = cheerfulness

A

allegro/**allegra** *adjective*
= cheerful

allenamento *noun, masculine*
l'allenamento = training

allenarsi *verb* [1] (**!** + *essere*)
= to train

allenatore/**allenatrice** *noun,
masculine/feminine*
un allenatore/un'allenatrice = a trainer

allergia *noun, feminine* (*plural* **allergie**)
un'allergia = an allergy

allergico/**allergica** *adjective* (*plural*
allergici/**allergiche**)
allergico/allergica a = allergic to

allevare *verb* [1]
• (*when it's children*) = to bring up
• (*when it's animals*) = to breed

allo ▶ a

alloggio *noun, masculine* (*plural* **alloggi**)
un alloggio = accommodation

allontanare *verb* [1]
1 = to move away
2 allontanarsi (**!** + *essere*)
allontanarsi = to move away

allora *adverb*
• = then
= at that time
• = well
= so

almeno *adverb*
= at least

Alpi *noun, feminine*
le Alpi = the Alps

alpinismo *noun, masculine*
l'alpinismo = mountaineering

alpino/**alpina** *adjective*
= Alpine

alt *exclamation*
alt! = stop!

alternativo/**alternativa** *adjective*
= alternative

altezza *noun, feminine*
l'altezza = the height

alto/**alta** *adjective*
• = high
• (*when it's a person*) = tall

altrettanto/**altrettanta**
1 *adjective*
= as much, as many
cento adulti e altrettanti bambini = a
hundred adults and the same number
of children
2 altrettanto *adverb*
= equally

altrimenti *adverb*
• = otherwise
• = differently

altro/**altra** *adjective*
= other
un altro/un'altra = another

altrui *adjective* (**!** *never changes*)
= other people's

alunno/**alunna** *noun,
masculine/feminine*
un alunno/un'alunna = a pupil

alzare *verb* [1]
1 = to raise
alzare il volume = to turn up the volume
2 alzarsi (**!** + *essere*)
alzarsi = to stand up
= to get up

amante *noun, masculine/feminine*
un amante/un'amante = a lover

amare *verb* [1]
= to love

amaro/**amara** *adjective*
= bitter

ambasciata *noun, feminine*
un'ambasciata = an embassy

ambientale *adjective*
= environmental

ambientare *verb* [1]
= to set
il film è ambientato a Firenze = the film
is set in Florence

ambiente *noun, masculine*
l'ambiente = the environment

ambiguo/**ambigua** *adjective*
= ambiguous

ambizione *noun, feminine*
l'ambizione = ambition

ambizioso/**ambiziosa** *adjective*
= ambitious

ambulanza *noun, feminine*
un'ambulanza = an ambulance

ambulatorio *noun, masculine* (*plural*
ambulatori)
un ambulatorio = a doctor's surgery, a
doctor's office

americano/**americana** *adjective*
= American

amichevole *adjective*
= friendly

amicizia *noun, feminine*
l'amicizia = friendship

amico/**amica** *noun, masculine/feminine*
(*plural* **amici**/**amiche**)
un amico/un'amica = a friend
un amico mio = a friend of mine

ammalato/**ammalata** *adjective*
= ill, sick

ammattire *verb* [9] (**!** + *essere*)
= to go crazy

ammazzare *verb* 1
• = to kill

ammesso/ammessa ▶ **ammettere**

ammettere *verb* 40
• = to admit
• = to allow (in)

amministrazione *noun, feminine*
l'amministrazione = the administration

ammirare *verb* 1
• = to admire

ammirazione *noun, feminine*
l'ammirazione = admiration

ammise ▶ **ammettere**

ammobiliato/ammobiliata
adjective
= furnished

amore *noun, masculine*
l'amore = love

ampio/ampia *adjective (plural*
**ampi/ampie)*
= wide

ampliare *verb* 6
• = to extend
• = to expand

anagrafe *noun, feminine*
l'anagrafe = the registry

analcolico/analcolica *adjective*
(*plural* **analcolici/analcoliche**)
= non-alcoholic

analisi *noun, feminine* (**!** *never changes*)
un'analisi = an analysis

analizzare *verb* 1
• = to analyse, to analyze

analogo/analoga *adjective (plural*
analogi/analoghe)
= similar

ananas *noun, masculine* (**!** *never changes*)
un ananas = a pineapple

anatomia *noun, feminine*
l'anatomia = anatomy

anatra *noun, feminine*
un'anatra = a duck

anche *conjunction*
• = also
= too
ci vado anch'io = I'm going too
• = even
anche se = even if
= although

ancora *adverb*
• = still
è ancora a letto = he's still in bed
• = yet
non è ancora arrivata = she hasn't arrived yet
• = even
ancora più difficile = even more difficult

• = again
ancora una volta = once again
• = more
ne vuoi ancora? = do you want some more?

ancora *noun, feminine*
l'ancora = the anchor

andare
1 *verb* 13 (**!** + *essere*)
• = to go
andare via = to go away
andare a sciare = to go skiing
• come va? = how are things?
va bene! = OK!
• non mi va di uscire = I don't want to go out
ti va bene? = is it OK for you?
• (*with the past participle*)
va fatto = it has to be done
2 **andarsene** *verb* 13 (**!** + *essere*)
andarsene = to go away
me ne vado = I'm off

andata *noun, feminine*
l'andata = the journey there
Siena, solo andata = a single to Siena, a one-way ticket to Siena
Bologna, andata e ritorno = a return to Bologna, a round-trip ticket to Bologna

andrà, andrò, etc ▶ **andare**

anello *noun, masculine*
un anello = a ring

angelo *noun, masculine*
un angelo = an angel

angolo *noun, masculine*
• un angolo = a corner
dietro l'angolo = (a)round the corner
• = an angle

angoscia *noun, feminine*
l'angoscia = anguish

anguria *noun, feminine*
un'anguria = a water melon

anima *noun, feminine*
l'anima = the soul

animale *noun, masculine*
un animale = an animal

animato/animata *adjective*
= lively

annaffiare *verb* 6
= to water

annata *noun, feminine*
un'annata = a vintage

annegare *verb* 5 (**!** + *essere* or *avere*)
= to drown

anniversario *noun, masculine* (*plural*
anniversari)
un anniversario = an anniversary

anno *noun, masculine*
un anno = a year
tutti gli anni = every year

····▶

quanti anni hai? = how old are you?
ho vent'anni = I'm twenty
gli anni 60 = the 60s
buon anno! = happy New Year!

annoiarsi *verb* ⑥ (**!** + *essere*)
= to get bored

annoiato/annoiata *adjective*
= bored

annuale *adjective*
= annual

annullare *verb* ①
= to cancel

annunciare *verb* ②
= to announce

annuncio *noun, masculine* (*plural* **annunci**)
• un annuncio = an advertisement
• = an announcement

annuo/annua *adjective*
= annual

ansia *noun, feminine*
l'ansia = anxiety
stare in ansia = to be worried

ansioso/ansiosa *adjective*
= anxious

Antartico *noun, masculine*
l'Antartico = the Antarctic Ocean

antenato/antenata *noun, masculine/feminine*
un antenato/un'antenata = an ancestor

antenna *noun, feminine*
un'antenna = an aerial

anteriore *adjective*
= front

antibiotico *noun, masculine* (*plural* **antibiotici**)
un antibiotico = an antibiotic

antichità *noun, feminine* (**!** *never changes*)
l'antichità = ancient times

anticipare *verb* ①
• = to bring forward
• = to advance

anticipo *noun, masculine*
• un anticipo = an advance
• in anticipo = in advance

antico/antica *adjective* (*plural* **antichi/antiche**)
• = ancient
• = antique

antiorario/antioraria *adjective* (*plural* **antiorari/antiorarie**)
in senso antiorario = anti-clockwise

antipasto *noun, masculine*
un antipasto = a starter, an appetizer

antipatico/antipatica *adjective* (*plural* **antipatici/antipatiche**)

= unpleasant
Elena mi è antipatica = I don't like Elena

antiquariato *noun, masculine*
l'antiquariato = antiques
un negozio di antiquariato = an antique shop

anzi *conjunction*
• ci vado lunedì, anzi martedì = I'm going on Monday, no, Tuesday
• = on the contrary

anziano/anziana *adjective*
= elderly

anziché *conjunction*
= rather than

anzitutto *adverb*
= first of all

ape *noun, feminine*
un'ape = a bee

aperitivo *noun, masculine*
un aperitivo = an aperitif

aperto/aperta
1 ▶ aprire
2 *adjective*
• = open
• (*when it's the gas, a tap, etc*) = on

apertura *noun, feminine*
l'apertura = the opening

apostrofo *noun, masculine*
un apostrofo = an apostrophe

appaio, appaiono, etc▶ apparire

apparecchiare *verb* ⑥
= to set the table

apparecchio *noun, masculine* (*plural* **apparecchi**)
un apparecchio = a machine

apparentemente *adverb*
= apparently

apparire *verb* ⑭ (**!** + *essere*)
= to appear

apparso/apparsa ▶ apparire

appartamento *noun, masculine*
un appartamento = a flat, an apartment

appartenere *verb* ⑦③
appartenere a = to belong to

appartengo, appartiene, apparterrà, etc ▶ appartenere

apparve, apparvi, etc ▶ apparire

appassionante *adjective*
= exciting

appassionato/appassionata *adjective*
• = passionate
• appassionato/appassionata di = keen on

appello *noun, masculine*
• un appello = an appeal
• fare l'appello = to call the register

appena
1 *adverb*
• = just
  sono appena arrivati = they've just arrived
• = scarcely
  ti sento appena = I can scarcely hear you
2 *conjunction*
  = as soon as
  appena finito = as soon as I've finished
  appena possibile = as soon as possible

appendere *verb* 53
  = to hang up

appendice *noun, feminine*
  un'appendice = an appendix
  l'appendice = the appendix

appendicite *noun, feminine*
  l'appendicite = appendicitis

appeso/appesa, appese, etc ▶
  appendere

appetito *noun, masculine*
  l'appetito = the appetite

appiccicare *verb* 4
  = to stick

appiccicoso/appiccicosa *adjective*
  = sticky

applaudire *verb* 9
  = to clap

applauso *noun, masculine*
  l'applauso = clapping

applicare *verb* 4
  = to apply

appoggiare *verb* 3
1 = to lean
  = to put down
2 **appoggiarsi** (! + *essere*)
  appoggiarsi a = to lean on

appoggio *noun, masculine* (*plural* **appoggi**)
  l'appoggio = support

apposta *adverb*
  = on purpose

apprendere *verb* 53
  = to learn

apprensivo/apprensiva *adjective*
  = apprehensive

appreso/appresa, apprese, etc ▶
  apprendere

apprezzare *verb* 1
  = to appreciate

approfittare *verb* 1
  approfittare di = to take advantage of

approfondire *verb* 9
  = to examine more closely
  = to go into detail

approfondito/approfondita
  adjective
  = close

approssimativo/approssimativa
  adjective
  = approximate

approvare *verb* 1
  = to approve (of)

approvazione *noun, feminine*
  l'approvazione = approval

appuntamento *noun, masculine*
  un appuntamento = an appointment

appunto
1 *noun, masculine*
  gli appunti = notes
2 *adverb*
  = exactly
  appunto! = exactly!

aprile *noun, masculine*
  = April

aprire *verb* 15
1 (! + *avere*)
• = to open
• (*when it's the gas, a tap, etc*) = to turn on
2 **aprirsi** (! + *essere*)
  aprirsi = to open

apriscatole *noun, masculine* (! *never changes*)
  un apriscatole = a tin opener, a can opener

aquila *noun, feminine*
  un'aquila = an eagle

arabo/araba *adjective*
  = Arabic

aragosta *noun, feminine*
  un'aragosta = a lobster

arancia *noun, feminine* (*plural* **arance**)
  un'arancia = an orange

aranciata *noun, feminine*
  l'aranciata = orangeade

arancione *adjective*
  = orange

arbitro *noun, masculine*
  l'arbitro = the referee

architetto *noun, masculine*
  un architetto = an architect

architettura *noun, feminine*
  l'architettura = architecture

arco *noun, masculine* (*plural* **archi**)
• **un arco** = an arch
• **un arco** = a bow

arcobaleno *noun, masculine*
  un arcobaleno = a rainbow

area *noun, feminine*
  l'area = the area

argento *noun, masculine*
  l'argento = silver

argomento *noun, masculine*
  = a topic
  cambiare argomento = to change the subject

aria *noun, feminine*
l'aria = air
all'aria aperta = in the open air

Ariete *noun, masculine*
= Aries

arma *noun, feminine (plural **armi**)*
• un'arma = a weapon
• le armi = arms

armadio *noun, masculine (plural armadi)*
• un armadio = a cupboard
• un armadio = a wardrobe, a closet

armato/armata *adjective*
= armed

armi ▶ **arma**

armonia *noun, feminine*
l'armonia = harmony

arrabbiarsi *verb* ⑥ (! + *essere*)
= to get angry

arrabbiato/arrabbiata *adjective*
= angry

arrampicarsi *verb* ④ (! + *essere*)
= to climb

arrestare *verb* ①
= to arrest

arrivare *verb* ① (! + *essere*)
= to arrive

arrivederci, arrivederla *exclamation*
arrivederci! = goodbye!

arrivo *noun, masculine*
l'arrivo = the arrival

arrogante *adjective*
= arrogant

arrossire *verb* ⑨ (! + *essere*)
= to blush

arrostire *verb* ⑨
= to roast

arrosto
1 *adjective* (! *never changes*)
= roast
agnello arrosto = roast lamb
2 *noun, masculine*
un arrosto = a roast

arrugginito/arrugginita *adjective*
= rusty

arte *noun, feminine*
l'arte = art

Artico *noun, masculine*
l'Artico = the Arctic Ocean

articolo *noun, masculine*
un articolo = an article

Artide *noun, feminine*
l'Artide = the Arctic

artificiale *adjective*
= artificial

artigiano/artigiana *noun, masculine/feminine*
un artigiano/un'artigiana = a craftsman/a craftswoman

artista *noun, masculine/feminine (plural artisti/artiste)*
un artista/un'artista = an artist

artistico/artistica *adjective (plural artistici/artistiche)*
= artistic

arto *noun, masculine*
un arto = a limb

ascensore *noun, masculine*
un ascensore = a lift, an elevator

asciugamano *noun, masculine*
un asciugamano = a towel

asciugare *verb* ⑤
= to dry

asciutto/asciutta *adjective*
= dry

ascoltare *verb* ①
= to listen to
ascoltami! = listen to me!

asiatico/asiatica *adjective (plural asiatici/asiatiche)*
= Asian

asilo *noun, masculine*
• l'asilo = nursery school, kindergarten
• l'asilo politico = political asylum

asino *noun, masculine*
un asino = a donkey

asma *noun, feminine*
l'asma = asthma

asparago *noun, masculine (plural asparagi)*
gli asparagi = asparagus

aspettare *verb* ①
1 = to wait for
aspettami! = wait for me!
2 aspettarsi (! + *essere*)
aspettarsi che = to expect that

aspetto *noun, masculine*
l'aspetto = the appearance

aspirapolvere *noun, masculine* (! *never changes*)
un aspirapolvere = a vacuum cleaner
passare l'aspirapolvere = to vacuum

aspirina *noun, feminine*
un'aspirina = an aspirin

aspro/aspra *adjective*
= sour

assaggiare *verb* ③
= to taste

assassinare *verb* ①
= to murder

assassino/assassina noun,
masculine/feminine
un assassino/un'assassina = a murderer

assegno noun, masculine
un assegno = a cheque, a check

assemblea noun, feminine
un'assemblea = an assembly

assente adjective
= absent

assenza noun, feminine
un'assenza = an absence

assessore noun, masculine
un assessore = a council(l)or

assicurare verb [1]
• = to insure
• = to assure

assicurazione noun, feminine
l'assicurazione = the insurance

assistente noun, masculine/feminine
un assistente/un'assistente = an assistant

assistenza noun, feminine
= assistance

assistere verb [16]
assistere a = to be present at

asso noun, masculine
un asso = an ace

associazione noun, feminine
un'associazione = an association

assolutamente adverb
• = absolutely
• assolutamente no = certainly not

assoluto/assoluta adjective
= absolute

assomigliare verb [6] (! + essere or
avere)
assomigliare a = to look like

assorbente
1 adjective
= absorbent
2 noun, masculine
un assorbente = a sanitary towel

assumere verb [17]
• = to hire
• = to assume

assunse, assunto/assunta, etc ▶
assumere

assurdo/assurda adjective
= absurd

asta noun, feminine
• un'asta = an pole
• un'asta = an auction

astratto/astratta adjective
= abstract

astrologia noun, feminine
l'astrologia = astrology

astronomia noun, feminine
l'astronomia = astronomy

astuccio noun, masculine (plural
astucci)
un astuccio = a case
= a pencil case

atlante noun, masculine
un atlante = an atlas

Atlantico noun, masculine
l'Atlantico = the Atlantic

atleta noun, masculine/feminine (plural
atleti/atlete)
un atleta/un'atleta = an athlete

atletica noun, feminine
l'atletica = athletics

atmosfera noun, feminine
l'atmosfera = the atmosphere

attaccare verb [4]
1 (! + avere)
• = to attack
• = to attach
= to stick
• = to hang up
2 attaccarsi (! + essere) = to stick

attacco noun, masculine (plural
attacchi)
un attacco = an attack

atteggiamento noun, masculine
un atteggiamento = an attitude

attendere verb [53]
= to await

attentato noun, masculine
un attentato = an attack
un attentato contro qualcuno = an
attempt on someone's life

attento/attenta adjective
= careful
stai attento! = be careful!

attenzione noun, feminine
= attention
fai attenzione! = pay attention!

atterraggio noun, masculine (plural
atterraggi)
un atterraggio = a landing

atterrare verb [1] (! + essere or avere)
= to land

attesa noun, feminine
un'attesa = a wait

attese, atteso/attesa, etc ▶
attendere

attimo noun, masculine
un attimo = a moment
un attimo! = just a moment!

attirare verb [1]
= to attract

attività noun, feminine (! never changes)
un'attività = an activity

attivo/**attiva** *adjective*
= active

atto *noun, masculine*
un atto = an act

attore/**attrice** *noun, masculine*/*feminine*
un attore/un'attrice = an actor/an actress

attorno ▶ **intorno**

attraente *adjective*
= attractive

attraversare *verb* [1]
= to cross

attraverso *preposition*
• = across
• = through

attrazione *noun, feminine*
un'attrazione = an attraction

attrezzatura *noun, feminine*
l'attrezzatura = the equipment

attrezzo *noun, masculine*
un attrezzo = a tool

attribuire *verb* [9]
= to attribute

attrice ▶ **attore**

attuale *adjective*
• = current
• = topical

attualità *noun, feminine* (**!** *never changes*)
l'attualità = current affairs
essere di attualità = to be topical

attualmente *adverb*
= at present

augurare *verb* [1]
= to wish

auguri *noun, masculine plural*
gli auguri = best wishes
tanti auguri! = all the best!

aula *noun, feminine*
un'aula = a classroom

aumentare *verb* [1] (**!** + *essere* or *avere*)
= to increase

aumento *noun, masculine*
un aumento = an increase

austriaco/**austriaca** *adjective* (*plural* austriaci/austriache)
= Austrian

autentico/**autentica** *adjective* (*plural* autentici/autentiche)
= authentic

autista *noun, masculine*/*feminine* (*plural* autisti/autiste)
un autista/un'autista = a driver

auto (**!** *never changes*), **automobile** *noun, feminine*
un'auto = a car

autobus *noun, masculine* (**!** *never changes*)
un autobus = a bus

autogrill *noun, masculine* (**!** *never changes*)
un autogrill = a motorway café, a freeway diner

automatico/**automatica** *adjective* (*plural* automatici/automatiche)
= automatic

automobile ▶ **auto**

autonoleggio *noun, masculine* (*plural* autonoleggi)
= car hire, car rental

autore/**autrice** *noun, masculine*/*feminine*
un autore/un'autrice = an author

autorevole *adjective*
= authoritative

autorità *noun, feminine* (**!** *never changes*)
un'autorità = an authority

autorizzare *verb* [1]
= to authorize

autostop *noun, masculine*
fare l'autostop = to hitch-hike

autostrada *noun, feminine*
un'autostrada = a motorway, a freeway

autrice ▶ **autore**

autunno *noun, masculine*
l'autunno = the autumn, the fall

avanti
1 *adverb*
• = forward
andare avanti = to go ahead
• (*when it's a clock*) = to be fast
2 *exclamation*
avanti! = come in!

avanzare *verb* [1] (**!** + *essere* or *avere*)
• = to advance
• = to be left over

avanzato/**avanzata** *adjective*
• = advanced
• = leftover

avanzi *noun, masculine plural*
gli avanzi = the leftovers

avaro/**avara** *adjective*
= miserly

avere *verb* [12] ▶ **12** *See the boxed note.*
ho vent'anni = I'm twenty
quanti ne abbiamo oggi? = what's the date today?
che cos'hai? = what's wrong with you?

avere

1 avere functions as an ordinary verb:

= to have

abbiamo un cane   = *we have a dog*

= to get

ho avuto il messaggio   = *I got your message*

2 avere is used as an auxiliary verb to form other tenses. The perfect tense uses the present tense of **avere** + the past participle. It is used to talk about events in the fairly recent past or that have had an effect on the present:

l'ho ricevuto ieri   = *I received it yesterday*
ho già visto questo film   = *I've already seen this film*

The pluperfect tense uses the imperfect tense of **avere** + the past participle. It is used to talk about events that happened before the event that is the main focus of attention:

l'avevo conosciuta prima = *I had met her before*

3 avere is used to talk about ages:

quanti anni hai?   = *how old are you?*
ho ventidue anni   = *I'm twenty-two*

4 avere is used to form many expressions such as **aver fame**. To find translations for these, look up the entry for the noun in the expression.

---

avesti, avrò, etc ▶ avere

avvelenare *verb* 1
   = to poison

avvenimento *noun, masculine*
   un avvenimento = an event

avvenga, avvengono, etc ▶
avvenire

avvenire *verb* 78 (**!** + *essere*)
   = to happen

avvenne, avvennero, etc ▶
avvenire

avventura *noun, feminine*
   un'avventura = an adventure

avversario/avversaria *noun,*
masculine/feminine (*plural*
avversari/avversarie)
   un avversario/un'avversaria = an
   opponent

avvertimento *noun, masculine*
   un avvertimento = a warning

avvertire *verb* 10
   = to notify
   = to warn

avviare *verb* 7
1 (**!** + *avere*)
   = to start (up)
2 avviarsi (**!** + *essere*)
   avviarsi = to set off

avvicinare *verb* 1
1 = to bring closer
2 avvicinarsi (**!** + *essere*)
   avvicinarsi = to come closer
   avvicinarsi a = to approach

avviene ▶ avvenire

avvisare *verb* 1
   = to notify

avviso *noun, masculine*
   un avviso = a notice

avvocato *noun, masculine*
   un avvocato = a lawyer

azienda *noun, feminine*
   un'azienda = a firm

azione *noun, feminine*
   • un'azione = an action
   • un'azione = a share

azzeccato/azzeccata *adjective*
   = exactly right

azzurro/azzurra *adjective*
   = blue

Bb

---

babbo *noun, masculine*
   • il babbo = the dad
   • Babbo Natale = Father Christmas, Santa
   Claus

baccalà *noun, masculine* (**!** *never*
changes)
   il baccalà = salt cod

baccano *noun, masculine*
   fare baccano = to make a racket

bacchetta *noun, feminine*
• una bacchetta = a stick
  = a baton
• una bacchetta magica = a magic wand

baciare *verb* 2
1 = to kiss
2 baciarsi (**!** + *essere*)
  baciarsi = to kiss (each other)

bacio *noun, masculine* (*plural* **baci**)
  un bacio = a kiss

badare *verb* 1
• badare a = to look after
• badare a = to pay attention to

baffi *noun, masculine plural*
  i baffi = a m(o)ustache

bagaglio *noun, masculine*
  il bagaglio = the luggage
  i bagagli = the luggage
  fare i bagagli = to pack

bagnare *verb* 1
1 = to wet
2 bagnarsi (**!** + *essere*)
  bagnarsi = to get wet

bagnato/bagnata *adjective*
  = wet

bagnino/bagnina *noun,*
  masculine/feminine
  un bagnino/una bagnina = a lifeguard

bagno *noun, masculine*
• (*a room*)
  il bagno = the bathroom
• fare il bagno
  (*in a bathtub*) = to have a bath
  (*in the sea*) = to have a swim

bagnoschiuma *noun, masculine*
  (**!** *never changes*)
  il bagnoschiuma = bubble bath

baia *noun, feminine*
  una baia = a bay

balcone *noun, masculine*
  un balcone = a balcony

balena *noun, feminine*
  una balena = a whale

ballare *verb* 1
  = to dance

ballerino/ballerina *noun,*
  masculine/feminine
  un ballerino/una ballerina = a dancer

balletto *noun, masculine*
  il balletto = ballet

ballo *noun, masculine*
  un ballo = a dance
  il ballo = dancing

balzo *noun, masculine*
  un balzo = a jump

bambino/bambina *noun,*
  masculine/feminine

un bambino/una bambina = a boy/a girl
  = a child

bambola *noun, feminine*
  una bambola = a doll

banale *adjective*
  = banal
  = trivial

banca *noun, feminine* (*plural* **banche**)
  una banca = a bank
  andare in banca = to go to the bank

bancarella *noun, feminine*
  una bancarella = a stall

bancario/bancaria (*plural*
  bancari/bancarie)
1 *adjective*
  = bank
2 *noun, masculine/feminine*
  un bancario/una bancaria = a bank clerk

bancarotta *noun, feminine*
  la bancarotta = bankruptcy

banchiere *noun, masculine*
  un banchiere = a banker

banco *noun, masculine* (*plural* **banchi**)
• (*at school*)
  un banco = a desk
• (*in a shop*)
  il banco = the counter

Bancomat® *noun, masculine* (**!** *never
  changes*)
  un Bancomat = a cash machine

banconota *noun, feminine*
  una banconota = a (bank)note, a bill

banda *noun, feminine*
  una banda = a band

bandiera *noun, feminine*
  una bandiera = a flag

barattolo *noun, masculine*
  un barattolo = a jar
  = a tin, a can

barba *noun, feminine*
• la barba = a beard
• farsi la barba = to shave

barbiere *noun, masculine*
  un barbiere = a barber

barbone/barbona *noun,*
  masculine/feminine
  un barbone/una barbona = a tramp, a
  bum

barca *noun, feminine* (*plural* **barche**)
• una barca = a boat
  una barca a vela = a yacht
• una barca di = loads of

barista *noun, masculine/feminine* (*plural*
  baristi/bariste)
  un/una barista = a bartender

barriera *noun, feminine*
  una barriera = a barrier

B

barzelletta *noun, feminine*
una barzelletta = a joke

basato/basata *adjective*
basato su = based on

base *noun, feminine*
una base = a base

basilico *noun, masculine*
il basilico = basil

basso/bassa *adjective*
• = low
• (when it's a person) = short

bastardo/bastarda✱ *noun, masculine/feminine*
un bastardo/una bastarda✱ = a bastard

bastare *verb* [1] (**!** + *essere*)
• = to be enough
  basta così! = that's enough!
  basta conoscere qualcuno = you just
    have to know someone
• basta che = as long as

bastone *noun, masculine*
un bastone = a stick

battaglia *noun, feminine* (*plural* **battaglie**)
una battaglia = a battle

battere *verb* [8]
• = to beat
• = to hit

batteria *noun, feminine*
• una batteria = a battery
• la batteria = the drums

battesimo *noun, masculine*
un battesimo = a christening

baule *noun, masculine*
• un baule = a trunk
• (of a car)
  il baule = the boot, the trunk

bebè *noun, masculine* (**!** *never changes*)
un bebè = a baby

beccare *verb* [4]
• = to peck
• = to get
  = to catch

becco *noun, masculine* (*plural* **becchi**)
il becco = the beak

Befana *noun, feminine*
• Befana = Epiphany (January 6)
• la Befana *an old woman who is supposed
  to bring presents to children on
  January 6*

begli, bei, bel ▶ **bello**

belga *adjective* (*plural* **belgi/belghe**)
= Belgian

Belgio *noun, masculine*
il Belgio = Belgium

bellezza *noun, feminine*
la bellezza = beauty

bello/bella *adjective*

> **!** *Before masculine nouns beginning
> with z, ps, gn, or s + another
> consonant,* **bello** *is used in the singular
> and* **begli** *in the plural. Before
> masculine nouns beginning with other
> consonants,* **bel** *is used in the singular
> and* **bei** *in the plural. Before all nouns
> beginning with a vowel,* **bell'** *is used in
> the singular and* **begli** *(masculine) or
> **belle** *(feminine) in the plural.*

• = beautiful
  = good-looking
• = nice
  un bel film = a good film
  bello caldo = nice and warm

benché *conjunction*
= although

bene
1 *adverb*
  = well
  stanno bene = they're well
  bene! = good!
  va bene! = OK!
  tutto bene? = is everything OK?
2 *noun, masculine*
  i beni = possessions

bensì *conjunction*
= but

bentornato/bentornata *adjective*
bentornato! = welcome back!

benvenuto/benvenuta *adjective*
benvenuto! = welcome!

benzina *noun, feminine*
la benzina = petrol, gas(oline)

bere *verb* [18]
= to drink

berrà, berrò, etc ▶ **bere**

bersaglio *noun, masculine* (*plural* **bersagli**)
un bersaglio = a target

bestemmia *noun, feminine*
una bestemmia = a curse

bestia *noun, feminine*
una bestia = an animal

bevanda *noun, feminine*
una bevanda = a drink

beve, bevuto, bevve, etc ▶ **bere**

biancheria *noun, feminine*
la biancheria = linen
la biancheria intima = underwear

bianco/bianca *adjective* (*plural* **bianchi/bianche**)
= white

Bibbia *noun, feminine*
la Bibbia = the Bible

✱ in informal situations   ✱ may be considered offensive

bibita *noun, feminine*
una bibita = a soft drink

biblioteca *noun, feminine* (*plural* biblioteche)
una biblioteca = a library
andare in biblioteca = to go to the library

bicchiere *noun, masculine*
un bicchiere = a glass
un bicchiere di plastica = a plastic cup

bici (! *never changes*), **bicicletta** *noun, feminine*
una bici = a bike
andare in bici = to cycle

bidello/bidella *noun, masculine/feminine*
un bidello/una bidella = a school caretaker, a janitor

bidone *noun, masculine*
il bidone dei rifiuti = the rubbish bin, the trashcan
fare il bidone a qualcuno✱ = to stand someone up

biglietto *noun, masculine*
• un biglietto = a ticket
• un biglietto = a note, a bill

bilancia *noun, feminine* (*plural* bilance)
• una bilancia = scales
• **Bilancia**
Bilancia = Libra

bilancio *noun, masculine* (*plural* bilanci)
un bilancio = a balance

bilingue *adjective*
= bilingual

bimbo/bimba *noun, masculine/feminine*
un bimbo/una bimba = a boy/a girl
= a child

binario *noun, masculine* (*plural* binari)
un binario = a platform

biografia *noun, feminine*
una biografia = a biography

biologia *noun, feminine*
la biologia = biology

biondo/bionda *adjective*
= blond
= blonde

birichino/birichina *adjective*
= naughty

birra *noun, feminine*
una birra = a beer

bis
1 *exclamation*
bis! = encore!
2 *noun, masculine* (! *never changes*)
il bis = an encore

biscotto *noun, masculine*
un biscotto = a biscuit, a cookie

bisnonno/bisnonna *noun, masculine/feminine*
il bisnonno/la bisnonna = the great-grandfather/the great-grandmother
i bisnonni = the great-grandparents

bisognare *verb* ⓵
bisogna [andare | aspettare | decidere] = we/you have to [go | wait | decide]
bisogna che studino = they have to study

bisogno *noun, masculine*
aver bisogno di = to need
ho bisogno di tempo = I need time
non c'è bisogno che tu gridi = you don't need to shout

bistecca *noun, feminine* (*plural* bistecche)
una bistecca = a steak

bloccare *verb* ⓸
1 = to block
2 bloccarsi (! + *essere*) = to get stuck

bloccato/bloccata *adjective*
rimanere bloccato/bloccata = to be stuck

blocco *noun, masculine* (*plural* **blocchi**)
un blocco = a block

bloc-notes *noun, masculine* (! *never changes*)
un bloc-notes = a notepad

blu *adjective* (! *never changes*)
= blue

bocca *noun, feminine* (*plural* **bocche**)
• la bocca = the mouth
• in bocca al lupo! = good luck!

boccata *noun, feminine*
una boccata d'aria = a breath of fresh air

bocciare *verb* ⓶
= to fail
= to reject
essere bocciato/bocciata = to fail

boccone *noun, masculine*
= a mouthful

bolla *noun, feminine*
una bolla = a bubble

bollente *adjective*
• = boiling
• = scalding

bolletta *noun, feminine*
una bolletta = a bill
la bolletta [della luce | del gas | del telefono] = the [electricity | gas | telephone] bill

bollire *verb* ⑩
= to boil

bollo *noun, masculine*
un bollo = a stamp

bomba *noun, feminine*
una bomba = a bomb

bombolone *noun, masculine*
un bombolone = a doughnut

bontà *noun, feminine*
la bontà = goodness

bordo *noun, masculine*
• il bordo = the edge
• salire a bordo = to go on board

borghese *adjective*
= middle-class

borghesia *noun, feminine*
la borghesia = the middle classes

borotalco *noun, masculine*
il borotalco = talcum powder

borsa *noun, feminine*
• una borsa = a handbag, a purse
  = a bag
• Borsa
  la Borsa = the Stock Exchange

borsaiolo/borsaiola *noun,*
masculine/feminine
un borsaiolo/una borsaiola = a pickpocket

borsellino *noun, masculine*
un borsellino = a purse

bosco *noun, masculine (plural* **boschi**)
un bosco = a wood

botanico/botanica
1 *adjective (plural* **botanici/botaniche**)
un giardino/un orto botanico = botanical
  gardens
2 *botanica noun, feminine*
la botanica = botany

botta *noun, feminine*
una botta = a blow

botte *noun, feminine*
una botte = a barrel

bottega *noun, feminine (plural*
botteghe)
una bottega = a shop

bottiglia *noun, feminine (plural*
bottiglie)
una bottiglia = a bottle

bottone *noun, masculine*
un bottone = a button

boxe *noun, feminine (! never changes)*
la boxe = boxing

braccio *noun, masculine (plural* **braccia**)
  ! Note that **braccia** is feminine.
il braccio = the arm

brace *noun, feminine*
la brace = embers
alla brace = grilled

brano *noun, masculine*
un brano = a passage

bravo/brava *adjective, exclamation*
= good
bravo a [disegnare | cantare | spiegare]
  = good at [drawing | singing | explaining]
bravo/brava! = well done!

breve *adjective*
= short

brezza *noun, feminine*
una brezza = a breeze

briciola *noun, feminine*
una briciola = a crumb

brillante *adjective*
• = shiny
• = brilliant

brillare *verb* 1
= to shine

brina *noun, feminine*
la brina = frost

brindare *verb* 1
= to toast

brindisi *noun, masculine (! never*
changes)
fare un brindisi = to drink a toast

britannico/britannica *adjective*
(*plural* **britannici/britanniche**)
= British

brivido *noun, masculine*
un brivido = a shiver

brocca *noun, feminine (plural* **brocche**)
una brocca = a jug

brodo *noun, masculine*
il brodo = stock
  = broth

brontolare *verb* 1
= to grumble

bronzo *noun, masculine*
il bronzo = bronze

bruciare *verb* 2
1 (! + *avere*)
• = to burn
• = to be very hot
2 bruciarsi (! + *essere*)
bruciarsi = to burn oneself

brufolo *noun, masculine*
un brufolo = a pimple

bruno/bruna *adjective*
= dark

brutto/brutta *adjective*
• = ugly
• = horrible

buca *noun, feminine (plural* **buche**)
una buca = a hole
la buca delle lettere = the postbox, the
  mailbox

bucare *verb* 4
= to make a hole in

bucato/bucata
1 *adjective*
= full of holes
2 bucato *noun, masculine*
il bucato = the washing

buccia *noun, feminine* (*plural* **bucce**)
la buccia = the peel
= the skin

buco *noun, masculine* (*plural* **buchi**)
un buco = a hole

budino *noun, masculine*
un budino = a pudding

bufera *noun, feminine*
una bufera = a storm

buffo/buffa *adjective*
= funny

bugia *noun, feminine* (*plural* **bugie**)
dire una bugia = to tell a lie

bugiardo/bugiarda
1 *adjective*
= lying
2 *noun, masculine/feminine*
un bugiardo/una bugiarda = a liar

buio/buia
1 *adjective* (*plural* **bui/buie**)
= dark
2 buio *noun, masculine*
il buio = the dark

buonanotte *exclamation*
buonanotte! = good night!

buonasera *exclamation*
buonasera! = good evening!

buongiorno *exclamation*
buongiorno! = good morning!

buono/buona *adjective*
1 *adjective*

> **!** *Before masculine singular nouns
> beginning with z, ps, gn, or s +
> another consonant, **buono** is used.
> Before masculine singular nouns
> beginning with other letters, **buon** is
> used. Before feminine singular nouns
> beginning with a vowel, **buon'** is used.*

= good
2 buono *noun, masculine*
un buono = a voucher

burattino *noun, masculine*
un burattino = a puppet

burocrazia *noun, feminine*
la burocrazia = bureaucracy

burro *noun, masculine*
il burro = butter

bussare *verb* ⟦1⟧
= to knock

bussola *noun, feminine*
una bussola = a compass

busta *noun, feminine*
una busta = an envelope
= a bag

bustarella *noun, feminine*
una bustarella = a bribe

bustina *noun, feminine*
una bustina = a bag
= a packet

buttare *verb* ⟦1⟧
= to throw (out)

Cc

cabina *noun, feminine*
una cabina = a cabin
= a beach hut
una cabina telefonica = a phone box

cacao *noun, masculine*
il cacao = cocoa

caccia *noun, feminine*
la caccia = shooting, hunting
andare a caccia = to go shooting, to go
hunting

cacciare *verb* ⟦2⟧
• (*when it's animals*) = to shoot, to hunt
• (*when it's a person*) = to throw out

cacciatore/cacciatrice *noun,
masculine/feminine*
un cacciatore/una cacciatrice = a hunter

cacciavite *noun, masculine*
un cacciavite = a screwdriver

cadavere *noun, masculine*
un cadavere = a corpse

cadde, caddero, etc ▶ **cadere**

cadere *verb* ⟦19⟧ (**!** + *essere*)
= to fall
lasciar cadere = to drop

cadrà, cadrò, etc ▶ **cadere**

caffè *noun, masculine* (**!** *never changes*)
un caffè = a coffee

calamaro *noun, masculine*
un calamaro = a squid

calamita *noun, feminine*
una calamita = a magnet

calare *verb* ⟦1⟧ (**!** + *essere*)
= to go down

calciatore *noun, masculine*
un calciatore = a footballer, a soccer
player

calcio *noun, masculine*
• il calcio = football, soccer
• (*plural* **calci**)
un calcio = a kick

calcolare *verb* ⟦1⟧
= to calculate

calcolatrice noun, feminine
una calcolatrice = a calculator

calcolo noun, masculine
un calcolo = a calculation

caldaia noun, feminine
una caldaia = a boiler

caldo/calda
1 adjective
= hot
= warm
2 **caldo** noun, masculine
il caldo = the heat
aver caldo = to be hot
far caldo = to be hot

calendario noun, masculine (plural
calendari)
un calendario = a calendar

calma noun, feminine
la calma = calm
mantenere la calma = to stay calm

calmare verb ①
1 = to calm
= to soothe
2 **calmarsi** (! + essere)
calmarsi = to calm down

calmo/calma adjective
= calm

calo noun, masculine
un calo = a drop

calore noun, masculine
il calore = heat
= warmth

caloria noun, feminine
una caloria = a calorie

calvo/calva adjective
= bald

calza noun, feminine
le calze = stockings
= tights, pantyhose

calzino noun, masculine
un calzino = a sock

cambiamento noun, masculine
un cambiamento = a change

cambiare verb ⑥ (! + essere or avere)
1 = to change
cambiare casa = to move house
2 **cambiarsi** (! + essere)
cambiarsi = to get changed

cambio noun, masculine
• il cambio = the exchange
• il tasso di cambio = the rate of exchange

camera noun, feminine
una camera = a room
= a bedroom

cameriere/cameriera noun,
masculine/feminine
un cameriere/una cameriera = a waiter/a
waitress

camicetta noun, feminine
una camicetta = a blouse

camicia noun, feminine (plural **camicie**)
una camicia = a shirt

camion noun, masculine (! never
changes)
un camion = a lorry, a truck

camionista noun, masculine/feminine
(plural **camionisti/camioniste**)
un/una camionista = a lorry driver, a
trucker

camminare verb ①
= to walk

campagna noun, feminine
• la campagna = the countryside
vivere in campagna = to live in the
country
• una campagna = a campaign

campana noun, feminine
una campana = a bell

campanello noun, masculine
un campanello = a bell
suonare il campanello = to ring the bell

campeggio noun, masculine (plural
campeggi)
un campeggio = a campsite, a
campground
andare in campeggio = to go camping

campionato noun, masculine
il campionato = the championship

campione/campionessa noun,
masculine/feminine
il campione/la campionessa = the
champion

campo noun, masculine
• un campo = a field
• un campo di calcio = a football pitch, a
soccer field

canadese adjective
= Canadian

canale noun, masculine
• un canale = a channel
cambiare canale = to change channels
• un canale = a canal

cancellare verb ①
= to erase

cancello noun, masculine
un cancello = a gate

cancro noun, masculine
1 il cancro = cancer
avere un cancro = to have cancer
2 **Cancro**
Cancro = Cancer

candela noun, feminine
una candela = a candle

candidato/candidata noun,
masculine/feminine
un candidato/una candidata = a candidate

cane *noun, masculine*
un cane = a dog

canestro *noun, masculine*
un canestro = a basket

cannuccia *noun, feminine* (*plural* **cannucce**)
una cannuccia = a straw

canoa *noun, feminine*
una canoa = a canoe

canottaggio *noun, masculine*
il canottaggio = rowing

canottiera *noun, feminine*
una canottiera = a vest, an undershirt

canotto *noun, masculine*
un canotto = a dinghy

cantante *noun, masculine/feminine*
un/una cantante = a singer

cantare *verb* [1]
= to sing

cantiere *noun, masculine*
un cantiere = a building site

cantina *noun, feminine*
la cantina = the cellar

canto *noun, masculine*
il canto = singing

cantone *noun, masculine*
un cantone = a canton

canzone *noun, feminine*
una canzone = a song

caos *noun, masculine*
il caos = chaos

caotico/caotica *adjective* (*plural* **caotici/caotiche**)
= chaotic

capace *adjective*
capace di = capable of

capacità *noun, feminine* (**!** *never changes*)
la capacità = the ability

capello *noun, masculine*
un capello = a hair
i capelli = the hair
ha i capelli neri = she has black hair

capire *verb* [9]
= to understand
ho capito = I see
capito? = you see?

capitale *noun, feminine*
una capitale = a capital

capitano *noun, masculine*
il capitano = the captain

capitare *verb* [1] (**!** + *essere*)
= to turn up
= to happen

capito ▶ **capire**

capitolo *noun, masculine*
un capitolo = a chapter

capo *noun, masculine*
• il capo = the boss
• il capo = the head

capodanno *noun, masculine*
= New Year's (Day)

capolavoro *noun, masculine*
un capolavoro = a masterpiece

cappella *noun, feminine*
una cappella = a chapel

cappello *noun, masculine*
un cappello = a hat

cappotto *noun, masculine*
un cappotto = a coat

cappuccio *noun, masculine* (*plural* **cappucci**)
un cappuccio = a hood

capra *noun, feminine*
una capra = a goat

capriccio *noun, masculine* (*plural* **capricci**)
• un capriccio = a whim
• fare i capricci = to be naughty

Capricorno *noun, masculine*
= Capricorn

carabiniere *noun, masculine*
un carabiniere = a policeman

caramella *noun, feminine*
una caramella = a sweet, a candy

carattere *noun, masculine*
il carattere = the character

caratteristica *noun, feminine* (*plural* **caratteristiche**)
una caratteristica = a characteristic

carbone *noun, masculine*
il carbone = coal

carcere *noun, masculine*
un carcere = a prison

carciofo *noun, masculine*
un carciofo = an artichoke

caricare *verb* [4]
• = to load
• = to charge

carico/carica *adjective* (*plural* **carichi/cariche**)
• = loaded
• = charged

carino/carina *adjective*
= nice

carne *noun, feminine*
la carne = meat

carnevale *noun, masculine*
il carnevale = carnival

caro/cara *adjective*
- = dear
  caro Flavio = dear Flavio
- = expensive

carota *noun, feminine*
  una carota = a carrot

carrello *noun, masculine*
  un carrello = a trolley, a cart

carriera *noun, feminine*
  una carriera = a career

carrozza *noun, feminine*
  una carrozza = a carriage

carrozzina *noun, feminine*
  una carrozzina = a pram, a baby carriage

carta *noun, feminine*
- la carta = paper
- una carta = a card
- una carta = a map
  una carta di credito = a credit card
  una carta d'identità = an identity card
  la carta igienica = toilet paper

cartello *noun, masculine*
  un cartello = a sign

cartoleria *noun, feminine*
  una cartoleria = a stationer's, an office
    supply store

cartolina *noun, feminine*
  una cartolina = a postcard

cartone *noun, masculine*
- il cartone = cardboard
- un cartone = a carton
  un cartone animato = a cartoon

casa *noun, feminine*
  una casa = a house
  a casa = at home
  andare a casa = to go home

casalinga *noun, feminine (plural*
  casalinghe)
  una casalinga = a housewife

cascare *verb* 4 (! + *essere*)
  = to fall

casco *noun, masculine (plural* **caschi)**
  un casco = a helmet

caserma *noun, feminine*
  una caserma = barracks

casino⁶ *noun, masculine*
- un casino = a mess
  che casino! = what a mess!
- un casino = a racket

casinò *noun, masculine* (! *never*
  changes)
  un casinò = a casino

caso *noun, masculine*
  un caso = a case
  a caso = at random
  per caso = by chance

---

cassa *noun, feminine*
- una cassa = a crate
- la cassa
  (*in a shop*) = a cash register
  (*in a supermarket*) = the checkout
  (*in a bank*) = the cashier's desk
- una cassa = a speaker

cassaforte *noun, feminine*
  una cassaforte = a safe

casseruola *noun, feminine*
  una casseruola = a saucepan

cassetta *noun, feminine*
  una cassetta = a cassette
  la cassetta delle lettere = the letter box,
    the mailbox

cassetto *noun, masculine*
  un cassetto = a drawer

castagna *noun, feminine*
  una castagna = a chestnut

castano/castana *adjective*
  = brown

castello *noun, masculine*
  un castello = a castle

casuale *adjective*
  = chance

catalogo *noun, masculine (plural*
  cataloghi)
  un catalogo = a catalog(ue)

catastrofe *noun, feminine*
  una catastrofe = a catastrophe

categoria *noun, feminine*
  una categoria = a category

catena *noun, feminine*
  una catena = a chain

cattedra *noun, feminine*
  la cattedra = the teacher's desk

cattedrale *noun, feminine*
  la cattedrale = the cathedral

cattivo/cattiva *adjective*
- = bad
- = naughty

cattolico/cattolica *adjective (plural*
  cattolici/cattoliche)
  = Catholic

catturare *verb* 1
  = to capture

causa *noun, feminine*
  una causa = a cause

causare *verb* 1
  = to cause

cautela *noun, feminine*
  la cautela = caution

cauto/cauta *adjective*
  = cautious

cava *noun, feminine*
  una cava = a quarry

✗ in informal situations ⁶ may be considered offensive

cavallo *noun, masculine*
un cavallo = a horse

cavarsela *verb* [1] (**!** + *essere*)
= to get on
= to get by
me la cavo bene = I'm getting on well

cavatappi *noun, masculine*
un cavatappi = a corkscrew

caviglia *noun, feminine*
la caviglia = the ankle

cavo/cava *adjective*
= hollow

cavolfiore *noun, masculine*
il cavolfiore = cauliflower

cavolo *noun, masculine*
• un cavolo = a cabbage
• che cavolo vuoi?✶ = what the heck do
   you want?

cazzo✶ *exclamation*
che cazzo vuoi?✶ = what the hell do you
want?

cella *noun, feminine*
una cella = a cell

cellula *noun, feminine*
una cellula = a cell

cellulare *noun, masculine*
un cellulare = a mobile phone, a cellular
phone

cemento *noun, masculine*
il cemento = cement

cena *noun, feminine*
la cena = dinner

cenere *noun, feminine*
la cenere = the ash

cent *noun, masculine*
un cent = a cent

centesimo/centesima
1 *adjective*
= hundredth
2 **centesimo** *noun, masculine*
un centesimo = a cent

centimetro *noun, masculine*
un centimetro = a centimetre, a
centimeter

centinaio *noun, masculine* (*plural*
centinaia)

> **!** *Note that* **centinaia** *is feminine.*

un centinaio = about a hundred
centinaia di persone = hundreds of
people

cento *number*
= a hundred

centrale *adjective*
= central

centralino *noun, masculine*
il centralino = the switchboard

centro *noun, masculine*
il centro = the centre, the center

cera *noun, feminine*
la cera = wax

cerca *noun, feminine*
in cerca di = in search of

cercare *verb* [4]
• = to look for
• cercare di fare qualcosa = to try to do
   something

cerchio *noun, masculine* (*plural* **cerchi**)
un cerchio = a circle

cerimonia *noun, feminine*
una cerimonia = a ceremony

cerotto *noun, masculine*
un cerotto = a plaster, a Band-Aid®

certamente *adverb*
= certainly

certezza *noun, feminine*
la certezza = certainty

certificato *noun, masculine*
un certificato = a certificate

certo/certa *adjective*
• = certain
• certo! = sure!

cervello *noun, masculine*
il cervello = the brain

cespuglio *noun, masculine* (*plural*
cespugli)
un cespuglio = a bush

cessare *verb* [1] (**!** + *essere* or *avere*)
= to cease

cestino *noun, masculine*
• un cestino = a basket
• un cestino = a waste-paper basket, a
   wastebasket

cesto *noun, masculine*
un cesto = a basket

che
1 *pronoun*
• (*in questions*) = what
   che fai? = what are you doing?
• (*in relative clauses*) = who
   = which
   = that
   la donna che è caduta = the woman who
      fell
   la macchina che ho comprato = the car I
      bought
2 *conjunction*
   = that
   mi ha detto che non viene = he told me
      he's not coming
   voglio che tu lo veda = I want you to see
      him

chi *pronoun*
• = who
   chi è? = who is it?   ····▸

di chi sono queste scarpe? = whose
shoes are these?
• = anyone who
ci saranno problemi per chi deve
viaggiare = there will be problems for
anyone who has to travel

chiacchierare verb 1
= to chat

chiacchierata noun, feminine
una chiacchierata = a chat

chiacchierone/chiacchierona
adjective
= talkative

chiamare verb 1
1 = to call
2 **chiamarsi** (! + essere)
chiamarsi = to be called
come ti chiami? = what's your name?
mi chiamo Elisa = my name's Elisa

chiamata noun, feminine
una chiamata = a call

chiaramente adverb
= clearly
= obviously

chiarezza noun, feminine
la chiarezza = clarity

chiarire verb 9
= to clarify

chiaro/chiara adjective
• = clear
è chiaro? = is that clear?
• = light
verde chiaro = light green

chiasso noun, masculine
un chiasso = a din

chiave noun, feminine
una chiave = a key

chicco noun, masculine (plural **chicchi**)
un chicco di riso = a grain of rice
un chicco di caffè = a coffee bean
un chicco d'uva = a grape

chiedere verb 20
1 (! + avere)
= to ask
chiedere il conto = to ask for the bill
chiedere a qualcuno di fare qualcosa
= to ask someone to do something
chiedere di qualcuno = to ask about
someone
2 **chiedersi** (! + essere)
chiedersi = to wonder

chiesa noun, feminine
una chiesa = a church

chiese, **chiesto/chiesta**, etc ▶
chiedere

chilo, **chilogrammo** noun, masculine
un chilo = a kilo

chilometro noun, masculine
un chilometro = a kilometre, a kilometer

chimica noun, feminine
la chimica = chemistry

chimico/chimica (plural **chimici/**
chimiche)
1 adjective
= chemical
2 noun, masculine|feminine
un chimico/una chimica = a chemist

chiocciola noun, feminine
una chiocciola = a snail

chiodo noun, masculine
un chiodo = a nail

chirurgia noun, feminine
la chirurgia = surgery

chirurgo noun, masculine (plural
chirurghi)
un chirurgo = a surgeon

chissà adverb
= who knows

chitarra noun, feminine
una chitarra = a guitar

chiudere verb 21
1 = to close, to shut
2 **chiudersi** (! + essere)
= to close, to shut

chiunque pronoun
= anyone

chiuse, **chiusero, etc** ▶ chiudere

chiuso/chiusa
1 ▶ chiudere
2 adjective
= closed, shut

ci (**ce** before lo/la, li/le, and ne)
1 pronoun
• = us
= to us
ci hanno visto = they've seen us
vuole conoscerci = he wants to meet us
• = to it
ci penso = I'll think about it
2 adverb
= here
= there
non ci vado = I'm not going
Flavio c'è? = is Flavio there?
c'è molto da fare = there's a lot to do
ci sono troppi turisti = there are too many
tourists

ciao exclamation
• (when arriving)
ciao! = hi!
• (when leaving)
ciao! = bye!

ciascuno/ciascuna adjective,
pronoun

! Note that before masculine nouns
beginning with z, ps, gn, or s +
another consonant **ciascuno** is used.
Ciascun is used before all other
masculine nouns.

····▶

= each
ciascuno di voi = each one of you

cibo noun, masculine
il cibo = food

cicatrice noun, feminine
una cicatrice = a scar

ciclismo noun, masculine
il ciclismo = cycling

cieco/cieca adjective (plural **ciechi/cieche**)
= blind

cielo noun, masculine
• il cielo = the sky
• il cielo = heaven

cifra noun, feminine
una cifra = a figure

ciglio noun, masculine (plural **ciglia**)

> **!** Note that ciglia is feminine.

il ciglio = the eyelash

ciliegia noun, feminine (plural **ciliege**)
una ciliegia = a cherry

cima noun, feminine
la cima = the top

cimitero noun, masculine
un cimitero = a cemetery

Cina noun, feminine
la Cina = China

cincin exclamation
cincin! = cheers!

cinema noun, masculine
il cinema = the cinema, the movie theater

cinese adjective
= Chinese

cinghiale noun, masculine
un cinghiale = a wild boar

cinico/cinica adjective (plural **cinici/ciniche**)
= cynical

cinquanta number
= fifty

cinquantesimo/cinquantesima adjective
= fiftieth

cinquantina noun, feminine
una cinquantina di chili = about fifty kilos

cinque number
= five

cinquecento
1 number
= five hundred
2 Cinquecento noun, masculine
il Cinquecento = the 16th century

cintura noun, feminine
una cintura = a belt
una cintura di sicurezza = a seat belt

ciò pronoun
= this
= that
ciò che fai non è giusto = what you're doing isn't right

cioccolata noun, feminine,
cioccolato noun, masculine
la cioccolata = chocolate

cioccolatino noun, masculine
un cioccolatino = a chocolate

cioè conjunction
= that is
= I mean

cipolla noun, feminine
una cipolla = an onion

circa adverb
= about, around

circo noun, masculine (plural **circhi**)
il circo = the circus

circolare
1 adjective
= circular
2 verb [1]
= to circulate

circondato/circondata adjective
circondato/circondata da = surrounded by

circostanza noun, feminine
una circostanza = a circumstance

citare verb [1]
= to quote

citazione noun, feminine
una citazione = a quotation

citofono noun, masculine
un citofono = an entry phone

città noun, feminine (**!** never changes)
una città = a town
= a city

cittadinanza noun, feminine
la cittadinanza = citizenship

cittadino/cittadina noun, masculine/feminine
un cittadino/una cittadina = a citizen

civile adjective
= civilized

civiltà noun, feminine (**!** never changes)
la civiltà = civilization

clacson noun, masculine (**!** never changes)
il clacson = the horn

clamoroso/clamorosa adjective
= outrageous

clandestino/clandestina noun, masculine/feminine
un clandestino/una clandestina = an illegal immigrant

classe noun, feminine
• una classe = a class, a grade
  che classe fai? = what class are you in?
• una classe = a classroom

classico/classica adjective (plural
  classici/classiche)
  = classic
  = classical

cliente noun, masculine/feminine
  un/una cliente = a customer

clima noun, masculine
  il clima = the climate

climatizzato/climatizzata adjective
  = air-conditioned

clinica noun, feminine (plural **cliniche**)
  una clinica = a clinic

cocco noun, masculine
  il cocco = coconut
  una noce di cocco = a coconut

coccodrillo noun, masculine
  un coccodrillo = a crocodile

coccolare verb [1]
  = to hug

cocomero noun, masculine
  un cocomero = a water melon

coda noun, feminine
• la coda = the tail
• una coda = a queue, a line
  fare la coda = to queue, to wait in line

codice noun, masculine
  un codice = a code

coetaneo/coetanea adjective
  sono coetanei = they're the same age

cofano noun, masculine
  il cofano = the bonnet, the hood

cogli ▶ con

cogliere verb [22]
  = to pick

coglioni* noun, masculine plural
  i coglioni = balls

cognato/cognata noun,
  masculine/feminine
  il cognato/la cognata = the brother-in-
  law/the sister-in-law

cognome noun, masculine
  un cognome = a surname

coi ▶ con

coincidenza noun, feminine
• una coincidenza = a coincidence
• (on the train)
  una coincidenza = a connection

coinvolgere verb [59]
  = to involve

**coinvolse, coinvolto/coinvolta,
  etc** ▶ coinvolgere

---

* may be considered offensive

col ▶ con

colare verb [1] (! + essere)
  = to drip

colazione noun, feminine
  la colazione = breakfast
  fare colazione = to have breakfast

colgo, colgono, etc ▶ cogliere

colino noun, masculine
  un colino = a strainer

colla ▶ con

colla noun, feminine
  la colla = glue

collaborazione noun, feminine
  la collaborazione = collaboration

collana noun, feminine
  una collana = a necklace

collant noun, masculine
  i collant = tights, pantyhose

collasso noun, masculine
  un collasso = a collapse

colle ▶ con

collega noun, masculine/feminine (plural
  colleghi/colleghe)
  un/una collega = a colleague

collegamento noun, masculine
  un collegamento = a connection

collegare verb [5]
  = to link
  essere collegato/collegata a = to be
  linked to

colletto noun, masculine
  un colletto = a collar

collezionare verb [1]
  = to collect

collezione noun, feminine
  una collezione = a collection

collina noun, feminine
  una collina = a hill

collo ▶ con

collo noun, masculine
  il collo = the neck

colloquio noun, masculine (plural
  colloqui)
  un colloquio di lavoro = a job interview

colomba noun, feminine
  una colomba = a dove

colonia noun, feminine
  una colonia = a colony

colonna noun, feminine
  una colonna = a column

colorare verb [1]
  = to colo(u)r (in)

colorato/colorata adjective
  = colo(u)red

colore *noun, masculine*
un colore = a colo(u)r

colpa *noun, feminine*
• la colpa = the blame
dare la colpa a qualcuno = to blame
  someone
• è colpa tua = it's your fault

colpevole *adjective*
= guilty

colpire *verb* ⑨
= to hit
= to strike

colpo *noun, masculine*
un colpo = a blow
un colpo di fortuna = a stroke of luck
un colpo di telefono = a phone call

colsi, **colse**, etc ▶ **cogliere**

coltello *noun, masculine*
un coltello = a knife

colto/colta
1 ▶ **cogliere**
2 *adjective*
= cultured

combattere *verb* ⑧
= to fight

combinazione *noun, feminine*
una combinazione = a combination

come

> **!** Note that before **è**, **era**, etc **com'** is
> used.

1 *adverb*
• (in questions) = how
come si dice 'pizza' in inglese? = how do
  you say 'pizza' in English?
come stai? = how are you?
com'è la casa? = what is the house like?
come? = what?
• (in exclamations)
com'è freddo! = it's so cold!
2 *conjunction*
(in comparisons) = like
= as
era come un sogno = it was like a dream
come sai = as you know
lavoro come barista = I work as a
  bartender
come sempre = as usual

comico/comica *adjective* (plural
comici/comiche)
= funny
un film comico = a comedy

cominciare *verb* ② (**!** + *essere* or
avere)
= to start
il film è cominciato = the film has started
cominciare a fare qualcosa = to start
  doing something

commedia *noun, feminine*
una commedia = a play

commento *noun, masculine*
un commento = a comment

commerciale *adjective*
= commercial

commercialista *noun,*
masculine/feminine (*plural*
commercialisti/commercialiste)
un/una commercialista = an accountant

commercio *noun, masculine*
il commercio = trade

commesso/commessa
1 ▶ **commettere**
2 *noun, masculine/feminine*
un commesso/una commessa = a shop
  assistant, a salesclerk

commestibile *adjective*
= edible

commettere *verb* ㊵
= to commit

commise, **commisero**, etc ▶
commettere

commissione *noun, feminine*
la commissione = commission

comò *noun, masculine* (**!** *never changes*)
un comò = a chest of drawers

comodo/comoda *adjective*
• = comfortable
• = convenient

compagnia *noun, feminine*
• una compagnia = a company
• fare compagnia a qualcuno = to keep
  someone company

compagno/compagna *noun,*
masculine/feminine
un compagno/una compagna = a
  companion
un compagno di classe = a classmate

compaio, **compaiono**, etc ▶
comparire

comparire *verb* ⑭ (**!** + *essere*)
= to appear

comparso/comparsa, **comparve**,
etc ▶ **comparire**

competente *adjective*
= competent

competizione *noun, feminine*
una competizione = a competition

compito *noun, masculine*
• un compito = a task
= a duty
• un compito in classe = a class test
i compiti = homework

compleanno *noun, masculine*
un compleanno = a birthday
buon compleanno! = happy birthday!

complessivo/complessiva
adjective
= total

complesso/complessa *adjective*
= complex

completamente *adverb*
= completely

completare *verb* 1
= to complete

completo/completa *adjective*
• = complete
• = full up

complicato/complicata *adjective*
= complicated

complicazione *noun, feminine*
una complicazione = a complication

complimento *noun, masculine*
un complimento = a compliment

compongo, compone, etc ►
comporre

comporre *verb* 50
• = to compose
• (*using the telephone*) = to dial

comportamento *noun, masculine*
il comportamento = the behavio(u)r

comportarsi *verb* 1 (! + *essere*)
= to behave
comportati bene! = behave yourself!

compose, composi, etc ►
comporre

compositore/compositrice *noun,
masculine/feminine*
un compositore/una compositrice = a
composer

composizione *noun, feminine*
una composizione = a composition

composto/composta
1 ► comporre
2 *adjective*
= compound

comprare *verb* 1
= to buy

comprendere *verb* 53
• = to include
• = to understand

comprensibile *adjective*
= understandable

comprensione *noun, feminine*
la comprensione = understanding

comprensivo/comprensiva
adjective
= understanding

comprese, compresi, etc ►
comprendere

compreso/compresa
1 ► comprendere
2 *adjective*
= including

compromesso *noun, masculine*
un compromesso = a compromise

comunale *adjective*
= council
= municipal
il consiglio comunale = the town council

comune
1 *adjective*
= common
2 *noun, masculine*
il comune = the town council
= the town hall

comunicare *verb* 4
= to communicate

comunicazione *noun, feminine*
la comunicazione = communication

comunione *noun, feminine*
la comunione = (first) communion

comunista *adjective* (*plural*
comunisti/comuniste)
= communist

comunità *noun, feminine* (! *never
changes*)
una comunità = a community

comunque
1 *adverb*
= anyway
2 *conjunction*
= however

con *preposition*
= with

> ! *Note that* con *sometimes combines
> with* il, la, *etc.* Con + il = col; con + l'
> = coll'; con + lo = collo; con + i = coi;
> con + gli = cogli; con + la = colla;
> con + le = colle.

concentrarsi *verb* 1 (! + *essere*)
= to concentrate

concentrato/concentrata
1 *adjective*
• = concentrated
• = immersed
2 concentrato *noun, masculine*
il concentrato di pomodoro = tomato
puré

concentrazione *noun, feminine*
la concentrazione = concentration

concepire *verb* 9
• = to conceive
• = to understand

concerto *noun, masculine*
un concerto = a concert

concessionaria *noun, feminine*
una concessionaria = a dealer

concetto *noun, masculine*
un concetto = a concept

conchiglia *noun, feminine*
una conchiglia = a shell

concludere *verb* 21
1 = to conclude
= to achieve
2 **concludersi** (**!** + *essere*)
concludersi = to end

concluse, conclusi, etc ▶
concludere

conclusione *noun, feminine*
una conclusione = a conclusion

concluso/conclusa ▶ concludere

concorrente *noun, masculine/feminine*
un/una concorrente = a competitor

concorrenza *noun, feminine*
la concorrenza = the competition

concorso *noun, masculine*
un concorso = a competition

concreto/concreta *adjective*
= concrete

condanna *noun, feminine*
una condanna = a sentence

condire *verb* 9
= to season
condire l'insalata = to dress the salad

condizione *noun, feminine*
una condizione = a condition

condominio *noun, masculine* (*plural*
condomini)
un condominio = a block of flats, an
apartment building

condotta *noun, feminine*
la condotta = conduct

condotto/condotta, conduce, etc
▶ condurre

condurre *verb* 54
• = to lead
• = to conduct

condusse, condussi, etc ▶
condurre

conferenza *noun, feminine*
• una conferenza = a lecture
• una conferenza = a conference
una conferenza stampa = a press
conference

conferma *noun, feminine*
una conferma = a confirmation

confermare *verb* 1
= to confirm

confessare *verb* 1
= to confess

confessione *noun, feminine*
una confessione = a confession

confetto *noun, masculine*
un confetto = a sugared almond

conficcare *verb* 4
= to drive

confidare *verb* 1
= to confide

confidenza *noun, feminine*
una confidenza = a secret

confine *noun, masculine*
un confine = a border

conflitto *noun, masculine*
un conflitto = a conflict

confondere *verb* 24
1 = to confuse
2 **confondersi** (**!** + *essere*)
confondersi = to get confused

confrontare *verb* 1
= to compare

confronto *noun, masculine*
un confronto = a comparison

confuse, confusi, etc ▶
confondere

confusione *noun, feminine*
• la confusione = confusion
• una confusione = a mess
= a racket

confuso/confusa
1 ▶ confondere
2 *adjective*
• = confused
• = confusing

congelato/congelata *adjective*
= frozen

congelatore *noun, masculine*
il congelatore = the freezer

congratulazioni *exclamation*
congratulazioni! = congratulations!

congresso *noun, masculine*
un congresso = a conference

coniglio *noun, masculine* (*plural* **conigli**)
un coniglio = a rabbit

cono *noun, masculine*
un cono = a cone

conobbe, conobbi, etc ▶
conoscere

conoscenza *noun, feminine*
la conoscenza = knowledge

conoscere *verb* 25
• = to know
• = to meet

conosciuto/conosciuta
1 ▶ conoscere
2 *adjective*
= well-known

conquista *noun, feminine*
una conquista = a conquest

conquistare *verb* [1]
= to conquer

consapevole *adjective*
consapevole di = aware of

consegna *noun, feminine*
una consegna = a delivery

consegnare *verb* [1]
= to deliver

conseguenza *noun, feminine*
una conseguenza = a consequence

consentire *verb* [10]
= to consent

conservante *noun, masculine*
un conservante = a preservative

conservare *verb* [1]
= to keep

conservatore/conservatrice
adjective
= conservative

conservatorio *noun, masculine (plural* conservatori)
un conservatorio = a music school

considerare *verb* [1]
= to consider

considerazione *noun, feminine*
la considerazione = consideration
prendere qualcosa in considerazione = to take something into consideration

consigliare *verb* [6]
• consigliare a qualcuno di fare qualcosa
= to advise someone to do something
• = to recommend

consiglio *noun, masculine (plural* consigli)
un consiglio = a piece of advice
dei consigli = some advice

consistere *verb* [16] (! + *essere*)
consistere di/in = to consist of

consolato *noun, masculine*
un consolato = a consulate

consonante *noun, feminine*
una consonante = a consonant

consulente *noun, masculine/feminine*
un/una consulente = a consultant

consultare *verb* [1]
= to consult

consumare *verb* [1]
• = to consume
• = to use up
• = to wear out

consumatore/consumatrice *noun,*
masculine/feminine
un consumatore/una consumatrice = a consumer

contabile *noun, masculine/feminine*
un/una contabile = an accountant

contabilità *noun, feminine*
la contabilità = accountancy

contadino/contadina *noun,*
masculine/feminine
un contadino/una contadina = a peasant

contaminare *verb* [1]
= to contaminate

contanti *noun, masculine plural*
i contanti = cash

contare *verb* [1]
= to count

contattare *verb* [1]
= to contact

contatto *noun, masculine*
il contatto = contact
mettersi in contatto con qualcuno = to get in touch with someone

contemporaneo/contemporanea
adjective
= contemporary

contenere *verb* [73]
= to contain

contengo, contengono, etc ▶
contenere

contenitore *noun, masculine*
un contenitore = a container

contento/contenta *adjective*
= pleased

contenuto/contenuta
1 ▶ contenere
2 contenuto *noun, masculine*
il contenuto = the content

contesto *noun, masculine*
il contesto = the context

contiene, contieni, etc ▶
contenere

continente *noun, masculine*
un continente = a continent

continuare *verb* [1] (! + *essere* or
avere)
= to continue
= to carry on

continuazione *noun, feminine*
la continuazione = the continuation
in continuazione = constantly

continuo/continua *adjective*
= continuous
= continual

conto *noun, masculine*
• il conto = the bill
• un conto = an account
• un conto = a calculation
• rendersi conto di qualcosa = to realize something

contorno *noun, masculine*
un contorno = a side dish

contrabbando *noun, masculine*
il contrabbando = smuggling

contraccettivo *noun, masculine*
un contraccettivo = a contraceptive

contraddizione *noun, feminine*
una contraddizione = a contradiction

contrae, **contraggo**, etc ▶
contrarre

contrario/contraria (*plural* contrari/
contrarie)
1 *adjective*
= opposite
2 **contrario** *noun, masculine*
il contrario = the opposite

contrarre *verb* 74
1 = to contract
2 contrarsi (**!** + *essere*)
= to contract

contrasse, **contrassero**, etc ▶
contrarre

contrasto *noun, masculine*
un contrasto = a contrast

contratto/contratta
1 ▶ contrarre
2 contratto *noun, masculine*
un contratto = a contract

contribuente *noun, masculine/feminine*
un/una contribuente = a taxpayer

contribuire *verb* 9
= to contribute

contributo *noun, masculine*
un contributo = a contribution

contro *preposition*
= against

controllare *verb* 1
= to check

controllo *noun, masculine*
un controllo = a check

controllore *noun, masculine*
un controllore = a ticket inspector

convegno *noun, masculine*
un convegno = a conference

convenga, **convengono**, etc ▶
convenire

conveniente *adjective*
= cheap

convenire *verb* 78 (**!** + *essere*)
• conviene aspettare = it's best to wait
ti conviene non dire niente = you'd better
not say anything
• = to be cheaper

convento *noun, masculine*
un convento = a convent

conversazione *noun, feminine*
una conversazione = a conversation

conviene, **convieni** ▶ convenire

convincere *verb* 79
= to convince
convincere qualcuno a fare qualcosa = to
persuade someone to do something

convinse, **convinsi**, etc ▶
convincere

convinto/convinta
1 ▶ convincere
2 *adjective*
essere convinto/convinta = to be sure

coperchio *noun, masculine* (*plural*
coperchi)
un coperchio = a lid

coperta *noun, feminine*
una coperta = a blanket

copertina *noun, feminine*
una copertina = a cover

coperto/coperta
1 ▶ coprire
2 *adjective*
• coperto/coperta di neve = covered with
snow
• un cielo coperto = a cloudy sky

copia *noun, feminine*
una copia = a copy

copiare *verb* 6
= to copy

coppa *noun, feminine*
• una coppa di spumante = a glass of
sparkling wine
• la coppa = the cup

coppia *noun, feminine*
una coppia = a couple

coprire *verb* 15
= to cover

coque *noun, feminine*
un uovo alla coque = a soft-boiled egg

coraggio *noun, masculine*
il coraggio = courage

coraggioso/coraggiosa *adjective*
= brave

corallo *noun, masculine*
il corallo = coral

corda *noun, feminine*
una corda = a rope

corna ▶ corno

cornetta *noun, feminine*
la cornetta = the receiver

cornice *noun, feminine*
una cornice = a frame

corno *noun, masculine*
un corno = a horn

> **!** When **corno** refers to the horns of an
> animal the plural is **corna** (*feminine*).

corona *noun, feminine*
una corona = a crown

corpo *noun, masculine*
un corpo = a body

correggere *verb* 39
= to correct

corrente
1 *adjective*
• = current
• = fluent
2 *noun, feminine*
una corrente = a current
una corrente d'aria = a draught, a draft

correre *verb* 26 (**!** + *essere* or *avere*)
= to run

corresse, **corressi**, **etc** ▶ **correggere**

corretto/corretta
1 ▶ **correggere**
2 *adjective*
= correct

correzione *noun, feminine*
una correzione = a correction

corridoio *noun, masculine* (*plural* **corridoi**)
un corridoio = a corridor

corrotto/corrotta *adjective*
= corrupt

corruzione *noun, feminine*
la corruzione = corruption

corsa *noun, feminine*
una corsa = a race
di corsa = quickly

corse, **corsi**, **etc** ▶ **correre**

corsia *noun, feminine*
una corsia = a lane

corso/corsa
1 ▶ **correre**
2 *corso noun, masculine*
un corso = a course

corte *noun, feminine*
una corte = a court

cortese *adjective*
= polite

cortesia *noun, feminine*
una cortesia = a favo(u)r
per cortesia = please

cortile *noun, masculine*
un cortile = a yard

corto/corta *adjective*
= short

cosa
1 *noun, feminine*
una cosa = a thing
dove sono le mie cose? = where are my things?
2 *pronoun*
= what

(che) cosa è successo? = what happened?

coscia *noun, feminine* (*plural* **cosce**)
• (*of a person*)
la coscia = the thigh
• (*of a chicken*)
una coscia = a leg

coscienza *noun, feminine*
la coscienza = the conscience

così
1 *adverb*
• = like this
= like that
fallo così = do it like this
• = so
così grande = so big
un film così lungo = such a long film
2 *conjunction*
= so
ho fatto tardi e così ho perso l'inizio del film = I was late so I missed the beginning of the film

cosiddetto/cosiddetta *adjective*
= so-called

coso/cosa *noun, masculine/feminine*
ho parlato con coso/cosa = I spoke to what's-his-name/what's-her-name

cosse, **cossi**, **etc** ▶ **cuocere**

costa *noun, feminine*
la costa = the coast

costante *adjective*
= constant

costare *verb* 1 (**!** + *essere*)
= to cost

costo *noun, masculine*
il costo = the cost

costola *noun, feminine*
una costola = a rib

costoletta *noun, feminine*
una costoletta = a cutlet

costoso/costosa *adjective*
= expensive

costretto/costretta ▶ **costringere**

costringere *verb* 71
costringere qualcuno a fare qualcosa
= to force someone to do something
fui costretto a fermarmi = I had to stop

costrinse, **costrinsi**, **etc** ▶ **costringere**

costruire *verb* 9
= to build

costume *noun, masculine*
• un costume = a costume
• un costume = a custom

cotoletta *noun, feminine*
una cotoletta = a chop, a cutlet

cotone *noun, masculine*
il cotone = cotton

✘ in informal situations

cotto/cotta
1 ▶ cuocere
2 adjective
   = ready

cottura noun, feminine
la cottura = the cooking

cozza noun, feminine
una cozza = a mussel

cravatta noun, feminine
una cravatta = a tie

creare verb [1]
   = to create

crebbe, crebbi, etc ▶ crescere

credenza noun, feminine
una credenza = a sideboard

credere verb [8]
   = to believe
   = to think
   credo che sia vero = I think it's true
   crede di sapere tutto = he thinks he
      knows everything
   credo di sì = I think so
   credo di no = I don't think so
   non ci credo! = I don't believe it!

credito noun, masculine
il credito = credit

crema noun, feminine
• una crema = a cream
• la crema = custard

crepa noun, feminine
una crepa = a crack

crepare verb [1] (! + essere)
1 ✱ = to snuff it
2 creparsi (! + essere)
   creparsi = to crack

crescere verb [27] (! + essere)
• = to grow
• = to grow up

crescita noun, feminine
la crescita = growth

cresciuto/cresciuta ▶ crescere

cretino/cretina noun,
   masculine/feminine
un cretino/una cretina = a cretin

criminale noun, masculine/feminine
un/una criminale = a criminal

criminalità noun, feminine
la criminalità = crime

crimine noun, masculine
un crimine = a crime

crisi noun, feminine (! never changes)
una crisi = a crisis

cristallo noun, masculine
un cristallo = a crystal

cristianesimo noun, masculine
il cristianesimo = Christianity

cristiano/cristiana adjective
   = Christian

criterio noun, masculine (plural **criteri**)
un criterio = a criterion

critica noun, feminine (plural **critiche**)
una critica = a criticism

criticare verb [4]
   = to criticize

critico/critica (plural **critici/critiche**)
1 adjective
   = critical
2 noun, masculine/feminine
   un critico/una critica = a critic

croccante adjective
   = crunchy

croce noun, feminine
una croce = a cross

crociera noun, feminine
una crociera = a cruise

crollare verb [1] (! + essere)
   = to collapse

crollo noun, masculine
un crollo = a collapse

crosta noun, feminine
una crosta = a crust

cruciverba noun, masculine (! never
   changes)
un cruciverba = a crossword

crudele adjective
   = cruel

crudeltà noun, feminine
la crudeltà = cruelty

crudo/cruda adjective
   = raw

cubetto noun, masculine
un cubetto di ghiaccio = an ice cube

cubo noun, masculine
un cubo = a cube

cuccetta noun, feminine
una cuccetta = a couchette

cucchiaino noun, masculine
un cucchiaino = a teaspoon

cucchiaio noun, masculine (plural
   cucchiai)
un cucchiaio = a spoon

cucciolo noun, masculine
un cucciolo = a pup
   = a cub

cucina noun, feminine
• la cucina = the kitchen
• una cucina = a cooker, a stove
• la cucina italiana = Italian cookery

cucinare verb [1]
   = to cook

cucire verb [10]
   = to sew

cucitrice *noun, feminine*
una cucitrice = a stapler

cuffia *noun, feminine*
• una cuffia = a cap
• una cuffia = headphones

cugino/cugina *noun, masculine/feminine*
un cugino/una cugina = a cousin

cui *pronoun*
• = whose
• = whom
= which

culla *noun, feminine*
una culla = a crib

culo *noun, masculine*
il culo = the arse, the ass

cultura *noun, feminine*
la cultura = culture

culturale *adjective*
= cultural

culturismo *noun, masculine*
il culturismo = body-building

cuocere *verb* 28
= to cook

cuoco/cuoca *noun, masculine/feminine* (*plural* **cuochi/cuoche**)
un cuoco/una cuoca = a cook

cuoio *noun, masculine*
il cuoio = leather

cuore *noun, masculine*
il cuore = the heart

cupola *noun, feminine*
una cupola = a dome

cura *noun, feminine*
• una cura = a cure
• la cura = treatment
prendersi cura di = to look after

curare *verb* 1
• = to treat
• = to cure

curiosità *noun, feminine*
la curiosità = curiosity

curioso/curiosa *adjective*
= curious

curriculum *noun, masculine* (**!** *never changes*)
un curriculum = a CV, a résumé

curva *noun, feminine*
una curva = a bend
= a curve

cuscino *noun, masculine*
un cuscino = a cushion
= a pillow

custode *noun, masculine/feminine*
un/una custode = a caretaker, a janitor

custodire *verb* 9
= to guard

Dd

da *preposition*

> **!** *Note that* da *combines with* il, la, *etc.*
> Da + il = dal; da + l' = dall'; da + lo = dallo; da + i = dai; da + gli = dagli; da + la = dalla; da + le = dalle.

• = from
da Roma a Milano = from Rome to Milan
• = at
= to
sarò da Giulia = I'll be at Giulia's
vado dal dentista = I'm going to the dentist's
• = by
è stata costruita dai pisani = it was built by the Pisans
• = for
= since
la conosco da anni = I've known her for years
lavoro qui dal 1996 = I've been working here since 1996
• (*other uses*)
qualcosa da mangiare = something to eat
un francobollo da 0,41 euro = a 0·41 euro stamp
da bambino/bambina = as a child

dà, da' ▶ dare

dado *noun, masculine*
• un dado = a dice
• un dado = a stock cube

dagli ▶ da

dai
1 ▶ dare
2 ▶ da

dal, dalla, dalle, etc ▶ da

dammi ▶ dare

danese *adjective*
= Danish

Danimarca *noun, feminine*
la Danimarca = Denmark

danneggiare *verb* 3
= to damage

danno
1 ▶ dare
2 *noun, masculine*
fare un danno = to cause damage
i danni = damage

dannoso/dannosa *adjective*
= harmful

danza *noun, feminine*
una danza = a dance

dappertutto *adverb*
= everywhere

✖ in informal situations   **☞** may be considered offensive

dare verb 29
• = to give
  dammi la chiave! = give me the key!
• **dare del tu a qualcuno** = to address someone using 'tu'
  dare del lei a qualcuno = to address someone using 'lei'
• **la finestra dà sulla piazza** = the window overlooks the square
• **dare un esame** = to take an exam
• **dare da mangiare a qualcuno** = to feed someone

data noun, feminine
  una data = a date

date ▶ **dare**

dato/data
1 ▶ **dare**
2 **dato** noun, masculine
  un dato = a piece of information
  i dati = information

datore/datrice noun, masculine/feminine
  un datore/una datrice di lavoro = an employer

dattilografo/dattilografa noun, masculine/feminine
  un dattilografo/una dattilografa = a typist

davanti
1 adverb
• = in front
  la macchina davanti = the car in front
• = opposite
  la stazione è davanti = the station is opposite
2 **davanti a** preposition
• = in front of
  incontriamoci davanti alla scuola = let's meet in front of the school
• = opposite
  la stazione è davanti alla chiesa = the station is opposite the church

davvero adverb
  = really

debito noun, masculine
  un debito = a debt

debole adjective
  = weak

decennio noun, masculine (plural **decenni**)
  un decennio = a decade

decente adjective
  = decent

decidere verb 30
  = to decide
  decidere di sposarsi = to decide to get married

decimo/decima adjective
  = tenth

decina noun, feminine
  una decina di studenti = about ten students

decisamente adverb
  = definitely

decise, decisi, etc ▶ **decidere**

decisione noun, feminine
  una decisione = a decision

deciso/decisa ▶ **decidere**

decollare verb 1
  = to take off

decollo noun, masculine
  un decollo = a take-off

decorare verb 1
  = to decorate

decorazione noun, feminine
  una decorazione = a decoration

dedicare verb 4
  = to dedicate

deduco, deduce, etc ▶ **dedurre**

dedurre verb 54
• = to deduct
• = to deduce

dedusse, dedotto/dedotta, etc ▶ **dedurre**

deficiente✶ adjective
  = stupid

definire verb 9
  = to define

definito/definita adjective
  = definite

definizione noun, feminine
  una definizione = a definition

degli ▶ **di**

degno/degna adjective
  = worthy

dei, del ▶ **di**

delfino noun, masculine
  un delfino = a dolphin

delicato/delicata adjective
  = delicate

delitto noun, masculine
  un delitto = a crime

delizioso/deliziosa adjective
  = delicious

della, delle, dello ▶ **di**

deludere verb 21
  = to disappoint

deluse, delusero, etc ▶ **deludere**

delusione noun, feminine
  una delusione = a disappointment

deluso/delusa
1 ▶ **deludere**
2 adjective
  = disappointed

democratico/democratica
adjective (plural
democratici/democratiche)
= democratic

democrazia noun, feminine
la democrazia = democracy

demolire verb [9]
= to demolish

denaro noun, masculine
il denaro = money

dente noun, masculine
un dente = a tooth

dentifricio noun, masculine
il dentifricio = toothpaste

dentista noun, masculine/feminine (plural
dentisti/dentiste)
un/una dentista = a dentist

dentro preposition, adverb
= inside

denuncia noun, feminine (plural
denunce)
una denuncia = a report

denunciare verb [2]
= to report

deodorante noun, masculine
il deodorante = deodorant

depliant noun, masculine (! never
changes)
un depliant = a leaflet

deposito noun, masculine
• un deposito = a deposit
• deposito bagagli = left luggage office

depresso/depressa adjective
= depressed

deprimente adjective
= depressing

derubare verb [1]
= to rob

descrisse, **descritto/descritta**,
etc ▶ descrivere

descrivere verb [65]
= to describe

descrizione noun, feminine
una descrizione = a description

deserto noun, masculine
un deserto = a desert

desiderare verb [1]
= to want

desiderio noun, masculine (plural
desideri)
esprimere un desiderio = to make a wish

destinatario/destinataria noun,
masculine/feminine (plural **destinatari/
destinatarie**)
il destinatario/la destinataria = the
addressee

destinazione noun, feminine
una destinazione = a destination

destino noun, masculine
il destino = destiny

destro/destra
1 adjective
= right
la mano destra = the right hand
2 **destra** noun, feminine
= right
a destra = on the right
girare a destra = to turn right

determinazione noun, feminine
la determinazione = determination

dettaglio noun, masculine (plural
dettagli)
un dettaglio = a detail

dette, **detti**, etc ▶ dare

detto/detta ▶ dire

deve, **devo**, etc ▶ dovere

di

> ! Note that di combines with il, la, etc.
> Di + il = del; di + l' = dell'; di + lo
> = dello; di + i = dei; di + gli = degli;
> di + la = della; di + le = delle.

1 preposition
• = of
la capitale d'Italia = the capital of Italy
la porta della cucina = the kitchen door
la macchina di Renato = Renato's car
• = from
sono di Dublino = they're from Dublin
• = than
tu sei più alto di me = you're taller than
me
• = by
un libro di Calvino = a book by Calvino
• = made of
è di legno = it's made of wood
2 del/della determiner
= some

> ! Before masculine nouns beginning
> with z, ps, gn, or s + another
> consonant, dello is used in the singular
> and degli in the plural. Before
> masculine nouns beginning with other
> consonants, del is used in the singular
> and dei in the plural. Before all nouns
> beginning with a vowel, dell' is used in
> the singular and degli (masculine) or
> delle (feminine) in the plural.

dell'acqua = some water
sono arrivate delle lettere = some letters
have arrived

di' ▶ dire

dia ▶ dare

diabetico/diabetica adjective (plural
diabetici/diabetiche)
= diabetic

diagnosi noun, feminine (**!** never changes)
una diagnosi = a diagnosis

dialetto noun, masculine
un dialetto = a dialect

dialogo noun, masculine (plural dialoghi)
un dialogo = a dialogue

diamo ▶ dare

diapositiva noun, feminine
una diapositiva = a slide

diario noun, masculine (plural diari)
un diario = a diary

diavolo noun, masculine
il diavolo = the devil

dibattito noun, masculine
un dibattito = a debate

dica, dice, dicevo, etc ▶ dire

dichiarare verb 1
= to declare

dichiarazione noun, feminine
una dichiarazione = a declaration

dici, diciamo ▶ dire

diciannove number
= nineteen

diciannovenne adjective
= nineteen-year-old

diciannovesimo/diciannovesima
adjective
= nineteenth

diciassette number
= seventeen

diciassettenne adjective
= seventeen-year-old

diciassettesimo/diciasettesima
adjective
= seventeenth

diciottenne adjective
= eighteen-year-old

diciottesimo/diciottesima
adjective
= eighteenth

diciotto number
= eighteen

dico, dicono ▶ dire

dieci number
= ten

diede, diedi, etc ▶ dare

dieta noun, feminine
una dieta = a diet
mettersi a dieta = to go on a diet

dietro
1 adverb
= behind
= in/at the back

2 noun, masculine
il dietro = the back
3 **dietro (a/di)** preposition
= behind
la macchina dietro di noi = the car behind us
dietro alla stazione = behind the station

difendere verb 53
= to defend

difesa noun, feminine
la difesa = defence, defense

difese, difeso/difesa, etc ▶ difendere

difetto noun, masculine
un difetto = a defect

differente adjective
= different

differenza noun, feminine
una differenza = a difference

difficile adjective
= difficult

difficilmente adverb
= with difficulty

difficoltà noun, feminine (**!** never changes)
una difficoltà = a difficulty

diffondere verb 24
1 = to spread
2 diffondersi (**!** + essere)
diffondersi = to spread

diffuso/diffusa, etc
1 ▶ diffondere
2 adjective
= common

digiuno/digiuna adjective
= on an empty stomach
essere digiuno/digiuna = not to have eaten

dignità noun, feminine
la dignità = dignity

dilettante noun, masculine/feminine
un/una dilettante = an amateur

dimagrire verb (**!** + essere)
= to lose weight

dimensione noun, feminine
una dimensione = a dimension

dimenticare verb 4
= to forget
ho dimenticato l'ombrello sul treno = I left my umbrella on the train

dimesso/dimessa ▶ dimettersi

dimettersi verb 40
= to resign

diminuire verb 9 (**!** + essere or avere)
= to decrease

dimise, **dimisi**, etc ▶ **dimettersi**

dimissioni noun, feminine plural
dare le dimissioni = to resign

dimmi ▶ **dire**

dimostrare verb [1]
= to show

dimostrazione noun, feminine
una dimostrazione = a demonstration

dinamico/dinamica adjective (plural
dinamici/dinamiche)
= dynamic

dintorni noun, masculine plural
i dintorni = the outskirts

dio/dea noun, masculine/feminine (plural
dei/dee)
1 un dio/una dea = a god/a goddess
2 **Dio** noun, masculine
Dio = God

dipartimento noun, masculine
un dipartimento = a department

dipendente noun, masculine/feminine
un/una dipendente = an employee

dipendere verb [53] (! + essere)
dipendere da = to depend on
dipende = it depends

dipingere verb [48]
= to paint

dipinse, **dipinsi**, etc ▶ **dipingere**

dipinto/dipinta
1 ▶ **dipingere**
2 **dipinto** noun, masculine
un dipinto = a painting

diploma noun, masculine (plural
diplomi)
un diploma = a diploma

dire verb [31]
= to say
= to tell
dire di sì/di no = to say yes/no
dimmi la verità! = tell me the truth!
dica! = yes?

diresse, **diressi**, etc ▶ **dirigere**

direttamente adverb
= directly
vado direttamente a casa = I'm going
straight home

diretto/diretta
1 ▶ **dirigere**
2 adjective
= direct

direttore/direttrice noun,
masculine/feminine
• un direttore/una direttrice = a director
= a manager
• un direttore/una direttrice = a
headteacher, a principal

direzione noun, feminine
• una direzione = a direction
• la direzione = the management

dirigente noun, masculine/feminine
un/una dirigente = a leader
= a manager

dirigere verb [32]
= to lead
= to run

diritto/diritta
1 adjective
= straight
2 **diritto** noun, masculine
un diritto = a right

disastro noun, masculine
un disastro = a disaster

discesa noun, feminine
la discesa = the descent

disciplina noun, feminine
la disciplina = discipline

disco noun, masculine (plural **dischi**)
un disco = a record
= a disc, a disk

discorso noun, masculine
• un discorso = a speech
• che discorsi! = what a stupid thing to
say!

discoteca noun, feminine (plural
discoteche)
una discoteca = a club

discreto/discreta adjective
= not bad

discriminazione noun, feminine
la discriminazione = discrimination

discussione noun, feminine
una discussione = an argument

discusse, **discussi**, etc ▶
discutere

discusso/discussa
1 ▶ **discutere**
2 adjective
= controversial

discutere verb [33]
= to discuss

disdetto/disdetta, **disdico**, etc ▶
disdire

disdire verb [31]
= to cancel

disegnare verb [1]
= to draw

disegno noun, masculine
un disegno = a drawing
= a design

disgrazia noun, feminine
una disgrazia = a terrible thing

disoccupato/disoccupata *adjective*
= unemployed

disoccupazione *noun, feminine*
la disoccupazione = unemployment

disordinato/disordinata *adjective*
= untidy

disordine *noun, masculine*
un disordine = a mess
in disordine = in a mess

disperato/disperata *adjective*
= desperate

disperazione *noun, feminine*
la disperazione = desperation

dispettoso/dispettosa *adjective*
= naughty

dispiacere
1 *verb* (**!** + *essere*)
• mi dispiace = I'm sorry
• se non le dispiace = if you don't mind
  ti dispiace abbassare la radio? = would
  you mind turning down the radio?
• non mi dispiace = I quite like it
2 *noun, masculine*
  un dispiacere = a disappointment

dispiaciuto/dispiaciuta
1 ▶ dispiacere
2 *adjective*
= sorry

dispone, dispongo, etc ▶ disporre

disponibile *adjective*
• = available
• (*when it's a person*) = helpful

disponibilità *noun, feminine*
la disponibilità = availability

disporre *verb* 50
= to arrange

dispose, disposi, etc ▶ disporre

disposto/disposta
1 ▶ disporre
2 *adjective*
  disposto/disposta a fare qualcosa
  = willing to do something

disse, dissi, etc ▶ dire

distante *adjective*
= far away

distanza *noun, feminine*
la distanza = the distance

distinguere *verb* 34
= to distinguish
= to make out

distinse, distinsi, etc ▶
distinguere

distinto/distinta
1 ▶ distinguere
2 *adjective*
• = distinct
• = distinguished

distinzione *noun, feminine*
una distinzione = a distinction

distribuire *verb* 9
= to distribute
= to hand out

distribuzione *noun, feminine*
la distribuzione = the distribution

distruggere *verb* 39
= to destroy

distrussi, distrusse, etc ▶
distruggere

distrutto/distrutta
1 ▶ distruggere
2 *adjective*
= exhausted

distruzione *noun, feminine*
la distruzione = destruction

disturbare *verb* 1
= to disturb

disturbo *noun, masculine*
• un disturbo = a disturbance
• un disturbo di stomaco = a stomach
  upset

dita ▶ dito

dite ▶ dire

dito *noun, masculine* (*plural* **dita**)

> **!** *Note that* dita *is feminine.*

un dito = a finger

ditta *noun, feminine*
una ditta = a firm

dittatore *noun, masculine*
un dittatore = a dictator

divano *noun, masculine*
un divano = a sofa
un divano letto = a sofa bed

diventare *verb* 1 (**!** + *essere*)
= to become

diverso/diversa *adjective*
• = different
• = several
  diverse volte = several times

divertente *adjective*
= enjoyable
= amusing

divertimento *noun, masculine*
il divertimento = fun

divertirsi *verb* 10 (**!** + *essere*)
= to have a good time

dividere *verb* 30
• = to divide
• = to share

divieto *noun, masculine*
un divieto = a ban

dovere

1 dovere functions as an ordinary verb:

= to owe

mi devi trenta euro	= *you owe me thirty euros*

2 dovere is used to talk about obligations and prohibitions:

devo andare	= *I have to go*
dobbiamo agire subito	= *we must do something at once*
abbiamo dovuto prendere un taxi	= *we had to get a taxi*
non si deve correre	= *you mustn't run*
non dovevi dirglielo	= *you weren't supposed to tell him*

3 dovere is used to make polite offers:

ti devo aiutare?	= *shall I help you?*

4 dovere is used when making a logical deduction:

ci deve essere una perdita	= *there must be a leak*
dev'essere il postino	= *it must be the postman*

5 dovere is used in the *conditional tense* to express the idea of 'ought to' or 'should'. The forms of this tense are:

dovrei
dovresti
dovrebbe
dovremmo
dovreste
dovrebbero

dovrei andare	= *I ought to go*
non dovrebbe fare quel rumore	= *it shouldn't make that noise*
dovrebbero arrivare alle undici	= *they should arrive at eleven*

---

divino/divina *adjective*
= divine

divisa *noun, feminine*
una divisa = a uniform

divise, **divisi**, **etc** ▶ **dividere**

divisione *noun, feminine*
una divisione = a division

diviso/divisa ▶ **dividere**

divorziato/divorziata *adjective*
= divorced

divorzio *noun, masculine* (*plural* **divorzi**)
un divorzio = a divorce

dizionario *noun, masculine* (*plural* **dizionari**)
un dizionario = a dictionary

do ▶ **dare**

dobbiamo ▶ **dovere**

doccia *noun, feminine* (*plural* **docce**)
una doccia = a shower
fare una doccia = to have a shower, to take a shower

documentario *noun, masculine* (*plural* **documentari**)
un documentario = a documentary

documento *noun, masculine*
un documento = a document

dodicenne *adjective*
= twelve-year-old

dodicesimo/dodicesima *adjective*
= twelfth

dodici *number*
= twelve

dogana *noun, feminine*
la dogana = customs

doganiere *noun, masculine*
un doganiere = a customs officer

dolce
1 *adjective*
• = sweet
• = gentle
2 *noun, masculine*
un dolce = a dessert
= a cake

dollaro *noun, masculine*
un dollaro = a dollar

dolore *noun, masculine*
un dolore = a pain

✖ in informal situations

domanda *noun, feminine*
  una domanda = a question
  fare una domanda = to ask a question
  una domanda di lavoro = a job
    application

domandare *verb* ①
  1 = to ask
  2 domandarsi (**!** + *essere*)
    domandarsi = to wonder

domani *adverb*
  = tomorrow
  domani l'altro = the day after tomorrow

domattina *adverb*
  = tomorrow morning

domenica *noun, feminine* (*plural*
  domeniche)
  = Sunday
  arrivo domenica = I'm arriving on Sunday
  la domenica = on Sundays

domestico/domestica *adjective*
  (*plural* **domestici/domestiche**)
  = household
  = domestic

donare *verb* ①
  = to donate

donna *noun, feminine*
  una donna = a woman

dono *noun, masculine*
  un dono = a gift

dopo
  1 *preposition*
    = after
  2 *adverb*
    = afterward(s)

dopodomani *adverb*
  = the day after tomorrow

doppio/doppia *adjective*
  = double

dormire *verb* ⑩
  = to sleep

dorso *noun, masculine*
  il dorso = the back

dose *noun, feminine*
  una dose = a dose

dottorato *noun, masculine*
  un dottorato = a doctorate

dottore/dottoressa *noun,*
  masculine|feminine
  un dottore/una dottoressa = a doctor

dove *adverb*
  = where
  dov'è Roberta? = where's Roberta?

dovere
  1 *verb*
    = must

    = to have to
    devo andare = I have to go
  2 *noun, masculine*
    il dovere = duty

dovette, **dovrà**, **dovrebbe**, **etc** ▶
  dovere

dovunque *adverb*
  = everywhere

dozzina *noun, feminine*
  una dozzina = a dozen

dramma *noun, masculine* (*plural*
  drammi)
  un dramma = a drama

drammatico/drammatica *adjective*
  (*plural* **drammatici/drammatiche**)
  = dramatic

dritto/dritta *adjective*
  = straight
  sempre dritto = straight on

droga *noun, feminine* (*plural* **droghe**)
  una droga = a drug
  la droga = drugs

drogarsi *verb* ⑤ (**!** + *essere*)
  = to take drugs

drogato/drogata✶ *noun,*
  masculine|feminine
  un drogato/una drogata = a junkie

dubbio *noun, masculine* (*plural* **dubbi**)
  un dubbio = a doubt
  senza dubbio = no doubt

dubitare *verb* ①
  = to doubt

due *number*
  = two

duecento
  1 *number*
    = two hundred
  2 Duecento *noun, masculine*
    il Duecento = the 13th century

duemila *number*
  = two thousand
  il duemila = the year 2000

dunque *conjunction*
  = so

duomo *noun, masculine*
  il duomo = the cathedral

durante *preposition*
  = during

durare *verb* ① (**!** + *essere*)
  = to last
  quanto dura? = how long does it last?

durata *noun, feminine*
  la durata = the length

duro/dura *adjective*
  = hard

Ee

e (sometimes **ed** *before a vowel*)
conjunction
= and
e gli altri? = what about the others?

è ▶ **essere**

ebbe, **ebbi**, etc ▶ **avere**

ebraico/ebraica *adjective* (*plural*
ebraici/ebraiche)
= Jewish

ebreo/ebrea *noun, masculine/feminine*
un ebreo/un'ebrea = a Jew

ecc *abbreviation*
= etc

eccellente *adjective*
= excellent

eccessivo/eccessiva *adjective*
= excessive

eccetera *adverb*
= et cetera

eccezionale *adjective*
= exceptional

eccezione *noun, feminine*
un'eccezione = an exception

eccitare *verb* [1]
= to arouse

ecco *adverb*
ecco! = here!
eccolo/eccola! = here he is/here she is!
eccomi! = here I am!

eco *noun, feminine* (*plural* **echi**)

> **!** *Note that* **echi** *is masculine.*

un'eco = an echo

ecologico/ecologica *adjective* (*plural*
ecologici/ecologiche)
• = ecological
• = green

economia *noun, feminine*
l'economia = the economy

economico/economica *adjective*
(*plural* **economici/economiche**)
= cheap

ed ▶ **e**

edicola *noun, feminine*
un'edicola = a newsagent's, a newsdealer's

edificio *noun, masculine* (*plural* **edifici**)
un edificio = a building

Edimburgo *noun*
= Edinburgh

editore/editrice *noun,*
masculine/feminine
un editore/un'editrice = a publisher

edizione *noun, feminine*
un'edizione = an edition

educare *verb* [4]
= to bring up

educato/educata *adjective*
= well-behaved

educazione *noun, feminine*
l'educazione = up-bringing

effettivamente *adverb*
= in fact

effettivo/effettiva *adjective*
= real

effetto *noun, masculine*
un effetto = an effect

efficace *adjective*
= effective

efficiente *adjective*
= efficient

egli *pronoun*
= he

egoista *adjective* (*plural*
egoisti/egoiste)
= selfish

elaborare *verb* [1]
= to work out

elefante *noun, masculine*
un elefante = an elephant

elegante *adjective*
= elegant
= smart, well-dressed

eleganza *noun, feminine*
l'eleganza = elegance

eleggere *verb* [39]
= to elect

elementare *adjective*
= elementary

elemento *noun, masculine*
un elemento = an element

elenco *noun, masculine* (*plural* **elenchi**)
un elenco = a list
l'elenco telefonico = the phone book

eletto/eletta ▶ **eleggere**

elettricista *noun, masculine/feminine*
(*plural* **elettricisti/elettriciste**)
un elettricista/un'elettricista = an
electrician

elettrico/elettrica *adjective* (*plural*
elettrici/elettriche)
= electric
= electrical

elettrodomestici *noun, masculine*
plural
gli elettrodomestici = electrical goods

elevato/elevata *adjective*
= high

elezione *noun, feminine*
un'elezione = an election

elicottero *noun, masculine*
un elicottero = a helicopter

eliminare *verb* [1]
= to eliminate

ella *pronoun*
= she

emarginato/emarginata *noun, masculine/feminine*
un emarginato/un'emarginata = an outcast

emergenza *noun, feminine*
un'emergenza = an emergency

emigrare *verb* [1] (**!** + *essere*)
= to emigrate

emigrato/emigrata *noun, masculine/feminine*
un emigrato/un'emigrata = an emigrant

emittente *noun, feminine*
un'emittente = a station

emozionante *adjective*
= exciting

emozionato/emozionata *adjective*
• = excited
• = nervous

emozione *noun, masculine*
l'emozione = the emotion
= the excitement

enciclopedia *noun, feminine*
un'enciclopedia = an encyclopedia

energia *noun, feminine*
l'energia = energy

ennesimo/ennesima *adjective*
= umpteenth

enorme *adjective*
= huge

ente *noun, masculine*
un ente = a body

entrambi/entrambe *adjective*
= both

entrare *verb* (**!** + *essere*)
• = to come in
= to go in
entrare in = to enter
• = to fit
• che c'entra? = what's that got to do with it?

entrata *noun, feminine*
l'entrata = the entrance

entro *preposition*
entro il 5 maggio = by May 5

entusiasmo *noun, masculine*
l'entusiasmo = enthusiasm

entusiasta *adjective* (*plural* entusiasti/entusiaste)
= enthusiastic

epoca *noun, feminine* (*plural* **epoche**)
un'epoca = a time
a quell'epoca = at that time

eppure *conjunction*
= yet

equatore *noun, masculine*
l'equatore = the equator

equilibrio *noun, masculine*
l'equilibrio = balance

equipaggio *noun, masculine* (*plural* equipaggi)
l'equipaggio = the crew

equivalente *adjective*
= equivalent

equo/equa *adjective*
= fair

era, **erano**, **eravamo**, etc ▶ essere

erba *noun, feminine*
• l'erba = grass
• un'erba = a(n) herb

erbaccia *noun, feminine* (*plural* erbacce)
un'erbaccia = a weed

erede *noun, masculine/feminine*
un erede/un'erede = an heir

ereditare *verb* [1]
= to inherit

eri, **ero** ▶ essere

eroe/eroina *noun, masculine/feminine*
un eroe/un'eroina = a hero/a heroine

eroina *noun, feminine*
l'eroina = heroin

errore *noun, masculine*
un errore = a mistake
fare un errore = to make a mistake

esagerare *verb* [1]
= to exaggerate

esame *noun, masculine*
un esame = an exam

esaminare *verb* [1]
= to examine

esatto/esatta
1 ▶ esigere
2 *adjective*
= exact
= correct
esatto! = exactly!

esaurito/esaurita *adjective*
• (*when it's a person*) = run-down
• (*when it's tickets, seats*) = sold out

esausto/esausta *adjective*
= exhausted

esca, **esce**, etc ▶ uscire

escludere *verb* [21]
= to exclude

essere

1 essere functions as an ordinary verb. It forms its perfect tense with **essere**:
= to be

è aperto	= *it's open*
sono io	= *it's me*
erano stanchi	= *they were tired*
dove sei stato?	= *where have you been?*

2 essere is used as an auxiliary verb to form other tenses of certain verbs, marked (**!** + *essere*) in this dictionary, and of all reflexive verbs. The perfect tense uses the present tense of **essere** + the past participle. It is used to talk about events that took place in the fairly recent past, or that have had an effect on the present:

siamo già passati di qua	= *we've already been this way*
ti sei divertita alla festa, Laura?	= *did you enjoy yourself at the party, Laura?*

The pluperfect tense uses the imperfect tense of **essere** + the past participle. It is used to talk about events that happened *before* the event that is the main focus of attention:

ci eravamo conosciuti prima	= *we had met before*

3 essere is used to form the passive:

i motori sono fabbricati in Germania	= *the engines are made in Germany*

4 essere is used with **ci** to mean 'there is', 'there are', etc.

c'è un problema	= *there's a problem*
ce n'erano troppi	= *there were too many*

---

escluse, **esclusi**, etc ▶ **escludere**

escluso/esclusa
1 ▶ **escludere**
2 *adjective*
  martedì escluso = excluding Tuesdays

esco, **escono** ▶ **uscire**

eseguire *verb* 10
  = to carry out

esempio *noun, masculine* (*plural* **esempi**)
  un esempio = an example
  per esempio, ad esempio = for example

esente *adjective*
  = exempt

esercito *noun, masculine*
  l'esercito = the army

esercizio *noun, masculine* (*plural* **esercizi**)
  un esercizio = an exercise

esigente *adjective*
  = demanding

esigenza *noun, feminine*
  un'esigenza = a need
  = a demand

esigere *verb* 36
  = to demand

esistenza *noun, feminine*
  l'esistenza = the existence

esistere *verb* 16 (**!** + *essere*)
  = to exist

esitare *verb* 1
  = to hesitate

esotico/esotica *adjective* (*plural* **esotici/esotiche**)
  = exotic

espansivo/espansiva *adjective*
  = outgoing

esperienza *noun, feminine*
  l'esperienza = experience

esperimento *noun, masculine*
  un esperimento = an experiment

esperto/esperta *noun, masculine/feminine*
  un esperto/un'esperta = an expert

esplodere *verb* 21 (**!** + *essere*)
  = to explode
  far esplodere una macchina = to blow up a car

esplorare *verb* 1
  = to explore

esplose, **esplosero**, etc ▶ **esplodere**

esplosione *noun, feminine*
  un'esplosione = an explosion

esploso/esplosa ▶ **esplodere**

esportazione *noun, feminine*
  l'esportazione = export

esposizione *noun, feminine*
  un'esposizione = an exhibition

espressione *noun, feminine*
  un'espressione = an expression

espresso/espressa
1 ▶ esprimere
2 *noun, masculine*
  un espresso = an espresso

esprimere *verb* 37
  = to express

essa ▶ esso

essenziale *adjective*
  = essential

essi/esse *pronoun*
  = they
  = them

essere ▶ 42 *See the boxed note.*
1 *verb* (**!** + *essere*)
  = to be
2 *noun, masculine*
  un essere = a being

esso/essa *pronoun*
  = it

est *noun, masculine*
  l'est = the east

estate *noun, feminine*
  l'estate = the summer
  d'estate = in summer

esterno/esterna *adjective*
  = outer

estero/estera
1 *adjective*
  = foreign
2 estero *noun, masculine*
  l'estero = overseas
  all'estero = abroad

esteso/estesa *adjective*
  = extensive

estetista *noun, masculine/feminine*
  (*plural* estetisti/estetiste)
  un estetista/un'estetista = a beautician

estinto/estinta *adjective*
  = extinct

estivo/estiva *adjective*
  = summer

estrae, estraggo, etc ▶ estrarre

estrarre *verb* 74
  = to extract

estrasse, estrassero, etc ▶
  estrarre

estratto/estratta
1 ▶ estrarre
2 estratto *noun, masculine*
  un estratto = an extract

estremamente *adverb*
  = extremely

estremo/estrema *adjective*
  = extreme

età *noun, feminine* (**!** *never changes*)
  l'età = age

etichetta *noun, feminine*
  un'etichetta = a label

etnico/etnica *adjective* (*plural*
  etnici/etniche)
  = ethnic

ettaro *noun, masculine*
  un ettaro = a hectare

etto *noun, masculine*
  un etto = a hundred grams

euro *noun, masculine*
  un euro = a euro

europeo/europea *adjective*
  = European

eventuale *adjective*
  = possible
  pagherò gli eventuali danni = I'll pay for
  any damage caused

eventualmente *adverb*
  eventualmente si può cambiare = you can
  change it if necessary

evidente *adjective*
  = obvious

evidentemente *adverb*
  = obviously

evidenza *noun, feminine*
  l'evidenza = the evidence

evitare *verb* 1
  = to avoid
  evitare di fare qualcosa = to avoid doing
  something

evviva *exclamation*
  evviva! = hurray!

Ff

fa
1 ▶ fare
2 *adverb*
  tre anni fa = three years ago
  quanto tempo fa? = how long ago?

fabbrica *noun, feminine* (*plural*
  fabbriche)
  una fabbrica = a factory

faccenda *noun, feminine*
  • una faccenda = a matter
  • fare le faccende = to do the housework

faccia *noun, feminine* (*plural* facce)
  la faccia = the face

faccia, facciamo ▶ fare

facciata *noun, feminine*
  la facciata = the façade

faccio, **facemmo**, **faceva**, etc ▶
fare

facile *adjective*
= easy

facoltà *noun, feminine* (! *never changes*)
una facoltà = a faculty

fagiolino *noun, masculine*
un fagiolino = a green bean

fagiolo *noun, masculine*
un fagiolo = a bean

fai ▶ **fare**

fai da te *noun, masculine*
il fai da te = DIY, do-it-yourself

falegname *noun, masculine*
un falegname = a carpenter

fallire *verb* 9 (! + *essere*)
• = to fail
• = to go out of business

fallito/**fallita** *adjective*
= unsuccessful

fallo *noun, masculine*
un fallo = a foul

falò *noun, masculine* (! *never changes*)
un falò = a bonfire

falso/**falsa** *adjective*
= false
= fake

fama *noun, feminine*
la fama = fame
avere la fama di = to have a reputation
for

fame *noun, feminine*
la fame = hunger
aver fame = to be hungry

famiglia *noun, feminine*
una famiglia = a family

familiare *adjective*
= familiar

famoso/**famosa** *adjective*
= famous

fanale *noun, masculine*
un fanale = a light

fango *noun, masculine*
il fango = mud

fanno ▶ **fare**

fantascienza *noun, feminine*
la fantascienza = science fiction

fantasia *noun, feminine*
• la fantasia = imagination
• una fantasia = a fantasy

fantasma *noun, masculine* (*plural*
fantasmi)
un fantasma = a ghost

fantastico/**fantastica** *adjective*
(*plural* **fantastici**/**fantastiche**)
= fantastic

farcire *verb* 9
= to stuff

fare *verb* 38

> ! You will find translations for phrases
> with **fare** such as **fare colazione**, **fare
> una domanda**, **fare un errore** etc under
> the words **colazione**, **domanda**, **errore**
> etc.

• = to make
  fare un dolce = to make a cake
  il vino si fa con l'uva = wine is made
  from grapes
• = to do
  cosa fai? = what are you doing?
  fare i compiti = to do one's homework
• = to have
  fare una doccia = to have a shower, to
  take a shower
  fare un picnic = to have a picnic
• (*talking about the weather*)
  fa freddo = it's cold
  fa bel tempo = it's nice weather
• (*with the infinitive*)
  l'hai fatto piangere = you made him cry
  mi hai fatto fare un errore = you've made
  me make a mistake
  fammi parlare! = let me speak!
  ho fatto riparare il cancello = I had the
  gate repaired
  mi sono fatta fare un vestito = I had a
  dress made

farfalla *noun, feminine*
una farfalla = a butterfly

farina *noun, feminine*
la farina = flour

farmacia *noun, feminine* (*plural*
farmacie)
una farmacia = a chemist's, a drugstore

faro *noun, masculine*
• un faro = a lighthouse
• i fari = the headlights

fascia *noun, feminine* (*plural* **fasce**)
una fascia = a band
= a bandage

fasciare *verb* 6
= to bandage

fascino *noun, masculine*
il fascino = charm

fascismo *noun, masculine*
il fascismo = Fascism

fascista *adjective* (*plural*
fascisti/**fasciste**)
= Fascist

fase *noun, feminine*
una fase = a phase

fastidio *noun, masculine*
dare fastidio a = to annoy

fatale *adjective*
= fatal

fate ▶ **fare**

fatica *noun, feminine*
una fatica = hard work

faticoso/faticosa *adjective*
= tiring

fatto/fatta
1 ▶ fare
2 **fatto** *noun, masculine*
un fatto = a fact
= an event

fattore *noun, masculine*
• un fattore = a factor
• un fattore = a farmer

fattoria *noun, feminine*
una fattoria = a farm

fattura *noun, feminine*
una fattura = an invoice

favola *noun, feminine*
una favola = a fairy tale

favoloso/favolosa *adjective*
= fabulous

favore *noun, masculine*
un favore = a favo(u)r
per favore = please

favorevole *adjective*
= favo(u)rable

fazzoletto *noun, masculine*
un fazzoletto = a handkerchief

febbraio *noun, masculine*
= February

febbre *noun, feminine*
avere la febbre = to have a temperature

fece, feci, etc ▶ fare

fede *noun, feminine*
• la fede = faith
• una fede = a wedding ring

fedele *adjective*
= faithful

fedeltà *noun, feminine*
la fedeltà = loyalty

federa *noun, feminine*
una federa = a pillowcase

fegato *noun, masculine*
il fegato = the liver

felice *adjective*
= happy

felicità *noun, feminine*
la felicità = happiness

felpa *noun, feminine*
una felpa = a sweatshirt

femmina
1 *adjective*
= female
2 *noun, feminine*
una femmina = a female
= a girl

femminile *adjective*
= female
= feminine

feriale *adjective*
un giorno feriale = a weekday

ferie *noun, feminine plural*
le ferie = the holidays, the vacation
in ferie = on holiday, on vacation

ferire *verb* 9
= to injure
= to wound

ferita *noun, feminine*
una ferita = an injury
= a wound

ferito/ferita
1 *adjective*
= injured
= wounded
2 *noun, masculine/feminine*
un ferito/una ferita = an injured person
i feriti = the injured

fermare *verb* 1
1 = to stop
2 **fermarsi** (! + essere)
fermarsi = to stop

fermata *noun, feminine*
una fermata = a stop

fermo/ferma *adjective*
= stationary
la macchina era ferma = the car wasn't
moving
stai fermo! = stay still!

feroce *adjective*
= fierce

Ferragosto *noun, masculine*
Ferragosto *Italian public holiday on
August 15*

ferro *noun, masculine*
• il ferro = iron
• un ferro (da stiro) = an iron

ferrovia *noun, feminine*
la ferrovia = the railway, the railroad

festa *noun, feminine*
• una festa = a holiday
• una festa = a party

festeggiare *verb* 3
= to celebrate

festivo/festiva *adjective*
un giorno festivo = a holiday

fetta *noun, feminine*
una fetta = a slice

fiamma *noun, feminine*
una fiamma = a flame

fiammifero *noun, masculine*
un fiammifero = a match

fianco *noun, masculine* (*plural* **fianchi**)
• il fianco = the side
• i fianchi = the hips

F

fiasco *noun, masculine* (*plural* **fiaschi**)
• un fiasco di vino = a flask of wine
• un fiasco = a flop

fiato *noun, masculine*
  il fiato = breath

ficcare *verb* [4]
  = to put

fico *noun, masculine* (*plural* **fichi**)
  un fico = a fig
  = a fig tree

fidanzato/fidanzata
1 *adjective*
  = engaged
2 *noun, masculine/feminine*
  un fidanzato/una fidanzata = a fiancé/a
    fiancée

fidarsi *verb* [1] (**!** + *essere*)
  fidarsi di qualcuno = to trust someone

fiducia *noun, feminine*
  la fiducia = trust

fiera *noun, feminine*
  una fiera = a fair

fiero/fiera *adjective*
  = proud

figlio/figlia *noun, masculine/feminine*
  (*plural* **figli/figlie**)
  un figlio/una figlia = a son/a daughter
  i figli = the children

figura *noun, feminine*
• una figura = a figure
• una figura = a picture

figurarsi *verb* [1] (**!** + *essere*)
  = to imagine
  figurati! = imagine that!

fila *noun, feminine*
• una fila = a row
• una fila = a queue, a line

film *noun, masculine* (**!** *never changes*)
  un film = a film, a movie

filmare *verb* [1]
  = to film

filo *noun, masculine*
• un filo = a string
  = a thread
• un filo = a wire

filosofia *noun, feminine*
  la filosofia = philosophy

finale
1 *adjective*
  = final
2 *noun, feminine*
  la finale = the final
3 *noun, masculine*
  il finale = the end

finalmente *adverb*
  = at last
  = finally

finanza *noun, feminine*
  la finanza = finance

finché *conjunction*
  = for as long as
  finché dura = for as long as it lasts
  finché (non) ne arrivano degli altri = until
    some more arrive

fine
1 *noun, feminine*
  la fine = the end
2 *noun, masculine*
  il fine = the aim
3 *adjective*
  = fine

fine settimana *noun, masculine*
  il fine settimana = the weekend

finestra *noun, feminine*
  una finestra = a window

fingere *verb* [48]
  = to pretend

finire *verb* [9] (**!** + *essere or avere*)
  = to finish
  hai finito di mangiare? = have you
    finished eating?

fino a *preposition*
  = until
  = as far as

finora *adverb*
  = so far

finse, **finsi**, **etc** ▶ **fingere**

finta *noun, feminine*
  fare finta di dormire = to pretend to be
    asleep

finto/finta
1 ▶ **fingere**
2 *adjective*
  = false

fiocco *noun, masculine* (*plural* **fiocchi**)
• un fiocco = a bow
  = a bow tie
• un fiocco = a flake

fioraio/fioraia *noun, masculine/feminine*
  (*plural* **fiorai/fioraie**)
  un fioraio/una fioraia = a florist

fiore *noun, masculine*
  un fiore = a flower

fiorentino/fiorentina *adjective*
  = Florentine

Firenze *noun*
  = Florence

firma *noun, feminine*
  una firma = a signature

firmare *verb* [1]
  = to sign

fischiare *verb* [6]
  = to whistle

fischio noun, masculine (plural **fischi**)
un fischio = a whistle

fisica noun, feminine
la fisica = physics

fisico/fisica adjective (plural
fisici/fisiche)
= physical

fissare verb [1]
• = to fix
• = to stare at

fisso/fissa adjective
= fixed
= steady

fitto/fitta adjective
= thick

fiume noun, masculine
un fiume = a river

flauto noun, masculine
un flauto = a flute

fodera noun, feminine
la fodera = the lining

foglia noun, feminine
una foglia = a leaf

foglio noun, masculine (plural **fogli**)
un foglio = a sheet of paper

fogna noun, feminine
una fogna = a drain

folla noun, feminine
una folla = a crowd

folle adjective
= mad, crazy

follia noun, feminine
la follia = madness

fon noun, masculine (**!** never changes)
un fon = a hairdryer

fondamentale adjective
= basic

fondare verb [1]
= to found

fondo noun, masculine
il fondo = the bottom
in fondo alla scatola = at the bottom of
the box
in fondo alla classe = at the back of the
classroom
in fondo al corridoio = at the end of the
corridor

fontana noun, feminine
una fontana = a fountain

fonte noun, feminine
• una fonte = a spring
• una fonte = a source

footing noun, masculine
fare footing = to go jogging

forbici noun, feminine plural
le forbici = scissors

forchetta noun, feminine
una forchetta = a fork

foresta noun, feminine
una foresta = a forest

forfora noun, feminine
la forfora = dandruff

forma noun, feminine
una forma = a form
= a shape
in forma = in good shape

formaggio noun, masculine (plural
formaggi)
il formaggio = cheese

formale adjective
= formal

formare verb [1]
= to form

formica noun, feminine (plural **formiche**)
una formica = an ant

formidabile adjective
= tremendous

fornaio/fornaia noun,
masculine/feminine (plural **fornai/fornaie**)
un fornaio/una fornaia = a baker

fornire verb [9]
= to supply

forno noun, masculine
un forno = an oven
un forno a microonde = a microwave

foro noun, masculine
un foro = a hole

forse adverb
= perhaps

forte
1 adjective
= strong
2 adverb
= hard
pioveva forte = it was raining heavily
parlare forte = to talk loudly

fortuna noun, feminine
la fortuna = luck
avere fortuna = to be lucky

fortunato/fortunata adjective
= lucky

forza noun, feminine
• la forza = strength
= force
• forza! = come on!

foschia noun, feminine
la foschia = mist

fossa noun, feminine
una fossa = a hole

fosso noun, masculine
un fosso = a ditch

fosti, **foste**, etc ▶ essere

F

foto noun, feminine (**!** never changes)
  una foto = a photo
  fare una foto a qualcuno = to take a
    photo of someone

fotocopia noun, feminine
  una fotocopia = a photocopy

fotocopiare verb [6]
  = to photocopy

fotografare verb [1]
  = to photograph

fotografia noun, feminine
  • **una fotografia** = a photograph
  • **la fotografia** = photography

fotografo/fotografa noun,
  masculine/feminine
  un fotografo/una fotografa = a
    photographer

foulard noun, masculine (**!** never
  changes)
  un foulard = a scarf

fra, tra preposition
  • = between
  = among
  • **fra due anni** = in two years' time
  fra poco = soon

fragile adjective
  = fragile

fragola noun, feminine
  una fragola = a strawberry

frana noun, feminine
  una frana = a landslide

francese adjective
  = French

Francia noun, feminine
  la Francia = France

franco/franca (plural
  franchi/franche)
1 adjective
  = frank
2 **franco** noun, masculine
  un franco = a franc

francobollo noun, masculine
  un francobollo = a stamp

frase noun, feminine
  una frase = a sentence

fratello noun, masculine
  un fratello = a brother
  i fratelli = brothers and sisters

frattempo noun, masculine
  nel frattempo = meanwhile

frattura noun, feminine
  una frattura = a fracture

fratturare verb [1]
  = to fracture

frazione noun, feminine
  una frazione = a fraction

freccia noun, feminine (plural **frecce**)
  • **una freccia** = an arrow
  • (on a car)
  la freccia = the indicator

freddo/fredda
1 adjective
  = cold
2 **freddo** noun, masculine
  il freddo = cold
  avere freddo = to be cold
  fa freddo = it's cold

fregare verb [5]
1 (**!** + avere)
  • = to rub
  • **✘** = to pinch, to swipe
  • **✘** = to cheat
2 **fregarsene✘** (**!** + essere)
  me ne frego = I don't give a damn

frenare verb [1]
  = to brake

freno noun, masculine
  un freno = a brake

frequentare verb [1]
  • = to go to
  • = to hang around with

frequente adjective
  = frequent

fresco/fresca adjective (plural
  freschi/fresche)
  • = fresh
  • = cool

fretta noun, feminine
  avere fretta = to be in a hurry
  in fretta = quickly

friggere verb [39]
  = to fry

frigorifero noun, masculine
  un frigorifero = a fridge

frittata noun, feminine
  una frittata = an omelet(te)

fritto/fritta
1 ▶ **friggere**
2 adjective
  = fried

frizione noun, feminine
  la frizione = the clutch

frizzante adjective
  = fizzy

fronte
1 noun, feminine
  la fronte = the forehead
2 noun, masculine
  un fronte = a front
3 **di fronte a** preposition
  = opposite
  di fronte alla banca = opposite the bank

frontiera noun, feminine
  la frontiera = the border

✘ in informal situations

frullato *noun, masculine*
  un frullato = a milk shake

frutta *noun, feminine*
  la frutta = fruit

fruttivendolo/**fruttivendola** *noun,*
masculine/feminine
  un fruttivendolo/una fruttivendola = a
  greengrocer

frutto *noun, masculine*
  un frutto = a piece of fruit

fu ▶ **essere**

fucile *noun, masculine*
  un fucile = a gun

fuga *noun, feminine (plural* **fughe)**
• una fuga = an escape
• una fuga = a leak

fuggire *verb* ⑩ (! + *essere*)
  = to flee

fui ▶ **essere**

fulminare *verb* ①
1 essere fulminato = to be struck by
  lightning
2 fulminarsi (! + *essere*)
  si è fulminata la lampadina = the bulb
  has gone

fulmine *noun, masculine*
  un fulmine = a flash of lightning
  i fulmini = lightning

fumare *verb* ①
  = to smoke

fumatore/**fumatrice** *noun,*
masculine/feminine
  un fumatore/una fumatrice = a smoker
  fumatori o non fumatori? = smoking or
  non-smoking?

fumetto *noun, masculine*
  un fumetto = a cartoon

fummo ▶ **essere**

fumo *noun, masculine*
• il fumo = smoke
• il fumo = smoking

funerale *noun, masculine*
  un funerale = a funeral

fungo *noun, masculine (plural* **funghi)**
  un fungo = a mushroom

funzionare *verb* ①
  = to work
  far funzionare = to operate

funzione *noun, feminine*
  una funzione = a function

fuoco *noun, masculine (plural* **fuochi)**
  un fuoco = a fire
  dare fuoco a una casa = to set fire to a
  house
i fuochi d'artificio = fireworks

fuori *adverb*
  = out
  = outside
  fuori dell'Italia = outside Italy

furbo/**furba** *adjective*
  = clever, smart
  = cunning

furgone *noun, masculine*
  un furgone = a van

furono ▶ **essere**

furto *noun, masculine*
  un furto = a theft

futuro/**futura**
1 *adjective*
  = future
2 futuro *noun, masculine*
  il futuro = the future

G

Gg

gabbia *noun, feminine*
  una gabbia = a cage

gabinetto *noun, masculine*
  il gabinetto = the toilet, the bathroom

galeraˣ *noun, feminine*
  in galera = in jail

galleggiare *verb* ③
  = to float

galleria *noun, feminine*
• una galleria = a gallery
• una galleria = a tunnel

Galles *noun, masculine*
  il Galles = Wales

gallese *adjective*
  = Welsh

gallina *noun, feminine*
  una gallina = a hen

gallo *noun, masculine*
  un gallo = a cock, a rooster

gamba *noun, feminine*
  una gamba = a leg

gamberetto *noun, masculine*
  un gamberetto = a shrimp

gambero *noun, masculine*
  un gambero = a prawn, a shrimp

gancio *noun, masculine (plural* **ganci)**
  un gancio = a hook

gara *noun, feminine*
  una gara = a race
  = a competition

garantire verb 9
= to guarantee

garanzia noun, feminine
una garanzia = a guarantee

gas noun, masculine (! never changes)
il gas = gas

gasolio noun, masculine
il gasolio = diesel

gassato/gassata adjective
= fizzy

gatto/gatta noun, masculine/feminine
un gatto/una gatta = a cat

gelare verb 1 (! + essere or avere)
= to freeze

gelateria noun, feminine
una gelateria = an ice cream parlo(u)r

gelato/gelata
1 adjective
= frozen
2 gelato noun, masculine
il gelato = ice cream

gelido/gelida adjective
= freezing

gelo noun, masculine
il gelo = frost

geloso/gelosa adjective
= jealous

gemello/gemella noun,
masculine/feminine
1 i gemelli = twins
2 Gemelli
= Gemini

generale
1 adjective
= general
2 noun, masculine
un generale = a general

generazione noun, feminine
una generazione = a generation

genere noun, masculine
un genere = a kind

genero noun, masculine
un genero = a son-in-law

generoso/generosa adjective
= generous

geniale adjective
= brilliant

genio noun, masculine (plural **geni**)
un genio = a genius

genitore noun, masculine
un genitore = a parent
i miei genitori = my parents

gennaio noun, masculine
= January

Genova noun
= Genoa

genovese adjective
= Genoese

gente noun, feminine (! never changes)
la gente = people
c'era troppa gente = there were too many
people

gentile adjective
= kind

gentilezza noun, feminine
la gentilezza = kindness

geografia noun, feminine
la geografia = geography

geometra noun, masculine/feminine
(plural **geometri/geometre**)
un/una geometra = a quantity surveyor

Germania noun, feminine
la Germania = Germany

gesso noun, masculine
il gesso = chalk

gestione noun, feminine
la gestione = the management

gestire verb 9
= to run

gesto noun, masculine
un gesto = a gesture

gettare verb 1
= to throw

gettone noun, masculine
un gettone = a telephone token

ghiaccio noun, masculine
il ghiaccio = ice

già adverb
= already
sono già partiti = they've already left

giacca noun, feminine (plural **giacche**)
una giacca = a jacket
una giacca a vento = a windcheater, a
windbreaker

giaccone noun, masculine
un giaccone = a jacket

giallo/gialla adjective
= yellow

Giappone noun, masculine
il Giappone = Japan

giapponese adjective
= Japanese

giardino noun, masculine
un giardino = a garden, a yard

gigante noun, masculine
un gigante = a giant

gilè noun, masculine (! never changes)
un gilè = a waistcoat, a vest

ginnastica noun, feminine
la ginnastica = gymnastics

ginocchio *noun, masculine (plural* **ginocchia***)*

> **!** *Note that* **ginocchia** *is feminine.*

un ginocchio = a knee

giocare *verb* 4
• = to play
  giocare a tennis = to play tennis
• = to bet
  = to gamble

giocatore/giocatrice *noun,*
masculine/feminine
• un giocatore/una giocatrice = a player
• un giocatore/una giocatrice = a gambler

giocattolo *noun, masculine*
un giocattolo = a toy

gioco *noun, masculine (plural* **giochi***)*
• un gioco = a game
  fare un gioco = to play a game
• il gioco = gambling

gioia *noun, feminine*
la gioia = joy

gioielleria *noun, feminine*
una gioielleria = a jewel(l)er's shop

gioiello *noun, masculine*
un gioiello = a jewel
i gioielli = jewel(l)ery

giornalaio/giornalaia *noun,*
masculine/feminine (plural
giornalai/giornalaie*)*
un giornalaio/una giornalaia = a
  newsagent, a newsdealer

giornale *noun, masculine*
un giornale = a newspaper

giornalismo *noun, masculine*
il giornalismo = journalism

giornalista *noun, masculine/feminine*
(plural **giornalisti/giornaliste***)*
un/una giornalista = a journalist

giornata *noun, feminine*
una giornata = a day

giorno *noun, masculine*
un giorno = a day

giovane
1 *adjective*
  = young
2 *noun, masculine/feminine*
  un/una giovane = a young person
  i giovani = the young

giovedì *noun, masculine (***!** *never*
changes)
  = Thursday
  arrivo giovedì = I'm arriving (on)
    Thursday
  il giovedì = on Thursdays

gioventù *noun, feminine*
la gioventù = youth

girare *verb* 1
1 (**!** + *avere*)

• = to turn (over)
• = to walk around
• mi gira la testa = I feel dizzy
• girare un film = to shoot a film
2 girarsi (**!** + *essere*)
  = to turn (around)

girasole *noun, masculine*
un girasole = a sunflower

giro *noun, masculine*
• un giro = a tour
  fare il giro di = to go around
• prendere in giro qualcuno = to make fun
    of someone

gironzolare *verb* 1
  = to hang around

gita *noun, feminine*
una gita = a trip

giù *adverb*
  = down
  porto giù la valigia = I'll take the case
    downstairs

giubbotto *noun, masculine*
un giubbotto = a jacket

giudicare *verb* 4
  = to judge

giudice *noun, masculine*
un giudice = a judge

giudizio *noun, masculine (plural* **giudizi***)*
un giudizio = a judg(e)ment

giugno *noun, masculine*
  = June

giungla *noun, feminine*
una giungla = a jungle

giurare *verb* 1
  = to swear

giuria *noun, feminine*
la giuria = the jury

giustizia *noun, feminine*
la giustizia = justice

giusto/giusta *adjective*
• = right
• = fair
  = just

gli ▶ **il**

gli/le *pronoun*
  = to him/to her

> **!** *Note that in spoken Italian* **gli** *is often
> used to mean 'to her' or 'to them'.*

gli ho detto la verità = I told
  him/her/them the truth

> **!** *When* **gli** *or* **le** *come immediately
> before* **lo/la**, **li/le**, *or* **ne**, *they combine
> to form* **glielo/gliela**, **glieli/gliele**, *and*
> **gliene**.

gliene ho dato un po' = I gave him some

glielo/gliela, glieli/gliele, gliene
▶ **gli**

goccia noun, feminine (plural **gocce**)
una goccia = a drop

goccio noun, masculine
un goccio di = a drop of

gocciolare verb [1]
= to drip

gol noun, masculine (! never changes)
un gol = a goal

gola noun, feminine
la gola = the throat

golf noun, masculine (! never changes)
• il golf = golf
• un golf = a cardigan

golfo noun, masculine
un golfo = a gulf

goloso/golosa adjective
= greedy

gomito noun, masculine
il gomito = the elbow

gomma noun, feminine
• la gomma = rubber
• una gomma = an eraser
• una gomma = a tyre, a tire

gonfiare verb [6]
1 = to inflate
2 **gonfiarsi** (! + essere)
= to swell (up)

gonfio/gonfia adjective
= swollen

gonna noun, feminine
una gonna = a skirt

gotico/gotica adjective (plural
gotici/gotiche)
= Gothic

governo noun, masculine
il governo = the government

gradevole adjective
= pleasant

gradino noun, masculine
un gradino = a step

grado noun, masculine
un grado = a degree
trenta gradi = 30°C

graduale adjective
= gradual

graffiare verb [6]
= to scratch

graffio noun, masculine (plural **graffi**)
un graffio = a scratch

grafico noun, masculine (plural **grafici**)
• un grafico = a graph
• un grafico = a graphic designer

grammatica noun, feminine
la grammatica = grammar

grammo noun, masculine
un grammo = a gram

gran ▶ grande

Gran Bretagna noun, feminine
la Gran Bretagna = Great Britain

granché pronoun
non era un granché = it was nothing
special

granchio noun, masculine (plural
granchi)
un granchio = a crab

grande adjective (! sometimes **gran**
before a noun)
• = big
• = great
• = grown-up

grandezza noun, feminine
la grandezza = size

grandinare verb [1]
= to hail

grandine noun, feminine
la grandine = hail

grano noun, masculine
• un grano = a grain
• il grano = wheat

granturco noun, masculine
il granturco = maize, corn

grappolo noun, masculine
un grappolo d'uva = a bunch of grapes

grasso/grassa adjective
• = fat
• = fatty
= greasy

gratis adverb
= free

grato/grata adjective
= grateful

grattugia noun, feminine (plural
grattugie)
una grattugia = a grater

grattugiare verb [3]
= to grate

gratuito/gratuita adjective
= free

grave adjective
= serious

gravidanza noun, feminine
la gravidanza = pregnancy

gravità noun, feminine
• la gravità = seriousness
• la gravità = gravity

grazia noun, feminine
la grazia = grace

grazie exclamation
grazie! = thank you!

grazioso/graziosa adjective
= pretty

Grecia noun, feminine
la Grecia = Greece

greco/greca adjective (plural
greci/greche)
= Greek

grida ▶ **grido**

gridare verb ①
= to shout

grido noun, masculine (plural **grida**)
❗ Note that **grida** is feminine.
un grido = a shout

grigio/grigia adjective (plural
grigi/grigie)
= grey, gray

griglia noun, feminine
una griglia = a grill
alla griglia = grilled

grillo noun, masculine
un grillo = a cricket

grosso/grossa adjective
= big

gruppo noun, masculine
un gruppo = a group

guadagnare verb ①
= to earn

guaio noun, masculine (plural **guai**)
un guaio = a problem
essere nei guai = to be in trouble

guancia noun, feminine (plural **guance**)
una guancia = a cheek

guanciale noun, masculine
un guanciale = a pillow

guanto noun, masculine
un guanto = a glove

guardare verb ①
• = to look at
= to watch
• guardare un bambino = to look after a
child

guardia noun, feminine
una guardia = a guard

guarire verb ⑨ (❗ + essere)
= to get better

guasto/guasta
1 adjective
= out of order
2 **guasto** noun, masculine
un guasto = a fault

guerra noun, feminine
una guerra = a war

gufo noun, masculine
un gufo = an owl

guida noun, feminine
• una guida = a guide
• la guida = driving

guidare verb ①
= to drive

gusto noun, masculine
• il gusto = taste
• un gusto = a flavo(u)r

Hh

ha, **hai** ▶ **avere**

handicappato/handicappata
adjective
= handicapped

hanno, **ho** ▶ **avere**

Ii

i ▶ **il**

idea noun, feminine
un'idea = an idea
non ne ho idea = I've no idea

ideale adjective
= ideal

identico/identica adjective (plural
identici/identiche)
= identical

identificare verb ④
= to identify

identità noun, feminine (❗ never
changes)
un'identità = an identity

idiota noun, masculine|feminine (plural
idioti/idiote)
un idiota/un'idiota = an idiot

idraulico noun, masculine (plural
idraulici)
un idraulico = a plumber

ieri adverb
= yesterday
ieri l'altro = the day before yesterday

igienico/igienica adjective (plural
igienici/igieniche)
= hygienic

ignorante adjective
= ignorant

ignorare verb [1]
• = to ignore
• = not to know

il determiner

> **!** Note that **il** can have the forms **lo**, **l'**,
> **la**, **i**, **gli**, **le**. Look at the notes on **the**,
> The human body, and Countries,
> cities, and continents for more detailed
> information.

• = the
  il Colosseo = the Colosseum
  la Torre Pendente = the Leaning Tower
  dove ho messo l'ombrello? = where did I
    put my umbrella?
  non ho la macchina = I don't have a car
  chiudi gli occhi! = close your eyes!

> **!** Note that **il**, **la**, etc are sometimes not
> translated.

  le sigarette sono care = cigarettes are
    expensive
  non mi piace il vino = I don't like wine
  la Francia = France
  il Vesuvio = Vesuvius
• **il lunedì** = on Mondays
• **le tre** = three o'clock
  sono le ventidue = it's 10 pm
• **nel 1265** = in 1265

illegale adjective
  = illegal

illuminare verb [1]
  = to light (up)

illusione noun, feminine
  un'illusione = an illusion

imbarazzato/imbarazzata adjective
  = embarrassed

imbarazzo noun, masculine
  l'imbarazzo = embarrassment
  mettere in imbarazzo = to embarrass

imbarco noun, masculine
  l'imbarco = boarding

imbecille noun, masculine/feminine
  un imbecille/un'imbecille = an idiot

imbiancare verb [4]
  = to paint

imbrogliare verb [6]
  = to cheat

imbroglio noun, masculine (plural
  imbrogli)
  un imbroglio = a trick

imbucare verb [4]
  = to post, to mail

imitare verb [1]
  = to imitate

imitazione noun, feminine
  un'imitazione = an imitation

immaginare verb [1]
  = to imagine

immaginazione noun, feminine
  l'immaginazione = imagination

immagine noun, feminine
  un'immagine = an image
    = a picture

immediato/immediata adjective
  = immediate

immenso/immensa adjective
  = huge

immersione noun, feminine
  un'immersione = a dive

immigrato/immigrata noun,
  masculine/feminine
  un immigrato/un'immigrata = an
    immigrant

imparare verb [1]
  = to learn
  imparare a guidare = to learn to drive

impaziente adjective
  = impatient

impazzire verb [9] (**!** + essere)
  = to go crazy

impedire verb [9]
• = to block
• **impedire a qualcuno di fare qualcosa**
    = to prevent someone from doing
    something

impegnarsi verb [1] (**!** + essere)
  = to work hard

impegnato/impegnata adjective
• = busy
• = committed

impegno noun, masculine
• **un impegno** = a commitment
  domani ho un impegno = I'm busy
    tomorrow
• **l'impegno** = determination
    = effort

imperatore/imperatrice noun,
  masculine/feminine
  un imperatore/un'imperatrice = an
    emperor/an empress

impermeabile noun, masculine
  un impermeabile = a raincoat

impero noun, masculine
  un impero = an empire

impiccare verb [4]
  = to hang

impiegare verb [5]
  = to use

impiegato/impiegata noun,
  masculine/feminine
  un impiegato/un'impiegata = an office
    worker

impiego noun, masculine (plural
  impieghi)
  un impiego = a job
  trovare impiego = to find work

imporre verb [50]
= to impose

importante adjective
= important

importanza noun, feminine
l'importanza = importance
non ha importanza = it's not important

importare verb [1]
• (! + essere) = to matter
non m'importa = I don't care
• (! + avere) = to import

importazione noun, feminine
un'importazione = an import

impossibile adjective
= impossible

imprenditore/imprenditrice noun,
masculine/feminine
un imprenditore/un'imprenditrice = a
businessman/a businesswoman

impresa noun, feminine
un'impresa = a business

impressionante adjective
= shocking

impressione noun, feminine
un'impressione = an impression

imprevisto/imprevista
1 adjective
= unforeseen
2 imprevisto noun masculine
gli imprevisti = unexpected things

improbabile adjective
= improbable

improvvisamente adverb
= suddenly

improvviso/improvvisa adjective
= sudden
d'improvviso = suddenly

in preposition

> ! Note that **in** combines with **il**, **la**, etc.
> **In** + **il** = **nel**; **in** + **l'** = **nell'**; **in** + **lo**
> = **nello**; **in** + **i** = **nei**; **in** + **gli** = **negli**;
> **in** + **la** = **nella**; **in** + **le** = **nelle**.

• = in
vivo in Italia = I live in Italy
• = to
vado in Svizzera = I'm going to
Switzerland
• (means of transport) = by
in bicicletta = by bike
• siamo in nove = there are nine of us

inaccettabile adjective
= unacceptable

incantevole adjective
= charming

incapace adjective
essere incapace di fare qualcosa = to be
incapable of doing something

incazzato/incazzata adjective
= pissed off

incendio noun, masculine (plural
incendi)
un incendio = a fire

incertezza noun, feminine
l'incertezza = uncertainty

incerto/incerta adjective
= uncertain

inchiesta noun, feminine
un'inchiesta = an enquiry

inchiostro noun, masculine
l'inchiostro = ink

inciampare verb [1]
inciampare in = to stumble over

incidente noun, masculine
un incidente = an accident

incinta adjective
= pregnant

incirca adverb
all'incirca = approximately

incluso/inclusa adjective
= included
= including

incollare verb [1]
= to stick

incomprensibile adjective
= incomprehensible

incontrare verb [1]
= to meet
= to encounter

incontro noun, masculine
un incontro = a meeting

incoraggiare verb [3]
= to encourage

incosciente adjective
= irresponsible

incredibile adjective
= incredible

incrocio noun, masculine (plural
incroci)
un incrocio = a junction

incubo noun, masculine
un incubo = a nightmare

indagare verb [5]
= to investigate

indagine noun, feminine
un'indagine = an investigation

indeciso/indecisa adjective
• = undecided
• = indecisive

indicare verb [4]
= to indicate

indicato/indicata adjective
= suitable

indicazione *noun, feminine*
• un'indicazione = an indication
• le indicazioni = directions

indice *noun, masculine*
• un indice = an index
• l'indice = the index finger

indietro *adverb*
essere indietro = to be behind
tornare indietro = to go back
all'indietro = backwards

indifferente *adjective*
= indifferent
per me è indifferente = it's all the same to
me

indipendente *adjective*
= independent

indipendenza *noun, feminine*
l'indipendenza = independence

indiretto/indiretta *adjective*
= indirect

indirizzo *noun, masculine*
un indirizzo = an address
un indirizzo email = an email address

individuale *adjective*
= individual

individuare *verb* 1
= to identify

individuo *noun, masculine*
un individuo = an individual

indizio *noun, masculine (plural indizi)*
un indizio = a clue

indossare *verb* 1
= to wear

indovinare *verb* 1
= to guess

industria *noun, feminine*
l'industria = industry

inevitabile *adjective*
= inevitable

infanzia *noun, feminine*
l'infanzia = childhood

infarto *noun, masculine*
un infarto = a heart attack

infastidire *verb* 9
= to irritate

infatti *conjunction*
= indeed
infatti! = exactly!

infelice *adjective*
= unhappy

inferiore *adjective*
= lower
= inferior

infermiere/infermiera *noun,*
masculine/feminine
un infermiere/un'infermiera = a nurse

inferno *noun, masculine*
l'inferno = hell

infezione *noun, feminine*
un'infezione = an infection

infine *adverb*
= finally

infinito/infinita *adjective*
= infinite

inflazione *noun, feminine*
l'inflazione = inflation

influenza *noun, feminine*
• un'inflenza = an influence
• l'influenza = flu

informale *adjective*
= informal

informare *verb* 1
1 = to inform
2 **informarsi** (! + *essere*)
informarsi di = to find out about

informatica *noun, feminine*
l'informatica = information technology

informazione *noun, feminine*
un'informazione = a piece of information
l'informazione = information

ingannare *verb* 1
= to trick

ingegnere *noun, masculine*
un ingegnere = an engineer

ingegneria *noun, feminine*
l'ingegneria = engineering

Inghilterra *noun, feminine*
l'Inghilterra = England

inghiottire *verb* 9
= to swallow

inglese *adjective*
= English

ingrandimento *noun, masculine*
un ingrandimento = an enlargement

ingrassare *verb* 1 (! + *essere*)
= to put on weight

ingrediente *noun, masculine*
un ingrediente = an ingredient

ingresso *noun, masculine*
l'ingresso = the entrance

iniziale
1 *adjective*
= initial
2 *noun, feminine*
le iniziali = the initials

iniziare *verb* 6 (! + *essere* or *avere*)
= to start

inizio *noun, masculine (plural inizi)*
l'inizio = the beginning

innamorarsi verb ① (! + *essere*)
= to fall in love

innamorato/innamorata adjective
essere innamorato/innamorata di qualcuno = to be in love with someone

innocente adjective
= innocent

inoltre adverb
= besides

inquilino/inquilina noun, *masculine/feminine*
un inquilino/un'inquilina = a tenant

inquinamento noun, *masculine*
l'inquinamento = pollution

inquinare verb ①
= to pollute

insalata noun, *feminine*
l'insalata = salad

insegna noun, *feminine*
un'insegna = a sign

insegnamento noun, *masculine*
l'insegnamento = teaching

insegnante noun, *masculine/feminine*
un insegnante/un'insegnante = a teacher

insegnare verb ①
= to teach

inserire verb ⑨
= to insert

insetto noun, *masculine*
un insetto = an insect

insieme adverb
= together
insieme a noi = together with us

insistere verb ⑯
insistere su = to insist on

insolito/insolita adjective
= unusual

insomma adverb
= well
insomma! = really!

insopportabile adjective
= unbearable

installare verb ①
= to install

insultare verb
= to insult

intanto adverb
= meanwhile

integrale adjective
• = complete
• **pane integrale** = wholemeal bread

intelligente adjective
= intelligent

intendere verb ㊾
• = to intend

• = to mean
• = to understand

intenditore/intenditrice noun, *masculine/feminine*
un intenditore/un'intenditrice = a connoisseur

intensivo/intensiva adjective
= intensive

intenso/intensa adjective
= intense

intenzione noun, *feminine*
un'intenzione = an intention
ho intenzione di smettere = I intend to stop

interessante adjective
= interesting

interessare verb ①
= to interest

interesse noun, *masculine*
• **l'interesse** = interest
• (*in a bank*)
gli interessi = interest

interiore adjective
= inner

internazionale adjective
= international

Internet noun, *masculine*
l'Internet = the Internet

interno/interna
1 adjective
= internal
= inside
2 interno noun, *masculine*
l'interno = the inside

intero/intera adjective
= whole

interpretare verb ①
= to interpret

interpretazione noun, *feminine*
un'interpretazione = an interpretation

interprete noun, *masculine/feminine*
• **un interprete/un'interprete** = an interpreter
• **un interprete/un'interprete** = a performer

interrogare verb ⑤
• = to interrogate
• (*in school*) = to test

interrompere verb ㊿
= to interrupt

interrotto/interrotta, **interruppe**, etc ▶ **interrompere**

interruttore noun, *masculine*
un interruttore = a switch

interruzione noun, *feminine*
un'interruzione = an interruption

interurbana noun, *feminine*
un'interurbana = a long-distance call

intervallo noun, masculine
un intervallo = an interval, an
   intermission

intervengo, **intervengono**, **etc** ▶
   intervenire

intervenire verb 78 (**!** + essere)
= to intervene
= to take part

intervento noun, masculine
• l'intervento = the intervention
• un intervento chirurgico = an operation

interviene, **intervenuto**/
   intervenuta, **etc** ▶ **intervenire**

intervista noun, feminine
un'intervista = an interview

intervistare verb 1
= to interview

intese, **inteso**/**intesa**, **etc**
1 ▶ **intendere**
2 adjective
   siamo intesi? = is that understood?

intimo/**intima** adjective
= intimate

intorno
1 adverb
   = around
2 **intorno a** preposition
   = around
   intorno al tavolo = around the table

introdotto/**introdotta** ▶ **introdurre**

introdurre verb 54
• = to introduce
• = to insert

introdusse, **introdussero**, **etc** ▶
   introdurre

introduzione noun, feminine
l'introduzione = the introduction

inutile adjective
= useless
   è inutile che tu piangi = it's a waste of
   time crying

invadere verb 46
= to invade

invasione noun, feminine
un'invasione = an invasion

invase, **invaso**/**invasa**, **etc** ▶
   invadere

invecchiare verb 6 (**!** + essere)
= to get old

invece adverb
= instead
   invece di = instead of

inventare verb 1
= to invent

invenzione noun, feminine
un'invenzione = an invention

invernale adjective
= winter

inverno noun, masculine
l'inverno = winter
d'inverno = in winter

investimento noun, masculine
un investimento = an investment

investire verb 9
• = to invest
• = to knock down

inviare verb 7
= to send

invidiare verb 6
= to envy

invisibile adjective
= invisible

invitare verb 1
= to invite

invitato/**invitata** noun,
   masculine/feminine
un invitato/un'invitata = a guest

invito noun, masculine
un invito = an invitation

io pronoun
= I
   sono io = it's me

ipotesi noun, feminine (**!** never changes)
un'ipotesi = a hypothesis

Irlanda noun, feminine
l'Irlanda = Ireland
l'Irlanda del Nord = Northern Ireland

irlandese adjective
= Irish

ironico/**ironica** adjective (plural
   ironici/**ironiche**)
= ironic

irregolare adjective
= irregular

irresistibile adjective
= irresistible

irresponsabile adjective
= irresponsible

irritare verb 1
= to irritate

iscritto/**iscritta**
1 ▶ **iscriversi**
2 noun, masculine/feminine
   un iscritto/un'iscritta = a member

iscriversi verb 65 (**!** + essere)
= to enrol(l)

iscrizione noun, feminine
l'iscrizione = enrol(l)ment

isola noun, feminine
un'isola = an island

isolato/isolata
1 *adjective*
= isolated
2 **isolato** *noun, masculine*
un isolato = a block

ispettore/ispettrice *noun,*
masculine/feminine
un ispettore/un'ispettrice = an inspector

ispezione *noun, feminine*
un'ispezione = an inspection

ispirare *verb* [1]
= to inspire

ispirazione *noun, feminine*
l'ispirazione = inspiration

istante *noun, masculine*
un istante = an instant

istinto *noun, masculine*
l'istinto = instinct

istituto *noun, masculine*
un istituto = an institute

istituzione *noun, feminine*
un'istituzione = an institution

istruzione *noun, feminine*
• l'istruzione = education
• le istruzioni = the instructions

Italia *noun, feminine*
l'Italia = Italy

italiano/italiana *adjective*
= Italian

IVA *noun, feminine*
l'IVA = VAT

Iugoslavia, etc ▶ Jugoslavia, etc

Jugoslavia *noun, feminine*
la Jugoslavia = Yugoslavia

jugoslavo/jugoslava *adjective*
= Yugoslavian

krapfen *noun, masculine* (**!** *never*
changes)
un krapfen = a doughnut

l'
1 ▶ il
2 ▶ lo/la

la
1 ▶ il
2 ▶ lo/la

là *adverb*
= there

labbro *noun, masculine* (*plural* **labbra**)
  ! *Note that* **labbra** *is feminine.*
il labbro = the lip

lacca *noun, feminine*
la lacca = hairspray

laccio *noun, masculine* (*plural* **lacci**)
i lacci = shoelaces

lacrima *noun, feminine*
una lacrima = a tear

ladro/ladra *noun, masculine/feminine*
un ladro/una ladra = a thief

laggiù *adverb*
= down there
= over there

lago *noun, masculine* (*plural* **laghi**)
un lago = a lake

lama *noun, feminine*
una lama = a blade

lamentarsi *verb* [1] (**!** + *essere*)
= to complain

lametta *noun, feminine*
una lametta = a razor blade

lampada *noun, feminine*
una lampada = a lamp

lampadina *noun, feminine*
una lampadina = a bulb

lampo *noun, masculine*
un lampo = a flash of lightning
i lampi = lightning

lampone *noun, masculine*
un lampone = a raspberry

lana *noun, feminine*
la lana = wool

lanciare *verb* [2]
• = to throw
• = to launch

larghezza *noun, feminine*
la larghezza = width

largo/larga *adjective* (*plural* **larghi/**
larghe)
= wide

J
K
L

lasciare verb [6]
- = to leave
  lasciami stare! = leave me alone!
- = to let
  lasciami passare! = let me past!

lassù adverb
= up there

laterale adjective
= side

latino noun, masculine
il latino = Latin

lato noun, masculine
un lato = a side

latte noun, masculine
il latte = milk

lattina noun, feminine
una lattina = a can

laurea noun, feminine
una laurea = a degree

laurearsi verb [1] (**!** + essere)
= to graduate

laureato/laureata adjective
essere laureato/laureata in lingue = to have a degree in languages

lavaggio noun, masculine (plural **lavaggi**)
il lavaggio = washing
il lavaggio a secco = dry cleaning

lavagna noun, feminine
la lavagna = the board

lavandino noun, masculine
un lavandino = a sink

lavare verb [1]
= to wash
mi sono lavato le mani = I washed my hands

lavastoviglie noun, feminine (**!** never changes)
una lavastoviglie = a dishwasher

lavatrice noun, feminine
una lavatrice = a washing machine

lavello noun, masculine
un lavello = a sink

lavorare verb [1]
= to work

lavoratore/lavoratrice noun, masculine/feminine
un lavoratore/una lavoratrice = a worker

lavoro noun, masculine
il lavoro = work
un lavoro = a job

le
1 ▶ **il**
2 ▶ **li/le**
3 ▶ **gli/le**

leccare verb [4]
= to lick

lega noun, feminine (plural **leghe**)
- **una lega** = a league
- **una lega** = an alloy

legale adjective
= legal

legame noun, masculine
un legame = a link

legare verb [5]
= to tie (up)

legge noun, feminine
la legge = the law

leggenda noun, feminine
una leggenda = a legend

leggere verb [39]
= to read

leggermente adverb
= slightly

leggero/leggera adjective
- = light
- = slight

legno noun, masculine
il legno = wood
una sedia di legno = a wooden chair

lei pronoun
- = she
  = her
- = you

lente noun, feminine
una lente = a lens
una lente a contatto = a contact lens

lenticchia noun, feminine
una lenticchia = a lentil

lento/lenta adjective
= slow

lenzuolo noun, masculine (plural **lenzuola**)

> **!** Note that **lenzuola** is feminine.

un lenzuolo = a sheet

leone/leonessa noun, masculine/feminine
1 **un leone/una leonessa** = a lion/a lioness
2 **Leone**
= Leo

lesse, **lessero**, etc ▶ **leggere**

lesso/lessa adjective
= boiled

lettera noun, feminine
una lettera = a letter

letteralmente adverb
= literally

letteratura noun, feminine
la letteratura = literature

lettino noun, masculine
un lettino = a cot, a crib

letto *noun, masculine*
un letto = a bed
andare a letto = to go to bed
un letto a una piazza = a single bed
un letto matrimoniale = a double bed

letto/letta ▶ **leggere**

lettore/lettrice *noun,*
masculine/feminine
un lettore/una lettrice = a reader
un lettore di compact disc = a CD player

lettura *noun, feminine*
la lettura = reading

levare *verb* ①
= to take off
= to remove

lezione *noun, feminine*
una lezione = a lesson

li/le *pronoun*
= them
li conosco benissimo = I know them
really well
li ho mangiati tante volte = I've eaten
them lots of times

> ! *Note that* **li** *and* **le** *combine with the
infinitive, the imperative and the
gerund.*

voglio conoscerli = I want to meet them

> ! *When the group referred to consists
of males and females,* **li** *is always
used.*

li *adverb*
= there

liberare *verb* ①
1 = to free
2 liberarsi (! + *essere*)
liberarsi di qualcosa = to get rid of
something

libero/libera *adjective*
= free

libertà *noun, feminine* (! *never changes*)
la libertà = freedom

libreria *noun, feminine*
una libreria = a bookshop, a bookstore

libro *noun, masculine*
un libro = a book

licenziare *verb* ⑥
= to sack

liceo *noun, masculine*
il liceo = secondary school, high school

lieto/lieta *adjective*
= glad
molto lieto/lieta! = pleased to meet you!

lieve *adjective*
= light

ligure *adjective*
= Ligurian

limitato/limitata *adjective*
= limited

limitazione *noun, feminine*
una limitazione = a limitation

limite *noun, masculine*
un limite = a limit

limonata *noun, feminine*
la limonata = lemonade

limone *noun, masculine*
un limone = a lemon

linea *noun, feminine*
una linea = a line

lingua *noun, feminine*
• la lingua = the tongue
• una lingua = a language

linguaggio *noun, masculine* (*plural*
linguaggi)
il linguaggio = language

lino *noun, masculine*
il lino = linen

liquidazione *noun, feminine*
una liquidazione = a sale

liquido *noun, masculine*
un liquido = a liquid

liquore *noun, masculine*
un liquore = a liqueur

lira *noun, feminine*
una lira = a lira
mille lire = a thousand lire

liscio/liscia *adjective* (*plural* **lisci/lisce**)
• = smooth
• avere i capelli lisci = to have straight hair
un whisky liscio = a straight whisky

lista *noun, feminine*
una lista = a list

litigare *verb* ⑤
= to quarrel

litigio *noun, masculine* (*plural* **litigi**)
un litigio = a quarrel

litro *noun, masculine*
un litro = a litre, a liter

livello *noun, masculine*
il livello = the level

livido *noun, masculine*
un livido = a bruise

lo ▶ **il**

lo/la *pronoun* (also **l'** *before a vowel or
mute h*)
= him/her
= it
lo conosco benissimo = I know him
really well
l'ho vista in città = I saw her in town
l'ho mangiato = I've eaten it

> ! *Note that* **lo** *and* **la** *combine with the
infinitive, the imperative and the
gerund.*

voglio conoscerla = I want to meet her

L

locale
1 *adjective*
= local
2 *noun, masculine*
un locale = a club

logico/logica *adjective (plural **logici/logiche**)*
= logical

Lombardia *noun, feminine*
la Lombardia = Lombardy

lombardo/lombarda *adjective*
= Lombard

londinese *adjective*
= London

Londra *noun*
= London

lontano/lontana *adjective*
= far
= distant
è lontano dal mare = it's a long way from the sea

lordo/lorda *adjective*
= gross

loro
1 *pronoun*
= they
= them
= to them
loro stanno a casa = they're staying at home
vado con loro = I'm going with them
2 *determiner*
= their
il loro cane/la loro casa = their dog/their house

lotta *noun, feminine*
una lotta = a struggle
= a fight
la lotta = wrestling

lottare *verb* ⃞1
= to struggle
= to fight

lotteria *noun, feminine*
una lotteria = a lottery

lucciola *noun, feminine*
una lucciola = a firefly, a glowworm

luce *noun, feminine*
la luce = light

lucertola *noun, feminine*
una lucertola = a lizard

lucidare *verb* ⃞1
= to polish

lucido/lucida *adjective*
= shiny

luglio *noun, masculine*
= July

lui *pronoun*

✶ in informal situations

= he
= him
lui è mio fratello = he's my brother
è per lui = it's for him

lumaca *noun, feminine*
una lumaca = a slug

luna *noun, feminine*
la luna = the moon

luna park *noun, masculine* (**!** *never changes*)
un luna park = a fair

lunedì *noun, masculine* (**!** *never changes*)
= Monday
arrivo lunedì = I'm arriving (on) Monday
il lunedì = on Mondays

lunghezza *noun, feminine*
la lunghezza = length

lungo/lunga (*plural **lunghi/lunghe***)
1 *adjective*
= long
è lungo cinque metri = it's five metres long
2 **lungo** *preposition*
= along
lungo la spiaggia = along the beach

lungomare *noun, masculine*
il lungomare = the promenade

luogo *noun, masculine* (*plural **luoghi***)
un luogo = a place
aver luogo = to take place

lupo *noun, masculine*
un lupo = a wolf

lusso *noun, masculine*
un lusso = a luxury

lussuoso/lussuosa *adjective*
= luxurious

lutto *noun, masculine*
il lutto = mourning

Mm

ma *conjunction*
= but

macchia *noun, feminine*
una macchia = a stain
= a spot

macchiare *verb* ⃞6
= to stain

macchiato/macchiata
1 *adjective*
= stained
2 **macchiato** *noun, masculine*
un macchiato = an espresso with milk

macchina *noun, feminine*
• una macchina = a machine
• una macchina = a car
una macchina fotografica = a camera
una macchina da cucire = a sewing
  machine
una macchina da scrivere = a typewriter

macedonia *noun, feminine*
  una macedonia = a fruit salad

macellaio/macellaia *noun,*
  masculine/feminine (plural **macellai/**
  macellaie)
  un macellaio/una macellaia = a butcher

macelleria *noun, feminine*
  una macelleria = a butcher's

macello✱ *noun, masculine*
  un macello = a mess

macerie *noun, feminine plural*
  le macerie = the rubble

macinapepe *noun, masculine (*! *never*
  changes)
  un macinapepe = a pepper mill

macinare *verb* [1]
  = to mince, to grind

macinato *noun, masculine*
  il macinato = mince, ground beef

madre *noun, feminine*
  la madre = the mother

madrina *noun, feminine*
  una madrina = a godmother

maestro/maestra *noun,*
  masculine/feminine
  un maestro/una maestra = a teacher

magari
1 *exclamation*
  magari! = I wish!
2 *adverb*
  = maybe

magazzino *noun, masculine*
  un magazzino = a warehouse
  = a store room
  i grandi magazzini = a department store

maggio *noun, masculine*
  = May

maggioranza *noun, feminine*
  una maggioranza = a majority

maggiore *adjective*
• = elder
  = eldest
• la maggior parte di = most
  la maggior parte della gente = most
  people

maggiorenne *adjective*
  essere maggiorenne = to be of age

magia *noun, feminine*
  la magia = magic

magico/magica *adjective (plural*
  magici/magiche)
  = magic

maglia *noun, feminine*
• la maglia = knitting
  fare la maglia = to knit
• (*in sport*)
  una maglia = a shirt

maglietta *noun, feminine*
  una maglietta = a T-shirt

maglione *noun, masculine*
  un maglione = a sweater

magnifico/magnifica *adjective (plural*
  magnifici/magnifiche)
  = wonderful

mago/maga *noun, masculine/feminine*
  (*plural* **maghi/maghe**)
  un mago/una maga = a magician

magro/magra *adjective*
  = thin
  = slim

mai *adverb*
• (*in negative sentences*) = never
  non ci sono mai stato = I've never been
    there
  non ci vado mai più = I'm never going
    there again
  non dice mai niente = he never says
    anything
• (*in questions*) = ever
  hai mai visto un lupo? = have you ever
    seen a wolf?
• come mai? = why?

maiale *noun, masculine*
  un maiale = a pig
  il maiale = pork

maionese *noun, feminine*
  la maionese = mayonnaise

mais *noun, masculine*
  il mais = maize, corn

maiuscolo/maiuscola *adjective*
  = capital
  S maiuscola = capital S

malato/malata *adjective*
  = ill, sick

malattia *noun, feminine*
  una malattia = an illness

male
1 *adverb*
  = badly
  è scritto male = it's spelt wrong
  mi sento male = I don't feel well
2 *noun, masculine*
• il male = evil
• fare male = to hurt
  mi fanno male i piedi = my feet hurt
• un mal di testa = a headache

maledetto/maledetta *adjective*
  = damned

M

maleducato/maleducata *adjective*
= badly-behaved

malgrado
1 *preposition*
= despite
2 *conjunction*
= although

maltempo *noun, masculine*
il maltempo = bad weather

mamma *noun, feminine*
la mamma = the mum, the mom

mancanza *noun, feminine*
• mancanza di = lack of
• sentire la mancanza di = to miss

mancare *verb* 4
• = to be lacking
= to be missing
chi manca? = who's missing?
ci manca il sale = there's not enough salt
• mancare di qualcosa = to lack something
• mancare a un appuntamento = to miss an
appointment
• mi manca mia sorella = I miss my sister

mancia *noun, feminine (plural* **mance**)
una mancia = a tip

manciata *noun, feminine*
una manciata di = a handful of

mancino/mancina *adjective*
= left-handed

mandare *verb* 1
= to send

mangiare *verb* 3
= to eat
a che ora si mangia? = what time are we
having dinner?
dopo mangiato = after dinner

mani ▶ **mano**

manica *noun, feminine (plural* **maniche**)
1 una manica = a sleeve
2 Manica
la Manica = the English Channel

manico *noun, masculine (plural* **manici**)
un manico = a handle

maniera *noun, feminine*
• una maniera = a way
• le maniere = manners

manifestazione *noun, feminine*
una manifestazione = a demonstration

manifesto *noun, masculine*
un manifesto = a poster

maniglia *noun, feminine*
una maniglia = a handle

mano *noun, feminine (plural* **mani**)
una mano = a hand
a mano = by hand
dare una mano a qualcuno = to give
someone a hand

mansarda *noun, feminine*
una mansarda = an attic

mantenere *verb* 73
= to keep

mantengo, **mantiene**, **etc** ▶
mantenere

manuale
1 *adjective*
= manual
2 *noun, masculine*
un manuale = a manual

mappa *noun, feminine*
una mappa = a map

marca *noun, feminine (plural* **marche**)
una marca = a brand
= a make

marcia *noun, feminine (plural* **marce**)
• una marcia = a march
• (*when it's a bicycle, car*)
una marcia = a gear
fare marcia indietro = to reverse

marciapiede *noun, masculine*
il marciapiede = the pavement, the
sidewalk

marcio/marcia *adjective (plural*
marci/marce)
= rotten

marco *noun, masculine (plural* **marchi**)
un marco tedesco = a German mark

mare *noun, masculine*
il mare = the sea
andare al mare = to go to the seaside

marea *noun, feminine*
la marea = the tide

margarina *noun, feminine*
la margarina = margarine

margherita *noun, feminine*
una margherita = a daisy

margine *noun, masculine*
• il margine = the edge
• un margine = a margin

marina *noun, feminine*
la marina = the navy

marinaio *noun, masculine (plural*
marinai)
un marinaio = a sailor

marinare *verb* 1
• = to marinade
• marinare la scuola = to play truant

marino/marina *adjective*
= marine
= sea

marito *noun, masculine*
il marito = the husband

marmellata *noun, feminine*
la marmellata = jam

marmo noun, masculine
il marmo = marble

marrone adjective
= brown (**!** never changes)

martedì noun, masculine (**!** never changes)
= Tuesday
arrivo martedì = I'm arriving (on) Tuesday
il martedì = on Tuesdays

martello noun, masculine
un martello = a hammer

marzo noun, masculine
= March

maschera noun, feminine
• una maschera = a mask
• una maschera = fancy-dress, costume

mascherarsi verb [1] (**!** + essere)
= to dress up

maschile adjective
= male
= masculine

maschio noun, masculine (plural maschi)
un maschio = a male

massa noun, feminine
una massa = a mass

massimo/massima
1 adjective
= maximum
al massimo = at the most
2 massima noun, feminine
una massima = a maximum temperature

masticare verb [4]
= to chew

matematica noun, feminine
la matematica = mathematics

materasso noun, masculine
un materasso = a mattress

materia noun, feminine
• la materia = matter
• una materia = a subject

materiale noun, masculine
il materiale = material

materno/materna adjective
= maternal
= motherly

matita noun, feminine
una matita = a pencil

matrigna noun, feminine
la matrigna = the stepmother

matrimonio noun, masculine (plural matrimoni)
un matrimonio = a wedding
= a marriage

mattina noun, feminine, **mattino** noun, masculine
la mattina = the morning
domani mattina = tomorrow morning

matto/matta adjective
= mad, crazy

mattone noun, masculine
un mattone = a brick

maturità noun, feminine
• la maturità = maturity
• la maturità = high school diploma

maturo/matura adjective
• = mature
• (when it's fruit) = ripe

mazza noun, feminine
• (in golf) una mazza = a club
• (in baseball, cricket) una mazza = a bat

mazzo noun, masculine
un mazzo di fiori = a bunch of flowers
un mazzo di chiavi = a bunch of keys
un mazzo di carte = a pack of cards, a deck of cards

me pronoun
= me
= to me
vieni con me? = are you coming with me?
me ne dai uno? = can you give me one?

meccanico/meccanica (plural meccanici/meccaniche)
1 adjective
= mechanical
2 meccanico noun, masculine
un meccanico = a mechanic

medaglia noun, feminine
una medaglia = a medal

medesimo/medesima adjective
il medesimo/la medesima = the same

medicina noun, feminine
la medicina = medicine

medico/medica (plural medici/mediche)
1 adjective
= medical
2 medico noun, masculine
un medico = a doctor

medievale adjective
= medieval

medio/media (plural medi/medie)
1 adjective
= average
2 media noun, feminine
• una media = an average
di media = on average
• le medie = middle school

Mediterraneo noun, masculine
il Mediterraneo = the Mediterranean

meglio adverb
= better
= best
Natascia guida meglio di me = Natascia drives better than me
chi cucina meglio? = who cooks the best?

M

mela *noun, feminine*
  una mela = an apple

melanzana *noun, feminine*
  una melanzana = an aubergine, an
  eggplant

melodia *noun, feminine*
  una melodia = a tune

melone *noun, masculine*
  un melone = a melon

membro *noun, masculine*
• (*plural* **membri**)
  un membro = a member
• (*plural* **membra**)

  ! *Note that* **membra** *is feminine.*

  un membro = a limb

memoria *noun, feminine*
  la memoria = the memory

meno *adverb*
• = less
  = least
  è meno alto di me = he's not as tall as me
  ho comprato le scarpe meno care = I
    bought the least expensive shoes
  mettici meno zucchero = put less sugar in
    it
  chi ha fatto meno errori? = who made the
    fewest mistakes?
• 9 meno 6 = 9 minus 6
• fare a meno di qualcosa = to do without
    something
• meno male! = thank goodness!
• a meno che = unless

mensa *noun, feminine*
  una mensa = a canteen

mensile *adjective*
  = monthly

menta *noun, feminine*
  la menta = mint

mentale *adjective*
  = mental

mentalità *noun, feminine*
  una mentalità = a mentality

mente *noun, feminine*
  la mente = the mind

mentire *verb* 9
  = to lie

mento *noun, masculine*
  il mento = the chin

mentre *conjunction*
  = while
  mentre aspettavo = while I was waiting

menù *noun, masculine* (**!** *never changes*)
  un menù = a menu

meraviglia *noun, feminine*
  una meraviglia = a wonder

meravigliarsi *verb* 6 (**!** + *essere*)
  = to be amazed

meraviglioso/meravigliosa
  adjective
  = marvel(l)ous

mercato *noun, masculine*
  un mercato = a market

merce *noun, feminine*
  la merce = the goods

merceria *noun, feminine*
  una merceria = a haberdasher's

mercoledì *noun, masculine* (**!** *never*
  changes)
  = Wednesday
  arrivo mercoledì = I'm arriving (on)
    Wednesday
  il mercoledì = on Wednesdays

merda *noun, feminine*
  la merda = shit
  merda! = shit!

merenda *noun, feminine*
  una merenda = a snack

meridionale *adjective*
  = southern

meritare *verb* 1
  = to deserve

mescolanza *noun, feminine*
  una mescolanza = a mixture

mescolare *verb* 1
  = to mix
  = to stir

mese *noun, masculine*
  un mese = a month
  due milioni al mese = two million lire a
    month

messa *noun, feminine*
  una messa = a mass

messaggio *noun, masculine* (*plural*
  messaggi)
  un messaggio = a message

messo/messa ▶ **mettere**

mestiere *noun, masculine*
  un mestiere = a trade

meta *noun, feminine*
  una meta = a goal

metà *noun, feminine* (**!** *never changes*)
  la metà della classe = half of the class
  dividere qualcosa a metà = to cut
    something in half

metallo *noun, masculine*
  il metallo = metal

metodo *noun, masculine*
  un metodo = a method

metro *noun, masculine*
• un metro = a metre, a meter
• un metro = a tape measure

metropolitana *noun, feminine*
  la metropolitana = the underground, the
    subway

mettere *verb* 40
1 (**!** + *avere*)
• = to put (on)
  metti le valigie qua = put the cases here
  mettere un CD = to put a CD on
  non so che mettermi = I don't know what
    to wear
• = to take
  quanto ci hai messo? = how long did you
    take?
  ci ho messo un'ora = I took an hour
2 **mettersi** (**!** + *essere*)
  si è messo a piovere = it's started to rain

mezzanotte *noun, feminine*
  = midnight

mezzo/mezza
1 *adjective*
  = half
  mezzo chilo di gamberetti = half a kilo of
    shrimps
  una mezz'ora = half an hour
2 **mezzo** *noun, masculine*
• il mezzo = the middle
  in mezzo alla piazza = in the middle of
    the square
• un mezzo = a means
  un mezzo di trasporto = a means of
    transport
• sono le tre e mezzo = it's half past three,
    it's three thirty

mezzogiorno *noun, masculine*
• = midday
• il mezzogiorno = the south

mi (**me** *before* lo/la, li/le, *and* ne) *pronoun*
  = me
  = to me
  = myself
  non mi ha creduto = he didn't believe me
  mi ha spiegato come funziona = he
    explained to me how it works
  non mi sono fatto male = I didn't hurt
    myself

mica *adverb*
  = not
  non è mica vero! = it's not true, you
    know!
  non vuoi mica andare a letto? = surely
    you don't want to go to bed?

microfono *noun, masculine*
  un microfono = a microphone

miei ▶ **mio**

miele *noun, masculine*
  il miele = honey

migliaio *noun, masculine* (*plural*
  migliaia)

  ┌───┐
  │ **!** *Note that* **migliaia** *is feminine.* │
  └───┘

un migliaio di persone = about a
    thousand people
  migliaia di insetti = thousands of insects

miglio *noun, masculine* (*plural* **miglia**)

  ┌───┐
  │ **!** *Note that* **miglia** *is feminine.* │
  └───┘

un miglio = a mile

migliorare *verb* 1 (**!** + *essere or avere*)
  = to improve

migliore *adjective*
  = better
  = best
  la mia macchina nuova è migliore di
    quella vecchia = my new car is better
    than the old one
  il mio migliore amico = my best friend

-mila ▶ **mille**

Milano *noun*
  = Milan

miliardario/miliardaria *noun,*
  masculine/feminine (*plural*
  miliardari/miliardarie)
  un miliardario/una miliardaria = a
    millionaire

miliardo *number*
  un miliardo = a thousand million, a
    billion
  un miliardo di euro = a billion euros

milione *number*
  un milione = a million
  un milione di stelle = a million stars

militare
1 *adjective*
  = military
2 *noun, masculine*
  un militare = a soldier
  fare il militare = to do one's military
    service

mille *number* (*plural* **-mila**)
  = a thousand
  diecimila = ten thousand

millimetro *noun, masculine*
  un millimetro = a millimetre, a millimeter

minaccia *noun, feminine* (*plural*
  minacce)
  una minaccia = a threat

minacciare *verb* 2
  = to threaten

minatore *noun, masculine*
  un minatore = a miner

minerale *noun, masculine*
  un minerale = a mineral

minestra *noun, feminine*
  la minestra = soup

miniera *noun, feminine*
  una miniera = a mine

minimo/minima
1 *adjective*
  = minimum   ····▶

M

2 minima *noun, feminine*
  una minima = a minimum temperature

ministero *noun, masculine*
  un ministero = a ministry

ministro *noun, masculine*
  un ministro = a minister

minoranza *noun, feminine*
  una minoranza = a minority

minore *adjective*
  = younger
  = youngest

minorenne *adjective*
  essere minorenne = to be under-age

minuscolo/minuscola *adjective*
  = small
  s minuscola = small s

minuto *noun, masculine*
  un minuto = a minute

mio/mia (*plural* **miei/mie**)
1 *adjective*
  = my
2 *pronoun*
  = mine
  il mio/la mia = my one

miracolo *noun, masculine*
  un miracolo = a miracle

mirare *verb* [1]
  = to aim

mirtillo *noun, masculine*
  un mirtillo = a bilberry

mischiare *verb* [6]
  = to mix (up)

mise ▶ **mettere**

miseria *noun, feminine*
  la miseria = poverty

misero, misi ▶ **mettere**

missile *noun, masculine*
  un missile = a missile
  = a rocket

missione *noun, feminine*
  una missione = a mission

misterioso/misteriosa *adjective*
  = mysterious

mistero *noun, masculine*
  un mistero = a mystery

misto/mista *adjective*
  = mixed

misura *noun, feminine*
  • **una misura** = a size
  • **le misure** = the measurements

misurare *verb* [1]
  = to measure
  misurarsi la febbre = to take one's
    temperature

✗ in informal situations

mite *adjective*
  = mild

mito *noun, masculine*
  un mito = a myth

mittente *noun, masculine/feminine*
  il/la mittente = the sender

mobile
1 *adjective*
  = mobile
2 *noun, masculine*
  un mobile = a piece of furniture
  i mobili = furniture

moda *noun, feminine*
  la moda = fashion

modello *noun, masculine*
  un modello = a model

moderno/moderna *adjective*
  = modern

modesto/modesta *adjective*
  = modest

modificare *verb* [4]
  = to modify

modo *noun, masculine*
  un modo = a way

modulo *noun, masculine*
  un modulo = a form

moglie *noun, feminine* (*plural* **mogli**)
  la moglie = the wife

mollare *verb* [1]
  • = to let go of
  • (*when it's a boyfriend or girlfriend*)✗ = to
    dump

molle *adjective*
  = soft

molo *noun, masculine*
  un molo = a pier

moltiplicare *verb* [4]
  = to multiply

molto/molta
1 *adjective, pronoun*
  molto/molta = much
  molti/molte = many
  c'era molto traffico = there was a lot of
    traffic
  hanno molti problemi = they have a lot of
    problems
  molto tempo fa = a long time ago
2 molto *adverb*
  • = a lot
  leggo molto = I read a lot
  • (*with adjectives and adverbs*) = very
  è molto caro = it's very expensive
  • (*with* **più**) = much
  molto più grande = much bigger

momento *noun, masculine*
  un momento = a moment

monastero *noun, masculine*
  un monastero = a monastery

mondiale *adjective*
= world

mondo *noun, masculine*
il mondo = the world

moneta *noun, feminine*
• una moneta = a coin
• una moneta = a currency

montagna *noun, feminine*
una montagna = a mountain
la montagna = mountains

montare *verb* 1
• (**!** + *avere*) = to assemble
• (**!** + *essere*) = to get in
= to get on

monte *noun, masculine*
un monte = a mountain

monumento *noun, masculine*
un monumento = a monument
visitare i monumenti = to see the sights

moquette *noun, feminine* (**!** *never changes*)
la moquette = fitted carpet

mora *noun, feminine*
una mora = a blackberry

morale
1 *adjective*
= moral
2 *noun, feminine*
la morale = the moral
3 *noun, masculine*
il morale = morale

morbido/morbida *adjective*
= soft

morbillo *noun, masculine*
il morbillo = measles

mordere *verb* 45
= to bite

morire *verb* 41 (**!** + *essere*)
= to die
morire di [fame | sete | noia] = to be dying
of [hunger | thirst | boredom]

morse, morsi, etc ▶ mordere

morso/morsa
1 ▶ mordere
2 morso *noun, masculine*
un morso = a bite

morte *noun, feminine*
la morte = death

morto/morta
1 ▶ morire
2 *adjective*
= dead

mosca *noun, feminine* (*plural* **mosche**)
una mosca = a fly

Mosca *noun*
= Moscow

mossa *noun, feminine*
una mossa = a move

mosse, mossi, etc ▶ muovere

mosso/mossa
1 ▶ muovere
2 *adjective*
• (*when it's hair*) = wavy
• (*when it's the sea*) = rough

mostra *noun, feminine*
una mostra = an exhibition

mostrare *verb* 1
= to show

mostro *noun, masculine*
un mostro = a monster

motivo *noun, masculine*
• un motivo = a reason
• un motivo = a pattern

moto
1 *noun, masculine*
il moto = movement
fare del moto = to take some exercise
2 *noun, feminine* (**!** *never changes*)
una moto = a motorcycle

motore *noun, masculine*
un motore = an engine
= a motor

motorino *noun, masculine*
un motorino = a moped

motoscafo *noun, masculine*
un motoscafo = a motor boat

movimento *noun, masculine*
un movimento = a movement

mucca *noun, feminine* (*plural* **mucche**)
una mucca = a cow

mucchio *noun, masculine* (*plural* **mucchi**)
un mucchio = a pile

mulino *noun, masculine*
un mulino = a mill

multa *noun, feminine*
una multa = a fine

municipio *noun, masculine* (*plural* **municipi**)
il municipio = the town hall
= the town council, the city council

muoio, muore, etc ▶ morire

muovere *verb* 42
1 = to move
2 muoversi (**!** + *essere*)
muoversi = to move

mura *noun, feminine plural*
le mura della città = the city walls

muratore *noun, masculine*
un muratore = a builder

muro *noun, masculine*
un muro = a wall

M

muscolo *noun, masculine*
un muscolo = a muscle

museo *noun, masculine*
un museo = a museum
= a gallery

musica *noun, feminine*
la musica = music

musicista *noun, masculine/feminine*
(*plural* **musicisti/musiciste**)
un/una musicista = a musician

muso *noun, masculine*
il muso
(*when it's an animal*) = the muzzle
(*when it's a person*)✖ = the face

musulmano/musulmana *noun,*
masculine/feminine
un musulmano/una musulmana = a
Muslim

mutande *noun, feminine plural*
le mutande = underpants

muto/muta *adjective*
• = dumb
• = silent

mutua *noun, feminine*
la mutua = the health service

mutuo *noun, masculine*
un mutuo = a mortgage

Nn

nacque, **nacquero**, etc ▶ nascere

napoletano/napoletana *adjective*
= Neapolitan

Napoli *noun*
= Naples

nascere *verb* 43 (❗ + *essere*)
= to be born
sono nato nel 1981 = I was born in 1981

nascita *noun, feminine*
una nascita = a birth

nascondere *verb* 58
1 (❗ + *avere*) = to hide
2 **nascondersi** (❗ + *essere*)
nascondersi = to hide

nascono ▶ nascere

nascose, **nascosi**, etc ▶
nascondere

nascosto/nascosta
1 ▶ nascondere
2 *adjective*

✖ in informal situations

= hiding
dov'era nascosta? = where was she
hiding?

naso *noun, masculine*
il naso = the nose

nastro *noun, masculine*
• un nastro = a ribbon
• un nastro = a tape

Natale *noun, masculine*
Natale = Christmas

nato/nata ▶ nascere

natura *noun, feminine*
la natura = nature

naturale *adjective*
= natural

naturalmente *adverb*
= of course

nave *noun, feminine*
una nave = a ship

nazionale *adjective*
= national

nazionalità *noun, feminine* (❗ *never*
changes)
una nazionalità = a nationality

nazione *noun, feminine*
una nazione = a nation

ne (**n'** *before* è, era, *etc*)
1 *pronoun*
= of it
= of them
ne ho tanti = I've got lots of them
quanto ce n'è? = how much is there?
non ne so niente = I don't know anything
about it
2 *adverb*
nessuno ne è uscito vivo = no one got
out of it alive
se n'è andato = he's gone away

né *conjunction*
né Carlo né Antonio = neither Carlo nor
Antonio

neanche *adverb*
• = neither
'non la conosco'—'neanch'io' = 'I don't
know her'—'neither do I'
• = not even
non mi ha neanche salutato = he didn't
even say hello

nebbia *noun, feminine*
la nebbia = fog

necessario/necessaria *adjective*
(*plural* **necessari/necessarie**)
= necessary

negare *verb* 5
= to deny

negativo/negativa *adjective*
= negative

negato/**negata** adjective
essere negato/negata per qualcosa = to be useless at something

negli ▶ in

negozio noun, masculine (plural **negozi**)
un negozio = a shop, a store

nei, **nel, nella** ▶ in

nemico/**nemica** noun, masculine/feminine (plural **nemici**/**nemiche**)
un nemico/una nemica = an enemy

nemmeno ▶ neanche

neonato/**neonata** noun, masculine/feminine
un neonato/una neonata = a newborn baby

neppure ▶ neanche

nero/**nera** adjective
= black

nervo noun, masculine
un nervo = a nerve

nervoso/**nervosa** adjective
= on edge

nessuno/**nessuna**
1 adjective
= no
non c'è nessun dubbio = there's no doubt

! Before masculine singular nouns beginning with z, ps, gn, or s + another consonant, **nessuno** is used. Before masculine singular nouns beginning with another consonant or a vowel, **nessun** is used. Before feminine singular nouns beginning with a vowel, **nessun'** is used.

2 pronoun
• = no one
non ha chiamato nessuno = no one called
• = none
nessuno di noi può aiutare = none of us can help
delle tre, nessuna era sposata = none of the three was married

neve noun, feminine
la neve = snow

nevicare verb 4 (! + essere or avere)
= to snow

nido noun, masculine
un nido = a nest

niente pronoun
• = nothing
non è successo niente = nothing happened
non voglio niente = I don't want anything
niente di speciale = nothing special
quasi niente = hardly anything
• di niente! = you're welcome!

nipote noun, masculine/feminine
• un/una nipote = a nephew/a niece
• un/una nipote = a grandson/a granddaughter
i nipoti = the grandchildren

no adverb
= no
dire di no = to say no
lei è contenta ma io no = she's pleased but I'm not
l'hai fatto, no? = you've done it, haven't you?

nocciola noun, feminine
una nocciola = a hazelnut

nocciolina noun, feminine
una nocciolina = a peanut

nocciolo noun, masculine
un nocciolo = a stone, a pit

noce noun, feminine
una noce = a walnut

nodo noun, masculine
un nodo = a knot
fare un nodo = to tie a knot

noi pronoun
= we
= us

noia noun, feminine
la noia = boredom
dare noia a qualcuno = to annoy someone

noioso/**noiosa** adjective
= boring
= annoying

noleggiare verb 3
= to hire, to rent

nome noun, masculine
un nome = a name
= a first name

non adverb
= not
non fumo = I don't smoke
non piangere! = don't cry!
credo che non verrò = I don't think I'll come
non è successo niente = nothing happened

nonno/**nonna** noun, masculine/feminine
il nonno/la nonna = the grandfather/the grandmother
i nonni = the grandparents

nono/**nona** adjective
= ninth

nonostante
1 preposition
= despite
2 conjunction
= although

nord noun, masculine
il nord = the north

N

nordest noun, masculine
il nordest = the north-east

nordovest noun, masculine
il nordovest = the north-west

normale adjective
= normal

nostalgia noun, feminine
la nostalgia = nostalgia
avere nostalgia di casa = to feel
homesick

nostro/nostra
1 adjective
= our
il nostro appartamento = our apartment
2 pronoun
= ours
il nostro/la nostra = our one

nota noun, feminine
una nota = a note

notare verb 1
• = to note
• = to notice

notevole adjective
= notable

notizia noun, feminine
una notizia = a piece of news
le notizie = the news

noto/nota adjective
= well-known

notte noun, feminine
una notte = a night
di notte = at night

novanta number
= ninety

novantesimo/novantesima
adjective
= ninetieth

nove number
= nine

novecento
1 number
= nine hundred
2 Novecento noun, masculine
il Novecento = the 20th century

novembre noun, masculine
= November

novità noun, feminine (**!** never changes)
una novità = a novelty

nozze noun, feminine plural
le nozze = the wedding

nubile adjective
= single

nucleare adjective
= nuclear

nudo/nuda adjective
= naked
= nude

nulla pronoun
= nothing
non vedo nulla = I can't see anything

numero noun, masculine
• un numero = a number
il mio numero di telefono = my phone
number
• (when talking about shoes)
un numero = a size

nuora noun, feminine
una nuora = a daughter-in-law

nuotare verb 1
= to swim

nuoto noun, masculine
il nuoto = swimming

nuovo/nuova adjective
• = new
• di nuovo = again

nuvola noun, feminine
una nuvola = a cloud

nuvoloso/nuvolosa adjective
= cloudy

o conjunction
= or
o domani o dopodomani = either
tomorrow or the day after

obbediente, ubbidiente adjective
= obedient

obbedire, ubbidire verb 9
obbedire a = to obey

obbligatorio/obbligatoria adjective
(plural **obbligatori/obbligatorie**)
= compulsory

obiettivo/obiettiva
1 adjective
= objective
2 obiettivo noun, masculine
• un obiettivo = an objective
• un obiettivo = a lens

obiezione noun, feminine
un'obiezione = an objection

oca noun, feminine (plural **oche**)
un'oca = a goose

occasione noun, feminine
• l'occasione = the opportunity
• un'occasione = an occasion
• un'occasione = a bargain

occhiali noun, masculine plural
gli occhiali = glasses
gli occhiali da sole = sunglasses

occhiata *noun, feminine*
dare un'occhiata a qualcosa = to take a
look at something

occhio *noun, masculine (plural **occhi**)*
un occhio = an eye
ha gli occhi azzurri = he has blue eyes
tenere d'occhio qualcosa = to keep an
eye on something

occidentale *adjective*
= western

occidente *noun, masculine*
l'occidente = the west

occorrere *verb* 26 (! + *essere*)
= to be necessary
ci occorre un chilo di farina = we need a
kilo of flour

occupare *verb* 1
1 (! + *avere*)
= to occupy
2 occuparsi (! + *essere*)
occuparsi di = to deal with

occupato/occupata *adjective*
= engaged, busy

oceano *noun, masculine*
un oceano = an ocean

oculista *noun, masculine|feminine (plural
oculisti/oculiste)*
un oculista/un'oculista = an eye specialist

odiare *verb* 6
= to hate

odio *noun, masculine*
l'odio = hatred

odore *noun, masculine*
un odore = a smell

offendere *verb* 53
1 (! + *avere*)
= to offend
2 offendersi (! + *essere*)
offendersi = to take offence, to take
offense

offensivo/offensiva *adjective*
= offensive

offerta *noun, feminine*
un'offerta = an offer

offerto/offerta ▶ offrire

offese, offeso/offesa, etc ▶
offendere

officina *noun, feminine*
un'officina = a garage
= a workshop

offrire *verb* 15
1 (! + *avere*)
= to offer
2 offrirsi (! + *essere*)
offrirsi di fare qualcosa = to offer to do
something

oggetto *noun, masculine*
un oggetto = an object

oggi *adverb*
= today

oggigiorno *adverb*
= nowadays

ogni *adjective*
= every
ogni anno = every year
ogni dieci anni = every ten years
ogni tanto = every so often

ognuno/ognuna *pronoun*
• = each one
ognuno di noi = every one of us
• ognuno = everyone

Olanda *noun, feminine*
l'Olanda = the Netherlands

olandese *adjective*
= Dutch

Olimpiadi *noun, feminine plural*
le Olimpiadi = the Olympics

olio *noun, masculine (plural **oli**)*
l'olio = oil

oliva *noun, feminine*
un'oliva = an olive

oltre *preposition*
• = beyond
• = over
oltre diciott'anni = over eighteen
• oltre a = as well as
= apart from

ombra *noun, feminine*
• un'ombra = a shadow
• l'ombra = the shade
ero seduto all'ombra = I was sitting in
the shade

ombrello *noun, masculine*
un ombrello = an umbrella

ombrellone *noun, masculine*
un ombrellone = a beach umbrella

omesso/omessa ▶ omettere

omettere *verb* 40
= to omit

omicida *noun, masculine|feminine (plural
omicidi/omicide)*
un omicida/un'omicida = a murderer

omicidio *noun, masculine (plural
omicidi)*
un omicidio = a murder

omise, omisi, etc ▶ omettere

omosessuale *noun, masculine|feminine*
un omosessuale/un'omosessuale = a
homosexual

onda *noun, feminine*
un'onda = a wave

onestà *noun, feminine*
l'onestà = honesty

onesto/onesta *adjective*
= honest

O

onore noun, masculine
un onore = an hono(u)r

ONU noun, feminine
l'ONU = the United Nations

opera noun, feminine
• un'opera = a work
un'opera d'arte = a work of art
• un'opera = an opera

operaio/operaia noun,
masculine/feminine (plural
operai/operaie)
un operaio/un'operaia = a worker

operare verb [1]
• = to operate
• operare qualcuno = to operate on
someone

operazione noun, feminine
un'operazione = an operation

opinione noun, feminine
un'opinione = an opinion

oppone, oppongo, etc ▶ opporsi

opporsi verb [50] (! + essere)
opporsi a qualcosa = to oppose
something

oppose, opposi, etc ▶ opporsi

opportunità noun, feminine (! never
changes)
un'opportunità = an opportunity

opposizione noun, feminine
l'opposizione = opposition

opposto/opposta
1 ▶ opporsi
2 adjective
= opposite

oppure conjunction
= or (else)

opuscolo noun, masculine
un opuscolo = a brochure

ora
1 noun, feminine
• un'ora = an hour
duecento chilometri all'ora = two
hundred kilometres an hour
• l'ora = the time
che ore sono? = what's the time?
l'ora di pranzo = lunchtime
• non vedere l'ora di fare qualcosa = to
look forward to doing something
non vedo l'ora di andare in vacanza = I'm
looking forward to going on holiday
l'ora di punta = rush hour
2 adverb
= now

orale adjective
= oral

orario/oraria (plural orari/orarie)
1 adjective
in senso orario = clockwise

2 **orario** noun, masculine
un orario = a timetable

ordinare verb [1]
= to order
ordinare a qualcuno di fare qualcosa = to
order someone to do something

ordinario/ordinaria adjective (plural
ordinari/ordinarie)
= ordinary

ordinato/ordinata adjective
= tidy

ordine noun, masculine
• l'ordine = order
mettere in ordine = to tidy up
• un ordine = an order

orecchino noun, masculine
un orecchino = an earring

orecchio noun, masculine (plural
orecchie)

! Note that **orecchie** is feminine.

un orecchio = an ear
mi fanno male le orecchie = my ears hurt

organizzare verb [1]
= to organize

organizzazione noun, feminine
un'organizzazione = an organization

organo noun, masculine
un organo = an organ

orgoglio noun, masculine
l'orgoglio = pride

orgoglioso/orgogliosa adjective
= proud

orientale adjective
= oriental
= eastern

oriente noun, masculine
l'oriente = the east

origano noun, masculine
l'origano = oregano

originale adjective
= original

origine noun, feminine
l'origine = the origin

orizzontale adjective
= horizontal

orizzonte noun, masculine
l'orizzonte = the horizon

orlo noun, masculine
• l'orlo = the edge
• un orlo = a hem

ormai adverb
= now
= by now

oro noun, masculine
l'oro = gold
un anello d'oro = a gold ring

orologio *noun, masculine*
un orologio = a watch
= a clock

oroscopo *noun, masculine*
un oroscopo = a horoscope

orrendo/orrenda *adjective*
= horrible

orribile *adjective*
= horrible

orrore *noun, masculine*
l'orrore = horror

orso *noun, masculine*
un orso = a bear

orto *noun, masculine*
un orto = a vegetable garden

ortografia *noun, feminine*
l'ortografia = spelling

osare *verb* 1
= to dare
come osi? = how dare you!

oscuro/oscura *adjective*
= obscure

ospedale *noun, masculine*
un ospedale = a hospital

ospitalità *noun, feminine*
l'ospitalità = hospitality

ospitare *verb* 1
ospitare qualcuno = to put someone up

ospite *noun, masculine/feminine*
• un ospite/un'ospite = a host
• un ospite/un'ospite = a guest

ossa ▶ osso

osservare *verb* 1
= to observe

osservazione *noun, feminine*
un'osservazione = a remark

ossigeno *noun, masculine*
l'ossigeno = oxygen

osso *noun, masculine (plural* **ossi** *or* **ossa***)*

> ! Note that **ossa** is feminine. It is used
> when referring to human bones.

un osso = a bone
mi fanno male le ossa = my bones hurt

ostacolo *noun, masculine*
un ostacolo = an obstacle

ostaggio *noun, masculine (plural* **ostaggi***)*
un ostaggio = a hostage

ostello *noun, masculine*
un ostello della gioventù = a youth hostel

ostile *adjective*
= hostile

ostinato/ostinata *adjective*
= obstinate

ostrica *noun, feminine (plural* **ostriche***)*
un'ostrica = an oyster

ottanta *number*
= eighty

ottantesimo/ottantesima *adjective*
= eightieth

ottavo/ottava *adjective*
= eighth

ottenere *verb* 73
= to obtain

ottengo, **ottiene**, etc ▶ **ottenere**

ottico *noun, masculine (plural* **ottici***)*
un ottico = an optician

ottimista *(plural* **ottimisti/ottimiste***)*
1 *adjective*
= optimistic
2 *noun, masculine/feminine*
un ottimista/un'ottimista = an optimist

ottimo/ottima *adjective*
= excellent

otto *number*
= eight

ottobre *noun, masculine*
= October

ottocento
1 *number*
= eight hundred
2 **Ottocento** *noun, masculine*
l'Ottocento = the 19th century

ovest *noun, masculine*
l'ovest = the west

ovunque *adverb*
= everywhere

ovvio/ovvia *adjective (plural* **ovvi/ovvie***)*
= obvious

P

Pp

pacchetto *noun, masculine*
un pacchetto = a packet, a pack

pacco *noun, masculine (plural* **pacchi***)*
un pacco = a parcel, a package

pace *noun, feminine*
la pace = peace

Pacifico *noun, masculine*
il Pacifico = the Pacific

padella *noun, feminine*
una padella = a frying pan

Padova *noun*
= Padua

pado̱va̱no/pado̱va̱na *adjective*
= Paduan

pa̱dre *noun, masculine*
il padre = the father

padri̱no *noun, masculine*
un padrino = a godfather

padro̱ne *noun, masculine*
un padrone = a master

paesa̱ggio *noun, masculine (plural*
paesa̱ggi)
il paesaggio = the landscape
= the scenery

pae̱se *noun, masculine*
• un paese = a country
• un paese = a village

pa̱ga *noun, feminine*
la paga = the pay

pagame̱nto *noun, masculine*
un pagamento = a payment

paga̱re *verb* ⑤
= to pay (for)
pagare il conto = to pay the bill
non ho pagato i biglietti = I haven't paid
for the tickets

pa̱gina *noun, feminine*
una pagina = a page

pa̱glia *noun, feminine*
la paglia = straw

paglia̱ccio *noun, masculine (plural*
paglia̱cci)
un pagliaccio = a clown

pagno̱tta *noun, feminine*
una pagnotta = a loaf

pa̱io *noun, masculine (plural* **pa̱ia**)

! Note that **paia** is feminine.

• un paio di scarpe = a pair of shoes
• un paio d'anni fa = a couple of years ago

pa̱iono ▶ **parere**

pala̱zzo *noun, masculine*
• un palazzo = a palace
• un palazzo = a block of flats, an
apartment building

palcosce̱nico *noun, masculine (plural*
palcosce̱nici)
il palcoscenico = the stage

pale̱stra *noun, feminine*
una palestra = a gym

pa̱lla *noun, feminine*
• una palla = a ball
• che palle!✶ = what a pain!
rompere le palle a qualcuno✶ = to get on
someone's nerves

pallacane̱stro *noun, feminine*
la pallacanestro = basketball

palla̱vo̱lo *noun, feminine*
la pallavolo = volleyball

pa̱llido/pa̱llida *adjective*
= pale

palli̱na *noun, feminine*
una pallina = a ball

palli̱no *noun, masculine*
un pallino = a polka-dot
un vestito a pallini = a polka-dot dress

pallonci̱no *noun, masculine*
un palloncino = a balloon

pallo̱ne *noun, masculine*
un pallone = a football

pallo̱ttola *noun, feminine*
una pallottola = a bullet

pa̱lma *noun, feminine*
una palma = a palm tree

pa̱lo *noun, masculine*
un palo = a pole
= a post

palu̱de *noun, feminine*
una palude = a marsh

pa̱nca *noun, feminine (plural* **pa̱nche**)
una panca = a bench

pance̱tta *noun, feminine*
la pancetta = bacon

pa̱ncia *noun, feminine (plural* **pa̱nce**)
la pancia = the belly

pa̱ne *noun, masculine*
il pane = bread

panifi̱cio *noun, masculine (plural*
panifi̱ci)
un panificio = a bakery

pa̱nico *noun, masculine*
il panico = panic
farsi prendere dal panico = to panic

pani̱no *noun, masculine*
un panino = a roll
un panino al formaggio = a cheese roll

pa̱nna *noun, feminine*
la panna = cream

pa̱nno *noun, masculine*
• un panno = a cloth
• i panni = the washing

panno̱lino *noun, masculine*
un pannolino = a nappy, a diaper

panora̱ma *noun, masculine (plural*
panora̱mi)
un panorama = a view

pantalo̱ni *noun, masculine plural*
i pantaloni = trousers

pa̱pa *noun, masculine (plural* **pa̱pi**)
il Papa = the Pope

papà *noun, masculine (! never changes)*
il papà = the dad

pappagallo *noun, masculine*
un pappagallo = a parrot

paradiso *noun, masculine*
il paradiso = paradise

paragonare *verb* 1
= to compare

paragone *noun, masculine*
un paragone = a comparison

paragrafo *noun, masculine*
un paragrafo = a paragraph

paralizzato/paralizzata *adjective*
= paralysed, paralyzed

parallelo/parallela *adjective*
= parallel

parcheggiare *verb* 3
= to park

parcheggio *noun, masculine (plural* parcheggi)
un parcheggio = a car park, a parking lot
= a parking space

parco *noun, masculine (plural* parchi)
un parco = a park

parecchio/parecchia
1 *adjective (plural* parecchi/parecchie)
= quite a lot of
parecchio traffico = quite a lot of traffic
parecchie volte = several times
2 **parecchio** *adverb*
= quite a lot
mi è costato parecchio = it cost me quite a lot

pareggio *noun, masculine (plural* pareggi)
un pareggio = a draw

parente *noun, masculine/feminine*
un/una parente = a relative

parentesi *noun, feminine* (! *never changes*)
fra parentesi = in brackets, in parentheses

parere
1 *verb* 44 (! + *essere*)
pare che = it seems that
mi pare che = I think that
mi pare [assurdo | giusto | logico] = I think it's [absurd | right | logical]
non ti pare? = don't you think so?
a quanto pare = apparently
2 *noun, masculine*
un parere = an opinion
a mio parere = in my opinion

parete *noun, feminine*
una parete = a wall

pari *adjective* (! *never changes*)
= even
un numero pari = an even number

Parigi *noun*
= Paris

parlamentare
1 *adjective*
= parliamentary
2 *noun, masculine/feminine*
un/una parlamentare = a member of parliament

parlamento *noun, masculine*
un parlamento = a parliament

parlare *verb* 1
= to speak
= to talk
il libro parla della sua infanzia = the book is about his childhood

parola *noun, feminine*
una parola = a word
le parole crociate = a crossword

parolaccia *noun, feminine (plural* parolacce)
una parolaccia = a bad word

parrà, parranno ▶ parere

parrocchia *noun, feminine*
una parrocchia = a parish

parrucca *noun, feminine*
una parrucca = a wig

parrucchiere/parrucchiera *noun, masculine/feminine*
un parrucchiere/una parrucchiera = a hairdresser

parso/parsa ▶ parere

parte
1 *noun, feminine*
• una parte = a part
= a share
• da tutte le parti = everywhere
da nessuna parte = nowhere
2 a parte = apart from

partecipare *verb* 1
partecipare a qualcosa = to take part in something

partenza *noun, feminine*
la partenza = the departure

particolare
1 *adjective*
= particular
2 *noun, masculine*
un particolare = a detail

partire *verb* 10 (! + *essere*)
• = to leave
• a partire da lunedì = starting from Monday

partita *noun, feminine*
una partita = a match, a game

partito *noun, masculine*
un partito politico = a political party

parve, parvero, etc ▶ parere

parziale *adjective*
= partial

P

Pasqua *noun, feminine*
  Pasqua = Easter

Pasquetta *noun, feminine*
  Pasquetta = Easter Monday

passaggio *noun, masculine (plural*
  passaggi)
• un passaggio = a passage
• dare un passaggio a qualcuno = to give
  someone a lift, a ride
  un passaggio a livello = a level crossing,
  a grade crossing

passante *noun, masculine/feminine*
  un/una passante = a passer-by

passaporto *noun, masculine*
  un passaporto = a passport

passare *verb* [1]
• (**!** + *avere*) = to pass
  mi passi il sale? = can you pass the salt?
• (**!** + *avere*)
  passare il tempo a fare qualcosa = to
  spend time doing something
• (**!** + *essere*) = to go past
  è passato davanti alla banca = he went
  past the bank
  non ci passo! = I can't get past!
  passa di qua! = come this way!

passato *noun, masculine*
  il passato = the past

passeggero/passeggera *noun,*
  masculine/feminine
  un passeggero/una passeggera = a
  passenger

passeggiare *verb* [3]
  = to stroll

passeggino *noun, masculine*
  un passeggino = a pushchair, a stroller

passione *noun, feminine*
  la passione = passion

passo *noun, masculine*
  un passo = a step
  a due passi da qui = a stone's throw from
  here

pasta *noun, feminine*
• la pasta = pasta
• la pasta = pastry
  = dough
• una pasta = a cake

pastasciutta *noun, feminine*
  la pastasciutta = pasta

pasticceria *noun, feminine*
  una pasticceria = a cake shop

pasticcio✶ *noun, masculine (plural*
  pasticci)
  un pasticcio = a mess

pasto *noun, masculine*
  un pasto = a meal

────────────────────
✶ in informal situations

pastore *noun, masculine*
  un pastore = a shepherd

patata *noun, feminine*
  una patata = a potato
  le patate fritte = chips, French fries

patatina *noun, feminine*
  una patatina = a crisp, a potato chip

patente *noun, feminine*
  una patente di guida = a driving licence,
  a driver's license

patrigno *noun, masculine*
  il patrigno = the stepfather

patrimonio *noun, masculine*
  un patrimonio = a fortune

pattinaggio *noun, masculine*
  il pattinaggio = skating

pattino *noun, masculine*
  un pattino = a skate

paura *noun, feminine*
  la paura = fear
  ho paura dei ragni = I'm afraid of spiders

pausa *noun, feminine*
  una pausa = a pause
  fare una pausa = to have a break

pavimento *noun, masculine*
  il pavimento = the floor

paziente
1 *adjective*
  = patient
2 *noun, masculine/feminine*
  un/una paziente = a patient

pazienza *noun, feminine*
  la pazienza = patience
  pazienza! = never mind!

pazzesco/pazzesca *adjective (plural*
  pazzeschi/pazzesche)
  = crazy

pazzo/pazza *adjective*
  = crazy

peccato *noun, masculine*
• un peccato = a sin
• che peccato! = what a pity!

Pechino *noun*
  = Beijing

pecora *noun, feminine*
  una pecora = a sheep

pedone *noun, masculine*
  un pedone = a pedestrian

peggio *adverb*
  = worse
  = worst
  poteva andare peggio = it could have
  been worse
  i peggio pagati = the worst paid

peggiorare *verb* [1] (**!** + *essere*)
  = to get worse

peggiore *adjective*
= worse
= worst
il clima è peggiore = the climate is worse
il momento peggiore = the worst time

pelato/pelata
1 *adjective*
= bald
2 pelati *noun, masculine plural*
i pelati = tinned tomatoes, canned tomatoes

pelle *noun, feminine*
• **la pelle** = the skin
• **la pelle** = leather

pelliccia *noun, feminine (plural* **pellicce***)*
una pelliccia = a fur

pellicola *noun, feminine*
una pellicola = a film

pelo *noun, masculine*
• **un pelo** = a hair
• **il pelo** = the coat
• **per un pelo** = by the skin of one's teeth

pena *noun, feminine*
• **la pena di morte** = the death penalty
• **valere la pena** = to be worth it

penisola *noun, feminine*
una penisola = a peninsula

penna *noun, feminine*
• **una penna** = a pen
• **una penna** = a feather

pennello *noun, masculine*
un pennello = a paintbrush

pensare *verb* 1
= to think
che pensi della casa? = what do you think of the house?
stavo pensando alle vacanze = I was thinking about the holidays
penso di partire domani = I think I'll go tomorrow
penso di sì = I think so
penso di no = I don't think so

pensiero *noun, masculine*
un pensiero = a thought
stare in pensiero = to be worried

pensionato/pensionata *noun, masculine/feminine*
un pensionato/una pensionata = a pensioner

pensione *noun, feminine*
• **una pensione** = a boarding house
• **andare in pensione** = to retire
mezza pensione = half board
pensione completa = full board

pentirsi *verb* 10 *(! + essere)*
pentirsi di aver fatto qualcosa = to regret doing something

pentola *noun, feminine*
una pentola = a pan

pepe *noun, masculine*
il pepe = pepper

peperoncino *noun, masculine*
un peperoncino = a chil(l)i

peperone *noun, masculine*
un peperone = a pepper

per *preposition*
• = for
è per te = it's for you
per tre notti = for three nights
• = in order to
per dormire = in order to sleep
• = times
tre per cinque = three times five

pera *noun, feminine*
una pera = a pear

perché
1 *adverb*
= why
perché non ti riposi? = why don't you have a rest?
perché no? = why not?
2 *conjunction*
= because

perciò *conjunction*
= therefore

perdere *verb* 45
• = to lose
• = to miss
• = to leak
• **lascia perdere!** = forget it!

perdita *noun, feminine*
• **la perdita** = the loss
• **una perdita** = a leak
• **una perdita di tempo** = a waste of time

perdonare *verb* 1
= to forgive

perfetto/perfetta *adjective*
= perfect

perfino *adverb*
= even

pericolo *noun, masculine*
il pericolo = danger

pericoloso/pericolosa *adjective*
= dangerous

periferia *noun, feminine*
la periferia di Varese = the outskirts of Varese

periodo *noun, masculine*
un periodo = a period

permanente *adjective*
= permanent

permanenza *noun, feminine*
una permanenza = a stay

P

permesso/permessa
1 ▶ **permettere**
2 **permesso** *noun, masculine*
• **il permesso** = permission
• **un permesso** = a permit

permettere *verb* 40
1 (**!** + *avere*)
permettere a qualcuno di fare qualcosa
= to allow someone to do something
permesso! = excuse me!
è permesso? = can I come in?
2 **permettersi** (**!** + *essere*)
non me lo posso permettere = I can't
afford it

però *conjunction*
= but
= however

perplesso/perplessa *adjective*
= perplexed

perse, **perso/persa**, **etc** ▶ **perdere**

persiana *noun, feminine*
una persiana = a shutter

persino ▶ **perfino**

persona *noun, feminine*
una persona = a person
trenta persone = thirty people

personaggio *noun, masculine* (*plural*
personaggi)
• **un personaggio** = a character
• **un personaggio** = a personality

personale
1 *adjective* = personal
2 *noun, masculine*
il personale = the staff

personalità *noun, feminine* (**!** *never*
changes)
la personalità = the personality

personalmente *adverb*
= personally

persuadere *verb* 46
= to persuade

pesante *adjective*
= heavy

pesare *verb* 1
= to weigh
quanto pesa? = how much does it weigh?

pesca[1] *noun, feminine* (*plural* **pesche**)
una pesca = a peach

pesca[2] *noun, feminine*
la pesca = fishing

pescare *verb* 4
= to fish
= to catch

pesce *noun, masculine*
• **un pesce** = a fish
mi piace il pesce = I like fish
• **Pesci** = Pisces

pescheria *noun, feminine*
una pescheria = a fishmonger's, a fish
shop

pescivendolo/pescivendola *noun,*
masculine/feminine
un pescivendolo/una pescivendola = a
fishmonger, a fish vendor

peso *noun, masculine*
il peso = the weight

pessimista (*plural* **pessimisti/**
pessimiste)
1 *adjective*
= pessimistic
2 *noun, masculine/feminine*
un/una pessimista = a pessimist

pessimo/pessima *adjective*
= dreadful

pestare *verb* 1
= to tread on

peste *noun, feminine*
• **la peste** = the plague
• **una peste** = a pest

petrolio *noun, masculine*
il petrolio = oil

pettinarsi *verb* 1 (**!** + *essere*)
= to comb one's hair

pettine *noun, masculine*
un pettine = a comb

petto *noun, masculine*
il petto = the chest
= the bust

pezzo *noun, masculine*
un pezzo = a piece

piaccia, **piacciono**, **etc** ▶ **piacere**

piacere
1 *verb* 47 (**!** + *essere*)
= to please
mi piace ballare = I like dancing
ti piacciono queste olive? = do you like
these olives?
2 *noun, masculine*
• **il piacere** = pleasure
piacere! = pleased to meet you!
• **un piacere** = a favo(u)r
per piacere = please

piacevole *adjective*
= pleasant

piaciuto/piaciuta, **piacque**, **etc** ▶
piacere

pianeta *noun, masculine* (*plural* **pianeti**)
un pianeta = a planet

piangere *verb* 48
= to cry

piano/piana
1 *adjective*
= level

────────
✗ in informal situations

....▶

2 piano *noun, masculine*
- un piano = a plan
- un piano = a piano
- un piano = a floor
  al piano terra (*in Britain*) = on the ground floor
  (*in the US*) = on the first floor
  al primo piano (*in Britain*) = on the first floor
  (*in the US*) = on the second floor

pianse, **piansi**, etc ▶ **piangere**

pianta *noun, feminine*
- una pianta = a plant
- una pianta = a plan

piantare *verb* 1
- = to plant
- ✶ = to ditch

pianterreno *noun, masculine*
  il pianterreno (*in Britain*) = the ground floor
  (*in the US*) = the first floor

pianto/pianta
1 ▶ **piangere**
2 pianto *noun, masculine*
  il pianto = crying

piattino *noun, masculine*
  un piattino = a saucer

piatto *noun, masculine*
  un piatto = a plate

piazza *noun, feminine*
  una piazza = a square

piccante *adjective*
  = spicy

picchiare *verb* 6
  = to hit

piccolo/piccola *adjective*
  = small

piede *noun, masculine*
  un piede = a foot
  a piedi = on foot

piegare *verb* 5
- = to bend
- = to fold

Piemonte *noun, masculine*
  il Piemonte = Piedmont

piemontese *adjective*
  = Piedmontese

pieno/piena *adjective*
  = full
  pieno di errori = full of mistakes

pietra *noun, feminine*
  una pietra = a stone

pigiama *noun, masculine*
  un pigiama = a pair of pyjamas

pigro/pigra *adjective*
  = lazy

pila *noun, feminine*
- una pila = a battery
- una pila di giornali = a pile of newspapers

pillola *noun, feminine*
  una pillola = a pill

pilota *noun, masculine/feminine* (*plural* **piloti/pilote**)
  un/una pilota
  (*of a plane*) = a pilot
  (*of a racing car*) = a driver

pino *noun, masculine*
  un pino = a pine tree

pioggia *noun, feminine* (*plural* **piogge**)
  la pioggia = the rain

piombo *noun, masculine*
  il piombo = lead

piovere *verb* 49 (**!** + *essere* or *avere*)
  = to rain
  piove = it's raining

piovve ▶ **piovere**

pipì✶ *noun, feminine*
  fare la pipì = to pee

piscina *noun, feminine*
  una piscina = a swimming pool

pisello *noun, masculine*
  i piselli = peas

pista *noun, feminine*
- una pista = a track
- una pista = a ski slope
- la pista = the runway

pistola *noun, feminine*
  una pistola = a gun

pittore/pittrice *noun, masculine/feminine*
  un pittore/una pittrice = a painter

pittura *noun, feminine*
- la pittura = painting
- la pittura = paint

più *adverb*
- = more
  = most
  è più alto di me = he's taller than me
  è il più alto della classe = he's the tallest in the class
  mettici più zucchero = put more sugar in it
  chi ha fatto più errori? = who made the most mistakes?
- = any more
  non esiste più = it doesn't exist any more
  non ci vado mai più = I'm never going there again
- = plus
  cinque più cinque = five plus five

piuma *noun, feminine*
  una piuma = a feather

piumone® *noun, masculine*
  un piumone = a duvet

P

piuttosto *adverb*
= rather
sono piuttosto stanco = I'm rather tired

plastica *noun, feminine*
la plastica = plastic
una bottiglia di plastica = a plastic bottle

po'
1 *noun, masculine*
un po' di = a little
un po' di vino = a little wine
dura un po' di tempo = it lasts some time
2 un po' *adverb*
= a bit, a little
un po' stanco = a bit tired, a little tired
ho dormito un po' = I slept a little

poco/poca *(plural* **pochi/poche***)*
1 *adjective*
poco tempo = not much time
pochi turisti = not many tourists
troppo poca pasta = not enough pasta
2 poco *adverb*
• *(with verbs)* = not much
ho dormito poco = I didn't sleep much
• *(with adjectives)* = not very
poco gentile = not very nice
poco profondo = shallow

poesia *noun, feminine*
• la poesia = poetry
• una poesia = a poem

poeta *noun, masculine (plural* **poeti***)*
un poeta = a poet

poi *adverb*
• = then
= next
prima o poi = sooner or later
da lunedì in poi = from Monday onward(s)
• = besides

poiché *conjunction*
= since

polacco/polacca *adjective (plural*
polacchi/polacche*)*
= Polish

polemica *noun, feminine*
una polemica = a controversy

politica *noun, feminine*
• la politica = politics
• una politica = a policy

politico/politica *(plural* **politici/**
politiche*)*
1 *adjective*
= political
2 politico *noun, masculine*
un politico = a politician

polizia *noun, feminine*
la polizia = the police

poliziotto *noun, masculine*
un poliziotto = a policeman

pollice *noun, masculine*
• un pollice = a thumb
• un pollice = an inch

pollo *noun, masculine*
un pollo = a chicken
mi piace il pollo = I like chicken

polmone *noun, masculine*
un polmone = a lung

Polonia *noun, feminine*
la Polonia = Poland

polpo *noun, masculine*
un polpo = an octopus

polso *noun, masculine*
• il polso = the wrist
• il polso = the pulse

poltrona *noun, feminine*
una poltrona = an armchair

polvere *noun, feminine*
• la polvere = powder
• la polvere = dust

pomeriggio *noun, masculine (plural*
pomeriggi*)*
un pomeriggio = an afternoon
nel pomeriggio = in the afternoon

pomodoro *noun, masculine*
un pomodoro = a tomato

pompelmo *noun, masculine*
un pompelmo = a grapefruit

pompiere *noun, masculine*
un pompiere = a firefighter
i pompieri = the fire brigade, the fire
department

pone, **pongo**, etc ▶ **porre**

ponte *noun, masculine*
un ponte = a bridge

popolare *adjective*
= popular

popolazione *noun, feminine*
la popolazione = the population

popolo *noun, masculine*
un popolo = a people

porcellana *noun, feminine*
la porcellana = china

porco *noun, masculine (plural* **porci***)*
un porco = a pig

porre *verb* 50
= to put

porta *noun, feminine*
una porta = a door

portacenere *noun, masculine* (**!** *never*
changes)
un portacenere = an ashtray

portafoglio *noun, masculine (plural*
portafogli*)*
un portafoglio = a wallet

portare *verb* 1
• = to carry
• = to bring
= to take
'da portar via' = 'to take away'

portata *noun, feminine*
- una portata = a course
- a portata di mano = within reach

portatile *adjective*
= portable

portato/portata *adjective*
essere portato/portata per le lingue = to be good at languages

portavoce *noun, masculine/feminine*
(**!** *never changes*)
un/una portavoce = a spokesperson

porto *noun, masculine*
un porto = a port

posate *noun, feminine plural*
le posate = cutlery

pose, **posi**, etc ▶ **porre**

positivo/positiva *adjective*
= positive

posizione *noun, feminine*
una posizione = a position

possa, **possano** ▶ **potere**

possedere *verb* 51
= to possess

possiamo ▶ **potere**

possibile *adjective*
= possible

possibilità *noun, feminine* (**!** *never changes*)
- una possibilità = a possibility
- una possibilità = a chance

possibilmente *adverb*
= if possible

possiede, **possiedo**, etc ▶ **possedere**

posso, **possono** ▶ **potere**

posta *noun, feminine*
la posta = the post, the mail

posta elettronica *noun, feminine*
una posta elettronica = an email

postino/postina *noun, masculine/feminine*
un postino/una postina = a postman/a postwoman, a letter carrier

posto *noun, masculine*
- un posto = a place
- un posto = a seat
- a posto = tidy
mettere a posto = to tidy up

posto/posta ▶ **porre**

potabile *adjective*
acqua potabile = drinking water

potente *adjective*
= powerful

potenza *noun, feminine*
la potenza = power

potere
1 *verb* 52
= to be able
= can
non posso venire = I can't come
lo posso provare? = can I try it on?
non si può fare così = you can't do that
2 *noun, masculine*
il potere = power

potrà, **potuto/potuta**, etc ▶ **potere**

povero/povera *adjective*
= poor
povero Renato! = poor Renato!

pranzo *noun, masculine*
il pranzo = lunch

pratica *noun, feminine*
la pratica = practice
in pratica = practically

praticamente *adverb*
= practically

pratico/pratica *adjective* (*plural* **pratici/pratiche**)
= practical

prato *noun, masculine*
- un prato = a meadow
- un prato = a lawn

precedente *adjective*
= previous

preciso/precisa *adjective*
= precise

preferenza *noun, feminine*
una preferenza = a preference

preferire *verb* 9
= to prefer

preferito/preferita *adjective*
= favo(u)rite

prefisso *noun, masculine*
- un prefisso = a prefix
- un prefisso telefonico = a dialling code, an area code

pregare *verb* 5
- = to pray
- pregare qualcuno di fare qualcosa = to ask someone to do something

preghiera *noun, feminine*
una preghiera = a prayer

pregiudizio *noun, masculine* (*plural* **pregiudizi**)
un pregiudizio = a prejudice

prego *exclamation*
- 'grazie!'—'prego!' = 'thank you!'—'you're welcome!'
- 'posso fumare?'—'prego!' = 'can I smoke?'—'please do!'

premere verb [8]
= to press

premio noun, masculine (plural **premi**)
un premio = a prize

prendere verb [53]
- = to take
  chi ha preso la mia borsa? = who took
  my bag?
  ho preso l'autobus = I took the bus
- = to get
  vai a prendere le posate! = go and get
  the cutlery!
- = to catch
  prendere la palla = to catch the ball
  prendere freddo = to catch cold
- (talking about food, drink) = to have
  prendi un caffè? = would you like a
  coffee?
- (in a car) = to pick up
  devo andare a prenderli alla stazione = I
  have to pick them up from the station

prenotare verb [1]
= to book

prenotazione noun, feminine
una prenotazione = a booking

preoccupare verb [1]
1 (! + avere)
= to worry
2 preoccuparsi (! + essere)
= to worry
= to be worried

preoccupato/preoccupata
adjective
= worried

preparare verb [1]
= to prepare
preparare la colazione = to fix breakfast

presa noun, feminine
una presa = a socket

prese, **presi** ▶ **prendere**

presentare verb [1]
- = to introduce
- = to present

presente
1 adjective
= present
2 noun, masculine
il presente = the present

preservativo noun, masculine
un preservativo = a condom

preside noun, masculine/feminine
il/la preside = the headteacher, the
principal

presidente/presidentessa noun,
masculine/feminine
il presidente/la presidentessa = the
president

preso/presa ▶ **prendere**

pressione noun, feminine
la pressione = the pressure

prestare verb [1]
= to lend

prestito noun, masculine
un prestito = a loan
prendere in prestito qualcosa = to borrow
something

presto adverb
- = early
- = soon
- fare presto = to be quick

prete noun, masculine
un prete = a priest

pretendere verb [53]
- = to demand
- = to expect

pretese, **preteso/pretesa**, **etc** ▶
pretendere

prevenzione noun, feminine
la prevenzione = prevention

previsione noun, feminine
una previsione = a forecast
le previsioni del tempo = the weather
forecast

previsto/prevista adjective
= expected

prezioso/preziosa adjective
= precious

prezzemolo noun, masculine
il prezzemolo = parsley

prezzo noun, masculine
un prezzo = a price

prigione noun, feminine
una prigione = a prison

prigioniero/prigioniera noun,
masculine/feminine
un prigioniero/una prigioniera = a
prisoner

prima adverb
- = before
- prima di = before
  prima della lezione = before the lesson
- prima che = before
  prima che se ne accorga = before he
  realizes

primavera noun, feminine
la primavera = spring

primo/prima
1 adjective
= first
il primo maggio = the first of May
2 primo noun, masculine
il primo = the first course

principale adjective
= principal
= main

principe/principessa *noun, masculine/feminine*
  un principe/una principessa = a prince/a princess

principiante *noun, masculine/feminine*
  un/una principiante = a beginner

principio *noun, masculine (plural* **principi**)
• **un principio** = a principle
• **il principio** = the beginning

privato/privata *adjective*
  = private

privilegio *noun, masculine (plural* **privilegi**)
  un privilegio = a privilege

privo/priva *adjective*
  privo di sintomi = without symptoms

probabile *adjective*
  = probable

probabilmente *adverb*
  = probably

problema *noun, masculine (plural* **problemi**)
  un problema = a problem
  non c'è problema! = no problem!

processo *noun, masculine*
• **un processo** = a process
• **un processo** = a trial

prodotto/prodotta
1 ▶ **produrre**
2 **prodotto** *noun, masculine*
  un prodotto = a product

produce, producono, etc ▶ **produrre**

produrre *verb* 54
  = to produce

produsse, produssi, etc ▶ **produrre**

professionale *adjective*
  = professional

professione *noun, feminine*
  una professione = a profession

professionista *noun, masculine/feminine (plural* **professionisti/professioniste**)
  un/una professionista = a professional

professore/professoressa *noun, masculine/feminine*
  un professore/una professoressa = a teacher

profondità *noun, feminine*
  la profondità = the depth

profondo/profonda *adjective*
  = deep

profugo/profuga *noun, masculine/feminine (plural* **profughi/profughe**)
  un profugo/una profuga = a refugee

profumo *noun, masculine*
  un profumo = a perfume

profumeria *noun, feminine*
  una profumeria = a perfumery

progetto *noun, masculine*
  un progetto = a plan
  = a project

programma *noun, masculine (plural* **programmi**)
• **un programma** = a program(me)
• **un programma** = a plan

progresso *noun, masculine*
  il progresso = progress
  fare progressi = to make progress

proibire *verb* 9
  = to forbid
  proibire a qualcuno di fare qualcosa = to forbid someone to do something

promessa *noun, feminine*
  una promessa = a promise

promesso/promessa ▶ **promettere**

promettere *verb* 40
  = to promise

promise, promisi, etc ▶ **promettere**

promosse, promosso/promossa, etc ▶ **promuovere**

promozione *noun, feminine*
  una promozione = a promotion

promuovere *verb* 42
• = to promote
• **essere promosso/promossa** = to be promoted
  (*at school*) = to go up a year

pronto/pronta
1 *adjective*
  = ready
2 **pronto** *exclamation*
  pronto? = hello!

pronuncia *noun, feminine (plural* **pronunce**)
  la pronuncia = pronunciation

pronunciare *verb* 2
  = to pronounce
  come si pronuncia? = how do you pronounce it?

propone, propongo, etc ▶ **proporre**

proporre *verb* 50
  = to propose
  = to suggest

propose, proposi, etc ▶ **proporre**

proposito *noun, masculine*
• **un proposito** = a purpose
• **a proposito** = by the way

P

proposta *noun, feminine*
una proposta = a proposal
= a suggestion

proposto/proposta ▶ **proporre**

proprietà *noun, feminine* (**!** *never changes*)
la proprietà = property

proprietario/proprietaria *noun, masculine|feminine* (*plural* **proprietari/proprietarie**)
il proprietario/la proprietaria = the owner

proprio/propria (*plural* **propri/proprie**)
1 *adjective*
la propria camera = one's own room
2 proprio *adverb*
• = just
proprio in quel momento = just at that moment
• = really
è proprio vero! = it's really true!

prosciutto *noun, masculine*
il prosciutto crudo = cured ham
il prosciutto cotto = cooked ham

prossimo/prossima *adjective*
= next
venerdì prossimo = next Friday

prostituto/prostituta *noun, masculine|feminine*
un prostituto/una prostituta = a prostitute

proteggere *verb* 39
= to protect

protesse, protessi, etc ▶ **proteggere**

protesta *noun, feminine*
una protesta = a protest

protestante *noun, masculine|feminine*
un/una protestante = a Protestant

protestare *verb* 1
= to protest

protetto/protetta ▶ **proteggere**

protezione *noun, feminine*
la protezione = protection

prova *noun, feminine*
• una prova = a trial
• le prove = the proof
• una prova = a rehearsal

provare *verb* 1
• = to try (on)
• provare a fare qualcosa = to try to do something
• = to rehearse

provincia *noun, feminine* (*plural* **province**)
una provincia = a province

provocare *verb* 4
= to cause

provvisorio/provvisoria *adjective*
= temporary

prudente *adjective*
= careful

psichiatra *noun, masculine|feminine* (*plural* **psichiatri/psichiatre**)
uno/una psichiatra = a psychiatrist

psicologia *noun, feminine*
la psicologia = psychology

psicologo/psicologa *noun masculine|feminine* (*plural* **psicologi/psicologhe**)
uno psicologo/una psicologa = a psychologist

pubblicare *verb* 4
= to publish

pubblicità *noun, feminine* (**!** *never changes*)
la pubblicità = advertising
una pubblicità = an advertisement

pubblico/pubblica (*plural* **pubblici/pubbliche**)
1 *adjective*
= public
2 pubblico *noun, masculine*
• il pubblico = the public
• il pubblico = the audience

pugilato *noun, masculine*
il pugilato = boxing

pugile *noun, masculine*
un pugile = a boxer

Puglia *noun, feminine*
la Puglia = Apulia

pugliese *adjective*
= Apulian

pugno *noun, masculine*
un pugno = a fist
= a punch

pulire *verb* 9
= to clean

pulito/pulita *adjective*
= clean

pulizia *noun, feminine*
fare le pulizie = to do the cleaning

pullman *noun, masculine* (**!** *never changes*)
un pullman = a coach, a bus

pungere *verb* 48
= to sting

punire *verb* 9
= to punish

punizione *noun, feminine*
una punizione = a punishment

punse, punsero, etc ▶ **pungere**

punta *noun, feminine*
una punta = a point

puntare *verb* 1
= to point

◆ may be considered offensive

puntata *noun, feminine*
una puntata = an episode

punteggiatura *noun, feminine*
la punteggiatura = punctuation

punteggio *noun, masculine (plural* **punteggi**)
il punteggio = the score

punto/punta
1 ▶ **pungere**
2 **punto** *noun, masculine*
• un punto = a point
• un punto = a stitch
• un punto = a full stop, a period
punto e virgola = semicolon
due punti = colon

puntuale *adjective*
= punctual
= on time

puntura *noun, feminine*
una puntura = an injection

può, **puoi** ▶ **potere**

purché *conjunction*
= as long as

pure *adverb*
• = as well
• fai pure! = go ahead!
si accomodi pure! = do sit down!

purè *noun, masculine*
il purè di patate = mashed potatoes

puro/pura *adjective*
= pure

purtroppo *adverb*
= unfortunately

puttana *noun, feminine*
una puttana = a whore

puzza *noun, feminine*
una puzza = a stink

puzzare *verb* 1
= to stink

puzzo *noun, masculine* ▶ **puzza**

qua *adverb*
= here
vieni qua! = come here!

quaderno *noun, masculine*
un quaderno = an exercise book

quadrato/quadrata
1 *adjective*
= square
2 **quadrato** *noun, masculine*
un quadrato = a square

quadro/quadra
1 *adjective*
un metro quadro = a square metre, a square meter
2 **quadro** *noun, masculine*
un quadro = a painting

qualche *adjective*
= a few
qualche ostrica = a few oysters
> ❗ Qualche *is always followed by a singular noun.*

qualcosa *pronoun*
= something
= anything
qualcosa di strano = something strange
c'è qualcosa che non va? = is there anything wrong?

qualcuno/qualcuna *pronoun*
1 = some
ne ho preso qualcuno = I took some
qualcuna è marcia = some of them are rotten
2 **qualcuno**
= someone
= anyone
qualcun altro = someone else
ha chiamato qualcuno? = did anyone call?

quale
1 *adjective*
= which
= what
quali scarpe mi metto? = which shoes shall I wear?
qual è il tuo numero di telefono? = what's your phone number?
2 *pronoun*
• = which (one)
= what
quale preferisci? = which one do you prefer?
qual è il mio? = which one is mine?
qual è il tuo colore preferito? = what's your favourite colour?
• il quale/la quale = who, whom
= which
del quale = whose

qualifica *noun, feminine (plural* **qualifiche**)
una qualifica = a qualification

qualità *noun, feminine* (❗ *never changes*)
una qualità = a quality

qualsiasi, **qualunque** *adjective*
= any
in qualsiasi momento = at any time
qualsiasi cosa = anything

quando
1 *adverb*
= when
quando sei arrivato? = when did you arrive?   ····▶

Q

2 *conjunction*
= when
quando lo leggerai, capirai tutto = you'll understand everything when you read it

quantità *noun, feminine* (**!** *never changes*)
una quantità = a quantity

quanto/quanta
1 *adjective*
• **quanto/quanta** = how much
quanti/quante = how many
quanto tempo hai? = how much time do you have?
quanti ne vuoi? = how many do you want?
quanti ne abbiamo oggi? = what's the date today?
• (*in exclamations*) = what a lot
quanta gente! = what a lot of people!
2 **quanto** *adverb*
• (*in questions*) = how much
quanto viene? = how much is it?
quanto ci hai messo? = how long did you take?
• (*in exclamations*)
quanto mi piace! = I like it so much!
quant'è bello! = it's so beautiful!
• (*with adjectives*) = how
quant'è lungo? = how long is it?

quaranta *number*
= forty

quarantesimo/quarantesima
adjective
= fortieth

quarantina *noun, feminine*
una quarantina di scioperanti = about forty strikers

quaresima *noun, feminine*
quaresima = Lent

quartiere *noun, masculine*
un quartiere = a neighbo(u)rhood

quarto/quarta *adjective*
= fourth

quasi *adverb*
= almost
quasi mai = hardly ever

quattordicenne *adjective*
= fourteen-year-old

quattordicesimo/quattordicesima
adjective
= fourteenth

quattordici *number*
= fourteen

quattrini *noun, masculine plural*
i quattrini = money

quattro *number*
= four

quattrocento
1 *number*
= four hundred

2 **Quattrocento** *noun, masculine*
il Quattrocento = the 15th century

quello/quella
1 *adjective*

> **!** *Before masculine nouns beginning with z, ps, gn, or s + another consonant,* **quello** *is used in the singular and* **quegli** *in the plural. Before masculine nouns beginning with other consonants,* **quel** *is used in the singular and* **quei** *in the plural. Before all nouns beginning with a vowel,* **quell'** *is used in the singular and* **quegli** (*masculine*) *or* **quelle** (*feminine*) *in the plural.*

quel/quella = that
quei/quelle = those
quell'informazione = that information
quegli uomini = those men
quel negozio lì = that shop
2 *pronoun*
• **quello/quella** = that (one)
quelli/quelle = those (ones)
voglio quello là = I want that one
• **quello rosso** = the red one
quelli verdi = the green ones
quello che ti piace = the one you like
• **quello che vorrei fare** = what I'd like to do

questione *noun, feminine*
una questione = an issue

questo/questa
1 *adjective* (*sometimes* **quest'** *before a vowel*)
questo/questa = this
questi/queste = these
quest'estate = this summer
2 *pronoun*
= this (one)
questo/questa = this (one)
questi/queste = these (ones)
voglio questi qui = I want these ones

questura *noun, feminine*
la questura = the police station

qui *adverb*
= here
voglio restare qui = I want to stay here

quindi
1 *conjunction*
= so
2 *adverb*
= then

quindicenne *adjective*
= fifteen-year-old

quindicesimo/quindicesima
adjective
= fifteenth

quindici *number*
= fifteen

quindicina *noun, feminine*
- **una quindicina di ragazzi** = about fifteen boys
- **una quindicina di giorni** = a fortnight, two weeks

quinto/quinta *adjective*
= fifth

quotidiano/quotidiana
1 *adjective*
= daily
2 quotidiano *noun, masculine*
un quotidiano = a daily newspaper

Rr

---

rabbia *noun, feminine*
- **la rabbia** = anger
- **la rabbia** = rabies

racchetta *noun, feminine*
una racchetta = a racket

raccogliere *verb* 22
= to pick (up)

raccolgo, **raccolse**, **etc** ▶ raccogliere

raccolta *noun, feminine*
- **la raccolta** = the harvest
- **una raccolta** = a collection

raccolto/raccolta
1 ▶ raccogliere
2 raccolto *noun, masculine*
il raccolto = the harvest

raccomandare *verb* 1
= to recommend

raccomandata *noun, feminine*
una raccomandata = a recorded-delivery letter, a certified letter

raccontare *verb* 1
= to tell

racconto *noun, masculine*
un racconto = a story

raddoppiare *verb* 6
= to double

radice *noun, feminine*
una radice = a root

radio *noun, feminine* (**!** *never changes*)
una radio = a radio
alla radio = on the radio

radiografia *noun, feminine*
una radiografia = an X-ray

raffinato/raffinata *adjective*
= refined

rafforzare *verb* 1
= to strengthen

raffreddarsi *verb* 1 (**!** + *essere*)
= to cool down
= to get cold

raffreddato/raffreddata *adjective*
essere raffreddato/raffreddata = to have a cold

raffreddore *noun, masculine*
un raffreddore = a cold

ragazzo/ragazza *noun, masculine/feminine*
un ragazzo/una ragazza = a boy/a girl
i ragazzi = the children

raggio *noun, masculine* (*plural* **raggi**)
un raggio = a ray

raggiungere *verb* 48
= to reach

raggiunse, **raggiunto/raggiunta**, **etc** ▶ raggiungere

ragione *noun, feminine*
- **una ragione** = a reason
- **aver ragione** = to be right

ragioneria *noun, feminine*
la ragioneria = accountancy

ragionevole *adjective*
= reasonable

ragioniere/ragioniera *noun, masculine/feminine*
un ragioniere/una ragioniera = an accountant

ragnatela *noun, feminine*
una ragnatela = a spider's web
= a cobweb

ragno *noun, masculine*
un ragno = a spider

rallentare *verb* 1
= to slow down

ramo *noun, masculine*
un ramo = a branch

rana *noun, feminine*
una rana = a frog

rapido/rapida *adjective*
= quick

rapina *noun, feminine*
una rapina = a robbery

rapinare *verb* 1
= to rob

rapinatore/rapinatrice *noun, masculine/feminine*
un rapinatore/una rapinatrice = a robber

rapire *verb* 9
= to kidnap

rapporto *noun, masculine*
un rapporto = a relationship

R

rappresentante *noun, masculine/feminine*
un/una rappresentante = a representative

rappresentare *verb* [1]
= to represent

raro/rara *adjective*
= rare

rasoio *noun, masculine (plural rasoi)*
un rasoio = a razor

rassicurare *verb* [1]
= to reassure

rata *noun, feminine*
una rata = an instal(l)ment

razza *noun, feminine*
• una razza = a race
• una razza canina = a breed of dog

razzismo *noun, masculine*
il razzismo = racism

razzista *noun, masculine/feminine (plural razzisti/razziste)*
un/una razzista = a racist

re *noun, masculine (! never changes)*
un re = a king

reagire *verb* [9]
= to react

reale *adjective*
• = real
• = royal

realista *noun, masculine/feminine (plural realisti/realiste)*
un/una realista = a realist

realizzare *verb* [1]
• = to achieve
• = to realize

realmente *adverb*
= really

realtà *noun, feminine*
la realtà = reality
in realtà = really

reazione *noun, feminine*
una reazione = a reaction

recente *adjective*
= recent
di recente = recently

recitare *verb* [1]
= to act

réclame *noun, feminine (! never changes)*
una réclame = an advert

reclamo *noun, masculine*
un reclamo = a complaint

recuperare *verb* [1]
= to get back

redattore/redattrice *noun, masculine/feminine*
un redattore/una redattrice = an editor

referenza *noun, feminine*
una referenza = a reference

regalare *verb* [1]
= to give

regalo *noun, masculine*
un regalo = a present

reggere *verb* [39]
1 (! + avere)
= to hold (up)
2 reggersi (! + essere)
reggersi in piedi = to stand up

reggiseno *noun, masculine*
un reggiseno = a bra

regina *noun, feminine*
una regina = a queen

regionale *adjective*
= regional

regione *noun, feminine*
una regione = a region

regista *noun, masculine/feminine (plural registi/registe)*
un/una regista = a director

registrare *verb* [1]
= to record

registratore *noun, masculine*
un registratore = a tape recorder

registrazione *noun, feminine*
una registrazione = a recording

registro *noun, masculine*
un registro = a register

regno *noun, masculine*
un regno = a kingdom

Regno Unito *noun, masculine*
il Regno Unito = the United Kingdom

regola *noun, feminine*
una regola = a rule

regolare
1 *adjective*
= regular
2 *verb* [1]
• = to regulate
• = to adjust
• = to settle

relativo/relativa *adjective*
= relative

relazione *noun, feminine*
• una relazione = a relationship
• una relazione = a report

religione *noun, feminine*
la religione = religion

religioso/religiosa *adjective*
= religious

rendere *verb* [53]
• = to give back
• = to make
rendere qualcuno felice = to make someone happy

reparto noun, masculine
un reparto = a department
(*in a hospital*) = a ward

replica noun, feminine (plural **repliche**)
una replica = a repeat

repubblica noun, feminine (plural
repubbliche)
una repubblica = a republic

reputazione noun, feminine
una reputazione = a reputation

requisito noun, masculine
un requisito = a condition

residente noun, masculine|feminine
un/una residente = a resident

resistente adjective
= strong
= tough

resistere verb 16
resistere a qualcosa = to resist something
= to withstand something

rese, **reso/resa**, etc ▶ **rendere**

respingere verb 48
= to reject
essere respinto/respinta = to fail

respinse, **respinto/respinta**, etc
▶ **respingere**

respirare verb 1
= to breathe

respiro noun, masculine
il respiro = breath

responsabile
1 adjective
• = responsible
• essere responsabile = to be in charge
2 noun, masculine|feminine
il/la responsabile = the person in charge

responsabilità noun, feminine (! never
changes)
una responsabilità = a responsibility

restare verb 1
• = to stay
• = to be left
me ne restano quattro = I have four left

restaurare verb 1
= to restore

restauro noun, masculine
un restauro = a restoration

restituire verb 9
= to give back

resto noun, masculine
• il resto del latte = the rest of the milk
• i resti = the leftovers
• il resto = the change

rete noun, feminine
• una rete = a net
• una rete = a network

retromarcia noun, feminine
la retromarcia = reverse gear

rettangolo noun, masculine
un rettangolo = a rectangle

retto/retta
1 ▶ **reggere**
2 adjective
= straight

riassumere verb 17
= to summarize

riassunto/riassunta
1 ▶ **riassumere**
2 **riassunto** noun, masculine
un riassunto = a summary

ribelle noun, masculine|feminine
un/una ribelle = a rebel

ribes noun, masculine (! never changes)
il ribes nero = blackcurrants
il ribes rosso = redcurrants

ricamare verb 1
= to embroider

ricattare verb 1
= to blackmail

riccio/riccia (plural **ricci/ricce**)
1 adjective
= curly
2 **riccio** noun, masculine
• un riccio = a curl
• un riccio = a hedgehog

ricco/ricca adjective (plural
ricchi/ricche)
= rich

ricerca noun, feminine (plural **ricerche**)
• la ricerca = research
fare delle ricerche = to do research
• una ricerca = a project

ricetta noun, feminine
• una ricetta = a recipe
• una ricetta medica = a prescription

ricevere verb 8
= to receive

ricevuta noun, feminine
una ricevuta = a receipt

richiamare verb 1
• = to call back
• = to attract

richiedere verb 20
= to require

richiese, **richiesi**, etc ▶
richiedere

richiesta noun, feminine
una richiesta = a request

richiesto/richiesta ▶ **richiedere**

riciclare verb 1
= to recycle

R

ricominciare *verb* [2] (**!** + *essere* or *avere*)
= to start again

riconobbe, **riconobbi**, **etc** ▶ **riconoscere**

riconoscere *verb* [25]
= to recognize

ricordare *verb* [1]
1 (**!** + *avere*)
• = to remember
• = to remind
2 ricordarsi (**!** + *essere*)
ricordarsi = to remember
ricordarsi di fare qualcosa = to remember to do something
non mi ricordo = I can't remember

ricordo *noun, masculine*
• un ricordo = a memory
• un ricordo = a souvenir

ricoverare *verb* [1]
1 (**!** + *avere*)
ricoverare qualcuno = to take someone into hospital
essere ricoverato/ricoverata = to be taken into hospital
2 ricoverarsi (**!** + *essere*)
ricoverarsi = to go into hospital

ridere *verb* [30]
= to laugh

ridicolo/**ridicola** *adjective*
= ridiculous

ridotto/**ridotta**, **riduce**, **etc** ▶ **ridurre**

ridurre *verb* [54]
= to reduce

riduzione *noun, feminine*
una riduzione = a reduction

riempire *verb* [55]
= to fill

riesce, **riesco**, **etc** ▶ **riuscire**

rifà, **rifaccio**, **etc** ▶ **rifare**

rifare *verb* [38]
• = to do again
• rifare il letto = to make the bed

rifatto/**rifatta** ▶ **rifare**

riferire *verb* [9]
1 (**!** + *avere*)
essere riferito a qualcosa = to refer to something
2 riferirsi (**!** + *essere*)
riferirsi a qualcosa = to refer to something

rifiutare *verb* [1]
1 (**!** + *avere*)
= to refuse
2 rifiutarsi (**!** + *essere*)
rifiutarsi di fare qualcosa = to refuse to do something

rifiuto *noun, masculine*
• un rifiuto = a refusal
• i rifiuti = rubbish, garbage

riflesso *noun, masculine*
un riflesso = a reflection

riflettere *verb* [8]
= to reflect

riforma *noun, feminine*
una riforma = a reform

rifornire *verb* [9]
= to supply

riga *noun, feminine* (*plural* **righe**)
• una riga = a line
• una riga = a stripe
una camicia a righe = a striped shirt
• una riga = a parting, a part

rigido/**rigida** *adjective*
= rigid
= stiff

riguardare *verb* [1]
= to concern
non ti riguarda! = it has nothing to do with you!

riguardo *noun, masculine*
• con riguardo = with respect
• **riguardo a**
riguardo all'annuncio = concerning the ad

rilasciare *verb* [6]
• = to release
• = to issue

rilassarsi *verb* [1] (**!** + *essere*)
= to relax

rima *noun, feminine*
una rima = a rhyme

rimandare *verb* [1]
• = to send back
• = to postpone

rimanere *verb* [56] (**!** + *essere*)
• = to stay
• = to be left
me ne rimangono tre = I have three left
• = to be
sono rimasto deluso = I was disappointed
rimanere male = to be offended

rimango, **rimarrà**, **rimase**, **etc** ▶ **rimanere**

rimasto/**rimasta**
1 ▶ **rimanere**
2 *adjective*
= left over

rimborso *noun, masculine*
un rimborso = a refund

rimpiangere *verb* [48]
= to regret

Rinascimento *noun, masculine*
il Rinascimento = the Renaissance

rinchiudere *verb* 21
  rinchiudere qualcuno = to shut someone
    up

rinfrescare *verb* 4
  = to refresh

ringraziare *verb* 6
  = to thank

rinnovare *verb* 1
  = to renew

rintracciare *verb* 2
  = to get in touch with

rinunciare *verb* 2
  rinunciare a qualcosa = to give
    something up
  ci rinuncio! = I give up!

rinviare *verb* 7
  = to postpone

riparare *verb* 1
1 (**!** + *avere*)
  = to repair
2 **ripararsi** (**!** + *essere*)
  ripararsi = to shelter

ripassare *verb* 1
  = to revise

ripetere *verb* 8
  = to repeat

ripetizione *noun, feminine*
  la ripetizione = repetition

ripiano *noun, masculine*
  un ripiano = a shelf

ripido/ripida *adjective*
  = steep

ripieno *noun, masculine*
  il ripieno = the stuffing

riposarsi *verb* 1 (**!** + *essere*)
  = to rest

riposo *noun, masculine*
  il riposo = rest

riprendere *verb* 53
• = to take back
  = to take again
• = to resume

riprese, **ripreso/ripresa**, etc ▶
  riprendere

riprodurre *verb* 54
  = to reproduce

risalga, **risalgono**, etc ▶ risalire

risalire *verb* 61
• (**!** + *essere* or *avere*) = to go back up
• (**!** + *essere*) risalire a = to date back to
  risale al Medioevo = it dates back to the
    Middle Ages

risata *noun, feminine*
  una risata = a laugh

riscaldamento *noun, masculine*
  il riscaldamento = the heating

riscaldare *verb* 1
  = to heat (up)
  = to warm (up)

rischiare *verb* 6
  = to risk

rischio *noun, masculine* (*plural* **rischi**)
  un rischio = a risk

rise, **risi**, etc ▶ ridere

riservare *verb* 1
  = to reserve

riso¹ ▶ ridere

riso² *noun, masculine*
  il riso = rice

risolse, **risolto/risolta**, etc ▶
  risolvere

risolvere *verb* 57
  = to solve

risorsa *noun, feminine*
  le risorse = resources

risparmiare *verb* 6
  = to save

risparmio *noun, masculine* (*plural*
  risparmi)
  un risparmio = a saving

rispettare *verb* 1
  = to respect

rispetto *noun, masculine*
  il rispetto = respect

rispondere *verb* 58
  rispondere a qualcuno = to answer
    someone

rispose, **risposi**, etc ▶ rispondere

risposta *noun feminine*
  una risposta = an answer
  = a reply

risposto/risposta ▶ rispondere

ristorante *noun, masculine*
  un ristorante = a restaurant

risultato *noun, masculine*
  un risultato = a result

ritardare *verb* 1
  = to delay
  = to be late

ritardo *noun, masculine*
  un ritardo = a delay
  arrivare in ritardo = to arrive late

ritenere *verb* 73
• = to consider
• = to hold back

ritengo, **ritiene**, etc ▶ ritenere

ritirare *verb* 1
• = to withdraw
• = to pick up

ritmo *noun, masculine*
  il ritmo = rhythm

R

ritorno *noun, masculine*
il ritorno = return

ritratto *noun, masculine*
un ritratto = a portrait

riunione *noun, feminine*
una riunione = a meeting

riunire *verb* 9
1 (**!** + *avere*) = to gather together
2 **riunirsi** (**!** + *essere*)
riunirsi = to meet

riuscire *verb* 75 (**!** + *essere*)
riuscire a fare qualcosa = to manage to
do something
non mi riesce, non ci riesco = I can't
manage

riuscita *noun, feminine*
la riuscita = the success

riuscito/riuscita *adjective*
= successful

riva *noun, feminine*
la riva = the bank

rivale *noun, masculine/feminine*
un/una rivale = a rival

rivista *noun, feminine*
una rivista = a magazine

rivolgere *verb* 59
1 (**!** + *avere*)
rivolgere la parola a qualcuno = to speak
to someone
2 **rivolgersi** (**!** + *essere*)
rivolgersi a qualcuno = to speak to
someone

rivolse, **rivolto/rivolta** ▶ rivolgere

rivoluzione *noun, feminine*
una rivoluzione = a revolution

roba *noun, feminine*
la roba = stuff

roccia *noun, feminine* (*plural* **rocce**)
una roccia = a rock

Roma *noun*
= Rome

romanico/romanica *adjective* (*plural*
romanici/romaniche)
= romanesque

romano/romana *adjective*
= Roman

romanzo *noun, masculine*
un romanzo = a novel

rompere *verb* 60
1 (**!** + *avere*)
= to break
2 **rompersi** (**!** + *essere*)
rompersi = to break
si è rotta la sedia = the chair broke

✗ in informal situations

rosa
1 *noun, feminine*
una rosa = a rose
2 *adjective* (**!** *never changes*)
= pink

rosmarino *noun, masculine*
il rosmarino = rosemary

rossetto *noun, masculine*
il rossetto = lipstick

rosso/rossa *adjective*
= red

rotolare *verb* 1
= to roll

rotondo/rotonda *adjective*
= round

rotto/rotta
1 ▶ rompere
2 *adjective*
= broken

rottura *noun, feminine*
• una rottura = a break
• che rottura!✗ = what a pain!

roulotte *noun, feminine* (**!** *never
changes*)
una roulotte = a caravan, a trailer

rovescia *noun, feminine*, **rovescio**
noun, masculine
alla rovescia, a rovescio = the wrong way
round

rovesciare *verb* 6
• = to overturn
• = to spill

rovinare *verb* 1
= to ruin

rubare *verb* 1
= to steal

rubinetto *noun, masculine*
un rubinetto = a tap, a faucet

ruga *noun, feminine* (*plural* **rughe**)
una ruga = a wrinkle

ruggine *noun, feminine*
la ruggine = rust

ruggire *verb* 9
= to roar

rullino *noun, masculine*
un rullino = a film

rumore *noun, masculine*
un rumore = a noise

rumoroso/rumorosa *adjective*
= noisy

ruolo *noun, masculine*
un ruolo = a role

ruota *noun, feminine*
una ruota = a wheel

ruppe, **ruppi**, **etc** ▶ rompere

ruscello noun, masculine
 un ruscello = a stream

russo/russa adjective
 = Russian

ruvido/ruvida adjective
 = rough

---

sa ▶ sapere

sabato noun, masculine
 = Saturday
 arrivo sabato = I'm arriving on Saturday
 il sabato = on Saturdays

sabbia noun, feminine
 la sabbia = sand

sacchetto noun, masculine
 un sacchetto = a bag

sacco noun, masculine (plural **sacchi**)
• un sacco = a bag
• un sacco di soldi = loads of money

sacro/sacra adjective
 = sacred

saggio/saggia (plural **saggi/sagge**)
1 adjective
 = wise
2 noun, masculine
• un saggio = a sage
• un saggio = an essay

Sagittario noun, masculine
 = Sagittarius

sai ▶ sapere

sala noun, feminine
 una sala = a living room
 una sala da pranzo = a dining room

salame noun, masculine
 il salame = salami

salario noun, masculine (plural **salari**)
 un salario = a salary

salato/salata adjective
• (when it's food)
 (having a lot of salt) = salty
 (not sweet) = savo(u)ry
• (when it's a price) = high

saldo/salda
1 adjective
 = steady
2 saldo noun, masculine
• il saldo = the balance
• i saldi = the sales

sale noun, masculine
 il sale = salt

salgo, **salgono**, etc ▶ salire

salire verb 61 (! + essere or avere)
• = to go up
 salire le scale = to go up the stairs
• (with vehicles)
 salire [sul treno | sull'autobus | sulla bici] = to
  get on [the train | the bus | the bike]
 salire in macchina = to get in the car

salita noun, feminine
• una salita = a climb
• una salita = a slope
 in salita = uphill

salmone noun, masculine
 il salmone = salmon

salotto noun, masculine
 il salotto = the living room

salsa noun, feminine
 una salsa = a sauce

salsiccia noun, feminine (plural
 salsicce)
 una salsiccia = a sausage

saltare verb 1 (! + essere or avere)
• = to jump
• far saltare un edificio = to blow up a
 building

salto noun, masculine
• un salto = a jump
• fare un salto da qualcuno = to drop in on
 someone

salumeria noun, feminine
 una salumeria = a delicatessen

salumi noun, masculine plural
 i salumi = cured meats

salutare verb 1
 = to say hello/goodbye
 salutami Gabriele = say hello to Gabriele
  for me
 ti saluta Iacopo = Iacopo says hello

salute noun, feminine
• la salute = health
• salute! = cheers!

saluto noun, masculine
• un saluto = a greeting
• (in a letter)
 tanti saluti, Elena = lots of love, Elena
 cordiali saluti = (yours) sincerely

salvare verb 1
 = to save
 = to rescue

salve exclamation
 salve! = hi!

salvo preposition
 = except

salvo/salva adjective
 = safe

sammarinese adjective
 = San Marinese

san ▶ santo

sandalo noun, masculine
un sandalo = a sandal

sangue noun, masculine
il sangue = blood
una bistecca al sangue = a rare steak

sanguinare verb [1]
= to bleed
mi sanguina il naso = my nose is
bleeding

sanno ▶ sapere

sano/sana adjective
= healthy
sano e salvo/sana e salva = safe and
sound

santo/santa
1 adjective
= holy
2 noun, masculine/feminine
• un santo/una santa = a saint
San Francesco/Santa Chiara = Saint
Francis/Saint Clare
• San Valentino = Valentine's Day
Santo Stefano = Boxing Day, December
26

sapere verb [62]
• = to know
so che verrà = I know he'll come
• = can
so nuotare = I can swim
• = to find out
• = to hear
ho saputo che ti sposi = I heard you're
getting married
• sapere di qualcosa = to smell of
something
= to taste of something
sa di pesce = it smells of fish

sapone noun, masculine
il sapone = soap

sapore noun, masculine
un sapore = a taste

sappiamo, **saprà**, etc ▶ sapere

sarà, **sarai**, etc ▶ essere

Sardegna noun, feminine
la Sardegna = Sardinia

sardo/sarda adjective
= Sardinian

saremo, **sarò**, etc ▶ essere

sasso noun, masculine
un sasso = a stone

sazio/sazia adjective (plural **sazi/sazie**)
= full
sono sazio = I'm full

sbagliare verb [6]
1 (! + avere)
ho sbagliato numero = I got the wrong
number

2 sbagliarsi (! + essere)
sbagliarsi = to make a mistake
mi sono sbagliato = I made a mistake

sbagliato/sbagliata adjective
= wrong

sbaglio noun, masculine (plural **sbagli**)
fare uno sbaglio = to make a mistake
per sbaglio = by mistake

sbattere verb [8]
• = to beat
• = to bang
la porta sbatteva = the door was banging

sbrigarsi verb [5] (! + essere)
= to hurry up
sbrigati! = hurry up!

sbucciare verb [2]
= to peel

scacchi noun, masculine plural
gli scacchi = chess

scadenza noun, feminine
una scadenza = a deadline

scadere verb [19] (! + essere)
= to expire
il tempo è scaduto = time is up

scaduto/scaduta adjective
= out-of-date

scaffale noun, masculine
uno scaffale = shelves

scala noun, feminine
• una scala = a ladder
• le scale = the stairs
• una scala = a scale

scaldare verb [1]
= to heat up
= to warm up

scalzo/scalza adjective
= barefoot

scambiare verb [6]
• = to exchange
• scambiare A per B = to mistake A for B

scambio noun, masculine (plural
scambi)
uno scambio = an exchange

scandalo noun, masculine
uno scandalo = a scandal

scappare verb [1] (! + essere)
• = to run away
• = to dash

scaricare
= to unload

scarico/scarica adjective (plural
scarichi/scariche)
(when it's a battery) = flat

scarpa noun, feminine
una scarpa = a shoe
= a boot
una scarpa da ginnastica = a trainer, a
sneaker

scarso/scarsa *adjective*
= scarse
visibilità scarsa = poor visibility

scartare *verb* 1
• = to discard
= to reject
• = to unwrap

scatenare *verb* 1
= to unleash

scatola *noun, feminine*
• **una scatola** = a box
• **una scatola** = a tin, a can

scatoletta *noun, feminine*
una scatoletta = a tin, a can

scattare *verb* 1
= to go off
scattare una foto = to take a picture

scatto *noun, masculine*
• **uno scatto** = a click
• **uno scatto** = a jerk
• **di scatto** = suddenly

scavare *verb* 1
= to dig

scegliere *verb* 22
= to choose

scelgo, **scelse**, etc ▶ **scegliere**

scelta *noun, feminine*
una scelta = a choice

scelto/scelta ▶ **scegliere**

scemo/scema* *adjective*
= stupid

scena *noun, feminine*
una scena = a scene

scendere *verb* 53 (**!** + *essere* or *avere*)
= to come down
= to go down

scese, **sceso/scesa** ▶ **scendere**

schedina *noun, feminine*
fare la schedina = to do the pools

scheletro *noun, masculine*
lo scheletro = the skeleton

schermo *noun, masculine*
uno schermo = a screen

scherzare *verb* 1
= to joke
ma scherzi! = you're joking!

scherzo *noun, masculine*
uno scherzo = a joke
fare uno scherzo a qualcuno = to play a
joke on someone

schiacciare *verb* 2
• = to squash
= to crush
• **schiacciare una noce** = to crack a walnut

schiaffo *noun, masculine*
uno schiaffo = a slap

schiavo/schiava *noun,*
masculine/feminine
uno schiavo/una schiava = a slave

schiena *noun, feminine*
la schiena = the back

schifo* *noun, masculine*
che schifo! = yuck!
fare schifo = to be disgusting
= to be awful

schifoso/schifosa* *adjective*
= disgusting
= horrible

schiuma *noun, feminine*
la schiuma = foam
= froth

schizzare *verb* 1
= to splash

sci *noun, masculine* (**!** *never changes*)
• **lo sci** = skiing
fare dello sci = to ski
lo sci acquatico/d'acqua/nautico = water-
skiing
• **uno sci** = a ski

sciare *verb* 7
= to ski

sciarpa *noun, feminine*
una sciarpa = a scarf

scientifico/scientifica *adjective*
(*plural* **scientifici/scientifiche**)
= scientific

scienza *noun, feminine*
la scienza = science

scienziato/scienziata *noun,*
masculine/feminine
uno scienziato/una scienziata = a
scientist

scimmia *noun, feminine*
una scimmia = a monkey

sciocchezza *noun, feminine*
• **una sciocchezza** = a silly thing
dire sciocchezze = to say something
stupid
• **costa una sciocchezza** = it costs next to
nothing

sciocco/sciocca *adjective* (*plural*
sciocchi/sciocche)
= silly

sciogliere *verb* 22
1 (**!** + *avere*)
• = to dissolve
• = to loosen
2 **sciogliersi** (**!** + *essere*)
• **sciogliersi** = to melt
• **sciogliersi** = to dissolve

sciolgo, **sciolto/sciolta**, etc ▶
sciogliere

sciopero *noun, masculine*
uno sciopero = a strike

S

sciroppo *noun, masculine*
uno sciroppo = a syrup

sciupare *verb* 1
= to spoil

scivolare *verb* 1 (**!** + *essere*)
= to slip
= to slide

scocciare✱ *verb* 2
= to annoy

scocciatura✱ *noun, feminine*
una scocciatura = a nuisance

scoglio *noun, masculine* (*plural* **scogli**)
uno scoglio = a rock

scolastico/scolastica *adjective*
(*plural* **scolastici/scolastiche**)
= school
l'anno scolastico = the school year

scommessa *noun, feminine*
una scommessa = a bet
fare una scommessa = to place a bet

scommettere *verb* 40
= to bet

scomodo/scomoda *adjective*
• = uncomfortable
• = inconvenient

scomparire *verb* 14 (**!** + *essere*)
= to disappear

scomparsa *noun, feminine*
la scomparsa = the disappearance

scomparso/scomparsa,
scomparve, etc ▶ scomparire

scompartimento *noun, masculine*
uno scompartimento = a compartment

sconcertare *verb* 1
= to disconcert

sconfitta *noun, feminine*
una sconfitta = a defeat

sconosciuto/sconosciuta
1 *adjective*
= unknown
2 *noun, masculine/feminine*
uno sconosciuto/una sconosciuta = a
stranger

sconsigliare *verb* 6
= to advise against

scontato/scontata *adjective*
• = reduced
• è scontato che = it goes without saying
that
dare per scontato qualcosa = to take
something for granted

sconto *noun, masculine*
uno sconto = a discount
sconti = reductions

scontrino *noun, masculine*
uno scontrino = a receipt

scontro *noun, masculine*
uno scontro = a crash

sconvolgente *adjective*
= upsetting

sconvolto/sconvolta *adjective*
= distraught

scopa *noun, feminine*
una scopa = a broom

scoperta *noun, feminine*
una scoperta = a discovery

scoperto/scoperta ▶ scoprire

scopo *noun, masculine*
uno scopo = a purpose

scoppiare *verb* 6 (**!** + *essere*)
• (*when it's a bomb*) = to explode
• (*when it's a tyre*) = to burst
• scoppiare dal caldo = to be boiling

scoppio *noun, masculine* (*plural* **scoppi**)
• uno scoppio = an explosion
• lo scoppio della guerra = the outbreak of
the war

scoprire *verb* 15
= to discover
= to find out

scoraggiare *verb* 3
= to discourage

scordare *verb* 1
1 (**!** + *avere*)
= to forget
2 scordarsi (**!** + *essere*)
mi sono scordato di spegnerlo = I forgot
to switch it off

scorpione *noun, masculine*
1 uno scorpione = a scorpion
2 Scorpione
Scorpione = Scorpio

scorrere *verb* 26
• (**!** + *essere*) = to flow
• (**!** + *avere*) = to glance through

scorretto/scorretta *adjective*
= improper

scorso/scorsa
1 ▶ **scorrere**
2 *adjective*
= last
l'anno scorso = last year

scortese *adjective*
= rude

scossa *noun, feminine*
• prendere la scossa = to get a shock
• una scossa = a tremor

scosse, scossi, etc ▶ scuotere

scosso/scossa
1 ▶ **scuotere**
2 *adjective*
= shocked

scotch® *noun, masculine*
lo scotch = Sellotape®, Scotch tape®

---

scottare verb [1]
1 = to burn
2 **scottarsi** (! + *essere*)
  scottarsi = to burn oneself
  = to get burnt

Scozia noun, feminine
  la Scozia = Scotland

scozzese adjective
  = Scottish

scrisse, **scritto/scritta**, etc ▶
  scrivere

scrittore/scrittrice noun, masculine/
  feminine
  uno scrittore/una scrittrice = a writer

scrittura noun, feminine
  la scrittura = the writing

scrivania noun, feminine
  una scrivania = a desk

scrivere verb [65]
  = to write
  c'è scritto 'privato' = it says 'private'

scultura noun, feminine
  una scultura = a sculpture

scuola noun, feminine
  una scuola = a school
  una scuola guida = a driving school
  una scuola materna = a nursery school
  una scuola media = a middle school

scuotere verb [66]
  = to shake

scuro/scura adjective
  = dark

scusa noun, feminine
• una scusa = an excuse
• le scuse = an apology

scusarsi verb [1] (! + *essere*)
  = to apologize

sdraio noun, feminine (! *never changes*)
  una sdraio = a deckchair

sdraiarsi verb [6] (! + *essere*)
  = to lie down

sdraiato/sdraiata adjective
  stare sdraiato/sdraiata = to be lying
    (down)

se
1 ▶ si
2 ▶ sé
3 *conjunction*
  = if
  se lo vedrò, glielo dirò = If I see him I'll
    tell him

sé pronoun
  = himself/herself
  = itself
  = themselves
  = yourself

vuole tenere tutto per sé = he wants to
  keep everything for himself

> **!** When *sé* comes before
> *stesso/stessa*, it is usually spelled **se**.

Francesca pensa solo a se stessa
  = Francesca thinks only of herself

sebbene conjunction
  = although

seccato/seccata adjective
  = annoyed

secchio noun, masculine (*plural* **secchi**)
  un secchio = a bucket

secco/secca adjective (*plural* **secchi/**
  secche)
  = dry

secolo noun, masculine
  un secolo = a century
  da secoli = for ages

secondo/seconda
1 *adjective*
  = second
2 **secondo** noun, masculine
• un secondo = a second
• il secondo = the main course
3 *preposition*
  secondo me = in my opinion
  secondo il dizionario = according to the
    dictionary

sedersi verb [51] (! + *essere*)
  = to sit down
  siediti! = sit down!

sedia noun, feminine
  una sedia = a chair
  una sedia a rotelle = a wheelchair
  una sedia a sdraio = a deckchair

sedicenne adjective
  = sixteen-year-old

sedicesimo/sedicesima adjective
  = sixteenth

sedici number
  = sixteen

sedile noun, masculine
  un sedile = a seat

seduto/seduta
1 ▶ sedersi
2 *adjective*
  = sitting
  era seduto per terra = he was sitting on
    the ground

segnalare verb [1]
  = to report

segnale noun, masculine
  un segnale = a signal
  = a sign

segnare verb [1]
• = to mark
• = to write down

S

segno *noun, masculine*
- un segno = a sign
- un segno = a mark

segretario/segretaria *noun,*
masculine/feminine (plural
segretari/segretarie)
un segretario/una segretaria = a secretary

segreteria *noun, feminine*
una segreteria = an office
una segreteria telefonica = an
    answering machine

segreto/segreta
1 *adjective*
= secret
2 **segreto** *noun, masculine*
un segreto = a secret

seguente *adjective*
= following

seguire *verb* 10
= to follow

sei
1 ▶ **essere**
2 *number*
= six

seicento
1 *number*
= six hundred
2 **Seicento** *noun*
il Seicento = the 17th century

sella *noun, feminine*
una sella = a saddle

sellino *noun, masculine*
un sellino = a saddle

selvaggina *noun, feminine*
la selvaggina = game

selvaggio/selvaggia *adjective (plural*
selvaggi/selvagge)
= wild

selvatico/selvatica *adjective (plural*
selvatici/selvatiche)
= wild

semaforo *noun, masculine*
il semaforo = the traffic lights

sembrare *verb* 1 (**!** + *essere*)
= to seem
= to look (like)
sembra impossibile = it seems impossible
sembri un pagliaccio = you look like a
    clown
mi sembra che abbia ragione tu = I think
    you're right
mi sembra di sì = I think so
mi sembrava di volare = I felt as I were
    flying

seme *noun, masculine*
un seme = a seed

seminare *verb* 1
= to sow

semplice *adjective*
- = simple
- = plain

sempre *adverb*
- = always
come sempre = as usual
per sempre = for ever
- = still
lavora sempre qui = he still works here

senato *noun, masculine*
il senato = the senate

senatore/senatrice *noun,*
masculine/feminine
un senatore/una senatrice = a senator

senese *adjective*
= Sienese

seno *noun, masculine*
un seno = a breast
il seno = the bust

sensato/sensata *adjective*
= sensible

sensazione *noun, feminine*
una sensazione = a sensation
ho la sensazione che... = I have a
    feeling that...

sensibile *adjective*
= sensitive

senso *noun, masculine*
- un senso = a sense
- un senso = a direction
'senso unico' = 'one way'

sentiero *noun, masculine*
un sentiero = a path

sentimentale *adjective*
= sentimental

sentire *verb* 10
1 (**!** + *avere*)
- = to feel
- = to hear
non ti sento = I can't hear you
- = to smell
- = to taste
2 **sentirsi** (**!** + *essere*)
sentirsi = to feel
mi sento male = I don't feel well

senz'altro *adverb*
= definitely

senza *preposition, conjunction*
= without
senza pensarci = without thinking about
    it

separare *verb* 1
= to separate

separato/separata *adjective*
- = separate
- (*when it's a couple*) = separated

seppe, seppi, etc ▶ **sapere**

sequestrare *verb* 1
= to seize
= to kidnap

sera *noun, feminine*
una sera = an evening

serale *adjective*
= evening

serata *noun, feminine*
una serata = an evening

sereno/serena *adjective*
• = peaceful
• = happy
• (*talking about the weather*) = clear

serie *noun, feminine* (**!** *never changes*)
una serie = a series

serio/seria *adjective* (*plural* **seri/serie**)
= serious
sul serio = seriously

serpente *noun, masculine*
un serpente = a snake

serra *noun, feminine*
una serra = a greenhouse

serratura *noun, feminine*
una serratura = a lock

servire *verb* 10
1 (**!** + *avere*)
• = to serve
• = to be useful
ti serve il coltello? = do you need the
knife?
non mi serve più = I don't need it any
more
2 **servirsi** (**!** + *essere*)
servirsi = to help oneself
serviti! = help yourself!

servizio *noun, masculine* (*plural* **servizi**)
il servizio = the service

sessanta *number*
= sixty

sessantesimo/sessantesima
adjective
= sixtieth

sesso *noun, masculine*
il sesso = sex

sessuale *adjective*
= sexual

sesto/sesta *adjective*
= sixth

seta *noun, feminine*
la seta = silk

sete *noun, feminine*
la sete = thirst
aver sete = to be thirsty

settanta *number*
= seventy

settantesimo/settantesima
adjective
= seventieth

sette *number*
= seven

settecento
1 *number*
= seven hundred
2 **Settecento** *noun, masculine*
il Settecento = the 18th century

settembre *noun, masculine*
= September

settentrionale *adjective*
= northern

settimana *noun, feminine*
una settimana = a week
una settimana bianca = a skiing holiday

settimanale *adjective*
= weekly

settimo/settima *adjective*
= seventh

severo/severa *adjective*
= strict

sezione *noun, feminine*
una sezione = a section

sfacciato/sfacciata *adjective*
= cheeky

sfidare *verb* 1
= to challenge

sfilata *noun, feminine*
una sfilata = a parade
una sfilata di moda = a fashion show

sfocato/sfocata *adjective*
= blurred

sfogliare *verb* 6
= to flick through

sfondo *noun, masculine*
uno sfondo = a background

sfortuna *noun, feminine*
la sfortuna = bad luck
avere sfortuna = to be unlucky

sfortunato/sfortunata *adjective*
= unlucky

sforzarsi *verb* 1 (**!** + *essere*)
= to make an effort

sforzo *noun, masculine*
uno sforzo = an effort
fare uno sforzo = to make an effort

sfruttare *verb* 1
= to take advantage of

sfuggire *verb* 10 (**!** + *essere*)
= to escape
mi sfugge il nome = the name escapes me

sgombrare *verb* 1
= to clear

S

si

Si is the reflexive pronoun of the third person singular and plural. It is also used with **lei** meaning 'you':

si sono divertiti   = *they enjoyed themselves*
si è divertita, signora Giusti?   = *did you enjoy yourself, Mrs Giusti?*

Si is the reciprocal pronoun for the third person plural, and can be translated as 'each other' or 'one another':

non si capiscono   = *they don't understand each other*

Si is also used with a verb as a less formal alternative to the passive:

l'olio si fa con le olive   = *oil is made from olives*
non si accettano carte di credito = *credit cards are not accepted*

and to form impersonal constructions:

in campagna si dorme bene   = *you sleep well in the country*

It sometimes also replaces the first person plural ('we'):

si prende un taxi?   = *shall we take a taxi?*

---

sgomento/sgomenta
1 *adjective*
= dismayed
2 sgomento *noun, masculine*
lo sgomento = dismay

sgradevole *adjective*
= unpleasant

sgridare *verb* [1]
= to tell off

sguardo *noun, masculine*
uno sguardo = a look

si (**se** before **lo/la, li/le**, and **ne**)
pronoun
▶ **102** | *See the boxed note.*
= (to) himself/herself
= (to) itself
= (to) themselves
= (to) yourself

sì *adverb*
= yes
dire di sì = to say yes
sì che mi piace = I do like it
Laura non è sposata ma Elena sì = Laura isn't married but Elena is

sia
1 ▶ **essere**
2 *conjunction*
sia Paolo che Luca = both Paolo and Luca
sia oggi che domani = either today or tomorrow

siamo, siano ▶ **essere**

sicché *conjunction*
= so

siccome *conjunction*
= since

Sicilia *noun, feminine*
la Sicilia = Sicily

siciliano/siciliana *adjective*
= Sicilian

sicuramente *adverb*
= certainly

sicurezza *noun, feminine*
la sicurezza = safety

sicuro/sicura *adjective*
• = sure
di sicuro = definitely
• = safe
• sicuro/sicura di sé = self-confident

siede, siedo, etc ▶ **sedersi**

siete ▶ **essere**

sigaretta *noun, feminine*
una sigaretta = a cigarette

sigaro *noun, masculine*
un sigaro = a cigar

significare *verb* [4]
= to mean
che significa questa parola? = what does this word mean?

significato *noun, masculine*
il significato = the meaning

signora *noun, feminine*
• una signora = a lady
• buongiorno, signora! = good morning, madam!
• la signora Martini = Mrs Martini

signore *noun, masculine*
• un signore = a gentleman
• buongiorno, signore! = good morning, sir!
buonasera, signori! = good evening, ladies and gentlemen!
• il signor Martini = Mr Martini
i signori Martini = Mr and Mrs Martini

signorina *noun, feminine*
• una signorina = a young lady   ····▶

- **buongiorno, signorina!** = good morning, miss!
- **la signorina Martini** = Miss Martini

sii ▶ **essere**

silenzio *noun, masculine*
il silenzio = silence

silenzioso/silenziosa *adjective*
= silent
= quiet

simile *adjective*
= similar
è simile a quello di Monica = it's similar to Monica's

simpatia *noun, feminine*
la simpatia = friendliness

simpatico/simpatica *adjective*
(*plural* **simpatici/simpatiche**)
= nice
mi è simpatica = I like her

sinceramente *adverb*
= honestly

sincero/sincera *adjective*
= sincere
a essere sincero/sincera = to be honest

sindacato *noun, masculine*
un sindacato = a union

sindaco *noun, masculine* (*plural* **sindaci**)
il sindaco = the mayor

singhiozzo *noun, masculine*
avere il singhiozzo = to have hiccups

singolare *adjective*
= singular

singolo/singola *adjective*
= single

sinistro/sinistra
1 *adjective*
= left
la mano sinistra = the left hand
2 **sinistra** *noun, feminine*
la sinistra = the left
girare a sinistra = to turn left

sino ▶ **fino**

sintomo *noun, masculine*
un sintomo = a symptom

sistema *noun, masculine* (*plural* **sistemi**)
un sistema = a system

sistemare *verb* ⬚1
= to sort out

sito web *noun, masculine*
un sito web = a website

situazione *noun, feminine*
una situazione = a situation

slip *noun, masculine* (**!** *never changes*)
uno slip = a pair of underpants

slogare *verb* ⬚5
= to sprain
mi sono slogato la caviglia = I sprained my ankle

smalto *noun, masculine*
lo smalto per le unghie = nail polish

smarrire *verb* ⬚9
1 = to lose
2 **smarrirsi** (**!** + *essere*)
smarrirsi = to get lost

smentire *verb* ⬚9
= to deny

smesso/smessa ▶ **smettere**

smettere *verb* ⬚40
= to stop
ha smesso di piovere = it's stopped raining
smettila! = stop it!

smise, **smisi**, **etc** ▶ **smettere**

smontare *verb* ⬚1
= to take apart

sms *noun, masculine*
uno sms = a text message

snello/snella *adjective*
= slim

so ▶ **sapere**

soccorso *noun, masculine*
il soccorso = help

sociale *adjective*
= social

società *noun, feminine* (**!** *never changes*)
- la società = society
- una società = a company

socievole *adjective*
= sociable

socio/socia *noun, masculine/feminine*
(*plural* **soci/socie**)
un socio/una socia = a member
= a partner

soddisfare *verb* ⬚38
= to satisfy

soddisfatto/soddisfatta
1 ▶ **soddisfare**
2 *adjective*
= satisfied

sodo/soda
1 *adjective*
= solid
un uovo sodo = a hard-boiled egg
2 **sodo** *adverb*
dormire sodo = to sleep soundly
lavorare sodo = to work hard

sofà *noun, masculine* (**!** *never changes*)
un sofà = a sofa

sofferto/sofferta ▶ **soffrire**

soffiare *verb* ⬚6
= to blow

S

soffitta *noun, feminine*
la soffitta = the attic

soffitto *noun, masculine*
il soffitto = the ceiling

soffocare *verb* 4
= to suffocate
= to choke

soffrire *verb* 10
= to suffer
= to be in pain
soffre di cuore = he has heart problems

soggetto *noun, masculine*
un soggetto = a subject

soggiorno *noun, masculine*
• un soggiorno = a stay
• un soggiorno = a living room

sognare *verb* 1
= to dream

sogno *noun, masculine*
un sogno = a dream

soldato *noun, masculine*
un soldato = a soldier

soldi *noun, masculine plural*
i soldi = money
quanti soldi hai? = how much money do
you have?

sole *noun, masculine*
il sole = the sun
c'è il sole = it's sunny

solido/solida *adjective*
= solid

solito/solita *adjective*
= usual
di solito = usually
come al solito = as usual

sollevare *verb* 1
= to lift

sollievo *noun, masculine*
il sollievo = relief

solo/sola
1 *adjective*
= alone
da solo/sola = on one's own
sentirsi solo/sola = to feel lonely
2 **solo** *adverb*
= only

soltanto *adverb*
= only

soluzione *noun, feminine*
una soluzione = a solution

sommare *verb* 1
• = to add up
• tutto sommato = all things considered

sondaggio *noun, masculine* (*plural*
sondaggi)
un sondaggio = a survey

sonno *noun, masculine*
il sonno = sleep
aver sonno = to be sleepy

sono ▶ **essere**

sopportare *verb* 1
= to put up with
non la sopporto = I can't stand her

sopra
1 *preposition*
= over
= on top of
= above
2 *adverb*
= on top
di sopra = upstairs

soprattutto *adverb*
= especially

sopravvissuto/sopravvissuta ▶
sopravvivere

sopravvivere *verb* 80 (! + *essere*)
= to survive

sordo/sorda *adjective*
= deaf

sorella *noun, feminine*
una sorella = a sister

sorellastra *noun, feminine*
una sorellastra = a step-sister

sorgente *noun, feminine*
una sorgente = a spring

sorgere *verb* 64 (! + *essere*)
• = to rise
• = to arise

sorpassare *verb* 1
= to overtake

sorprendente *adjective*
= surprising

sorprendere *verb* 53
= to surprise

sorpresa *noun, feminine*
una sorpresa = a surprise

sorprese, sorpresi ▶ sorprendere

sorpreso/sorpresa
1 ▶ sorprendere
2 *adjective*
= surprised

sorridere *verb* 30
= to smile

sorrise, sorrisi ▶ sorridere

sorriso
1 ▶ sorridere
2 *noun, masculine*
un sorriso = a smile

sorte *noun, feminine*
la sorte = fate

sorto/sorta ▶ sorgere

sospettare verb [1]
= to suspect

sospetto/sospetta
1 adjective
= suspicious
2 **sospetto** noun, masculine
• un sospetto = a suspicion
• un sospetto = a suspect

sospiro noun, masculine
un sospiro = a sigh

sosta noun, feminine
una sosta = a stop
= a break

sostanza noun, feminine
una sostanza = a substance

sostenere verb [73]
• = to support
• = to maintain

sostengo, **sostengono**, etc ▶
sostenere

sostenitore/sostenitrice noun,
masculine/feminine
un sostenitore/una sostenitrice = a
supporter

sostenuto/sostenuta, **sostiene**,
etc ▶ sostenere

sostituire verb [9]
= to substitute
= to change

sottile adjective
• = subtle
• = thin

sotto
1 preposition
= under
= below
2 adverb
= underneath
di sotto = downstairs

sottofondo noun, masculine
un sottofondo = a background

sottolineare verb [1]
= to underline

sottotitolo noun, masculine
i sottotitoli = subtitles

spaccare verb [4]
= to break

spada noun, feminine
una spada = a sword

Spagna noun, feminine
la Spagna = Spain

spagnolo/spagnola adjective
= Spanish

spago noun, masculine
lo spago = string

spalla noun, feminine
la spalla = the shoulder

sparare verb [1]
sparare a qualcuno = to shoot someone

spargere verb [68]
• = to scatter
• spargere la voce = to spread the word

sparire verb [9] (! + essere)
= to disappear

sparse, **sparso/sparsa** ▶ spargere

spaventare verb [1]
= to scare

spavento noun, masculine
prendere uno spavento = to get a fright

spaventoso/spaventosa adjective
= terrifying

spazio noun, masculine (plural **spazi**)
lo spazio = space

spazzare verb [1]
= to sweep

spazzatura noun, feminine
la spazzatura = rubbish, garbage

spazzola noun, feminine
una spazzola = a brush

spazzolare verb [1]
= to brush
spazzolarsi i capelli = to brush one's hair

spazzolino noun, masculine
uno spazzolino = a toothbrush

specchio noun, masculine (plural
specchi)
uno specchio = a mirror

speciale adjective
= special

specialità noun, feminine (! never
changes)
una specialità = a speciality, a specialty

specializzato/specializzata
adjective
= specialized

specialmente adverb
= especially

specie noun, feminine (! never changes)
• una specie = a species
• una specie di = a kind of

specifico/specifica adjective (plural
specifici/specifiche)
= specific

spedire verb [9]
= to send

spegnere verb [69]
1 = to switch off
= to blow out
2 **spegnersi** (! + essere)
spegnersi = to go out

spendere verb [53]
= to spend

S

spense, **spensi** ▶ spegnere

spento/spenta
1 ▶ spegnere
2 *adjective*
 = off
 = out

speranza *noun, feminine*
 la speranza = hope

sperare *verb* 1
 = to hope
 spero di vederti presto = I hope to see
 you soon

spesa *noun, feminine*
• una spesa = an expense
• fare la spesa = to do the shopping

spese, **speso/spesa**, etc ▶
 spendere

spesso/spessa
1 *adjective*
 = thick
2 **spesso** *adverb*
 = often

spettacolo *noun, masculine*
 uno spettacolo = a show

spettatore/spettatrice *noun,*
 masculine/feminine
 uno spettatore/una spettatrice = a
 spectator
 gli spettatori = the audience

spezia *noun, feminine*
 una spezia = a spice

spia *noun, feminine*
 una spia = a spy

spiacevole *adjective*
 = unpleasant

spiaggia *noun, feminine (plural* **spiagge**)
 una spiaggia = a beach

spiccioli *noun, masculine plural*
 gli spiccioli = small change

spiegare *verb* 5
 = to explain

spiegazione *noun, feminine*
 una spiegazione = an explanation

spilla *noun, feminine*
 una spilla = a brooch

spillo *noun, masculine*
 uno spillo = a pin

spina *noun, feminine*
• una spina = a thorn
• una spina di pesce = a fish bone
• una spina = a plug

spinaci *noun, masculine plural*
 gli spinaci = spinach

spingere *verb* 48
 = to push

spinse, **spinsi**, etc ▶ spingere

spinto/spinta
1 ▶ spingere
2 *adjective*
 = risqué

spirito *noun, masculine*
 lo spirito = the spirit

spiritoso/spiritosa *adjective*
 = witty

splendido/splendida *adjective*
 = splendid
 = beautiful

spogliarsi *verb* 6 (**!** + *essere*)
 = to strip

spogliatoio *noun, masculine (plural*
 spogliatoi)
 uno spogliatoio = a changing room

spolverare *verb* 1
 = to dust

sporcare *verb* 4
1 = to dirty
2 **sporcarsi** (**!** + *essere*)
 sporcarsi = to get dirty

sporco/sporca *adjective (plural*
 sporchi/sporche)
 = dirty

sport *noun, masculine* (**!** *never changes*)
 lo sport = sport, sports

sportello *noun, masculine*
• (*of a car*)
 uno sportello = a door
• (*in a bank*)
 uno sportello = a counter

sportivo/sportiva *adjective*
 = sporty

sposare *verb* 1
1 = to marry
2 **sposarsi** (**!** + *essere*) = to get married

sposato/sposata *adjective*
 = married
 è sposato con una pittrice = he's married
 to a painter

sposo/sposa *noun, masculine/feminine*
 lo sposo/la sposa = the bridegroom/the
 bride
 gli sposi = the bride and groom

spostare *verb* 1
1 = to move
2 **spostarsi** (**!** + *essere*) = to move

spot *noun, masculine* (**!** *never changes*)
 uno spot pubblicitario = an advert

sprecare *verb* 4
 = to waste

spreco *noun, masculine (plural* **sprechi**)
 uno spreco = a waste

spremuta *noun, feminine*
 una spremuta d'arancia = a fresh orange
 juice

spruzzare verb ①
= to spray

spugna noun, feminine
una spugna = a sponge

spumante noun, masculine
lo spumante = sparkling wine

spuntino noun, masculine
uno spuntino = a snack

sputare verb ①
= to spit (out)

squadra noun, feminine
una squadra = a team

squalo noun, masculine
uno squalo = a shark

squillare verb ①
= to ring

sta, **sta'** ▶ stare

stabilire verb ⑨
1 = to establish
2 stabilirsi (! + essere)
  stabilirsi = to settle (down)

staccare verb ④
1 (! + avere)
• = to remove
• = to unplug
2 staccarsi (! + essere)
  staccarsi = to come off

stadio noun, masculine (plural stadi)
• uno stadio = a stage
• uno stadio = a stadium

stagione noun, feminine
una stagione = a season

stai ▶ stare

stalla noun, feminine
una stalla = a stable

stamani, **stamattina** adverb
= this morning

stampa noun, feminine
la stampa = the press

stampante noun, feminine
una stampante = a printer

stampare verb ①
= to print

stampatello noun, masculine
scrivere in stampatello = to print

stanchezza noun, feminine
la stanchezza = tiredness

stanco/stanca adjective (plural
stanchi/stanche)
= tired

stanno ▶ stare

stanotte adverb
• = tonight
• = last night

stanza noun, feminine
una stanza = a room

stappare verb ①
= to open

stare verb ⑦⓪ (! + essere)
• = to stay
  voglio stare a casa = I want to stay at
  home
• = to be
  come stai? = how are you?
  sto benissimo = I'm very well
• = to suit
  ti sta benissimo! = it really suits you!
• = to fit
  le scarpe non mi stanno più = my shoes
  don't fit me any more
• (with the gerund)
  sto lavorando = I'm working
  stavano mangiando = they were eating
• stare per fare qualcosa = to be about to
  do something
  stavo per dirtelo = I was just about to tell
  you

starnutire verb ⑨
= to sneeze

stasera adverb
= this evening

statale adjective
= state

state ▶ stare

statistica noun, feminine (plural
statistiche)
la statistica = statistics
una statistica = a statistic

Stati Uniti noun, masculine plural
gli Stati Uniti = the United States

stato noun, masculine
uno stato = a state

stato/stata
1 ▶ essere
2 ▶ stare

statua noun, feminine
una statua = a statue

stazione noun, feminine
una stazione = a station
una stazione di servizio = a service area

stella noun, feminine
una stella = a star
un albergo a tre stelle = a three-star hotel

stendere verb ⑤③
• = to spread out
• stendere il bucato = to hang out the
  washing

sterlina noun, feminine
una sterlina = a pound

sterzare verb ①
• = to steer
• = to swerve

S

steso/**stesa**
1 ▶ **stendere**
2 *adjective*
= lying

stesso/**stessa**
1 *adjective*
• = same
 lo stesso giorno = the same day
• **il presidente stesso** = the president himself
 se stesso/**se stessa** = himself/herself
 se stessi = themselves
2 *pronoun*
= the same one
3 **lo stesso**
• = anyway
 ha continuato lo stesso = he carried on anyway
• **per me è lo stesso** = it's all the same to me

stette, **stia**, etc ▶ **stare**

stile *noun, masculine*
uno stile = a style

stilista *noun, masculine/feminine (plural* **stilisti**/**stiliste***)*
uno/**una stilista** = a designer

stimare *verb* [1]
= to respect

stipendio *noun, masculine (plural* **stipendi***)*
uno stipendio = a salary

stirare *verb* [1]
= to iron

stivale *noun, masculine*
uno stivale = a boot

sto ▶ **stare**

stoffa *noun, feminine*
la stoffa = material

stomaco *noun, masculine (plural* **stomachi***)*
lo stomaco = the stomach

storia *noun, feminine*
• **una storia** = a story
• **la storia** = history

storico/**storica** *adjective (plural* **storici**/**storiche***)*
= historic
= historical

storto/**storta** *adjective*
= crooked

straccio *noun, masculine (plural* **stracci***)*
• **uno straccio** = a rag
• **uno straccio** = a cloth

strada *noun, feminine*
una strada = a road

strage *noun, feminine*
una strage = a massacre

straniero/**straniera**
1 *adjective*
= foreign
2 *noun, masculine/feminine*
uno straniero/**una straniera** = a foreigner

strano/**strana** *adjective*
= strange

straordinario/**straordinaria** *adjective (plural* **straordinari**/**straordinarie***)*
= extraordinary

strappare *verb* [1]
= to tear

strategia *noun, feminine*
una strategia = a strategy

strato *noun, masculine*
uno strato = a layer

strega *noun, feminine (plural* **streghe***)*
una strega = a witch

stressante *adjective*
= stressful

stressato/**stressata** *adjective*
essere stressato/**stressata** = to be under stress

stretto/**stretta**
1 ▶ **stringere**
2 *adjective*
• = narrow
• = tight

strillare *verb* [1]
= to scream

stringa *noun, feminine (plural* **stringhe***)*
una stringa = a lace

stringere *verb* [71]
= to squeeze
stringere la mano a qualcuno = to shake someone's hand

strinse, **strinsi**, etc ▶ **stringere**

striscia *noun, feminine (plural* **strisce***)*
una striscia = a strip
= a stripe

strofinare *verb* [1]
= to rub

stronzo/**stronza**⬥ *noun, masculine/feminine*
uno stronza/**una stronza** = a bastard

stronzata⬥ *noun, feminine*
una stronzata = bullshit

strozzare *verb* [1]
= to strangle

strumento *noun, masculine*
uno strumento = an instrument

struttura *noun, feminine*
una struttura = a structure

⬥ may be considered offensive

studente/studentessa *noun,*
masculine/feminine
uno studente/una studentessa = a
student

studiare *verb* [6]
= to study

studio *noun, masculine (plural* **studi**)
• lo studio = study
• uno studio = a studio
= a study

stufa *noun, feminine*
una stufa = a stove
una stufa elettrica = an electric fire

stufarsi *verb* [1] (! + *essere*)
= to get fed up

stufo/stufa *adjective*
essere stufo/stufa di qualcosa = to be fed
up of something

stupendo/stupenda *adjective*
= fantastic

stupido/stupida *adjective*
= stupid

stupire *verb* [9]
= to amaze

su
1 *preposition*

> ! *Note that* su *combines with* il, la, *etc.*
> Su + il = sul; su + l' = sull'; su + lo
> = sullo; su + i = sui; su + gli = sugli;
> su + la = sulla; su + le = sulle.

• = on
su un aereo per New York = on a plane
for New York
sulla destra = on the right
• sul giornale = in the newspaper
• nove su dieci = nine out of ten
• un libro sulla Toscana = a book about
Tuscany
2 *adverb*
• = up
• = upstairs

subire *verb* [9]
= to undergo

subito *adverb*
= immediately

succedere *verb* [23] (! + *essere*)
= to happen
non succede niente = nothing's
happening
cos'è successo? = what's happened?

successe, **successero**, **etc** ▶
succedere

successo/successa
1 ▶ **succedere**
2 successo *noun, masculine*
il successo = success

succhiare *verb* [6]
= to suck

succo *noun, masculine (plural* **succhi**)
il succo = juice

sud *noun, masculine*
il sud = the south

Sudafrica *noun, masculine*
il Sudafrica = South Africa

sudare *verb* [1]
= to sweat

sudest *noun, masculine*
il sudest = the south-east

sudicio/sudicia *adjective (plural*
sudici/sudice)
= dirty

sudore *noun, masculine*
il sudore = sweat

sudovest *noun, masculine*
il sudovest = the south-west

sufficiente *adjective*
= sufficient

suggerimento *noun, masculine*
un suggerimento = a suggestion

suggerire *verb* [9]
= to suggest

sugli ▶ **su**

sugo *noun, masculine (plural* **sughi**)
il sugo = sauce
= gravy

sui ▶ **su**

suicidarsi *verb* [1] (! + *essere*)
= to commit suicide

suicidio *noun, masculine (plural* **suicidi**)
il suicidio = suicide

sul, **sulla**, **sullo**, **etc** ▶ **su**

suo/sua
1 *adjective (plural* **suoi/sue**)
= his/her
= its
2 *pronoun*
= his/hers
il suo/la sua = his one
= her one

suocero/suocera *noun,*
masculine/feminine
il suocero/la suocera = the father-in-
law/the mother-in-law
i suoceri = the in-laws

suoi ▶ **suo**

suola *noun, feminine*
una suola = a sole

suonare *verb* [1]
• = to sound
suonare il clacson = to sound one's horn
• = to ring
il telefono suona = the telephone is
ringing   ····▶

S

suonare il campanello = to ring the bell
• = to play
suono il violino = I play the violin

suono noun, masculine
un suono = a sound

suora noun, feminine
una suora = a nun

superare verb $\boxed{1}$
• = to overcome
• = to overtake

superficiale adjective
= superficial

superficie noun, feminine (**!** never changes)
una superficie = a surface

superiore adjective
= superior
= upper

supermercato noun, masculine
un supermercato = a supermarket

supplemento noun, masculine
un supplemento = a supplement

suppone, **suppongo**, **etc** ▶ supporre

supporre verb $\boxed{50}$
= to suppose, to guess
suppongo di sì = I suppose so, I guess so

suppose, **supposto/supposta**, **etc** ▶ supporre

surgelato adjective
= frozen

susina noun, feminine
una susina = a plum

sussurrare verb $\boxed{1}$
= to whisper

svantaggio noun, masculine (plural svantaggi)
uno svantaggio = a disadvantage

sveglia noun, feminine
una sveglia = an alarm clock

svegliarsi verb $\boxed{6}$ (**!** + essere)
= to wake up

sveglio/sveglia adjective (plural svegli/sveglie)
= awake

svelto/svelta adjective
= quick

svenga, **svengo**, **etc** ▶ svenire

svenire verb $\boxed{78}$ (**!** + essere)
= to faint

svenne, **svenuto/svenuta**, **etc** ▶ svenire

svestirsi verb $\boxed{10}$ (**!** + essere)
= to undress

× in informal situations

sviluppare verb $\boxed{1}$
= to develop

sviluppo noun, masculine
uno sviluppo = a development

Svizzera noun, feminine
la Svizzera = Switzerland

svizzero/svizzera adjective
= Swiss

svolgere verb $\boxed{59}$
= to carry out

svolta noun, feminine
• una svolta = a turning
• una svolta = a turning point

svolto/svolta ▶ svolgere

svuotare verb $\boxed{1}$
= to empty

Tt

tabaccaio/tabaccaia noun, masculine/feminine (plural tabaccai/tabaccaie)
un tabaccaio/una tabaccaia = a tobacconist

tabaccheria noun, feminine
una tabaccheria = a tobacconist's, a smoke shop

tabacco noun, masculine
il tabacco = tobacco

tacchino noun, masculine
un tacchino = a turkey

taccio, **tacciono**, **etc** ▶ tacere

tacco noun, masculine (plural tacchi)
un tacco = a heel

tacere verb $\boxed{72}$
= to be silent

taciuto/taciuta ▶ tacere

taglia noun, feminine
una taglia = a size

tagliare verb $\boxed{6}$
= to cut
mi sono tagliato un dito = I've cut my finger

tagliente adjective
= sharp

taglio noun, masculine (plural tagli)
un taglio = a cut

tailleur noun, masculine (**!** never changes)
un tailleur = a suit

tale
1 *adjective*
= such
un tale successo = such as success
2 *pronoun*
un tale = someone
quel tale = that person

talento *noun, masculine*
il talento = talent

tallone *noun, masculine*
un tallone = a heel

talmente *adverb*
= so
talmente stupido = so stupid

tamburo *noun, masculine*
un tamburo = a drum

Tamigi *noun, masculine*
il Tamigi = the Thames

tangente *noun, feminine*
una tangente = a bribe

tanto/tanta
1 *adjective, pronoun*
tanto/tanta = so much
tanti/tante = so many
è successo tante volte = it's happened lots of times
tanto tempo fa = a long time ago
2 **tanto** *adverb*
= so (much)
= a lot
tanto caldo = so hot
mi piace tanto = I really like it

tappeto *noun, masculine*
un tappeto = a carpet
= a rug

tappo *noun, masculine*
un tappo = a top
= a cork

tardi *adverb*
= late
fare tardi = to be late

targa *noun, feminine (plural* **targhe***)*
una targa = a number plate, a license plate

tartaruga *noun, feminine (plural* **tartarughe***)*
una tartaruga = a tortoise
= a turtle

tasca *noun, feminine (plural* **tasche***)*
una tasca = a pocket

tassa *noun, feminine*
una tassa = a tax

tassista *noun, masculine/feminine (plural* **tassisti/tassiste***)*
un/una tassista = a taxi driver

tasso *noun, masculine*
il tasso = the rate

tasto *noun, masculine*
un tasto = key

tavola *noun, feminine*
• **una tavola** = a table
• **una tavola** = a plank

tavolo *noun, masculine*
un tavolo = a table

tazza *noun, feminine*
una tazza = a cup

tazzina *noun, feminine*
una tazzina = a coffee cup

te *pronoun*
1 ▶ **ti**
2 = you
= to you
= yourself
è per te = it's for you

tè *noun, masculine (*❗ *never changes)*
il tè = tea

teatro *noun, masculine*
un teatro = a theatre, a theater

tecnico/tecnica *adjective (plural* **tecnici/tecniche***)*
= technical

tecnologia *noun, feminine*
la tecnologia = technology

tedesco/tedesca *adjective (plural* **tedeschi/tedesche***)*
= German

tela *noun, feminine*
la tela = canvas

telecomando *noun, masculine*
il telecomando = the remote control

telefonare *verb* 1
telefonare a = to phone

telefonata *noun, feminine*
una telefonata = a phone call

telefonino✗ *noun, masculine*
un telefonino = a mobile phone, a cellphone

telefono *noun, masculine*
un telefono = a telephone

telegiornale *noun, masculine*
il telegiornale = the news

televisione *noun, feminine*
la televisione = television
che c'è alla televisione? = what's on TV?

televisore *noun, masculine*
un televisore = a TV

tema *noun, masculine (plural* **temi***)*
• **il tema** = the theme
• **un tema** = an essay

temere *verb* 8
= to be afraid

temperatura *noun, feminine*
la temperatura = the temperature

tempio noun, masculine (plural **templi**)
un tempio = a temple

tempo noun, masculine
• il tempo = time
  tanto tempo fa = a long time ago
  il tempo libero = spare time
• il tempo = the weather
  che tempo fa? = what's the weather like?

temporale noun, masculine
un temporale = a storm

tenda noun, feminine
• una tenda = a tent
• le tende = curtains, drapes

tendenza noun, feminine
una tendenza = a tendency

tendere verb 53
• = to hold out
• tende a parlare troppo = he tends to
  speak too much

tenere verb 73
• = to hold
• = to keep
• tieni! = here you are!

tenero/tenera adjective
= tender

tengo, tengono ▶ tenere

tennista noun, masculine/feminine (plural
tennisti/tenniste)
un/una tennista = a tennis player

tensione noun, feminine
la tensione = tension

tentare verb 1
• = to tempt
• tentare di fare qualcosa = to attempt to
  do something

tentativo noun, masculine
un tentativo = an attempt

tenuto/tenuta ▶ tenere

teoria noun, feminine
una teoria = a theory

teppista noun, masculine/feminine (plural
teppisti/teppiste)
un/una teppista = a hooligan

terapia noun, feminine
la terapia = therapy

terme noun, feminine plural
le terme = the baths

terminare verb 1
= to end

termine noun, masculine
• un termine = a term
• il termine = the end

terra noun, feminine
la terra = the earth
= the land
per terra = on the ground

✗ in informal situations

terrazza noun, feminine, **terrazzo**
noun, masculine
un terrazzo = a balcony

terremoto noun, masculine
un terremoto = an earthquake

terreno noun, masculine
il terreno = land
un terreno = a piece of land

terribile adjective
= terrible

territorio noun, masculine (plural
territori)
un territorio = a territory

terrore noun, masculine
il terrore = terror

terrorismo noun, masculine
il terrorismo = terrorism

terrorista noun, masculine/feminine
(plural **terroristi/terroriste**)
un/una terrorista = a terrorist

terzo/terza adjective
= third

teso/tesa adjective
= tense

tesoro noun, masculine
• il tesoro = treasure
• ciao, tesoro = hi, darling

tessera noun, feminine
una tessera = a membership card

tessuto noun, masculine
un tessuto = a fabric

testa noun, feminine
• la testa = the head
• sei sterline a testa = six pounds each

testamento noun, masculine
un testamento = a will

testardo/testarda adjective
= stubborn

testimone noun, masculine/feminine
un/una testimone = a witness

testo noun, masculine
un testo = a text

tetto noun, masculine
un tetto = a roof

Tevere noun, masculine
il Tevere = the Tiber

ti (**te** before lo/la, li/le, and ne) pronoun
= you
= to you
= yourself
non ti credo! = I don't believe you!
ti spiego come funziona = I'll explain to
  you how it works
ti sei fatto male? = did you hurt yourself?
te lo apro = I'll open it for you

ticket noun, masculine (**!** never changes)
il ticket = the prescription charge

tiene, **tieni** ▶ tenere

tifare verb $\boxed{1}$
tifare per la Juve = to support Juventus

tifoso/tifosa noun, masculine/feminine
un tifoso/una tifosa = a supporter

tigre noun, feminine
una tigre = a tiger

timbrare verb $\boxed{1}$
= to stamp

timbro noun, masculine
un timbro = a stamp

timido/timida adjective
= shy

tinello noun, masculine
il tinello = the dining room

tingere verb $\boxed{48}$
= to dye

tinse, **tinsi**, etc ▶ tingere

tinta noun, feminine
la tinta = dye
= paint

tinto/tinta ▶ tingere

tintoria noun, feminine
una tintoria = a dry-cleaner's

tipico/tipica adjective (plural
tipici/tipiche)
= typical

tipo noun, masculine
• un tipo di = a kind of
• quel tipo✶ = that guy

tirare verb $\boxed{1}$
• = to pull
• = to throw

tiro noun, masculine
un tiro = a throw

titolare noun, masculine/feminine
il/la titolare = the owner

titolo noun, masculine
un titolo = a title
un titolo di studio = a qualification

tivù noun, feminine (! never changes)
la tivù = the TV

tizio/tizia✶ noun, masculine/feminine
(plural tizi/tizie)
un tizio/una tizia = a guy/a girl

toccare verb $\boxed{4}$
= to touch

togliere verb $\boxed{22}$
= to remove
mi sono tolto le scarpe = I took off my
shoes

toilette noun, feminine (! never changes)
una toilette = a toilet, a bathroom

tolgo, **tolgono**, etc ▶ togliere

tollerare verb $\boxed{1}$
= to tolerate

tolse, **tolto/tolta**, etc ▶ togliere

tomba noun, feminine
una tomba = a grave

tondo/tonda adjective
= round

tonnellata noun, feminine
una tonnellata = a tonne

tonno noun, masculine
il tonno = tuna

tono noun, masculine
un tono = a tone

topo noun, masculine
un topo = a mouse

torinese adjective
= Turinese

Torino noun
= Turin

tornare verb $\boxed{1}$ (! + essere)
• = to come back
= to go back
• non torna = it doesn't add up

toro noun, masculine
1 un toro = a bull
2 Toro = Taurus

torre noun, feminine
una torre = a tower

torta noun, feminine
una torta = a cake

Toscana noun, feminine
la Toscana = Tuscany

toscano/toscana adjective
= Tuscan

tossicodipendente noun,
masculine/feminine
un/una tossicodipendente = a drug addict

tosse noun, feminine
la tosse = a cough

tossire verb $\boxed{9}$
= to cough

totale
1 adjective
= total
2 noun, masculine
il totale = the total

totocalcio noun, masculine
il totocalcio = the football pools

tournée noun, feminine (! never
changes)
una tournée = a tour

tovaglia noun, feminine
una tovaglia = a tablecloth

tovagliolo noun, masculine
un tovagliolo = a napkin

tra ▶ fra

T

traccia noun, feminine (plural **tracce**)
una traccia = a trace
le tracce = the trail

tradire verb [9]
= to betray

tradizionale adjective
= traditional

tradizione noun, feminine
una tradizione = a tradition

tradotto/tradotta ▶ tradurre

tradurre verb [54]
= to translate

tradusse, tradussi, etc ▶ tradurre

traduttore/traduttrice noun,
masculine/feminine
un traduttore/una traduttrice = a
translator

traduzione noun, feminine
una traduzione = a translation

trae, traete, etc ▶ trarre

traffico noun, masculine
il traffico = the traffic

tragedia noun, feminine
una tragedia = a tragedy

traggo, traggono, etc ▶ trarre

traghetto noun, masculine
un traghetto = a ferry

tragico/tragica adjective (plural
tragici/tragiche)
= tragic

trai, traiamo, etc ▶ trarre

trama noun, feminine
la trama = the plot

tramite preposition
= by means of
= through

tramonto noun, masculine
il tramonto = sunset

tranello noun, masculine
un tranello = a trap

tranne preposition
= except

tranquillo/tranquilla adjective
• = peaceful
• = happy

trapano noun, masculine
un trapano = a drill

trapianto noun, masculine
un trapianto = a transplant

trappola noun, feminine
una trappola = a trap

trapunta noun, feminine
una trapunta = a quilt

trarre verb [74]
= to draw
trarre una conclusione = to draw a
conclusion
il film è stato tratto da un romanzo = the
film was taken from a novel

trascinare verb [1]
= to drag

trascorrere verb [26]
= to spend

trascorse, trascorso/trascorsa
▶ trascorrere

trascurare verb [1]
= to neglect

trasferire verb [9]
1 = to transfer
2 **trasferirsi** (! + essere)
trasferirsi = to move

trasformare verb [1]
1 = to transform
2 **trasformarsi** (! + essere)
trasformarsi in qualcosa = to change into
something

trasloco noun, masculine (plural
traslochi)
un trasloco = a removal

trasmesso/trasmessa ▶
trasmettere

trasmettere verb [40]
= to broadcast

trasmise, trasmisi, etc ▶
trasmettere

trasmissione noun, feminine
una trasmissione = a program(me)

trasparente adjective
= transparent

trasporto noun, masculine
il trasporto = transport, transportation

trasse, trassi, etc ▶ trarre

trattamento noun, masculine
un trattamento = a treatment

trattare verb [1]
1 (! + avere)
• = to treat
• trattare con qualcuno = to deal with
someone
2 **trattarsi** (! + essere)
si tratta di = it's about

trattenere verb [73]
= to hold (back)
trattenere il respiro = to hold one's breath

trattengo, trattiene ▶ trattenere

tratto/tratta ▶ trarre

traversa noun, feminine
una traversa = a side street

tre *number*
= three

trecento
1 *number*
= three hundred
2 **Trecento** *noun, masculine*
il Trecento = the 14th century

tredicenne *adjective*
= thirteen-year-old

tredicesimo/tredicesima *adjective*
= thirteenth

tredici *number*
= thirteen

tremare *verb* [1]
= to shake

tremendo/tremenda *adjective*
= awful

treno *noun, masculine*
un treno = a train

trenta *number*
= thirty

trentesimo/trentesima *adjective*
= thirtieth

trentina *noun, feminine*
una trentina di macchine = about thirty cars

triangolo *noun, masculine*
un triangolo = a triangle

tribù *noun, feminine* (**!** *never changes*)
una tribù = a tribe

tribunale *noun, masculine*
un tribunale = a court

trimestre *noun, masculine*
un trimestre = a term

triste *adjective*
= sad

tristezza *noun, feminine*
la tristezza = sadness

tritare *verb* [1]
= to chop

trofeo *noun, masculine*
un trofeo = a trophy

tromba *noun, feminine*
una tromba = a trumpet

tronco *noun, masculine* (*plural* **tronchi**)
un tronco = a trunk

troppo/troppa
1 *adjective, pronoun*
troppo/troppa = too much
troppi/troppe = too many
troppo zucchero = too much sugar
troppe mosche = too many flies

2 **troppo** *adverb*
• = too much
parli troppo = you talk too much
• (*with adjectives and adverbs*) = too
è troppo caldo = it's too hot

trovare *verb* [1]
1 = to find
non trovo i miei occhiali = I can't find my glasses
2 **trovarsi** (**!** + *essere*)
• trovarsi = to be
dove si trova il cinema? = where is the cinema?
• trovarsi = to meet
dove ci troviamo? = where shall we meet?

truccare *verb* [4]
1 = to rig
2 **truccarsi** (**!** + *essere*) = to put on one's make-up

trucco *noun, masculine* (*plural* **trucchi**)
• un trucco = a trick
• il trucco = make-up

truffare *verb* [1]
= to swindle

truppe *noun, feminine plural*
le truppe = troops

tu *pronoun*
= you
tu dove vuoi andare? = where do you want to go?

tubo *noun, masculine*
• un tubo = a tube
• un tubo = a pipe

tuffare *verb* [1]
1 = to dip
2 **tuffarsi** (**!** + *essere*)
tuffarsi = to dive

tuffo *noun, masculine*
fare un tuffo = to go for a dip

tuo/tua
1 *adjective* (*plural* **tuoi/tue**)
= your
2 *pronoun*
= yours
il tuo/la tua = your one

tuono *noun, masculine*
un tuono = a clap of thunder
i tuoni = thunder

turismo *noun, masculine*
il turismo = tourism

turista *noun, masculine/feminine* (*plural* **turisti/turiste**)
un/una turista = a tourist

turistico/turistica *adjective* (*plural* **turistici/turistiche**)
= tourist

T

turno noun, masculine
  un turno = a turn
  = a shift

tuta noun, feminine
• **una tuta** = a suit
• **una tuta** = overalls, coveralls
  una tuta da ginnastica = a tracksuit

tuttavia conjunction
  = but

tutto/tutta
1 adjective
  = all
  tutto il tempo = all the time
  tutti i ragazzi/tutte le ragazze = all the
    boys/all the girls
  tutto il giorno = all day
  tutti i giorni = every day
2 **tutto** pronoun
  = everything
  non è tutto = that's not all
3 **tutti** pronoun
  = everyone
  tutti vogliono la stessa cosa = everyone
    wants the same thing

ubbidire, etc ▶ **obbedire**, **etc**

ubriaco/ubriaca adjective (plural
  ubriachi/ubriache)
  = drunk

uccello noun, masculine
  un uccello = a bird

uccidere verb 30
  = to kill

uccise, **ucciso/uccisa**, **etc** ▶
  uccidere

UE noun, feminine
  l'UE = the EU

ufficiale
1 adjective
  = official
2 noun, masculine
  un ufficiale = an officer

ufficio noun, masculine (plural **uffici**)
  un ufficio = an office
  in ufficio = in the office

uguale adjective
  = the same
  è uguale a quello vecchio = it's the same
    as the old one
  per me è uguale = it's all the same to me

ulteriore adjective
  = further

ultimamente adverb
  = recently

ultimo/ultima adjective
  = last
  = latest
  l'ultimo dell'anno = New Year's Eve

umano/umana adjective
  = human

umbro/umbra adjective
  = Umbrian

umidità noun, feminine
  l'umidità = dampness

umido/umida adjective
  = damp
  = humid

umore noun, masculine
  un umore = a mood
  di buon umore = in a good mood

umorismo noun, masculine
  l'umorismo = humo(u)r

un, **un'** ▶ **uno/una**

undicenne adjective
  = eleven-year-old

undicesimo/undicesima adjective
  = eleventh

undici number
  = eleven

unghia noun, feminine (plural **unghie**)
  un'unghia = a nail

unico/unica adjective (plural
  unici/uniche)
• = only
  l'unico problema = the only problem
  figlio unico = an only child
• = unique

unione noun, feminine
  un'unione = a union

unire verb 9
  = to unite

unità noun, feminine (! never changes)
• **l'unità** = unity
• **un'unità** = a unit

università noun, feminine (! never
  changes)
  un'università = a university

universitario/universitaria
  adjective (plural
  universitari/universitarie)
  = university

universo noun, masculine
  l'universo = the universe

uno/una
1 number

! Before masculine singular nouns
beginning with z, ps, gn, or s +
another consonant, **uno** is used. Before
masculine singular nouns beginning
with another consonant or a vowel, **un**
is used. Before feminine singular nouns
beginning with a vowel, **un'** is used.

····▶

= one
ne voglio uno solo = I just want one
un giorno = one day
un'altra volta = another time
2 *determiner*
= a, an
vuoi un gelato? = do you want an ice
cream?

unto/unta *adjective*
= oily
= greasy

uomo *noun, masculine (plural* **uomini***)*
un uomo = a man

uovo *noun, masculine (plural* **uova***)*

> **!** *Note that* **uova** *is feminine.*

un uovo = an egg

uragano *noun, masculine*
un uragano = a hurricane

urgente *adjective*
= urgent

urlare *verb* [1]
= to shout
= to scream

urlo *noun, masculine (plural* **urli** *and* **urla***)*

> **!** *Note that* **urla** *is feminine. It is used
> when talking about the shouts of a
> crowd.*

un urlo = a shout
= a scream

urtare *verb* [1]
• = to bump into
• **urtare contro qualcosa** = to crash into
  something

usanza *noun, feminine*
un'usanza = a custom

usare *verb* [1]
= to use

usato/usata *adjective*
= used

uscire *verb* [75] (**!** + *essere*)
= to go out
= to come out
= to get out

uscita *noun, feminine*
l'uscita = the exit

uso *noun, masculine*
un uso = a use

utile *adjective*
= useful

utilizzare *verb* [1]
= to use

uva *noun, feminine*
l'uva = grapes
un chicco d'uva = a grape

va, **va'** ▶ **andare**

vacanza *noun, feminine*
una vacanza = a holiday, a vacation
in vacanza = on holiday, on vacation

vada, **vado**, **etc** ▶ **andare**

vago/vaga *adjective*
= vague

vagone *noun, masculine*
un vagone = a carriage, a car

vai ▶ **andare**

valanga *noun, feminine (plural*
valanghe*)*
• **una valanga** = an avalanche
• **una valanga di lettere** = a flood of letters

valere *verb* [76] (**!** + *essere*)
• = to be worth
  quanto vale? = how much is it worth?
  non vale la pena = it's not worth it
• **non vale!** = it's not fair!

valgo, **valgono**, **etc** ▶ **valere**

valido/valida *adjective*
= valid

valigia *noun, feminine (plural* **valigie** *or*
valige*)*
una valigia = a suitcase
fare le valigie = to pack
disfare le valigie = to unpack

valle *noun, feminine*
una valle = a valley

valore *noun, masculine*
il valore = the value

valse, **valso/valsa**, **etc** ▶ **valere**

valuta *noun, feminine*
la valuta = currency

vanga *noun, feminine (plural* **vanghe***)*
una vanga = a spade

vanitoso/vanitosa *adjective*
= vain

vanno ▶ **andare**

vantaggio *noun, masculine (plural*
vantaggi*)*
un vantaggio = an advantage

vantarsi *verb* [1] (**!** + *essere*)
= to boast

vapore *noun, masculine*
il vapore = steam

variabile *adjective*
= variable
= changeable

V

varietà *noun, feminine* (**!** *never changes*)
la varietà = variety

vario/varia *adjective* (*plural* **vari/varie**)
• = various
• = several

varrà, **varranno**, etc ▶ **valere**

vasca *noun, feminine* (*plural* **vasche**)
una vasca da bagno = a bath, a bathtub

vaso *noun, masculine*
un vaso = a vase

vassoio *noun, masculine* (*plural* **vassoi**)
un vassoio = a tray

ve ▶ **vi**

vecchiaia *noun, feminine*
la vecchiaia = old age

vecchio/vecchia *adjective* (*plural* **vecchi/vecchie**)
= old

vedere *verb* 77
= to see
non vedo niente = I can't see anything
non ci vedo = I can't see

vedovo/vedova *noun, masculine/feminine*
un vedovo/una vedova = a widower/a widow

vedrà, **vedremo**, etc ▶ **vedere**

veicolo *noun, masculine*
un veicolo = a vehicle

vela *noun, feminine*
• una vela = a sail
• la vela = sailing

veleno *noun, masculine*
il veleno = poison

velenoso/velenosa *adjective*
= poisonous

veloce *adjective, adverb*
= fast

velocemente *adverb*
= fast

velocità *noun, feminine*
la velocità = speed

vendemmia *noun, feminine*
la vendemmia = the grape harvest

vendere *verb* 8
= to sell
'vendesi' = 'for sale'

vendicarsi *verb* 4 (**!** + *essere*)
= to take revenge

vendita *noun, feminine*
una vendita = a sale

venerdì *noun, masculine* (**!** *never changes*)
= Friday

arrivo venerdì = I'm arriving on Friday
il venerdì = on Fridays

Venezia *noun*
= Venice

veneziano/veneziana *adjective*
= Venetian

venga, **vengo**, etc ▶ **venire**

venire *verb* 78 (**!** + *essere*)
• = to come
da dove viene? = where does he come from?
• = to cost
viene cinquantamila euro = it's fifty thousand euros
• (*with the past participle*) = to be
le bottiglie vengono riciclate = the bottles are recycled

venne, **venni**, etc ▶ **venire**

ventenne *adjective*
= twenty-year-old

ventesimo/ventesima *adjective*
= twentieth

venti *number*
= twenty

ventina *noun, feminine*
una ventina di studenti = about twenty students

vento *noun, masculine*
il vento = the wind
c'è vento = it's windy

venuto/venuta ▶ **venire**

veramente *adverb*
= really

verde *adjective*
= green

verdura *noun, feminine*
la verdura = vegetables

Vergine *noun, feminine*
Vergine = Virgo

vergogna *noun, feminine*
la vergogna = shame
che vergogna! = how embarrassing!

vergognarsi *verb* 1 (**!** + *essere*)
• = to be ashamed
• = to be embarrassed

verifica *noun, feminine* (*plural* **verifiche**)
una verifica = a check
= a test

verità *noun, feminine* (**!** *never changes*)
la verità = the truth

vernice *noun, feminine*
la vernice = paint

vero/vera *adjective*
• = true
• = real

····▶

- **(non è) vero?**
  è tuo, (non è) vero? = it's yours, isn't it?
  verrai, (non è) vero? = you'll come, won't you?

verrà, **verremo**, **etc** ▶ **venire**

versare *verb* 1
- = to pour
- = to spill

verso *preposition*
- = toward(s)
- **verso le nove** = at about nine o'clock

verticale *adjective*
= vertical

vescovo *noun, masculine*
un vescovo = a bishop

vespa *noun, feminine*
- **una vespa** = a wasp
- **una vespa**® = a scooter

vestire *verb* 10
1 = to dress
2 vestirsi (**!** + *essere*)
vestirsi = to get dressed

vestito *noun, masculine*
- **un vestito**
  (*when it's a woman's*) = a dress
  (*when it's a man's*) = a suit
- **i vestiti** = clothes

vetrina *noun, feminine*
una vetrina = a shop window, a store window

vetro *noun, masculine*
il vetro = glass
un vetro = a pane of glass

vi (**ve** *before* **lo/la**, **li/le**, *and* **ne**)
1 *pronoun*
= you
= to you
= yourselves
vi aspetto là = I'll be waiting for you there
divertitevi! = enjoy yourselves!
2 *adverb*
= there

via
1 *noun, feminine*
una via = a street
2 *adverb*
= away
va' via! = go away!

viaggiare *verb* 3
= to travel

viaggio *noun, masculine* (*plural* **viaggi**)
un viaggio = a journey
= a trip
un viaggio di nozze = a honeymoon

vicino/vicina
1 *adjective*
= near
la primavera è vicina = spring is near

un paese vicino al mare = a village near the sea
2 vicino *adverb*
= near
= nearby
3 *noun, masculine/feminine*
un vicino/una vicina = a neighbo(u)r

vide, **vidi**, **etc** ▶ **vedere**

videoregistratore *noun, masculine*
un videoregistratore = a video recorder

viene, **vieni** ▶ **venire**

vietare *verb* 1
= to forbid
vietato fumare = no smoking

vigile *noun, masculine*
un vigile (urbano) = a traffic warden
i vigili del fuoco = the fire brigade, the fire department

vigilia *noun, feminine*
la vigilia = the day before
la Vigilia di Natale = Christmas Eve

vincere *verb* 79
- = to win
- = to beat

vincitore/vincitrice *noun, masculine/feminine*
il vincitore/la vincitrice = the winner

vino *noun, masculine*
il vino = wine

vinse, **vinto/vinta**, **etc** ▶ **vincere**

viola *adjective* (**!** *never changes*)
= purple

violentare *verb* 1
= to rape

violento/violenta *adjective*
= violent

violenza *noun, feminine*
la violenza = violence

violino *noun, masculine*
un violino = a violin

virgola *noun, feminine*
- **una virgola** = a comma
- **due virgola cinque** = two point five

virgolette *noun, feminine plural*
le virgolette = quotation marks
fra virgolette = in quotation marks

visibile *adjective*
= visible

visita *noun, feminine*
- **una visita** = a visit
- **una visita medica** = a medical examination

visitare *verb* 1
= to visit

viso *noun, masculine*
il viso = the face

V

volere

1 volere functions as an ordinary verb:

= to want

vuole un cagnolino	= *he wants a puppy*
voglio dormire	= *I want to sleep*
voglio che tu mi dica la verità	= *I want you to tell me the truth*

! Note that the subjunctive is used after **volere che**.

2 volere is used with **ci** to form **ci vuole, ci vogliono**, etc:

volerci (**!** + *essere*)	= *to be necessary*
ci vuole pazienza	= *you need patience*
mi ci vogliono delle olive	= *I need some olives*
c'è voluto un po' di tempo	= *it took some time*

3 volere is used in the *conditional tense* to form polite requests and offers. The forms of this tense are:

vorrei
vorresti
vorrebbe
vorremmo
vorreste
vorrebbero

vorrei un caffè	= *I'd like a coffee*
vorremmo prenotare due posti	= *we'd like to book two seats*

---

visse, **vissuto/vissuta**, **etc** ▶
  vivere

vista noun, feminine
• la vista = eyesight
  farsi controllare la vista = to have one's
  eyes tested
• la vista = the view

visto/vista
1 ▶ vedere
2 **visto** noun, masculine
  un visto = a visa

vita noun, feminine
• la vita = life
• la vita = the waist

vite noun, feminine
• una vite = a screw
• una vite = a vine

vitello noun, masculine
  un vitello = a calf
  il vitello = veal

vittima noun, feminine
  una vittima = a victim

vittoria noun, feminine
  una vittoria = a victory

vivace adjective
  = lively

vivere verb 80 (**!** + *essere*)
  = to live

vivo/viva adjective
  = alive
  = living

vizio noun, masculine (plural **vizi**)
  un vizio = a vice

vocabolario noun, masculine (plural
  vocabolari)
  un vocabolario = a dictionary

voce noun, feminine
  una voce = a voice
  leggere ad alta voce = to read aloud

voglia noun, feminine
  una voglia = a desire
  aver voglia di fare qualcosa = to feel like
    doing something
  non ho voglia = I don't feel like it

vogliamo, **voglio**, **etc** ▶ volere

voi pronoun
  = you
  voi altri = you lot, you guys

volante noun, masculine
  il volante = the steering wheel

volare verb 1 (**!** + *essere* or *avere*)
  = to fly

volentieri adverb
  = willingly
  vengo volentieri = I'd love to come

volere verb 81
  ▶ **120** See the boxed note.
  voler dire = to mean
  voglio dire = I mean
  che vuol dire? = what does it mean?

volle, **volli**, **etc** ▶ volere

volo *noun, masculine*
un volo = a flight
un volo di linea = a scheduled flight

volpe *noun, feminine*
una volpe = a fox

volta *noun, feminine*
la volta = the time
la prima volta = the first time
una volta = once
due volte = twice
ancora una volta = once again

voltare *verb* ⬚
1 (**!** + *avere*)
= to turn
2 **voltarsi** (**!** + *essere*)
voltarsi = to turn round

volto *noun, masculine*
il volto = the face

volume *noun, masculine*
il volume = the volume

vongola *noun, feminine*
una vongola = a clam

vorrà, **vorrebbe**, **vorrei**, etc ▶
volere

vostro/vostra
1 *adjective*
= your
i vostri cugini = your cousins
a casa vostra = at your house
2 *pronoun*
= yours
il vostro/la vostra = your one

votare *verb* ⬚
= to vote

voto *noun, masculine*
• un voto = a vote
• (*at school*)
un voto = a mark, a grade

vulcano *noun, masculine*
un vulcano = a volcano

vuoi, **vuole** ▶ volere

vuotare *verb* ⬚
= to empty

vuoto/vuota *adjective*
= empty

Web *noun, masculine*
il Web = the Web

würstel *noun, masculine* (**!** *never changes*)
un würstel = a frankfurter, a wiener

Zz

zaino *noun, masculine*
uno zaino = a backpack

zampa *noun, feminine*
una zampa = a paw

zanzara *noun, feminine*
una zanzara = a mosquito

zero *number*
= zero
= nought
abbiamo vinto tre a zero = we won three-nil

zingaro/zingara *noun, masculine/feminine*
uno zingaro/una zingara = a gypsy

zio/zia *noun, masculine/feminine* (*plural* **zii/zie**)
uno zio/una zia = an aunt/an uncle
gli zii = uncle and aunt
tutti gli zii = all my aunts and uncles

zitto/zitta *adjective*
stare zitto/zitta = to be quiet
stai zitto! = shut up!

zona *noun, feminine*
una zona = an area

zucchero *noun, masculine*
lo zucchero = sugar

zucchino *noun, masculine*
uno zucchino = a courgette, a zucchini

zuppa *noun, feminine*
la zuppa = soup
la zuppa inglese = trifle

W
Z

Numbers

Cardinal numbers in Italian

1	uno	100	cento
2	due	101	centouno
3	tre	102	centodue
4	quattro	103	centotré
5	cinque	108	centootto
6	sei	200	duecento
7	sette	300	trecento
8	otto	1000	mille
9	nove	2000	duemila
10	dieci	3000	tremila
11	undici	10 000	diecimila
12	dodici	100 000	centomila
13	tredici	1 000 000	un milione
14	quattordici	2 000 000	due milioni
15	quindici	1 000 000 000	un miliardo
16	sedici		
17	diciassette		
18	diciotto		
19	diciannove		
20	venti		
21	ventuno		
22	ventidue		
23	ventitré		
28	ventotto		
29	ventinove		
30	trenta		
40	quaranta		
50	cinquanta		
60	sessanta		
70	settanta		
80	ottanta		
90	novanta		

Note the following points:

One is **uno** when counting. Before a noun, **un** is used in the masculine (but **uno** before **z**, **ps**, **gn**, or **s** + another consonant) and **una** in the feminine (but **un'** before a vowel):

one year	= un anno
one copy	= una copia
one student	= uno studente
one unit	= un'unità

In numbers, the plural of **mille** is **–mila**. It is only used in combination with other numbers.

When **un milione**, **un miliardo**, etc is followed by a noun, **di** is used:

fifty million euros	= cinquanta milioni di euro

When writing large numbers in figures Italian uses a period, never a comma:

30,000	= 30.000
25,000,000	= 25.000.000

Italian uses the ending **–ina** with some numbers to show that they are only approximate (**cento** and **mille** have their own forms):

about twenty customers	= una ventina di clienti
about fifty kilometres	= una cinquantina di chilometri
hundreds of letters	= centinaia di lettere
thousands of stars	= migliaia di stelle

Ordinal numbers in Italian

1st	primo/prima
2nd	secondo/seconda
3rd	terzo/terza
4th	quarto/quarta
5th	quinto/quinta
6th	sesto/sesta
7th	settimo/settima
8th	ottavo/ottava
9th	nono/nona
10th	decimo/decima
11th	undicesimo/undicesima
12th	dodicesimo/dodicesima
13th	tredicesimo/tredicesima
14th	quattordicesimo/quattordicesima
15th	quindicesimo/quindicesima
16th	sedicesimo/sedicesima
17th	diciassettesimo/diciassettesima
18th	diciottesimo/diciottesima
19th	diciannovesimo/diciannovesima
20th	ventesimo/ventesima
21st	ventunesimo/ventunesima
22nd	ventiduesimo/ventiduesima
23rd	ventitreesimo/ventitreesima
30th	trentesimo/trentesima
40th	quarantesimo/quarantesima
50th	cinquantesimo/cinquantesima
60th	sessantesimo/sessantesima
70th	settantesimo/settantesima
80th	ottantesimo/ottantesima
90th	novantesimo/novantesima
100th	centesimo/centesima
101st	centunesimo/centunesima
102nd	centoduesimo/centoduesima
200th	duecentesimo/duecentesima
300th	trecentesimo/trecentesima
1000th	millesimo/millesima
2000th	duemillesimo/duemillesima
3000th	tremillesimo/tremillesima
10 000th	diecimillesimo/diecimillesima
100 000th	centomillesimo/centomillesima
1 000 000th	milionesimo/milionesima
2 000 000th	duemilionesimo/duemilionesima
1 000 000 000th	miliardesimo/miliardesima

Fractions

Fractions are formed by taking the masculine form of the ordinal number. The only exception is a **half**:

$\frac{1}{2}$	un mezzo
$\frac{1}{3}$	un terzo
$\frac{2}{3}$	due terzi
$\frac{1}{4}$	un quarto
$\frac{3}{4}$	tre quarti
$\frac{1}{100}$	un centesimo

Note that in decimal fractions the decimal point is replaced by the comma:

2.5 = 2,5 (say due virgola cinque)

a, **an** *determiner*
  a, **an** = un/una (**!** uno *before a masculine noun beginning with z, ps, gn, or s + another consonant;* un' *before a feminine noun beginning with a vowel*)
  a boy/a girl = un ragazzo/una ragazza
  a Scotsman/a Scotswoman = uno scozzese/una scozzese
  an Englishman/an Englishwoman = un inglese/un'inglese
  my mother's a doctor = mia madre fa il dottore

able *adjective*
• (*having the possibility*)
  he's able to walk now = ora può camminare
• (*having the skill or knowledge*)
  to be able to [drive | read | type] = saper [guidare | leggere | battere a macchina]
• (*failure*)
  I wasn't able to do it = non ho potuto farlo

aboard *adverb*
  to go aboard = salire a bordo (**!** + *essere*)

about

> **!** *Often* **about** *occurs in combinations with verbs, for example:* **bring about**, **run about**, *etc. To find the correct translations for this type of verb, look up the separate dictionary entries at* **bring**, **run**, *etc.*

1 *preposition*
  it's a book about Italy = è un libro sull'Italia
  to talk about something = parlare di qualcosa
2 *adverb*
  = circa
  I have about 20 euros left = mi sono rimaste circa 20 euro
  we arrived at about midnight = siamo arrivati verso mezzanotte
3 to be about to = stare per
  to be about to [leave | cry | fall asleep] = stare per [partire | piangere | addormentarsi]

above
1 *preposition*
  = sopra
  their apartment is above the shop = il loro appartamento è sopra il negozio
2 above all = soprattutto

abroad *adverb*
  = all'estero
  we're going abroad = andiamo all'estero

absent *adjective*
  = assente

accent *noun*
  an accent = un accento

accept *verb*
  = accettare

accident *noun*
• (*causing injury or damage*)
  an accident = un incidente
• **I heard about it by accident** = l'ho saputo per caso

accommodation *noun*
  I'm looking for accommodation = devo trovare un alloggio

accompany *verb*
  = accompagnare

account *noun*
• (*in a bank or post office*)
  an account = un conto
  there's no money in my account = non ho soldi sul conto
• **to take travelling expenses into account** = tenere conto delle spese di viaggio

accountant *noun* ▶ 281|
  an accountant = un ragioniere/una ragioniera

accuse *verb*
  to accuse someone of cheating = accusare qualcuno di imbrogliare

across *preposition*
• **to walk across the street** = attraversare la strada
  to run across the street = attraversare la strada di corsa
  to swim across the Channel = attraversare la Manica a nuoto
  a journey across Africa = un viaggio attraverso l'Africa
• (*on the other side of*) = dall'altra parte di
  he lives across the road = abita dall'altra parte della strada

act *verb*
• (*to do something*) = agire
• (*to play a role*) = recitare

activity *noun*
  an activity = un'attività

actor *noun* ▶ 281|
  an actor = un attore

actress *noun* ▶ 281|
  an actress = un'attrice

actually *adverb*

> **!** *Note that* **actually** *is not translated by* **attualmente.**

did she actually say that? = ha
veramente detto così?
actually, I'm rather tired = veramente sono
piuttosto stanco

adapt *verb*
to adapt something = adattare qualcosa
to adapt to something = adattarsi a
qualcosa (**!** + *essere*)

add *verb*
• (*to put in*) = aggiungere
• (*in arithmetic*) = sommare

address *noun*
an address = un indirizzo

admire *verb*
= ammirare

admit *verb*
• (*to recognize as being true*) = riconoscere
• (*to own up*) = confessare
• **to be admitted to (the) hospital** = essere
ricoverato/ricoverata in ospedale

adolescent *noun*
an adolescent = un
adolescente/un'adolescente

adopt *verb*
= adottare

adult *noun*
an adult = un adulto/un'adulta

advantage *noun*
• (*a positive point*)
an advantage = un vantaggio
• **to take advantage of a situation**
= approfittare di una situazione

adventure *noun*
an adventure = un'avventura

advertisement *noun*
• (*on TV, in the cinema*)
an advertisement = una pubblicità
• (*in a newspaper*)
an advertisement = un annuncio

advertising *noun*
advertising = la pubblicità

advice *noun*
a piece of advice = un consiglio
advice = dei consigli (*plural*)

advise *verb*
to advise someone to rest = consigliare a
qualcuno di riposare
I've been advised not to go there = mi
hanno consigliato di non andarci

aerial *noun*
an aerial = un'antenna

aerobics *noun* ▶ 178 |
aerobics = l'aerobica (*singular*)

affect *verb*
the farmers have been affected by the
drought = gli agricoltori sono stati
colpiti dalla siccità
the war will affect tourism = la guerra
avrà un effetto negativo sul turismo

afford *verb*
I can't afford a car = non posso
permettermi la macchina

afraid *adjective*
to be afraid of spiders = avere paura dei
ragni

Africa *noun* ▶ 151 |
Africa = l'Africa

African ▶ 199 |
1 *adjective*
= africano/africana
2 *noun*
the Africans = gli africani

after
1 *preposition*
= dopo
we'll leave after breakfast = partiamo
dopo colazione
the day after tomorrow = dopodomani
2 *conjunction*
after I had ironed my shirts, I put them
away = dopo aver stirato le camicie le
ho messe via
after we had eaten, we went out = dopo
mangiato siamo usciti
3 after all = dopotutto

afternoon *noun* ▶ 146 |, ▶ 267 |
an afternoon = un pomeriggio

afterwards, **afterward** (*US English*)
adverb
= dopo

again *adverb*
= di nuovo
are you going camping again this year?
= vai di nuovo in campeggio
quest'anno?

> **!** *Note that there will very often be a
> specific Italian verb to translate the
> idea of doing something again -* **to
> start again** = *ricominciare,* **to do the
> work again** = *rifare il lavoro,* **to see
> someone again** = *rivedere qualcuno.*

against *preposition*
= contro

age *noun* ▶ 125 |
age = l'età (*feminine*)
he's my age, he's the same age as me
= ha la mia età

aged *adjective*
a boy aged 13 = un ragazzo di 13 anni

ago *adverb*
two weeks ago = due settimane fa
a long time ago = molto tempo fa

Age

Note that, where English says **to be X years old**, Italian says **avere X anni**.

How old?

*how old **are you**?* = quanti anni **hai**?
*what age **is he**?* = quanti anni **ha**?

The word **anni** is not dropped:

*he is forty-two (**years old**)* = ha quarantadue **anni**
*the house is a hundred **years old*** = la casa ha cent'**anni**

To say **twenty-year-old**, **thirty-year old**, etc Italian uses the ending –**enne** added to the number. Note that not all numbers can take this ending: those which commonly take it are given in this dictionary.

*an **eighteen-year-old** girl* = una ragazza **diciottenne**
twelve-year-olds = i **dodicenni**

Comparing ages

I'm older than you = sono più vecchia di te
she's younger than him = è più giovane di lui
Anne's two years younger = Anne ha due anni di meno
Tom's five years older than Jo = Tom ha cinque anni più di Jo

Approximate ages

he is about fifty = è sulla cinquantina
she's just over sixty = ha appena superato i sessanta

---

agree *verb*
• (*to have the same opinion*) = essere d'accordo
  I don't agree with you = non sono d'accordo con te
• (*to be prepared to do something*)
  to agree to come a week later = accettare di venire una settimana dopo
• (*to reach a decision*) = rimanere d'accordo (**!** + *essere*)
  we agreed to meet = siamo rimasti d'accordo di vederci

agriculture *noun*
  agriculture = l'agricoltura

ahead *adverb*
  to go ahead = andare avanti (**!** + *essere*)

Aids *noun* ▶ **193** |
  Aids = l'Aids (*masculine*)

aim
1 *noun*
  an aim = uno scopo
2 *verb*
• (*to be directed at*)
  it's aimed at young people = è rivolto ai giovani
• (*when using a weapon*)
  to aim a rifle at someone = puntare un fucile contro qualcuno

air *noun*
  air = l'aria
  to throw a ball up in the air = lanciare una palla in aria

air force *noun*
  the air force = l'aeronautica militare

air hostess *noun* ▶ **281** | (*British English*)
  an air hostess = un'assistente di volo

airmail *noun*
  to send a letter by airmail = spedire una lettera per posta aerea

airport *noun*
  an airport = un aeroporto

alarm clock *noun*
  an alarm clock = una sveglia

alcohol *noun*
  alcohol = l'alcol (*masculine*)

alive *adjective*
  = vivo/viva

all
1 *determiner*
  = tutto/tutta (+ *singular*)
  = tutti/tutte (+ *plural*)
  I worked all week = ho lavorato tutta la settimana
  all the guests have left = tutti gli invitati sono andati via
2 *pronoun*
  = tutto
  that's all = è tutto
3 *adverb*
  all alone = tutto solo/tutta sola

allow *verb*
  to allow someone to [watch TV | play | go
    out] = permettere a qualcuno di [guardare
    la TV | giocare | uscire]
  I'm not allowed to smoke at home = non
    mi fanno fumare in casa
  smoking is not allowed = non è permesso
    fumare

all right *adjective*
• (*when giving your opinion*)
  the film was all right = il film non era
    male
• (*when talking about health*)
  are you all right? = tutto bene?
• (*when making arrangements*)
  is it all right if I come later? = va bene se
    vengo più tardi?
  all right! = va bene!

almost *adverb*
  = quasi
  I've almost finished = ho quasi finito

alone
1 *adjective*
  = solo/sola
  to be all alone = essere tutto solo/tutta
    sola
  leave me alone! = lasciami in pace!
2 *adverb*
  [to work | to live | to travel] alone = [lavorare |
    abitare | viaggiare] da solo/da sola

along *preposition*
  = lungo
  there are seats all along the canal = ci
    sono panchine lungo tutto il canale

aloud *adverb*
  to read aloud = leggere ad alta voce

already *adverb*
  = già
  it's ten o'clock already = sono già le dieci
  have you finished already? = hai già
    finito?

also *adverb*
  = anche

although *conjunction*
  = anche se
  although she's strict, she's fair = anche
    se è severa, è giusta

always *adverb*
  = sempre
  I always go to Italy in (the) summer
    = vado sempre in Italia d'estate

amazed *adjective*
  to be amazed = rimanere stupito/stupita
    (**!** + *essere*)

amazing *adjective*
  = incredibile

ambition *noun*
  an ambition = un'aspirazione

ambitious *adjective*
  = ambizioso/ambiziosa

ambulance *noun*
  an ambulance = un'ambulanza

America *noun* ▶ 151 |
  America = l'America

American ▶ 199 |
1 *adjective*
  = americano/americana
2 *noun*
  the Americans = gli americani

among, **amongst** *preposition*
  = fra, tra
  unemployment among young people = la
    disoccupazione tra i giovani

amount *noun*
  an amount = una quantità

amusement arcade *noun*
  an amusement arcade = una sala giochi

amusement park *noun*
  an amusement park = un parco dei
    divertimenti

an ▶ **a**

ancestor *noun*
  an ancestor = un antenato/un'antenata

and *conjunction*
• and = e

  > **!** *Note that before a vowel, especially*
  > *before e, **ed** is also possible.*

  a red and white sweater = un maglione
    rosso e bianco
  she stood up and went out = si è alzata
    ed è uscita
  faster and faster = sempre più veloce
• (*in numbers* and *is not translated*)
  three hundred and sixty-five
    = trecentosessantacinque

anger *noun*
  anger = la rabbia

angry *adjective*
  = arrabbiato/arrabbiata
  to be angry with someone = essere
    arrabbiato con qualcuno
  to get angry = arrabbiarsi (**!** + *essere*)

animal *noun*
  an animal = un animale

ankle *noun* ▶ 137 |
  the ankle = la caviglia

announcement *noun*
  an announcement = un annuncio

annoy *verb*
  to annoy someone = dare fastidio a
    qualcuno

annoyed *adjective*
  to be annoyed with someone = essere
    seccato/seccata con qualcuno

another
1 *determiner*
  another = un altro/un'altra   ····▶

another cup of coffee? = un altro caffè?
2 *pronoun*
there are some pears left—would you like another? = sono rimaste delle pere—ne vuoi un'altra?

! *Note that it is necessary to use* **ne**, *which might be translated as* 'of it' *or* 'of them', *with pronouns like* **another**. *See also* **any**, **a few**, **a lot**, *etc for this use of* **ne**.

answer
1 *noun*
an answer = una risposta
there's no answer (*at the door*) = non c'è nessuno
(*on the phone*) = non risponde nessuno
2 *verb*
= rispondere
to answer a question = rispondere a una domanda
to answer the phone = rispondere al telefono

answering machine *noun*
an answering machine = una segreteria telefonica

ant *noun*
an ant = una formica

antique *noun*
an antique = un pezzo d'antiquariato
an antique shop = un negozio d'antiquariato

anxious *adjective*
= preoccupato/preoccupata
to get anxious = preoccuparsi (! + *essere*)

any
1 *determiner*
• (*in questions*) = del/della (+ *singular*)
= dei/delle (+ *plural*)

! *Before masculine nouns beginning with z, ps, gn, or s + another consonant,* **dello** *is used in the singular and* **degli** *in the plural. Before masculine and feminine singular nouns beginning with a vowel,* **dell'** *is used. Degli is used before masculine plural nouns beginning with a vowel.*

is there any tea? = c'è del tè?
have you got any money? = hai soldi?
• (*with the negative*)
I didn't find any mistakes = non ho trovato nessun errore
we don't have any bread = non abbiamo pane
I didn't have any friends = non avevo amici
• (*whatever*) = qualsiasi
you can take any bus to go into town = per andare in città puoi prendere qualsiasi autobus

2 *pronoun*
do you have any? = ne hai?
he doesn't have any = non ne ha

! *Note that it is necessary to use* **ne**, *which might be translated as* 'of it' *or* 'of them', *with pronouns like* **any**. *See also* **another**, **a few**, **a lot**, *etc for this use of* **ne**.

anyone *pronoun* (*also* **anybody**)
• (*in questions*) = qualcuno
does anyone have an umbrella? = qualcuno ha un ombrello?
• (*with the negative*) = nessuno
there isn't anyone at home = non c'è nessuno in casa
• (*everyone*)
anyone can go = chiunque può andarci

anything *pronoun*
• (*in questions*) = qualcosa
do you need anything? = ha bisogno di qualcosa?
• (*with the negative*) = niente
she didn't say anything = non ha detto niente
• (*everything*) = tutto
I like anything to do with sports = mi piace tutto quello che ha a che fare con lo sport

anyway *adverb*
= in ogni modo

anywhere *adverb*
• (*in questions*) = da qualche parte
can you see a phone booth anywhere? = vedi una cabina telefonica da qualche parte?
• (*with the negative*) = da nessuna parte
you're not going anywhere = non vai da nessuna parte
• (*any place*)
we can meet anywhere you like = ci possiamo incontrare dovunque vuoi

apart
1 *adjective*
they don't like being apart = a loro non piace stare lontani
2 apart from = a parte

apartment *noun*
an apartment = un appartamento
an apartment block = un palazzo

apologize *verb*
= scusarsi (! + *essere*)
apology *noun*
an apology = delle scuse (*plural*)
to make an apology = scusarsi (! + *essere*)

appear *verb*
• (*to seem*)
= sembrare (! + *essere*)
• (*to come into view*) = apparire (! + *essere*)

appetite *noun*
  the appetite = l'appetito
  to have a good appetite = avere un
    ottimo appetito

apple *noun*
  an apple = una mela
  apple juice = il succo di mela

application *noun*
  a job application = una domanda di
    lavoro

apply *verb*
  to apply for a job = fare una domanda di
    lavoro

appointment *noun*
  an appointment = un appuntamento
  to make an appointment = prendere un
    appuntamento

appreciate *verb*
  he appreciates good food = gli piace la
    buona tavola
  I'd appreciate it = te ne sarei grato

approach *verb*
  = avvicinarsi a (**!** + *essere*)

approve *verb*
  to approve of someone = vedere
    qualcuno di buon occhio

apricot *noun*
  an apricot = un'albicocca

April *noun* ▶ **155**
  April = aprile (*masculine*)

Aquarius *noun*
  Aquarius = Acquario

architect *noun* ▶ **281**
  an architect = un architetto

area *noun*
  an area = una zona

area code *noun* (*US English*)
  the area code = il prefisso telefonico

argue *verb*
  = litigare
  to argue about money = litigare per una
    questione di soldi

argument *noun*
  an argument = una discussione
  to have an argument with someone
    = litigare con qualcuno

Aries *noun*
  Aries = Ariete (*masculine*)

arm *noun* ▶ **137**
  the arm = il braccio

  > **!** Note that the plural of **braccio** is
  > **braccia**. It is masculine in the singular
  > and feminine in the plural.

  she's hurt her arm = si è fatta male al
    braccio
  my arms hurt = mi fanno male le braccia

armchair *noun*
  an armchair = una poltrona

armed *adjective*
  = armato/armata

arms *noun*
  arms = le armi

army *noun*
  the army = l'esercito

around

  > **!** Often **around** occurs in combinations
  > with verbs, for example: **run around**,
  > **turn around**, etc. To find the correct
  > translations for this type of verb, look
  > up the separate dictionary entries at
  > **run**, **turn**, etc.

1 *preposition*
  = intorno a
  the people around me were speaking
    Italian = la gente intorno a me parlava
    italiano
  to walk around the room = camminare
    per la stanza
  to go around the world = fare il giro del
    mondo
2 *adverb*
• (*with numbers*) = circa
  it costs around £200 = costa circa 200
    sterline
• (*with times*) = verso
  we'll be there at around four o'clock
    = saremo lì verso le quattro

arrange *verb*
  to arrange a break in Italy = organizzare
    una vacanza in Italia
  we arranged to have lunch together = ci
    siamo accordati per pranzare insieme

arrest *verb*
  = arrestare

arrive *verb*
  = arrivare (**!** + *essere*)
  we arrived at the station at noon = siamo
    arrivati alla stazione a mezzogiorno

arrow *noun*
  an arrow = una freccia

art *noun*
• art = l'arte (*feminine*)
• (*as a school subject*)
  art = l'educazione artistica

art gallery *noun*
  an art gallery = un museo

artificial *adjective*
  = artificiale

artist *noun* ▶ **281**
  an artist = un artista/un'artista

as
1 *conjunction*
• as = come
  as you know, we're leaving = come sai, ce
    ne andiamo
• (*at the time when*)
  the phone rang as I was getting out of
    the bath = il telefono ha squillato
    mentre uscivo dalla vasca   ····▶

I used to live there as a child = da
bambino abitavo là
• (British English) (because, since)
  = siccome
  as you were out, I left a message
  = siccome eri fuori, ho lasciato un
  messaggio
2 preposition
  she's got a job as a teacher = lavora
  come insegnante
  he was dressed as a sailor = era vestito
  da marinaio
3 adverb
  as [intelligent | rich | strong] **as** = tanto
  [intelligente | ricco | forte] quanto
  I have as much work as you = ho tanto
  lavoro quanto te
  he plays as well as his sister = suona
  bene quanto la sorella
  as soon as possible = il più presto
  possibile
4 as usual = come al solito

ashamed adjective
  to be ashamed = vergognarsi (**!** + essere)

ashtray noun
  an ashtray = un portacenere

Asia noun ▶ 151 |
  Asia = l'Asia

Asian adjective ▶ 199 |
  = asiatico/asiatica

ask verb
• **to ask** = chiedere
  she asked him his name = gli ha chiesto
  come si chiamava
  to ask someone to [phone | leave a message
  | do the shopping] = chiedere a qualcuno
  di [telefonare | lasciare un messaggio | fare la
  spesa]
  I'll ask her if she wants to come = le
  chiederò se vuole venire
  I asked for a coffee = ho chiesto un caffè
  to ask to speak to someone = chiedere di
  parlare con qualcuno
  to ask someone a question = fare una
  domanda a qualcuno
• (to invite) = invitare
  to ask some friends to dinner = invitare
  degli amici a cena
  he asked her out = le ha chiesto di uscire
  con lui

asleep adjective
  to be asleep = dormire
  to fall asleep = addormentarsi (**!** +
  essere)

assistant noun
  an assistant = un assistente/un'assistente

at preposition
  ! There are many verbs which involve
  the use of **at**, like **look at**, **laugh at**,
  point at, etc. For translations, look up
  the entries at **look**, **laugh**, **point**, etc.

• (when talking about a position or place)
  = a
  ! Note that before a vowel, especially
  before a, **ad** is also possible.

  we met at a concert = ci siamo conosciuti
  a un concerto
  she's at an exhibition = è a una mostra
  at the = al/alla (**!** + singular)
  = ai/alle (+ plural)

  ! Before masculine nouns beginning
  with z, ps, gn, or s + another
  consonant, **allo** is used in the singular
  and **agli** in the plural. Before masculine
  and feminine singular nouns beginning
  with a vowel, **all'** is used.

  they're at the station = sono alla stazione
  to be [at home | at school | at work] = essere
  [a casa | a scuola | al lavoro]
• (at the house, shop, practice of) = da
  we'll be at Francesca's = saremo da
  Francesca
  he's got an appointment at the dentist's
  = ha un appuntamento dal dentista
  at the office = in ufficio
• (when talking about time) = a
  the film starts at nine o'clock = il film
  comincia alle nove
• (when talking about age) = a
  she was able to read at four years of age
  = sapeva leggere a quattro anni

athlete noun ▶ 281 |
  an athlete = un atleta/un'atleta

athletics noun ▶ 178 |
  athletics (in Britain) = l'atletica
  (in the US) = lo sport

Atlantic noun
  the Atlantic = l'Atlantico

atmosphere noun
  the atmosphere = l'atmosfera

attach verb
  = attaccare
  to be attached to the suitcase = essere
  attaccato alla valigia

attack verb
  to attack a town = attaccare una città
  to attack someone in the street
  = aggredire qualcuno per strada

attempt
1 verb
  to attempt to break the record = tentare
  di battere il record
2 noun
  an attempt = un tentativo

attend verb
  to attend the village school = frequentare
  la scuola del paese
  to attend evening classes = seguire corsi
  serali

attention noun
  attention = l'attenzione (feminine)   ····▶

to get someone's attention = attrarre
l'attenzione di qualcuno
to pay attention to the teacher = ascoltare
l'insegnante
pay attention to what you're doing! = fai
attenzione a quello che stai facendo!

attic *noun*
an attic = una soffitta

attitude *noun*
an attitude = un atteggiamento
**he has a strange attitude toward(s)
people** = ha un atteggiamento strano
con la gente

attract *verb*
(*a person*) = attrarre
(*insects*) = attirare

attractive *adjective*
= attraente

auburn *adjective* ▶ 147│
= ramato/ramata

audience *noun*
the audience = il pubblico

August *noun* ▶ 155│
August = agosto

aunt *noun*
an aunt = una zia

au pair *noun*
an au pair = una ragazza alla pari

Australia *noun* ▶ 151│
Australia = l'Australia

Australian ▶ 199│
1 *adjective*
= australiano/australiana
2 *noun*
the Australians = gli australiani

Austria *noun* ▶ 151│
Austria = l'Austria

Austrian ▶ 199│
1 *adjective*
= austriaco/austriaca
2 *noun*
the Austrians = gli austriaci

author *noun* ▶ 281│
an author = un autore/un'autrice

automatic *adjective*
= automatico/automatica

autumn *noun*
autumn = l'autunno
in (the) autumn = d'autunno

available *adjective*
• (*on sale*) = disponibile
tickets for the concert are still available
= ci sono ancora biglietti per il concerto
• (*free*) = libero/libera
are you available? = sei libero?

average *adjective*
= medio/media
the average teenager = il tipico teenager

avoid *verb*
= evitare
to avoid spending money = evitare di
spendere

awake *adjective*
to be awake = essere sveglio/sveglia
to keep someone awake = tenere sveglio
qualcuno

award *noun*
an award = un premio

aware *adjective*
to be aware of the [problem | danger | risk]
= essere consapevole del [problema |
pericolo | rischio]

away *adverb*
• (*absent*)
to be away = essere via
she's away on business = è via per
lavoro
• (*in its place*)
= via
to put something away = mettere via
qualcosa
• (*when talking about distances*)
to be far away = essere lontano/lontana
London is 40 km away = Londra è a 40
km

awful *adjective*
• (*no good*) = brutto/brutta
the film was awful = il film era brutto
• (*causing shock*) = terribile
• **I feel awful** = non mi sento affatto bene

awkward *adjective*
(*describing a situation, a problem*)
= difficile
I feel awkward about telling him = mi
imbarazza dirglielo

axe, ax (*US English*) *noun*
an axe = un'ascia

baby *noun*
a baby = un bambino/una bambina

babysitter *noun*
= un/una babysitter

back

> **!** *Often* **back** *occurs in combinations
> with verbs, for example:* **come back,
> get back, give back,** *etc. To find the
> correct translations for this type of
> verb, look up the separate dictionary
> entries at* **come, get, give,** *etc.*

1 *noun*
• (*part of the body*) ▶ 137│   ····▶

the back = la schiena
I've hurt my back = mi sono fatto male
 alla schiena
- (*the rear*)
 at the back of the classroom = in fondo
 all'aula
 to sit in the back of the car = sedere
 dietro
2 *adverb*
- to be back = tornare (**!** + *essere*)
 I'll be back in five minutes = torno tra
 cinque minuti
- (*before in time*)
 back in January = a gennaio

background *noun*
- (*of a person*)
 he's from a comfortable background = è
 di famiglia piuttosto benestante
- (*of a picture*)
 the background = lo sfondo
 in the background = sullo sfondo

backpack *noun*
 a backpack = uno zaino

back to front *adverb*
 = al contrario
 he put his sweater on back to front = si è
 messo il maglione al contrario

backwards, **backward** (*US English*)
adverb
 = all'indietro

bacon *noun*
 bacon = la pancetta

bad *adjective*
- (*unpleasant, serious*) = brutto/brutta
 a bad film = un brutto film
 I have some bad news = ho brutte
 notizie
 a bad accident = un brutto incidente
 to have a bad cold = avere un brutto
 raffreddore
 smoking is bad for you = fumare fa male
- (*incompetent*)
 to be bad [at maths | at tennis | at chess]
 = non essere bravo/brava [in matematica |
 a tennis | con gli scacchi]
- (*naughty, wicked*) = cattivo/cattiva
 a bad boy = un bambino cattivo
- (*talking about quality*)
 a bad idea = una cattiva idea
 'how was the film?'—'not bad' = 'com'era
 il film?'—'non era male'
- (*when talking about food*) = guasto/guasta

badly *adverb*
- (*not well*) = male
 she slept badly = ha dormito male
- (*seriously*) = gravemente
 he was badly injured = era ferito
 gravemente

badminton *noun* ▶ **178**
 badminton = il badminton

bad-tempered *adjective*
 = irascibile

bag *noun*
- a bag = una borsa
- (*made of paper, plastic*)
 a bag = un sacchetto

baggage *noun*
 baggage = i bagagli (*plural*)

bake *verb*
 to bake bread = fare il pane
 to bake a cake = fare un dolce

baker *noun* ▶ **281**
 a baker = un fornaio/una fornaia

bakery *noun* ▶ **281**
 a bakery = un panificio

balance *noun*
 balance = l'equilibrio
 to lose one's balance = perdere
 l'equilibrio

balcony *noun*
 a balcony = un terrazzo

bald *adjective*
 = calvo/calva

ball *noun*
 a ball (*in football, rugby, or basketball*)
 = un pallone
 (*in tennis, golf, or cricket*) = una pallina
 (*in billiards*) = una palla
 to play ball = giocare a pallone

ballet *noun*
 ballet = la danza

balloon *noun*
- a balloon = un palloncino
- a hot air balloon = un pallone aerostatico

ban *verb*
 = proibire

banana *noun*
 a banana = una banana

band *noun*
 a band = un gruppo
 a rock band = un gruppo rock

bandage *noun*
 a bandage = una fascia

bang
1 *noun*
- (*a loud noise*)
 a bang = un colpo
- (*US English*) (*a fringe*)
 bangs = la frangia (*singular*)
2 *verb*
- (*to close with a bang*) = sbattere
- (*to hit*)
 to bang one's fist on the table = battere il
 pugno sul tavolo
 to bang one's head on the wall = battere
 la testa contro il muro

bank *noun*
 a bank = una banca
 a bank account = un conto in banca
 a bank manager = un direttore/una
 direttrice di banca

bank holiday noun (*British English*)
  a bank holiday = un giorno festivo

bar noun
• (*a place*)
  a bar = un bar
• (*made of metal*)
  a bar = una sbarra
• (*other uses*)
  a bar of soap = una saponetta
  a bar of chocolate = una tavoletta di
  cioccolata

barbecue noun
  a barbecue = una grigliata

barely adverb
  = a malapena
  he was barely able to walk = riusciva a
  malapena a camminare

bargain noun
  a bargain = un affare

bark verb
  = abbaiare

barrel noun
  a barrel = un barile

base verb
  to be based on a true story = essere
  basato/basata su una storia vera

baseball noun ▶ 178 |
  baseball = il baseball

basement noun
  a basement = un seminterrato

basically adverb
  = fondamentalmente

basket noun
  a basket = un cesto

basketball noun ▶ 178 |
  basketball = la pallacanestro

bat noun
• (*in cricket or baseball*)
  a bat = una mazza
• (*an animal*)
  a bat = un pipistrello

bath noun
• to have a bath = fare il bagno
  he's in the bath = sta facendo il bagno
• (*a bathtub*)
  a bath = una vasca

bathroom noun
  a bathroom = un bagno
  to go to the bathroom = andare in bagno
  (**!** + *essere*)

battery noun
  a battery (*for a torch*) = una pila
  (*for a car*) = una batteria

battle noun
  a battle = una battaglia

bay noun
  a bay = un'insenatura

be verb
▶ *See the boxed note on* **be** *for more
information and examples.*
• to be = essere
  to be intelligent = essere intelligente
  he is tall = è alto
  be polite! = sii gentile!
  it's Monday = è lunedì
  it's past midnight = è mezzanotte passata
  I've never been to Spain = non sono mai
  stato in Spagna
  the house has been sold = la casa è stata
  venduta
• (*when talking about jobs*) ▶ 281 |
  she is a lawyer = fa l'avvocato
• (*when describing a physical or mental
  state*)
  to be [cold | hungry | afraid] = avere [freddo |
  fame | paura]
  my feet are cold = ho i piedi freddi
  I am 18 = ho diciotto anni
• (*when describing the weather*)
  the weather is [fine | awful | cold] = fa [bello
  | brutto | freddo]
  it's raining = piove
• (*when talking about health*)
  how are you? = come stai?
  I'm very well = sto benissimo
• (*when talking about prices*)
  how much is that umbrella? = quant'è
  quell'ombrello?
  how much is it all together? = quanto fa
  in tutto?
  that's 9 euros = fa 9 euro
• (*in continuous tenses*)
  he is reading = sta leggendo
  it was snowing = stava nevicando
  I'm coming = arrivo
• (*in questions and short answers*)
  it's a lovely house, isn't it? = è una bella
  casa, non è vero?
  'he's not here'—'yes he is' = 'non
  c'è'—'sì, c'è'

beach noun
  a beach = una spiaggia

beak noun
  a beak = un becco

bean noun
  a bean = un fagiolo

bear
1 noun
  a bear = un orso
2 verb
  = sopportare
  I can't bear him = non lo sopporto

beard noun
  a beard = una barba

beat verb
• (*to hit hard*) = picchiare
• (*in cooking*) = sbattere   ····▶

be

As an ordinary verb

When **be** is used as a simple verb in *subject* + *verb* sentences, it is usually translated by **essere** (**!** + *essere*):

> *I'm tired* = **sono** stanco
> *the kids **have been** very good* = i bambini **sono stati** proprio bravi

But note some expressions where italian uses **avere**:

> *she's twenty* = **ha** vent'anni
> *I'm hungry* = **ho** fame

As an auxiliary verb in progressive tenses

In English, **be** can be used in combination with another verb to form a progressive tense which allows us to express an idea of duration, of something happening over a period of time. To express the same idea in Italian there are also progressive forms using **stare** + **-ando/-endo**:

> *I'm looking for my glasses* = **sto cercando** gli occhiali
> *they **were waiting** for me* = mi **stavano aspettando**

However, these forms are only used to emphasize the fact that the action is continuing. Often the simple present and imperfect tenses are used to translate the progressive in English:

> *where **are** you **going**?* = dove vai?
> *it **was snowing*** = nevicava

As part of the passive

In Italian the passive is formed using the verb **essere**, in a similar way to English:

> *wine **is made** from grapes* = il vino **è fatto** con l'uva
> *she **was arrested*** = **è stata** arrestata

However, in spoken Italian the construction with **si** is more often used to express the same idea:

> *oil **is made** from olives* = l'olio **si fa** con le olive

---

- (*to win against*) = battere
  Scotland beat England two nil = la Scozia ha battuto l'Inghilterra due a zero
beat up = picchiare

beautiful *adjective*
  = bello/bella

> **!** *Note that before masculine nouns beginning with z, ps, gn or s + another consonant, **bello** is used in the singular and **begli** in the plural. Before masculine nouns beginning with other consonants, **bel** is used in the singular and **bei** in the plural. Before all nouns beginning with a vowel, **bell'** is used in the singular and **begli** (masculine) or **belle** (feminine) in the plural.*

  a beautiful girl = una bella ragazza
  a beautiful place = un bel posto
  they are beautiful cities = sono belle città

beauty *noun*
  beauty = la bellezza

because
1 *conjunction*
  = perché
  he did it because he had to = lo ha fatto perché era necessario
2 **because of** = a causa di

  we didn't go out because of the rain = non siamo usciti a causa della pioggia

become *verb*
  = diventare (**!** + *essere*)

bed *noun*
  a bed = un letto
  to go to bed = andare a letto (**!** + *essere*)

bedroom *noun*
  a bedroom = una camera

bee *noun*
  a bee = un'ape

beef *noun*
  beef = il manzo

beer *noun*
  beer = la birra
  a beer = una birra

before
1 *preposition*
  = prima di
  before the holidays = prima delle vacanze
  the day before yesterday = ieri l'altro
2 *adverb*
  = prima
  two months before = due mesi prima
  the day before = il giorno prima
  have you been to Venice before? = sei già stato a Venezia?   ⋯▶

3 *conjunction*
I'd like to see him before I go = vorrei
vederlo prima di andare via
I'd like to see him before he goes
= vorrei vederlo prima che vada via

> **!** *Note that the subjunctive is used after*
> **prima che**.

beggar *noun*
a beggar = un/una mendicante

begin *verb*
= cominciare
to begin to [laugh | cry | rain] = cominciare
a [ridere | piangere | piovere]

beginner *noun*
a beginner = un/una principiante

beginning *noun*
the beginning = l'inizio
at the beginning of May = all'inizio di
maggio

behave *verb*
= comportarsi (**!** + *essere*)
he behaved badly = si è comportato male
to be well behaved = essere
beneducato/beneducata
behave yourself! = comportati bene!

behaviour (*British English*), **behavior**
(*US English*) *noun*
behaviour = il comportamento

behind *preposition*
= dietro
behind the chair = dietro la sedia
behind me = dietro di me

Belgian ▶ 199 ⌋
1 *adjective*
= belga
2 *noun*
the Belgians = i belgi

Belgium *noun* ▶ 151 ⌋
Belgium = il Belgio

believe *verb*
= credere
to believe someone = credere a qualcuno

bell *noun*
• (*in a church*)
a bell = una campana
• (*on a door or bicycle*)
a bell = un campanello

belong *verb*
• (*to be the property of*)
to belong to someone = appartenere a
qualcuno
that book belongs to me = quel libro è
mio
• (*to be a member of*)
to belong to a club = fare parte di un
club

below *preposition*
= sotto

belt *noun*
a belt = una cintura

bench *noun*
a bench = una panca
(*in a park*) = una panchina

bend
1 *verb* = piegare
to bend one's knees = piegare le
ginocchia
2 *noun*
a bend = una curva
bend down = piegarsi (**!** + *essere*)

beneath *preposition*
= sotto

beside *preposition*
• (*next to*) = accanto a
he is sitting beside me = è seduto
accanto a me
• (*near*) = vicino a
I live beside the harbour = abito vicino al
porto

best
1 *noun*
the best = il/la migliore
to be the best at Italian = essere il/la
migliore in italiano
who is the best at drawing? = chi disegna
meglio?
I'm doing my best = faccio del mio
meglio
2 *adjective*
= migliore
the best hotel in town = il migliore
albergo della città
my best friend = il mio migliore amico/la
mia migliore amica
the best book I've ever read = il miglior
libro che abbia mai letto

> **!** *Note that the subjunctive is used after*
> **il migliore … che**.

3 *adverb*
= meglio
the best-dressed man = l'uomo meglio
vestito
I like tennis best = preferisco il tennis

bet *verb*
= scommettere

better
1 *adjective*
= migliore
her new film is better than the others = il
suo nuovo film è migliore degli altri
he is better at sports than me = nelle
attività sportive è più bravo di me
the weather is going to get better = il
tempo migliorerà
he was ill but now he's better = era
malato ma ora sta meglio
2 *adverb*
= meglio
he speaks French better than I do
= parla francese meglio di me ····➤

we'd better go = sarà meglio andare
it's better to [phone | write | check] = è
  meglio [telefonare | scrivere | controllare]

between
1 *preposition*
  = fra
  there is a wall between the two gardens
  = c'è un muro tra i due giardini
2 in between = in mezzo

beyond *preposition*
  = oltre
  beyond the mountains = oltre le
  montagne

bicycle *noun*
  a bicycle = una bicicletta

big *adjective*
• (*large*) = grande
  a big garden = un giardino grande
  a big party = una grande festa
• (*heavy, thick, serious*) = grosso/grossa
  a big parcel = un grosso pacco
  a big book = un libro grosso
  to make a big mistake = fare un grosso
  sbaglio

bill *noun*
• (*for gas, electricity, telephone*)
  a bill = una bolletta
• (*in a restaurant, hotel*)
  a bill = un conto
  could we have the bill please? = il conto,
  per favore
• (*US English*) (*money*)
  a bill = una banconota

billiards *noun* ▶ **178**|
  billiards = il biliardo

bin *noun* (*British English*)
  a bin = una pattumiera

biology *noun*
  biology = la biologia

bird *noun*
  a bird = un uccello

birth *noun*
  a birth = una nascita
  place of birth = luogo di nascita

birthday *noun*
  a birthday = un compleanno
  happy birthday! = buon compleanno!

biscuit *noun* (*British English*)
  a biscuit = un biscotto

bit
1 *noun*
  (*of cheese, bread, wood*) = un pezzo
2 a bit (*British English*)
  a bit [early | hot | odd] = un po' [presto | caldo
  | strano]

bite *verb*
  = mordere

bitter *adjective*
  = amaro/amara

black *adjective* ▶ **147**|
  = nero/nera

blackberry *noun*
  a blackberry = una mora

blackboard *noun*
  the blackboard = la lavagna

blackcurrant *noun*
  blackcurrants = il ribes nero (*singular*)

blade *noun*
• (*of a knife, a sword*)
  a blade = una lama
• a razor blade = una lametta
• a blade of grass = un filo d'erba

blame *verb*
  to blame someone = dare la colpa a
  qualcuno

blank *adjective*
  (*describing a page*) = bianco/bianca
  (*describing a cassette*) = vuoto/vuota

blanket *noun*
  a blanket = una coperta

bleed *verb*
  = sanguinare
  my nose is bleeding = mi sanguina il
  naso

blind
1 *adjective*
  = cieco/cieca
2 *noun*
  a roller blind = un avvolgibile
  a venetian blind = una veneziana

blister *noun*
  a blister = una vescica

block
1 *noun*
• (*a building*)
  a block of apartments = un palazzo
• (*a group of houses*) = un isolato
• (*a large piece*)
  a block = un blocco
2 *verb*
  = bloccare
  to block a road = bloccare una strada

blond, blonde *adjective* ▶ **147**|
  = biondo/bionda
  he has blond hair = ha i capelli biondi
  my sister's blonde = mia sorella è bionda

blood *noun*
  blood = il sangue

blouse *noun*
  a blouse = una camicetta

blow
1 *verb*
• (*if it's the wind*) = soffiare
  the wind blew the door shut = un colpo
  di vento ha chiuso la porta
• (*if it's a person*)
  to blow a whistle = fischiare
  to blow one's nose = soffiarsi il naso
  (**!** + *essere*)   ····▶

- (*if it's a light bulb*) = saltare (**!** + *essere*)

2 *noun*
 a blow = un colpo

blow away
 to be blown away = essere portato/portata
 via dal vento

blow down
 to be blown down = essere
 abbattuto/abbattuta dal vento

blow out = spegnere
 to blow out a candle = spegnere una
 candela

blow up
- (*to destroy*) = far saltare
 to blow up a car = far saltare una
 macchina
- (*to be destroyed*) = esplodere (**!** + *essere*)
- (*to put air into*) = gonfiare

blue *adjective* ▶ **147** |
- = blu (**!** *never changes*)
- (*when it's eyes, the sky*) = azzurro/azzurra

blush *verb*
 = arrossire (**!** + *essere*)

board

1 *noun*
- (*a piece of wood*)
 a board = una tavola
- (*for games*)
 a board = una scacchiera
- (*a blackboard*)
 a board = una lavagna

2 *verb*
 to board a ship = salire a bordo di una
 nave (**!** + *essere*)

3 on board = a bordo

boast *verb*
 = vantarsi (**!** + *essere*)

boat *noun*
 a boat = una barca

body *noun*
 the body = il corpo
 a dead body = un cadavere

boil *verb*
- (*if it's a person*)
 to boil water = far bollire l'acqua
 to boil an egg = far bollire un uovo
 a boiled egg
 (*soft*) = un uovo alla coque
 (*hard*) = un uovo sodo
- (*if it's water, milk*) = bollire

boiler *noun*
 a boiler = una caldaia

boiling *adjective*
 = bollente

bomb *noun*
 a bomb = una bomba

bone *noun* ▶ **137** |
 a bone (*in the body, in meat*) = un osso
 ! *Look at the note at* **osso**.

 (*in fish*) = una lisca

bonnet *noun* (*British English*)
 the bonnet (*in a car*) = il cofano

book

1 *noun*
 a book = un libro

2 *verb*
 = prenotare
 to book a room = prenotare una stanza
 the flight is fully booked = il volo è
 completo

booking *noun*
 a booking = una prenotazione

bookshop, bookstore *noun* ▶ **281** |
 a bookshop, a bookstore = una libreria

boot *noun*
- (*worn on the feet*)
 a boot = uno stivale
- (*British English*) (*of a car*)
 the boot = il bagagliaio

border *noun*
 a border = una frontiera
 to cross the border = passare la frontiera

bore *verb*
 = annoiare

bored *adjective*
 to be bored, to get bored = annoiarsi (**!** +
 essere)

boring *adjective*
 = noioso/noiosa

born *adjective*
 to be born = nascere (**!** + *essere*)
 he was born in 1988 = è nato nel 1988
 she was born in Italy = è nata in Italia

borrow *verb*
 = prendere in prestito
 to borrow some money from someone
 = prendere in prestito dei soldi da
 qualcuno

boss *noun*
 the boss = il capo

both

1 *determiner*
 both girls are blonde = entrambe le
 ragazze sono bionde
 both my sons = i miei due figli
 both Anne and Brian came = sono venuti
 sia Anne che Brian

2 *pronoun*
 = entrambi/entrambe
 you are both wrong, both of you are
 wrong = avete torto entrambi

bother *verb*
- (*to take the trouble*)
 don't bother to call back = non importa
 che tu richiami
- (*to annoy, to upset*) = dare fastidio a
- (*in polite apologies*) = disturbare
 I'm sorry to bother you = scusi se la
 disturbo

The human body

Note the use of **il/la**, etc in Italian where English uses **my**, **your**, etc.

*he raised **his** hand*	= ha alzato **la** mano
*she closed **her** eyes*	= ha chiuso **gli** occhi
***my** eye hurts*	= mi fa male l'occhio

For expressions which involve more than the simple movement of a body part, use a reflexive verb in Italian:

*she has broken **her** leg*	= **si** è rotta **la** gamba
*he was washing **his** hands*	= **si** lavava **le** mani

Note also the following:

*she broke **his** nose*	= **gli** ha rotto **il** naso

Describing people

Here are some ways of describing people in Italian:

his hair is long/he has long hair	= ha i capelli lunghi
a boy with long hair	= un ragazzo con i capelli lunghi
her eyes are blue/she has blue eyes	= ha gli occhi azzurri
the girl with blue eyes	= la ragazza con gli occhi azzurri

▶ For further expressions with terms referring to the body, look at the note on **illnesses, aches, and pains**.

---

bottle *noun*
  a bottle = una bottiglia

bottle-opener *noun*
  a bottle-opener = un apribottiglie

bottom
1 *noun*
• (*the lowest part*)
  at the bottom of [the page | the stairs | the sea] = in fondo [alla pagina | alle scale | al mare]
• (*at the lowest level*)
  to be bottom of the class = essere l'ultimo/l'ultima della classe
• (*part of the body*) ▶ **137** |
  the bottom = il sedere
2 *adjective*
  the bottom [shelf | drawer | cupboard] = [lo scaffale | il cassetto | l'armadietto] in basso

bound: **to be bound to** *verb*
  she's bound to complain = si lamenterà di sicuro
  it was bound to happen = doveva succedere

bow[1] *noun*
• (*a knot*)
  a bow = un fiocco
• (*a weapon*)
  a bow = un arco

bow[2] *verb*
  = fare un inchino

bowl *noun*
  a bowl = una ciotola

bowling *noun* ▶ **178** |
  bowling = il bowling

box *noun*
  a box = una scatola

boxing *noun* ▶ **178** |
  boxing = il pugilato

boy *noun*
  a boy = un bambino
  (*a teenager*) = un ragazzo

boyfriend *noun*
  a boyfriend = un ragazzo

bra *noun*
  a bra = un reggiseno

bracelet *noun*
  a bracelet = un braccialetto

brain *noun* ▶ **137** |
  the brain = il cervello

brake
1 *noun*
  a brake = un freno
2 *verb*
  = frenare

branch *noun*
  a branch = un ramo

brand-new *adjective*
  = nuovo/nuova di zecca

brandy *noun*
  brandy = il cognac

brave *adjective*
  = coraggioso/coraggiosa

Brazil *noun* ▶ **151** |
  Brazil = il Brasile

bread *noun*
  bread = il pane

break
1 *verb*
• (*to be damaged*) = rompersi (**!** + *essere*)
  the chair broke = la sedia si è rotta ····▶

- (*to smash or damage*) = rompere
  to break an egg = rompere un uovo
- (*to injure*)
  to break one's leg = rompersi la gamba
  (**!** + *essere*)
  she broke her arm = si è rotta un braccio
- (*not to keep*)
  to break a promise = non mantenere una
  promessa
  to break the rules = non rispettare le
  regole
2 *noun*
- (*a short rest*)
  a break = una pausa
  to take a break = fare una pausa
- (*at school*)
  the break = l'intervallo
break down
- (*if it's a TV, a car*) = rompersi (**!** + *essere*)
- (*to get upset*) = crollare (**!** + *essere*)
break out
  = scoppiare (**!** + *essere*)
break up
- (*if it's a crowd*) = sciogliersi (**!** + *essere*)
- (*if it's a couple*) = lasciarsi (**!** + *essere*)
  to break up with someone = lasciarsi da
  qualcuno
- (*to put an end to*) = mettere fine a

breakfast *noun*
  breakfast = la colazione
  to have breakfast = fare colazione

breast *noun* ▶ 137 |
  a breast = un seno

breath *noun*
  breath = il respiro
  to be out of breath = essere senza fiato
  to hold one's breath = trattenere il
  respiro

breathe *verb*
  = respirare

breeze *noun*
  a breeze = una brezza

brick *noun*
  a brick = un mattone

bride *noun*
  a bride = una sposa

bridegroom *noun*
  a bridegroom = uno sposo

bridge *noun*
  a bridge = un ponte

brief *adjective*
  = breve

bright *adjective*
- (*describing colours*) = vivace
- (*having plenty of light*)
  = luminoso/luminosa
  a bright spell = una schiarita
  to get brighter = schiarire (**!** + *essere*)
- (*intelligent*) = sveglio/sveglia

✗ in informal situations

brilliant *adjective*
- (*very intelligent*) = brillante
- (*British English*) (*used for emphasis*)
  = fantastico/fantastica

bring *verb*
  = portare
  to bring someone a present = portare un
  regalo a qualcuno
  he brought his sister to the party = ha
  portato sua sorella alla festa
bring about
  to bring about a change = portare un
  cambiamento
bring back = riportare
  he brought me back my book = mi ha
  riportato il libro
bring up = allevare
  to bring up a child = allevare un bambino

Britain *noun* ▶ 151 |
  Britain = la Gran Bretagna

British ▶ 199 | *adjective*
  = britannico/britannica
  a British passport = un passaporto
  britannico

  > **!** *Note that* **britannico/britannica** *is not
  > very common in Italian. For most
  > purposes it is more natural to use*
  > **inglese**, **scozzese**, **gallese**, *or*
  > **irlandese** *to describe oneself. Look at
  > the entries for* **English**, **Scot**, **Welsh**,
  > *and* **Irish** *to see how to refer to the
  > people.*

broad *adjective*
  = ampio/ampia

broadcast *verb*
  = trasmettere

brochure *noun*
  a brochure = un depliant

broke *adjective*
  = al verde✗

broken *adjective*
  = rotto/rotta

bronze *noun*
  bronze = il bronzo

brother *noun*
  a brother = un fratello

brother-in-law *noun*
  a brother-in-law = un cognato

brown *adjective* ▶ 147 |
- (*in colour*) = marrone
  to have brown eyes = avere gli occhi
  marroni
- (*describing hair*) = castano/castana
- (*tanned*) = abbronzato/abbronzata

bruise *noun* ▶ 193 |
  a bruise = un livido

brush
1 *noun*
- (*for hair, clothes or shoes*)
  a brush = una spazzola
- (*for sweeping up*)
  a brush = una scopa
- (*for painting*)
  a brush = un pennello
2 *verb*
  to brush one's hair = spazzolarsi i capelli
    (**!** + *essere*)
  to brush one's teeth = lavarsi i denti (**!** +
    essere)

Brussels *noun* ▶ 151 |
  Brussels = Bruxelles

bubble *noun*
  a bubble = una bolla

bucket *noun*
  a bucket = un secchio

budgerigar, budgie *noun*
  a budgerigar = un pappagallino

build *verb*
  = costruire
  to build a house = costruire una casa

building *noun*
  a building = un edificio

bull *noun*
  a bull = un toro

bullet *noun*
  a bullet = una pallottola

bully *noun*
  a bully = un/una prepotente

bump *verb*
  to bump one's head = sbattere la testa
bump into
- (*to hit*) = sbattere contro
- (*to meet*) = imbattersi in (**!** + *essere*)

bunch *noun*
  a bunch of flowers = un mazzo di fiori
  a bunch of grapes = un grappolo d'uva
  a bunch of keys = un mazzo di chiavi

burger *noun*
  a burger = un hamburger

burglar *noun*
  a burglar = un ladro/una ladra

burn
1 *verb*
- = bruciare
  to burn rubbish = bruciare l'immondizia
- (*to injure*)
  to burn oneself = bruciarsi (**!** + *essere*)
  to burn one's finger = bruciarsi un dito
- (*in the sun*)
  to burn easily = bruciare facilmente
2 *noun*
  a burn = una bruciatura
burn down = incendiare

burst *verb*
  = scoppiare (**!** + *essere*)

burst into
  to burst into tears = scoppiare a piangere
burst out
  to burst out laughing = scoppiare a ridere

bury *verb*
  = seppellire

bus *noun*
  a bus = un autobus

bus driver *noun* ▶ 281 |
  a bus driver = un autista/un'autista

bush *noun*
  a bush = un cespuglio

business *noun*
- (*commercial activities*)
  business = gli affari
  I'm going to London on business = vado
    a Londra per affari
- (*a company*)
  a business = un'impresa
- (*when protecting one's privacy*)
  it's none of your business = non sono
    affari tuoi

businessman *noun* ▶ 281 |
  a businessman = un imprenditore

businesswoman *noun* ▶ 281 |
  a businesswoman = un'imprenditrice

bus station *noun*
  a bus station = un deposito degli autobus

bus stop *noun*
  a bus stop = una fermata dell'autobus

busy *adjective*
  = impegnato/impegnata
  to be busy packing = essere impegnato a
    fare i bagagli
  to have a busy day = avere una giornata
    piena
  to lead a busy life = fare una vita attiva

but *conjunction*
  = ma
  **he understands Italian but he doesn't
    speak it** = capisce l'italiano, ma non lo
    parla

butcher *noun* ▶ 281 |
  a butcher = un macellaio/una macellaia

butter *noun*
  butter = il burro

butterfly *noun*
  a butterfly = una farfalla

button *noun*
  a button = un bottone

buy *verb*
  = comprare
  to buy a present for someone = comprare
    un regalo a qualcuno
  she bought herself a new coat = si è
    comprata un cappotto nuovo

by *preposition*
- **by** = da   ····▶

he was bitten by a dog = è stato morso
   da un cane
- (on one's own)
   by oneself = da solo/sola
- (using)
   to travel by bus = viaggiare in autobus
   we went there by bicycle = ci siamo
      andati in bicicletta
   to pay by cheque = pagare con un
      assegno
   to book by phone = prenotare per
      telefono
   to come in by the back door = entrare
      dalla porta di dietro
- (as a result of)
   she got in by breaking a window = è
      entrata spaccando un vetro
- (beside) = vicino a
   by the sea
   (when it's a town) = sul mare
   (when it's a house) = al mare
   by the side of the road = sul ciglio della
      strada
- (indicating the author or painter) = di
   a book by Dickens = un libro di Dickens
- (when talking about time)
   by next Thursday = per giovedì prossimo
   he should be here by now = a quest'ora
      dovrebbe essere qui
- (when talking about figures, rates)
   to increase by 20% = aumentare del 20%
   8 metres by 4 metres = 8 metri per 4
   one by one = uno per uno

cab noun
   a cab = un taxi

cabbage noun
   cabbage = il cavolo

café noun
   a café = un bar

cake noun
   a cake = una torta

calculator noun
   a calculator = una calcolatrice

calendar noun
   a calendar = un calendario

calf noun
- (the animal)
   a calf = un vitello
- (part of the leg) ▶ 137
   the calf = il polpaccio

call verb
- = chiamare

to call the doctor = chiamare il dottore
he's called Michael = si chiama Michael
what's this called in Italian? = come si
   chiama questo in italiano?
- (to phone) = chiamare
   who's calling? = chi parla?
- (to pay a visit) = passare (❗ + essere)
   they called yesterday = sono passati ieri
call back
- (to come back) = ripassare (❗ + essere)
- (to phone back) = richiamare
call off = annullare

calm
1 adjective
   = calmo/calma
2 verb
   = calmare
calm down = calmarsi (❗ + essere)

camcorder noun
   a camcorder = una videocamera

camel noun
   a camel = un cammello

camera noun
   a camera (for taking photos) = una
      macchina fotografica
   (in a studio, for videos) = una telecamera

camp
1 noun
   a camp = un campeggio
2 verb
   = accamparsi (❗ + essere)
   to go camping = andare in campeggio
      (❗ + essere)

campsite noun
   a campsite = un campeggio

can¹ verb
- (to have the possibility) = potere
   can you come? = puoi venire?
   where can I buy stamps? = dove posso
      comprare dei francobolli?
   he can't sleep when it's hot = non riesce
      a dormire quando fa caldo
- (when talking about seeing, hearing,
   understanding, can is not usually
   translated)
   I can hear you better now = ora ti sento
      meglio
   can they see us? = ci vedono?
- (to be allowed to)
   can I smoke? = posso fumare?
   we can't turn right here = qui non si può
      girare a destra
- (to know how to) = sapere
   she can swim = sa nuotare
   can you speak Italian? = parli italiano?
- (when asking, offering or suggesting)
   can we borrow your car? = possiamo
      prendere la tua macchina?
   can I help you? = posso esserti d'aiuto?
   you can phone back later if you like
      = puoi telefonare più tardi, se vuoi

can² noun
   a can

(*for drinks*) = una lattina
(*for food*) = una scatoletta

Canada *noun* ▶ **151**|
Canada = il Canada

Canadian ▶ **199**|
1 *adjective*
= canadese
2 *noun*
the Canadians = i canadesi

canal *noun*
a canal = un canale

cancel *verb*
= annullare

cancer *noun* ▶ **193**|
cancer = il cancro

candle *noun*
a candle = una candela

candy *noun* (*US English*)
• candy = i dolciumi
• (*a sweet*)
a candy = una caramella

canoe *noun*
a canoe = una canoa

canoeing *noun* ▶ **178**|
canoeing = il canottaggio

can-opener *noun*
a can-opener = un apriscatole

canteen *noun*
a canteen = una mensa

cap *noun*
a cap = un berretto
a baseball cap = un berretto da baseball

capable *adjective*
• to be capable of looking after oneself
= essere capace di badare a se stesso
• (*having ability, skill*) = abile

capital
1 *noun*
the capital = la capitale
Rome is the capital of Italy = Roma è la
capitale d'Italia
2 *adjective*
= maiuscolo/maiuscola
capital P = P maiuscola

captain *noun*
a captain = un capitano

car *noun*
a car = una macchina

caravan *noun* (*British English*)
a caravan = una roulotte

card *noun*
• (*for sending to someone*)
a card = un biglietto
• (*for playing games*)
a card = una carta
to play cards = giocare a carte

care
1 *noun*
• to take care = fare attenzione
take care crossing the street! = fai
attenzione quando attraversi la strada!
• to take care of someone = prendersi cura
di qualcuno (**!** + *essere*)
to take care of something = trattare bene
qualcosa
2 *verb*
I don't care = non me ne importa
to care about the environment = tenere
all'ambiente

career *noun*
a career = una carriera

careful *adjective*
to be careful = stare attento/attenta
be careful crossing the street! = stai
attento quando attraversi la strada!
to be careful not to make mistakes
= stare attento a non fare errori

careless *adjective*
= incurante

carnival *noun*
• (*British English*) (*a festival*)
a carnival = un carnevale
• (*US English*) (*a fair*)
a carnival = un luna park

car park *noun* (*British English*)
a car park = un parcheggio

carpet *noun*
the carpet = la moquette

carrot *noun*
a carrot = una carota

carry *verb*
= portare
carry on = continuare

cartoon *noun*
a cartoon (*a comic strip*) = un fumetto
(*a film*) = un cartone animato

case¹: in case *conjunction*
= in caso
keep the bike in case you need it = tieni
la bici in caso ti serva

> **!** *Note that the subjunctive is used after*
> **in caso**.

case² *noun*
• (*a box*)
a case = una cassa
• (*a suitcase*)
a case = una valigia

cash
1 *noun*
• (*coins or bills*)
I don't have any cash on me = non ho
contanti
to pay in cash = pagare in contanti
• (*money in general*)
cash = soldi (*masculine plural*)   ····▶

2 *verb*
= incassare

cash dispenser *noun*
a cash dispenser = un Bancomat®

cassette *noun*
a cassette = una cassetta

cassette player *noun*
a cassette player = un mangiacassette

castle *noun*
a castle = un castello

cat *noun*
a cat = un gatto/una gatta

catch *verb*
• (*to capture, to hold*) = prendere
to catch a fish = prendere un pesce
• (*to pinch, to stick*)
he caught his finger in the door = si è
chiuso un dito nella porta
• to catch the train = prendere il treno
• (*to become ill with*)
to catch flu = prendere l'influenza
• to catch fire = prendere fuoco
catch up
to catch up with someone = raggiungere
qualcuno

caterpillar *noun*
a caterpillar = un bruco

cathedral *noun*
a cathedral = una cattedrale

cauliflower *noun*
cauliflower = il cavolfiore

cause *verb*
= causare
it's going to cause delays = causerà dei
ritardi
to cause damage = fare dei danni

cautious *adjective*
= cauto/cauta

cave *noun*
a cave = una caverna

CD *noun*
a CD = un CD
a CD player = un lettore CD

ceiling *noun*
the ceiling = il soffitto

celebrate *verb*
= festeggiare

cell *noun*
a prison cell = una cella

cellar *noun*
a cellar = una cantina

cement *noun*
cement = il cemento

cemetery *noun*
a cemetery = un cimitero

cent *noun*
a cent (*of dollar*) = un centesimo
(*of euro*) = un cent, un centesimo

centimetre (*British English*),
centimeter (*US English*) *noun* ▶ **202** |
a centimetre = un centimetro

central heating *noun*
central heating = il riscaldamento
autonomo

centre (*British English*), **center** (*US
English*) *noun*
• (*a place for activities, meetings*)
a centre = un centro
a leisure centre = un centro sportivo
• (*the middle*)
the centre = il centro

century *noun* ▶ **267** |
a century = un secolo

certain *adjective*
= certo/certa

certainly *adverb*
= certamente

chain *noun*
a chain = una catena

chair *noun*
a chair = una sedia

chalk *noun*
chalk = il gesso

champion *noun*
a champion = un campione/una
campionessa
a tennis champion = un campione/una
campionessa di tennis

chance *noun*
• (*when talking about a possibility*)
there is a chance that she'll get a job in
Turin = c'è la possibilità che trovi un
lavoro a Torino

> ! Note that the subjunctive is used after
> c'è la possibilità che.

• (*an opportunity*)
a chance = un'occasione
to have the chance to meet people
= avere l'opportunità di incontrare della
gente
• by chance = per caso

change
1 *noun*
• a change = un cambiamento
• (*a different experience*)
let's go to the beach for a change = per
cambiare andiamo al mare
• (*cash*)
change = gli spiccioli
have you got change for 10 euros? = ha
da cambiare 10 euro?
• (*money given back after paying*)
the change = il resto
2 *verb*
• (*to make different, to replace*) = cambiare
(**!** + *avere*)   ····▶

I've changed my mind = ho cambiato idea

she keeps changing channels = continua a cambiare canale

to change a wheel = cambiare una ruota

to change dollars into lire = cambiare i dollari in lire

- (*to become different*) = cambiare (**!** + *essere*)

  the town has changed a lot = la città è molto cambiata

- (*to exchange in a shop*) = cambiare (**!** + *avere*)

  change a shirt for a smaller size = cambiare una camicia con una più piccola

- (*when talking about one's clothes*) = cambiarsi (**!** + *essere*)

  to get changed = cambiarsi (**!** + *essere*)

- (*when using transport*) = cambiare (**!** + *avere*)

channel *noun*
　a TV channel = un canale televisivo

Channel *noun*
　the (English) Channel = la Manica

chapter *noun*
　a chapter = un capitolo

charge
1 *verb*
　they'll charge you for the damage = ti faranno pagare i danni
2 *noun*
- (*a price, a fee*)
　a charge = una tariffa
　there's no charge = è gratis
3 in charge = responsabile
　to be in charge of the money = essere responsabile dei soldi

charming *adjective*
　= incantevole

chase *verb*
　= inseguire
chase away = cacciare via

chat
1 *verb*
　= chiacchierare
2 *noun*
　a chat = una chiacchierata
chat up (*British English*) = abbordare

cheap *adjective*
- (*not expensive*) = economico/economica
　it's cheap = non costa molto
　it's cheaper to take the bus = costa meno prendere l'autobus
- (*of poor quality*) = scadente

cheat *verb*
　= imbrogliare

check
1 *verb*
　= controllare
　you should check whether it's true = dovresti controllare se è vero

2 *noun*
- (*US English*) (*a bill*)
　a check = un conto
- (*US English*) (*a cheque*)
　a check = un assegno
check in
- (*at the airport*) = fare il check-in
- (*at a hotel*) = firmare il registro
check out = andare via (**!** + *essere*)

checkbook *noun* (*US English*)
　a checkbook = un libretto degli assegni

checkers *noun* ▶ **178|** (*US English*)
　checkers = la dama

check-in *noun*
　the check-in = il check-in

checkout *noun*
　the checkout = la cassa

cheek *noun* ▶ **137|**
　the cheek = la guancia

cheeky *adjective*
　= sfacciato/sfacciata

cheerful *adjective*
　= allegro/allegra

cheese *noun*
　cheese = il formaggio

chef *noun* ▶ **281|**
　a chef = un cuoco/una cuoca

chemist *noun* ▶ **281|**
- (*in a shop*)
　a chemist = un/una farmacista
- (*the shop*)
　a chemist = una farmacia
- (*in a laboratory*)
　a chemist = un chimico/una chimica

chemistry *noun*
　chemistry = la chimica

cheque *noun* (*British English*)
　a cheque = un assegno
　to write a cheque for £50 = fare un assegno da 50 sterline

cheque book *noun* (*British English*)
　a cheque book = un libretto degli assegni

cherry *noun*
　a cherry = una ciliegia

chess *noun* ▶ **178|**
　chess = gli scacchi

chest *noun* ▶ **137|**
　the chest = il petto

chew *verb*
　= masticare

chewing gum *noun*
　chewing gum = il chewing-gum

chicken *noun*
　a chicken = un pollo
　chicken = il pollo

chickenpox *noun*
　chickenpox = la varicella

C

child *noun*
a child = un bambino/una bambina

chilly *adjective*
it's chilly = fa freddo

chimney *noun*
a chimney = un camino

chin *noun* ▶ 137 ⏐
the chin = il mento

China *noun* ▶ 151 ⏐
China = la Cina

Chinese ▶ 199 ⏐
1 *adjective*
= cinese
2 *noun*
• (*the people*)
the Chinese = i cinesi
• (*the language*)
Chinese = il cinese

chips *noun*
• (*British English*) (*French fries*)
chips = le patate fritte
• (*US English*) (*crisps*)
(potato) chips = le patatine

chocolate *noun*
chocolate = il cioccolato
a chocolate = un cioccolatino
a box of chocolates = una scatola di
cioccolatini

choice *noun*
a choice = una scelta
we had no choice = non avevamo scelta

choir *noun*
a choir = un coro

choke *verb*
= soffocare

choose *verb*
= scegliere

chore *noun*
to do the chores = fare le faccende

Christian *adjective*
= cristiano/cristiana

Christian name *noun*
a Christian name = un nome di battesimo

Christmas *noun*
Christmas (Day) = il Natale
merry Christmas!, happy Christmas!
= buon Natale!

Christmas Eve *noun*
Christmas Eve = la Vigilia di Natale

Christmas tree *noun*
a Christmas tree = un albero di Natale

church *noun*
a church = una chiesa

cider *noun*
cider = il sidro

cigar *noun*
a cigar = un sigaro

cigarette *noun*
a cigarette = una sigaretta

cinema *noun* (*British English*)
a cinema = un cinema

circle *noun*
a circle = un cerchio
we were sitting in a circle = eravamo
seduti in cerchio

circus *noun*
a circus = un circo

citizen *noun*
a citizen = un cittadino/una cittadina

city *noun*
a city = una città

civil servant *noun* ▶ 281 ⏐
a civil servant = un
impiegato/un'impiegata statale

clap *verb*
= applaudire

class *noun*
• (*a group of students*)
a class = una classe
• (*a lesson*)
a class = una lezione
a history class = una lezione di storia
• (*a social group*)
a (social) class = una classe (sociale)

classical music *noun*
classical music = la musica classica

classmate *noun*
a classmate = un compagno/una
compagna di classe

classroom *noun*
a classroom = un'aula

clean
1 *adjective*
= pulito/pulita
my hands are clean = ho le mani pulite
to keep the house clean = tenere la casa
pulita
2 *verb*
= pulire
to have a jacket cleaned = far lavare una
giacca

clear
1 *adjective*
• = chiaro/chiara
is that clear? = è chiaro?
a clear voice = una voce chiara
your writing must be clear = la calligrafia
deve essere chiara
• (*with no rain or cloud*) = sereno/serena
on a clear day = quando è sereno
2 *verb*
• (*to empty, to remove from*)
to clear the table = sgombrare la tavola
to clear the snow off the road
= sgombrare la strada dalla neve
• (*if it's fog, mist*) = schiarire (❗ + *essere*)

clever *adjective*
- (*intelligent*) = intelligente
- (*smart*) = furbo/furba

cliff *noun*
  a cliff = una scogliera

climate *noun*
  a climate = un clima

climb *verb*
- to climb (up) a tree = arrampicarsi su un albero (**!** + *essere*)
  to climb a mountain = scalare una montagna
  to climb over a wall = scavalcare un muro
- (*to rise higher*) = salire (**!** + *essere*)

climbing *noun* ▶ 178|
  climbing = l'arrampicata

clinic *noun*
  a clinic = una clinica

cloakroom *noun*
  a cloakroom = un guardaroba

clock *noun*
  a clock = un orologio
  (*in sporting events*) = un cronometro

close¹
1 *adjective*
- = vicino/vicina
  the station is quite close = la stazione è abbastanza vicina
  is the house close to the school? = la casa è vicina alla scuola?
- (*as a friend*) = intimo/intima
2 *adverb*
  to live close (by) = abitare vicino
  to come closer = avvicinarsi (**!** + *essere*)

close² *verb*
  = chiudere
  close your eyes = chiudi gli occhi
  the shop closes at noon = il negozio chiude a mezzogiorno
  the door closed suddenly = la porta si è chiusa all'improvviso
  close down = chiudere

closed *adjective*
  = chiuso/chiusa

cloth *noun*
- (*material*)
  cloth = la stoffa
- a cloth = uno straccio

clothes *noun*
  clothes = i vestiti
  to put on one's clothes = vestirsi (**!** + *essere*)
  to take off one's clothes = spogliarsi (**!** + *essere*)
  to have no clothes on = essere nudo/nuda

cloud *noun*
  a cloud = una nuvola

clown *noun*
  a clown = un pagliaccio

club *noun*
- a club = un circolo
  a tennis club = un circolo di tennis
  to be in a club = essere socio/socia di un club
- (*a nightclub*)
  a club = un locale

clue *noun*
  a clue = un indizio

clumsy *adjective*
  = goffo/goffa

coach
1 *noun* (*British English*)
- (*a bus*)
  a coach = un pullman
  a coach station = una stazione dei pullman
- (*of a train*)
  a coach = una carrozza
2 *verb*
  = allenare

coal *noun*
  coal = il carbone

coast *noun*
  the coast = la costa

coat *noun*
- a coat = un cappotto
- (*of an animal*)
  the coat = il pelo

coat hanger *noun*
  a coat hanger = un attaccapanni

cock *noun*
  a cock = un gallo

cocoa *noun*
- (*the drink*)
  cocoa = la cioccolata calda
- (*the product*)
  cocoa = il cacao

coconut *noun*
  coconut = il cocco
  a coconut = una noce di cocco

cod *noun*
  cod = il merluzzo

coffee *noun*
  coffee = il caffè
  a coffee = un caffè

coin *noun*
  a coin = una moneta
  a 2 euro coin = una moneta da 2 euro

coincidence *noun*
  a coincidence = una coincidenza

cold
1 *adjective*
  = freddo/fredda
  to be cold, to feel cold = avere freddo
  I'm very cold = ho molto freddo
  it's cold = fa freddo
  to go cold = raffreddarsi (**!** + *essere*) ····▶

The clock

What time is it?

what time is it?	= che ore sono?
could you tell me the time?	= mi sa dire che ore sono?
it's exactly four o'clock	= sono le quattro in punto
it's 1.00	= è l'una
it's 4.00	= sono le quattro
it's 4 am	= sono le quattro di mattino
it's 4 pm	= sono le quattro di pomeriggio
it's 8 pm	= sono le otto di sera
it's 4.05	= sono le quattro e cinque
it's 4.10	= sono le quattro e dieci
it's 4.15	= sono le quattro e un quarto
it's 4.20	= sono le quattro e venti
it's 4.25	= sono le quattro e venticinque
it's 4.30	= sono le quattro e mezzo
it's 4.35	= sono le quattro e trentacinque
it's 4.40	= sono le quattro e quaranta
it's 4.45	= sono le quattro e quarantacinque
it's 4.50	= sono le quattro e cinquanta
it's 4.55	= sono le quattro e cinquantacinque
it's 12 (noon)	= è mezzogiorno
it's midnight	= è mezzanotte

The twenty-four hour clock is always used in timetables and fairly often in speech, so that **5.00 pm** is **le diciassette**.

When?

Italian uses the preposition **a** to say what time something happens:

at one	= **all'**una
at five	= **alle** cinque
at midnight	= **a** mezzanotte

Italian always uses the preposition **a** (or another preposition like **verso** or **dopo**) even where it is often omitted in English:

what time did it happen?	= **a** che ora è successo?
*it happened **at** two*	= è successo **alle** due
*he'll come **at** one*	= verrà **all'**una
at about five	= **verso** le cinque
*it must be ready **by** ten*	= deve essere pronto **per** le dieci
*closed **from** 1.00 **to** 2.00*	= chiuso **dall'**una **alle** due

---

2 *noun*
- *(the lack of heat)*
  the cold = il freddo
- *(a common illness)*
  a cold = un raffreddore

collapse *verb*
(if it's a building, a wall) = crollare (**!** + *essere*)
(if it's a chair) = cadere (**!** + *essere*)

collar *noun*
- *(on a shirt or jacket)*
  a collar = un collo
- *(for a pet)*
  a collar = un collare

colleague *noun*
a colleague = un/una collega

collect *verb*
- *(to gather)* = raccogliere

to collect the exercise books
= raccogliere i quaderni
- *(to make a collection of)* = collezionare
  he collects stamps = colleziona francobolli
- *(to take away)*
  to collect the post = ritirare la posta
  to collect the rubbish = portare via la spazzatura

collection *noun*
- *(a set)*
  a collection = una collezione
- *(money collected)*
  a collection = una colletta

college *noun*
a college = un istituto superiore
I'm at college = vado all'università

colour *(British English)*, **color** *(US English)* *noun* ····▶

Colours

Most colours agree with the noun they are describing:

*a **red** hat*	= un cappello **rosso**
*a **red** shirt*	= una camicia **rossa**
*a **green** shoe*	= una scarpa **verde**
***green** shoes*	= scarpe **verdi**

There are exceptions, labelled (**!** *never changes*) in the dictionary. Even with a plural noun, this type of adjective remains the same:

*a **blue** jacket*	= una giacca **blu**
*a **pink** dress*	= un vestito **rosa**

Describing the colour of something

what colour is your car?	= di che colore è la tua macchina?
it's green	= è verde

---

a colour = un colore
what colour is the car? = di che colore è la macchina?

colourful (*British English*), **colorful** (*US English*) *adjective*
  a colourful shirt = una camicia dai colori vivaci

comb
1 *noun*
  a comb = un pettine
2 *verb*
  to comb one's hair = pettinarsi (**!** + *essere*)

come *verb*
• **to come** = venire (**!** + *essere*)
  she's coming today = viene oggi
  come to Padua with us = vieni a Padova con noi
  we came by bike = siamo venuti in bicicletta
  come and see! = vieni a vedere!
  I'm coming! = vengo!
  is the bus coming? = sta arrivando l'autobus?
  be careful when you come down the stairs = stai attento quando scendi le scale
  he came into the house = è entrato in casa
• (*to reach*)
  turn left when you come to the traffic lights = gira a sinistra quando arrivi al semaforo
• (*to be a native or a product of*)
  she comes from Italy = è italiana
  I come from Dublin = sono di Dublino
  where do you come from? = di dove sei?
  the strawberries come from Spain = le fragole vengono dalla Spagna
• (*in a contest*)
  to come first = arrivare primo/prima (**!** + *essere*)
come around ▶ **come round**
come back = tornare (**!** + *essere*)
  she came back home = è tornata a casa

come in
• (*to enter*) = entrare (**!** + *essere*)
• (*if it's a plane, a train*) = arrivare (**!** + *essere*)
• **the tide's coming in** = si sta alzando la marea
come off
  (*if it's a cover, a lid*) = venire via (**!** + *essere*)
  (*if it's a button, a label*) = staccarsi (**!** + *essere*)
come on
• (*to start to work*) = accendersi (**!** + *essere*)
• (*when encouraging someone*)
  come on, hurry up! = dai, sbrigati!
  come on, you can do better than that! = forza, puoi fare meglio di così
come out
• (*to leave a place*) = uscire (**!** + *essere*)
  I saw him as I was coming out of the shop = l'ho visto mentre uscivo dal negozio
• (*if it's a film, a book*) = uscire (**!** + *essere*)
• (*to wash out*) = venire via (**!** + *essere*)
• (*if it's a photo*) = venire (**!** + *essere*)
come round
• (*to visit*) = passare (**!** + *essere*)
• (*after a faint*) = rinvenire (**!** + *essere*)
come to
  lunch came to 40 euros = il pranzo è costato 40 euro
  how much does it come to? = quant'è?

comfortable *adjective*
• (*if it's a chair, a bed*) = comodo/comoda
  are you comfortable? = stai comodo?
• (*relaxed*)
  I don't feel comfortable here = non mi sento a mio agio qui
• (*having enough money*) = agiato/agiata

comic strip *noun*
  a comic strip = un fumetto

commercial
1 *adjective*
  = commerciale

2 *noun*
  a commercial = uno spot pubblicitario

commit *verb*
  to commit a crime = commettere un crimine

common *adjective*
  = comune

communicate *verb*
  = comunicare

community *noun*
  a community = una comunità

company *noun*
• (*a business*)
  a company = una ditta
• (*a group of actors*)
  a theatre company = una compagnia teatrale
• (*other people*)
  company = la compagnia
  to keep someone company = fare compagnia a qualcuno

compare *verb*
  to compare France with Italy = paragonare la Francia all'Italia

competition *noun*
• **competition** = la concorrenza
  there's a lot of competition between the schools = c'è molta concorrenza tra le scuole
• (*a contest*)
  a competition = un concorso

competitive *adjective*
  to be competitive = avere spirito di competizione

complain *verb*
• = lamentarsi (**!** + *essere*)
  to complain about the weather = lamentarsi del tempo
• (*to make a complaint*) = fare reclamo
  he complained about the service = ha fatto reclamo per il servizio

complete
1 *adjective*
  it was a complete disaster = è stato un disastro totale
  this is a complete waste of time = è una totale perdita di tempo
2 *verb*
  = finire
  she completed the course = ha finito il corso

completely *adverb*
  = completamente

complicate *verb*
  = complicare

complicated *adjective*
  = complicato/complicata

× in informal situations

compliment
1 *noun*
  a compliment = un complimento
2 *verb*
  to compliment someone = congratularsi con qualcuno (**!** + *essere*)

comprehensive *noun* (*British English*)
  a comprehensive = una scuola superiore statale

compulsory *adjective*
  = obbligatorio/obbligatoria

computer *noun*
  a computer = un computer

computer game *noun*
  a computer game = un gioco per computer

computer studies *noun*
  computer studies = l'informatica

concentrate *verb*
  = concentrarsi (**!** + *essere*)

concert *noun*
  a concert = un concerto

concrete *noun*
  concrete = il cemento

condition
1 *noun*
  a condition = una condizione
  in a terrible condition = in pessime condizioni
  the car is in good condition = la macchina è in buone condizioni
2 on condition that = a condizione che
  you can go on condition that her parents drive you home = puoi andare a condizione che i suoi genitori ti riaccompagnino a casa
  ! *Note that the subjunctive is used after* **a condizione che.**

condom *noun*
  a condom = un preservativo

conductor *noun* ▶ 281|
  a conductor = un direttore d'orchestra

cone *noun*
  a cone = un cono

conference *noun*
  a conference = una conferenza

confidence *noun*
• **confidence** = la sicurzza
• (*trust*)
  to have confidence in someone = avere fiducia in qualcuno

confident *adjective*
  = sicuro/sicura di sé
  she's a confident girl = è una ragazza sicura di sé
  ! *Note that* **sé** *will change to* **me, te,** *etc, depending on the person or people being described.*

confidential adjective
= riservato/riservata

conflict noun
a conflict = un conflitto

confused adjective
= confuso/confusa
to get confused = confondersi (! + essere)

congratulate verb
= congratularsi con (! + essere)

congratulations noun (also exclamation)
congratulations! = congratulazioni!

connection noun
a connection = una relazione
it has no connection with the strike = non ha nessuna relazione con lo sciopero

conscientious adjective
= diligente

conscious adjective
• (aware) = consapevole
• (after an operation) = cosciente

construct verb
= costruire

consult verb
= consultare

contact
1 noun
to be in contact with someone = essere in contatto con qualcuno
to lose contact = perdere contatto
2 verb
= contattare

contact lens noun
a contact lens = una lente a contatto

contain verb
= contenere

content adjective
= soddisfatto/soddisfatta

contest noun
a contest = un concorso

continent noun
• (a large mass of land)
a continent = un continente
• (British English) (Europe)
the Continent = l'Europa continentale

continue verb
to continue to talk, to continue talking = continuare a parlare

continuous adjective
= continuo/continua
the continuous noise of the traffic = il continuo rumore del traffico

contraception noun
contraception = la contraccezione

contract noun
a contract = un contratto

contradict verb
= contraddire

contradiction noun
a contradiction = una contraddizione

contrast noun
a contrast = un contrasto

contribute verb
• (to give money) = contribuire
• to contribute to the discussion = partecipare alla discussione

control
1 noun
to take control of a situation = prendere il controllo della situazione
to lose control of a car = perdere il controllo della macchina
2 verb
to control a region = controllare una regione

convenient adjective
• (useful, practical) = comodo/comoda
it's more convenient to take the bus = conviene prendere l'autobus
• (suitable) = adatto/adatta
it's a convenient place to meet = è un posto adatto per incontrarsi
it's not convenient for me = a me non va bene

conversation noun
a conversation = una conversazione
to have a conversation = parlare

convince verb
= convincere

cook
1 verb
• (to prepare food) = cucinare
to cook a meal = fare da mangiare
• (to boil, fry, roast) = cuocere
to cook vegetables = cuocere le verdure
2 noun ▶ 281 |
a cook = un cuoco/una cuoca

cooker noun (British English)
a cooker = una cucina

cookie noun (US English)
a cookie = un biscotto

cooking noun
cooking = la cucina
to do the cooking = cucinare

cool adjective
• (fresh, not hot) = fresco/fresca
a cool drink = una bibita fresca
it's much cooler today = oggi fa più fresco
• (calm) = calmo/calma
• (fashionable) = figo/figa✖
• (relaxed) = calmo/calma
cool down = raffreddarsi (! + essere)

cooperate verb
= collaborare

cope *verb*
- (*to manage*) = cavarsela (**!** + *essere*)
- **to cope with pain** = sopportare il dolore

copy
1 *noun*
  a copy = una copia
2 *verb*
  = copiare
copy down, copy out = ricopiare

cork *noun*
- **a cork** = un tappo
- **cork** = il sughero

corkscrew *noun*
  a corkscrew = un cavatappi

corner *noun*
- (*of a street, a building*)
  the corner = l'angolo
  the shop on the corner = il negozio
    all'angolo
  to go around the corner = girare l'angolo
- (*in football*)
  a corner = un calcio d'angolo

correct
1 *adjective*
  = esatto/esatta
  the correct answer = la risposta esatta
  that's correct! = esatto!
2 *verb*
  = correggere

correction *noun*
  a correction = una correzione

corridor *noun*
  a corridor = un corridoio

cost *verb*
  = costare (**!** + *essere*)
  how much does it cost? = quanto costa?
  it costs a lot of money = costa tanto

costume *noun*
  a costume = un costume

cosy *adjective* (*British English*)
  a cosy room = una stanza accogliente

cot *noun* (*British English*)
  a cot = un lettino

cottage *noun*
  a cottage = una villetta

cotton *noun*
  cotton = il cotone

cotton wool *noun* (*British English*)
  cotton wool = il cotone idrofilo

couch *noun*
  a couch = un divano

cough
1 *verb*
  = tossire
2 *noun*
  to have a cough = avere la tosse

could *verb*
- (*had the possibility*)
  I couldn't move = non potevo muovermi
  he couldn't sleep for weeks = non ha
    potuto dormire per settimane
- (*knew how to*)
  she could read at the age of three
    = sapeva leggere all'età di tre anni
  he couldn't type = non sapeva battere a
    macchina
  I couldn't speak any German = non
    sapevo parlare tedesco
- (*when talking about* **seeing, hearing,**
  understanding, could *is not translated*)
  I couldn't see a thing = non vedevo
    niente
  he could hear them = li sentiva
  they couldn't understand me = non mi
    capivano
- (*when implying that something did not
  happen*)
  she could have become a doctor
    = poteva diventare un medico
  you could have apologized! = potevi
    scusarti!
- (*when indicating a possibility*)
  they could be wrong = potrebbero
    sbagliarsi
- (*when asking, offering or suggesting*)
  could I speak to Annie? = posso parlare
    con Annie?
  could you help me? = può darmi una
    mano?

count *verb*
  = contare
count on
  to count on someone = contare su
    qualcuno

counter *noun*
  a counter (*in a shop*) = un banco
  (*in a bank, a post office*) = uno sportello
  (*in a bar*) = un banco

country *noun*
- (*a state*)
  a country = un paese
- (*the countryside*)
  the country = la campagna
  to live in the country = vivere in
    campagna

countryside *noun*
  the countryside = la campagna

couple *noun*
- **a couple of days**
  (*a few days*) = un paio di giorni
- (*two people*)
  a couple = una coppia

courage *noun*
  courage = il coraggio

course
1 *noun*
- (*a series of lessons or lectures*)
  a course = un corso   ····▶

Countries, cities, and continents

Countries and continents

The definite article **il/la**, etc is used when talking about countries and continents in Italian:

I like Italy/Japan   = mi piace **l'**Italia/**il** Giappone
to visit the United States   = visitare **gli** Stati Uniti

Names of countries and continents can be masculine or feminine, and some are plural.

In, to, and from somewhere

In is used in Italian for both **in** and **to** in English. When **in** is used the article is generally omitted:

*to live **in** Italy*   = vivere **in** Italia
*to go **to** China*   = andare **in** Cina
*to live **in** Mexico*   = vivere **in** Messico
*to go **to** Brazil*   = andare **in** Brasile

but note:

*to live **in the** United States*   = vivere **negli** Stati Uniti
*to go **to the** United States*   = andare **negli** Stati Uniti
*to live **in the** Czech Republic* = vivere **nella** Repubblica Ceca

Da followed by the definite article is used to express **from**:

***from** France*   = **dalla** Francia
***from** Australia*   = **dall'**Australia

Towns and cities

For **in** and **to** with the name of a town, use **a** (or **ad** before a vowel). For **from** use **da**. If the Italian name includes the definite article, it combines with **a** or **da**:

*to live **in** Pavia*   = vivere **a** Pavia
*to go **to** Ancona*   = andare **ad** Ancona
*to live **in La** Spezia*   = vivere **alla** Spezia
*to arrive **from** Cairo*   = arrivare **dal** Cairo

---

an Italian course = un corso d'italiano
• (*part of a meal*)
  a course = una portata
  what's the main course? = cosa c'è come piatto principale?
2 of course = certo
  of course not! = certo che no!

court *noun*
• (*of law*)
  a court = un tribunale
• (*for playing sports*)
  a tennis court = un campo da tennis
  a basketball court = un campo di pallacanestro

cousin *noun*
  a cousin = un cugino/una cugina

cover
1 *verb*
  to cover = coprire
  to be covered in spots = essere coperto/coperta di brufoli
2 *noun*
• (*a lid*)
  a cover = un coperchio
• (*for a cushion, a quilt*)
  a cover = una fodera

• (*a blanket*)
  a cover = una coperta
• (*on a book, a magazine, an exercise book*)
  the cover = la copertina

cow *noun*
  a cow = una mucca

coward *noun*
  a coward = un vigliacco/una vigliacca

cowboy *noun*
  a cowboy = un cowboy

cozy *adjective* (*US English*)
  a cozy room = una stanza accogliente

crab *noun*
  a crab = un granchio

crack *verb*
  = incrinarsi (**!** + *essere*)

cramp *noun*
  a cramp = un crampo

crash
1 *noun*
  a crash = uno scontro   ····▶

2 *verb*
  to crash into a tree = andare a sbattere contro un albero (**!** + *essere*)
  the plane crashed = l'aereo è precipitato

crazy *adjective*
  = pazzo/pazza

cream *noun*
  cream = la panna

create *verb*
  = creare

credit card *noun*
  a credit card = una carta di credito

cricket *noun* ▶ 178|
  cricket = il cricket

crime *noun*
  a crime = un crimine
  crime = la crminalità

criminal
1 *noun*
  a criminal = un/una criminale
2 *adjective*
  = criminale

crisis *noun*
  a crisis = una crisi

crisps *noun* (*British English*)
  crisps = le patatine

critical *adjective*
  = critico/critica

criticize *verb*
  = criticare

crocodile *noun*
  a crocodile = un coccodrillo

crooked *adjective*
  = storto/storta
  the picture is crooked = il quadro è storto

cross
1 *verb*
• (*to go across*) = attraversare
  to cross the road = attraversare la strada
  to cross the Channel = attraversare la Manica
• (*other uses*)
  to cross one's legs = accavallare le gambe
  our letters crossed = le nostre lettere si sono incrociate
2 *noun*
  a cross = una croce
3 *adjective*
  = arrabbiato/arrabbiata
  to get cross = arrabbiarsi (**!** + *essere*)
  cross out = cancellare

crossroads *noun*
  a crossroads = un incrocio

crossword puzzle *noun*
  a crossword puzzle = un cruciverba

crowd *noun*
• (*a large number of people*)

a crowd = una folla
  crowds of people = una gran folla
• (*watching a game*)
  the crowd = il pubblico

crown *noun*
  a crown = una corona

cruel *adjective*
  = crudele

cruelty *noun*
  cruelty = la crudeltà

cruise *noun*
  a cruise = una crociera

crush *verb*
  = schiacciare

crutch *noun*
  a crutch = una stampella

cry
1 *verb*
  = piangere
2 *noun*
  a cry = un grido

cub *noun*
  a cub = un cucciolo

cucumber *noun*
  a cucumber = un cetriolo

cuddle *noun*
  to give someone a cuddle = fare le coccole a qualcuno

culprit *noun*
  the culprit = il/la colpevole

cultural *adjective*
  = culturale

culture *noun*
  culture = la cultura

cunning *adjective*
  (*describing a person*) = astuto/astuta
  (*describing a plan*) = ingegnoso/ingegnosa

cup *noun*
• **a cup** = una tazza
  a cup of coffee = un caffè
• (*in sport*)
  a cup = una coppa

cupboard *noun*
  a cupboard = un armadio

curb *noun* (*US English*)
  the curb = il bordo del marciapiede

cure
1 *verb*
  = guarire
2 *noun*
  a cure = una cura

curious *adjective*
  = curioso/curiosa

curly *adjective*
  = riccio/riccia
  to have curly hair = avere i capelli ricci

currency *noun*
a currency = una valuta

curry *noun*
a curry = una pietanza al curry

curtain *noun*
a curtain = una tenda

cushion *noun*
a cushion = un cuscino

custard *noun* (*British English*)
custard = la crema

custom *noun*
a custom = un'usanza

customer *noun*
a customer = un/una cliente

customs *noun*
customs = la dogana
to go through customs = passare la dogana

customs officer *noun* ▶ 281
a customs officer = un doganiere

cut
1 *verb*
= tagliare
to cut an apple in half = tagliare una mela a metà
to cut [one's finger | one's knee | one's foot]
= tagliarsi [un dito | un ginocchio | un piede] (**!** + *essere*)
she cut herself = si è tagliata
to have one's hair cut = tagliarsi i capelli (**!** + *essere*)
I got my hair cut = mi sono tagliata i capelli
2 *noun*
a cut = un taglio
cut down = tagliare
cut out
to cut a photo out of a magazine
= ritagliare una foto da una rivista
cut up = fare a pezzetti

cute *adjective*
= carino/carina

CV *noun*
a CV = un curriculum

cycle *verb*
I cycle to school = vado a scuola in bicicletta
to go cycling = andare in bicicletta (**!** + *essere*)

cycling *noun* ▶ 178
cycling = il ciclismo

cyclist *noun*
a cyclist = un/una ciclista

cynical *adjective*
= cinico/cinica

Czech Republic *noun* ▶ 151
the Czech Republic = la Repubblica Ceca

Dd

dad, **Dad** *noun*
a dad = un papà

damage
1 *verb*
• to damage = danneggiare
the building was damaged by the fire
= l'edificio è stato danneggiato dall'incendio
• (*to harm*) = nuocere a
it can damage your health = può nuocere alla salute
2 *noun*
damage = i danni
to cause damage = danneggiare

damp *adjective*
= umido/umida

dance
1 *verb*
= ballare
2 *noun*
a dance = un ballo

dancer *noun* ▶ 281
a dancer = un ballerino/una ballerina

dancing *noun*
dancing = il ballo

danger *noun*
danger = il pericolo
to be in danger = essere in pericolo

dangerous *adjective*
= pericoloso/pericolosa

Danish ▶ 199
1 *adjective*
= danese
2 *noun*
Danish = il danese

dare *verb*
• (*to have the courage*) = osare
• (*when testing someone*)
to dare someone to play a trick = sfidare qualcuno a fare uno scherzo
• (*when expressing anger*)
don't dare speak to me like that! = come ti permetti di usare questo tono con me?

dark
1 *adjective*
• (*lacking light*) = buio/buia
it's getting dark = si sta facendo buio
• (*describing a colour, clothes*) ▶ 147
= scuro/scura
a dark blue dress = un vestito blu scuro
• (*describing a person*) = bruno/bruna
2 *noun*
the dark = il buio

darts noun ▶ 178 |
darts = le freccette

date ▶ 155 | noun
• (in a calendar)
a date = una data
what date is today? = quanti ne abbiamo
oggi?
• (with a friend)
a date = un appuntamento

daughter noun
a daughter = una figlia

daughter-in-law noun
a daughter-in-law = una nuora

dawn noun
dawn = l'alba
at dawn = all'alba

day noun ▶ 267 |

> ! Note that **day** is usually translated by
> **giorno** in Italian. However it is
> sometimes translated by **giornata**,
> which refers to all the things that
> happen during the day.

a day = un giorno
what day is it today? = che giorno è oggi?
during the day = durante il giorno
we had a very nice day = abbiamo
passato una bella giornata
the next day, the day after = il giorno
dopo
the day before = il giorno prima

daylight noun
daylight = la luce del giorno

dazzle verb
= abbagliare

dead adjective
= morto/morta
he is dead = è morto

deaf adjective
= sordo/sorda

deal
1 noun
• a deal = un affare
• a great deal [of money | of time | of energy]
= [molti soldi | molto tempo | molta energia]
2 verb
to deal the cards = dare le carte
deal with = occuparsi di (! + essere)
to deal with a problem = affrontare un
problema

dear
1 adjective
• (in letters) = caro/cara
Dear Anne = Cara Anne
Dear Anne and Paul = Cari Anne e Paul
Dear Sir/Madam = Gentile
Signore/Signora
• (expensive) = caro/cara
2 exclamation
oh dear! = oh Dio!

death noun
death = la morte

debate noun
a debate = un dibattito

debt noun
a debt = un debito
to be in debt = avere dei debiti

decade noun
a decade = un decennio

decaffeinated adjective
= decaffeinato/decaffeinata

deceive verb
= ingannare

December noun ▶ 155 |
December = dicembre (masculine)

decide verb
= decidere
he decided [to accept | to stay | to get
married] = ha deciso [di accettare | di
restare | di sposarsi]

decision noun
a decision = una decisione
to make a decision = prendere una
decisione

deck noun
a deck = un ponte
on deck = sul ponte

deckchair noun
a deckchair = una sedia a sdraio

decorate verb
• (with ornaments) = decorare
• (with wallpaper) = mettere la carta da
parati
(to paint) = dipingere

decoration noun
a decoration = una decorazione

deep adjective ▶ 202 |
= profondo/profonda
how deep is the lake? = quanto è
profondo il lago?
the hole is three metres deep = la buca è
profonda tre metri

deer noun
a deer = un cervo

defeat
1 verb
= sconfiggere
to defeat an enemy = sconfiggere un
nemico
the team was defeated = la squadra è
stata sconfitta
2 noun
a defeat = una sconfitta

defence (British English), **defense** (US
English) noun
defence = la difesa

defend verb
= difendere

Dates, days, and months

The days of the week

Note that Italian uses lower-case letters for the names of the days. All the days are masculine except **domenica**.

Monday	= lunedì
Tuesday	= martedì
Wednesday	= mercoledì
Thursday	= giovedì
Friday	= venerdì
Saturday	= sabato
Sunday	= domenica

In the examples below, **lunedì** can be replaced by any day (but be careful with **domenica**, which the adjective and the article should agree with). Note the use of **il** for weekly occurrences and no article for one-off occurrences:

on Monday	= lunedì
on Mondays	= il lunedì
every Monday	= ogni lunedì
Monday evening	= lunedì sera
last/next Monday	= lunedì scorso/prossimo
early on Monday	= lunedì presto

The months of the year

As with the days of the week, do not use capitals to spell the names of the months in Italian. All the months are masculine.

January	= gennaio
February	= febbraio
March	= marzo
April	= aprile
May	= maggio
June	= giugno
July	= luglio
August	= agosto
September	= settembre
October	= ottobre
November	= novembre
December	= dicembre

May in the notes below stands for any month: they all work the same way.

in May	= a maggio
the middle of May	= metà maggio
the end of May	= fine maggio

Dates

On is not translated when giving dates:

(on) May 1	= il primo maggio
(on) May 2	= il due maggio
(on) May 8	= l'otto maggio
from 3rd to 11th May	= dal tre all'undici maggio
Monday May 1st	= lunedì primo maggio
what's the date?	= quanti ne abbiamo oggi?
it's the tenth of May	= è il 10 maggio
in 1968	= nel 1968 (*say* millenovecentosessantotto)
in the year 2000	= nel duemila

Centuries

There are two ways to refer to centuries in Italian. The first is as in English **the 20th century**. The second is similar to the English **the 1900s** and can be used only for the centuries from the 13th to the 20th:

the 20th century	= il ventesimo secolo
in the 15th century	= nel Quattrocento

definite *adjective*
• (*obvious, visible*) = netto/netta
  a definite improvement = un netto
  miglioramento
• (*describing a plan*) = preciso/precisa

definitely *adverb*
  = di sicuro
  they're definitely lying = stanno
  mentendo di sicuro
  I'm definitely coming = vengo di sicuro
  definitely! = certamente!

defy *verb*
  = sfidare

degree *noun*
• (*from a university*)
  a degree = una laurea
• (*in measurements*)
  a degree = un grado

delay
1 *verb*
  = ritardare
2 *noun*
  a delay = un ritardo

deliberately *adverb*
  = apposta
  he did it deliberately = l'ha fatto apposta

delicious *adjective*
  = squisito/squisita

delighted *adjective*
  = contentissimo/contentissima
  I'm delighted with the present = sono
  contentissimo del regalo

deliver *verb*
  = consegnare

demand *verb*
  = esigere

demolish *verb*
  = demolire

demonstration *noun*
  a demonstration = una manifestazione

denim *noun*
  a denim jacket = un giubbotto di jeans

Denmark *noun* ▶ 151|
  Denmark = la Danimarca

dentist *noun* ▶ 281|
  a dentist = un/una dentista

deny *verb*
  = negare

department *noun*
  a department (*in a firm, a store*) = un
  reparto
  (*in a school, university*) = un dipartimento

department store *noun*
  a department store = un grande
  magazzino

depend *verb*
  = dipendere

to depend on someone = dipendere da
  qualcuno
  it depends = dipende

depressed *adjective*
  = depresso/depressa

depressing *adjective*
  = deprimente

depth *noun* ▶ 202|
  depth = la profondità

describe *verb*
  = descrivere

description *noun*
  a description = una descrizione

desert *noun*
  a desert = un deserto

deserve *verb*
  = meritare
  he deserves to be punished = si merita
  di essere punito

design
1 *verb*
• (*to plan*) = progettare
  the house was designed for a hot climate
  = la casa è stata progettata per un clima
  caldo
• (*in fashion*)
  to design clothes = disegnare degli abiti
2 *noun*
• (*a subject of study*)
  (fashion) design = la moda
• (*a pattern*)
  a design = un motivo

desk *noun*
  a desk = una scrivania
  (*at school*) = un banco

desperate *adjective*
  = disperato/disperata

dessert *noun*
  a dessert = un dessert

destroy *verb*
  = distruggere

detail *noun*
  a detail = un particolare

detective *noun* ▶ 281|
  a detective = un
  investigatore/un'investigatrice
  a private detective = un investigatore
  privato/un'investigatrice privata

detective story *noun*
  a detective story = un poliziesco

determined *adjective*
  = deciso/decisa
  to be determined to go = essere deciso ad
  andare

develop *verb*
• (*when it's a photograph*) = sviluppare
• (*to change*) = svilupparsi (! + *essere*)

development *noun*
a development = uno sviluppo

diagram *noun*
a diagram = uno schema

dial *verb*
to dial a number = fare un numero

dialling code *noun* (*British English*)
a dialling code = un prefisso telefonico

dialling tone (*British English*), **dial tone** (*US English*) *noun*
a dialling tone = un segnale di libero

diamond *noun*
a diamond = un diamante

diary *noun*
• (*for personal thoughts*)
  a diary = un diario
• (*for appointments*)
  a diary = un'agenda

dice *noun*
a dice = un dado

dictionary *noun*
a dictionary = un dizionario

die *verb*
• to die = morire (**!** + *essere*)
  he died in the war = è morto in guerra
• (*used for emphasis*)
  I'm dying to go on holiday = muoio dalla
  voglia di andare in ferie**✱**

diet *noun*
a diet = una dieta
to go on a diet = mettersi a dieta (**!** +
essere)

difference *noun*
a difference = una differenza
I can't tell the difference = non vedo la
differenza
it won't make any difference = non farà
nessuna differenza
what difference does it make? = che
differenza fa?

different *adjective*
= diverso/diversa

difficult *adjective*
= difficile
Spanish is not difficult to learn = lo
spagnolo non è difficile da imparare
he's difficult to get along with = è
difficile andarci d'accordo

difficulty *noun*
a difficulty = una difficoltà
to have difficulty concentrating = avere
difficoltà a concentrarsi

dig *verb*
= scavare

diner *noun* (*US English*)
a diner = una tavola calda

dinghy *noun*
a dinghy = un gommone

dining room *noun*
a dining room = una sala da pranzo

dinner *noun*
a dinner = una cena
dinner's ready! = è pronto!

dip *verb*
= immergere

direct
1 *adjective*
= diretto/diretta
2 *verb*
• (*when talking about directions*)
  could you direct me to the station?
  = potrebbe indicarmi la strada per la
  stazione?
• (*in cinema or theatre*) = dirigere

direction *noun*
a direction = una direzione
is this the right direction? = è questa la
direzione giusta?
they were going in the other direction
= andavano nell'altra direzione

directions *noun*
directions = le indicazioni
to give someone directions = indicare la
strada a qualcuno
to ask someone for directions = chiedere
la strada a qualcuno

director *noun* ▶ 281 |
• (*of a film or play*)
  a director = un/una regista
• (*of a company*)
  a director = un direttore/una direttrice

dirt *noun*
dirt = lo sporco

dirty
1 *adjective*
= sporco/sporca
to get dirty = sporcarsi (**!** + *essere*)
2 *verb*
= sporcare

disabled *adjective*
= disabile

disadvantage *noun*
a disadvantage = uno svantaggio

disagree *verb*
= non essere d'accordo
I disagree with you = non sono d'accordo
con te

disappear *verb*
= scomparire (**!** + *essere*)

disappoint *verb*
= deludere

disappointed *adjective*
= deluso/delusa

disappointing *adjective*
= deludente

disappointment *noun*
disappointment = una delusione

disapprove *verb*
to disapprove of someone = disapprovare qualcuno

disaster *noun*
a disaster = un disastro

discipline *noun*
discipline = la disciplina

disco *noun*
a disco = una discoteca

disconnect *verb*
• (to pull out a plug) = staccare
• (to cut off) = tagliare

discourage *verb*
= scoraggiare

discover *verb*
= scoprire

discovery *noun*
a discovery = una scoperta

discreet *adjective*
= discreto/discreta

discrimination *noun*
discrimination = la discriminazione

discuss *verb*
= discutere di
to discuss politics = discutere di politica

discussion *noun*
a discussion = una discussione

disease *noun* ▶ 193|
a disease = una malattia

disguise
1 *noun*
a disguise = un travestimento
to wear a disguise = essere travestito/travestita
2 *verb*
to disguise oneself as a woman
= travestirsi da donna (! + essere)

disgusting *adjective*
= disgustoso/disgustosa

dish *noun*
• (food)
a dish = un piatto
• the dishes = i piatti
to wash the dishes = lavare i piatti

dishonest *adjective*
= disonesto/disonesta

dishwasher *noun*
a dishwasher = una lavapiatti

dislike *verb*
I dislike him = non mi piace

dismiss *verb*
= licenziare

disobedient *adjective*
= disobbediente

disobey *verb*
to disobey someone = disobbedire a qualcuno

dispute *noun*
a dispute = una disputa

disqualify *verb*
= squalificare

disrupt *verb*
= disturbare

dissatisfied *adjective*
= scontento/scontenta

distance *noun*
a distance = una distanza
in the distance = in lontananza
to keep one's distance = mantenere le distanze

distinct *adjective*
= distinto/distinta

distinguish *verb*
= distinguere

distract *verb*
= distrarre
to distract someone from working
= distrarre qualcuno dal lavoro

distressed *adjective*
= angosciato/angosciata

distribute *verb*
= distribuire

disturb *verb*
= disturbare

disturbing *adjective*
= inquietante

dive *verb* ▶ 178|
= tuffarsi (! + essere)
to go diving = fare delle immersioni

divide *verb*
= dividere

diving board *noun*
a diving board = un trampolino

divorce
1 *noun*
a divorce = un divorzio
2 *verb*
= divorziare

DIY *noun* (British English)
DIY = il fai da te

dizzy *adjective*
I feel dizzy = mi gira la testa

do *verb*
▶ See the boxed note on **do** for more information and examples.
• to do = fare
to do the cooking = fare da mangiare
to do one's homework = fare i compiti
what has he done with the newspaper?
= cosa ne ha fatto del giornale?
what has she done to her hair? = cosa si è fatta ai capelli? ····▶

do

Usually the Italian equivalent of **do** is **fare**:

*what **are** you **doing?*** = cosa **stai facendo?**
*I'm **doing** a crossword* = **sto facendo** le parole crociate

As an auxiliary verb

English uses **do** to form questions, negative statements and other constructions; Italian has no equivalent for this.

D

do you come here often? = ci vieni spesso?
*yes, I **do**/no, I **don't*** = sì/no
*I **don't** remember* = non mi ricordo
*so **do** I* = anch'io
*nor **do** I* = neanch'io
*I **do** like it!* = come mi piace!
don't shout! = non gridare!
*you cheated, **didn't** you?* = hai imbrogliato, non è vero?
*you **don't** eat meat, **do** you?* = non mangi la carne, vero?
do sit down! = si accomodi!

---

do as you're told = fai come ti si dice
• (*in questions, negatives*)
do you like cats? = ti piacciono i gatti?
I don't like cats = non mi piacciono i gatti
I didn't do anything = non ho fatto niente
don't shout! = non gridare!
• (*in short answers and tag questions*)
'do you like strawberries?'—'yes, I do' = 'ti piacciono le fragole?'—'sì'
'I never said I liked him'—'yes, you did' = 'non ho mai detto che mi piaceva'—'sì che l'hai detto'
'I live in the country'—'so do I' = 'vivo in campagna'—'anch'io'
'who wrote it?'—'I did' = 'chi l'ha scritto?'—'io'
he lives in London, doesn't he? = abita a Londra, no?
Martina didn't phone, did she? = Martina non ha mica telefonato?
'may I sit down?'—'yes, please do' = 'posso sedermi?'—'prego'
• (*to be enough*) = bastare (**!** + *essere*)
ten pounds will do = dieci sterline basteranno
• (*to be suitable*) = andare bene (**!** + *essere*)
that box will do = quella scatola andrà bene
• (*to perform*)
he did well = se l'è cavata bene
he did badly = gli è andata male
do up (*British English*)
to do up one's buttons = abbottonarsi (**!** + *essere*)
to do up a house = rimettere a nuovo una casa
do with
it's got something to do with computers = ha qualcosa a che fare con i computer
it has nothing to do with him = lui non c'entra niente

do without = fare a meno di
I can do without a television = posso fare a meno della televisione

dock *noun*
a dock = una darsena

doctor *noun* ▶ **281**|
a doctor = un dottore

document *noun*
a document = un documento

documentary *noun*
a documentary = un documentario

dog *noun*
a dog = un cane

doll *noun*
a doll = una bambola

dollar *noun*
a dollar = un dollaro

dolphin *noun*
a dolphin = un delfino

dominoes *noun* ▶ **178**|
dominoes = il domino

donkey *noun*
a donkey = un asino

door *noun*
a door = una porta

doorbell *noun*
a doorbell = un campanello

dose *noun*
a dose = una dose

double
1 *adjective*   ····▶
- (*of an amount*) = doppio/doppia
  a double helping of strawberries = una doppia porzione di fragole
- (*when spelling or giving a number*)
  Anna is spelled with a double 'n' = Anna si scrive con due 'n'
  three double five (*British English*) = trecentocinquantacinque
2 *verb*
= raddoppiare

double bass *noun*
a double bass = un contrabbasso

double bed *noun*
a double bed = un letto matrimoniale

double-decker *noun*
a double-decker = un autobus a due piani

double room *noun*
a double room = una camera doppia

doubt
1 *noun*
a doubt = un dubbio
I've no doubt that it's true = sono certo che è vero
2 *verb*
= dubitare
I doubt if she'll come = dubito che venga
> **!** *Note that the subjunctive is used after* **dubitare che.**

doughnut, donut (*US English*) *noun*
a doughnut = un bombolone

down
> **!** *Often* **down** *occurs in combinations with verbs, for example:* **calm down, let down, slow down** *etc. To find the correct translations for this type of verb, look up the separate dictionary entries at* **calm, let, slow** *etc.*

1 *preposition*
he ran down the hill = è corso giù per la collina
the kitchen is down those stairs = la cucina è in fondo alle scale
2 *adverb*
she's down in the cellar = è giù in cantina
down in Brighton = a Brighton
to go down = scendere (**!** + *essere*)
to fall down = cadere (**!** + *essere*)
down there = laggiù

downstairs *adverb*
= di sotto
I'm going downstairs = vado giù
to bring the boxes downstairs = portare giù le scatole

dozen *noun* ▶ 233 |
a dozen = una dozzina
a dozen eggs = una dozzina di uova

draft *noun* (*US English*)
a draft = una corrente d'aria

drag *verb*
= trascinare

drain *verb*
- (*when cooking*) = scolare (**!** + *avere*)
- (*if it's water*)
  to drain (away) = scolare (**!** + *essere*)

drama *noun*
drama = l'arte drammatica

dramatic *adjective*
= spettacolare

drapes *noun* (*US English*)
the drapes = le tende

draught *noun* (*British English*)
a draught = una corrente d'aria

draughts *noun* ▶ 178 | (*British English*)
draughts = la dama

draw
1 *verb*
- (*with a pen or pencil*) = disegnare
  to draw a rabbit = disegnare un coniglio
  to draw a picture = fare un disegno
  to draw a line = tracciare una riga
  she drew his portrait = gli ha fatto il ritratto
- (*to pull*) = tirare
  to draw the curtains = tirare le tende
- (*to take out*) = tirare fuori
  to draw a knife = tirare fuori un coltello
- (*to attract*) = attirare
- (*British English*) (*in sport*) = pareggiare
- **Christmas is drawing near** = il Natale si avvicina
2 *noun*
- (*in sport*)
  a draw = un pareggio
- (*in a lottery*)
  a draw = un'estrazione a sorte
draw aside
  to draw someone aside = tirare qualcuno in disparte

drawer *noun*
a drawer = un cassetto

drawing *noun*
drawing = il disegno
a drawing = un disegno

dread *verb*
= avere il terrore di

dreadful *adjective*
= spaventoso/spaventosa

dream
1 *noun*
a dream = un sogno
to have a dream = fare un sogno
2 *verb*
= sognare
to dream of going to Japan = sognare di andare in Giappone

dress
1 *noun*
  a dress = un vestito
2 *verb*
  • (*to put one's own clothes on*) = vestirsi
    (**!** + *essere*)
  • (*to put clothes on someone*) = vestire
dress up
  • (*in good clothes*) = mettersi elegante (**!** +
    essere)
  • (*in a disguise*) = mascherarsi (**!** + *essere*)
  she dressed up as a clown = si è
    mascherata da pagliaccio

dressing gown *noun*
  a dressing gown = una vestaglia

drill
1 *noun*
  a drill = un trapano
2 *verb*
  to drill a hole = fare un buco col trapano
  to drill through the wall = trapanare il
    muro

drink
1 *verb*
  = bere
2 *noun*
  a drink = una bevanda
  a drink of water = un bicchier d'acqua
  let's go for a drink = andiamo a bere
    qualcosa

drive
1 *verb*
  • (*in a car*) = guidare
  to learn to drive = imparare a guidare
  he drives to work = va al lavoro in
    macchina
  to drive someone home = accompagnare
    qualcuno a casa in macchina
  • (*to make*)
  to drive someone mad = fare impazzire
    qualcuno
2 *noun*
  a drive = un giro in macchina
  let's go for a drive = andiamo a fare un
    giro in macchina
drive away
  • (*in a car*) = andare via (**!** + *essere*)
  • (*to chase away*) = cacciare

driver *noun*
  a driver = un
    automobilista/un'automobilista
  (*of a bus*) = un autista/un'autista

driver's license (*US English*),
driving licence (*British English*) *noun*
  a driver's license = una patente di guida

drizzle *verb*
  = piovigginare (**!** + *essere* or *avere*)

drop
1 *verb*
  • (*to come down*) = abbassarsi (**!** + *essere*)
  the temperature has dropped = la
    temperatura si è abbassata

  • (*to let fall*) = lasciar cadere
  she dropped her ring = le è caduto
    l'anello
  • (*to fall*) = cadere (**!** + *essere*)
2 *noun*
  • (*a fall*)
  a drop = un abbassamento
  a drop in temperature = un abbassamento
    di temperatura
  • (*of liquid*)
  a drop = una goccia
drop in = passare (**!** + *essere*)
  he dropped in to see me = è passato a
    trovarmi
drop off = lasciare
  could you drop me off at the station?
    = mi puoi lasciare alla stazione?
drop out
  to drop out of school = abbandonare gli
    studi
  to drop out of the race = abbandonare la
    gara

drought *noun*
  a drought = la siccità

drown *verb*
  = annegare (**!** + *essere*)

drug
1 *noun*
  • (*for illegal use*)
  drugs = la droga
  to be on drugs = drogarsi (**!** + *essere*)
  • (*for medical use*)
  a drug = un medicinale
2 *verb*
  to drug someone = drogare qualcuno

drug addict *noun*
  a drug addict = un/una tossicodipendente

drum *noun*
  a drum = un tamburo
  to play drums = suonare la batteria

drunk *adjective*
  = ubriaco/ubriaca

dry
1 *adjective*
  • (*after being wet*) = asciutto/asciutta
  the clothes are dry = la biancheria è
    asciutta
  • (*having no moisture*) = secco/secca
  dry leaves = foglie secche
  dry white wine = vino bianco secco
  a dry day = una giornata senza pioggia
2 *verb*
  = asciugare
  to dry oneself = asciugarsi (**!** + *essere*)
  he dried his hands = si è asciugato le
    mani
  to dry the dishes = asciugare i piatti

duck
1 *noun*
  a duck = un'anatra

····▶

2 *verb*
= abbassare la testa

due
1 due to = a causa di
the game was cancelled due to rain = la
   partita è stata annullata a causa della
   pioggia
2 *adjective*
• (*expected*)
   the train is due (in) at two o'clock = il
   treno dovrebbe arrivare alle due
• (*owed*) = dovuto/dovuta
   the amount due = la somma dovuta

dull *adjective*
• (*describing a person or book*)
   = noioso/noiosa
• (*describing a colour*) = spento/spenta
• (*describing the weather or a landscape*)
   = grigio/grigia

dumb *adjective*
• (*unable to speak*) = muto/muta
• (*stupid*) = scemo/scema✖

dump
1 *verb*
= buttare
2 *noun*
   a dump = una discarica

during *preposition*
= durante
during the summer = durante l'estate

dust
1 *noun*
   dust = la polvere
2 *verb*
   = spolverare

dustbin *noun* (*British English*)
   a dustbin = un bidone della spazzatura

dustman *noun* (*British English*)
   a dustman = un netturbino

Dutch ▶ 199|
1 *adjective*
   = olandese
2 *noun*
   the Dutch = gli olandesi

duty *noun*
• (*a task, part of one's job*)
   a duty = un compito
• (*of a soldier, a nurse*)
   to be on duty = essere di servizio
• (*what one must do*)
   duty = il dovere
• (*a tax*)
   customs duties = diritti di dogana

dye *verb*
   = tingere
   to dye one's hair = tingersi i capelli (✱ +
   essere)

✖ in informal situations

each
1 *determiner*
   = ogni
   each time I see him = ogni volta che lo
   vedo
2 *pronoun*
   = ognuno/ognuna
   each of the boys = ognuno dei ragazzi
   **each of them has a car, they each have a
   car** = hanno tutti la macchina

each other *pronoun*
> ❗ *Note that* **each other** *is very often
> translated by using a reflexive pronoun
> like* **si**, **ci** *or* **vi**.

   they know each other already = si
   conoscono già
   we write to each other every year = ci
   scriviamo tutti gli anni

eager *adjective*
   = entusiasta

eagle *noun*
   an eagle = un'aquila

ear *noun* ▶ 137|
   an ear = un orecchio

early *adverb*
• **early** = presto
   I got up early = mi sono alzato presto
   early in the afternoon = nel primo
   pomeriggio
• (*ahead of time*) = in anticipo
   we arrived early = siamo arrivati in
   anticipo

earn *verb*
   = guadagnare

earring *noun*
   an earring = un orecchino

earth *noun*
• (*the planet*)
   the earth = la terra
• (*soil*)
   earth = terra

easily *adverb*
   = facilmente

east
1 *noun*
   the east = l'est (*masculine*)
   in the east of France = nell'est della
   Francia
2 *adverb*
   to go east = andare a est (✱ + *essere*)
   to live east of Turin = abitare a est di
   Torino   ....➤

3 *adjective*
= est (**!** *never changes*)
to work in east London = lavorare nella zona est di Londra

Easter *noun*
Easter = Pasqua
happy Easter! = buona Pasqua!
an Easter egg = un uovo di Pasqua

easy *adjective*
= facile
it's easy to fix = è facile da riparare
it's not easy to find work here = non è facile trovare lavoro qui

eat *verb*
= mangiare
eat out = mangiar fuori

EC *noun*
the EC = la Comunità Europea

echo *noun*
an echo = un'eco

economic *adjective*
= economico/economica

economics *noun*
economics = economia

economy *noun*
the economy = l'economia

edge *noun*
• (*of a road, table, an object*)
the edge = il bordo
the edge of the lake = la riva del lago
at the edge of the town = ai margini della città
• (*of a blade or knife*)
the edge = il filo

educate *verb*
he was educated in Paris = ha studiato a Parigi

education *noun*
education = l'istruzione (*feminine*)
to get a good education = ricevere una buona istruzione

effect *noun*
an effect = un effetto

effective *adjective*
= efficace

efficient *adjective*
= efficiente

effort *noun*
an effort
= uno sforzo
to make an effort = fare uno sforzo

egg *noun*
an egg = un uovo
how many eggs? = quante uova?

eight *number* **▶ 122 |**, **▶ 146 |**
eight = otto
eight apples = otto mele
I've got eight (of them) = ne ho otto

eighteen *number* **▶ 122 |**, **▶ 146 |**
eighteen = diciotto

eighteenth *number*
• (*in a series*) = diciottesimo/diciottesima
• (*in dates*) **▶ 155 |**
the eighteenth of August = il diciotto agosto

eighth *number*
• (*in a series*) = ottavo/ottava
• (*in dates*) **▶ 155 |**
the eighth of August = l'otto agosto

eighty *number* **▶ 122 |**
eighty = ottanta

either
1 *conjunction*
either Fiona or Kate = o Fiona o Kate
they're coming on either Tuesday or Wednesday = arrivano martedì o mercoledì
he didn't contact either Helen or Paul = non ha cercato né Helen né Paul
2 *pronoun*
take either (of them) = prendi uno dei due/una delle due
I don't know either (of them) = non conosco nessuno dei due/nessuna delle due
3 *determiner*
take either road = prendi una delle due strade
I don't want to live in either country = non voglio vivere in nessuno dei due paesi
4 *adverb*
= nemmeno
she can't do it either = non lo sa fare nemmeno lei

elbow *noun* **▶ 137 |**
the elbow = il gomito

elder *adjective*
= maggiore

elderly *adjective*
= anziano/anziana

eldest *adjective*
= maggiore
the eldest daughter = la figlia maggiore

elect *verb*
= eleggere

election *noun*
an election = un'elezione
to win an election = vincere le elezioni

electric *adjective*
= elettrico/elettrica

electrician *noun* **▶ 281 |**
an electrician = un elettricista

electricity *noun*
electricity = l'elettricità
the electricity has gone off = è andata via la luce

E

elephant *noun*
an elephant = un elefante

elevator *noun* (*US English*)
an elevator = un ascensore

eleven *number* ▶ 122 |, ▶ 146 |
eleven = undici
eleven apples = undici mele
I've got eleven (of them) = ne ho undici

eleventh *number*
• (*in a series*) = undicesimo/undicesima
• (*in dates*) ▶ 155 |
the eleventh of May = l'undici maggio

else
1 *adverb*
= altro/altra
someone else = qualcun
altro/qualcun'altra
nothing else = nient'altro
what else did he say? = che altro ha
detto?
something else = qualcos'altro
everything else = tutto il resto
2 or else = altrimenti
be quiet or else I'll get angry = fate
silenzio altrimenti mi arrabbio

elsewhere *adverb*
= da qualche altra parte

email *noun*
an email = una posta elettronica
an email address = un indirizzo email

embarrassed *adjective*
= imbarazzato/imbarazzata

embarrassing *adjective*
= imbarazzante

embassy *noun*
an embassy = un'ambasciata

emergency *noun*
an emergency = un'emergenza
in an emergency = in caso di emergenza

emergency exit *noun*
an emergency exit = un'uscita di
sicurezza

emigrate *verb*
= emigrare

emotion *noun*
• (*a feeling*)
an emotion = un sentimento
• (*strong feeling*)
emotion = l'emozione (*feminine*)

emotional *adjective*
• (*describing a scene or moment*)
= commovente
• (*describing a person*) = emotivo/emotiva

employed *adjective*
to be employed = lavorare

employee *noun*
an employee = un/una dipendente

employer *noun*
an employer = un datore/una datrice di
lavoro

employment *noun*
employment = il lavoro

empty
1 *adjective*
= vuoto/vuota
2 *verb*
= vuotare

encourage *verb*
= incoraggiare

end
1 *noun*
• (*the final part*)
the end = la fine
at the end of May = alla fine di maggio
in the end = alla fine
• (*the furthest part*)
the end = il fondo
at the end of the street = in fondo alla
strada
2 *verb*
• (*to come to an end*) = finire (! + *essere*)
• (*to put an end to*) = mettere fine a
to end the war = mettere fine alla guerra
end up
to end up in London = finire a Londra

ending *noun*
the ending = la fine

enemy *noun*
an enemy = un nemico/una nemica

energetic *adjective*
= attivo/attiva

energy *noun*
energy = l'energia

engaged *adjective*
• to get engaged = fidanzarsi (! + *essere*)
to be engaged = essere
fidanzato/fidanzata
• (*British English*) (*describing a phone,
toilet*) = occupato/occupata

engine *noun*
• (*of a car*)
an engine = un motore
• (*for a train*)
an engine = una locomotiva

engineer *noun* ▶ 281 |
an engineer = un ingegnere

England *noun* ▶ 151 |
England = l'Inghilterra

English ▶ 199 |
1 *adjective*
= inglese
2 *noun*
• (*the people*)
the English = gli inglesi
• (*the language*)
English = l'inglese (*masculine*)

enjoy *verb*
* (*to like*)
  he enjoys fishing = gli piace pescare
  did you enjoy your holiday? = ti sei
    divertito in vacanza?
* (*to have a good time*)
  to enjoy oneself = divertirsi (**!** + *essere*)

enjoyable *adjective*
= piacevole

enormous *adjective*
= enorme

enough
1 *determiner*
= abbastanza
I don't have enough [money | time] = non
  ho abbastanza [soldi | tempo]
there's enough room for everyone = c'è
  posto per tutti
2 *adverb*
= abbastanza
is it big enough? = è grande abbastanza?
you're not old enough = non sei grande
  abbastanza
3 *pronoun*
= abbastanza
we have enough to eat = abbiamo
  abbastanza da mangiare
I've had enough = ne ho abbastanza
that's enough = basta così

enquire *verb*
= informarsi (**!** + *essere*)
I'll enquire about the price = m'informerò
  sul prezzo

enter *verb*
* (*to go into*) = entrare in (**!** + *essere*)
* (*to take part in*) = partecipare a

entertain *verb*
= divertire

entertaining *adjective*
= divertente

entertainment *noun*
entertainment = il divertimento

enthusiasm *noun*
enthusiasm = l'entusiasmo

enthusiastic *adjective*
= entusiasta

entrance *noun*
an entrance = un ingresso

envelope *noun*
an envelope = una busta

environment *noun*
the environment = l'ambiente (*masculine*)

envy
1 *noun*
envy = l'invidia
2 *verb*
= invidiare

episode *noun*
an episode = una puntata

equal
1 *adjective*
= uguale
to fight for equal rights = lottare per la
  parità di diritti
2 *verb*
= fare
six and four equals ten = sei più quattro
  fa dieci

equality *noun*
equality = la parità

equator *noun*
the equator = l'equatore (*masculine*)

equipment *noun*
equipment = l'attrezzatura

eraser *noun*
an eraser = una gomma

escalator *noun*
an escalator = una scala mobile

escape *verb*
* (*to get away*) = fuggire (**!** + *essere*)
  he escaped from prison = è fuggito di
    prigione
* (*to avoid*) = sfuggire a (**!** + *essere*)
  to escape death = scampare la morte

especially *adverb*
= specialmente

essay *noun*
an essay = un tema

essential *adjective*
= essenziale

ethnic *adjective*
= etnico/etnica

euro *noun*
a euro = un euro

Europe *noun* ▶ **151** |
Europe = l'Europa

European *adjective* ▶ **199** |
= europeo/europea

European Union *noun*
the European Union = l'Unione europea

evacuate *verb*
to evacuate a building = sgomberare un
  edificio

even¹
1 *adverb*
* (*when expressing surprise*) = perfino
  she even works on weekends = lavora
    perfino il fine settimana
  he didn't even try = non ha neanche
    provato
* (*in comparisons*) = ancora
  it's even colder today = oggi fa ancora
    più freddo   ····▶

2 even though = anche se
  he was bored even though he was on
    holiday = si annoiava anche se era in
    vacanza

even² *adjective*
• (*flat, smooth*) = regolare
• (*when talking about numbers*)
  an even number = un numero pari

evening *noun* ▶ **146** , ▶ **267**
  an evening = una sera
  at eight o'clock in the evening = alle otto
    di sera
  to spend the evening at home = passare
    la sera in casa

event *noun*
  an event = un avvenimento

eventually *adverb*

> **!** *Note that* **eventually** *is never*
> *translated by* **eventualmente**.

  = alla fine

ever *adverb*
• (*at any time*)
  nothing ever happens = non succede mai
    niente
  no one will ever know = non lo saprà mai
    nessuno
  have you ever been to Greece? = sei mai
    stato in Grecia?
  I hardly ever go there = non ci vado quasi
    mai
• (*always*)
  he's as lazy as ever = è pigro come
    sempre

every *determiner* ▶ **267**
  = ogni
  every house was different = ogni casa era
    diversa
  every time I meet her = tutte le volte che
    la vedo
  every day = tutti i giorni
  every second day, every other day = un
    giorno sì e uno no
  two out of every three people = due
    persone su tre

everyone *pronoun* (*also* **everybody**)
  = tutti/tutte
  everyone was sleeping = tutti dormivano
  everyone else = tutti gli altri/tutte le
    altre

> **!** *Note that* **tutte** *is only used when all*
> *the people referred to are female. If*
> *there are males in the group, use* **tutti.**
> **Tutti/tutte** *is plural.*

everything *pronoun*
  = tutto

everywhere *adverb*
  = dappertutto
  everywhere else = da ogni altra parte

evidence *noun*
  a piece of evidence = una prova

evil *noun*
  evil = il male

exact *adjective*
  = esatto/esatta

exactly *adverb*
  = esattamente
  exactly! = esatto!

exaggerate *verb*
  = esagerare

exam *noun*
  an exam = un esame
  to take an exam = dare un esame

examine *verb*
  = esaminare

example *noun*
  an example = un esempio
  for example = per esempio

excellent *adjective*
  = eccellente

except *preposition*
  = eccetto

exchange rate *noun*
  the exchange rate = il tasso di cambio

excited *adjective*
  = entusiasta

exciting *adjective*
  = emozionante

exclude *verb*
  = escludere

excuse
1 *noun*
  an excuse = una scusa
  to make excuses = trovare delle scuse
2 *verb*
  = scusare
  excuse me! = scusi!

exercise *noun*
• (*to keep fit*)
  an exercise = un esercizio
  to take exercise, to do exercise = fare
    moto
• (*a piece of work*)
  an exercise = un esercizio

exercise book *noun*
  an exercise book = un quaderno

exhausted *adjective*
  = esausto/esausta

exhibition *noun*
  an exhibition = una mostra

exit *noun*
  an exit = un'uscita

expect *verb*
• (*to be prepared for*) = aspettarsi (**!** +
    essere) ····▶

Useful everyday expressions in Italian

Where appropriate, the familiar **tu** form is given before the more formal **lei** form.

When things are going well

well done!	= bravo/brava!	*good luck!*	= buona fortuna!
congratulations!	= complimenti!		= in bocca al lupo!

When things are not so good

oh dear!	= mamma mia!✖	*shit!*	= merda!✖
damn!	= accidenti!✖	*yuck!*	= che schifo!✖
ouch!	= ahi!	*phew!*	= meno male!

E

Coming

can I come in?	= è permesso?	*good afternoon,*	
come in!	= avanti!	*good evening!*	= buonasera!
pleased to meet you!	= piacere!	*hi!*	= ciao!
hello! (face to face)	= buongiorno!		= salve!
(on the phone)	= pronto?		

Going

goodbye	= arrivederci!	*see you tomorrow!*	= ci vediamo domani!
bye!	= ciao!	*look after yourself!*	= stammi bene!
see you soon!	= a presto!	*speak to you soon!*	= ci sentiamo
see you later!	= a dopo!		

Please and thank you

please	= per favore	*please do!*	= prego!
	= per piacere	*yes please!*	= volentieri!
	= per cortesia	*thank you!*	= grazie!
can I help you?	= dimmi, dica!	*no thank you!*	= no grazie!
	= prego!	*you're welcome!*	= prego!
I'd like...	= vorrei...	*don't mention it!*	= figurati, si figuri!
	= mi dai..., mi dà...	*no problem, not at all!*	= di niente!

Attracting attention

excuse me!	= scusa, mi scusi!
	= senti, senta!

Apologizing

I'm sorry!	= mi dispiace!	*sorry? (when one has*	
	= scusami, mi scusi!	*not heard)*	= come?
excuse me! (to get past)	= permesso!		

Wishing someone well

have a nice day!	= buona giornata!	*have a great time!*	= divertiti, si diverta!
have a nice evening!	= buona serata!	*have a good trip!*	= buon viaggio!
have a great holiday			
or vacation!	= buone vacanze!		

Special greetings

happy birthday!	= buon compleanno!	*happy New Year!*	= buon anno!
happy Christmas!	= buon Natale!		

Eating and drinking

enjoy your meal!	= buon appetito!
cheers!	= cin cin!
	= salute!

Sneezing

bless you, gesundheit!	= salute!

Sleeping

good night!	= buonanotte!	*sweet dreams!*	= sogni d'oro!

to **expect bad news** = aspettarsi cattive notizie
they expect to win = si aspettano di vincere
- (*to wait for*) = aspettare
- (*to want*) = aspettarsi (**!** + *essere*)
they expect us to do it = si aspettano che lo facciamo noi

> **!** Note that the subjunctive is used after **aspettarsi che**.

expensive *adjective*
= caro/cara

experience *noun*
an experience = un'esperienza

experienced *adjective*
= esperto/esperta

experiment
1 *noun*
an experiment = un esperimento
2 *verb*
= sperimentare

expert *noun*
an expert = un esperto/un'esperta
a computer expert = un esperto di computer

explain *verb*
= spiegare

explanation *noun*
an explanation = una spiegazione

explode *verb*
= esplodere (**!** + *essere*)

exploit *verb*
= sfruttare

explosion *noun*
an explosion = un'esplosione

export *verb*
= esportare

express
1 *verb*
= esprimere
2 *adverb*
to send a letter express = spedire una lettera per espresso

expression *noun*
an expression = un'espressione

extinct *adjective*
(*describing an animal*) = estinto/estinta
(*describing a volcano*) = spento/spenta

extra
1 *adjective*
= in più
an extra bed = un letto in più
to pay an extra ten pounds = pagare dieci sterline in più
2 *adverb*
to pay extra = pagare un supplemento

extraordinary *adjective*
= straordinario/straordinaria

extreme *adjective*
= estremo/estrema

extremely *adverb*
= estremamente

eye *noun* ▶ **137** |
an eye = un occhio
to have green eyes = avere gli occhi verdi

eyebrow *noun* ▶ **137** |
an eyebrow = un sopracciglio
the eyebrows = le sopracciglia

eyelash *noun* ▶ **137** |
an eyelash = un ciglio
the eyelashes = le ciglia

eyelid *noun* ▶ **137** |
an eyelid = una palpebra

eye shadow *noun*
eye shadow = l'ombretto

eyesight *noun*
eyesight = la vista
to have good eyesight = avere la vista buona

Ff

face
1 *noun*
the face = il viso, la faccia
to make a face = fare una smorfia
2 *verb*
- (*to be opposite*) = essere di fronte a
she was facing me = era di fronte a me
- (*to have to deal with*)
I can't face seeing them again = non ho il coraggio di rivederli
- (*to look toward(s)*)
my room faces the sea = la mia camera dà sul mare
face up to = affrontare

fact
1 *noun*
a fact = un fatto
2 in fact = in realtà

factory *noun*
a factory = una fabbrica

fade *verb*
= scolorire (**!** + *essere*)

fail *verb*
= non riuscire (**!** + *essere*)
to fail an exam = non passare un esame

failure *noun*
a failure = un fallimento

faint *verb*
= svenire (**!** + *essere*)

fair
1 *adjective*
• (*just*) = giusto/giusta
  it's not fair = non è giusto
• (*in colour*)
  to have fair hair = avere i capelli biondi
  to have fair skin = avere la pelle chiara
2 *noun*
• (*British English*) (*a funfair*)
  a fair = un luna park
• (*a display of goods*)
  a (trade) fair = una fiera

fairly *adverb*
  = abbastanza

faith *noun*
  faith = la fede

faithful *adjective*
  = fedele

fall
1 *verb*
• (*if it's a person*) = cadere (**!** + *essere*)
  she fell to the ground = è caduta a terra
• (*to come down, to be reduced*) = scendere
  (**!** + *essere*)
• (*other uses*)
  to fall asleep = addormentarsi (**!** +
  essere)
  to fall ill = ammalarsi (**!** + *essere*)
  to fall in love with someone
    = innamorarsi di qualcuno (**!** + *essere*)
2 *noun*
• (*in prices, temperature*)
  a fall = un calo
  a fall in prices = un calo dei prezzi
• (*US English*) (*autumn*)
  fall = l'autunno
fall down
• = cadere (**!** + *essere*)
fall off = cadere (**!** + *essere*)
  to fall off a chair = cadere da una sedia
fall out
• (*from somewhere*) = cadere (**!** + *essere*)
  the letter fell out of his pocket = la lettera
  gli è caduta dalla tasca
• (*to quarrel*) = litigare
fall over = cadere (**!** + *essere*)
fall through = fallire (**!** + *essere*)

false *adjective*
  = falso/falsa

false teeth *noun*
  false teeth = una dentiera (*singular*)

familiar *adjective*
  = familiare

family *noun*
  a family = una famiglia

famous *adjective*
  = famoso/famosa

fan *noun*
• (*of a pop star, an actor*)
  a fan = un/una fan
• (*of a team*)
  a fan = un tifoso/una tifosa

• (*for cooling*)
  a fan (*electric*) = un ventilatore
  (*hand-held*) = un ventaglio

fancy dress party *noun* (*British English*)
  a fancy dress party = una festa
  mascherata

fantastic *adjective*
  = fantastico/fantastica

far
1 *adverb*
• ▶ **202**|
  far (away) = lontano
  how far is it to London? = quanto è
  lontano Londra?
  how far is Oxford from London?
    = quanto è lontano Oxford da Londra?
  we went as far as the coast = siamo
  arrivati fino alla costa
• (*in time*)
  as far back as 1950 = già nel 1950
• (*very much*)
  you're eating far too much bread = mangi
  troppo pane
  we know far fewer people here
    = conosciamo molta meno gente qui
2 *adjective*
  at the far side of the room = dall'altra
  parte della stanza
3 so far = finora

fare *noun*
  the fare (*on a bus or train*) = il (prezzo
  del) biglietto

farm *noun*
  a farm = una fattoria

farmer *noun* ▶ **281**|
  a farmer = un contadino/una contadina

fascinating *adjective*
  = affascinante

fashion *noun*
  fashion = la moda
  to be in fashion = essere di moda
  to go out of fashion = passare di moda
  (**!** + *essere*)

fashionable *adjective*
  = alla moda

fast
1 *adjective*
• (*describing movement*) = veloce
• **to be fast** = andare avanti (**!** + *essere*)
  my watch is ten minutes fast = il mio
  orologio va avanti di dieci minuti
2 *adverb*
  = rapidamente

fasten *verb*
  to fasten a seatbelt = allacciare una
  cintura di sicurezza

fat *adjective*
  = grasso/grassa
  to get fat = ingrassare (**!** + *essere*)

fatal *adjective*
= mortale

father *noun*
a father = un padre

Father Christmas *noun* (*British English*)
Father Christmas = Babbo Natale

father-in-law *noun*
a father-in-law = un suocero

faucet *noun* (*US English*)
a faucet = un rubinetto

fault *noun*
to be someone's fault = essere colpa di qualcuno
it's not my fault = non è colpa mia
whose fault was it? = di chi era la colpa?

favour (*British English*), **favor** (*US English*)
1 *noun*
a favour = un favore
to do someone a favour = fare un favore a qualcuno
to ask someone a favour = chiedere un favore a qualcuno
2 **in favour of**
to be in favour of a change in the law = essere a favore di un cambiamento di legge

favourite (*British English*), **favorite** (*US English*) *adjective*
= preferito/preferita
it's my favourite film = è il mio film preferito

fax *noun*
a fax = un fax

fear *noun*
fear = la paura

feather *noun*
a feather = una piuma

February *noun* ▶ 155|
February = febbraio

fed up *adjective*
to be fed up with something = essere stufo/stufa di qualcosa

feed *verb*
= dare da mangiare a
I must feed the children = devo dare da mangiare ai bambini

feel *verb*
• (*to have a feeling*) = sentirsi (! + *essere*)
to feel ill = sentirsi male
to feel [hot | cold | sleepy] = avere [caldo | freddo | sonno]
to feel happy = essere contento/contenta
to feel afraid = avere paura
I feel as if I'm being followed = ho l'impressione che qualcuno mi segua

! *Note that* avere l'impressione che *is followed by the subjunctive.*

• (*to be aware of*)
to feel a draught = sentire una corrente
I don't feel a thing = non sento niente
• (*describing how something seems*)
the box felt very heavy = la scatola era pesante
the room feels very cold = la stanza è molto fredda
it feels like winter = sembra inverno
it feels good to be back home = è bello riessere a casa
• (*to touch*) = toccare
• to feel like [going out | eating | dancing] = avere voglia di [uscire | mangiare | ballare]
I don't feel like it = non ne ho voglia

feeling *noun*
• (*physical*)
a feeling = una sensazione
• (*emotional*)
to hurt someone's feelings = ferire qualcuno
• (*an idea*) I have a feeling he's right = ho la sensazione che abbia ragione lui

! *Note that* avere la sensazione che *is followed by the subjunctive.*

female *adjective*
• (*in biology*) = femmina
• (*relating to women*) = femminile

feminine *adjective*
= femminile

fence *noun*
a fence = uno steccato

fencing *noun* ▶ 178|
fencing = la scherma

festival *noun*
a festival = un festival

fetch *verb*
= prendere
go and fetch some water = vai a prendere dell'acqua

fever *noun*
to have a fever = avere la febbre

few ▶ 233|
1 **a few**
a few [people | houses | books] = qualche [persona | casa | libro]

! *Note that* qualche *is followed by the singular.*

a few of the houses = alcune delle case
a few of them speak Greek = qualcuno di loro parla greco
I would like a few more = ne vorrei qualcun altro/qualcun'altra

! *Note that it is necessary to use* ne, *which may be translated as 'of them', with phrases like* a few. *See also* another, a lot, none *etc for this use of* ne.

····▶

2 *determiner*
• (*not many*) = pochi/poche
  few [visitors | letters | meals] = [pochi visitatori
  | poche lettere | pochi pasti]
3 *pronoun*
  = pochi/poche
  few of us succeeded = pochi di noi ce
    l'hanno fatta
  there are so few of them (*of people*) = ce
    ne sono pochi

fewer ▶ 233 |
1 *determiner*
  = meno
  fewer shops = meno negozi
2 *pronoun*
  = meno
  fewer than ten people = meno di dieci
    persone

fewest
1 *determiner*
  the fewest = meno
  who has the fewest cards? = chi ha
    meno carte?
2 *pronoun*
  the fewest = meno

field *noun*
  a field = un campo

fifteen *number* ▶ 122 |, ▶ 146 |
  fifteen = quindici

fifteenth *number*
• (*in a series*) = quindicesimo/quindicesima
• (*in dates*) ▶ 155 |
  the fifteenth of May = il quindici maggio

fifth *number*
• (*in a series*) = quinto/quinta
• (*in dates*) ▶ 155 |
  the fifth of June = il cinque giugno

fifty *number* ▶ 122 |, ▶ 146 |
  fifty = cinquanta

fight
1 *verb*
• **to fight (against) prejudice** = lottare
    contro i pregiudizi
  to fight for justice = lottare per la
    giustizia
• (*in war*) = combattere
  to fight the enemy = combattere il
    nemico
• (*physically*) = lottare
• (*to quarrel*) = litigare
2 *noun*
  a fight = una lotta
fight back = difendersi (**!** + *essere*)

figure *noun*
• (*a number*)
  a figure = una cifra
• **to have a good figure** = avere un bel
    corpo

file *noun*
• **a file** (*for documents*) = una cartella
  (*in a computer*) = un file
• **in single file** = in fila indiana

fill *verb*
• (*to make full*) = riempire
• (*to become full*) = riempirsi (**!** + *essere*)
fill in = riempire

film
1 *noun*
• (*in cinema or on TV*)
  a film = un film
• (*for a camera*)
  a film = una pellicola
2 *verb*
  = filmare

filthy *adjective*
  = sporco/sporca

final
1 *adjective*
  = finale
2 *noun*
  the final = la finale

finally *adverb*
  = finalmente

find *verb*
  = trovare
  I can't find it = non lo trovo
find out
  to find out the truth = scoprire la verità

fine
1 *adjective*
• (*very good, excellent*) = bello/bella
  the weather is fine = è bel tempo
• (*in good health*)
  I feel fine = sto bene
• (*expressing agreement*)
  (that's) fine = va bene
2 *noun*
  a fine = una multa

finger *noun* ▶ 137 |
  a finger = un dito
  the fingers = le dita

finish
1 *verb*
• (*to complete*) = finire (**!** + *avere*)
  to finish writing a letter = finire di
    scrivere una lettera
• (*to come to an end*) = finire (**!** + *essere*)
2 *noun*
  the finish (*in a race*) = il traguardo

Finland *noun* ▶ 151 |
  Finland = la Finlandia

fire
1 *noun*
  a fire (*for heat*) = un fuoco
  (*causing damage*) = un incendio
  to catch fire = prendere fuoco
  to be on fire = essere in fiamme
2 *verb*
• (*to shoot*) = sparare
• (*to dismiss*) = licenziare

fire alarm *noun*
  a fire alarm = un allarme antincendio

fire brigade (*British English*), **fire department** (*US English*) *noun*
the fire brigade = i vigili del fuoco (*plural*)

fire engine *noun*
a fire engine = un'autopompa

fireman *noun* ▶ 281 |
a fireman = un vigile del fuoco

fire station *noun*
a fire station = una caserma dei vigili del fuoco

fireworks *noun*
fireworks = i fuochi d'artificio

firm
1 *noun*
a firm = un'azienda
2 *adjective*
= solido/solida

first
1 *adjective*
= primo/prima
the first time = la prima volta
the first three weeks = le prime tre settimane
2 *adverb*
• (*to begin with*) = prima
first of all = prima di tutto
• (*for the first time*) = per la prima volta
• we arrived first = siamo arrivati primi noi
3 *noun*
• (*in a series or group*)
the first = il primo/la prima
he was the first to congratulate us = è stato il primo a congratularsi con noi
• (*in dates*) ▶ 155 |
the first of June = il primo giugno
4 at first = all'inizio

first aid *noun*
first aid = il pronto soccorso

first class *adverb*
to travel first class = viaggiare in prima classe

first floor *noun*
the first floor (*in Britain*) = il primo piano (*in the US*) = il pianterreno

first name *noun*
a first name = un nome

fish
1 *noun*
a fish = un pesce
2 *verb*
to go fishing = andare a pescare (**!** + *essere*)

fisherman *noun* ▶ 281 |
a fisherman = un pescatore

fishing *noun* ▶ 178 |
fishing = la pesca

fishing rod *noun*
a fishing rod = una canna da pesca

fist *noun* ▶ 137 |
the fist = il pugno

fit
1 *verb*
the shoes don't fit me = le scarpe non mi stanno
the photo won't fit into the envelope = la foto non sta nella busta
will the table fit here? = il tavolo ci starà qui?
2 *adjective*
• (*suitable, capable*)
the house isn't fit to live in = la casa non è abitabile
to be fit to drive = essere in grado di guidare
• (*healthy*)
to be fit = essere in forma

fit in
• (*in a room or car*)
can you all fit in? = ci state tutti?
• (*in a group or team*) = integrarsi (**!** + *essere*)

fitness *noun*
(physical) fitness = la forma (fisica)

five *number* ▶ 122 |, ▶ 146 |
five = cinque
five apples = cinque mele
I've got five (of them) = ne ho cinque

fix *verb*
• (*to decide on, to set*) = fissare
• (*to repair*) = riparare
to get a watch fixed = far riparare un orologio
• (*to prepare*) = preparare

flag *noun*
a flag = una bandiera

flame *noun*
a flame = una fiamma
to go up in flames = andare in fiamme (**!** + *essere*)

flash
1 *noun*
a flash (*for a camera*) = un flash
2 *verb*
to flash (on and off) = lampeggiare

flashlight *noun*
a flashlight = una torcia

flask *noun*
a flask = un thermos®

flat
1 *noun* (*British English*)
a flat = un appartamento
2 *adjective*
= piatto/piatta
to have a flat tyre = avere una gomma a terra

flavour (*British English*), **flavor** (*US English*) *noun*
a flavour (*of food*) = un sapore
(*of ice cream, yogurt*) = un gusto

flight *noun*
a flight = un volo

flight attendant *noun* ▶ 281 |
  a flight attendant = un
    assistente/un'assistente di volo

float *verb*
  = galleggiare

flock *noun*
• (*of sheep, goats*)
  a flock = un gregge
• (*of birds*)
  a flock = uno stormo

flood *noun*
  a flood = un'alluvione

floor *noun*
• (*a surface*)
  the floor = il pavimento
  to sit on the floor = sedere per terra
• (*a storey*)
  a floor = un piano

florist *noun* ▶ 281 |
  a florist = un fioraio/una fioraia

flour *noun*
  flour = la farina

flow *verb*
  = scorrere (**!** + *essere*)

flower
1 *noun*
  a flower = un fiore
2 *verb*
  = fiorire (**!** + *essere*)

flu *noun* ▶ 193 |
  flu = l'influenza

fluently *adverb*
  = correntemente

flush *verb*
  to flush the toilet = tirare lo sciacquone

flute *noun*
  a flute = un flauto

fly
1 *noun*
  a fly = una mosca
2 *verb*
• (*if it's a bird, a kite, a plane, an insect*)
  = volare
• (*if it's a passenger*) = viaggiare in aereo
  I flew from London to Pisa = sono andato
    da Londra a Pisa in aereo
• to fly a plane = pilotare un aereo
• (*if it's a flag*) = sventolare
  fly away = volare via (**!** + *essere*)

fog *noun*
  fog = la nebbia

fold *verb*
• to fold a shirt = piegare una camicia
• to fold one's arms = incrociare le braccia

folder *noun*
  a folder (*for work*) = una cartellina
  (*in computing*) = una cartella

follow *verb*
  = seguire

following *adjective*
  = seguente

fond *adjective*
  I'm very fond of you = ti sono molto
  affezionata

food *noun*
  food = il cibo
  the food is good here = qui si mangia
    bene
  Chinese food = la cucina cinese
  do we have enough food? = abbiamo
    abbastanza da mangiare?

fool *verb*
  = ingannare

foot *noun*
• (*part of the leg*) ▶ 137 |
  the foot = il piede
  on foot = a piedi
• (*of an animal*)
  the foot = la zampa
• (*in measurements*) ▶ 202 |
  a foot = un piede
     ! *Note that a* **foot** = *30.48 cm.*

football *noun* ▶ 178 |
• football (*soccer*) = il calcio
  (*American football*) = il football americano
• (*a ball*)
  a football = un pallone

footballer (*British English*), *noun*
  ▶ 281 |
  a footballer = un calciatore

footprint *noun*
  a footprint = un'impronta

footstep *noun*
  a footstep = un passo

for *preposition*
• for = per
  the letter is for you = la lettera è per te
  to work for a company = lavorare per una
    ditta
  he cooked dinner for us = ci ha preparato
    la cena
• (*when talking about time, distance*)
  we've been living here for two years
    = viviamo qui da due anni
  he's going to Paris for a year = va a
    Parigi per un anno
  she read for two hours = ha letto per due
    ore
  I've been waiting for three hours = sono
    tre ore che aspetto
  we drove for 80 kilometres = abbiamo
    guidato per 80 chilometri
• (*when talking about money*)
  he bought it for £50 = l'ha comprato per
    50 sterline
  a cheque for £20 = un assegno da 20
    sterline
• (*in favour (of)*) = per
• (*other uses*)
  T for Tom = T come Tom   ····▶

what is the Italian for 'ant'? = come si
dice 'ant' in italiano?
we went [**for a swim** | **for a run** | **for a walk**]
= siamo andati a [nuotare | correre | fare
una passeggiata]

forbid verb
= proibire
to forbid someone to go out = proibire a
qualcuno di uscire
smoking is forbidden = è vietato fumare

force
1 verb
= costringere
to force someone to leave = costringere
qualcuno a uscire
2 noun
force = la forza
by force = con la forza

forecast noun
the forecast = le previsioni
the forecast is for rain = secondo le
previsioni piove

forehead noun ▶ 137 |
the forehead = la fronte

foreign adjective
= straniero/straniera

foreigner noun
a foreigner = uno straniero/una straniera

forest noun
a forest = una foresta

forever, for ever adverb
= per sempre

forget verb
= dimenticare
to forget to do something = dimenticarsi
di fare qualcosa (**!** + essere)
we forgot about him = ci siamo
dimenticati di lui

forgive verb
to forgive someone = perdonare qualcuno

fork noun
a fork = una forchetta

form
1 noun
• (a shape)
a form = una forma
• (a document)
a form = un modulo
• (referring to mood or fitness)
to be in good form = essere in forma
• (British English) (a class)
a form = una classe
to be in the sixth form = essere all'ultimo
anno

──────────
✖ in informal situations

2 verb
• (to create, to make) = formare
to form a circle = formare un cerchio
• (to start, to set up) = creare

formal adjective
• = formale
• **to wear formal dress** = essere in abito da
sera
• (official) = ufficiale

former adjective
the former president = l'ex presidente

fortnight noun ▶ 267 | (British English)
a fortnight = quindici giorni

fortunately adverb
= fortunatamente

fortune noun
• **a fortune** = un patrimonio
to make a fortune = fare i soldi a palate✖
• **to tell someone's fortune** = predire il
futuro a qualcuno

forty number ▶ 122 |, ▶ 146 |
forty = quaranta

forward
1 adverb
= avanti
to step forward = fare un passo avanti
2 verb
to forward a letter to someone = inoltrare
una lettera a qualcuno

found verb
= fondare

fountain noun
a fountain = una fontana

four number ▶ 122 |, ▶ 146 |
four = quattro
four apples = quattro mele
I've got four (of them) = ne ho quattro

fourteen number ▶ 122 |, ▶ 146 |
fourteen = quattordici

fourteenth number
• (in a series)
= quattordicesimo/quattordicesima
• (in dates) ▶ 155 |
the fourteenth of July = il quattordici
luglio

fourth number
• (in a series) = quarto/quarta
• (in dates) ▶ 155 |
the fourth of July = il quattro luglio

fox noun
a fox = una volpe

fragile adjective
= fragile

frame noun
a frame = una cornice

France noun ▶ 151 |
France = la Francia

Forms of address (Miss, Mrs, Mr)

When speaking to or about someone
When the surname of the person one is addressing is not known it is possible to address him or her using **signore**, **signora** or **signorina**:

good morning, **Mr** Jones	= buongiorno, **signor** Jones
good morning, **sir**	= buongiorno, **signore**
excuse me, **madam**	= scusi, **signora**
come in, **miss**	= avanti, **signorina**

When talking about someone the definite article is used:

I saw **Mrs** Lucchesi	= ho visto **la signora** Lucchesi
Is **Mr** Fowler in?	= **il signor** Fowler è in casa?

Professional titles
Professional titles are often used:

Doctor Bellato	= **il dottor** Bellato
Mrs Cortopassi *(the teacher)*	= **la professoressa** Cortopassi

▶ There is no Italian equivalent of **Ms**. Use **signora** or **signorina**.

---

frank *adjective*
= franco/franca

freckle *noun*
a freckle = una lentiggine

free
1 *adjective*
- *(costing nothing)* = gratuito/gratuita
- *(independent, able to come and go)* = libero/libera
he is free to do what he likes = è libero di fare quello che vuole
- *(not occupied, available)* = libero/libera
are you free on Monday? = sei libero lunedì?
2 *verb*
= liberare
3 *adverb*
= gratis

freedom *noun*
freedom = la libertà

freeway *noun* (*US English*)
a freeway = un'autostrada

freeze *verb*
- *(in cold weather)* = ghiacciare (**!** + *essere*)
the river froze = il fiume è ghiacciato
the ground was frozen = la terra era ghiacciata
- *(in a freezer)* = congelare
- to freeze to death = morire di freddo (**!** + *essere*)

freezer *noun*
a freezer = un congelatore

freezing *adjective*
it's freezing = è freddissimo

this room is freezing = questa stanza è gelata
to be freezing (*if it's a person*) = morire di freddo (**!** + *essere*)

French ▶ 199 |
1 *adjective*
= francese
2 *noun*
- *(the people)*
the French = i francesi
- *(the language)*
French = il francese

French fries *noun*
French fries = le patatine fritte

fresh *adjective*
= fresco/fresca

Friday *noun* ▶ 155 |
Friday = venerdì (*masculine*)

fridge *noun*
a fridge = un frigorifero

fried *adjective*
= fritto/fritta

friend *noun*
a friend = un amico/un'amica
to make friends with someone = fare amicizia con qualcuno

friendly *adjective*
= simpatico/simpatica

fright *noun*
to get a fright = prendersi uno spavento (**!** + *essere*)
to give someone a fright = far prendere uno spavento a qualcuno

frightened *adjective*
to be frightened = avere paura

fringe noun (British English)
 a fringe = una frangia

from preposition

> ! There are many verbs which involve the use of **from**, like **borrow from**, **escape from**, etc. For translations, look up the entries at **borrow**, **escape**, etc.

- from = da
 there's a message from Paul = c'è un messaggio di Paul
 from the = dal/dalla (! + singular)
 = dai/dalle (+ plural)

> ! Before masculine nouns beginning with z, ps, gn, or s + another consonant, **dallo** is used in the singular and **dagli** in the plural. Before masculine and feminine singular nouns beginning with a vowel, **dall'** is used.

 we live ten minutes from the city centre = abitiamo a dieci minuti dal centro
 she came back from the office = è tornata dall'ufficio
- (belonging to a place)
 where is she from? = di dov'è?
 the boy from London = il ragazzo di Londra
- (when talking about time) = da
 the shop is open from eight to six = il negozio è aperto dalle otto alle sei
 from Monday to Saturday = dal lunedì al sabato
 from April on = da Aprile in poi
 from then on = da allora in poi
 fifty years from now = tra cinquant'anni
- (British English) (in arithmetic)
 5 from 8 leaves 3 = otto meno cinque tre

front
1 noun
- (of a building)
 the front of the house = la facciata della casa
- (of a car, a train or queue)
 at the front of the bus = nella parte davanti dell'autobus
 at the front of the queue = in cima alla fila
2 in front of = davanti a

front door noun
 the front door = la porta davanti

front page noun
 the front page = la prima pagina

front seat noun
 the front seat = il posto davanti

frost noun
 frost = la brina

frozen adjective
 = congelato/congelata

fruit noun
 fruit = la frutta
 a piece of fruit = un frutto

fry verb
 = friggere

frying pan noun (British English)
 a frying pan = una padella

full adjective
- (not empty) = pieno/piena
 the streets were full of people = le strade erano piene di gente
- (describing a flight, a hotel) = completo/completa
- (maximum)
 at full speed = a tutta velocità
 to get full marks = prendere il massimo dei voti
- (complete)
 to pay the full fare = pagare il biglietto intero
 his full name = il suo nome e cognome

full-time adverb
 = a tempo pieno
 to work full-time = lavorare a tempo pieno

fun noun
 it's fun = è divertente
 skiing is fun = sciare è divertente
 to have fun = divertirsi (! + essere)
 she's fun = è simpatica

function verb
 = funzionare

funeral noun
 a funeral = un funerale

funfair noun (British English)
 a funfair = un luna park

funny adjective
- (amusing) = divertente
- (odd) = buffo/buffa

fur noun
 a fur = una pelliccia

furious adjective
 = furioso/furiosa

furniture noun
 a piece of furniture = un mobile
 furniture = i mobili

further adverb
 = più lontano
 he lives further away from the school = abita più lontano dalla scuola
 how much further is it? = quanto manca ancora?

fuss noun
 to make a fuss = fare storie

> ! Note that **storie** is plural.

future
1 noun
 the future = il futuro
 in the future = in futuro
 in future, let us know = in futuro, informaci
2 adjective
 = futuro/futura

game *noun*
  a game = un gioco
  a game of tennis = una partita di tennis

games *noun* (*British English*)
  games = lo sport

game show *noun*
  a game show = un gioco a premi

gang *noun*
  a gang = una banda

gap *noun*
• a gap (*in a fence or hedge*) = un buco
  (*between buildings, cars*) = uno spazio
• (*a period of time*)
  a gap = un intervallo di tempo

garage *noun*
• (*where the car is kept*)
  a garage = un garage
• (*where cars are repaired*)
  a garage = un'autofficina

garbage *noun* (*US English*)
  garbage = la spazzatura

garden *noun*
  a garden = un giardino

gardener *noun* ▶ 281
  a gardener = un giardiniere/una
  giardiniera

gardening *noun*
  gardening = il giardinaggio
  to do some gardening = fare del
  giardinaggio

garlic *noun*
  garlic = l'aglio

gas *noun*
• (*for cooking, heating*)
  gas = il gas
• (*US English*) (*gasoline*)
  gas = la benzina

gas station *noun* (*US English*)
  a gas station = una stazione di servizio

gate *noun*
  a gate = un cancello

gather *verb*
• (*to come together*) = radunarsi (**!** +
  essere)
• (*to collect*)
  to gather wood = raccogliere la legna

gay *adjective*
  = gay (**!** never changes)

gear *noun*
• (*in a car or bus, on a bike*)
  a gear = una marcia
• (*equipment*)
  gear = l'attrezzatura

  fishing gear = l'attrezzatura da pesca
• (*clothes*)
  my football gear = la mia tenuta da calcio
  your swimming gear = la tua roba per il
  nuoto

Gemini *noun*
  Gemini = Gemelli (*masculine plural*)

general
1 *noun*
  a general = un generale
2 *adjective*
  = generale
3 in general = in generale

generation *noun*
  a generation = una generazione

generous *adjective*
  = generoso/generosa

genius *noun*
  a genius = un genio

gentle *adjective*
  = dolce

gentleman *noun*
  a gentleman = un signore

geography *noun*
  geography = la geografia

germ *noun*
  a germ = un microbo

German ▶ 199
1 *adjective*
  = tedesco/tedesca
2 *noun*
• (*the people*)
  the Germans = i tedeschi
• (*the language*)
  German = il tedesco

Germany *noun* ▶ 151
  Germany = la Germania

get *verb*
▶ See the boxed note on **get** for more
information and examples.

get away
• (*to escape*) = fuggire (**!** + essere)
• he won't get away with it = non la
  passerà liscia
get back
• (*to return*) = tornare (**!** + essere)
• (*to have back*) = recuperare
  I got my bike back = ho recuperato la
  bicicletta
  he got his money back = è stato
  rimborsato
get down
• (*to come or go down*) = scendere (**!** +
  essere)
  he can't get down from the tree = non
  riesce a scendere dall'albero
• (*to take down*)
  I got the box down from the shelf = ho
  preso la scatola dallo scaffale   ····➤

Games and sports

Games and sports have the definite article in Italian. When talking about playing a game, use
giocare a without the article:

tennis	= **il** tennis
chess	= **gli** scacchi
to play soccer	= giocare **a** calcio
to go hang-gliding	= fare **il** deltaplano

Players

Sometimes there is a special word in Italian for the player:

a tennis-player	= un/una tennista
a soccer-player	= un calciatore

but:

a golfer	= un giocatore/una giocatrice di golf

- (*to depress*) = deprimere
  it gets him down = lo deprime
  get in = entrare (**!** + *essere*)
  get off
- (*to leave a bus or train*) = scendere (**!** +
  essere)
  he fell as he was getting off the train = è
  caduto mentre scendeva dal treno
- (*to remove*) = togliere
  to get a stain off = togliere una macchia
  get on
- (*to climb on board a bus or train*) = salire
  (**!** + *essere*)
  to get on the bus = salire sull'autobus
- **to get on well** = andare d'accordo (**!** +
  essere)
  I get on well with her = con lei vado
  d'accordo
- (*in polite enquiries*)
  how did you get on? = come è andata?
  how is she getting on at school? = come
  va a scuola?
  get out
- (*to leave*) = uscire (**!** + *essere*)
  she got out of the building = è uscita dal
  palazzo
- (*to take out*) = portare fuori
  to get the furniture out of the house
  = portare i mobili fuori
  get over
  to get over the shock = superare lo shock
  get through to
  to get through to someone = rintracciare
  qualcuno
  get together = riunirsi (**!** + *essere*)
  get up = alzarsi (**!** + *essere*)

ghost *noun*
  a ghost = un fantasma

ginger *adjective* ▶ **147**
  = rosso/rossa
  to have ginger hair (*British English*)
  = avere i capelli rossi

girl *noun*
  a girl = una bambina
  (*a teenager*) = una ragazza

girlfriend *noun*
  a girlfriend (*in a couple*) = una ragazza
  (*a female friend*) = un'amica

give *verb*

> **!** *For translations of expressions like* **to
> give someone a lift, to give someone
> an injection, to give someone a fright,**
> *etc, look up the entries* **lift, injection,
> fright.**

- **to give** = dare
  I gave him the photos = gli ho dato le
  foto
  give me the newspapers! = dammi i
  giornali!
  he gave us a present = ci ha dato un
  regalo
- (*as a present*) = regalare
  to give someone a book = regalare un
  libro a qualcuno
  give away
- (*to make a present of*) = dare via
- **to give away a secret** = svelare un segreto
  give back = restituire
  give in
- (*to relent*) = cedere
- (*to abandon an attempt*) = rinunciare
  give out
  to give out the exercise books
  = distribuire i quaderni
  give up
- (*to abandon an attempt*) = rinunciare
  we gave up looking for her = abbiamo
  abbandonato le ricerche
- (*to stop*)
  to give up smoking = smettere di fumare
- **to give oneself up to the police**
  = costituirsi alla polizia (**!** + *essere*)

glad *adjective*
  = contento/contenta

glass *noun*
- (*the material*)
  glass = il vetro
- (*for drinking*)
  a glass = un bicchiere

get

A multi-purpose verb

The word **get** in English has many meanings, and has no Italian equivalent that will be suitable for all occasions. It can be helpful to think of an English word with a similar meaning and find the translation for that.

   *go and **get** (or **fetch**) some water*   = vai a **prendere** dell'acqua
   ***we got to** (or **arrived at**) the station at noon* = **siamo arrivati** alla stazione a mezzogiorno

meaning 'to become'

Get can be translated by **diventare** (**!** + *essere*) when it means 'become':

   *she's **got** even cheekier*   = **è diventata** ancora più sfacciata

But remember that there is often a specific verb in Italian to express the type of change:

   *things **have got worse***   = le cose **sono peggiorate**
   *he's **got** much **older***   = **è invecchiato** molto

meaning 'to receive'

Use **ricevere**:

   *I **got** a postcard*   = **ho ricevuto** una cartolina

meaning 'to obtain'

Use **prendere**:

   *I **got** a new car*   = **ho pres**o una macchina nuova
   *remember **to get** the bread*   = non dimenticare di **prendere** il pane

meaning 'to persuade, to make'

Use **fare** followed by an infinitive:

   *he **got** me to wash up*   = mi **ha fatto** lavare i piatti

when using transport

Use **prendere**:

   *to **get** a taxi*   = **prendere** un taxi

when getting things done

Use **fare** followed by an infinitive:

   *to **get** the car **fixed***   = **far riparare** la macchina

but note:

   *to **get** one's hair **cut***   = **tagliarsi** i capelli

with illnesses

Use **prendere**:

   *she **got** chickenpox*   = **ha preso** la varicella

when cooking

Use **preparare**:

   *to **get** dinner*   = **preparare** la cena

▶ For translations of expressions containing **get**, look up the entry for the noun or adjective in the expression:

   *to get a **shock***   = avere uno **shock**

▶ For translations of phrasal verbs (for example **get down**, **get away**), look in the entry for **get**.

▶ For translations of **have got**, look in the entry and the note for **have**.

go

▶ You will find translations for phrasal verbs like **go away**, **go back**, etc in the entry for **go**.

getting from A to B

Generally **go** is translated by **andare** (**!** + *essere*):

we went to the cinema	=	**siamo andati** al cinema
to go into town	=	**andare** in città
to go to the dentist's	=	**andare** dal dentista

Translating verbs of movement

Where English uses two separate words like **go in** to indicate the direction of the movement, Italian often has specific verbs for each kind of movement:

to go into a room	=	**entrare in** una stanza (**!** + *essere*)
to go home	=	**tornare a casa** (**!** + *essere*)
to go out	=	**uscire** (**!** + *essere*)
to go up	=	**salire** (**!** + *essere*)
to go down	=	**scendere** (**!** + *essere*)

Talking about the future

To talk about things that one is going to do or that are going to happen, use the future tense or **avere intenzione di**:

I'm going to learn Italian	=	**ho intenzione di** imparare l'italiano
it's going to rain	=	**pioverà**

Meaning 'to become'

Diventare (**!** + *essere*) can often be used:

to go deaf	=	**diventare** sordo/sorda (**!** + *essere*)

but remember there is often a specific verb in Italian to express the type of change:

to go red	=	**arrossire** (**!** + *essere*)
to go mad	=	**impazzire** (**!** + *essere*)

---

glasses *noun*
glasses = gli occhiali

glove *noun*
a glove = un guanto

glue
1 *noun*
glue = la colla
2 *verb*
= incollare

go *verb*
▶ *See the boxed note on* **go** *for more information and examples.*
go across = attraversare
go after = seguire
go ahead
• (*if it's an event*)
the concert's going ahead after all = alla fine il concerto si farà
• (*if it's a person*)
go ahead, there's no one there = vai, non c'è nessuno
go around = go round
go around with = go round with
go away = andare via (**!** + *essere*)
go away! = via!

go back = ritornare (**!** + *essere*)
Gary went back to Paris = Gary è ritornato a Parigi
to go back to sleep = riaddormentarsi (**!** + *essere*)
go by = passare (**!** + *essere*)
go down
• = scendere (**!** + *essere*)
the temperature went down = la temperatura è scesa
• (*if it's the sun*) = calare (**!** + *essere*)
• (*if it's a computer*) = guastarsi (**!** + *essere*)
go in
• (*to enter*) = entrare (**!** + *essere*)
go off
• (*to explode*) = esplodere (**!** + *essere*)
• (*to ring*) (*if it's an alarm clock*) = suonare (*if it's an alarm*) = scattare (**!** + *essere*)
• (*to leave*) = andarsene (**!** + *essere*)
• the milk will go off = il latte andrà a male
• (*to be switched off*) = spegnersi (**!** + *essere*)
go on
• (*to continue*)
to go on talking = continuare a parlare
• (*to happen*)
what's going on? = cosa succede? ····▶

* (*to keep talking*)
  he goes on (and on) about his work
  = parla sempre del lavoro
* (*to be switched on*) = accendersi (**!** +
  essere)

go out
* (*to leave the house*) = uscire (**!** + *essere*)
  are you going out this evening? = esci
  stasera?
* (*as a boyfriend, a girlfriend*)
  to go out with someone = stare insieme a
  qualcuno (**!** + *essere*)
* (*to be switched off, to stop burning*)
  = spegnersi (**!** + *essere*)
* **the tide's going out** = la marea sta
  calando

go over
* (*to check*) = controllare
* (*to revise*) = ripassare

go round
* (*British English*) (*to call on*) = passare (**!** +
  essere)
  to go round to see someone = passare a
  trovare qualcuno
* (*to walk around, to visit*) = visitare
  we went round the museums = abbiamo
  visitato i musei
  we went round the shops = abbiamo
  fatto un giro per i negozi
* (*to be enough*)
  is there enough bread to go round? = c'è
  abbastanza pane per tutti?

go round with
* (*British English*) (*to spend time with*)
  = frequentare

go through
* (*to have, to live through*)
  to go through a difficult time
  = attraversare un periodo difficile
  I don't want to go through that again
  = non voglio rivivere un'esperienza del
  genere
* (*to search*) = perquisire
* (*to check*) = controllare

go up
* (*if it's a person*) = salire (**!** + *essere*)
  he went up the stairs = ha salito le scale
  to go up to the top of the hill = salire in
  cima alla collina
  he went up to bed = è andato a letto
* (*if it's a price, a salary*) = aumentare (**!** +
  essere)

go with
  **the trousers don't really go with your
  jacket** = i pantaloni non stanno tanto
  bene con la giacca

goal *noun*
* (*in sport*)
  a goal = un gol
* (*an aim in life*)
  a goal = una meta

goalkeeper *noun*
  a goalkeeper = un portiere

goat *noun*
  a goat = una capra

god *noun*
  a god = un dio
  God = Dio

goddaughter *noun*
  a goddaughter = una figlioccia

godfather *noun*
  a godfather = un padrino

godmother *noun*
  a godmother = una madrina

godson *noun*
  a godson = un figlioccio

gold
1 *noun*
  gold = l'oro
2 *adjective*
  = d'oro
  a gold ring = un anello d'oro

goldfish *noun*
  a goldfish = un pesce rosso

golf *noun* ▶ **178**
  golf = il golf
  a golf course = un campo di golf

good
1 *adjective*
* = buono/buona
  we've got some good news = abbiamo
  buone notizie
  it's a good time to buy a house = è un
  buon momento per comprare casa
* (*enjoyable*) = bello/bella
  a good film = un bel film
  a good party = una bella festa
  I had a good time = mi sono divertito
* (*talented*)
  to be good [at chemistry | at drawing | at
  chess] = essere bravo/brava [in chimica | a
  disegnare | a schacchi]
* (*healthy*)
  exercise is good for you = il moto fa
  bene
  I don't feel too good = non mi sento
  tanto bene
* (*kind*) = gentile
  it's very good of you = è molto gentile da
  parte tua
2 *noun*
  it's no good shouting = non serve a
  niente gridare
  to be no good at Latin = non essere
  affatto bravo/brava in latino
  the change will do you good = cambiare
  ti farà bene
3 *exclamation*
* (*when pleased*)
  good! = bene!
* (*when praising*)
  good! = bravo/brava!
4 for good = per sempre

good afternoon *exclamation*
  good afternoon! = buonasera!

goodbye *exclamation*
goodbye! = arrivederci!

good evening *exclamation*
good evening! = buonasera!

good-looking *adjective*
= bello/bella
a good-looking guy = un bell'uomo

good morning *exclamation*
good morning! = buongiorno!

good night *exclamation*
good night! = buonanotte!

goods *noun*
goods = la merce (*singular*)

goose *noun*
a goose = un'oca

gooseberry *noun*
gooseberries = l'uva spina (*singular*)

gossip *verb*
= spettegolare

got: **to have got** *verb*
▶ *See the boxed note on* **have** *for
information and examples.*

government *noun*
a government = un governo

GP *noun* ▶ 281 | (*British English*)
a GP = un medico generico

grab *verb*
= afferrare
he tried to grab my handbag = ha
provato a strapparmi la borsa

grade *noun*
• (*a mark*)
a grade = un voto
• (*US English*) (*a class*)
a grade = una classe

grade school *noun* (*US English*)
grade school = una scuola elementare

gradually *adverb*
= poco a poco

gram(me) *noun* ▶ 202 |
a gram = un grammo

grammar *noun*
grammar = la grammatica

grandchild *noun*
a grandchild = un/una nipote
the grandchildren = i nipoti

granddaughter *noun*
a granddaughter = una nipote

grandfather *noun*
a grandfather = un nonno

grandmother *noun*
a grandmother = una nonna

grandparents *noun*
grandparents = i nonni

grandson *noun*
a grandson = un nipote

grapefruit *noun*
a grapefruit = un pompelmo

grapes *noun*
grapes = l'uva (*singular*)
a grape = un chicco d'uva
a bunch of grapes = un grappolo d'uva

grass *noun*
grass = l'erba
to cut the grass = tagliare l'erba

grasshopper *noun*
a grasshopper = una cavalletta

grateful *adjective*
= grato/grata

grave *noun*
a grave = una tomba

gray (*US English*) ▶ **grey**

grease *noun*
grease = il grasso

greasy *adjective*
= unto/unta

great *adjective*
• (*stressing size, amount, importance*)
= grande
the guide book was a great help = la
guida è stata di grande aiuto
to have great difficulty reading = avere
molte difficoltà a leggere
a great improvement = un grosso
miglioramento
• (*showing enthusiasm*)
that's great! = fantastico!
I had a great time = mi sono divertito un
sacco

Great Britain *noun* ▶ 151 |
Great Britain = la Gran Bretagna

great grandfather *noun*
a great grandfather = un bisnonno

great grandmother *noun*
a great grandmother = una bisnonna

Greece *noun* ▶ 151 |
Greece = la Grecia

greedy *adjective*
= goloso/golosa

Greek ▶ 199 |
1 *adjective*
= greco/greca
2 *noun*
• (*the people*)
the Greeks = i greci
• (*the language*)
Greek = il greco

green *adjective* ▶ 147 |
= verde

greenhouse *noun*
a greenhouse = una serra

grey (*British English*), **gray** (*US English*)
  adjective ▶ **147** |
  = grigio/grigia
  to have grey hair = avere i capelli grigi

grill *verb*
  = cuocere alla griglia

grin *verb*
  = fare un sorriso da un orecchio all'altro

grocery *noun* ▶ **281** |
  a grocery = un alimentari

ground *noun*
• (*the surface of the earth*)
  the ground = la terra
  to throw papers on the ground = gettare
    la carta per terra
• (*earth*)
  the ground = la terra
  the ground is hard in winter = la terra è
    dura d'inverno
• (*land used for sports*)
  a sports ground = un campo sportivo

ground floor *noun* (*British English*)
  the ground floor = il pianterreno

group *noun*
  a group = un gruppo

grow *verb*
• (*to get big, strong*) = crescere (**!** + *essere*)
• (*as a gardener, a farmer*) = coltivare
  to grow tomatoes = coltivare pomodori
• (*to let grow*)
  he's grown a beard = si è fatto crescere la
    barba
• (*to become*) = diventare (**!** + *essere*)
  she's grown cynical = è diventata cinica
  to grow old = invecchiare (**!** + *essere*)
• (*to increase in size*) = aumentare (**!** +
    essere)
  the population will grow = la popolazione
    aumenterà
grow up = crescere (**!** + *essere*)
  when I grow up, I'm going to be a doctor
    = da grande farò il dottore

grumble *verb*
  = brontolare

guard *noun*
• (*in a prison, at a bank*)
  a guard = una guardia
• (*in the army*)
  a guard = una sentinella
  to be on guard = essere di guardia

guard dog *noun*
  a guard dog = un cane da guardia

guess *verb*
• = indovinare
• (*to suppose*)
  I guess you're right = credo che tu abbia
    ragione

    | **!** Note that the subjunctive is used after
    | **credere che**.

guest *noun*
• (*a person invited to stay*)
  a guest = un ospite/un'ospite
• (*at a hotel*)
  a guest = un/una cliente

guesthouse *noun*
  a guesthouse = una pensione

guide
1 *noun*
• (*a person, a book*)
  a guide = una guida
• (*British English*) (*a Girl Guide*)
  a guide = una Guida
2 *verb*
  = guidare

guided tour *noun*
  a guided tour = una visita guidata

guilty *adjective*
  = colpevole
  to feel guilty = sentirsi in colpa (**!** +
    essere)

guinea pig *noun*
  a guinea pig = una cavia

guitar *noun*
  a guitar = una chitarra

gum *noun*
  the gum = la gengiva

gun *noun*
  a gun (*a rifle*) = un fucile
  (*a revolver*) = una pistola

gym *noun*
  a gym = una palestra
  I go to the gym = vado in palestra

gymnasium *noun*
  a gymnasium = una palestra

gymnastics *noun* ▶ **178** |
  gymnastics = la ginnastica

H

Hh

habit *noun*
  a habit = un'abitudine

hail *noun*
  hail = la grandine

hair *noun*
  hair (*on the head*) = i capelli
  (*on the body*) = i peli

hairbrush *noun*
  a hairbrush = una spazzola

hairdresser *noun* ▶ **281** |
  a hairdresser = un parrucchiere/una
    parrucchiera

hairdryer *noun*
a hairdryer = un asciugacapelli

hairstyle *noun*
a hairstyle = un'acconciatura

half ▶ 233 |
1 *noun*
• a half = una metà
to cut a melon in half = tagliare un melone a metà
• (*in a game*)
the first half = il primo tempo
2 *adjective*
half a litre of milk = un mezzo litro di latte
3 *pronoun*
• (*when talking about quantities, numbers*)
half the pupils speak French = metà degli studenti parla francese
• (*when talking about time, age*) ▶ 146 |, ▶ 125 |
an hour and a half = un'ora e mezzo
he's three and a half = ha tre anni e mezzo
it's half (past) three (*British English*) = sono le tre e mezzo
4 *adverb*
Sam's half Italian half Irish = Sam è metà italiano e metà irlandese

half hour *noun* ▶ 267 |
a half hour = una mezz'ora

half term *noun* (*British English*)
half term = le vacanze di metà trimestre

hall *noun*
• (*in a house, an apartment*)
a hall = un ingresso
• (*for public events*)
a hall = una sala

ham *noun*
ham = il prosciutto

hamburger *noun*
a hamburger = un hamburger

hammer *noun*
a hammer = un martello

hamster *noun*
a hamster = un criceto

hand *noun*
• (*the part of the body*) ▶ 137 |
the hand = la mano
my hands are cold = ho le mani fredde
he had a pencil in his hand = aveva in mano una matita
to hold someone's hand = tenere qualcuno per mano
• (*help*)
to give somone a hand = dare una mano a qualcuno
• (*on a clock or watch*)
a hand = una lancetta

✱ in informal situations

• (*when judging a situation or subject*)
on the one hand..., on the other... = da un lato..., dall'altro...

handbag *noun*
a handbag = una borsa

handball *noun* ▶ 178 |
handball = la pallamano

handicapped *adjective*
= handicappato/handicappata

handkerchief *noun*
a handkerchief = un fazzoletto

handle *noun*
• (*on a cup, pan*)
a handle = un manico
• (*on a door*)
a handle = una maniglia

handsome *adjective*
= bello/bella
a handsome man = un bell'uomo

handwriting *noun*
handwriting = la calligrafia

handy *adjective*
= comodo/comoda
my mobile phone comes in handy = il telefonino mi fa comodo

hang *verb*
• (*on a hook, a coat hanger, a line*)
to hang a picture (up) on the wall = appendere un quadro alla parete
to hang clothes (up) in the wardrobe = appendere gli abiti nell'armadio
to hang clothes on a line = stendere il bucato
• (*to be attached*)
to be hanging from the ceiling = essere appeso/appesa al soffitto
• (*to kill*) = impiccare
hang around
• (*to wait*) = aspettare
• (*to waste time, to do nothing*) = gironzolare✱
hang on to = aggrapparsi a (**!** + *essere*)
she was hanging on to the rope = era aggrappata alla fune
hang up
• (*on a hook, a coat hanger, a line*)
to hang up one's coat = appendere il cappotto
to hang clothes up to dry = stendere il bucato
• your coat's hanging up in the hall = il tuo cappotto è appeso nell'ingresso
• (*when phoning*) = riagganciare

hang-gliding *noun* ▶ 178 |
hang-gliding = il deltaplano

happen *verb*
= succedere (**!** + *essere*)
what happened? = cosa è successo?
something odd happened to me = mi è successa una cosa strana

happy *adjective*
- (*contented*) = felice
  they were happy to hear from you = sono stati felici di avere tue notizie
- (*satisfied*) = contento/contenta
  he's happy with the language course = è contento del corso di lingue
- (*in greetings*)
  happy birthday! = buon compleanno!
  happy New Year! = buon anno!

hard
1 *adjective*
- (*firm, stiff*) = duro/dura
  the ground is hard = la terra è dura
- (*difficult, tough*) = difficile
  a hard question = una domanda difficile
  it's not hard to change a light bulb = non è difficile cambiare una lampadina
  it's hard to understand = è difficile capirlo
  I find it hard to concentrate = mi è difficile concentrarmi
  to be having a hard time = attraversare un periodo difficile
2 *adverb*
  to work hard = lavorare duro
  they hit him hard = l'hanno colpito forte
  to try hard to concentrate = fare uno sforzo per concentrarsi

hardly *adverb*
  = a malapena
  I hardly know them = li conosco a malapena

hardware *noun*
  hardware (*for computers*) = l'hardware (*masculine*)

hard-working *adjective*
  = diligente

harm *verb*
  to harm someone = fare del male a qualcuno
  to harm the environment = danneggiare l'ambiente

harmful *adjective*
  = dannoso/dannosa

harmless *adjective*
  = innocuo/innocua

harvest *noun*
  the harvest (*the job, the time*) = il raccolto
  (*what is picked*) = la raccolta
  (*of grapes*) = la vendemmia

hat *noun*
  a hat = un cappello

hate *verb*
  = odiare
  I hate cooking = odio cucinare

hatred *noun*
  hatred = l'odio

have
1 *verb*
▶ *See the boxed note on* **have** *for more information and examples.*
- (*to eat, to drink*)
  to have a sandwich = mangiare un panino
  to have a glass of wine = bere un bicchiere di vino
  to have dinner = cenare
- (*to get*)
  I had a letter from Bob yesterday = ho ricevuto una lettera di Bob ieri
  I'll let you have the money soon = ti farò presto avere i soldi
- (*to hold or organize*)
  to have a party = fare una festa
  to have a competition = fare una gara
- (*to spend*)
  we had a nice day at the beach = abbiamo passato una bella giornata al mare
  I'll have a good time in Rimini = mi divertirò a Rimini
- (*to suffer*)
  to have [flu | a headache | a toothache] = avere [l'influenza | il mal di testa | il mal di denti]
- (*to get something done*)
  to have the house painted = far dipingere la casa
- **to have a baby** = avere un bambino
2 *auxiliary verb*
  ! *For a detailed note on the use of* **have** *as an auxiliary verb, see the boxed note on* **have**. *All verbs which do not take* **avere** *as an auxiliary verb are marked* (**!** + **essere**) *in this dictionary.*
  you've seen her, haven't you? = l'hai vista, no?
  he hasn't called, has he? = non ha mica telefonato?
  'I've no money'—'yes you have!' = 'non ho soldi'—'sì che ne hai'
3 **to have to** = dovere
  I have to [study | pay | go home] = devo [studiare | pagare | andare a casa]

hay *noun*
  hay = il fieno

hay fever *noun*
  hay fever = il raffreddore da fieno

he *pronoun*
  he = lui
  ! *Note that the subject pronoun is usually omitted in Italian. It is used for emphasis, to express a contrast, or when it is necessary to avoid ambiguity.*
  he's coming next week = arriva la settimana prossima
  he does all the work here = qui fa tutto lui ····▶

have

As an ordinary verb

When **have** or **have got** is used as an ordinary verb meaning 'possess', it can generally be translated by **avere**:

I *have* a brother	= **ho** un fratello
do you have a ticket?	= **hai** un biglietto?

For examples and special problems see the entry **have**.

As an auxiliary verb

When **have** is used in English with a past participle, the perfect tense, formed with **avere** or **essere**, is used in Italian. In this dictionary verbs which require **essere** are marked (**!** + *essere*). Note that when **essere** is used as an auxiliary, the past participle must agree with the subject:

I*'ve* found my glasses	= **ho** trovato gli occhiali
has she hurt herself?	= si **è** fatta male?
we*'ve* arrived	= **siamo** arrivati

to have to

To **have** to meaning 'must' is usually translated by **dovere**:

I *have to* get up early	= **devo** alzarmi presto
I *don't have to* work today	= oggi **non devo** lavorare

but other translations are possible:

I *have to* see it first	= bisogna che lo veda prima
you *don't have to* help me	= non c'è bisogno che tu mi aiuti
you *don't have to* shout	= non c'è bisogno che tu gridi
it *has to* be done immediately	= va fatto subito

I work in London but he doesn't = io lavoro a Londra ma lui no
there he is! = eccolo!

head
1 *noun*
• (*the part of the body, the mind*) ▶ **137**
the head = la testa
• (*the person in charge*)
the head = il responsabile/la responsabile
a head of state = un capo di stato
2 *verb*
• (*to be in charge of*)
to head a team = essere a capo di una squadra
• (*in soccer*)
to head the ball = colpire di testa la palla
head for = dirigersi verso (**!** + *essere*)

headache *noun* ▶ **193**
to have a headache = avere mal di testa

headlamp, headlight *noun*
a headlamp = un faro

headline *noun*
a headline = un titolo
the news headlines = il sommario del telegiornale

headquarters *noun*
the headquarters
(*of a company*) = la sede centrale
(*of an army*) = il quartier generale

headteacher *noun* ▶ **281**
the headteacher
(*of a junior school*) = il direttore/la direttrice
(*of a high school*) = il preside/la preside

health *noun*
health = la salute

healthy *adjective*
• (*in good health*) = in buona salute
• (*good for the health*) = salutare

hear *verb*
• to hear = sentire
he can't hear anything = non sente niente
I heard someone coming in = ho sentito entrare qualcuno
• (*to learn, to discover*) = sapere
have you heard the news? = hai saputo?
I've heard about that school = ho sentito parlare di quella scuola
we've heard a lot about you = abbiamo sentito molto parlare di te
hear from = avere notizie di
have you heard from Cathy? = hai notizie di Cathy?
hear of = sentire parlare di
I've never heard of it = non ne ho mai sentito parlare

heart *noun*
• (*part of the body*) ▶ **137**
the heart = il cuore   ····▶

- (*the centre*)
  right in the heart of London = proprio nel cuore di Londra
- **by heart** = a memoria

heart attack *noun* ▶ **193**
  a heart attack = un infarto

heat
1 *verb*
  = riscaldare
2 *noun*
- **the heat** = il calore
- (*warm weather*)
  I can't stand the heat = non sopporto il caldo
- (*on a cooker*)
  to cook at a low heat = cuocere a fuoco basso
- (*in a sporting contest*)
  a heat = una prova eliminatoria
heat up = riscaldare

heater *noun*
  a heater = una stufa

heating *noun*
  heating = il riscaldamento

heatwave *noun*
  a heatwave = un'ondata di caldo

heaven *noun*
  heaven = il paradiso

heavy *adjective*
- (*in weight*) ▶ **202** = pesante
- (*in quantity, intensity*)
  the traffic is very heavy = il traffico è molto intenso
  to be a heavy smoker = fumare molto

hedge *noun*
  a hedge = una siepe

heel *noun* ▶ **137**
- (*part of the foot*)
  the heel = il tallone
- (*part of a shoe*)
  a heel = un tacco

height *noun* ▶ **202**
  height = l'altezza
  to be afraid of heights = soffrire di vertigini

helicopter *noun*
  a helicopter = un elicottero

hell *noun*
  hell = l'inferno

hello *exclamation*
  hello! (*when greeting someone*) = ciao!
  (*on the phone*) = pronto!

helmet *noun*
  a helmet = un casco

help
1 *verb*
- **to help** = aiutare
  to help someone to [**walk** | **do the housework** | **escape**] = aiutare qualcuno a [camminare | fare le faccende | fuggire]

- (*at a meal*)
  to help oneself = servirsi (**!** + *essere*)
  help yourself! = serviti!
- **I can't help thinking about it** = non riesco a non pensarci
2 *exclamation*
  help! = aiuto!
3 *noun*
  help = l'aiuto
  to ask someone for help = chiedere aiuto a qualcuno
  to shout for help = gridare aiuto
help out = aiutare

helpful *adjective*
- (*ready to help*) = disponibile
- (*useful*) = utile

helping *noun*
  a helping = una porzione

helpless *adjective*
- (*having no power*) = impotente
- (*because of weakness, ill health*) = indifeso/indifesa

hen *noun*
  a hen = una gallina

her
1 *pronoun*
- = la

  > **!** Note that *la* combines with the infinitive, the gerund, and the imperative. **Lei** is used for emphasis.

  I know her = la conosco
  he's seen her = l'ha vista
  help her! = aiutala!
  don't help her! = non aiutarla!
  don't help HER! = non aiutare lei!
- (*to her*) = le

  > **!** Note that *le* combines with the infinitive, the gerund, and the imperative. **A lei** is used for emphasis. *Le* also combines with **lo/la, li/le,** and **ne** to form **glielo/gliela, glieli/gliele,** and **gliene.**

  I gave her the book = le ho dato il libro
  write to her! = scrivile!
  don't show it to her! = non farglielo vedere!
  don't show it to HER! = non farlo vedere a lei!
- (*after a preposition*) = lei
  he did it for her = l'ha fatto per lei
  stand in front of her = mettiti davanti a lei
- **it's her** = è lei
2 *determiner*
  her = il suo/la sua (+ *singular*)
  = i suoi/le sue (+ *plural*)

  > **!** Note that the definite article *il/la*, etc is generally used except when talking about a close family member.

····▶

I hate her dog = non sopporto il suo cane
did you see all her CDs? = hai visto tutti
i suoi CD?
her brother/her sister = suo fratello/sua
sorella
what do you think of her house? = cosa
ne pensi di casa sua?
she licked her plate = ha leccato il piatto
she broke her leg = si è rotta la gamba

> ! *Note that, when talking about parts of
> the body,* **suo/sua** *is not used. See the
> usage note on* **The human body**
> ▶ **137** *for further examples.*

herd *noun*
a herd = una mandria

here *adverb*
- (*when talking about location*) = qui, qua
is it far from here? = è lontano da qui?
tell him I'm not here = digli che non ci
sono
I'm up here = sono quassù
- (*when drawing attention*)
here's my telephone number = ecco il
mio numero di telefono
here they are = eccoli
here comes the train = ecco il treno
- **here you are** = tieni

hers *pronoun*
hers = il suo/la sua (*singular*)
= i suoi/le sue (*plural*)

> ! *Note that* **il/la**, *etc is used when
> comparing things belonging to different
> people, but not when saying who
> something belongs to.*

my jacket is red but hers is green = la
mia giacca è rossa ma la sua è verde
my parents are younger than hers = i
miei genitori sono più giovani dei suoi
the green pen is hers = la penna verde è
sua
a friend of hers = un suo amico

herself *pronoun*
- (*when used as a reflexive pronoun*) = si

> ! *Note that* **si** *combines with the
> infinitive and the gerund.* **Si** *beomes* **se**
> *before* **lo/la, li/le,** *and* **ne.**

she's cut herself with a knife = si è
tagliata con un coltello
she wants to enjoy herself = vuole
divertirsi
- (*when used for emphasis*)
she said it herself = l'ha detto lei stessa
she did it all by herself = l'ha fatto tutto
da sé

hesitate *verb*
= esitare

hi *exclamation*
hi! = ciao!

hiccups *noun*
to have hiccups = avere il singhiozzo

hidden *adjective*
= nascosto/nascosta

hide *verb*
- (*to avoid showing*) = nascondere
- (*to avoid being seen*) = nascondersi (**!** +
essere)

hi-fi *noun*
a hi-fi = uno stereo

high *adjective* ▶ **202**
- = alto/alta
prices are high = i prezzi sono alti
at high speed = ad alta velocità
- (*describing a voice, a note*) = acuto/acuta

high-rise block *noun*
a high-rise block = un palazzone

high school *noun*
a high school = un liceo

hijack *verb*
= dirottare

hiking *noun* ▶ **178**
hiking = l'escursionismo
to go hiking = fare dell'escursionismo

hill *noun*
a hill = una collina
(*a rise in the road*) = un pendio

him *pronoun*
- = lo

> ! *Note that* **lo** *combines with the
> infinitive, the gerund, and the
> imperative.* **Lui** *is used for emphasis.*

I know him = lo conosco
she's seen him = l'ha visto
help him! = aiutalo!
don't help him! = non aiutarlo!
don't help HIM! = non aiutare lui!
- (*to him*) = gli

> ! *Note that* **gli** *combines with the
> infinitive, the gerund, and the
> imperative.* **A lui** *is used for emphasis.*
> **Gli** *also combines with* **lo/la, li/le,** *and*
> **ne** *to form* **glielo/gliela, glieli/gliele,** *and*
> **gliene.**

I gave him the book = gli ho dato il libro
write to him! = scrivigli!
don't show it to him! = non farglielo
vedere!
don't show it to HIM! = non farlo vedere a
lui!
- (*after a preposition*) = lui
she did it for him = l'ha fatto per lui
stand in front of him = mettiti davanti a
lui
- **it's him** = è lui

himself *pronoun*
- (*when used as a reflexive pronoun*) = si

> ! *Note that* **si** *combines with the infinitive and the gerund.* **Si** *beomes* **se** *before* **lo/la, li/le.** *and* **ne.**

  he's cut himself with a knife = si è tagliato con un coltello
  he wants to enjoy himself = vuole divertirsi
- (*when used for emphasis*)
  he said it himself = l'ha detto lui stesso
  he did it all by himself = l'ha fatto tutto da sé

hip *noun* ▶ **137 |**
  the hip = l'anca

hire *verb*
- (*to employ*) = assumere
- (*British English*) (*to rent*) = noleggiare
  to hire a car = noleggiare una macchina
- (*to lend for a fee*) = noleggiare
  they hire skates = noleggiano i pattini

his
1 *determiner*
  his = il suo/la sua (+ *singular*)
  = i suoi/le sue (+ *plural*)

> ! *Note that the definite article* **il/la**, *etc is generally used except when talking about a close family member.*

  I hate his dog = non sopporto il suo cane
  did you see all his CDs? = hai visto tutti i suoi CD?
  his brother/his sister = suo fratello/sua sorella
  what do you think of his house? = cosa pensi di casa sua?
  he licked his plate = ha leccato il piatto
  he broke his arm = si è rotto il braccio

> ! *Note that, when talking about parts of the body,* **il suo, la sua, i suoi,** *and* **le sue** *are not used. See the usage note on* **The human body** ▶ **137 |** *for further examples.*

2 *pronoun*
  his = il suo/la sua (*singular*)
  = i suoi/le sue (*plural*)

> ! *Note that* **il/la**, *etc is used when comparing things belonging to different people, but not when saying who something belongs to.*

  my shirt is white but his is yellow = la mia camicia è bianca ma la sua è gialla
  my brother is taller than his = mio fratello è più alto del suo
  the blue pen is his = la penna blu è sua
  a friend of his = un suo amico

history *noun*
  history = la storia

hit
1 *verb*
- (*to strike*) = colpire
  to hit someone on the head = colpire qualcuno in testa

to hit one's head on a chair = battere la testa sulla sedia
- (*to crash into*)
  to hit a wall = urtare un muro
  to hit a pedestrian = investire un pedone
2 *noun*
  a hit = un successo

hitchhike *verb*
  = fare l'autostop

hitchhiker *noun*
  a hitchhiker = un autostoppista/un'autostoppista

hoarse *adjective*
  = rauco/rauca

hobby *noun*
  a hobby = un hobby

hockey *noun* ▶ **178 |**
  field hockey = l'hockey
  ice hockey = l'hockey sul ghiaccio

> ! *Note that* **hockey** *is masculine.*

hold
1 *verb*
- to hold = tenere
- (*to arrange*)
  to hold a competition = organizzare un concorso
- (*other uses*)
  to hold the world record = detenere il record mondiale
  to hold someone responsible = ritenere qualcuno responsabile
  to hold, to hold the line = restare in linea
  (! + *essere*)
2 *noun*
- to get hold of the ball = prendere la palla
- to get hold of someone (*to find*) = trovare qualcuno
  (*by phone*) = rintracciare qualcuno
hold on
- (*to wait*) = aspettare
- hold on tight! = tieniti forte!
hold on to = aggrapparsi a (! + *essere*)
hold up
- (*to raise*) = alzare
  to hold up one's hand = alzare la mano
- (*to delay*)
  to hold someone up = trattenere qualcuno
  to hold up the traffic = rallentare il traffico

hole *noun*
  a hole = un buco
  (*in the ground*) = una buca

holiday *noun*
- (*British English*) (*a vacation*)
  a holiday = una vacanza
  the holidays = le vacanze
  to go on holiday = andare in vacanza (! + *essere*)
- (*a national or religious festival*)
  a (public) holiday = un giorno festivo ····➤

- (*British English*) (*time taken off work*)
  a day's holiday = un giorno di ferie
  to take two weeks' holiday = prendere due settimane di ferie

Holland *noun* ▶ 151 |
  Holland = l'Olanda

home
1 *noun*
- **a home** = una casa
  he left home = è andato via di casa
- (*for elderly, ill or disabled people*)
  a home for handicapped children = un istituto per bambini handicappati
  an old people's home = una casa di riposo
2 *adverb*
  to go home = andare a casa (**!** + *essere*)
  on my way home = tornando a casa
  to be home (*from school, work*) = essere rincasato/rincasata
  I can take you home = posso accompagnarti a casa
3 **at home**
- (*in one's house*) = a casa
  he lives at home = abita con i genitori
- **to feel at home** = sentirsi a casa (**!** + *essere*)
- (*when talking about a sports team*) = in casa

homeless *adjective*
  to be homeless = essere senzatetto
  homeless people = i senzatetto

homesick *adjective*
  to be homesick = avere nostalgia di casa

homework *noun*
  homework = i compiti per casa

honest *adjective*
  = onesto/onesta
  to be honest, I'd rather stay here = francamente, preferisco restare

honestly *adverb*
  = onestamente

honey *noun*
  honey = il miele

honeymoon *noun*
  a honeymoon = un viaggio di nozze

hood *noun*
- (*to cover the head*)
  a hood = un cappuccio
- (*US English*) (*of a car*)
  the hood = il cofano

hook *noun*
- (*for hanging clothes, pictures*)
  a hook = un gancio
- (*for fishing*)
  a hook = un amo

hooligan *noun*
  a hooligan = un/una teppista
  a football hooligan = un hooligan

hoover *verb* (*British English*)
  to hoover the house = passare l'aspirapolvere in casa

hope
1 *verb*
  = sperare
  I hope you don't mind = spero che non ti dispiaccia

  > **!** Note that, when talking about the future, **sperare che** is followed by the subjunctive.

  we hope to meet lots of people = speriamo di conoscere tanta gente
  I hope so = lo spero
2 *noun*
  hope = la speranza
  to give up hope = abbandonare le speranze

hopeless *adjective*
- (*without hope of success*) = disperato/disperata
- (*without any ability*) = negato/negata
  to be hopeless at cooking = essere negato per cucinare

horn *noun*
- (*on a car, a bus*)
  a horn = un clacson
  to blow the horn = suonare il clacson
- (*of an animal*)
  a horn = un corno
  a bull's horns = le corna di un toro
- (*an instrument*)
  a horn = un corno

horoscope *noun*
  the horoscope = l'oroscopo

horrible *adjective*
  = orrendo/orrenda

horror film *noun*
  a horror film = un film dell'orrore

horse *noun*
  a horse = un cavallo

horseracing *noun* ▶ 178 |
  horseracing = le corse dei cavalli

horseriding *noun* ▶ 178 |
  horseriding = l'equitazione (*feminine*)

hospital *noun*
  a hospital = un ospedale
  he's still in hospital = è ancora in ospedale
  to be taken to hospital = essere ricoverato/ricoverata
  to go into hospital = ricoverarsi (**!** + *essere*)

host *noun*
  a host = un ospite/un'ospite

hostage *noun*
  a hostage = un ostaggio

hostess *noun*
  a hostess = un'ospite

hot *adjective*
- (*very warm*) = caldo/calda
  to be hot, to feel hot = aver caldo
  I'm very hot = ho molto caldo
  it's too hot in the office = è troppo caldo in ufficio
- (*spicy*) = piccante

hotel *noun*
  a hotel = un albergo

hour *noun* ▶ **146**|, ▶ **267**|
  an hour = un'ora
  I earn eight pounds an hour = guadagno otto sterline all'ora

house *noun*
  a house = una casa
  let's go to Jill's house = andiamo a casa di Jill
  the bike is at my house = la bicicletta è a casa mia

housewife *noun* ▶ **281**|
  a housewife = una casalinga

housework *noun*
  to do the housework = fare le faccende

housing estate (*British English*), **housing development** (*US English*) *noun*
  a housing estate = una zona residenziale

how *adverb*
- (*in what way*) = come
  how did you find us? = come hai fatto a trovarci?
  how do you get there? = come ci si arriva?
  I know how [to swim | to ride a horse | to cook lasagna] = io so [nuotare | andare a cavallo | fare le lasagne]
- (*in polite questions*)
  how are you? = come stai?
  how was your holiday? = com'è andata la vacanza?
- (*in questions requiring specific information*)
  how tall are you? = quanto sei alto?
  how old is he? = quanti anni ha?
  how long will it take? = quanto ci vorrà?
- (*when making a suggestion*)
  how would you like to eat out? = che ne dici di andare a mangiare fuori?

however *adverb*
  = comunque

how many ▶ **233**|
1 *pronoun*
  = quanti/quante
  how many do you want? = quanti ne vuoi?
  how many of you are there? = quanti siete?
2 *determiner*
  = quanti/quante
  how many children are going on the trip? = quanti ragazzi andranno in gita?

how much ▶ **233**|
1 *pronoun*
  = quanto/quanta
  how much does it come to? = quanto viene?
  how much is the jacket? = quanto costa la giacca?
2 *determiner*
  = quanto/quanta
  how much time do you have left? = quanto tempo ti è rimasto?

huge *adjective*
  = enorme

human being *noun*
  a human being = un essere umano

humour (*British English*), **humor** (*US English*) *noun*
  humour = l'umorismo
  to have a sense of humour = avere il senso dell'umorismo

hundred *number* ▶ **122**|
  one hundred, a hundred = cento
  three hundred = trecento
  five hundred and fifty euros = cinquecentocinquanta euro
  about a hundred people = un centinaio di persone

Hungary *noun* ▶ **151**|
  Hungary = l'Ungheria

hungry *adjective*
  to be hungry = avere fame
  I'm very hungry = ho molta fame

hunt *verb* ▶ **178**|
  = cacciare
  to go hunting = andare a caccia (**!** + *essere*)

hurrah, **hurray** *exclamation*
  hurrah! = urrà!

hurry
1 *verb*
- = sbrigarsi (**!** + *essere*)
  I hurried home = sono andato a casa di corsa
- **to hurry someone** = mettere fretta a qualcuno
2 *noun*
  to be in a hurry = avere fretta
  there's no hurry = non c'è fretta
hurry up = sbrigarsi (**!** + *essere*)

hurt *verb*
- (*to injure*)
  to hurt oneself = farsi male (**!** + *essere*)
  to hurt one's leg = farsi male alla gamba
- (*to be painful*)
  my throat hurts = mi fa male la gola
  that hurts = così fa male
- (*to upset*) = ferire
  to hurt someone's feelings = ferire qualcuno

husband *noun*
  a husband = un marito

H

I i

I *pronoun*
I = io

> **!** *Note that the subject pronoun is usually omitted in Italian. It is used for emphasis, to express a contrast, or when it is necessary to avoid ambiguity.*

I'm coming next week = arrivo la settimana prossima
I do all the work here = qui faccio tutto io
he works in London but I don't = lui lavora a Londra ma io no
here I am! = eccomi!

ice *noun*
ice = il ghiaccio

ice cream *noun*
an ice cream = un gelato

ice rink *noun*
an ice rink = una pista di pattinaggio sul ghiaccio

ice-skating *noun* ▶ **178**
ice-skating = il pattinaggio sul ghiaccio

icing *noun*
icing = la glassa

idea *noun*
an idea = un'idea
what a good idea! = buona idea!

identity card *noun*
an identity card = la carta d'identità

idiot *noun*
an idiot = un idiota/un'idiota

if *conjunction*
= se
if you like = se vuoi
if it rains, we won't go = se piove, non andiamo
I wonder if they'll come = chissà se verranno

ignore *verb*
= ignorare

ill *adjective*
= malato/malata

illegal *adjective*
= illegale

illness *noun*
an illness = una malattia

imagination *noun*
imagination = l'immaginazione (*feminine*)

imagine *verb*
= immaginare

imitate *verb*
= imitare

immediately *adverb*
= subito

impatient *adjective*
= impaziente

import *verb*
= importare

important *adjective*
= importante
it is important to eat well = è importante mangiare bene

impossible *adjective*
= impossibile
it's impossible to argue with him = è impossibile discutere con lui

impress *verb*
= colpire

impression *noun*
an impression = un'impressione
to make a good impression = fare una buona impressione

improve *verb*
• (*to make better*) = migliorare (**!** + *avere*)
I want to improve my Italian = voglio migliorare il mio italiano
• (*to get better*) = migliorare (**!** + *essere*)

improvement *noun*
an improvement = un miglioramento

in

> **!** *Often in occurs in combinations with verbs, for example: drop in, fit in, move in , etc. To find the correct translations for this type of verb, look up the separate dictionary entries at drop, fit, move, etc.*

1 *preposition*
• (*inside*) = in
in the = nel/nella (+ *singular*)
= nei/nelle (+ *plural*)

> **!** *Before masculine nouns beginning with z, ps, gn, or s + another consonant, nello is used in the singular and negli in the plural. Before masculine and feminine singular nouns beginning with a vowel, nell' is used.*

there's a letter in the envelope = c'è una lettera nella busta
the woman in the photograph = la donna nella foto
in the house = in casa
there's a letter in it = c'è dentro una lettera
• (*when talking about countries or cities*)
to live in Ireland = abitare in Irlanda
to live in Paris = abitare a Parigi
• (*dressed in*) = con
the woman in a hat = la donna col cappello

····▶

Illnesses, aches, and pains

Where does it hurt?

where does it hurt?	= dove fa male?
my leg hurts	= **mi** fa male **la** gamba

Note that Italian uses the definite article where English uses a possessive adjective:

he has a pain in his leg	= ha un dolore alla gamba

Accidents

she broke her leg	= **si** è rotta **la** gamba
I sprained my ankle	= **mi** sono slogato **la** caviglia

Being ill

Italian mostly uses the definite article with the name of an illness:

to have chickenpox	= avere **la** varicella

but:

to have cancer	= avere **un** cancro

For small complaints, use **avere mal di**:

to have a headache	= avere mal di testa
to have a sore throat	= avere mal di gola

---

to be dressed in black = essere vestito/vestita in nero
• (*showing the way in which something is done*)
written in Italian = scritto in italiano
we paid in cash = abbiamo pagato in contanti
they were sitting in a circle = erano seduti in cerchio
in ink = a penna
• (*during*)
in October = in ottobre
in the night = di notte
in the morning = di mattina
• (*within*) = fra, tra
I'll be ready in ten minutes = sarò pronto tra dieci minuti
she'll be back in half an hour = sarà di ritorno tra mezz'ora
• (*other uses*)
I learned German in school = ho studiato il tedesco a scuola
in the countryside = in campagna
to stay in the rain = stare sotto la pioggia
I read it in the newspaper = l'ho letto sul giornale
she's in her twenties = ha tra venti e trent'anni
one in ten = uno su dieci
to cut an apple in two = tagliare una mela a metà
2 *adverb*
(*at home, available*)
tell her I'm not in = dille che non ci sono

inch *noun* ▶ 202|
an inch = un pollice
| **!** *Note that an inch = 2.54 cm.* |

include *verb*
= comprendere
service is included in the bill = il servizio è compreso nel conto

including *preposition*
= compreso/compresa
they were all invited, including the children = sono stati invitati tutti, compresi i bambini

income *noun*
an income = un reddito

income tax *noun*
income tax = l'imposta sul reddito

inconvenient *adjective*
it's an inconvenient place to meet = è un posto scomodo per incontrarci
an inconvenient time = un momento inopportuno

increase
1 *verb*
= aumentare (**!** + *essere*)
to increase in value = aumentare di valore
to increase by 10% = aumentare del 10%
2 *noun*
an increase = un aumento

incredible *adjective*
= incredibile

independent *adjective*
= indipendente

India *noun* ▶ 151|
= l'India

Indian ▶ 199 |
1 *adjective*
  = indiano/indiana
2 *noun*
  the Indians = gli indiani

indicate *verb*
  = indicare

indigestion *noun* ▶ 193 |
  to have indigestion = avere problemi di
    digestione

individual
1 *adjective*
  = individuale
2 *noun*
  an individual = un individuo

indoor *adjective*
  = al coperto
  an indoor swimming pool = una piscina
    coperta

indoors *adverb*
  = in casa

industry *noun*
  industry = l'industria

inevitable *adjective*
  = inevitabile

infant school *noun* (*British English*)
  an infant school = una scuola elementare

infection *noun*
  an infection = un'infezione

influence
1 *noun*
  an influence = un'influenza
2 *verb*
  • = influenzare
  to influence someone = influenzare
    qualcuno

inform *verb*
  to inform the police of an accident
    = informare la polizia di un incidente
  to keep someone informed = tenere
    informato qualcuno

informal *adjective*
  = informale

information *noun*
  a piece of information = un'informazione
  the information is correct = le
    informazioni sono giuste

information technology *noun*
  information technology = l'informatica

ingredient *noun*
  an ingredient = un ingrediente

inhabitant *noun*
  an inhabitant = un abitante/un'abitante

injection *noun*
  an injection = una puntura
  to give someone an injection = fare una
    puntura a qualcuno

injured *adjective*
  = ferito/ferita

injury *noun*
  an injury = una ferita

ink *noun*
  ink = l'inchiostro

innocent *adjective*
  = innocente

insect *noun*
  an insect = un insetto

inside
1 *preposition*
  = dentro
  inside the house = dentro la casa
2 *adverb*
  = dentro
  he's inside = è dentro
  I looked inside = ho guardato dentro
  let's bring the chairs inside = portiamo
    dentro le sedie
3 *noun*
  the inside = l'interno
4 *adjective*
  = interno/interna
5 inside out = alla rovescia
  to put one's shirt on inside out = mettersi
    la camicia alla rovescia (**!** + *essere*)

inspect *verb*
  • (*if it's an official*) = ispezionare
  • (*if it's a conductor*) = controllare

inspector *noun*
  • (*of a school*)
    an inspector = un ispettore/un'ispettrice
  • (*on a bus, a train*)
    an inspector = un controllore
  • (*in the police*)
    a police inspector = un
      ispettore/un'ispettrice di polizia

instantly *adverb*
  = subito

instead
1 instead of
  • (*rather than*) = invece di
    instead of working he's watching TV
      = invece di lavorare sta guardando la TV
  • (*in place of*) = al posto di
    use oil instead of butter = usa l'olio al
      posto del burro
2 *adverb*
  I don't feel like going to the cinema—let's
    stay at home instead = non ho voglia
    di andare al cinema—restiamo a casa

instruction *noun*
  an instruction = un'istruzione
  the instructions for use = le istruzioni per
    l'uso

instrument *noun*
  an instrument = uno strumento
  to play an instrument = suonare uno
    strumento

insult *verb*
  = insultare

insurance *noun*
insurance = l'assicurazione (*feminine*)

insure *verb*
= assicurare

intelligent *adjective*
= intelligente

intend *verb*
he intends [to leave | to learn Spanish] = ha intenzione di [andarsene | imparare lo spagnolo]

intense *adjective*
= intenso/intensa

interest
1 *noun*
• (*enthusiasm*)
interest = l'interesse (*masculine*)
to have an interest in music = avere interesse per la musica
• (*financial*)
interest = gli interessi
2 *verb*
= interessare

interested *adjective*
= interessato/interessata
to be interested [in politics | in sport | in painting] = interessarsi di [politica | sport | pittura] (**!** + *essere*)
are you interested? = ti interessa?

interesting *adjective*
= interessante

interfere *verb*
• (*to get involved in*)
to interfere in someone's business = intromettersi negli affari di qualcuno (**!** + *essere*)
• (*to have a bad effect on*)
it's going to interfere with his work = interferirà con il suo lavoro

international *adjective*
= internazionale

Internet *noun*
the Internet = l'Internet

interpreter *noun* ▶ 281 |
an interpreter = un interprete/un'interprete

interrupt *verb*
= interrompere

interval *noun*
an interval = un intervallo
at regular intervals = a intervalli regolari

interview
1 *noun*
an interview (*for a job*) = un colloquio di lavoro
(*with a journalist*) = un'intervista
2 *verb*
to interview someone (*if it's an employer*) = fare un colloquio di lavoro a qualcuno
(*if it's a journalist*) = fare un'intervista a qualcuno
(*if it's the police*) = interrogare qualcuno

into *preposition*
(*when talking about a location*) = in
let's go into the garden = andiamo in giardino
she got into bed = è andata a letto
to translate a letter into Italian = tradurre una lettera in italiano

introduce *verb*
• (*to bring in*) = introdurre
• (*when people meet*) = presentare
he introduced me to Peter = mi ha presentato a Peter
• (*on radio or television*) = presentare
to introduce a programme = presentare un programma

invade *verb*
= invadere

invent *verb*
= inventare

invention *noun*
an invention = un'invenzione

investigate *verb*
to investigate a crime = indagare su un crimine

investigation *noun*
an investigation = un'indagine

invisible *adjective*
= invisibile

invitation *noun*
an invitation = un invito

invite *verb*
= invitare
to invite someone to a party = invitare qualcuno a una festa

involved *adjective*
to be involved in an accident = essere coinvolto/coinvolta in un incidente

Ireland *noun* ▶ 151 |
Ireland = l'Irlanda

Irish ▶ 199 |
1 *adjective*
= irlandese
2 *noun*
the Irish = gli irlandesi

iron
1 *noun*
• iron = il ferro
• an iron = un ferro da stiro
2 *verb*
= stirare

island *noun*
an island = un'isola

it *pronoun*
• (*when it's the subject*)   ····▶

! Note that **it** *is not usually translated when it is the subject of the sentence.*

'where is it?'—'it's here' = 'dov'è?'—'è qui'
'who is it?'—'it's me' = 'chi è?'—'sono io'
it's a nice house = è una bella casa
it is [**difficult** | **easy** | **complicated**] = è [difficile | semplice | complicato]
it doesn't matter = non importa
it's [**cold** | **warm** | **nice**] = fa [freddo | caldo | bello]
• (*when it's the object*) = lo/la

! Note that **lo/la** *combines with the infinitive, the gerund, and the imperative.*

I can see it = lo/la vedo
she's seen it = l'ha visto/l'ha vista
do it! = fallo!
don't do it! = non farlo!
• (*to it*) = gli/le

! Note that **gli** *and* **le** *combine with the infinitive, the gerund, and the imperative.* **Gli** *and* **le** *also combine with* **lo/la, li/le,** *and* **ne** *to form* **glielo/gliela, glieli/gliele,** *and* **gliene.**

I gave it the bone = gli/le ho dato l'osso
give the bone to it! = dagli/dalle l'osso!
don't give it to it! = non dargielo!
• (*after a preposition*)
I've heard about it = ne ho sentito parlare
did you go to it? = ci sei andato?
stand in front of it = mettiti davanti
the key was under it = la chiave era sotto

Italian ▶ 199 |
1 *adjective*
= italiano/italiana
2 *noun*
• (*the people*)
the Italians = gli italiani
• (*the language*)
Italian = l'italiano

Italy *noun* ▶ 151 |
Italy = l'Italia

its *determiner*
its = suo/sua (+ *singular*)
= suoi/sue (+ *plural*)
the cat is washing its paws with its tongue = il gatto si lava le zampe con la lingua

itself *pronoun*
• (*when used as a reflexive pronoun*) = si

! Note that **si** *combines with the infinitive and the gerund.*

the cat's hurt itself = il gatto si è fatto male
it can defend itself = può difendersi
• (*when used for emphasis*)
the house itself = la casa stessa
the heating comes on by itself = il riscaldamento si accende da sé

jacket *noun*
a jacket = una giacca
(*gathered at the waist*) = un giubbotto
(*heavy*) = un giaccone

jail *noun*
a jail = un carcere

jam *noun* (*British English*)
jam = la marmellata

Jamaica *noun* ▶ 151 |
Jamaica = la Giamaica

January *noun* ▶ 155 |
January = gennaio

Japan *noun* ▶ 151 |
Japan = il Giappone

Japanese ▶ 199 |
1 *adjective*
= giapponese
2 *noun*
• (*the people*)
the Japanese = i giapponesi
• (*the language*)
Japanese = il giapponese

jaw *noun* ▶ 137 |
the jaw = la mascella

jazz *noun*
jazz = il jazz

jealous *adjective*
= geloso/gelosa
he is jealous of her = è geloso di lei

jeans *noun*
jeans = i jeans

jelly *noun*
• (*US English*) (*jam*)
jelly = la marmellata
• (*British English*) (*a dessert*)
jelly = la gelatina

jet *noun*
a jet = un jet

jewellery (*British English*), jewelry (*US English*) *noun*
a piece of jewellery = un gioiello
jewellery = i gioielli (*plural*)

Jewish *adjective*
= ebreo/ebrea

jigsaw puzzle *noun*
a jigsaw puzzle = un puzzle

job *noun*
• (*work*)
a job = un lavoro
to look for a job = cercare lavoro
• (*a task*)
a job = un compito

jogging noun ▶ 178 |
to go jogging = fare footing

join verb
- (meet up with) = raggiungere
I'll join you in half an hour = ti raggiungo tra mezz'ora
- (become a member of)
to join a club = iscriversi a un club (**!** + essere)
to join a company = entrare in una ditta (**!** + essere)

join in
to join in a game = partecipare a un gioco

joke
1 noun
to tell a joke = raccontare una barzelletta
to play a joke on someone = fare uno scherzo a qualcuno
2 verb
= scherzare

journalist noun ▶ 281 |
a journalist = un/una giornalista

journey noun
a journey = un viaggio
to go on a journey = fare un viaggio

joy noun
joy = la gioia

judge
1 noun ▶ 281 |
a judge = un giudice
2 verb
= giudicare

judo noun ▶ 178 |
judo = il judo

jug noun
a jug = una caraffa

juice noun
juice = il succo
fruit juice = il succo di frutta

July noun ▶ 155 |
July = luglio

jump verb
- = saltare
to jump across the stream = attraversare il ruscello con un salto
to jump out of the window = buttarsi dalla finestra (**!** + essere)
- to jump the queue (British English) = passare avanti (**!** + essere)

jumper noun (British English)
a jumper = un maglione

June noun ▶ 155 |
June = giugno

junior high school noun (US English)
a junior high school ≈ una scuola media

junior school noun (British English)
a junior school = una scuola elementare

jury noun
the jury = la giuria

just¹ adverb
- (very recently)
I have just arrived = sono appena arrivato
- (at this or that very moment)
I was just about to phone you = stavo giusto per telefonarti
I arrived just as he was leaving = sono arrivato proprio mentre stava uscendo
- (only) = solo
just two days ago = solo due giorni fa
he's just a child = è solo un bambino
- (barely) = appena
I got there just in time = sono arrivato lì appena in tempo
she's just 18 = ha appena 18 anni
I arrived just before him = sono arrivato poco prima di lui
- (when comparing)
she is just as intelligent as he is = è intelligente quanto lui

just² adjective
= giusto/giusta

justice noun
justice = la giustizia

Kk

karate noun ▶ 178 |
karate = il karatè

keen adjective
a keen student = uno studente entusiasta
to be keen on swimming = amare il nuoto

keep verb
- = tenere
we keep the wine in the cellar = teniamo il vino in cantina
this sweater will keep you warm = questo maglione ti terrà caldo
to keep someone waiting = fare aspettare qualcuno
- (to delay) = trattenere
what kept you? = cosa ti ha trattenuto?
I won't keep you long = non ti tratterrò tanto
- (not to break, not to reveal)
to keep a promise = mantenere una promessa
to keep a secret = tenere un segreto
- (to continue)
to keep [walking | talking | running] = continuare a [camminare | parlare | correre]
to keep going = continuare
- to keep calm = mantenere la calma   ····▶

keep away = stare lontano (**!** + *essere*)
  keep away from the fire! = stai lontano
    dal fuoco!
keep back = trattenere
keep on
  to keep on [talking | walking | singing]
    = continuare a [parlare | camminare |
    cantare]
keep out
  keep out of the sun! = non stare al sole!
  to keep the rain out = proteggere dalla
    pioggia
keep up = tenersi al passo (**!** + *essere*)
  to keep up with the other pupils = tenersi
    al passo con gli altri studenti
kerb *noun* (*British English*)
  the kerb = il bordo del marciapiede
kettle *noun*
  a kettle = un bollitore
key *noun*
  a key = una chiave
kick *verb*
  to kick someone = dare un calcio a
    qualcuno
  he kicked the ball = ha dato un calcio
    alla palla
kick off = dare il calcio d'inizio
kick out
  to kick someone out = cacciare fuori
    qualcuno
kidnap *verb*
  = rapire
kill *verb*
  = uccidere
  to kill oneself = ammazzarsi (**!** + *essere*)
kilo *noun* ▶ **202**|
  a kilo = un chilo
kilometre (*British English*), **kilometer**
  (*US English*) *noun* ▶ **202**|
  a kilometre = un chilometro
kind
1 *noun*
  it's a kind of fish = è un tipo di pesce
  what kind of film is it? = che tipo di film
    è?
2 *adjective*
  = gentile
king *noun*
  a king = un re
kiss
1 *verb*
  to kiss someone = baciare qualcuno
  to kiss (each other) = baciarsi (**!** +
    essere)
2 *noun*
  a kiss = un bacio
kitchen *noun*
  a kitchen = una cucina
  in the kitchen = in cucina
kite *noun*
  a kite = un aquilone

kitten *noun*
  a kitten = un gattino
knee *noun* ▶ **137**|
  the knee = il ginocchio
  the knees = le ginocchia
kneel down *verb*
  = inginocchiarsi (**!** + *essere*)
knife *noun*
  a knife = un coltello
knit *verb*
  = lavorare a maglia
knock
1 *verb*
  to knock on the door = bussare alla porta
2 *noun*
  a knock = un colpo
knock down
  • (*in an accident*) = investire
  • (*to demolish*) = demolire
knock out
  = mettere qualcuno k.o.
knock over = far cadere
knot *noun*
  a knot = un nodo
know *verb*
  • (*when talking about facts, information*)
    = sapere
  I know why he phoned = so perché ha
    telefonato
  she knows how to swim = sa nuotare
  I don't know the Italian word for it = non
    so come si dice in italiano
  let me know = fammi sapere
  does he know about the party? = sa della
    festa?
  to know all about art = sa tutto sull'arte
  • (*when talking about people, places*)
    = conoscere
  do you know Paris? = conosci Parigi?
  to get to know someone = conoscere
    qualcuno
knowledge *noun*
  knowledge = la conoscenza

Ll

laboratory *noun*
  a laboratory = un laboratorio
lace *noun*
  • (*the material*)
    lace = il pizzo
  • (*for shoes*)
    a lace = un laccio
    to tie one's laces = allacciarsi le scarpe
    (**!** + *essere*)

Languages and nationalities

Languages

The names of languages in Italian are always masculine, and are written with a small letter. They are usually used with the definite article:

to learn Italian   = imparare l'italiano

but this is omitted when it is the name of an academic subject. It is also omitted after **in** and **di** and sometimes after **parlare**:

I studied Italian at university	= ho studiato italiano all'università
the film was in English	= il film era in inglese
an Italian lesson	= una lezione d'italiano
they speak German there	= là parlano tedesco
they were speaking Albanian	= parlavano in albanese

Nationalities

Adjectives and nouns relating to nationalities never have a capital letter in Italian:

an Italian student	= uno studente italiano/una studentessa italiana
a Czech	= un ceco/una ceca

The adjective and the noun are always the same:

a Scottish taxi-driver	= un tassista scozzese
a Scot	= uno/una scozzese

---

lack
1 *noun*
a lack [of food | of money | of interest] = una mancanza [di cibo | di soldi | di interesse]
2 *verb*
he lacks confidence = gli manca la fiducia in se stesso

ladder *noun*
a ladder = una scala

lady *noun*
a lady = una signora

lake *noun*
a lake = un lago

lamb *noun*
a lamb = un agnello

lamp *noun*
a lamp = una lampada

lampshade *noun*
a lampshade = un paralume

land
1 *noun*
• land = la terra
• (*property*)
a piece of land = un terreno
to own land = possedere dei terreni
2 *verb*
• (*to fall*) = cadere (**!** + *essere*)
• (*if it's a plane*) = atterrare (**!** + *essere*)
• (*if it's a passenger*) = sbarcare

landscape *noun*
a landscape = un paesaggio

language *noun*
• a language = una lingua
foreign languages = lingue straniere
• to use bad language = dire parolacce

language laboratory *noun*
a language laboratory = un laboratorio linguistico

large *adjective*
• (*big*) = grande
a large garden = un grande giardino
a large house = una casa grande
• a large number of people = molta gente
a large sum of money = una grossa somma
• (*bulky*) = grosso/grossa
a large parcel = un grosso pacco

last
1 *adjective*
• = ultimo/ultima
that's the last time I saw her = è stata l'ultima volta che l'ho vista
• (*that has just passed*)
last week = la settimana scorsa
2 *adverb*
• (*most recently*)
when I was last here = l'ultima volta che ero qui
• (*at the end*) = per ultimo
I'll do the dishes last (of all) = laverò i piatti per ultimi
• (*in final position*)
he came last in the race = è arrivato ultimo nella gara
3 *pronoun*
the last = l'ultimo/l'ultima
they were the last to arrive = sono arrivati per ultimi
the night before last = ieri l'altro notte
4 *verb*
= durare (**!** + *essere*)
the film lasts two hours = il film dura due ore

late
1 *adverb*
= tardi
it's getting late = si sta facendo tardi
2 *adjective*
= in ritardo
to be late for work = arrivare tardi al
lavoro
the train was two hours late = il treno
aveva due ore di ritardo
to make someone late = far ritardare
qualcuno

later *adverb*
= dopo
I'll call back later = richiamerò
see you later! = a più tardi!

latest
1 *adjective*
= ultimo/ultima
the latest news = le ultime notizie
2 **at the latest** = al più tardi

laugh
1 *verb*
= ridere
to make someone laugh = far ridere
qualcuno
to laugh at someone = ridere di qualcuno
2 *noun*
a laugh = una risata

laundry *noun*
the laundry = il bucato
to do the laundry = fare il bucato

law *noun*
the law = la legge
it's against the law = è illegale
a law = una legge
she studied law at university = ha fatto
legge all'università

lawn *noun*
a lawn = un prato

lawnmower *noun*
a lawnmower = un tagliaerba

lawyer *noun* ▶ 281
a lawyer = un avvocato

lay *verb*
• (*to put*) = mettere
lay some newspapers on the floor
= mettere dei giornali sul pavimento
• **to lay the table** = apparecchiare
• (*of a chicken*)
to lay an egg = fare un uovo
lay off = licenziare

lazy *adjective*
= pigro/pigra

lead¹ *verb*
• (*to guide*) = portare
• (*in a match*) = condurre
(*in a race*) = essere in testa
• **to lead a busy life** = fare una vita molto
attiva
• (*to have as a result*)

to lead to an accident = causare un
incidente

lead² *noun*
lead = il piombo

leader *noun*
a leader (*of a political party*) = un/una
leader
(*of a state*) = un capo di stato

leaf *noun*
a leaf = una foglia

leak *verb*
• (*if it's a container*) = perdere
the pipe leaks = il tubo perde
• (*if it's a boat*) = fare acqua

lean
1 *verb*
• (*to support oneself*)
to lean against the wall = appoggiarsi al
muro (**!** + *essere*)
• (*to put*)
to lean a bicycle against the wall
= appoggiare una bicicletta al muro
• **to lean out of the window** = sporgersi
dalla finestra (**!** + *essere*)
2 *adjective*
= magro/magra
lean back = piegarsi all'indietro (**!** +
essere)
lean forward = piegarsi in avanti (**!** +
essere)
lean on = appoggiarsi a (**!** + *essere*)

learn *verb*
= imparare
to learn how to drive = imparare a
guidare

leash *noun*
a leash = un guinzaglio

least
1 *determiner*
the least = meno
they have the least money = hanno meno
soldi di tutti
2 *adverb*
the least = meno
Claudio speaks the least = Claudio è
quello che parla di meno
the least expensive shop = il negozio
meno caro
the least difficult question = la domanda
meno difficile
4 **at least**
= almeno
he's at least thirty = ha almeno trent'anni
he's gone out—at least, I think so = è
uscito—almeno credo

leather *noun*
leather = la pelle

leave *verb*
• = lasciare
to leave school = lasciare la scuola   ····▶

she left her husband = ha lasciato il
marito
he didn't leave a message = non ha
lasciato un messaggio
• (to go away) = partire (**!** + essere)
he left the next day = è partito il giorno
dopo
• (to go out of) = uscire da (**!** + essere)
she left the room = è uscita dalla stanza
• (to remain)
there's nothing left = non è rimasto
niente
we've got ten minutes left = ci restano
dieci minuti
leave behind = dimenticare
he left his belongings behind = ha
dimenticato le sue cose
leave out
• (not to show or talk about) = tralasciare
• (to exclude) = escludere
to feel left out = sentirsi escluso/esclusa
(**!** + essere)
leave over
there was not much left over = non è
avanzato molto
there is some food left over = sono
rimasti degli avanzi

lecture noun
a lecture (to students) = una lezione
(to the public) = una conferenza

left
1 noun
the left = la sinistra
the first street on the left = la prima
strada a sinistra
2 adjective
= sinistro/sinistra
his left hand = la mano sinistra
3 adverb
= a sinistra
to turn left = girare a sinistra

leg noun
• (of a person) ▶ **137** |
the leg = la gamba
• (of animals)
the leg = la zampa
• (of meat)
a leg of lamb = un coscio d'agnello

legal adjective
= legale

leisure noun
leisure = il tempo libero

lemon noun
a lemon = un limone

lemonade noun
lemonade = la limonata

lend verb
= prestare
to lend someone money = prestare dei
soldi a qualcuno

length noun ▶ **202** |
• (in measurements)

the length = la lunghezza
• **the length** (of a film, an event) = la durata

less ▶ **233** |
1 determiner
= meno
less [money | food | time] = meno [soldi | cibo
| tempo]
I have less work than he does = ho meno
lavoro di lui
2 pronoun
= meno
to cost less = costare meno
he reads less than she does = legge
meno di lei
they have less than you = hanno meno
di te
3 adverb
= meno
we travel less in winter = viaggiamo
meno d'inverno
4 preposition
(minus) = meno
5 less and less = sempre meno
6 less than = meno di
in less than half an hour = in meno di
mezz'ora

lesson noun
a lesson = una lezione
a riding lesson = una lezione di
equitazione

let[1] verb
• (when making suggestions)
let's go home = andiamo a casa
• (to allow) = fare
to let someone in = far entrare qualcuno
he let me help him = si è fatto aiutare
she lets him do what he likes = gli fa fare
quel che vuole
he's letting his hair grow = si fa crescere i
capelli
let down = deludere
let go
• (to stop holding) = lasciare
let go of me! = lasciami!
• (to release) = rilasciare
let in
= far entrare
he let me in = mi ha fatto entrare
let out
• (to allow to go out) = far uscire
let me out! = fammi uscire!
• **to let out a scream** = cacciare un urlo
let through
to let someone through = far passare
qualcuno

let[2] verb (British English)
= affittare

letter noun
a letter = una lettera

letter box noun (British English)
the letter box (for mailing letters) = la
buca delle lettere　　　　　　　····▶

Length and weight measurements

Note that Italian has a comma where English has a decimal point:

  5.75   = 5,75 (*say* cinque virgola settantacinque)

Length

  how long is the rope?   = quanto è lunga la corda?
  it's five metres long   = è lunga cinque metri

Height

  how tall are you?   = quanto sei alto?
  he's six feet tall   = è alto un metro e ottanta

Distance

  how far is it from Rome to Arezzo?   = quanto dista Arezzo da Roma?
  we live fifty kilometres from Birmingham = abitiamo a cinquanta chilometri da Birmingham

Width

  how wide is the river?   = quanto è largo il fiume?
  it's seven metres wide   = è largo sette metri

Depth

  how deep is the lake?   = quanto è profondo il lago?
  it's four metres deep   = è profondo quattro metri

Weight

  How much does it weigh?   = quanto pesa?
  it weighs four kilos   = pesa quattro chili

(*for delivering letters*) = la cassetta delle lettere

lettuce *noun*
  a lettuce = una lattuga

level
1 *noun*
  a level = un livello
2 *adjective*
  = piano/piana

library *noun*
  a library = una biblioteca

licence (*British English*), **license** (*US English*) *noun*
  a licence = un permesso

license plate *noun* (*US English*)
  a license plate = una targa

lick *verb*
  = leccare

lid *noun*
  a lid = un coperchio

lie
1 *verb*
• (*on the ground, on a bed*) = sdraiarsi (**!** + *essere*)
  he lay down on the sofa = si è sdraiato sul divano

he was lying on the sofa = era sdraiato sul divano
• (*to be situated*) = trovarsi (**!** + *essere*)
• (*not to tell the truth*) = mentire
2 *noun*
  a lie = una bugia
  to tell a lie = dire una bugia
lie around = essere in giro
  he always leaves his keys lying around = lascia sempre le chiavi in giro
lie down = sdraiarsi (**!** + *essere*)

life *noun*
  life = la vita

lift
1 *verb*
  = alzare
  to lift one's arm = alzare un braccio
2 *noun*
• (*British English*) (*an elevator*)
  a lift = un ascensore
• (*in a car*)
  he gave me a lift to the station = mi ha dato un passaggio alla stazione
lift up = sollevare

light
1 *noun*
• (*from the sun, moon*)
  light = la luce
• (*in a room, on a machine*)   ····▶

a light = una luce
to switch on a light = accendere una luce
* (for traffic)
the lights = il semaforo
* (in a street)
a light = un lampione
* have you got a light? = hai da accendere?
2 adjective
* (not dark) ▶ **147** = chiaro/chiara
it's still light outside = è ancora giorno
fuori
a light green dress = un vestito verde
chiaro
* (not heavy) = leggero/leggera
3 verb
= accendere
he lit a cigarette = ha acceso una sigaretta

light bulb noun
a light bulb = una lampadina

lighter noun
a lighter = un accendino

lighthouse noun
a lighthouse = un faro

lightning noun
a flash of lightning = un fulmine

like¹ preposition
= come
people like you = gente come te
what's it like? = com'è?

like² verb
* (when expressing an interest)
I like [swimming | reading | dancing] = mi
piace [nuotare | leggere | ballare]
I like it! = mi piace!
do you like America? = ti piace
l'America?
* (when expressing a wish)
I'd like a coffee please = vorrei un caffè
per favore
I'd like to help you = vorrei aiutarti

! See the boxed note on **volere** for
more information and examples.

limit noun
a limit = un limite

line
1 noun
* a line = una linea
* (US English) (a queue)
a line = una fila
to stand in line = fare la fila
* (a row)
a line = una fila
* the line is bad = la linea è disturbata
2 verb
a street lined with trees = una strada
alberata

link verb
= collegare
the two murders are linked = i due
omicidi sono collegati

lion noun
a lion = un leone

lip noun
a lip = un labbro
to have dry lips = avere le labbra secche

lipstick noun
lipstick = il rossetto

list noun
a list = una lista

listen verb
= ascoltare
to listen to someone = ascoltare qualcuno

litre (British English), **liter** (US English)
noun
a litre = un litro

little¹
1 determiner
▶ See the boxed note on **little** for more
information and examples.
* (not much, a very small quantity)
= poco/poca
little [sugar | wine | time] = poco [zucchero |
vino | tempo]
there is very little water = c'è pochissima
acqua
* (some) = un po' di
a little wine = un po' di vino
2 pronoun
a little = un po'
I only ate a little = ne ho mangiato solo
un po'

! Note that it is necessary to use **ne**,
which might be translated as 'of it',
with pronouns like **a little**. See also **a
lot**, **more**, **none**, etc for this use of **ne**.

3 adverb
= poco
4 a little (bit) = un po'
5 little by little = poco a poco

little² adjective
= piccolo/piccola

live¹ verb
* (to have one's home) = abitare
he lives in London = abita a Londra
* (to be alive) = vivere

live² adjective
* (alive) = vivo/viva
* (of a match, a show) = in diretta

lively adjective
= vivace

living room noun
a living room = un soggiorno

load noun
* (on a truck, being carried)
a load = un carico
* loads of money = un sacco di soldi

loaf noun
a loaf (of bread) = una pagnotta

little

Italian has a word for 'little', **piccolo/piccola**.

    a little car   = una macchina **piccola**

But Italians often express the idea of 'smallness' by using an ending. There are two very common ones: **-ino/-ina** and **-etto/-etta**. These also tend to express an affectionate attitude towards the person or thing, and can be used humorously:

    a little brother/sister   = un **fratellino**/una **sorellina**
    a little job   = un **lavoretto**
    a little problem   = un **problemino**

Be careful however: sometimes these endings change the meaning of the word in unexpected ways. In addition, the gender sometimes changes from feminine to masculine:

    a saddle (for a horse) = una sella
    a saddle (for a bicycle) = un sellino
    a disc, a disk   = un disco
    a floppy disk   = un dischetto

---

loan *noun*
  a loan = un prestito
lobster *noun*
  a lobster = un'aragosta
local *adjective*
  a local newspaper = un giornale locale
  the local people = la gente del posto
lock
1 *verb*
  = chiudere a chiave
  she locked the door = ha chiuso la porta
    a chiave
2 *noun*
  • a lock = una serratura
  • a bicycle lock = un lucchetto per la
    bicicletta
lock in
  to lock someone in = chiudere dentro
    qualcuno
  to lock oneself in = chiudersi dentro (**!** +
    essere)
locker *noun*
  a locker = un armadietto
logical *adjective*
  = logico/logica
London *noun* ▶ 151 |
  = Londra
lonely *adjective*
  to feel lonely = sentirsi solo/sola (**!** +
    essere)
long
1 *adjective* ▶ 202 |
  = lungo/lunga
  a long letter = una lunga lettera
  to have long hair = avere i capelli lunghi
  the film is two hours long = il film dura
    due ore
  I haven't seen him for a long time = non
    lo vedo da tanto tempo
2 *adverb*
  I don't want to stay long = non voglio
    stare tanto

long ago = tanto tempo fa
  you can stay as long as you like = puoi
    rimanere quanto vuoi
  I won't be long = torno subito
3 as long as = a condizione che
  as long as you work hard = a condizione
    che lavori sodo

> **!** *Note that the subjunctive is used after*
> **a condizione che**.

look
1 *verb*
  • = guardare
    to look at a photo = guardare una foto
    to look out of the window = guardare
      fuori dalla finestra
  • (*to appear*)
    to look tired = avere l'aria stanca
    you look well = ti trovo bene
    he looks young = sembra giovane
    she looks like her mother = assomiglia a
      sua madre
    what does he look like? = com'è?
2 *noun*
  a look = uno sguardo
look after = badare a
  to look after a child = badare a un
    bambino
look down
  • (*to lower one's eyes*) = abbassare lo
    sguardo
  • to look down on someone = disprezzare
    qualcuno
look for = cercare
  he is looking for a job = sta cercando
    lavoro
look forward to
  I am looking forward to meeting her
    = non vedo l'ora di conoscerla
look onto = dare su
  my bedroom looks onto the garden = la
    mia camera dà sul giardino
look out = stare attento/attenta
look through
  to look through a book = scorrere un
    libro
                ····➤

look up
• to look up a word in the dictionary
  = cercare una parola sul dizionario
• (*to raise one's eyes*) = alzare lo sguardo

loose *adjective*
• (*describing clothes*) = largo/larga
• (*describing a screw*) = allentato/allentata

lorry *noun* (*British English*)
  a lorry = un camion

lose *verb*
  = perdere

lost *adjective*
  = perso/persa
  to get lost = perdersi (**!** + *essere*)

lot *pronoun* ▶ 233 |
  a lot = molto/molta (+ *singular*)
  = molti/molte (+ *plural*)
  he eats a lot = mangia molto
  a lot [of money | of time | of books] = [molti
  soldi | molto tempo | molti libri]
  there's not a lot left = non ne è rimasto
  molto

> **!** *Note that it is necessary to use* **ne**,
> *which may be translated as* '**of it**' *or* '**of
> them**', *with pronouns like* **a lot**. *See
> also* **another, a few, any,** *etc for this
> use of* **ne**.

lottery *noun*
  a lottery = una lotteria

loud *adjective*
  = forte
  to talk in a loud voice = parlare a voce
  alta

lounge *noun*
  a lounge = una sala

love
1 *verb*
  = amare
  to love each other = amarsi (**!** + *essere*)
2 *noun*
  love = l'amore (*masculine*)
  to be in love = essere
  innamorato/innamorata
  to make love = fare l'amore

lovely *adjective*
• (*beautiful*) = bello/bella
  a lovely apartment = un
  bell'appartamento
• (*very nice, kind*) = carino/carina

low
1 *adjective*
  = basso/bassa
  to speak in a low voice = parlare a voce
  bassa
2 *adverb*
  = basso
  to turn the lights down low = abbassare le
  luci

lower *verb*
  = abbassare

loyal *adjective*
  = fedele

luck *noun*
  luck = la fortuna
  good luck! = buona fortuna!
  it'll bring you (good) luck = ti porterà
  fortuna

lucky *adjective*
  = fortunato/fortunata

lunch *noun*
  lunch = il pranzo

lung *noun*
  a lung = un polmone

Luxembourg *noun* ▶ 151 |
  Luxembourg = il Lussemburgo

luxury
1 *noun*
  a luxury = un lusso
2 *adjective*
  a luxury hotel = un albergo di lusso

machine *noun*
  a machine = una macchina

mad *adjective*
• (*crazy*) = pazzo/pazza
  to go mad = impazzire (**!** + *essere*)
• (*very angry*) = furioso/furiosa
• to be mad about someone = impazzire
  per qualcuno

magazine *noun*
  a magazine = una rivista

magic *adjective*
  = magico/magica

maiden name *noun*
  the maiden name = il nome da ragazza

mail
1 *noun*
  mail = la posta
2 *verb* (*US English*)
  to mail a letter to someone = mandare
  una lettera a qualcuno

mailbox *noun* (*US English*)
  a mailbox
  (*for delivering letters*) = una cassetta delle
  lettere
  (*for posting letters*) = una buca delle
  lettere

mailman *noun* ▶ 281 | (*US English*)
  a mailman = un postino

main *adjective*
= principale
the main course = il piatto principale

major
1 *adjective*
= importante
a major event = un avvenimento importante
2 *noun*
a major = un maggiore

majority *noun*
a majority = una maggioranza

make *verb*

> **!** *Note that the word* **make** *can often be translated by* **fare**. *This entry covers the most frequent uses of* **make**, *but to find translations for other expressions like* **to make a mess**, **to make a mistake**, **to make sure** *etc*, *look up the entries at* **mess, mistake, sure,** *etc.*

• **to make** = fare
to make [wine | a film | a coffee] = fare [il vino | un film | un caffè]
to make breakfast = preparare la colazione
to be made of gold = essere fatto/fatta d'oro
to be made in Italy = essere fabbricato/fabbricata in Italia
• (*to cause a particular reaction*)
to make someone happy = rendere felice qualcuno
to make someone angry = fare arrabbiare qualcuno
to make someone [cry | laugh | eat] = fare [piangere | ridere | mangiare] qualcuno
• (*to earn*)
to make a lot of money = fare un sacco di soldi
to make a living = guadagnarsi da vivere (**!** + *essere*)
make do = arrangiarsi (**!** + *essere*)
make out
to make out a list = fare un elenco
to make a cheque out to someone = intestare un assegno a qualcuno
make up
• (*to be friends again*) = fare la pace
• **to make up an excuse** = inventare una scusa

make-up *noun*
make-up = il trucco
to put on make-up = truccarsi (**!** + *essere*)

male *adjective*
• (*in biology*) = maschio
• (*relating to men*) = maschile

man *noun*
• **a man** = un uomo
• **man** = l'uomo

manage *verb*
• (*to run*) = gestire
• = riuscire (**!** + *essere*)

to manage to finish one's homework
= riuscire a finire i compiti

manager *noun* ▶ 281 |
a manager (*of a company, a bank*) = un direttore/una direttrice
(*of a shop*) = un gestore
(*of a football team*) = un manager

manners *noun*
manners = le maniere
it's bad manners not to say hello = è maleducazione non salutare

manufacture *verb*
= fabbricare

many ▶ 233 |
1 *determiner*
• (*a lot of*) = molti/molte
were there many tourists? = c'erano molti turisti?
there weren't many students there = non c'erano molti studenti
• (*when used with* how, too, so, as)
how many cases have you got? = quante valigie hai?
you eat too many chips = mangi troppe patate fritte
there are so many things to do = ci sono tante cose da fare
I got as many presents as you did = ho ricevuto tanti regali quanto te
2 *pronoun*
are there many left? = ce ne sono rimasti molti?
I've got too many = ne ho troppi

> **!** *Note that it is necessary to use* ne, *which might be translated as 'of them', with pronouns like* **many**. *See also* **another, a few, a lot** *etc for this use of* **ne**.

many (of them) speak English = molti (di loro) parlano inglese

map *noun*
a map (*of a country or region*) = una cartina
(*of a town or a transport system*) = una pianta

marble *noun*
marble = il marmo

march *verb*
• (*in the army*) = marciare
• (*in a demonstration*) = manifestare

March *noun* ▶ 155 |
March = marzo

margarine *noun*
margarine = la margarina

mark
1 *noun*
• **a mark** (*on a surface*) = una macchia
• (*British English*) (*a grade*)
a mark = un voto   ····▶

to get good marks = prendere dei bei voti
2 *verb*
- (*to stain*) = macchiare
- **to mark the homework** = correggere i
  compiti
- (*to indicate*) = indicare

market *noun*
- (*the place*)
  a market = un mercato
  a flea market = un mercatino delle pulci
- (*the system*)
  the market = il mercato

marmalade *noun*
  marmalade = la marmellata d'arance

marriage *noun*
  marriage = il matrimonio

married *adjective*
  = sposato/sposata
  to be married to someone = essere
  sposato/sposata con qualcuno
  to get married = sposarsi (**!** + *essere*)

marry *verb*
  to marry someone = sposare qualcuno

masculine *adjective*
  = maschile

mashed potatoes *noun*
  mashed potatoes = il purè di patate

mask *noun*
  a mask = una maschera

mat *noun*
  a mat = un tappetino

match
1 *noun*
- (*British English*) (*a game*)
  a match = una partita
  a football match = una partita di calcio
- (*a matchstick*)
  a match = un fiammifero
2 *verb*
  the shoes match the belt = le scarpe sono
  intonate alla cintura

mate *noun* (*British English*)
  a mate = un amico/un'amica

material *noun*
- (*things, stuff*)
  a material = un materiale
- (*a fabric*)
  a material = una stoffa

mathematics *noun*
  mathematics = la matematica

matter
1 *noun*
  what's the matter? = che cosa c'è?
  what's the matter with her? = che cos'ha?
2 *verb*
  does it really matter? = che importanza
  ha?
  it doesn't matter = non importa

maximum
1 *adjective*
  the maximum price = il prezzo massimo
  a maximum temperature of 80 degrees
  = una temperatura massima di 80 gradi
2 *noun*
  the maximum = il massimo

may *verb*
- (*when talking about a possibility*)
  they may be able to come = forse
  potranno venire
  she may not have seen him = forse non
  l'ha visto
  it may rain = forse pioverà
- (*when asking for permission*)
  may I come in? = posso entrare?

May *noun* ▶ 155 |
  May = maggio

maybe *adverb*
  = forse

mayor *noun* ▶ 281 |
  the mayor = il sindaco

me *pronoun*
- = mi

> **!** *Note that* mi *combines with the*
> *infinitive, the gerund, and the*
> *imperative.* Me *is used for emphasis.*

  they know me = mi conoscono
  he's seen me = mi ha visto
  help me! = aiutami!
  don't help me! = non aiutarmi!
  don't help ME! = non aiutare me!
- (*to me*) = mi

> **!** *Note that* mi *combines with the*
> *infinitive, the gerund, and the*
> *imperative.* A me *is used for emphasis.*
> Mi *beomes* me *before* lo/la, li/le, *and*
> ne.

  she gave me the book = mi ha dato il
  libro
  write to me! = scrivimi!
  don't show it to me! = non farmelo
  vedere!
  don't show it to ME! = non farlo vedere a
  me!
- (*after a preposition*) = me
  he did it for me = l'ha fatto per me
  stand in front of me = mettiti davanti a
  me
- **it's me** = sono io

meal *noun*
  a meal = un pasto

mean
1 *verb*
- **to mean** = voler dire
  what does that mean? = cosa vuol dire?
  what does 'falò' mean? = cosa vuol dire
  'falò'?
- (*to have as a result*)
  it means giving up my job = significa che
  dovrò lasciare il lavoro   ····➤

M

- (*to intend*)
  she didn't mean to upset you = non voleva offenderti
- (*to intend to say*) = voler dire
  what do you mean? = cosa vuoi dire?
- **her work means a lot to her** = il lavoro è molto importante per lei
  money doesn't mean much to him = i soldi non contano niente per lui

2 *adjective*
- (*British English*) (*not generous*) = avaro/avara
- **to be mean to someone** = essere cattivo/cattiva con qualcuno

meaning *noun*
  a meaning = un significato

means *noun*
  a means = un mezzo
  a means of transport = un mezzo di trasporto
  a means of earning money = un mezzo per guadagnare soldi

meant: **to be meant to** *verb*
▶ *See the boxed note on* **dovere** *for more information and examples.*
  the light is meant to come on = la luce dovrebbe accendersi

meanwhile *adverb*
  = nel frattempo

measles *noun* ▶ **193**
  measles = il morbillo

measure *verb*
  = misurare

meat *noun*
  meat = la carne

mechanic *noun* ▶ **281**
  a mechanic = un meccanico

medal *noun*
  a medal = una medaglia
  the gold medal = la medaglia d'oro

media *noun*
  the media = i mass media (*plural*)

medicine *noun*
  a medicine = una medicina

Mediterranean *noun*
  the Mediterranean = il Mediterraneo

medium *adjective*
  = medio/media

meet *verb*
- (*by accident or appointment*) = incontrare
  she met him in town = l'ha incontrato in città
  to meet (each other) = incontrarsi (**!** + *essere*)
  to meet again = rivedersi (**!** + *essere*)
- (*to be introduced to*) = conoscere
  she met him at a wedding = l'ha conosciuto ad un matrimonio
  have you met Tom? = conosci Tom?
  we met in 1995 = ci siamo conosciuti nel 1995

- (*to fetch*)
  can you meet me at the station? = puoi venire a prendermi alla stazione?
- (*to have a meeting*) = riunirsi (**!** + *essere*)

meeting *noun*
  a meeting = una riunione

melon *noun*
  a melon = un melone

melt *verb*
- = sciogliersi (**!** + *essere*)
  the snow is starting to melt = la neve comincia a sciogliersi

member *noun* ▶ **281**
  a member = un socio/una socia

memory *noun*
- **memory** = la memoria
  to have a good memory = avere buona memoria
  he's got a bad memory = non ha memoria
- (*of a person, a place or time*)
  a memory = un ricordo

mend *verb*
- (*to fix*) = riparare
- (*by sewing*) = rammendare

menu *noun*
  a menu = un menù

mess *noun*
  a mess = il disordine
  what a mess! = che disordine!
  your room is in a mess = la tua camera è in disordine
  to make a mess in the kitchen = fare disordine in cucina

message *noun*
  a message = un messaggio

metal *noun*
  a metal = un metallo

method *noun*
  a method = un metodo

metre (*British English*), **meter** (*US English*) *noun* ▶ **202**
  a metre = un metro

Mexico *noun* ▶ **151**
  Mexico = il Messico

microphone *noun*
  a microphone = un microfono

microwave *noun*
  a microwave = un forno a microonde

midday *noun* ▶ **146**, ▶ **267**
  it's midday = è mezzogiorno
  at midday = a mezzogiorno

middle *noun*
  the middle = il mezzo
  in the middle of the road = in mezzo alla strada

middle-aged *adjective*
  = di mezz'età

midnight *noun* ▶ 146 |, ▶ 267 |
  it's midnight = è mezzanotte (*feminine*)
  at midnight = a mezzanotte

might *verb*
• (*when talking about a possibility*)
  she might be right = forse ha ragione
  they might have got lost = forse si sono
    smarriti
  'will you come?'—'I might' = 'vieni?'
    —'può darsi'
• (*when implying something didn't happen*)
  you might have been killed! = potevi farti
    ammazzare!
  she might have warned us! = poteva
    avvertirci!
• (*when making suggestions*)
  it might be better to wait = forse è meglio
    aspettare

mild *adjective*
  the weather's mild = il clima è mite

mile *noun* ▶ 202 |
  a mile = un miglio
  450 miles = 450 miglia
  ❗ Note that a mile = 1609 m.

milk *noun*
  milk = il latte

milkman *noun* ▶ 281 |
  a milkman = un lattaio

million *number*
  one million, a million = un milione
  three million dollars = tre milioni di
    dollari
  a million inhabitants = un milione di
    abitanti

mind
1 *noun*
• the mind = la mente
  I have a lot on my mind = ho un sacco di
    preoccupazioni
• to make up one's mind = decidersi (❗ +
    essere)
  to change one's mind = cambiare idea
2 *verb*
• (*when expressing an opinion*)
  'where shall we go?'—'I don't mind'
    = 'dove andiamo?'—'per me fa lo
    stesso'
  she doesn't mind the heat = non le dà
    fastidio il caldo
• (*in polite questions or requests*)
  do you mind if I smoke? = le dispiace se
    fumo?
  would you mind coming? = ti dispiace
    venire?
  I wouldn't mind some cake = ho voglia di
    mangiare un po' di torta
• (*to be careful*)
  mind the step! = attenzione al gradino!
  mind you don't break the plates!
    = attento a non rompere i piatti!

• (*to take care of*) = guardare
• never mind, she'll get the next train
    = non importa, prenderà il prossimo
    treno

mine¹ *pronoun*
  mine = il mio/la mia (*singular*)
    = i miei/le mie (*plural*)
  ┌──────────────────────────────────┐
  │ ❗ Note that il/la, etc is used when │
  │ comparing things belonging to different │
  │ people, but not when saying who │
  │ something belongs to. │
  └──────────────────────────────────┘
  her coat is brown but mine is green = il
    suo cappotto è marrone ma il mio è
    verde
  her brother is taller than mine = suo
    fratello è più alto del mio
  the green pen is mine = la penna verde è
    mia
  a friend of mine = un mio amico

mine² *noun*
  a mine = una miniera

miner *noun* ▶ 281 |
  a miner = un minatore

mineral water *noun*
  mineral water = l'acqua minerale

minimum
1 *adjective*
  the minimum price = il prezzo minimo
  a minimum temperature of 15 degrees
    = una temperatura minima di 15 gradi
2 *noun*
  the minimum = il minimo

minister *noun* ▶ 281 |
• (*in government*)
  a minister = un ministro
• (*in religion*)
  a minister = un sacerdote/una
    sacerdotessa

minor *adjective*
  = poco importante
  a minor injury = una lieve ferita

minority *noun*
  a minority = una minoranza

minus *preposition*
  = meno
  it's minus four outside = fuori ci sono
    quattro gradi sotto zero

minute *noun* ▶ 146 |, ▶ 267 |
  a minute = un minuto
  they'll be here any minute now = saranno
    qui a momenti

mirror *noun*
  a mirror (*on a wall*) = uno specchio
    (*on a car*) = uno specchietto

miserable *adjective*
  to feel miserable = sentirsi giù (❗ +
    essere)
  miserable weather = un tempo
    deprimente

M

miss *verb*
* (*to fail to hit*)
  to miss the target = mancare il bersaglio
  the stone just missed his head = il sasso gli ha sfiorato il capo
* (*to fail to see*)
  you can't miss it = non puoi non vederlo
* (*to feel sad not to see*)
  I miss you = mi manchi
  we'll miss Oxford = ci mancherà Oxford
  to miss an opportunity = lasciarsi sfuggire un'occasione (**!** + *essere*)
* (*other uses*)
  don't miss this film = non perdere questo film
  she missed her plane = ha perso l'aereo

Miss *noun*
▶ See the boxed note on **Forms of address**.
  Miss = signorina

missing *adjective*
  to be missing = mancare (**!** + *essere*)
  there's a book missing = manca un libro

mist *noun*
  mist = la foschia

mistake *noun*
  a mistake = un errore
  a spelling mistake = un errore d'ortografia
  to make a mistake = sbagliare

mix *verb*
* = mescolare
* **to mix with the other students** = frequentare gli altri studenti
  mix up = confondere
  to get the two languages mixed up = fare confusione tra le due lingue
  I'm always mixing him up with his brother = lo confondo sempre con suo fratello

mixture *noun*
  a mixture = un miscuglio

mobile phone *noun*
  a mobile phone = un cellulare, un telefonino

model *noun*
* (*of a train, a car, a building*)
  a model = un modellino
* ▶ **281**|
  a (fashion) model = un indossatore/un'indossatrice

modern *adjective*
  = moderno/moderna

mom, **Mom** *noun* (*US English*)
  a mom = una mamma

moment *noun*
  a moment = un momento
  there's no one there at the moment = al momento non c'è nessuno

Monday *noun* ▶ **155**|
  Monday = lunedì (*masculine*)

money *noun*
  money = i soldi (*plural*)

monkey *noun*
  a monkey = una scimmia

month *noun* ▶ **267**|
  a month = un mese

monument *noun*
  a monument = un monumento

mood *noun*
  to be in a good mood = essere di buon umore
  I'm in a very bad mood = sono di pessimo umore

moon *noun*
  the moon = la luna

moped *noun*
  a moped = un motorino

moral *adjective*
  = morale

more ▶ **233**|
1 *determiner*
  = più
  more [time | books | CDs] = più [tempo | libri | CD]
  I have more work than him = ho più lavoro di lui
  there's no more bread = non c'è più pane
  there's more tea = c'è ancora tè
  would you like more coffee? = vuoi ancora caffè?
  he bought two more tickets = ha comprato altri due biglietti
  there were more than 20 people there = c'erano più di venti persone lì
2 *pronoun*
  = più
  they cost more = costano di più
  I did more than you = ho fatto più di te
  I can't tell you any more = non posso dirti altro
  we need more (of them) = ce ne occorrono di più
  we need more (of it) = ce ne occorre di più

  > **!** *Note that it is necessary to use* **ne**, *which might be translated as* '**of it**' *or* '**of them**', *with pronouns like* **more**. *See also* **another**, **a few**, **a lot** *etc for this use of* **ne**.

3 *adverb*
* (*when comparing*) = più
  it's more complicated than that = è più complicato di così
* (*when talking about time*)
  he doesn't live there any more = non abita più lì
4 more and more = sempre di più
  more and more expensive = sempre più caro
5 more or less = più o meno

morning noun ▶ 146 |, ▶ 267 |

> **!** Note that **morning** is usually translated by **mattino** in Italian. However it is sometimes translated by **mattinata**, which implies all the things that happen during the morning.

a morning = un mattino
at three o'clock in the morning = alle tre del mattino
to spend the morning reading = passare la mattinata a leggere

mosquito noun
a mosquito = una zanzara

most
1 determiner
• (the majority of) = la maggior parte di
most schools will be closed = la maggior parte delle scuole chiuderà
• (in superlatives)
the most = più
who has the most money? = chi ha più soldi?
2 pronoun
= la maggior parte
most of the time = la maggior parte del tempo
most (of them) speak Greek = la maggior parte (di loro) parla greco
3 adverb
= più
the most expensive shop in London = il negozio più caro di Londra
the most beautiful town in Italy = la più bella città d'Italia
4 at (the) most = al massimo
5 most of all = soprattutto

mostly adverb
= per lo più

mother noun
a mother = una madre

mother-in-law noun
a mother-in-law = una suocera

motor noun
a motor = un motore

motorbike noun
a motorbike = una moto

motorcyclist noun
a motorcyclist = un/una motociclista

motorist noun
a motorist = un automobilista/un'automobilista

motor racing noun ▶ 178 |
motor racing = l'automobilismo

motorway noun (British English)
a motorway = un'autostrada

mountain noun
a mountain = una montagna
to go camping in the mountains = andare in campeggio in montagna (**!** + essere)

mountain bike noun
a mountain bike = una mountain bike

mountain climbing noun ▶ 178 |
mountain climbing = l'alpinismo

mouse noun
a mouse = un topo

moustache, mustache (US English) noun
a moustache = i baffi (plural)

mouth noun ▶ 137 |
• (of a person)
the mouth = la bocca
• (of a river)
the mouth = la foce

move verb
• (to make a movement) = muoversi (**!** + essere)
don't move! = non muoverti!
• (to put elsewhere) = spostare
to move the car = spostare la macchina
• (to make a movement with) = muovere
I couldn't move my leg = non riuscivo a muovere la gamba
• to move (house) = traslocare
to move to Bologna = trasferirsi a Bologna (**!** + essere)
move away
• (to live elsewhere) = trasferirsi (**!** + essere)
• (to make a movement away) = allontanarsi (**!** + essere)
to move away from the window = allontanarsi dalla finestra
move back = indietreggiare (**!** + essere)
move forward = avanzare (**!** + essere)
move in = traslocare
I'm moving in with my friends = vado ad abitare con gli amici
move out = trasferirsi (**!** + essere)
move over = spostarsi (**!** + essere)
move over please! = spostati per favore!

movement noun
a movement = un movimento

movie noun (US English)
a movie = un film
to go to the movies = andare al cinema (**!** + essere)

movie theater noun (US English)
a movie theater = un cinema

moving adjective
= commovente

mow verb
to mow the lawn = tagliare l'erba

MP noun ▶ 281 | (British English)
an MP = un deputato

Mr noun
▶ See the boxed note on **Forms of address**.
Mr = (il) signor

M

Mrs noun
▶ See the boxed note on **Forms of
address**.
  Mrs = (la) signora

much ▶ **233** |
1 adverb
• (a lot) = molto
  her work is much more tiring = il suo
    lavoro è molto più faticoso
  he doesn't read much = non legge molto
• (often) = molto spesso
  they don't go out much = non escono
    molto spesso
• (when used with **very**, **too** or **so**)
  he misses her very much = lei gli manca
    moltissimo
  you talk too much = parli troppo
  she loves him so much = lo ama così
    tanto
2 pronoun = molto
  is there much to be done? = c'è molto da
    fare?
  he didn't eat much = non ha mangiato
    molto
3 determiner
• (a lot of) = molto/molta
  I haven't got much time = non ho molto
    tempo
  do you have much work? = hai molto
    lavoro?
• (when used with **how**, **very**, **too**, **so** or **as**)
  how much material have you got?
    = quanta stoffa hai?
  she doesn't eat very much meat = non
    mangia molta carne
  I spent too much money = ho speso
    troppo
  don't use so much salt = non usare così
    tanto sale
  she has as much work as me = ha tanto
    lavoro quanto me

mud noun
  mud = il fango

mug
1 noun
  a mug = un tazzone
2 verb
  to be mugged = essere derubato/derubata

multiply verb
  = moltiplicare

mum, Mum noun (British English)
  a mum = una mamma

mumps noun ▶ **193** |
  mumps = gli orecchioni (plural)

murder
1 noun
  a murder = un omicidio
2 verb
  = ammazzare

murderer noun
  a murderer = un omicida/un'omicida

muscle noun
  a muscle = un muscolo

museum noun
  a museum = un museo

mushroom noun
  a mushroom = un fungo

music noun
  music = la musica

musical noun
  a musical = un musical

musical instrument noun
  a musical instrument = uno strumento
    musicale

musician noun ▶ **281** |
  a musician = un/una musicista

Muslim adjective
  = musulmano/musulmana

mussel noun
  a mussel = una cozza

must verb
▶ See the boxed note on **dovere** for more
information and examples.
• (when stressing the importance of
  something)
  you must go to the doctor = devi andare
    dal medico
  we mustn't tell anyone = non dobbiamo
    dirlo a nessuno
• (when talking about a rule)
  visitors must go to (the) reception = i
    visitatori devono presentarsi alla
    reception
• (when assuming that something is true)
  it must be nice to live there = dev'essere
    bello abitare lì
  you must be David's sister = tu devi
    essere la sorella di David

mustard noun
  mustard = la senape

my determiner
  my = il mio/la mia (+ singular)
    = i miei/le mie (+ plural)

  ! Note that the definite article **il/la**, etc
  is generally used except when talking
  about a close family member.

  they hate my dog = non sopportano il
    mio cane
  I sold all my CDs = ho venduto tutti i
    miei CD
  my brother/my sister = mio fratello/mia
    sorella
  what do you think of my house? = cosa
    pensi di casa mia?
  I licked my plate = ho leccato il piatto
  I broke my leg = mi sono rotto la gamba

  ! Note that, when talking about parts of
  the body, **il mio/la mia** is not used. See
  the usage note on **The human body**
  ▶ **137** | for further examples.

myself *pronoun*
- (*when used as a reflexive pronoun*) = mi
  > ! *Note that* **mi** *combines with the infinitive, the gerund, and the imperative.* **Mi** *beomes* **me** *before* **lo/la, li/le,** *and* **ne.**

  I didn't hurt myself = non mi sono fatto male
  I want to enjoy myself = voglio divertirmi
- (*when used for emphasis*)
  I told them myself = gliel'ho detto io stesso
  I did it all by myself = l'ho fatto tutto da me

mystery *noun*
  a mystery = un mistero

nail *noun* ▶ **137**|
- (*for use in attaching, repairing*)
  a nail = un chiodo
- (*on the fingers or toes*)
  a nail = un'unghia

nail polish *noun*
  nail polish = lo smalto

naked *adjective*
  = nudo/nuda

name *noun*
- (*of a person*)
  a name = un nome
  what's your name? = come ti chiami?
  my name is James = mi chiamo James
- (*of a book, a play or film*)
  a name = un titolo

narrow *adjective*
  = stretto/stretta

nasty *adjective*
  = cattivo/cattiva

national *adjective*
  = nazionale

natural *adjective*
  = naturale

naturally *adverb*
  = naturalmente

nature *noun*
  nature = la natura

naughty *adjective*
  = birichino/birichina

navy *noun*
  the navy = la marina

navy blue *adjective* ▶ **147**|
  = blu scuro

near
1 *preposition*
  = vicino a
  he was sitting near us = sedeva vicino a noi
2 *adverb*
  they live quite near = abitano abbastanza vicino
3 *adjective*
  = vicino/vicina
  the school is quite near = la scuola è abbastanza vicina

nearby *adverb*
  = vicino

nearly *adverb*
  = quasi
  we're nearly there = siamo quasi arrivati

neat *adjective*
  = ordinato/ordinata

necessary *adjective*
  = necessario/necessaria

neck *noun* ▶ **137**|
  the neck = il collo

necklace *noun*
  a necklace = una collana

need *verb*
- (*(to) have to*)
  you don't need to ask permission = non c'è bisogno di chiedere il permesso
  they'll need to come early = bisogna che vengano presto
  > ! *Note that the subjunctive is used after* **bisogna che.**
- (*to want*) = avere bisogno di
  they need [money | help | friends] = hanno bisogno di [soldi | aiuto | amici]

needle *noun*
  a needle = un ago

negative
1 *adjective*
  = negativo/negativa
2 *noun*
  a negative = un negativo

neighbour (*British English*), **neighbor** (*US English*) *noun*
  a neighbour = un vicino/una vicina

neither
1 *conjunction*
- (*in* neither... nor *sentences*) = né... né...
  she speaks neither Italian nor English = non parla né italiano né inglese
- (*nor*)
  'I can't sleep'—'neither can I' = 'non riesco a dormire'—'nemmeno io'
2 *determiner*
  = nessuno dei due/nessuna delle due
  neither girl answered = nessuna delle due ragazze ha risposto   ····➤

N

3 *pronoun*
= né l'uno/l'una né l'altro/l'altra
neither of them is coming = non viene né l'uno né l'altro

> **!** Note that the negative **non** is used together with **né** or **nessuno/nessuna**, except when they come at the beginning of the sentence.

nephew *noun*
a nephew = un nipote

nerves *noun*
nerves = i nervi
to get on someone's nerves = dare sui nervi a qualcuno

nervous *adjective*
= ansioso/ansiosa
to feel nervous = essere ansioso/ansiosa

nest *noun*
a nest = un nido

net *noun*
a net = una rete

Netherlands *noun* ▶ 151 |
the Netherlands = i Paesi Bassi

network *noun*
a network = una rete

neutral *adjective*
= neutrale

never *adverb*

> **!** Note that the negative **non** is used together with **mai**.

* (*not ever*) = mai
  they never come to see us = non vengono mai a trovarci
  she has never been to the opera = non è mai stata all'opera
  I'll never go back there again = non tornerò mai più lì
* (*when used for emphasis*)
  she never even apologized = non si è nemmeno scusata

nevertheless *adverb*
= comunque

new *adjective*
= nuovo/nuova
a new bike = una bicicletta nuova
a new computer = un nuovo computer

news *noun*
* a piece of news = una notizia
  the news = le notizie
  have you heard the news? = hai saputo la notizia?
  that's good news! = che bella notizia!
  have you any news of John? = hai notizie di John?
* the news
  (*on the radio*) = il giornale radio
  (*on TV*) = il telegiornale

newsagent's *noun* ▶ 281 | (*British English*)
a newsagent's = un'edicola

newspaper *noun*
a newspaper = un giornale

New Year *noun*
the New Year = l'anno nuovo
happy New Year! = buon anno!

New Year's Day, **New Year's** (*US English*) *noun*
New Year's (Day) = Capodanno

New Year's Eve *noun*
New Year's Eve = San Silvestro

New Zealand *noun* ▶ 151 |
New Zealand = la Nuova Zelanda

next
1 *adjective*
* (*when talking about what is still to come*)
  = prossimo/prossima
  I'll take the next train to London = prendo il prossimo treno per Londra
  he'll be here next week = arriverà la prossima settimana
* (*when talking about what followed*)
  = successivo/successiva
  I took the next train = ho preso il treno successivo
  they arrived the next day = sono arrivati il giorno successivo
* (*in a queue*)
  who's next? = a chi tocca?
  I'm next = tocca a me
2 *adverb*
* (*in the past*) = poi
  what happened next? = e poi cos'è successo?
* (*in the future*)
  when you next go to Trieste, give Gary a call = la prossima volta che vai a Trieste, fai una telefonata a Gary
3 next to = accanto a

nice *adjective*
* (*enjoyable, attractive*) = bello/bella
  it's nice to relax = è bello rilassarsi
* (*kind, friendly*) = carino/carina
  to be nice to someone = essere carino con qualcuno

nickname *noun*
a nickname = un soprannome

niece *noun*
a niece = una nipote

night *noun* ▶ 267 |
* (*as opposed to day*)
  a night = una notte
  last night = ieri notte
  all night = tutta la notte
* (*evening*)
  a night = una sera
  last night = ieri sera

nightclub *noun*
a nightclub = un locale

nightdress *noun*
a nightdress = una camicia da notte

nightmare *noun*
a nightmare = un incubo
to have a nightmare = avere un incubo

nil *noun*
nil = zero

nine *number* ▶ 122 |, ▶ 146 |
nine = nove
nine books = nove libri
I have nine (of them) = ne ho nove

nineteen *number* ▶ 122 |, ▶ 146 |
nineteen = diciannove

nineteenth *number*
• (in a series)
    = diciannovesimo/diciannovesima
• (in dates) ▶ 155 |
    the nineteenth of July = il diciannove
    luglio

ninety *number* ▶ 122 |
ninety = novanta

ninth *number*
• (in a series) = nono/nona
• (in dates) ▶ 155 |
    the ninth of December = il nove dicembre

no
1 *adverb*
• no = no
    no thanks = no grazie
• he no longer works here = non lavora più
    qui
2 *determiner*
• (not any) = nessun/nessuna

    ! Nessuno *is used before a masculine
    noun beginning with z, ps, gn, or s +
    another consonant.* Nessun' *is used
    before a feminine noun beginning with
    a vowel. Note that the negative* non *is
    used together with* nessuno/nessuna
    to translate no, *except when it comes
    at the beginning of the sentence.*

    no man/no woman = nessun
    uomo/nessuna donna
    I found no mistakes = non ho trovato
    nessun errore
    we have no money = non abbiamo soldi
    there are no trains = non ci sono treni
• (when refusing permission)
    no smoking = vietato fumare
    no talking! = silenzio!
• (when used for emphasis)
    this is no time to argue = non è il
    momento di discutere
    it's no problem = non c'è problema

nobody ▶ no one

noise *noun*
a noise = un rumore
to make a noise = fare chiasso

noisy *adjective*
= rumoroso/rumorosa

none *pronoun*

    ! Note that the negative* non *is used
    together with* nessuno/nessuna *to
    translate* none, *except when it comes
    at the beginning of the sentence.*

none = nessuno/nessuna
none of the girls went to school
    = nessuna delle ragazze è andata a
    scuola
none of [us | you | them] can speak
    German = nessuno di [noi | voi | loro]
    parla tedesco
there's none left = non ce n'è più
I've got none, I have none = non ne ho
    nessuno

    ! Note that it is necessary to use* ne
    *which might be translated as 'of it' or
    'of them', with pronouns like* none. *See
    also* another, a few, a lot *etc for this
    use of* ne.

nonsense *noun*
that's nonsense! = che assurdità!

noon *noun* ▶ 146 |, ▶ 267 |
noon = mezzogiorno
at noon = a mezzogiorno

no one *pronoun* (*also* **nobody**)

    ! Note that the negative* non *is used
    together with* nessuno *to translate* no
    one, *except when it comes at the
    beginning of the sentence.*

no one = nessuno
no one tells me anything = nessuno mi
    dice niente
no one saw him = non l'ha visto nessuno
there's no one else in the office = in
    ufficio non c'è nessun altro

nor *conjunction*

    ! For translations of* nor *when used in
    combination with* neither, *look at the
    entry for* neither *in this dictionary.*

'I don't smoke'—'nor do I' = 'non
    fumo'—'neanch'io'

normal *adjective*
= normale

normally *adverb*
= normalmente

north
1 *noun*
    the north = il nord
    in the north of Italy = nel nord d'Italia
2 *adverb*
    to go north = andare verso nord
    to live north of Grosseto = abitare a nord
    di Grosseto
3 *adjective*
    = nord (**!** *never changes*)
    to work in north London = lavorare nella
    zona nord di Londra

N

North America noun ▶ 151 |
North America = l'America del nord

northeast noun
the northeast = il nordest

Northern Ireland noun ▶ 151 |
Northern Ireland = l'Irlanda del Nord

northwest noun
the northwest = il nordovest

Norway noun ▶ 151 |
Norway = la Norvegia

Norwegian ▶ 199 |
1 adjective
= norvegese
2 noun
the Norwegians = i norvegesi

nose noun ▶ 137 |
the nose = il naso

not
1 adverb
= non
she's not at home = non è a casa
hasn't he phoned you? = non ti ha
telefonato?
I hope not = spero di no
not everyone likes football = non a tutti
piace il calcio
2 not at all
• (in no way) = per niente
he's not at all worried = non è per niente
preoccupato
• 'thanks a lot'—'not at all' = 'mille
grazie'—'di niente'

note
1 noun
• (to remind oneself)
a note = un appunto
• (a message)
a note = un biglietto
I left you a note = ti ho lasciato un
biglietto
• (British English) (money)
a note = una banconota
a 50 euro note = una banconota da
50 euro
• (in music)
a note = una nota
2 verb
to note (down) = annotare

notebook noun
a notebook = un taccuino

nothing pronoun
nothing = niente, nulla

> ! Note that the negative **non** is used
> together with **niente** or **nulla** to
> translate **nothing**, except when they
> come at the beginning of the sentence.

nothing has changed = non è cambiato
niente
there's nothing left = non è rimasto
niente
she said nothing = non ha detto niente

I knew nothing about it = non ne sapevo
nulla
there's nothing we can do about it = non
possiamo farci niente
I had nothing to do with it! = io non
c'entro niente!
it's nothing to do with us = non ci
riguarda

notice
1 verb
= notare
2 noun
• (a written sign)
a notice = un cartello
• (warning people)
notice = un avviso
a month's notice = un preavviso di un
mese
to be cancelled at short notice = essere
cancellato all'ultimo minuto
• don't take any notice, take no notice
= non farci caso

novel noun
a novel = un romanzo

November noun ▶ 155 |
November = novembre (masculine)

now
1 adverb
= ora, adesso
we have to do it now = dobbiamo farlo
adesso
I'm phoning her now = sto per telefonarle
ora
do it right now = fallo adesso
it hasn't been a problem until now
= finora non è stato un problema
from now on = d'ora in poi
2 now and again, now and then = di
tanto in tanto

nowhere adverb
= da nessuna parte
I go nowhere without my dog = non vado
da nessuna parte senza il mio cane
there's nowhere to sit = non c'è posto per
sedersi

nuclear adjective
= nucleare

nuisance noun
a nuisance = una seccatura
it's a nuisance having to pay in cash = è
una seccatura dover pagare in contanti

number noun
• a number = un numero
to dial the wrong number = sbagliare
numero
• (when talking about quantities) ▶ 233 |
a number of times = un certo numero di
volte
a small number of tourists = pochi turisti

number plate noun (British English)
a number plate = una targa

nun *noun* ▶ **281**|
  a nun = una suora

nurse *noun* ▶ **281**|
  a nurse = un infermiere/un'infermiera

nursery school *noun*
  a nursery school = una scuola materna

nut *noun*
  a nut = una nocciolina

nylon *noun*
  nylon = il nailon

oar *noun*
  an oar = un remo

obedient *adjective*
  = obbediente

obey *verb*
  = obbedire
  to obey someone = obbedire a qualcuno
  to obey the law = rispettare la legge

object
1 *noun*
  an object = un oggetto
2 *verb*
  = opporsi (**!** + *essere*)

obtain *verb*
  = ottenere

obvious *adjective*
  = ovvio/ovvia

obviously *adverb*
  = ovviamente

occasion *noun*
  an occasion = un'occasione
  on special occasions = nelle grandi
    occasioni

occasionally *adverb*
  = ogni tanto

occupy *verb*
• (*to take over*) = occupare
• (*to keep busy*)
  to keep oneself occupied = tenersi
    occupato (**!** + *essere*)
  to keep the children occupied = tenere
    occupati i bambini

occur *verb*
  = accadere (**!** + *essere*)

ocean *noun*
  the ocean = l'oceano

o'clock *adverb* ▶ **146**|
  it's five o'clock = sono le cinque
  at one o'clock = all'una
  at five o'clock = alle cinque

October *noun* ▶ **155**|
  October = ottobre (*masculine*)

odd *adjective*
• (*strange*) = strano/strana
• (*not matching*) = spaiato/spaiata
• (*when talking about numbers*)
  an odd number = un numero dispari

odour (*British English*), **odor** (*US
English*) *noun*
  an odour = un odore

of *preposition*
• of = di
  the sound of an engine = il rumore di un
    motore
  a photo of the dog = una foto del cane
  half of the salad = metà dell'insalata
  the names of the pupils = i nomi degli
    alunni
• (*when talking about quantities*) ▶ **233**|
  of = di
  a kilo of potatoes = un chilo di patate
  a bottle of mineral water = una bottiglia
    d'acqua minerale
  there are six of them in the family = sono
    in sei in famiglia
  have you heard of it? = ne hai sentito
    parlare?
  there were too many of them = ce n'erano
    troppi

> **!** *Note that* ne *is used to translate* 'of it'
> *or* 'of them'.

off

> **!** *Often* off *occurs in combinations with
> verbs, for example:* get off, go off, take
> off *etc. To find the correct translations
> for this type of verb, look up the
> separate dictionary entries at* get, go,
> take *etc.*

1 *adverb*
• (*leaving*)
  I'm off (*British English*) = io me ne vado
  they're off to Italy tomorrow = partono
    per l'Italia domani
• (*away*)
  the coast is a long way off = la costa è
    piuttosto lontana
  we could see them from a long way off
    = li vedevamo da lontano
• (*free*)
  to take a day off = prendere un giorno di
    riposo
  today's her day off = oggi non lavora
• (*not working, switched off*)
  = spento/spenta
  the lights are all off = tutte le luci sono
    spente
2 *adjective*
  the milk is off = il latte è guasto

o

offence (*British English*), **offense** (*US English*) *noun*
• (*a crime*)
 an offence = un reato
• **to take offence** = offendersi (**!** + *essere*)

offend *verb*
 = offendere

offer *verb*
 to offer someone a job = offrire un lavoro a qualcuno
 to offer to do something = offrirsi di fare qualcosa (**!** + *essere*)
 she offered to water the plants = si è offerta di annaffiare le piante

office *noun*
 an office = un ufficio

officer *noun*
 an officer (*in the army or navy*) = un ufficiale
 (*in the police*) = un agente

office worker *noun* ▶ 281 |
 an office worker = un impiegato/un'impiegata

official *adjective*
 = ufficiale

often *adverb*
 = spesso

oil *noun*
• (*for heating, energy*)
 oil = il petrolio
• (*for a car, for cooking*)
 oil = l'olio

okay, **OK**
1 *adjective*
• (*when asking or giving opinions*)
 is it okay if I come later? = va bene se vengo più tardi?
• (*when talking about health*)
 to feel okay = sentirsi bene (**!** + *essere*)
 are you okay? = tutto bene?
2 *adverb*
 okay = va bene

old *adjective*
• (*not new, not young*) = vecchio/vecchia
 old houses = delle vecchie case
 old people = gli anziani
 an old man/woman = un vecchio/una vecchia
• (*when talking about a person's age*)
 ▶ 125 |
 how old are you? = quanti anni hai?
 a three-year old girl = una bambina di tre anni
 she's eight years older than her brother = ha otto anni più di suo fratello
 to be the oldest = essere il/la maggiore
 to be old enough to go out at night = essere grande abbastanza per uscire la sera
• (*previous*) = vecchio/vecchia (**!** *before the noun*)

 that's my old address = quello è il mio vecchio indirizzo
 in the old days = ai vecchi tempi

old-fashioned *adjective*
 (*describing attitudes, ideas*) = antiquato/antiquata
 (*describing people*) = all'antica

olive
1 *noun*
 an olive = un'oliva
2 *adjective* ▶ 147 |
 = verde oliva (**!** *never changes*)

olive oil *noun*
 olive oil = l'olio d'oliva

Olympics *noun*
 the Olympics = le Olimpiadi

omelette *noun*
 an omelette = una frittata

on

> **!** *Often* **on** *occurs in combinations with verbs, for example:* **count on**, **get on**, **keep on** *etc. To find the correct translations for this type of verb, look up the separate dictionary entries for* **count**, **get**, **keep** *etc.*

1 *preposition*
• **on** = su
 on the = sul/sulla (**!** + *singular*)
 = sui/sulle (+ *plural*)

> **!** *Before masculine nouns beginning with* z, ps, gn, *or* s + *another consonant,* **sullo** *is used in the singular and* **sugli** *in the plural. Before masculine and feminine singular nouns beginning with a vowel,* **sull'** *is used.*

 it's on the table = è sul tavolo
 it's on top of the wardrobe = è sull'armadio
 you've got a spot on your nose = hai un brufolo sul naso
 to fall on the floor = cadere per terra (**!** + *essere*)
 there's a picture on the wall = c'è un quadro appeso al muro
 to live on Park Avenue = abitare a Park Avenue
• (*when talking about transport*)
 to travel on the bus = viaggiare in autobus
 I'm on my bike today = sono in bici oggi
• (*about*) = su
 a book on Africa = un libro sull'Africa
• (*when talking about time*)
 she was born on the sixth of December = è nata il sei dicembre
 I'll be there on Saturday = arriverò sabato
• (*when talking about the media*)
 on television = alla televisione
 I saw it on the news = l'ho visto al telegiornale
2 *adverb*   ····▶

- (*when talking about what one wears*)
  to have a sweater on = indossare un maglione
  to have make-up on = essere truccato/truccata
- (*working, switched on*)
  why are all the lights on? = perché le luci sono accese?
- (*showing*)
  what's on? (*on TV*) = cosa c'è alla televisione?
  (*in the cinema?*) = cosa danno al cinema?
- (*when talking about time*)
  from Tuesday on, I'll be here = a partire da martedì sarò qui
  a little later on = un po' più tardi

once
1 *adverb*
  = una volta
  once a day = una volta al giorno
  once there were fields here = una volta qui c'erano dei campi
2 *conjunction*
  = non appena
  it'll be easier once we've found a house = sarà più facile non appena avremo trovato casa
3 at once = subito

one
1 *number*
  = un/una (**! uno** *before a masculine noun beginning with z, ps, gn, or s + another consonant;* **un'** *before a feminine noun beginning with a vowel*) ▶ **122** , ▶ **146**
  one, two, three = uno, due, tre
  one child = un figlio/una figlia
  one of my colleagues = uno dei miei colleghi
  one hundred = cento
2 *determiner*
- (*the only*)
  she's the one person who can help me = è l'unica persona che può aiutarmi
- (*the same*)
  to take three exams in the one day = fare tre esami nello stesso giorno
3 *pronoun*
- (*when referring to something generally*)
  I need an umbrella—have you got one? = mi serve un ombrello—ne hai uno?

  > **!** *Note that it is necessary to use* **ne**, *which might be translated as* 'of them', *with pronouns like* **one**. *See also* **any, a few, many** *etc for this use of* **ne**.

- (*when referring to a specific person or thing*)
  I like the new house but she prefers the old one = a me piace la nuova casa, ma lei preferisce quella vecchia
  the one you like = quello che piace a te
  which one? = quale?
  this one = questo/questa
- (*when used to mean 'you' or 'people'*)
  one never knows = non si sa mai

4 one by one = uno a uno/una a una

one another *pronoun*
▶ *See the boxed note on* **si** *for more information and examples.*

  > **!** *Note that* **one another** *is very often translated by using a reflexive pronoun like* **si**, **ci** *or* **vi**.

  they love one another = si amano
  we don't like being apart from one another = odiamo essere separati

oneself *pronoun*
  = se stesso
  to enjoy oneself = divertirsi (**!** + *essere*)
  to hurt oneself = farsi male (**!** + *essere*)

onion *noun*
  an onion = una cipolla

only
1 *adverb*
  only = solo
  it's only a game = è solo un gioco
  they've only met once = si sono incontrati solo una volta
  he only hit his elbow = ha solo sbattuto il gomito
  you only have to ask = basta chiedere
2 *adjective*
  = unico/unica
  the only problem is that I can't drive = l'unico problema è che non so guidare
  she was the only one who didn't speak Italian = era l'unica che non parlava italiano
  an only child = un figlio unico/una figlia unica
3 only just
  I've only just arrived = sono appena arrivato

onto *preposition*
  = su

open
1 *verb*
  to open = aprire
  to open a letter = aprire una lettera
  the shop opens at eight = il negozio apre alle otto
  the door opens very easily = la porta si apre facilmente
2 *adjective*
- (*not closed*) = aperto/aperta
  to leave the door open = lasciare la porta aperta
- (*frank*) = onesto/onesta
3 *noun*
  out in the open = all'aperto

open-minded *adjective*
  to be open-minded = essere aperto/aperta

opera *noun*
  an opera = un'opera

operate *verb*
- (*to make something work*) = far funzionare   ····▶

O

- (*to carry out an operation*) = operare
  to operate on someone = operare
  qualcuno
  to operate on someone's leg = operare
  qualcuno alla gamba

operation *noun*
  an operation = un'operazione
  to have an operation = farsi operare (**!** +
  essere)

operator *noun* ▶ **281 |**
  an operator = un/una centralinista

opinion *noun*
  an opinion (*a point of view*) = un parere
  (*when judging a person, a situation*)
  = un'opinione
  in my opinion, they're lying = secondo me
  mentono

opponent *noun*
  an opponent = un
  avversario/un'avversaria

opportunity *noun*
  an opportunity = un'occasione
  to take the opportunity to visit Vicenza
  = cogliere l'occasione per visitare
  Vicenza

oppose *verb*
  to oppose a plan = opporsi a un piano
  (**!** + *essere*)
  to be opposed to nuclear weapons
  = essere contro le armi nucleari

opposite
  1 *preposition*
  = di fronte a
  she was sitting opposite me = era seduta
  di fronte a me
  2 *adjective*
  he was walking in the opposite direction
  = camminava nella direzione opposta
  3 *adverb*
  = di fronte
  4 *noun*
  the opposite = il contrario
  it's the exact opposite = è tutto il
  contrario

optician *noun* ▶ **281 |**
  an optician = un ottico

optimistic *adjective*
  = ottimistico/ottimistica

or *conjunction*
- **or** = o
  once or twice a week = una o due volte
  alla settimana
  we'll stay either here or at Marta's
  = staremo qui o da Marta
  do you have any brothers or sisters?
  = hai fratelli?
- (*in negative sentences*)
  I can't come today or tomorrow = non
  posso venire né oggi né domani
- (*otherwise*) = se no
  be careful or you'll break the cups = stai
  attento se no rompi le tazze

oral *adjective*
  = orale

orange
  1 *noun*
  an orange = un'arancia
  orange juice = il succo d'arancia
  2 *adjective* ▶ **147 |**
  = arancione (**!** *never changes*)

orchestra *noun*
  an orchestra = un'orchestra

order
  1 *verb*
- (*to tell*)
  to order someone to go = ordinare a
  qualcuno di andarsene
- (*to ask for*) = ordinare
  to order goods from a catalogue
  = ordinare degli articoli da un catalogo
  2 *noun*
- (*an instruction*)
  an order = un ordine
  to give orders = dare ordini
- **the right order** = l'ordine giusto
  the list is in alphabetical order = l'elenco
  è in ordine alfabetico
  3 in order to = per
  **I phoned them in order to change the
  date** = ho telefonato per cambiare la
  data

ordinary *adjective*
  = ordinario/ordinaria
  just an ordinary family = una famiglia
  qualunque

organ *noun*
  an organ = un organo

organization *noun*
  an organization = un'organizzazione

organize *verb*
  = organizzare
  to get organized = organizzarsi (**!** +
  essere)

original *adjective*
- (*first*) = originario/originaria
- (*true, real*) = originale
- (*new, fresh*) = originale

ornament *noun*
  an ornament = un soprammobile

orphan *noun*
  an orphan = un orfano/un'orfana

other
  1 *adjective*
  = altro/altra (+ *singular*)
  = altri/altre (+ *plural*)
  not that dress, the other one = non
  questo vestito, l'altro
  they sold the other car = hanno venduto
  l'altra macchina
  to annoy the other pupils = dar fastidio
  agli altri studenti
  **some people like driving, other people
  don't** = ad alcuni piace guidare, ad altri
  no

····▶

every other Saturday = un sabato sì e
uno no

2 *pronoun*

he makes the others laugh = fa ridere gli
altri

some students learn Italian easily, others
have problems = alcuni studenti
imparano facilmente l'italiano, altri
fanno più difficoltà

they came in one after the other = sono
entrati uno alla volta

otherwise *conjunction*
= altrimenti

ought *verb*

▶ *See the boxed note on* **dovere** *for more
information and examples.*

• you ought not to say things like that
= non dovresti dire cose del genere
you ought to be in bed = dovresti essere a
letto

they ought to arrive tomorrow
= dovrebbero arrivare domani

• (*when saying something didn't happen*)
you ought to have gone with them
= dovevi accompagnarli

our *determiner*

our = il nostro/la nostra (+ *singular*)
= i nostri/le nostre (+ *plural*)

> **!** *Note that the definite article* **il**/**la**, *etc
> is generally used except when talking
> about a close family member.*

he ran over our dog = ha investito il
nostro cane

we've sold all our CDs = abbiamo
venduto tutti i nostri CD

our mother = nostra madre

what do you think of our house? = cosa
pensi di casa nostra?

> **!** *Note that, when talking about parts of
> the body,* **suo**/**sua** *is not used. See the
> usage note on* **The human body**
> ▶ **137 |** *for more information.*

ours *pronoun*

ours = il nostro/la nostra (*singular*)
= i nostri/le nostre (*plural*)

> **!** *Note that* **il**/**la**, *etc is used when
> comparing things belonging to different
> people, but not when saying who
> something belongs to.*

their garden is big but ours is small = il
loro giardino è grande ma il nostro è
piccolo

their children are younger than ours = i
loro figli sono più piccoli dei nostri

the red car is ours = la macchina rossa è
nostra

a friend of ours = un amico nostro

ourselves *pronoun*

• (*when used as a reflexive pronoun*) = ci

> **!** *Note that* **ci** *combines with the
> infinitive and the gerund, and the
> imperative.* **Ci** *beomes* **ce** *before* **lo**/**la**,
> **li**/**le**, *and* **ne**.

we want to enjoy ourselves = vogliamo
divertirci

we didn't hurt ourselves = non ci siamo
fatti male

• (*when used for emphasis*)
we did it all by ourselves = abbiamo fatto
tutto da noi

out

> **!** *Often* **out** *occurs in combinations with
> verbs, for example:* **blow out**, **come
> out**, **find out**, **give out** *etc. To find the
> correct translations for this type of
> verb, look up the separate dictionary
> entries at* **blow**, **come**, **find**, **give** *etc.*

1 *adverb*

• (*outside*) = fuori
they're out there = sono là fuori
don't stay out in the rain = non restare
fuori sotto la pioggia
she's out in the garden = è in giardino
I'm looking for the way out = sto
cercando l'uscita

• (*absent*)
she's out = è uscita
someone called while you were out
= qualcuno ha telefonato quando eri
fuori

• (*not lighting, not on*)
to be out = essere spento/spenta
all the lights were out = tutte le luci
erano spente

2 out of

to walk out of the building = uscire dal
palazzo (**!** + *essere*)

to get out of the city = uscire dalla città
(**!** + *essere*)

to take a pencil out of the drawer
= prendere una matita dal cassetto

outdoor *adjective*
= all'aperto
an outdoor swimming pool = una piscina
scoperta

outdoors *adverb*
= all'aria aperta

outer space *noun*
outer space = lo spazio

outside

1 *preposition*

• (*in front of*) = davanti
to wait outside the school = aspettare
davanti alla scuola

• (*beyond*)
outside the city = fuori città

2 *adverb*
= fuori
let's go outside = andiamo fuori
let's bring the chairs outside = portiamo
fuori le sedie

3 *noun*
the outside = l'esterno
the outside of the building = l'esterno del
palazzo   ····▶

4 *adjective*
= esterno/esterna

oven *noun*
an oven = un forno

over

> **!** *Often* over *occurs in combinations with verbs, for example:* get over, move over *etc. To find the correct translations for this type of verb, look up the separate dictionary entries at* get, move *etc.*

1 *preposition*
- over = sopra
  to climb over a wall = scavalcare un muro
- (*across*)
  over there = laggiù
  come over here = vieni qua
- (*above*) = sopra
  the picture over the piano = il quadro sopra il piano
  young people over 18 = i ragazzi oltre i diciotto anni
- (*during*)
  we saw them over the weekend = li abbiamo visti durante il fine settimana
- (*everywhere*)
  I've looked all over the house for my keys = ho cercato le chiavi dappertutto in casa
2 *adverb*
- (*finished*)
  is the film over? = è finito il film?
- (*to one's home*)
  to ask someone over = invitare qualcuno
- to start over again = ricominciare da capo

overdose *noun*
an overdose = un'overdose

overtake *verb*
= sorpassare

overweight *adjective*
= sovrappeso (**!** *never changes*)

owe *verb*
= dovere
to owe money to someone = dovere soldi a qualcuno

owl *noun*
an owl = un gufo

own
1 *adjective*
you should clean your own room = dovresti pulire la tua camera
he'd like his own car = vorrebbe una macchina tutta sua
2 *pronoun*
I didn't use his pencil—I've got my own = non ho usato la sua matita, ho la mia
they have a house of their own = hanno una casa tutta loro
3 *verb*
= avere

he owns a shop in town = ha un negozio in città
who owns that dog? = di chi è quel cane?
4 on one's own = da solo/sola
own up = confessare
to own up to something = ammettere qualcosa

owner *noun*
an owner = un proprietario/una proprietaria

oxygen *noun*
oxygen = l'ossigeno

oyster *noun*
an oyster = un'ostrica

Pp

Pacific *noun*
the Pacific = il Pacifico

pack
1 *verb*
= fare i bagagli
I've got to pack my suitcase = devo fare la valigia
2 *noun*
a pack = un pacchetto
a pack of cigarettes = un pacchetto di sigarette
a pack of cards = un mazzo di carte

package *noun*
a package = un pacco

packed *adjective*
= affollato/affollata

packet *noun*
a packet = un pacchetto

page *noun*
a page = una pagina
on page six = a pagina sei

pain *noun*
pain = il dolore
I've got a pain in my back = ho un dolore alla schiena
to be in pain = soffrire

painful *adjective*
it's painful = fa male

paint
1 *noun*
paint = la pittura
2 *verb*
= dipingere
to paint something green = dipingere qualcosa di verde

paintbrush *noun*
a paintbrush = un pennello

painter *noun* ▶ 281
- *(a decorator)*
  a painter = un imbianchino
- *(an artist)*
  a painter = un pittore/una pittrice

painting *noun*
- *(a picture)*
  a painting = un quadro
- *(the activity)*
  painting = la pittura

pair *noun*
  a pair = un paio
  a pair of shoes = un paio di scarpe
  two pairs of shoes = due paia di scarpe

pajamas *noun* *(US English)*
  pajamas = un pigiama *(singular)*

Pakistan *noun* ▶ 151
  Pakistan = il Pakistan

palace *noun*
  a palace = un palazzo

pale *adjective*
  = pallido/pallida
  to go pale, to turn pale = impallidire (**!** +
  essere)

pancake *noun*
  a pancake = una crêpe

panic *verb*
  = farsi prendere dal panico (**!** + *essere*)

pants *noun*
- *(British English)* *(underwear)*
  a pair of pants = uno slip
- *(US English)* *(trousers)*
  pants = i pantaloni

pantyhose *noun* *(US English)*
  pantyhose = il collant

paper *noun*
- *(for writing or drawing on)*
  paper = la carta
  a sheet of paper = un foglio di carta
- *(a newspaper)*
  a paper = un giornale

parachuting *noun* ▶ 178
  parachuting = il paracadutismo

parade *noun*
  a parade = una sfilata

paralysed *(British English)*,
paralyzed *(US English)* *adjective*
  = paralizzato/paralizzata

parcel *noun*
  a parcel = un pacco

parents *noun*
  parents = i genitori

  ! Note that **parenti** means 'relatives'.

Paris *noun* ▶ 151
  Paris = Parigi

park
1 *noun*
  a park = un parco
2 *verb*
  to park a car = parcheggiare una
  macchina
  to park near the office = parcheggiare
  vicino all'ufficio

parking lot *noun* *(US English)*
  a parking lot = un parcheggio

parliament *noun*
  a parliament = un parlamento

parrot *noun*
  a parrot = un pappagallo

part
- a part = una parte
  part of the [book | film | time] = una parte
  del [libro | film | tempo]
  it's part of the job = fa parte del lavoro
- *(a piece for a machine, a car)*
  a part = un pezzo
- *(in a series)*
  a part = un episodio
- *(a role)*
  a part = una parte
  to play the part of Evita = recitare la
  parte di Evita

participate *verb*
  to participate in something = partecipare
  a qualcosa

particular
1 *adjective*
  = particolare
2 in particular = in particolare

partner *noun*
- *(in a relationship, dancing)*
  a partner = un compagno/una compagna
- *(in business)*
  a partner = un socio/una socia

part-time *adverb*
  = part time
  to work part-time = lavorare part time

party *noun*
- *(a social event)*
  a party = una festa
  a birthday party = una festa di
  compleanno
- a political party = un partito politico

pass *verb*
- *(to go past)* = passare (**!** + *essere*)
  to pass the school = passare davanti alla
  scuola
  to pass a car = sorpassare una macchina
  to pass someone in the street
  = incrociare qualcuno per strada
- *(to give)* = passare (**!** + *avere*)
  pass me the salt = passami il sale
- *(to spend)* = passare (**!** + *avere*)
  to pass the time [reading | painting | listening
  to the radio] = passare il tempo [a leggere |
  a dipingere | ad ascoltare la radio]   ····▶

- (*to succeed in an exam*) = passare (**!** + *essere* or *avere*)
  I passed the exam! = ho passato l'esame!
  I passed! = sono passato!
pass around
  to pass around the biscuits = passare i biscotti
pass on = passare
  to pass on a message to someone = passare un messaggio a qualcuno

passenger *noun*
  a passenger = un passeggero/una passeggera

passport *noun*
  a passport = un passaporto

past
1 *noun*
  the past = il passato
  in the past = in passato
2 *adjective*
  = scorso/scorsa
  the past few days have been difficult = i giorni scorsi sono stati difficili
3 *preposition*
- (*when talking about time*) ▶ **146**|
  it's twenty past four = sono le quattro e venti
  it's past midnight = è mezzanotte passata
- (*by*)
  to go past someone = passare davanti a qualcuno (**!** + *essere*)
  she ran past me = mi è passata davanti correndo
- (*beyond*) = oltre
  it's just past the traffic lights = è appena oltre il semaforo
4 *adverb*
  to go past, to walk past = passare (**!** + *essere*)

pasta *noun*
  pasta = la pasta

pastry *noun*
- (*for baking*)
  pastry = la pasta
- (*a cake*)
  a pastry = un pasticcino

path *noun*
  a path = un sentiero

patience *noun*
  patience = la pazienza
  to lose patience with someone = perdere la pazienza con qualcuno

patient
1 *noun*
  a patient = un/una paziente
2 *adjective*
  = paziente

pattern *noun*
- (*a design*)
  a pattern = un motivo

- (*when making garments*)
  a pattern (*for knitting*) = un modello
  (*for sewing*) = un cartamodello

pavement *noun* (*British English*)
  the pavement = il marciapiede

paw *noun*
  a paw = una zampa

pay
1 *verb*
- **to pay** = pagare
  to pay the bills = pagare le bollette
  to pay for the shopping = pagare la spesa
  he paid for my meal = mi ha pagato il pranzo
- (*when talking about wages*)
  the work doesn't pay very well = il lavoro è mal pagato
  I'm paid eight pounds an hour = mi pagano otto sterline l'ora
- (*to give*)
  to pay attention to the teacher = ascoltare l'insegnante
  to pay someone a visit = fare visita a qualcuno
  to pay someone a compliment = fare un complimento a qualcuno
2 *noun*
  pay = la paga
  the pay is good = la paga è buona
pay back = rimborsare

PE *noun*
  PE = l'educazione fisica

pea *noun*
  a pea = un pisello

peace *noun*
  peace = la pace

peach *noun*
  a peach = una pesca

peanut *noun*
  a peanut = una nocciolina

pear *noun*
  a pear = una pera

pearl *noun*
  a pearl = una perla

pebble *noun*
  a pebble = un ciottolo

pedestrian *noun*
  a pedestrian = un pedone

pedestrian crossing *noun*
  a pedestrian crossing = un attraversamento pedonale

peel *verb*
  = sbucciare

pen *noun*
  a pen = una penna

penalty *noun*
  a penalty (*in soccer*) = un rigore
  (*in rugby*) = una penalità

pencil *noun*
a pencil = una matita

pencil case *noun*
a pencil case = un portamatite

pencil sharpener *noun*
a pencil sharpener = un temperamatite

penfriend (*British English*), **penpal** *noun*
a penfriend = un amico/un'amica di penna

penknife *noun*
a penknife = un temperino

pensioner *noun*
a pensioner = un pensionato/una pensionata

people *noun*
people (*in general*) = la gente
(*if counting*) = le persone
we met very nice people = abbiamo conosciuto gente molto simpatica
most people don't know what's going on = la maggior parte della gente non sa cosa succede
there were three people at the meeting = alla riunione c'erano tre persone
there are too many people here = qui c'è troppa gente
to help other people = aiutare gli altri

pepper *noun*
• (*the spice*)
  pepper = il pepe
• (*the vegetable*)
  a pepper = un peperone

per *preposition*
per person = a persona

per cent, **percent** (*US English*) *noun*
per cent = per cento

perfect *adjective*
= perfetto/perfetta
to speak perfect Italian = parlare un italiano perfetto
it's the perfect place for a picnic = è il posto ideale per un picnic

perform *verb*
• (*to do*)
  to perform a task = svolgere un compito
• (*to act*) = recitare
  (*to play music*) = suonare

perfume *noun*
perfume = il profumo

perhaps *adverb*
= forse

period *noun*
• (*in time*)
  a period = un periodo
• (*in history*)
  a period = un'epoca
• (*for women*)
  a period = le mestruazioni

to have one's period = avere le mestruazioni
• (*a school lesson*)
  a period = un'ora

permanent *adjective*
= permanente

permission *noun*
permission = il permesso
to get permission to leave the country = ottenere il permesso di lasciare il paese

person *noun*
a person = una persona
an old person = una persona anziana
he's not a very patient person = non è molto paziente

personal *adjective*
= personale

personality *noun*
a personality = una personalità

perspire *verb*
= sudare

persuade *verb*
= convincere
to persuade someone to buy a car = convincere qualcuno a comprare una macchina

pessimist *noun*
a pessimist = un/una pessimista

pessimistic *adjective*
= pessimista

pet *noun*
a pet = un animale domestico
do you have any pets? = hai qualche animale a casa?

petrol *noun* (*British English*)
petrol = la benzina
to run out of petrol = restare senza benzina (**!** + *essere*)

petrol station *noun* (*British English*)
a petrol station = una stazione di servizio

pet shop *noun* ▶ 281|
a pet shop = un negozio di animali

phone
1 *noun*
a phone = un telefono
the phone's ringing = sta squillando il telefono
to answer the phone = rispondere al telefono
he's on the phone = è al telefono
2 *verb*
to phone someone = telefonare a qualcuno

phone book *noun*
the phone book = l'elenco telefonico

phone booth *noun*
a phone booth = una cabina telefonica

P

phone call *noun*
  a phone call = una telefonata
  to make a phone call = fare una telefonata

phone card *noun*
  a phone card = una scheda telefonica

phone number *noun*
  a phone number = un numero di telefono

photo *noun*
  a photo = una foto

photocopier *noun*
  a photocopier = una fotocopiatrice

photocopy *noun*
  a photocopy = una fotocopia

photograph *noun*
  a photograph = una fotografia
  to take a photograph of someone = fare una fotografia a qualcuno

photographer *noun* ▶ 281 |
  a photographer = un fotografo/una fotografa

physical *adjective*
  = fisico/fisica

physics *noun*
  physics = la fisica

piano *noun*
  a piano = un piano

pick *verb*
• (*to choose*) = scegliere
  to pick a number = scegliere un numero
• (*to collect*) = raccogliere
  to pick blackberries = raccogliere le more
• (*to take*)
  to pick a book off the shelf = prendere un libro dallo scaffale
pick on
  to pick on someone = prendersela con qualcuno (**!** + *essere*)
pick out = scegliere
pick up
• (*to lift*) = raccogliere
  to pick the clothes up off the floor = raccogliere i vestiti da terra
  to pick a baby up = prendere in braccio un bambino
  to pick up the phone = alzare il ricevitore
• (*to collect*)
  he's coming to pick me up = viene a prendermi
• (*to buy*) = prendere
  I stopped to pick up some milk = mi sono fermato a prendere del latte
• (*to learn*)
  to pick up a little German = imparare un po' di tedesco

picnic *noun*
  a picnic = un picnic
  let's have a picnic = andiamo a fare un picnic

picture *noun*
• a picture (*painted*) = un quadro
  (*drawn*) = un disegno
  to paint someone's picture = fare il ritratto a qualcuno
• (*a photograph*)
  a picture = una foto
• the pictures = il cinema (*singular*)

piece *noun*
• (*a bit*)
  a piece = un pezzo
  a piece of cheese = un pezzo di formaggio
  to fall to pieces = cadere a pezzi (**!** + *essere*)
• (*a coin*)
  a 50-pence piece = una moneta da 50 penny
• (*other uses*)
  a piece of furniture = un mobile
  a piece of information = un'informazione
  a piece of advice = un consiglio

pig *noun*
  a pig = un maiale

pigeon *noun*
  a pigeon = un piccione

pile
• a pile = una pila
  (*untidy*) = un mucchio
• (*lots*)
  piles of [toys | records | books] = un mucchio di [giocattoli | dischi | libri]

pill *noun*
• (*a tablet*)
  a pill = una pillola
• (*a method of contraception*)
  the pill = la pillola

pillow *noun*
  a pillow = un cuscino

pilot *noun* ▶ 281 |
  a pilot = un/una pilota

pin *noun*
  a pin = uno spillo

pinball *noun* ▶ 178 |
  pinball = il flipper

pinch *verb*
• to pinch = pizzicare
  he pinched my arm, he pinched me on the arm = mi ha pizzicato il braccio
• (*to hurt by being too tight*) = stringere
  my shoes are pinching = le scarpe mi stringono

pineapple *noun*
  a pineapple = un ananas

pine tree *noun*
  a pine tree = un pino

pink *adjective* ▶ 147 |
  = rosa (*never changes*)

pint *noun*
* (*the quantity*)
  a pint = una pinta

  > **!** *Note that a* **pint** = *0.57 l in Britain and*
  > *0.47 l in the US.*

  a pint of milk ≈ un mezzo litro di latte
* (*British English*) (*a drink*)
  let's go for a pint = andiamo a bere una
  birra

pipe *noun*
* (*for gas, water*)
  a pipe = un tubo
* (*for smoking*)
  a pipe = una pipa

Pisces *noun*
  Pisces = Pesci (*masculine plural*)

pitch *noun* (*British English*)
  a football pitch = un campo di calcio

pity
1 *noun*
* **to take pity on someone** = avere pietà di
  qualcuno
* (*when expressing regret*)
  what a pity! = che peccato!
  it's a pity you can't come = è un peccato
  che tu non possa venire

  > **!** *Note that the subjunctive is used after*
  > **è un peccato che**.

2 *verb*
  = compatire

place *noun*
* **a place** = un posto
  they came from all over the place = sono
  venuti da tutte le parti
* (*where something happens*)
  place of birth = luogo di nascita
  a public place = un luogo pubblico
* (*a home*)
  at Alison's place = da Alison
  I'd like a place of my own = vorrei una
  casa tutta mia
* (*in a queue, on a bus, in a car park*)
  a place = un posto
  is this place free? = è libero questo
  posto?
  to take someone's place = prendere il
  posto di qualcuno
  to find a place to park = trovare un
  parcheggio
* (*on a team, a course, in a firm*)
  a place = un posto
  to get a place on a course = ottenere un
  posto nel corso
* (*in a contest*)
  a place = un posto
  to take first place = classificarsi al primo
  posto (**!** + *essere*)

plain
1 *adjective*
* (*simple*) = semplice
  a plain dress = un vestito semplice
* (*not good-looking*) = brutto/brutta

2 *noun*
  a plain = una pianura

plan
1 *noun*
  a plan = un piano
  do you have any plans for the future?
    = hai progetti per il futuro?
  I don't have any plans for tonight = non
  ho programmi per stasera
2 *verb*
* (*to prepare, to organize*)
  to plan a trip = organizzare una gita
* (*to intend*) = avere intenzione di
  I'm planning to visit Scotland = ho
  intenzione di visitare la Scozia

plane *noun*
  a plane = un aereo

planet *noun*
  a planet = un pianeta

plant
1 *noun*
  a plant = una pianta
2 *verb*
  = piantare

plaster *noun* (*British English*)
  a plaster = un cerotto

plastic
1 *noun*
  plastic = la plastica
2 *adjective*
  a plastic spoon
    = un cucchiaio di plastica

plate *noun*
  a plate = un piatto

platform *noun*
  a platform = un binario

play
1 *verb*
* (*to have fun*) = giocare
  to play with friends = giocare con gli
  amici
* (*when talking about games, sports*)
  ▶ 178 | = giocare
  to play cards = giocare a carte
  to play [**football** | **cricket** | **tennis**] = giocare [a
  calcio | a cricket | a tennis]
  Italy is playing (against) Scotland
  = l'Italia gioca contro la Scozia
* (*when talking about music*) = suonare
  to play [**the piano** | **the flute** | **drums**]
  = suonare [il piano | il flauto | la batteria]
* (*to put on*) = mettere
  to play [**a video** | **a CD** | **a record**] = mettere
  [una videocassetta | un CD | un disco]
* (*when talking about theatre, cinema*)
  to play the role of Juliet = recitare il
  ruolo di Giulietta
2 *noun*
  a play = una commedia   ····▶

P

play around = fare lo sciocco/la sciocca
play back
  to play back a tape = riascoltare un
    nastro

player noun ▶ 178|
  a player = un giocatore/una giocatrice
  a tennis player = un/una tennista

playground noun
  a playground = un parco giochi
  the school playground = il cortile della
    scuola

please adverb
  = per favore
  please come in = entrate, prego
  'more cake?'—'yes please' = 'ancora
    torta?'—'sì, grazie'

pleased adjective
  = contento/contenta
  I was very pleased with myself = ero
    proprio contento di me
  pleased to meet you! = piacere!

plenty pronoun
  to have plenty [of time | of money | of
    friends] = avere un sacco di [tempo | soldi |
    amici]

plot noun
• (a plan)
  a plot = un complotto
• (the story in a film, a novel, a play)
  the plot = la trama

plug noun
• (on an appliance)
  a plug = una spina
  to pull out the plug = staccare la spina
• (in a sink or bath)
  a plug = un tappo
plug in
  to plug in the TV = inserire la spina della
    TV

plum noun
  a plum = una susina

plumber noun ▶ 281|
  a plumber = un idraulico

plus preposition
  = più
  three plus three are six = tre più tre fa sei

pocket noun
  a pocket = una tasca

pocket money noun
  pocket money = la paghetta

poem noun
  a poem = una poesia

point
1 noun
• (the sharp end)
  the point = la punta
  the point of a pencil = la punta di una
    matita
• (in a contest, a game)
  a point = un punto

• (a statement in a discussion)
  a point = un'osservazione
  to make a point = fare un'osservazione
• (the most important idea)
  the point = la questione
  that's not the point = la questione è
    un'altra
• (use)
  there's no point in shouting = è inutile
    urlare
• (when talking about time)
  to be on the point of [moving | leaving |
    selling the house] = stare per [traslocare |
    partire | vendere la casa]
2 verb
• (to indicate)
  to point (one's finger) at someone
    = indicare qualcuno con il dito
  to point the way to the station = indicare
    la strada per la stazione
• (to aim)
  to point a gun at someone = puntare una
    pistola a qualcuno
point out = indicare

poison
1 noun
  poison = il veleno
2 verb
  = avvelenare

Poland noun ▶ 151|
  Poland = la Polonia

pole noun
  a pole = un palo

police noun
  the police = la polizia

policeman noun ▶ 281|
  a policeman = un poliziotto

police station noun
  the police station = la questura

policewoman noun ▶ 281|
  a policewoman = una poliziotta

polish verb
  = lucidare

polite adjective
  = educato/educata

political adjective
  = politico/politica

politician noun ▶ 281|
  a politician = un politico

politics noun
  politics = la politica

pollute verb
  = inquinare

pollution noun
  pollution = l'inquinamento

pond noun
  a pond = uno stagno

pony noun
  a pony = un pony

ponytail noun
  a ponytail = la coda di cavallo
pool noun
• (a swimming pool)
  a pool = una piscina
• (on the ground, the floor)
  a pool of water = una pozza d'acqua
• (the game) ▶ **178** |
  pool = il biliardo

poor adjective
• (not wealthy) = povero/povera
• (not satisfactory) = scarso/scarsa
  to be poor at languages = essere scarso in
    lingue
• (expressing sympathy) = povero/povera
  (**!** before the noun)
  the poor boy is exhausted = il povero
    ragazzo è esausto

popular adjective
  a popular actor = un attore popolare
  a popular hobby = un hobby diffuso
  to be popular with the boys = avere
    successo con i ragazzi

population noun
  the population = la popolazione

pork noun
  pork = il maiale

port noun
  a port = un porto

portrait noun
  a portrait = un ritratto

Portugal noun ▶ **151** |
  Portugal = il Portogallo

Portuguese ▶ **199** |
  1 adjective
  = portoghese
  2 noun
• (the people)
  the Portuguese = i portoghesi
• (the language)
  Portuguese = il portoghese

positive adjective
  = positivo/positiva

possibility noun
  a possibility = una possibilità

possible adjective
  = possibile
  they came as quickly as possible = sono
    venuti prima possibile
  I did as much as possible = ho fatto
    tutto il possibile

post (British English)
  1 noun
  the post = la posta
  2 verb
  to post a letter = imbucare una lettera

postbox noun (British English)
  a postbox = una buca delle lettere

postcard noun
  a postcard = una cartolina

postcode noun (British English)
  a postcode = un codice postale

poster noun
  a poster (giving information) = un
    manifesto
  (used as a picture) = un poster

postman noun ▶ **281** | (British English)
  a postman = un postino

post office noun
  a post office = un ufficio postale

postpone verb
  to postpone a concert = rinviare un
    concerto
  let's postpone the party until next week
    = rimandiamo la festa alla prossima
    settimana

pot noun
• (a container)
  a pot = un vasetto
• (a saucepan)
  a pot = una pentola

potato noun
  a potato = una patata

pottery noun
  pottery = la ceramica

pound noun
• (the currency)
  a pound = una sterlina
• (the measurement)
  a pound = una libbra
  | **!** Note that a pound = 453.6 g. |
  two pounds of apples ≈ un chilo di mele

pour verb
• (from a container) = versare
  to pour someone a gin = versare un gin a
    qualcuno
• (to flow) = riversarsi (**!** + essere)
  the water was pouring into the kitchen
    = l'acqua si riversava nella cucina
• (to escape)
  there is smoke pouring out of the
    window = esce fumo dalla finestra
• (to rain)
  it's pouring (with rain) = sta piovendo a
    dirotto

powder noun
  a powder = una polvere

power noun
• (control)
  power = il potere
  to be in power = essere al potere
• (electricity)
  power = la corrente

practical adjective
  = pratico/pratica

practise (British English), **practice**
  (US English) verb
  (at the piano, guitar) = esercitarsi (**!** +
  essere)   ····▶

to practise the violin = esercitarsi al violino
(*at a sport*) = allenarsi (**!** + *essere*)
(*for a play, a concert*) = fare le prove

praise *verb*
= lodare

prawn *noun* (*British English*)
a prawn = un gambero

prayer *noun*
a prayer = una preghiera

precaution *noun*
a precaution = una precauzione

precious *adjective*
= prezioso/preziosa

precise *adjective*
= preciso/precisa

prefer *verb*
= preferire
to prefer tea to coffee = preferire il tè al caffè
I'd prefer to phone = preferisco telefonare

pregnant *adjective*
= incinta

prejudice *noun*
a prejudice = un pregiudizio

prepare *verb*
• (*to get something or someone ready*) = preparare
• (*to get ready*) = prepararsi (**!** + *essere*)
to prepare for an exam = prepararsi per un esame

prepared *adjective*
= pronto/pronta
I'm prepared to wait = sono pronto ad attendere
to be prepared for an exam = essere pronto per un esame

prescription *noun*
a prescription = una ricetta

present
1 *noun*
• (*a gift*)
a present = un regalo
• (*now*)
the present = il presente
I'm staying here for the present = sto qui per il momento
2 *verb*
• (*to give*)
to present a prize to someone = consegnare un premio a qualcuno
• (*on radio or TV*)
to present a programme = presentare un programma

president *noun* ▶ 281
the president = il presidente/la presidentessa

press
1 *verb*
= premere

to press the bell = suonare il campanello
2 *noun*
the press = la stampa

pressure *noun*
pressure = la pressione
to put pressure on someone = fare pressione su qualcuno

pretend *verb*
= fingere
he's pretending to be annoyed = finge di essere seccato

pretty
1 *adjective*
= carino/carina
2 *adverb*
= abbastanza
it's pretty old = è abbastanza antico
that's pretty good! = niente male!

prevent *verb*
to prevent a war = evitare una guerra
to prevent someone from [working | having fun | sleeping] = impedire a qualcuno di [lavorare | divertirsi | dormire]

previous *adjective*
= precedente

price *noun*
a price = un prezzo

pride *noun*
pride = l'orgoglio

priest *noun* ▶ 281
a priest (*Catholic*) = un prete
(*other faiths*) = un sacerdote/una sacerdotessa

primary school *noun*
a primary school = una scuola elementare
a primary school teacher = un maestro/una maestra

prime minister *noun* ▶ 281
the prime minister = il primo ministro

prince *noun*
a prince = un principe

princess *noun*
a princess = una principessa

principal *noun*
a principal (*in a senior school*) = un/una preside
(*in a junior school*) = un direttore/una direttrice

print
1 *verb*
= stampare
2 *noun*
• (*of a photo*)
a print = una foto
• (*of a finger, a foot*)
a print = un'impronta

prison *noun*
a prison = una prigione
in prison = in prigione

prisoner *noun*
a prisoner = un prigioniero/una
prigioniera

private
1 *adjective*
= privato/privata
2 in private = in privato

prize *noun*
a prize = un premio

probably *adverb*
= probabilmente

problem *noun*
a problem = un problema
no problem! = non c'è problema!

process *noun*
a process = un procedimento
I'm in the process of selling my house
= sto vendendo la casa

produce
1 *verb*
• (*to make*) = produrre
• (*to create*)
to produce a film = produrre un film
to produce a play = mettere in scena una
commedia
2 *noun*
produce = i prodotti (*plural*)

product *noun*
a product = un prodotto

production *noun*
production = la produzione

profession *noun*
a profession = una professione

professional *adjective*
= professionale

professor *noun* ▶ 281 |
a professor = un professore/una
professoressa

profit *noun*
to make a profit = ricavare un utile

program
1 *noun*
• (*for a computer*)
a program = un programma
• (*US English*) ▶ **programme**
2 *verb*
= programmare

programme (*British English*),
program (*US English*)
1 *noun*
a programme = un programma
a programme about China = un
programma sulla Cina
2 *verb*
= programmare

progress *noun*
progress = il progresso
to make progress = fare progressi

project *noun*
a project = un progetto
(*at school*) = una ricerca

promise
1 *verb*
= promettere
to promise [to write | to pay | to say nothing]
= promettere [di scrivere | di pagare | di non
dire niente]
2 *noun*
a promise = una promessa

pronounce *verb*
= pronunciare
how do you pronounce 'chiacchierata'?
= come si pronuncia 'chiacchierata'?

proof *noun*
proof = le prove (*plural*)

properly *adverb*
= correttamente

property *noun*
property = la proprietà

protect *verb*
= proteggere

protest *verb*
• (*to complain*) = protestare
• (*to demonstrate*) = manifestare

protester *noun*
a protester = un/una manifestante

proud *adjective*
= orgoglioso/orgogliosa
she's proud of her work = è orgogliosa
del suo lavoro

prove *verb*
= provare

provide *verb*
to provide meals = fornire dei pasti
to provide a service = offrire un servizio

provided *conjunction*
I'll help you provided you pay me = ti
aiuto a condizione che mi paghi

> ! *Note that the subjunctive is used after*
> a condizione che.

psychiatrist *noun* ▶ 281 |
a psychiatrist = uno/una psichiatra

psychologist *noun* ▶ 281 |
a psychologist = uno psicologo/una
psicologa

pub *noun* (*British English*)
a pub = un pub

public
1 *noun*
the public = il pubblico
2 *adjective*
= pubblico/pubblica
a public library = una biblioteca
comunale
3 in public = in pubblico

P

public holiday noun
  a public holiday = un giorno festivo

public transport noun
  public transport = i trasporti pubblici
  (plural)

pudding noun (British English)
  a pudding = un dolce

puddle noun
  a puddle = una pozzanghera

pull verb
• to pull = tirare
  to pull someone's hair = tirare i capelli a
  qualcuno
  to pull (on) a rope = tirare una fune
• (to take out)
  to pull a handkerchief out of one's pocket
  = tirare fuori un fazzoletto dalla tasca
  to pull someone out of the river = tirare
  fuori qualcuno dal fiume
• to pull a face (British English) = fare una
  smorfia
pull down
• (to knock down) = demolire
• (to lower) = abbassare
pull out = tirare fuori
pull up
• (to stop) = fermarsi (! + essere)

pullover noun
  a pullover = un maglione

pump noun
  a pump = una pompa
pump up = gonfiare

pumpkin noun
  a pumpkin = una zucca

punch verb
  = dare un pugno
  she punched him in the face = gli ha
  dato un pugno in faccia

puncture noun
  I've got a puncture = ho bucato

punish verb
  = punire

pupil noun
  a pupil = uno studente/una studentessa

puppy noun
  a puppy = un cucciolo

pure adjective
  = puro/pura

purple adjective ▶ 147
  = viola (never changes)

purpose
1 noun
  a purpose = uno scopo
2 on purpose = apposta
  you did it on purpose! = l'hai fatto
  apposta!

purse noun
• (for money)
  a purse = un borsellino

• (US English) (a handbag)
  a purse = una borsa

push verb
• to push = spingere
  to push someone down the stairs
  = spingere qualcuno giù per le scale
  to push past someone = spingere
  qualcuno per passare
• (to sell) = spacciare
  to push drugs = spacciare droga

pushchair noun (British English)
  a pushchair = un passeggino

put verb
  = mettere
  don't put sugar in my coffee = non
  mettere zucchero nel mio caffè
  to put someone in a bad mood = mettere
  qualcuno di malumore
put away = mettere via
put back
• (to return to its place) = rimettere
  to put a book back on the shelf
  = rimettere un libro sullo scaffale
• (to change the time)
  to put the clocks back = mettere indietro
  l'orologio
put down
• (on a surface) = posare
  put your cases down here = posa qui le
  valigie
• (when phoning)
  to put the phone down = mettere giù il
  telefono
• (British English) (to give an injection to)
  = abbattere
  our dog had to be put down = abbiamo
  dovuto far abbattere il cane
put forward = anticipare
  to put the clocks forward = mettere
  avanti l'orologio
put off
• (to delay) = rinviare
• (to switch off) = spegnere
put on
• (when dressing) = mettersi (! + essere)
  to put jeans on = mettersi i jeans
• (to switch on)
  to put the heating on = accendere il
  riscaldamento
  to put a CD on = mettere un CD
• to put on weight = mettere su peso
• (to organize, to produce) = organizzare
  to put on a play = mettere in scena una
  commedia
put out
• to put out a cigarette = spegnere una
  sigaretta
• (to take out) = mettere fuori
  to put the trash out = mettere fuori la
  spazzatura
put up
• to put up one's hand = alzare la mano
• (to attach)
  to put a sign up = mettere un cartello
• (when camping)

Quantities

The following examples show the use of **ne** ('of it' or 'of them'). Note that **ne** becomes **n'** before
è, **era**, etc. This word must be included when you are mentioning quantities but the thing you
are talking about is not expressed. However, **ne** is not needed when the commodity is specified
(*there is a lot of butter* = c'è molto burro).

How much?

how much is there?	= quanto ce **n'**è?
there's a lot	= ce **n'**è molto
there's not much	= non ce **n'**è molto
there isn't any	= non ce **n'**è
there's two kilos	= ce **n'**è due chili
how much paint do you have?	= quanta vernice hai?
I have a lot	= **ne** ho molta

How many?

how many are there?	= quanti ce **ne** sono?
there are a lot	= ce **ne** sono molti
there aren't many	= non ce **ne** sono molti
there are twenty	= ce **ne** sono venti
how many children do you have?	= quanti figli hai?
I have three	= **ne** ho tre

Relative quantities

*how much is it **a** litre?*	= quanto costa **al** litro?
*it costs five pounds **a** litre*	= costa cinque sterline **al** litro

---

to put up a tent = montare una tenda
- (*British English*) (*to raise*) = aumentare
  to put the rent up = aumentare l'affitto
- (*to give someone a place to stay*)
  = ospitare
put up with = sopportare

puzzle *noun*
  a puzzle = un puzzle

pyjamas *noun* (*British English*)
  pyjamas = un pigiama (*singular*)

qualified *adjective*
- (*having studied*) = diplomato/diplomata
- (*having experience, skills*)
  = specializzato/specializzata

quality *noun*
  quality = la qualità

quantity *noun*
  a quantity = una quantità

quarrel
1 *noun*
  a quarrel = un litigio
2 *verb*
  = litigare

quarter
1 *noun*
  a quarter = un quarto
  a quarter of an hour = un quarto d'ora
  to cut the tomatoes in quarters = tagliare
  i pomodori in quattro
2 *pronoun*
- (*when talking about quantities,
  numbers*) ▶ **233** |
  a quarter of the population = un quarto
  della popolazione
- (*when talking about time*) ▶ **146** |
  an hour and a quarter = un'ora e un
  quarto
  it's (a) quarter past five = sono le cinque
  e un quarto

quay *noun*
  a quay = un molo

queen *noun*
  a queen = una regina

question
1 *noun*
- (*a request for information*)
  a question = una domanda   ····▶

Q

to ask someone a question = fare una
  domanda a qualcuno
• (*a problem, a matter*)
  a question = una questione
2 *verb*
  = interrogare

queue (*British English*)
1 *noun*
  a queue = una coda
  to join the queue = mettersi in coda (**!** +
    essere)
2 *verb*
  = fare la coda

quick *adjective*
  = rapido/rapida
  a quick answer = una risposta rapida
  it's quicker to go by train = è più rapido
    andare in treno

quiet
1 *adjective*
• (*silent*) = silenzioso/silenziosa
  be quiet! = fai silenzio!
• (*not talkative*) = taciturno/taciturna
• (*calm*) = tranquillo/tranquilla
  it's a quiet village = è un paese tranquillo
2 *noun*
  quiet = il silenzio
  quiet please! = silenzio, per favore!

quietly *adverb*
  to speak quietly = parlare piano
  to [play | sit | read] quietly = [giocare | stare
    seduto | leggere] in silenzio

quit *verb*
• (*to resign*) = licenziarsi (**!** + *essere*)
• (*US English*) (*to give up*)
  to quit [smoking | drinking | working]
    = smettere di [fumare | bere | lavorare]

quite *adverb*
• (*rather*) = abbastanza
  they go back to Italy quite often
    = ritornano in Italia abbastanza spesso
  I quite like Chinese food = mi piace
    abbastanza la cucina cinese
  she earns quite a lot of money
    = guadagna abbastanza
• (*completely*)
  it's not quite ready yet = non è ancora del
    tutto pronto
  you're quite right = hai perfettamente
    ragione
  are you quite sure? = sei sicurissimo?
• (*exactly*)
  'is it true?'—'not quite' = 'è vero?'—'non
    esattamente'
  I don't quite know what he does = non so
    esattamente cosa faccia

quiz *noun*
  a quiz = un quiz

Rr

rabbit *noun*
  a rabbit = un coniglio

race
1 *noun*
• (*a contest*)
  a race = una corsa
• (*for horse-racing*)
  the races = le corse
2 *verb*
• (*to compete with*)
  to race (against) someone = fare a gara
    con qualcuno
  I'll race you to the car = facciamo a gara
    fino alla macchina
• (*to take part in a contest*) = gareggiare

racism *noun*
  racism = il razzismo

racket, racquet *noun*
  a racket = una racchetta

radiator *noun*
  a radiator = un radiatore

radio *noun*
  a radio = una radio
  on the radio = alla radio

rage *noun*
  rage = la rabbia
  to fly into a rage = arrabbiarsi (**!** +
    essere)

raid *verb*
  to raid a bank = rapinare una banca
  the police raided the building = la polizia
    ha fatto irruzione nell'edificio

rail *noun*
• (*for holding on to*)
  a rail = un corrimano
• (*for trains*)
  the rails = i binari

railway (*British English*), **railroad** (*US
  English*) *noun*
• (*a track*)
  a railway = una strada ferrata
• (*the rail system*)
  the railway = la ferrovia

rain
1 *noun*
  rain = la pioggia
  in the rain = sotto la pioggia
2 *verb*
  = piovere (**!** + *essere* or *avere*)
  it's raining = piove

rainbow *noun*
  a rainbow = un arcobaleno

raincoat *noun*
  a raincoat = un impermeabile

raise *verb*
- (*to lift*) = sollevare
- (*to increase*) = aumentare
  to raise prices = aumentare i prezzi
- **to raise one's voice** = alzare la voce
- **to raise a subject** = sollevare una
  questione
- (*to bring up*)
  to raise children = allevare dei bambini

range *noun*
- (*a selection*)
  a range = una gamma
- (*of mountains*)
  a range = una catena
- (*US English*) (*for cooking*)
  a range = una cucina

rare *adjective*
- (*not common*) = raro/rara
- (*very slightly cooked*) = al sangue

rarely *adverb*
= raramente

raspberry *noun*
  a raspberry = un lampone

rat *noun*
  a rat = un ratto

rather *adverb*
- (*when saying what one would prefer*)
  I'd rather [**leave** | **stay here** | **read the paper**]
  = preferisco [andarmene | restare qui |
  leggere il giornale]
  I'd rather you came with me = preferisco
  che tu venga con me

  ! *Note that the subjunctive is used after*
  preferisco che.

- (*quite*) = piuttosto
  I think he's rather nice = lo trovo
  piuttosto simpatico

raw *adjective*
= crudo/cruda

razor *noun*
  a razor = un rasoio

razor blade *noun*
  a razor blade = una lametta

reach *verb*
- (*to arrive at*) = arrivare a (! + *essere*)
  they reached the town at midnight = sono
  arrivati in città a mezzanotte
  the letter never reached him = la lettera
  non gli è mai arrivata
- (*by stretching*)
  to reach up = allungare il braccio
  I can't reach the shelf = non arrivo allo
  scaffale
- (*to come to*) = arrivare a (! + *essere*)
  to reach a decision = arrivare a una
  decisione
- (*to contact by phone*) = contattare
  I can be reached at this number = mi
  puoi contattare a questo numero
reach out = allungare il braccio

react *verb*
= reagire

read *verb*
= leggere
read out
  to read out the names = leggere i nomi
  ad alta voce

reading *noun*
  reading = la lettura

ready *adjective*
- (*prepared*) = pronto/pronta
  are you ready to leave? = siete pronti a
  partire?
  to get ready = prepararsi (! + *essere*)
  to get lunch ready = preparare il pranzo
- (*happy*) = pronto/pronta
  I'm ready to help them = sono pronto ad
  aiutarli

real *adjective*
- = vero/vera
  are they real diamonds? = sono diamanti
  veri?
- **it's a real shame** = è un vero peccato

reality *noun*
  reality = la realtà

realize *verb*
= rendersi conto (! + *essere*)
  I didn't realize (that) he was your boss
  = non mi ero reso conto che era il tuo
  capo

really *adverb*
- (*in reality*) = veramente
  what really happened? = cos'è successo
  veramente?
- **it's really easy** = è facile davvero
  really? = davvero?

reason *noun*
  a reason = un motivo
  that's a good reason to learn Italian = è
  un buon motivo per imparare l'italiano
  **is there any reason why you shouldn't
  drive?** = c'è qualche motivo per cui non
  devi guidare?
  tell me the reason why = dimmi perché

reassure *verb*
= rassicurare

receipt *noun*
  a receipt = una ricevuta
  a till receipt = uno scontrino

receive *verb*
- (*to get*) = ricevere
- (*to meet*) = accogliere

recent *adjective*
= recente

recently *adverb*
= recentemente

reception *noun*
- (*in a hotel, a hospital, a company*)
  the reception = la reception   ····▶

R

- (*a formal event*)
a reception = un ricevimento

receptionist *noun* ▶ 281 |
a receptionist = un/una receptionist

recipe *noun*
a recipe = una ricetta

recognize *verb*
= riconoscere

recommend *verb*
= consigliare

record
1 *noun*
- (*information*)
the records (*historical, public*) = gli archivi
(*personal, medical*) = la pratica (*singular*)
- (*for playing music*)
a record = un disco
- (*in sport*)
a record = un record
to break the world record = battere il record mondiale
2 *verb*
= registrare

recover *verb*
= ristabilirsi (**!** + *essere*)
to recover from an illness = ristabilirsi dopo una malattia

recycle *verb*
= riciclare

red *adjective* ▶ 147 |
= rosso/rossa
to go red, to turn red = arrossire (**!** + *essere*)
to have red hair = avere i capelli rossi

reduce *verb*
to reduce prices = abbassare i prezzi
to reduce the number of employees = ridurre il numero di dipendenti
to reduce speed = rallentare

reduction *noun*
a reduction = una riduzione
(*a discount*) = uno sconto

redundant *adjective* (*British English*)
to be made redundant = essere licenziato per esubero di personale

referee *noun* ▶ 281 |
a referee = un arbitro

reflection *noun*
a reflection = un riflesso

refreshing *adjective*
= rinfrescante

refrigerator *noun*
a refrigerator = un frigorifero

refugee *noun*
a refugee = un profugo/una profuga

refuse *verb*
= rifiutare

to refuse [to listen | to stop | to pay]
= rifiutare [di ascoltare | di fermarsi | di pagare]

regards *noun*
give her my regards = dalle i miei saluti

region *noun*
a region = una regione

regional *adjective*
= regionale

register *noun*
the register = il registro
to take the register = fare l'appello

regret *verb*
= rimpiangere
I regret changing my mind = rimpiango di aver cambiato idea
he regrets that he can't come = gli dispiace di non poter venire

regular *adjective*
regular = regolare

regularly *adverb*
= regolarmente

rehearsal *noun*
a rehearsal = una prova

rehearse *verb*
= fare le prove

reject *verb*
to reject someone's advice = ignorare i consigli di qualcuno
to reject a candidate = scartare un candidato

relationship *noun*
- **a relationship** = un rapporto
she has a good relationship with her parents = ha un bel rapporto con i genitori
- (*an affair*)
a relationship = una relazione

relative *noun*
a relative = un parente

relax *verb*
= rilassarsi (**!** + *essere*)

relaxed *adjective*
= rilassato/rilassata

relay race *noun*
a relay race = una corsa a staffetta

release *verb*
= liberare

reliable *adjective*
= affidabile

relieved *adjective*
= sollevato/sollevata

religion *noun*
religion = la religione

religious education, RE (*British English*) *noun*
religious education = l'istruzione religiosa

rely verb
   to rely on someone = contare su
      qualcuno
   can we rely on you? = possiamo contare
      su di te?

remain verb
   = rimanere (**!** + essere)

remark noun
   a remark = un'osservazione

remarkable adjective
   = notevole

remember verb
   = ricordarsi (**!** + essere)
   do you remember her? = ti ricordi di lei?
   to remember to [write the letter | water the
      plants | turn off the lights] = ricordarsi di
      [scrivere la lettera | annaffiare le piante |
      spegnere le luci]

remind verb
   = ricordare
   to remind someone to buy milk
      = ricordare a qualcuno di comprare il
      latte
   she reminds me of my sister = mi ricorda
      mia sorella

remote control noun
   a remote control = un telecomando

remove verb
   = togliere

rent
1 verb
   = affittare
   to rent an apartment = affittare un
      appartamento
2 noun
   the rent = l'affitto
   rent out = affittare

repair verb
   = riparare
   to have a bicycle repaired = far riparare
      una bicicletta

repeat verb
   = ripetere

replace verb
   = sostituire
   they replaced the fence with a wall
      = hanno sostituito lo steccato con un
      muro

reply
1 verb
   = rispondere
   to reply to a letter = rispondere a una
      lettera
2 noun
   a reply = una risposta

report
1 verb
• (to tell about) = denunciare
   to report an accident = denunciare un
      incidente
• (in the news)
   to report on an event = fare un servizio
      su un avvenimento
2 noun
• (in the news)
   a report = un servizio
• (an official document)
   a report = un rapporto
• (British English) (from school)
   a (school) report = la pagella

represent verb
   = rappresentare

republic noun
   a republic = una repubblica

request noun
   a request = una richiesta

rescue verb
   = salvare

resemble verb
   = assomigliare a

resent verb
   to resent someone = avercela con
      qualcuno
   he resents her for winning = ce l'ha con
      lei perché ha vinto

reservation noun
   a reservation = una prenotazione

reserve verb
   = prenotare

resign verb
   = dimettersi (**!** + essere)

resist verb
   = resistere (a)

respect
1 verb
   = rispettare
2 noun
   respect = il rispetto
   out of respect = per rispetto

responsibility noun
   responsibility = la responsabilità

responsible adjective
• (the cause of) = responsabile
   to be responsible for the damage = essere
      responsabile dei danni
• (in charge) = responsabile
   to be responsible for organizing a trip
      = essere incaricato/incaricata di
      organizzare un viaggio

rest
1 noun
• (what is left)
   the rest = il resto
• (time to recover)
   rest = il riposo
   he needs rest = ha bisogno di riposo
• (a break)
   a rest = una pausa
   to have a rest = riposarsi (**!** + essere)····➤

R

2 *verb*
= riposarsi (**!** + *essere*)

restaurant *noun*
a restaurant = un ristorante

result *noun*
a result = un risultato
the exam results = i risultati degli esami
as a result of an accident = in seguito a
un incidente

résumé *noun* (*US English*)
a résumé = un curriculum

retire *verb*
= andare in pensione (**!** + *essere*)

return *verb*
• (*to go back*) = ritornare (**!** + *essere*)
• (*to give back*) = restituire
can you return my book? = mi puoi
restituire il libro?
• (*to send back*) = rispedire
to return goods = rispedire delle merci
• (*to start again*) = tornare (**!** + *essere*)
to return to work = tornare al lavoro
to return to school = tornare a scuola

return ticket *noun*
a return ticket = un biglietto di andata e
ritorno

reveal *verb*
to reveal a secret = svelare un segreto

revolution *noun*
a revolution = un rivoluzione

reward
1 *noun*
a reward = una ricompensa
2 *verb*
= ricompensare

rewind *verb*
= riavvolgere

rhythm *noun*
rhythm = il ritmo

rib *noun* ▶ **137** |
a rib = una costola

rice *noun*
rice = il riso

rich *adjective*
= ricco/ricca
to get rich = arricchirsi (**!** + *essere*)

rid: **to get rid of** *verb*
= sbarazzarsi di (**!** + *essere*)

ride
1 *verb* ▶ **178** |
to ride, to go riding = andare a cavallo
(**!** + *essere*)
to ride a bike = andare in bicicletta (**!** +
essere)
2 *noun*
to go for a ride (*in a car, on a bike*)
= andare a fare un giro (**!** + *essere*)
(*on a horse*) = andare a fare una cavalcata
(**!** + *essere*)

ridiculous *adjective*
= ridicolo/ridicola

rifle *noun*
a rifle = un fucile

right
1 *adjective*
• (*not left*) = destro/destra
his right hand = la mano destra
• (*good, desirable*) = giusto/giusta
to do the right thing = fare la cosa giusta
is this the right direction? = è questa la
direzione giusta?
• (*factually correct*) = esatto/esatta
the right answer = la risposta esatta
what's the right time? = hai l'ora esatta?
you're right = hai ragione
that's right! = esattamente!
2 *noun*
• (*the direction*)
the right = la destra
the first street on the right = la prima
strada a destra
• (*what one is entitled to*)
a right = un diritto
human rights = i diritti dell'uomo
3 *adverb*
= a destra
to turn right = girare a destra

ring
1 *verb*
• (*British English*) (*to phone*) = telefonare a
to ring for a taxi = chiamare un taxi
• (*to make a sound*) = suonare
to ring the bell = suonare il campanello
the doorbell rang = hanno suonato alla
porta
• (*when it's the telephone*) = squillare
the phone's ringing = sta squillando il
telefono
2 *noun*
• (*a piece of jewellery*)
a ring = un anello
a wedding ring = una fede
• (*a circle*)
a ring = un cerchio

rinse *verb*
= sciacquare

ripe *adjective*
= maturo/matura

rise *verb*
• (*if it's smoke, water*) = salire (**!** + *essere*)
• (*if it's a price*) = aumentare (**!** + *essere*)
• (*if it's the sun or moon*) = sorgere (**!** +
essere)

risk
1 *noun*
a risk = un rischio
2 *verb*
= rischiare
to risk losing one's job = rischiare di
perdere il lavoro

river *noun*
a river = un fiume

road *noun*
a road = una strada
the road to London = la strada per
   Londra

road sign *noun*
a road sign = un segnale stradale

roadworks *noun*
roadworks = i lavori stradali

roar *verb*
   (*if it's a lion*) = ruggire
   (*if it's a person*) = urlare
   (*if it's an engine*) = rombare

roast
1 *verb*
   = arrostire
2 *adjective*
   = arrosto (*never changes*)
   roast pork = maiale arrosto
3 *noun*
   a roast = un arrosto

rob *verb*
   to rob someone = derubare qualcuno
   to rob a bank = rapinare una banca

robbery *noun*
   a robbery = una rapina

robot *noun*
   a robot = un robot

rock *noun*
• (*the material*)
   rock = la roccia
• (*a large stone*)
   a rock = una pietra
• (*music*)
   rock = il rock

rocket *noun*
   a rocket = un razzo

role *noun*
   a role = un ruolo

roll
1 *verb*
   = rotolare (**!** + *essere*)
   the ball rolled under a car = la palla è
      rotolata sotto una macchina
2 *noun*
• (*of paper, cloth, plastic*)
   a roll = un rotolo
   a roll of film = un rullino
• (*bread*)
   a roll = un panino
• (*US English*) (*at school*)
   to call the roll = fare l'appello
   roll about, roll around (*if it's an object*)
   = rotolare (**!** + *essere*)
roll over = rigirarsi (**!** + *essere*)
roll up = arrotolare
   to roll up a newspaper = arrotolare un
      giornale

roller coaster *noun*
   a roller coaster = le montagne russe

roller-skate *noun*
   a roller-skate = un pattino a rotelle

roller-skating *noun* ▶ 178⌐
   roller-skating = il pattinaggio a rotelle

romantic *adjective*
   = romantico/romantica

roof *noun*
   a roof = un tetto

room *noun*
• a room = una stanza
   (*in a hotel*) = una camera
• (*space*)
   room = il posto
   is there room? = c'è posto?
   to make room = fare posto

root *noun*
   a root = una radice

rope *noun*
   a rope = una corda

rose *noun*
   a rose = una rosa

rotten *adjective*
   = marcio/marcia

rough *adjective*
• (*not smooth*) = ruvido/ruvida
• (*not gentle, tough*) = violento/violenta
   we live in a rough area = viviamo in un
      quartiere violento
• (*not exact, precise*)
   a rough figure = una cifra approssimativa
• (*difficult*) = difficile
   to have a rough time = attraversare un
      periodo difficile
• (*caused by bad weather*)
   a rough sea = un mare agitato

round

> **!** Often **round** *occurs in combinations
> with verbs. For more information, see
> the note at* **around**.

1 *preposition*
   = intorno a
   to be sitting round a table = sedere
      intorno alla tavola
   to sail round the world = fare il giro del
      mondo in barca
   to go round Oxford = visitare Oxford
2 *adverb*
   let's go round to John's = andiamo da
      John
   to invite someone round = invitare
      qualcuno a casa propria
3 *adjective*
   = rotondo/rotonda

roundabout *noun*
• (*British English*) (*in a fair*)
   a roundabout = una giostra
• (*for traffic*)
   a roundabout = una rotatoria

R

route noun
  a route = un itinerario
  a bus route = una linea d'autobus

routine noun
  a routine = una routine

row[1]
1 noun
• a row = una fila
  the students were sitting in rows = gli studenti erano seduti in file
• (when talking about frequency)
  she's been absent five days in a row = è stata assente cinque giorni di fila
2 verb
  (as an activity) = remare
  (as a sport) ▶ **178** = fare canottaggio

row[2] noun (British English)
  a row = un litigio
  to have a row with someone = litigare con qualcuno

rowing noun ▶ **178**
  rowing = il canottaggio

rowing boat (British English),
rowboat (US English) noun
  a rowing boat = una barca a remi

royal adjective
  = reale

rub verb
  to rub a stain = sfregare una macchia
  to rub one's eyes = sfregarsi gli occhi (**!** + essere)
rub out (British English) = cancellare

rubber noun
• (the material)
  rubber = la gomma
• (British English) (an eraser)
  a rubber = una gomma

rubbish noun (British English)
• (refuse)
  rubbish (household) = la spazzatura
  (in the street, in a dump) = l'immondizia
• (poor quality goods)
  rubbish = robaccia

rubbish bin noun (British English)
  a rubbish bin = un bidone della spazzatura

rucksack noun
  a rucksack = uno zaino

rude adjective
• (not polite) = maleducato/maleducata
  to be rude to someone = essere maleducato con qualcuno
• (vulgar) = volgare
  a rude word = una parolaccia

rug noun
  a rug = un tappeto

rugby noun ▶ **178**
  rugby = il rugby

ruin
1 verb
  = rovinare
2 noun
  a ruin = un rudere

rule
1 noun
  a rule (of a game, a language) = una regola
  (in a school, an organization) = un regolamento
  it's against the rules = è contro il regolamento
2 verb
  (if it's a leader) = governare
  (if it's a king, queen) = regnare
  (if it's a party) = dirigere

ruler noun
  a ruler = un righello

rumour (British English), **rumor** (US English) noun
  a rumour = una voce

run
1 verb
• to run = correre (**!** + essere or avere)
  to run after someone = rincorrere qualcuno
  to run across the street = attraversare la strada di corsa
• (from danger) = scappare (**!** + essere)
• (to manage) = gestire
• (to work, to operate) = funzionare
  the car runs on diesel = la macchina va a gasolio
  the system is running well = il sistema funziona bene
• (when talking about transport) = circolare
  the buses don't run after midnight = gli autobus non circolano dopo mezzanotte
• (to flow) = scorrere (**!** + essere)
• (to fill with water)
  to run a bath = riempire la vasca
• (to come off) (when talking about dyes) = stingere
  (when talking about make-up) = colare (**!** + essere)
• (in an election)
  to run for president = candidarsi alla presidenza (**!** + essere)
• (other uses)
  to be running late = essere in ritardo
2 noun
  a run = una corsa
  I'm going for a run = vado a correre
run about, run around = correre (**!** + avere)
run away = scappare (**!** + essere)
run off = fuggire (**!** + essere)

rush
1 verb
• (to hurry) = affrettarsi (**!** + essere)
  to rush to finish one's homework = affrettarsi a finire i compiti   ····▶

he rushed into the shop = è entrato di
corsa nel negozio
I rushed out of the house = sono uscito
di corsa dalla casa
she was rushed to the hospital = è stata
ricoverata d'urgenza all'ospedale
- (*to put pressure on*)
  to rush someone = mettere fretta a
  qualcuno
2 *noun*
  to be in a rush = avere fretta
  to do one's homework in a rush = fare i
  compiti in fretta

rush hour *noun*
  the rush hour = l'ora di punta

Russia *noun* ▶ 151 |
  Russia = la Russia

Russian ▶ 199 |
1 *adjective*
  = russo/russa
2 *noun*
- (*the people*)
  the Russians = i russi
- (*the language*)
  Russian = il russo

rusty *adjective*
  = arrugginito/arrugginita

Ss

---

sad *adjective*
  = triste

saddle *noun*
  a saddle = una sella
  (*on a bicycle*) = un sellino

safe
1 *adjective*
- (*free from danger*) = sicuro/sicura
  a safe place = un posto sicuro
  to feel safe = sentirsi al sicuro (**!** +
  essere)
  your car is safe here = la tua macchina
  qui è al sicuro
  it's not safe for children = è pericoloso
  per i bambini
  is it safe to go there? = ci si può andare
  senza pericolo?
- (*out of danger*) = salvo/salva
2 *noun*
  a safe = una cassaforte

safety *noun*
  safety = la sicurezza

Sagittarius *noun*
  Sagittarius = Sagittario

sail
1 *noun*
  a sail = una vela
  to set sail = salpare (**!** + *essere*)
2 *verb*
  to sail around the world = fare il giro del
  mondo in barca
  to go sailing = fare della vela

sailing *noun* ▶ 178 |
  sailing = la vela

sailing boat (*British English*),
sailboat (*US English*) *noun*
  a sailing boat = una barca a vela

sailor *noun* ▶ 281 |
  a sailor = un marinaio

saint *noun*
  a saint = un santo/una santa

salad *noun*
  a salad = un'insalata

salary *noun*
  a salary = uno stipendio

sale *noun*
- **to be on sale** (*British English*) = essere in
  vendita
  for sale = vendesi
- **the sales** = i saldi

sales assistant *noun* ▶ 281 | (*British
English*)
  a sales assistant = un commesso/una
  commessa

salmon *noun*
  a salmon = un salmone

salt *noun*
  salt = il sale

same
1 *adjective*
- = stesso/stessa
  they go to the same school
  = frequentano la stessa scuola
  things aren't the same without them
  = non è la stessa cosa senza di loro
  it's all the same to me = per me fa lo
  stesso
- **to be the same** = essere uguale
  it's the same as the car I had before = è
  uguale alla macchina che avevo prima
  her coat is the same as mine = ha il
  cappotto uguale al mio
  the houses all look the same = le case
  sono tutte uguali
2 *pronoun*
  the same = lo stesso
  I'll have the same = prendo lo stesso
  to do the same as the others = fare come
  gli altri
  'happy New Year!'—'the same to you!'
  = 'buon anno'—'altrettanto!'

sand *noun*
  sand = la sabbia

S

sandal *noun*
a sandal = un sandalo

sandwich *noun*
a sandwich = un tramezzino
a ham sandwich = un tramezzino al prosciutto

Santa (Claus) *noun*
Santa (Claus) = Babbo Natale

sardine *noun*
a sardine = una sardina

satellite TV *noun*
satellite TV = la TV via satellite

satisfactory *adjective*
= soddisfacente

satisfied *adjective*
= soddisfatto/soddisfatta

Saturday *noun* ▶ 155 |
Saturday = sabato

sauce *noun*
a sauce = una salsa

saucepan *noun*
a saucepan = una pentola

saucer *noun*
a saucer = un piattino

sausage *noun*
a sausage = una salsiccia

save *verb*
• (*to rescue*) = salvare
they saved his life = gli hanno salvato la vita
• (*to avoid spending*)
to save (up) = risparmiare
to save money = risparmiare dei soldi
• (*to avoid wasting*)
to save [time | energy | money]
= risparmiare [tempo | fatica | soldi]
• (*to keep*) = mettere da parte
save me a piece of cake = mettimi da parte un pezzo di torta
• to save a file = salvare un file
• (*to spare*)
to save someone a lot of work = far risparmiare un sacco di lavoro a qualcuno
it will save us from having to drive all night = ci eviterà di dover guidare tutta la notte

savings *noun*
savings = i risparmi

saw *noun*
a saw = una sega

say *verb*
= dire
to say goodbye = salutare
she says (that) she can't go out tonight = dice che non può uscire stasera
he said to wait here = ha detto di aspettare qui

they say she's very rich = dicono che sia molto ricca

! *Note that the subjunctive is used after* **dicono che**.

she wouldn't say = non l'ha detto
what does the message say? = cosa dice il messaggio?
it says here that smoking is not allowed = qui dice che non è permesso fumare
let's say three o'clock = diciamo alle tre

scandal *noun*
a scandal = uno scandalo

scare *verb*
= spaventare
you scared me! = mi hai spaventato!
scare away = far scappare

scared *adjective*
to be scared = avere paura

scarf *noun*
a scarf (*long*) = una sciarpa
(*square*) = un foulard

scenery *noun*
scenery = il paesaggio

school
1 *noun*
a school = una scuola
to be at school = essere a scuola
2 *adjective*
= scolastico/scolastica
a school trip = una gita scolastica

schoolbag *noun*
a schoolbag = una cartella

science *noun*
science = la scienza
to study science = studiare scienze

scientist *noun* ▶ 281 |
a scientist = uno scienziato/una scienziata

scissors *noun*
scissors = le forbici
a pair of scissors = un paio di forbici

score *verb*
to score a goal = segnare un gol

Scorpio *noun*
Scorpio = Scorpione (*masculine*)

Scot *noun* ▶ 151 |
a Scot = uno/una scozzese
the Scots = gli scozzesi

Scotland *noun* ▶ 151 |
Scotland = la Scozia

Scottish *adjective* ▶ 199 |
= scozzese

scratch *verb*
• (*when itchy*) = grattarsi (! + *essere*)
to scratch one's arm = grattarsi il braccio
• (*to hurt, to damage*) = graffiare

scream *verb*
= strillare

screen noun
  a screen = uno schermo

screw noun
  a screw = una vite

sea noun
  a sea = un mare
  a city by the sea = una città sul mare
  a house beside the sea = una casa al
    mare

seagull noun
  a seagull = un gabbiano

search verb
• to search = cercare
  to search for someone = cercare
    qualcuno
• (to examine a place, a person)
    = perquisire

seashell noun
  a seashell = una conchiglia

seasick adjective
  to be seasick = avere il mal di mare

seaside noun
  at the seaside = al mare
  to go to the seaside = andare al mare
    (**!** + essere)

season noun
  a season = una stagione
  strawberries are in season = è la stagione
    delle fragole

seat noun
• (a chair)
  a seat = una sedia
  have a seat! = si accomodi!
• (on transport, in a theatre)
  a seat = un posto
• (in a car)
  a seat = un sedile

seatbelt noun
  a seatbelt = una cintura di sicurezza

second
1 adjective
    = secondo/seconda
  it's the second time I've called her = è la
    seconda volta che la chiamo
2 noun
• (in a series)
  the second = il secondo/la seconda
• (in time)
  a second = un secondo
  (a very short time) = un attimo
• (in dates) ▶ **155**
  the second of May = il due maggio
3 adverb
  to come second = arrivare
    secondo/seconda (**!** + essere)

secondary school noun
  a secondary school = una scuola
    secondaria

second-hand adjective
  a second-hand [car | coat | book] = [una
    macchina | un cappotto | un libro] di
    seconda mano

secret
1 adjective
    = segreto/segreta
2 noun
  a secret = un segreto
  to tell someone a secret = rivelare un
    segreto a qualcuno
3 in secret = in segreto

secretary noun ▶ **281**
  a secretary = un segretario/una segretaria

see verb
• to see = vedere
  I can't see them = non li vedo
  he saw them come in = li ha visti entrare
  do they see each other often? = si
    vedono spesso?
  see you tomorrow! = a domani!
  I'll go and see = vado a vedere
• (to accompany)
  I'll see you home = ti accompagno a casa

seem verb
• (to appear)
  he seems [happy | annoyed | tired] = ha
    l'aria [felice | seccata | stanca]
• (when talking about one's impressions)
    = sembrare (**!** + essere)
  it seems (that) there are a lot of problems
    = sembra che ci siano un sacco di
    problemi
  they seem to be looking for someone
    = sembra che cerchino qualcuno

  ! Note that the subjunctive is used after
  sembra che.

  it seems strange (to me) = mi sembra
    strano

seldom adverb
    = raramente

self-confident ▶ confident

selfish adjective
    = egoista

sell verb
    = vendere
  to sell books to the students = vendere
    libri agli studenti
  he sold me his car = mi ha venduto la
    sua macchina
  water is sold in bottles = l'acqua si vende
    in bottiglie

send verb
    = mandare
  to send a package to someone
    = mandare un pacco a qualcuno
  he sent her a letter = le ha mandato una
    lettera
  to send a pupil home from school
    = mandare a casa uno studente
send away = mandare via   ····➤

S

send back = rimandare
send for = far venire
  to send for the doctor = far venire il
  medico
send off
  to send a player off = espellere un
  giocatore

senior high school (*US English*),
  senior school (*British English*) *noun*
  a senior (high) school ≈ un liceo

sense *noun*
• **(common) sense** = il buonsenso
  to have the sense to go home = avere il
  buonsenso di andare a casa
• (*allowing one to see, hear, smell etc*)
  a sense = un senso
  the sense of taste = il gusto
• (*a meaning*)
  a sense = un senso
  it doesn't make sense = non ha senso
  it makes sense to check first = è una
  buona idea controllare prima

sensible *adjective*

> **!** *Note that* **sensible** *in English is never
> translated by* **sensibile** *in Italian.*

  = sensato/sensata
  (*describing clothes*) = pratico/pratica

sensitive *adjective*
  (*describing a person*) = sensibile
  (*describing a situation*) = delicato/delicata

sentence
1 *noun*
• (*in grammar*)
  a sentence = una frase
• (*for a crime*)
  a (prison) sentence = una condanna
2 *verb*
  **to sentence someone to one year in
  prison** = condannare qualcuno ad un
  anno di reclusione

separate
1 *adjective*
  a separate room = una stanza separata
  there are two separate problems = ci
  sono due problemi distinti
2 *verb*
• **to separate** = separare
• (*if it's a couple*) = separarsi (**!** + *essere*)

separated *adjective*
  = separato/separata

separately *adverb*
  = separatamente

September *noun* ▶ 155 |
  September = settembre (*masculine*)

serial *noun*
  a serial = uno sceneggiato

series *noun*
  a series = una serie

serious *adjective*
• (*causing worry*) = grave

a serious accident = un grave incidente
• (*describing a personality*) = serio/seria
• **to be serious about football** = prendere il
  calcio sul serio

serve *verb*
• (*in a shop, at table*) = servire
  are you being served? = la stanno
  servendo?
• (*in sport*) = servire

service *noun*
• (*which people need or find useful*)
  a service = un servizio
• (*in a shop, a restaurant*)
  service = il servizio
• (*in a church*)
  a service = una funzione

service station *noun*
  a service station = una stazione di
  servizio

set
1 *noun*
• (*a collection*)
  a set of glasses = un servizio di bicchieri
• (*in tennis*)
  a set = un set
2 *verb*
• (*to decide on*) = fissare
  to set a date = fissare una data
• (*for a particular time*)
  to set the alarm clock = mettere la sveglia
  to set the video (*British English*)
    = programmare il videoregistratore
• (*in school*)
  to set homework = dare dei compiti a
  casa
  to set an exam = preparare il testo di un
  esame
• (*to be responsible for*)
  to set a record = stabilire un record
  to set a good example to someone
    = dare il buon esempio a qualcuno
• (*when talking about a story, a film*)
  the film is set in Sicily = il film è
  ambientato in Sicilia
• (*when talking about the sun*) = tramontare
  (**!** + *essere*)
• (*other uses*)
  to set the table = apparecchiare
  to set fire to a house = dare fuoco a una
  casa
  to set someone free = liberare qualcuno
set off
• (*to leave*) = partire (**!** + *essere*)
• (*to cause to go off*)
  to set off a burglar alarm = far scattare
  un allarme
set up = avviare
  to set up a company = avviare una ditta

settle *verb*
• (*to end*)
  to settle an argument = risolvere una
  disputa   ····▶

- (*to decide on*) = decidere
  nothing is settled yet = non c'è ancora niente di deciso
- (*to make one's home*) = stabilirsi (**!** + *essere*)

settle down

- (*to get comfortable*) = ambientarsi (**!** + *essere*)
- (*to marry*) = sistemarsi (**!** + *essere*)

settle in = ambientarsi (**!** + *essere*)

seven *number* ▶ **122**, ▶ **146**
  seven = sette
  seven exams = sette esami
  I've got seven (of them) = ne ho sette

seventeen *number* ▶ **122**, ▶ **146**
  seventeen = diciassette

seventeenth *number*
- (*in a series*)
  = diciassettesimo/diciassettesima
- (*in dates*) ▶ **155**
  the seventeenth of May = il diciassette maggio

seventh *number*
- (*in a series*) = settimo/settima
- (*in dates*) ▶ **155**
  the seventh of July = il sette luglio

seventy *number* ▶ **122**
  seventy = settanta

several *determiner*
  = parecchi/parecchie

severe *adjective*
- (*serious*) = grave
- (*harsh*) = severo/severa

sew *verb*
  = cucire

sewing *noun*
  sewing = il cucito

sewing machine *noun*
  a sewing machine = una macchina da cucire

sex *noun*
  sex = il sesso
  to have sex = avere rapporti sessuali

shade *noun*
- (*out of the sun*)
  shade = l'ombra
  to sit in the shade = sedere all'ombra
- (*a colour*)
  a shade = una tonalità
- (*for a lamp*)
  a shade = un paralume

shadow *noun*
  a shadow = un'ombra

shake *verb*
- **to shake** = scuotere
  the earthquake shook the building = il terremoto ha fatto tremare il palazzo
  to shake a bottle = agitare una bottiglia
  to shake hands with someone = stringere la mano a qualcuno

- (*when saying no*)
  to shake one's head = scuotere la testa
- (*a person, a building*) = tremare
  he was shaking with fear = tremava dalla paura

shall *verb*
- (*when talking about the future*)
  we shall know tomorrow = lo sapremo domani
- (*when making suggestions*)
  shall I set the table? = apparecchio?
  shall we go to the cinema? = andiamo al cinema?

shame *noun*
- **shame** = la vergogna
  shame on you! = vergognati!
- (*when expressing regret*)
  that's a shame = è un peccato

shampoo *noun*
  shampoo = lo shampoo

shape *noun*
- (*a form*)
  a shape = una forma
- (*when talking about health*)
  to be in good shape = essere in forma
  to get in shape = rimettersi in forma (**!** + *essere*)

share
1 *verb*
  = dividere
  to share a house = dividere una casa
2 *noun*
  a share = una parte

shark *noun*
  a shark = uno squalo

sharp *adjective*
- (*used for cutting*) = affilato/affilata
- (*with a point*) = appuntito/appuntita
- (*sudden*) = brusco/brusca
  a sharp bend = una curva stretta
- (*intelligent*) = sveglio/sveglia
- (*in taste*) = aspro/aspra

shave *verb*
  = farsi la barba (**!** + *essere*)

she *pronoun*
  she = lei

> **!** Note that the subject pronoun is usually omitted in Italian. It is used for emphasis, to express a contrast, or when it is necessary to avoid ambiguity.

  she's coming next week = arriva la settimana prossima
  she does all the work here = qui fa tutto lei
  he works in London but she doesn't = lui lavora a Londra ma lei no
  there she is! = eccola!

sheep *noun*
  a sheep = una pecora

S

sheet noun
- (for a bed)
  a sheet = un lenzuolo
- (a piece)
  a sheet (of paper) = un foglio
  (of glass) = una lastra

shelf noun
  a shelf (for books, ornaments) = una
  mensola
  (in a shop) = un ripiano
  a set of shelves = uno scaffale

shell noun
  a shell (of an egg, a nut, a tortoise) = un
  guscio
  (of a shellfish) = una conchiglia

shelter
1 noun
- (from rain, danger)
  a shelter = un riparo
- (for homeless people)
  a shelter = un rifugio
2 verb
- (to take shelter) = ripararsi (**!** + essere)
- (to help) = dare rifugio a

shine verb
- (to give out light) = brillare
  the light is shining in my eyes = ho la
  luce negli occhi
- (to point)
  to shine a torch at someone = fare luce a
  qualcuno con la torcia

ship noun
  a ship = una nave

shirt noun
  a shirt = una camicia

shiver verb
  = tremare

shock
1 noun
- (an upsetting experience)
  a shock = uno shock
  to get a shock = avere uno shock
  to give someone a shock = far venire un
  colpo a qualcuno
- (the medical state)
  to be in shock = essere in stato di shock
- (from electricity)
  a shock = una scossa
  to get a shock = prendere la scossa
2 verb
  = scioccare

shoe noun
  a shoe (for a person) = una scarpa
  (for a horse) = un ferro

shoot verb
- (using a weapon) = sparare
  to shoot someone = sparare a qualcuno
  they shot him in the leg = gli hanno
  sparato alla gamba
- (to move very fast)
  to shoot past = sfrecciare (**!** + essere)

- (to make)
  to shoot a film = girare un film

shop
1 noun
  a shop = un negozio
2 verb
  to go shopping = andare a fare spese (**!** +
  essere)

shop assistant noun ▶ **281**| (British
English)
  a shop assistant = un commesso/una
  commessa

shopkeeper noun ▶ **281**|
  a shopkeeper = un/una negoziante

shopping noun
  shopping = la spesa
  to do the shopping = fare la spesa

shopping centre (British English),
  shopping mall (US English) noun
  a shopping centre, a shopping mall = un
  centro commerciale

shop window noun
  a shop window = una vetrina

shore noun
- (the edge of the sea)
  the shore = la riva
- (dry land)
  the shore = la terra

short
1 adjective
- (not lasting long) = breve
  a short speech = un discorso breve
  the days are getting shorter = le giornate
  si stanno accorciando
- (not long) = corto/corta
  a short skirt = una gonna corta
  to have short hair = avere i capelli corti
- (not tall) = basso/bassa
- **to be short of** [money | food | ideas] = essere
  a corto di [soldi | cibo | idee]
2 in short = in breve

short cut noun
  a short cut = una scorciatoia

shortly adverb
- (soon) = presto
- **shortly before** = poco prima
  shortly after = poco dopo

shorts noun
- (British English) (short trousers)
  shorts = gli shorts
- (US English) (underpants)
  shorts = le mutande

shot noun
- (from a gun)
  a shot = uno sparo
  to fire a shot at someone = sparare a
  qualcuno
- (in sports) ▶ **178**|
  a shot (in football) = un tiro
  (in tennis, golf, cricket) = un colpo

should *verb*
▶ *See the boxed note on* **dovere** *for more information and examples.*

> **!** *Note that, in general,* **should** *is translated by the conditional tense of* **dovere**. *For more information and examples, see the note at* **dovere**.

- (*when talking about what is right, what one ought to do*)
  she should learn to drive = dovrebbe imparare a guidare
- (*when saying something may happen*)
  we should be there by midday
  = dovremmo essere lì per mezzogiorno
- (*when asking for advice or permission*)
  should I call the doctor? = chiamo il medico?

shoulder *noun* ▶ 137 |
  the shoulder = la spalla
  to wear a sweater over one's shoulders
  = portare un maglione sulle spalle

shout
1 *verb*
  = gridare
  to shout at someone = sgridare qualcuno
2 *noun*
  a shout = un grido
shout out = gridare

shovel *noun*
  a shovel = una pala

show
1 *verb*
- (*to let someone see*)
  to show someone a photo = far vedere una foto a qualcuno
  I'll show you how it works = ti faccio vedere come funziona
- (*to go with*)
  I'll show you to your room
  = l'accompagno alla sua stanza
- (*to point to, to indicate*)
  to show someone where to go = indicare a qualcuno dove andare
- (*to be on TV, at the cinema*)
  the film is showing at the Phoenix
  = danno il film al Phoenix
2 *noun*
- (*on a stage*) = uno spettacolo
  (*on TV, radio*) = una trasmissione
- (*an exhibition*)
  a show = una mostra
show off = mettersi in mostra (**!** + *essere*)
show round
  to show someone around the town = far visitare la città a qualcuno
show up = farsi vivo/viva (**!** + *essere*)

shower *noun*
- (*for washing*)
  a shower = una doccia
  to have a shower = fare la doccia
- (*rain*)
  a shower = un acquazzone

shrimp *noun*
  a shrimp = un gamberetto
shrink *verb*
  = restringere

shut
1 *adjective*
  = chiuso/chiusa
  my eyes were shut = avevo gli occhi chiusi
2 *verb*
  = chiudere
  to shut the windows = chiudere le finestre
  the door doesn't shut properly = la porta non chiude bene
shut down = chiudere
  the factory shut down in May = la fabbrica ha chiuso a maggio
shut out
  to shut someone out = chiudere fuori qualcuno
shut up
- (*to be quiet*) = stare zitto/zitta (**!** + *essere*)
  shut up! = sta' zitto!
- (*to lock inside*) = rinchiudere

shy *adjective*
  = timido/timida

sick *adjective*
- (*ill*) = malato/malata
  to get sick = ammalarsi (**!** + *essere*)
  to feel sick = sentirsi male (**!** + *essere*)
  to be sick (*British English*) (*to vomit*)
  = vomitare
- (*fed up*) = stufo/stufa
  he's sick of the neighbours = è stufo dei vicini

sickness *noun*
  a sickness = una malattia

side *noun*
- **a side** = un lato
  it's an apartment block with shops on either side = è un palazzo con dei negozi sui lati
  to be driving on the wrong side of the road = guidare sul lato sbagliato della strada
  he works on the other side of London
  = lavora dall'altra parte di Londra
- (*of a person's body*)
  the side = il fianco
  to be lying on one's side = essere sdraiato/sdraiata su un fianco
  on my right side = sulla mia destra
- (*in a conflict, a contest*)
  a side = una parte
- (*a team*)
  a side = una squadra
side with = schierarsi con (**!** + *essere*)

sidewalk *noun* (*US English*)
  the sidewalk = il marciapiede
sigh *verb*
  = sospirare

S

sight *noun*
  sight = la vista
  to catch sight of someone = scorgere
    qualcuno
  to be out of sight = non essere più visibile

sightseeing *noun*
  sightseeing = il turismo

sign
1 *noun*
• (*a mark*)
  a sign = un segno
  the dollar sign = il simbolo del dollaro
• (*for traffic*)
  a sign = un segnale
• (*a notice*)
  a sign = un cartello
2 *verb*
  = firmare
sign on (*British English*) = iscriversi
  all'ufficio di collocamento (**!** + *essere*)

signal
1 *noun*
  a signal = un segnale
2 *verb*
  = segnalare
  to signal to someone to come = fare
    segno a qualcuno di venire

signature *noun*
  a signature = una firma

silence *noun*
  silence = il silenzio

silent *adjective*
• (*quiet*) = silenzioso/silenziosa
• (*without sound or words*) = muto/muta

silk *noun*
  silk = la seta

silly *adjective*
  = sciocco/sciocca

silver
1 *noun*
  silver = l'argento
2 *adjective*
  = d'argento
  a silver ring = un anello d'argento

simple *adjective*
  = semplice

since
1 *preposition*

> **!** Note that, when *since* is used to
> describe an event or an action that is
> still going on, rather than an event or
> an action that belongs to the past and
> has finished, the present tense + **da** is
> used in Italian.

  = da
  I haven't seen him since yesterday = non
    lo vedo da ieri
  I haven't been feeling well since Monday
    = non mi sento bene da lunedì
  she has been living in Italy since 1988
    = vive in Italia dal 1988

2 *conjunction*
• (*from the time when*) = da quando
  since she left = da quando è partita
  I've lived here since I was ten = abito qui
    da quando avevo dieci anni
  it's ten years since she died = sono dieci
    anni che è morta
• (*because*) = siccome
  since she was ill, she couldn't go
    = siccome era malata non è potuta
    andare
3 *adverb*
  = da allora

sincere *adjective*
  = sincero/sincera

sincerely *adverb*
  = sinceramente
  yours sincerely (*British English*),
  sincerely yours (*US English*) = Distinti
    saluti
  (*less formal*) = cordiali saluti

sing *verb*
  = cantare

singer *noun* ▶ 281 |
  a singer = un/una cantante

singing *noun*
  singing = il canto

single *adjective*
• (*one*) = solo/sola
  we visited three towns in a single day
    = abbiamo visitato tre città in una sola
    giornata
• (*when used for emphasis*)
  every single day = tutti i santi giorni
  I didn't see a single person = non ho
    visto anima viva
• (*without a partner*) = single (**!** *never*
    changes)

single bed *noun*
  a single bed = un letto singolo

single room *noun*
  a single room = una camera singola

single ticket *noun* (*British English*)
  a single ticket = un biglietto di sola
    andata

sink
1 *noun*
  a sink = un lavandino
2 *verb*
  = andare a fondo (**!** + *essere*)

sister *noun*
  a sister = una sorella

sister-in-law *noun*
  a sister-in-law = una cognata

sit *verb*
• (*to take a seat*) = sedersi (**!** + *essere*)
  to be sitting on the floor = essere
    seduto/seduta per terra   ····▶

- (*British English*) (*to take*)
  to sit an exam = sostenere un esame
sit down = sedersi (**!** + *essere*)
  to be sitting down = essere seduto/seduta

sitting room *noun*
  a sitting room = un salotto

situated *adjective*
  = situato/situata
  situated near the town centre = situato vicino al centro

situation *noun*
  a situation = una situazione

six *number* ▶ **122 |** , ▶ **146 |**
  six = sei
  six weeks = sei settimane
  I've got six (of them) = ne ho sei

sixteen *number* ▶ **122 |** , ▶ **146 |**
  sixteen = sedici

sixteenth *number*
- (*in a series*) = sedicesimo/sedicesima
- (*in dates*) ▶ **155 |**
  the sixteenth of July = il sedici luglio

sixth *number*
- (*in a series*) = sesto/sesta
- (*in dates*) ▶ **155 |**
  the sixth of February = il sei febbraio

sixty *number* ▶ **122 |**
  sixty = sessanta

size *noun*
- (*when talking about a person*)
  a size = una taglia
  what's your size? (*in clothes*) = che taglia porti?
  (*in shoes*) = che numero porti?
  she's about your size = è pressappoco come te
- (*when talking about clothes*)
  a size (*of garment*) = una misura
  (*of shoes*) = un numero
  I'd like this in a smaller size = lo vorrei in una misura più piccola
- (*when talking about how big something is*)
  the size = le dimensioni (*plural*)

skateboard *noun* ▶ **178 |**
  a skateboard = uno skateboard

skating *noun* ▶ **178 |**
  skating = il pattinaggio

skating rink *noun*
  a skating rink = una pista di pattinaggio

sketch *noun*
- (*a drawing*)
  a sketch = uno schizzo
- (*a funny scene*)
  a sketch = una scenetta

ski
1 *noun*
  a ski = uno sci (**!** *never changes*)
2 *verb*
  to go skiing = andare a sciare (**!** + *essere*)

skiing *noun* ▶ **178 |**
  skiing = lo sci

skilful (*British English*), **skillful** (*US English*) *adjective*
  = abile

skill *noun*
- (*the quality*)
  skill = abilità
- (*a particular ability*)
  a skill = una tecnica

skin *noun*
  the skin = la pelle

skinny *adjective*
  = magro/magra

skip *verb*
- (*to give little jumps*) = saltellare
- (*with a rope*) = saltare con la corda
- **to skip classes** = saltare le lezioni

ski resort *noun*
  a ski resort = una stazione sciistica

skirt *noun*
  a skirt = una gonna

sky *noun*
  the sky = il cielo
  a clear sky = un cielo sereno

slap *verb*
  to slap someone = schiaffeggiare qualcuno

sled, **sledge** (*British English*) *noun*
  a sled = una slitta

sleep
1 *noun*
  sleep = il sonno
  to go to sleep = addormentarsi (**!** + *essere*)
  to go back to sleep = riaddormentarsi (**!** + *essere*)
  to put someone to sleep = far addormentare qualcuno
2 *verb*
- (*to be asleep*) = dormire
- **to sleep with someone** = andare a letto con qualcuno (**!** + *essere*)
sleep in = dormire fino a tardi

sleeping bag *noun*
  a sleeping bag = un sacco a pelo

sleepy *adjective*
  to be sleepy, to feel sleepy = avere sonno

sleet *noun*
  sleet = il nevischio

sleeve *noun*
  a sleeve = una manica
  to roll up one's sleeves = rimboccarsi le maniche (**!** + *essere*)

slice
1 *noun*
  a slice = una fetta
2 *verb*
  to slice bread = affettare il pane

S

slide
1 *verb*
= scivolare (**!** + *essere*)
the plates slid off the table = i piatti sono scivolati dal tavolo
2 *noun*
• (*an image*)
a slide = una diapositiva
• (*in a playground*)
a slide = uno scivolo

slim
1 *adjective*
= magro/magra
2 *verb* (*British English*)
= dimagrire (**!** + *essere*)

slip *verb*
• (*to slide*) = scivolare (**!** + *essere*)
• **the glass slipped out of my hands** = il bicchiere mi è scivolato di mano

slipper *noun*
a slipper = una pantofola

slippery *adjective*
= scivoloso/scivolosa

slot machine *noun*
a slot machine = una macchinetta mangiasoldi

slow *adjective*
• = lento/lenta
• (*describing a watch, a clock*)
to be slow = essere indietro
the clock is 20 minutes slow = l'orologio è indietro di 20 minuti
slow down
(*to make slower*) = rallentare (**!** + *avere*)
(*to get slower*) = rallentare (**!** + *essere*)

slowly *adverb*
= lentamente

sly *adjective*
= astuto/astuta

small *adjective*
= piccolo/piccola
a small car = una macchina piccola
a small quantity = una piccola quantità

smart *adjective*
• (*British English*) (*elegant*) = elegante
• (*intelligent*) = intelligente
• (*expensive*) = chic (**!** *never changes*)

smash *verb*
• (*to break*) = frantumare
• (*to get broken*) = frantumarsi (**!** + *essere*)
smash up = sfasciare

smell
1 *noun*
• (*an odour*)
a smell = un odore
• (*the sense*)
the sense of smell = l'olfatto
2 *verb*
= sentire odore di
I can't smell anything = non sento nessun odore

that smells nice = ha un buon odore
I can smell burning = sento odore di bruciato

smile
1 *verb*
= sorridere
to smile at someone = sorridere a qualcuno
2 *noun*
a smile = un sorriso

smoke
1 *noun*
smoke = il fumo
2 *verb*
= fumare

smooth *adjective*
(*not rough*) = liscio/liscia
a smooth crossing = una traversata senza problemi

snack *noun*
a snack = uno spuntino

snail *noun*
a snail = una chiocciola

snake *noun*
a snake = un serpente

sneaker *noun*
a sneaker = una scarpa da ginnastica

sneeze *verb*
= starnutire

snobbish *adjective*
= snob (**!** *never changes*)

snooker *noun* ▶ **178**
snooker = il biliardo

snore *verb*
= russare

snow
1 *noun*
snow = la neve
2 *verb*
= nevicare
it's snowing = sta nevicando

snowball *noun*
a snowball = una palla di neve

snowman *noun*
a snowman = un pupazzo di neve

so
1 *adverb*
• **so** = così
he's so [happy | stupid | smart] = è così [felice | stupido | intelligente]
it's so much easier = è talmente più facile
she has so many clothes = ha così tanti vestiti
I've so much work to do = ho così tanto lavoro da fare
• (*also*)
I'm fifteen and so is he = ho quindici anni e lui pure

····▶

if you go, so will I = se tu vai ci vado
anch'io
- (*other uses*)
I think so = penso di sì
I'm afraid so = temo di sì
I told you so = te l'avevo detto
so what? = e allora?
and so on = e così via
2 so (that) = così che
be quiet so I can work = fai silenzio, così
che possa lavorare

> **!** *Note that the subjunctive is used after* **così che***.*

3 so as = così da
we left early so as not to miss the train
= siamo partiti presto così da non
perdere il treno

soap *noun*
- (*for washing*)
soap = il sapone
- (*on TV*)
a soap = una soap opera

soccer *noun* ▶ **178** |
soccer = il calcio

social *adjective*
= sociale

social studies *noun*
social studies = le scienze sociali

social worker *noun* ▶ **281** |
a social worker = un
assistente/un'assistente sociale

sock *noun*
a sock = un calzino

sofa *noun*
a sofa = un divano

soft *adjective*
- (*not hard or tough*) = morbido/morbida
- (*not harsh or severe*) = delicato/delicata
- (*not strict*) = indulgente

software *noun*
software = il software

soldier *noun* ▶ **281** |
a soldier = un soldato

sole *noun*
- the sole (of the foot) = la pianta del piede
- (*of a shoe*)
a sole = una suola

solicitor *noun* ▶ **281** | (*British English*)
a solicitor = un avvocato

solution *noun*
a solution = una soluzione

solve *verb*
= risolvere
to solve a problem = risolvere un
problema

some
1 *determiner*
- (*an amount or a number of*) = del/della (+
singular)
= dei/delle (+ *plural*)

> **!** *Note that* **dello** *and* **degli** *are used
before singular and plural masculine
nouns beginning with z, ps, gn or s +
another consonant. Before a singular
noun beginning with a vowel* **dell'** *is
used.*

we bought some beer = abbiamo
comprato della birra
she ate some strawberries = ha mangiato
delle fragole
we visited some beautiful towns
= abbiamo visitato delle città bellissime
I have to buy some bread = devo
comprare il pane
have some water = prendi un po' d'acqua
- (*certain*) = alcuni/alcune
some houses are empty = alcune case
sono disabitate
2 *pronoun*
- (*an amount or a number of*) = ne
I know where you can find some = so
dove puoi trovarne
have some more! = prendine ancora!

> **!** *Note that it is necessary to use* **ne***,
which might be translated as* 'of it' *or*
'of them'*, with pronouns like* **some***. See
also* **any***,* **a few***,* **a lot** *etc for this use of*
ne*.*

- (*certain people or things*)
some are quite expensive = alcuni sono
costosi
some (of them) are Italian = alcuni di
loro sono italiani

someone *pronoun* (*also* **somebody**)
= qualcuno
someone famous = qualcuno di famoso

something *pronoun*
= qualcosa
I saw something interesting = ho visto
qualcosa di interessante

sometimes *adverb*
= a volte

somewhere *adverb*
= da qualche parte
they live somewhere in Ireland = vivono
da qualche parte in Irlanda
it must be somewhere = dev'essere da
qualche parte
let's go somewhere else = andiamo da
qualche altra parte

son *noun*
a son = un figlio

song *noun*
a song = una canzone

son-in-law *noun*
a son-in-law = un genero

S

soon *adverb*
- (*in a short time*) = presto
  see you soon! = a presto!
- (*early*)
  the sooner the better = prima è meglio è
  as soon as possible = al più presto
    possibile
  come as soon as you can = vieni prima
    che puoi

sore *adjective*
  to have a sore throat = avere mal di gola
  to have a sore leg = avere un dolore alla
    gamba
  it's very sore = mi fa molto male

sorry
1 *exclamation*
- (*when apologizing*)
  sorry! = scusa!
- (*when asking someone to repeat*)
  sorry? = come, scusa?
2 *adjective*
- (*when apologizing*)
  I'm sorry I'm late = scusa il ritardo
  to say sorry = chiedere scusa
- (*when expressing pity, regret*)
  I feel sorry for him = mi dispiace per lui
  I'm sorry you can't come = mi dispiace
    che tu non possa venire

  > **!** Note that the subjunctive is used after
  > dispiacere che.

sort
1 *noun*
  it's a sort of [bird | computer | loan] = è un
    tipo di [uccello | computer | prestito]
  he's not that sort of person = non è il
    tipo
2 *verb*
  to sort the books into piles = dividere i
    libri in pile
sort out
- (*to solve*) = risolvere
  to sort out a problem = risolvere un
    problema
- (*to deal with*) = occuparsi di (**!** + *essere*)
  I'll sort it out = me ne occupo io
- (*to organize*) = riordinare
  to sort out the documents = riordinare i
    documenti

sound
1 *noun*
- **a sound** (*a noise*) = un rumore
  (*of an instrument, a bell*) = un suono
  I heard the sound of voices = ho sentito
    delle voci
- (*of a radio, a television*)
  the sound = l'audio
  to turn the sound up = aumentare il
    volume
2 *verb*
  it sounds [dangerous | odd | interesting]
    = sembra [pericoloso | strano | interessante]
  it sounds like a piano = sembra un piano

soup *noun*
  a soup = una minestra

sour *adjective*
  = acido/acida
  to go sour = inacidire (**!** + *essere*)

south
1 *noun*
  the south = il sud
  in the south of Italy = nel sud d'Italia
2 *adverb*
  to go south = andare verso sud
  to live south of Rome = abitare a sud di
    Roma
3 *adjective*
  = sud (**!** *never changes*)
  to work in south London = lavorare nella
    zona sud di Londra

South Africa *noun* ▶ **151**
  South Africa = il Sudafrica

South America *noun* ▶ **151**
  South America = il Sudamerica

southeast *noun*
  the southeast = il sudest

southwest *noun*
  the southwest = il sudovest

souvenir *noun*
  a souvenir = un souvenir

space *noun*
- (*room*)
  space = lo spazio
  to take up space = occupare spazio
- (*an area of land*)
  an open space = uno spiazzo
- (*outer space*)
  space = lo spazio
- (*a gap*)
  a space = uno spazio

Spain *noun* ▶ **151**
  Spain = la Spagna

Spanish ▶ **199**
1 *adjective*
  = spagnolo/spagnola
2 *noun*
  Spanish = lo spagnolo

spare *adjective*
- (*extra*) = in più
  I've got a spare ticket = ho un biglietto
    in più
- (*available*) = disponibile
  are there any spare seats? = ci sono dei
    posti disponibili?

spare part *noun*
  a spare part = un pezzo di ricambio

spare room *noun*
  the spare room = la stanza degli ospiti

spare time *noun*
  spare time = il tempo libero

speak *verb*
= parlare
to speak German = parlare tedesco
they're not speaking (to each other)
= non si rivolgono la parola
who's speaking, please? = chi parla?
generally speaking = in generale
speak up = parlare più forte

special *adjective*
= speciale
a special offer = un'offerta speciale
she's a special friend = è un'amica
carissima

speciality (*British English*), **specialty**
(*US English*) *noun*
a speciality = una specialità

specially *adverb*
= specialmente

spectator *noun*
a spectator = uno spettatore/una
spettatrice

speech *noun*
a speech = un discorso
to make a speech = fare un discorso

speed
1 *noun*
speed = la velocità
2 *verb*
(*to drive too fast*) = andare troppo veloce
(**!** + *essere*)
to get a fine for speeding = prendere una
multa per eccesso di velocità
speed up = accelerare

speed limit *noun*
a speed limit = un limite di velocità

spell *verb*
how do you spell it? = come si scrive?
it's spelt with a small 'c' = si scrive con la
'c' minuscola

spelling *noun*
spelling = l'ortografia

spend *verb*
• (*to pay money*) = spendere
• (*to pass*)
to spend time [reading | painting | writing]
= passare il tempo a [leggere | dipingere |
scrivere]

spider *noun*
a spider = un ragno

spill *verb*
• (*if it's a person*) = versare
• (*if it's a liquid*) = versarsi (**!** + *essere*)

spinach *noun*
spinach = gli spinaci (*plural*)

spit *verb*
= sputare

spite: **in spite of** *preposition*
= nonostante

we went out in spite of the weather
= siamo usciti nonostante il maltempo

spiteful *adjective*
= dispettoso/dispettosa

spoil *verb*
• (*to ruin*) = rovinare
to spoil the evening = rovinare la serata
• (*as a parent*) = viziare
to spoil a child = viziare un bambino

sponge *noun*
a sponge = una spugna

spoon *noun*
a spoon = un cucchiaio

sport *noun* ▶ 178|
a sport = uno sport
to be good at sports = essere
portato/portata per lo sport

sports centre (*British English*),
sports center (*US English*) *noun*
a sports centre = un centro sportivo

sports club *noun*
a sports club = un club sportivo

spot
1 *noun*
• (*on an animal*)
a spot = una macchia
• (*British English*) (*on the face or body*)
a spot = un brufolo
• (*a place*)
a spot = un posto
on the spot (*there and then*) = lì per lì
2 *verb*
• (*to see*) = scorgere
• (*to recognize*) = notare

sprain *verb*
to sprain one's wrist = slogarsi il polso
(**!** + *essere*)

spring *noun*
spring = la primavera
in spring = in primavera

spy *noun*
a spy = una spia

square
1 *noun*
• (*the shape*)
a square = un quadrato
• (*in a town*)
a square = una piazza
2 *adjective*
= quadrato/quadrata

squash
1 *noun* ▶ 178|
squash = lo squash
2 *verb*
= schiacciare

squeak *verb*
(*if it's a door, a wheel*) = cigolare
(*if it's a shoe, a chair*) = scricchiolare

S

squeeze *verb*
to squeeze a lemon = strizzare un limone
to squeeze someone's hand = stringere
la mano a qualcuno

stable *noun*
a stable = una stalla

stadium *noun*
a stadium = uno stadio

staff *noun*
the staff (*of a company*) = il personale
(*of a school, a college*) = il personale
insegnante

stage *noun*
a stage = un palco

stain
1 *noun*
a stain = una macchia
2 *verb*
= macchiare

stairs *noun*
the stairs = le scale
he fell down the stairs = è caduto giù per
le scale

stamp *noun*
• (*for an envelope*)
a stamp = un francobollo
a 0·41 euro stamp = un francobollo da
0,41 euro
• (*on a document, a passport*)
a stamp = un timbro

stamp-collecting *noun*
stamp-collecting = la filatelia

stand *verb*
• to be standing = essere in piedi
to be able to stand = reggersi in piedi
(**!** + *essere*)
you're standing in my way = mi blocchi il
passaggio
• (*to put*)
to stand a vase on a table = mettere un
vaso sul tavolo
• (*to step*)
to stand on a nail = mettere il piede su
un chiodo
• (*to bear*)
I can't stand her = non la sopporto
• (*other uses*)
to stand for election (*British English*)
= candidarsi alle elezioni (**!** + *essere*)
to stand trial = essere processato/
processata
stand back = tirarsi indietro (**!** + *essere*)
stand for
• (*to represent*) = rappresentare
• (*to mean*) = significare
stand out
(*if it's a person*) = distinguersi (**!** +
essere)
stand up
• to stand up = alzarsi in piedi (**!** + *essere*)
• to stand someone up = dare bidone a
qualcuno

stand up for = difendere
to stand up for oneself = difendersi (**!** +
essere)
stand up to
to stand up to someone = tenere testa a
qualcuno

star *noun*
• (*in space*)
a star = una stella
• (*a famous person*)
a star = una star

stare *verb*
to stare at someone = fissare qualcuno

start
1 *verb*
• (*to begin doing something*) = cominciare
(**!** + *avere*)
to start [working | writing | running]
= cominciare a [lavorare | scrivere | correre]
• (*to begin to happen*) = cominciare (**!** +
essere)
the film has already started = il film è
già cominciato
• (*to cause*) = causare
to start a war = causare una guerra
• (*to begin working*) = partire (**!** + *essere*)
the car won't start = la macchina non
parte
• (*to put into action*)
to start a car = mettere in moto una
macchina
to start a machine = mettere in funzione
una macchina
2 *noun*
a start = un inizio
at the start of the week = all'inizio della
settimana
start off = cominciare (**!** + *avere* or
essere)
start over (*US English*) = ricominciare (**!** +
avere)

starter *noun* (*British English*)
a starter = un antipasto

state *noun*
• (*a country, part of a country*)
a state = uno stato
• (*a government*)
the State = lo Stato
• (*a condition*)
a state = uno stato
to be in a bad state (of repair) = essere in
cattivo stato
she's in no state to work = non è in
condizioni di lavorare

statement *noun*
a statement = una dichiarazione
(*official*) = un comunicato

station *noun*
• (*for trains*)
a station = una stazione
• a TV station = una televisione
a radio station = una radio

statue *noun*
a statue = una statua

stay
1 *verb*
- (*to remain*) = restare (**!** + *essere*)
  do you want to stay at home? = vuoi restare a casa?
- (*to have accommodation*) = alloggiare
  to stay with friends = alloggiare presso amici
2 *noun*
a stay = un soggiorno
stay away from = evitare
stay in = restare a casa (**!** + *essere*)
stay out
to stay out late = rientrare tardi (**!** + *essere*)
stay up = restare alzato/alzata (**!** + *essere*)

steady *adjective*
- (*continuous*)
  to make steady progress = fare progressi regolari
- (*not likely to move*) = stabile

steak *noun*
a steak = una bistecca

steal *verb*
= rubare
to steal money from someone = rubare dei soldi a qualcuno

steam *noun*
steam = il vapore

steel *noun*
steel = l'acciaio

steep *adjective*
= ripido/ripida

steering wheel *noun*
a steering wheel = un volante

step
1 *noun*
- (*when walking*)
  a step = un passo
  to take a step = fare un passo
- (*in stairs, at a door*)
  a step = un gradino
- (*a series of actions*)
  to take steps = prendere provvedimenti
2 *verb*
to step in a puddle = passare in una pozzanghera (**!** + *essere*)

stepbrother *noun*
a stepbrother = un fratellastro

stepfather *noun*
a stepfather = un patrigno

stepmother *noun*
a stepmother = una matrigna

stepsister *noun*
a stepsister = una sorellastra

stereo *noun*
a stereo = uno stereo

stewardess *noun* ▶ **281** |
a stewardess = una hostess

stick
1 *verb*
- (*using glue or tape*) = attaccare
- (*to become attached*) = appiccicarsi (**!** + *essere*)
- (*to get blocked*) = bloccarsi (**!** + *essere*)
  the door is stuck = la porta si è bloccata
2 *noun*
- (*a piece of wood*)
  a stick = un rametto
- (*for walking*)
  a stick = un bastone
stick at
to stick at a task = perseverare in un compito
stick out = sporgere
there's a nail sticking out = c'è un chiodo che sporge
his ears stick out = ha le orecchie a sventola

sticky tape *noun* (*British English*)
sticky tape = lo scotch®

stiff *adjective*
- (*not soft, not supple*) = rigido/rigida
  to have stiff legs (*after sport, walking*) = avere le gambe indolenzite
- (*not easy to use*) = duro/dura
  to be stiff (*if it's a door, a drawer*) = essere duro da aprire
  (*if it's a handle*) = essere duro da girare

still¹ *adverb*
= ancora, sempre
I still don't understand why you left = ancora non capisco perché te ne sei andato
she could still win = potrebbe ancora vincere
does she still play the piano? = suona sempre il piano?

still²
1 *adverb*
to sit still = stare seduto/seduta immobile
2 *adjective*
= tranquillo/tranquilla

sting *verb*
= pungere
I've been stung by a wasp = mi ha punto una vespa

stir *verb*
= mescolare

stomach *noun* ▶ **137** |, ▶ **193** |
the stomach = lo stomaco
to have a pain in one's stomach = avere mal di stomaco

stone *noun*
a stone = una pietra
(*a pebble*) = un sasso

S

stop

1 *verb*
- (*to make something stop*) = fermare
  to stop a taxi = fermare un taxi
- (*to come to a halt*) = fermarsi (**!** + *essere*)
  the bus didn't stop = l'autobus non si è fermato
- (*to cease*) = smettere
  to stop [smoking | laughing | working]
    = smettere di [fumare | ridere | lavorare]
  stop it! = smettila!
  it's stopped raining = ha smesso di piovere
- (*to prevent*)
  to stop someone from [leaving | winning | talking] = impedire a qualcuno di [partire | vincere | parlare]

2 *noun*
  a (bus) stop = una fermata dell'autobus

store *noun*
  a store = un negozio

storey (*British English*), story (*US English*) *noun*
  a storey = un piano

storm *noun*
  a storm = una tempesta
  (*with thunder*) = un temporale

story *noun*
- **a story** = una storia
  a true story = una storia vera
  (*in a book*) = un racconto
  a ghost story = un racconto di fantasmi
- (*in a newspaper*)
  a story = un servizio
- (*a rumour*)
  a story = una voce
- (*US English*) ▶ **storey**

stove *noun* (*US English*)
  a stove = una cucina

straight

1 *adjective*
- **straight** = diritto/diritta
  a straight line = una linea retta
- (*not curly*) = liscio/liscia
  to have straight hair = avere i capelli lisci
- (*in the right position*) = dritto/dritta
  the picture isn't straight = il quadro non è dritto
- (*honest*) = onesto/onesta

2 *adverb*
- **straight** = dritto
  to stand up straight = stare ben dritto
  straight ahead = sempre dritto
- (*without delay*) = immediatamente
  I'm going straight home = vado dritto a casa

strange *adjective*
- (*odd*) = strano/strana
- (*unknown*) = sconosciuto/sconosciuta

stranger *noun*
  a stranger = uno sconosciuto/una sconosciuta

straw *noun*
- (*for feeding animals*)
  straw = la paglia
- (*for drinking*)
  a straw = una cannuccia

strawberry *noun*
  a strawberry = una fragola

stream *noun*
  a stream = un ruscello

street *noun*
  a street = una strada

streetlamp *noun*
  a streetlamp = un lampione

strength *noun*
  strength = la forza

stressful *adjective*
  = stressante

stretch *verb*
  = stiracchiarsi (**!** + *essere*)
  to stretch one's legs = sgranchirsi le gambe (**!** + *essere*)

strict *adjective*
  = severo/severa

strike *noun*
  a strike = uno sciopero
  to go on strike = scioperare

string *noun*
  string = lo spago

striped *adjective*
  = a righe
  a striped shirt = una camicia a righe

stroke *verb*
  = accarezzare

stroller *noun* (*US English*)
  a stroller = un passeggino

strong *adjective*
- (*having strength*) = forte
  a strong wind = un vento forte
- (*not easily damaged*) = resistente
- (*obvious, noticeable*) = forte (**!** *before the noun*)
  a strong German accent = un forte accento tedesco
  a strong smell of garlic = un forte odore d'aglio
- (*having military power*) = potente

stubborn *adjective*
  = ostinato/ostinata

student *noun* ▶ 281
  a student = uno studente/una studentessa

study

1 *verb*
  to study history = studiare storia
  to study for an exam = prepararsi per un esame (**!** + *essere*) ⋯⋯➤

2 *noun*
a study = uno studio

stuff
1 *noun*
stuff = la roba
2 *verb*
to stuff a suitcase with clothes
= riempire una valigia di vestiti
to stuff oneself = rimpinzarsi (**!** +
essere)

stuffing *noun*
a stuffing = un ripieno

stupid *adjective*
= stupido/stupida

style *noun*
• (*a way of dressing, behaving*)
a style = uno stile
to have style = avere stile
• (*a design, a type*)
a style = un modello
• (*a fashion*)
a style = una moda

stylish *adjective*
= elegante

subject *noun*
• (*of a conversation, an essay*)
a subject = un argomento
to change the subject = cambiare
argomento
• (*being studied*)
a subject = una materia

suburb *noun*
the suburbs = la periferia (*singular*)

subway *noun*
• (*US English*) (*the underground*)
the subway = la metropolitana
• (*British English*) (*an underground
passage*)
a subway = un sottopassaggio

succeed *verb*
= riuscire (**!** + *essere*)

success *noun*
success = il successo
to be a success (*if it's a party*) = riuscire
(**!** + *essere*)
(*if it's a film, a book*) = avere successo

successful *adjective*
to be successful (*in an attempt*) = riuscire
(**!** + *essere*)
(*describing a film, a book*) = avere
successo
a successful businesswoman
= un'imprenditrice di successo

such
1 *determiner*
there's no such thing = non esiste
2 *adverb*
they have such a lot of money = hanno
talmente tanti soldi

she's such a strange person = è una tipa
così strana
I've never seen such a mess = non ho
mai visto un tale casino✱

suddenly *adverb*
= improvvisamente

suffer *verb* ▶ 193 |
= soffrire
to suffer from hay fever = soffrire di
raffreddore da fieno

sugar *noun*
sugar = lo zucchero

suggestion *noun*
a suggestion = una proposta

suicide *noun*
to commit suicide = suicidarsi (**!** +
essere)

suit
1 *noun*
a suit (*a man's*) = un abito
(*a woman's*) = un tailleur
2 *verb*
• (*to be convenient*) = andare bene (**!** +
essere)
does Friday suit you? = ti va bene
venerdì?
• (*to look well on*)
the hat suits you = il cappello ti sta bene

suitable *adjective*
= adatto/adatta
to be suitable for children = essere adatto
ai bambini

suitcase *noun*
a suitcase = una valigia

sum *noun*
• a sum of money = una somma di denaro
• a sum = un'addizione
sum up = riassumere

summer *noun*
summer = l'estate (*feminine*)
in summer = d'estate

summer holiday (*British English*),
summer vacation (*US English*)
noun
the summer holiday = le vacanze estive
(*from school*) = le vacanze scolastiche

> **!** Note that **vacanze** is plural.

sun *noun*
the sun = il sole
to sit in the sun = sedere al sole

sunbathe *verb*
= prendere il sole

sunburned *adjective*
to get sunburned = scottarsi (**!** + *essere*)

Sunday *noun* ▶ 155 |
Sunday = domenica

sunglasses *noun*
sunglasses = gli occhiali da sole

S

sunny *adjective*
= soleggiato/soleggiata
it's going to be sunny = ci sarà il sole

sunset *noun*
sunset = il tramonto

sunshade *noun*
a sunshade = un ombrellone

sunshine *noun*
sunshine = il sole

suntan *noun*
a suntan = un'abbronzatura
to get a suntan = abbronzarsi (! +
  essere)
a suntan oil = un olio solare

supermarket *noun*
a supermarket = un supermercato

supper *noun*
a supper = una cena

support *verb*
• (*to agree with, to help*) = appoggiare
  I support the strike = io appoggio lo
    sciopero
• (*to keep*)
  to support a family = mantenere una
    famiglia
  to support oneself = mantenersi (! +
    essere)
• (*to hold, to help physically*) = sostenere

supporter *noun*
a supporter (*of a team*) = un tifoso/una
  tifosa
(*of a party*) = un sostenitore/una
  sostenitrice

suppose *verb*
• (*to imagine*) = supporre
  I suppose you know? = suppongo che tu
    lo sappia, no?

  ! *Note that the subjunctive is used after*
  supporre che.

• (*to be meant to*)
  I'm supposed to be home by midnight
    = devo essere a casa per mezzanotte

sure *adjective*
• (*certain*) = sicuro/sicura
  I'm sure he said nine o'clock = sono
    sicura che ha detto le nove
  are you sure? = sei sicuro?
  I'm not sure if she's coming = non sono
    sicura se viene
  to make sure = assicurarsi (! + *essere*)
  make sure that the door is closed
    = assicurati che la porta sia chiusa

  ! *Note that the subjunctive is used after*
  assicurarsi che.

• (*bound*)
  he's sure to win = vincerà di sicuro
• sure of oneself = sicuro/sicura di sé

  ! *Note that* **sé** *will change to* **me, te,**
  etc, depending on the person or
  people being described.

surf *verb* ▶ **178**
to go surfing = fare il surf

surface
1 *noun*
  a surface = una superficie
2 *verb*
  = risalire in superficie (! + *essere*)

surfboard *noun*
a surfboard = un surf

surgeon *noun* ▶ **281**
a surgeon = un chirurgo

surgery *noun*
• to have surgery = farsi operare (! +
    essere)
• (*British English*) (*the place*)
  a surgery = un ambulatorio

surname *noun*
a surname = un cognome

surprise
1 *noun*
  a surprise = una sorpresa
  to take someone by surprise = prendere
    qualcuno di sorpresa
2 *verb*
  = sorprendere

surprised *adjective*
= sorpreso/sorpresa
I'm not surprised = non mi sorprende

surrender *verb*
= arrendersi (! + *essere*)

surround *verb*
= circondare
to be surrounded by trees = essere
  circondato/circondata da alberi

survey *noun*
a survey = un sondaggio

survive *verb*
= sopravvivere (! + *essere*)
to survive the winter = sopravvivere
  all'inverno
to survive an accident = sopravvivere ad
  un incidente

suspect
1 *verb*
  = sospettare
  to suspect someone of stealing
    = sospettare qualcuno di furto
2 *noun*
  a suspect = un sospetto/una sospetta

suspicious *adjective*
= sospettoso/sospettosa
to be suspicious of someone = sospettare
  di qualcuno

swan *noun*
a swan = un cigno

swap *verb*
= fare scambio
we swapped bags = abbiamo fatto
  scambio di borse

sweat *verb*
= sudare

sweater *noun*
a sweater = un maglione

sweatshirt *noun*
a sweatshirt = una felpa

Sweden *noun* ▶ 151 |
Sweden = la Svezia

Swedish ▶ 199 |
1 *adjective*
= svedese
2 *noun*
Swedish = lo svedese

sweep *verb*
= spazzare

sweet
1 *adjective*
• = dolce
  (*tasting of sugar*) = zuccherato/zuccherata
  to have a sweet tooth = essere
  goloso/golosa di dolci
• (*kind, cute*) = carino/carina
2 *noun* (*British English*)
a sweet = una caramella

swim
1 *verb*
= nuotare
to swim across a lake = attraversare un
lago a nuoto
2 *noun*
a swim = una nuotata
to go for a swim (*in the sea*) = fare il
bagno

swimming *noun* ▶ 178 |
swimming = il nuoto

swimming pool *noun*
a swimming pool = una piscina

swimsuit *noun*
a swimsuit = un costume da bagno

swing
1 *verb*
• (*to move back and forth*) = dondolarsi
  (**!** + *essere*)
  to swing on a gate = dondolarsi su un
  cancello
• (*to move something back and forth*)
  = dondolare
  to swing one's legs = ciondolare le
  gambe
2 *noun*
a swing = un'altalena

Swiss ▶ 199 |
1 *adjective*
= svizzero/svizzera
2 *noun*
the Swiss = gli svizzeri

switch
1 *noun*
a switch (*for a light*) = un interruttore
(*on a radio, an appliance*) = un pulsante

2 *verb*
• (*to exchange*) = cambiare
  to switch seats = cambiare posto
• (*to change*) = passare (**!** + *essere*)
  to switch from English to Italian = passare
  dall'inglese all'italiano
switch off = spegnere
  to switch off the light = spegnere la luce
switch on = accendere
  to switch the radio on = accendere la
  radio

Switzerland *noun* ▶ 151 |
Switzerland = la Svizzera

sympathetic *adjective*
= comprensivo/comprensiva

syringe *noun*
a syringe = una siringa

system *noun*
a system = un sistema

table *noun*
a table = un tavolo

tablet *noun*
a tablet = una pastiglia

table tennis *noun* ▶ 178 |
table tennis = il ping-pong®

tail *noun*
a tail = una coda

take *verb*
• (*to get, to have*) = prendere
  I took my umbrella = ho preso l'ombrello
  to take a book off the shelf = prendere un
  libro dallo scaffale
  to take someone by the hand = prendere
  per mano qualcuno
• (*to carry to a place, to accompany*)
  = portare
  I'll take the letters to Jack = porterò le
  lettere a Jack
  to take the children for a walk = portare i
  bambini a fare una passeggiata
  to take someone home = accompagnare a
  casa qualcuno
• (*talking about time*)
  it took two hours = ci sono volute due ore
  it takes two hours to get to Rome = ci
  vogliono due ore per andare a Roma
  I took two hours = ci ho messo due ore
  I took a long time to do my homework
  = ci ho messo molto tempo a fare i
  compiti
• (*to cope with, to bear*) = sopportare
  he can't take the pain = non sopporta il
  dolore   ····➤

I can't take any more = non ne posso più
- (when talking about what is necessary)
  it takes [time | courage | patience] = ci vuole [tempo | coraggio | pazienza]
  it won't take long = non ci vorrà molto
- (to accept) = accettare
- (to react to) = prendere
  he took the news badly = ha preso male la notizia
- (to use when travelling) = prendere
  to take a taxi = prendere un taxi
  take the first turn on the right = prendere la prima svolta a destra
- (to do)
  to take an exam = sostenere un esame
- (to have) = fare
  to take [a vacation | a bath | a shower] = fare [una vacanza | il bagno | una doccia]
  I don't take sugar = non prendo zucchero
- (to wear)
  to take a size 10 (in clothes) = portare la 40
  to take a size 5 (in shoes) = portare il 38
take apart = smontare
take away
  to take away the rubbish = portare via i rifiuti
take back = riportare
  I had to take the dress back = ho dovuto riportare indietro il vestito
take down
- (to remove)
  to take a poster down = togliere un poster
  to take down a tent = smontare una tenda
- (to write down) = annotare
take hold of = prendere
take off
- (from an airport) = decollare
- (to remove) = togliere
  I took off my shoes = mi sono tolto le scarpe
  to take off one's clothes = spogliarsi (! + essere)
take out
- (from a box, a bag) = tirare fuori
  he took a pen out of his pocket = ha tirato fuori una penna dalla tasca
- (from a bank account) = ritirare
  to take money out = ritirare dei soldi
- (to be nasty to)
  to take it out on someone = prendersela con qualcuno (! + essere)
take part
  to take part in a game = partecipare a un gioco
take place = svolgersi (! + essere)
take up
- (as a hobby)
  to take up windsurfing = cominciare a fare del windsurf
- (to occupy) = prendere
  to take up space = prendere spazio

talented adjective
= dotato/dotata

talk
1 verb
= parlare
  to talk on the phone = parlare al telefono
  to talk in Italian = parlare in italiano
  to talk to someone = parlare con qualcuno
  I talked to them about the trip = ho parlato a loro della gita
  they were talking about you = parlavano di te
2 noun
- (a conversation)
  a talk = una conversazione
- (about a special subject)
  a talk = una conferenza
- (discussions)
  talks = i negoziati

talkative adjective
= chiacchierone/chiacchierona

tall adjective ▶ 202 |
= alto/alta
  he's six feet tall ≈ è alto un metro e ottanta

tan noun
  a tan = un'abbronzatura
  to get a tan = abbronzarsi (! + essere)

tanned adjective
= abbronzato/abbronzata

tap
1 noun (British English)
  a tap = un rubinetto
  to turn the tap off = chiudere il rubinetto
2 verb
  to tap someone on the shoulder = dare un colpetto sulla spalla a qualcuno

tape
1 noun
- a tape (for a tape recorder) = una cassetta (for a video) = una videocassetta
- (for repairs, for sticking)
  tape = lo scotch®
2 verb
= registrare

tape recorder noun
  a tape recorder = un registratore

target noun
  a target = un bersaglio

tart noun (British English)
  a tart = una crostata
  an apple tart = una crostata di mele

task noun
  a task = un compito

taste
1 noun
- (when eating, drinking)
  a taste = un sapore

····▶

- (*when talking about preferences*)
  taste = il gusto
  to have good taste = avere buon gusto
  2 *verb*
- (*when describing a flavour*)
  to taste good = avere un buon sapore
  to taste awful = avere un cattivo sapore
  it tastes like cabbage = ha sapore di
  cavolo
- (*when eating, drinking*) = assaggiare

Taurus *noun*
  Taurus = Toro

tax *noun*
  tax = le tasse (*plural*)

taxi *noun*
  a taxi = un taxi

taxi rank (*British English*), **taxi stand**
  (*US English*) *noun*
  a taxi rank = un posteggio dei taxi

tea *noun*
- tea = il tè
  a tea = un tè
- (*British English*) (*a meal*)
  tea (*in the afternoon*) = il tè
  (*in the evening*) = la cena

teach *verb*
  = insegnare
  to teach someone [to read | to drive | to ride
  a horse] = insegnare a qualcuno [a leggere
  | a guidare | a cavalcare]
  to teach Italian to adults = insegnare
  italiano agli adulti

teacher *noun* ▶ **281**|
  a teacher = un insegnante/un'insegnante
  (*in a primary school*) = un maestro/una
  maestra
  (*in a secondary school*) = un
  professore/una professoressa

team *noun*
  a team = una squadra

teapot *noun*
  a teapot = una teiera

tear¹ *verb*
- (*to cause damage to*) = strappare
  to tear a page out of a book = strappare
  una pagina da un libro
- (*to get damaged*) = strapparsi (**!** +
  essere)
  tear off = staccare
  tear up = strappare

tear² *noun*
  a tear = una lacrima
  to burst into tears = scoppiare in lacrime
  (**!** + essere)

tease *verb*
  = stuzzicare

teaspoon *noun*
  a teaspoon = un cucchiaino

technical *adjective*
  = tecnico/tecnica

teenager *noun*
  a teenager = un
  adolescente/un'adolescente

telephone *noun*
  a telephone = un telefono

telephone directory *noun*
  a telephone directory = un elenco
  telefonico

telescope *noun*
  a telescope = un telescopio

television *noun*
- television = la televisione
  on television = alla televisione
- (*a TV set*)
  a television = un televisore

tell *verb*
- (*to say to*) = dire a
  did you tell your parents? = l'hai detto ai
  tuoi genitori?
  don't tell anyone = non dirlo a nessuno
  to tell someone about a problem
  = parlare di un problema con qualcuno
- (*to relate*) = raccontare
  to tell a joke = raccontare una barzelletta
- (*when giving orders or instructions*)
  to tell someone to be quiet = dire a
  qualcuno di stare zitto
  to tell someone not to smoke = dire a
  qualcuno di non fumare
- (*to work out, to know*)
  you can tell he's lying = si vede che
  mente
- (*when making distinctions*)
  to tell the twins apart = distinguere i
  gemelli
  I can't tell which is which = non riesco a
  distinguerli
  tell off
  to tell someone off = sgridare qualcuno

temper *noun*
  to be in a temper = essere in collera
  to lose one's temper = andare in collera
  (**!** + essere)

temperature *noun* ▶ **193**|
  the temperature = la temperatura
  to have a temperature = avere la febbre

temporary *adjective*
  (*describing a job*)
  = temporaneo/temporanea
  (*describing a situation*)
  = provvisorio/provvisoria

ten *number* ▶ **122**|, ▶ **146**|
  ten = dieci
  ten houses = dieci case
  I've got ten (of them) = ne ho dieci

tennis *noun* ▶ **178**|
  tennis = il tennis
  a tennis court = un campo da tennis

tense *adjective*
  = teso/tesa

T

tent *noun*
  a tent = una tenda

tenth *number*
• (*in a series*) = decimo/decima
• (*in dates*) ▶ **155|**
  the tenth of December = il dieci dicembre

term *noun*
  a term = un trimestre

terrible *adjective*
• (*expressing shock*)
  = spaventoso/spaventosa
• (*used for emphasis*) = terribile

terrified *adjective*
  = atterrito/atterrita
  to be terrified of something = avere il
    terrore di qualcosa

terror *noun*
  terror = il terrore

terrorist *noun*
  a terrorist = un/una terrorista

test
1 *verb*
• (*to try out*) = provare
• (*in exams*) = esaminare
2 *noun*
• a test = un test
  (*in school, college*) (*written*) = un compito
    in classe
  (*oral*) = un'interrogazione
  a driving test = un esame di guida
• to have an eye test = farsi controllare la
    vista (**!** + *essere*)

text message *noun*
  a text message = uno sms

than
1 *preposition*
  = di
  to be [stronger | more intelligent] than
    = essere [più forte | più intelligente] di
  I've got more money than you = ho più
    soldi di te
  more than half of the pupils are absent
    = più della metà degli alunni sono
    assenti
  it's worth less than £100 = vale meno di
    100 sterline
2 *conjunction*
  = che
  it's colder than in Aberdeen = fa più
    freddo che ad Aberdeen

thank *verb*
  = ringraziare

thanks to *preposition*
  = grazie a

thank you *adverb*
  = grazie
  thank you for coming = grazie per essere
    venuti
  thank you for the roses = grazie delle
    rose

that
1 *determiner*
  that = quel/quella

> **!** *Note that before a vowel* **quell'** *is
> used.* **Quello** *is used before a
> masculine noun beginning with z, ps,
> gn or s + another consonant.*

  do you know that place? = conosci quel
    posto?
  who is that woman? = chi è quella
    signora?

> **!** *If a clear distinction is to be made,
> the word* **là** *or* **lì** *is added.*

  I prefer that hotel = preferisco
    quell'albergo là
  I like that one = mi piace quello lì
2 *pronoun*
• = quello/quella
  what's that? = quello cos'è?
  who's that? = quello chi è?
  is that Gaia? = è Gaia?
  that's how they make butter = il burro si
    fa così
  that's not true = non è vero
• (*used as a relative pronoun*) = che
  the man that stole my bag = l'uomo che
    mi ha rubato la borsa
3 *conjunction*
  = che
  he says that he'll do it = ha detto che lo
    farà

the *determiner*
▶ *See the boxed note on* **the** *for detailed
information and examples.*

theatre (*British English*), **theater** (*US
English*) *noun*
  a theatre = un teatro

their *determiner*
  their = il loro/la loro (+ *singular*)
  = i loro/le loro (+ *plural*)

> **!** *Note that the definite article* **il/la**, *etc
> is generally used.*

  I hate their dog = non sopporto il loro
    cane
  they're selling their CDs = stanno
    vendendo i loro CD
  their brother/their sister = il loro
    fratello/la loro sorella
  what do you think of their house? = cosa
    pensi di casa loro?

theirs *pronoun*
  theirs = il loro/la loro (*singular*)
  = i loro/le loro (*plural*)

> **!** *Note that* **il/la**, *etc is used when
> comparing things belonging to different
> people, but not when saying who
> something belongs to.*

  my car is red but theirs is green = la mia
    macchina è rossa ma la loro è verde ····▶

the

● In Italian the definite article agrees with the noun which follows it:

il + masculine singular:

| *the* dog | = **il** cane |

la + feminine singular:

| *the* city | = **la** città |

l' + masculine or feminine singular beginning with a vowel:

| *the* east | = **l'**est |
| *the* air | = **l'**aria |

lo + masculine singular beginning with **z**, **ps**, **gn**, or **s** + another consonant:

| *the* sugar | = **lo** zucchero |
| *the* strike | = **lo** sciopero |

i + masculine plural:

| *the* meals | = **i** pasti |

le + feminine plural:

| *the* cups | = **le** tazze |

gli + masculine plural beginning with a vowel or with **z**, **ps**, **gn**, or **s** + another consonant:

| *the* inhabitants | = **gli** abitanti |
| *the* aunts and uncles | = **gli** zii |

● Remember that when the definite article follows the prepositions **a**, **da**, **di**, **in**, **su** and sometimes **con**, it combines with them:

| *the end **of the** course* | = la fine **del** corso |
| *he jumped **from the** train* | = si è buttato **dal** treno |

▶ Look at the entries for the individual prepositions for more information and examples.

The in English can usually be translated by the definite article in Italian. Look at the notes on **the clock**, **the human body**, **countries**, **dates**, **forms of address**, **games and sports**, **illnesses**, and **languages** for special uses of the definite article in Italian.

the door is banging	= **la** porta sta sbattendo
*switch on **the** computer*	= accendi **il** computer
the Thames	= **il** Tamigi
the Clintons	= **i** Clinton

but note:

| *Elizabeth **the** Second* | = Elisabetta II (*say* Elisabetta Seconda) |

---

our parents are younger than theirs = i nostri genitori sono più giovani dei loro
the new house is theirs = la nuova casa è loro
a friend of theirs = un loro amico

them *pronoun*
● = li/le

> **!** *Note that* **li/le** *combines with the infinitive, the gerund, and the imperative.* **Loro** *is used for emphasis.*

we know them = li conosciamo
we've seen them = li abbiamo visti
help them! = aiutalii!
don't help them! = non aiutarli!
don't help THEM! = non aiutare loro!
● (*to them*) = loro

> **!** *Note that* **loro** *never combines with the infinitive, the gerund, or the imperative.* **A** **loro** *is used for emphasis. In spoken Italian,* **loro** *is often replaced by* **gli**.

she gave them the book = ha dato loro il libro
write to them! = scrivi loro!
don't show it to them! = non farlo vedere a loro!
● (*after a preposition*) = loro
he did it for them = l'ha fatto per loro
stand in front of them! = mettiti davanti a loro!
● **it's them!** = sono loro!

themselves *pronoun*
● (*when used as a reflexive pronoun*) = si

> **!** *Note that* **si** *combines with the infinitive and the gerund.* **Si** *beomes* **se** *before* **lo/la**, **li/le**, *and* **ne**.

they want to enjoy themselves = vogliono divertirsi
they didn't hurt themselves = non si sono fatti male
● (*when used for emphasis*)
they said it themselves = l'hanno detto loro stessi ⋯▶

T

they did it all by themselves = l'hanno
fatto da soli

then adverb
• (at that point in time) = allora
  I was living in Rome then = allora abitavo
  a Roma
  from then on = da allora in poi
• (after, next) = poi
  I went for a drink and then had dinner
  = sono andato a bere qualcosa e poi ho
  cenato

there
1 pronoun
  there is a problem = c'è un problema
  there aren't any shops = non ci sono
  negozi
  there was no room = non c'era spazio
  there will be a lot of people = ci sarà un
  sacco di gente
2 adverb
• (when talking about location) = là
  the train wasn't there = il treno non c'era
  they don't go there very often = non ci
  vanno molto spesso
  it's over there = è laggiù
  when do we get there? = quando
  arriviamo?
• (when drawing attention)
  there's [the sea | my watch | Natalia] = ecco
  [il mare | il mio orologio | Natalia]
  there they are = eccoli
  there you are, there you go = ecco

therefore adverb
  = quindi

these
1 determiner
  these = questi/queste
  these books aren't mine = questi libri
  non sono miei
2 pronoun
  what are these? = cosa sono questi?
  these are your things = queste sono le
  tue cose
  these are my friends = questi sono i miei
  amici
  I prefer these = preferisco queste qui

they pronoun
  they = loro

! Note that the subject pronoun is
usually omitted in Italian. It is used for
emphasis, to express a contrast, or
when it is necessary to avoid
ambiguity.

  they're coming next week = arrivano la
  settimana prossima
  they do all the work here = qui fanno
  tutto loro
  we work in London but they don't = noi
  lavoriamo a Londra ma loro no
  there they are! = eccoli!

that's how they make yogurt = così si fa
lo yogurt

! Note that when talking in an
impersonal or vague way about
people, Italian uses si. Look at the
notes at you and si for more
information..

thick adjective
• = spesso/spessa
• (when it's fog, snow) = fitto/fitta

thief noun
  a thief = un ladro/una ladra

thigh noun ▶ 137|
  the thigh = la coscia

thin adjective
  = sottile
  (when it's a person) = magro/magra
  to get thin = dimagrire (! + essere)

thing noun
• a thing = una cosa
  I've got things to do = ho da fare
  that was a stupid thing to do = quella è
  stata una stupidaggine
  the best thing is to call him = la cosa
  migliore da fare è chiamarlo
  I can't hear a thing = non sento niente
• (belongings)
  my things = la mia roba (singular)

think verb
• (to reflect, to have in mind) = pensare
  to think about someone = pensare a
  qualcuno
  we didn't think of closing the window
  = non abbiamo pensato a chiudere la
  finestra
  think hard before answering = pensaci
  bene prima di rispondere
• (to believe, to have an opinion) = credere
  I think it's unfair = credo che sia ingiusto
  'will they come?'—'I don't think so'
  = 'verranno?'—'non credo'
  who do you think will win? = chi credi
  che vincerà?
  what do you think of it? = cosa ne pensi?
• (to remember)
  I can't think of his name = mi sfugge il
  nome
• (to have vague plans to)
  to be thinking of changing jobs = pensare
  di cambiare lavoro
• (to have an idea about)
  to think of a solution = trovare una
  soluzione

third
1 adjective
  = terzo/terza
2 noun
• (in a series)
  the third = il terzo/la terza
• (in dates) ▶ 155| ····▶

the third of June = il tre giugno
- *(when talking about quantities)* ▶ **233** |
  a third of the population = un terzo della
  popolazione
3 *adverb*
  to come third = arrivare terzo/terza

thirsty *adjective*
  to be thirsty = avere sete
  I'm very thirsty = ho molta sete

thirteen *number* ▶ **122** |, ▶ **146** |
  thirteen = tredici

thirteenth *number*
- *(in a series)* = tredicesimo/tredicesima
- *(in dates)* ▶ **155** |
  Friday the thirteenth = venerdì tredici

thirty *number* ▶ **122** |, ▶ **146** |
  thirty = trenta

this
1 *determiner*
  this = questo/questa
  do you know this place? = conosci questo
  posto?
  who is this woman? = chi è questa
  signora?

  ! *If a clear distinction is to be made,
  the word* **qui** *is added.*

  I prefer this hotel = preferisco questo
  albergo qui
  I like this one = mi piace questo qui
2 *pronoun*
  what's this? = cos'è questo?
  who's this? = chi è questo?
  this is my sister = questa è mia sorella

thorn *noun*
  a thorn = una spina

those
1 *determiner*
  those = quei/quelle

  ! *Note that* **quegli** *is used before
  masculine nouns beginning with a
  vowel or z, ps, gn, or s + another
  consonant.*

  those books are yours = quei libri sono
  tuoi
2 *pronoun*
  what are those? = cosa sono quelli?
  those are my letters = quelle sono le mie
  lettere
  those are my cousins = quelli sono i miei
  cugini
  I prefer those = preferisco quelli là

though
1 *conjunction*
  = nonostante
  though it's expensive, it's still a good buy
  = nonostante sia caro è pur sempre un
  affare

  ! *Note that the subjunctive is used after*
  nonostante.

2 *adverb*
  = però

it's too small, though = è troppo piccolo
però

thought *noun*
  a thought = un pensiero

thousand *number*
  one thousand, a thousand = mille
  four thousand pounds = quattromila
  sterline
  thousands of times = migliaia di volte

thread *noun*
  thread = il filo

threat *noun*
  a threat = una minaccia

threaten *verb*
  = minacciare

three *number* ▶ **122** |, ▶ **146** |
  three = tre
  three sisters = tre sorelle
  I've got three (of them) = ne ho tre

throat *noun* ▶ **137** |
  the throat = la gola

through

  ! *Often* **through** *occurs in combinations
  with verbs, for example:* **go through, let
  through, read through** *etc. To find the
  correct translations for this type of
  verb, look up the separate dictionary
  entries at* **go, let, read** *etc.*

preposition
- *(from one side to the other)* = attraverso
  to see through the fog = vedere attraverso
  la nebbia
  to go through the town centre = passare
  per il centro (! + *essere*)
  to go through a red light = passare col
  rosso (! + *essere*)
  to go through customs = passare la
  dogana (! + *avere*)
  to drive through the desert = attraversare
  il deserto in macchina
  to look through the window = guardare
  dalla finestra
- *(when talking about time)*
  right through the day = tutta la giornata
  from Friday through (to) Sunday = dal
  venerdì alla domenica

throw *verb*
  = tirare
  to throw stones at someone = tirare sassi
  a qualcuno
  throw me the ball = tirami la palla
  to throw a book on the floor = buttare un
  libro per terra
throw away, throw out = gettare

thumb *noun* ▶ **137** |
  the thumb = il pollice

thunder *noun*
  thunder = i tuoni (*plural*)
  a thunder clap = un tuono

T

thunderstorm noun
  a thunderstorm = un temporale

Thursday noun ▶ 155⌋
  Thursday = giovedì (masculine)

ticket noun
  a ticket = un biglietto

tide noun
  the tide = la marea
  the tide is out = c'è la bassa marea
  the tide is coming in = la marea si sta
    alzando

tidy adjective
  = ordinato/ordinata
tidy up = riordinare

tie
1 verb
  = legare
  to tie a dog to a tree = legare un cane ad
    un albero
  to tie a parcel (up) with string = legare un
    pacco con lo spago
2 noun
• (worn with a shirt)
  a tie = una cravatta
• (in sport)
  a tie = un pareggio
tie up = legare

tiger noun
  a tiger = una tigre

tight adjective
  = stretto/stretta

tights noun (British English)
  tights = i collant

till¹ ▶ until

till² noun
  a till = una cassa

time noun
• time = il tempo
  I don't have time to go there = non ho
    tempo di andarci
  we haven't seen them for some time
    = non li abbiamo visti da un po' di
    tempo
  a long time ago = molto tempo fa
• (when talking about a specific hour or
    period of time)
  the time = l'ora
  what's the time?, what time is it? = che
    ore sono?
  what time does the film start? = a che ora
    comincia il film?
  to arrive on time = essere puntuale
  in [five days' | a week's | six months'] time
    = tra [cinque giorni | una settimana | sei
    mesi]
  this time last year = l'anno scorso in
    questo periodo
  this time next week = fra una settimana
    esatta
  it's time we left = è ora di andar via
• (an occasion)

the first time we met = la prima volta che
  ci siamo incontrati
from time to time = di tanto in tanto
at times = a volte
• (a moment)
a time = un momento
at the right time = al momento giusto
this is no time to argue = non è il
  momento di discutere
any time now = a momenti
for the time being = per il momento
• (a period in the past)
a time = un'epoca
they didn't know each other at the time
  = all'epoca non si conoscevano
• (an experience)
to have a good time = divertirsi (! +
  essere)
to have a hard time concentrating = avere
  difficoltà a concentrarsi
• (when comparing)
three times more expensive = tre volte
  più caro

timetable noun
  a timetable = un orario

tin noun
• (the metal)
  tin = lo stagno
• (British English) (a can)
  a tin = una scatoletta
  a tin of tuna = una scatoletta di tonno

tin opener noun (British English)
  a tin opener = un apriscatole

tiny adjective
  = piccolino/piccolina

tip noun
• the tip = la punta
  on the tips of one's toes = in punta di
    piedi
• (given in a hotel, a restaurant)
  a tip = una mancia
• (a piece of advice)
  a tip = un consiglio

tire noun (US English)
  a tire = una gomma

tired adjective
• (needing rest) = stanco/stanca
  to get tired = stancarsi (! + essere)
• (needing a change) = stufo/stufa
  I'm tired of being a waitress = sono stufa
    di fare la cameriera

tiring adjective
  = stancante

tissue noun
  a tissue = un fazzolettino

to preposition ▶ 146⌋
▶ See the boxed note on **to**. There are
many adjectives like **mean**, **nice**, **rude** etc
and verbs like **belong**, **write** etc which
involve the use of **to**. For translations, look
up the adjective entries at **mean**, **nice**, **rude**
or the verb entries at **belong**, **write**.

Talking about time

How long?

how long does it take?	= quanto tempo ci vuole?
it takes five minutes	= ci vogliono cinque minuti
how long did you take?	= quanto tempo ci hai messo?
I took an hour	= ci ho messo un'ora
I did it in five minutes	= l'ho fatto in cinque minuti

The idea of **for** is expressed by **per** in Italian, but this is often omitted:

*I worked there **for** five years*	= ci ho lavorato **per** cinque anni
*I lived there **for** a year*	= ci sono vissuto un anno

But when the action is still continuing, **da** is used with the present tense to express **for** and **since**:

*I've known her **for** six months*	= la conosco **da** sei mesi
*we've been up **since** 5 o'clock*	= siamo in piedi **dalle** cinque

When?

Use **fra** or **tra** to say how far in the future something will happen. **Fra** and **tra** are usually interchangeable, but it is best to avoid combinations that are difficult to say, like **tra trentatré anni**.

*I'll do it **in** five minutes*	= lo farò **tra** cinque minuti
*we're leaving **in** a week*	= ce ne andiamo **fra** una settimana

To ask and say how long ago, use **fa**:

*how long **ago** did it happen?*	= quanto tempo **fa** è successo?
*we met three years **ago***	= ci siamo conosciuti tre anni **fa**

How often?

*how many times **a** week?*	= quante volte **alla** settimana?
*twice **a** week*	= due volte **alla** settimana
*how many times **a** day?*	= quante volte **al** giorno?
*once **a** day*	= una volta **al** giorno

How much an hour, a day, etc

*how much do you earn **an** hour?*	= quanto guadagni **all'**ora?
*I earn ten pounds **an** hour*	= guadagno dieci sterline **all'**ora
*a thousand euros **a** month*	= mille euro **al** mese
*two hundred kilometres **an** hour*	= duecento chilometri **all'**ora

---

toast *noun*
 toast = il pane tostato
 a piece of toast = una fetta di pane tostato

toaster *noun*
 a toaster = un tostapane

today *adverb* ▶ **267**|
 = oggi

toe *noun* ▶ **137**|
 the toe = il dito del piede
 my toes hurt = mi fanno male le dita del piede

together *adverb*
 = insieme

toilet *noun*
 a toilet = un gabinetto

toilet paper *noun*
 toilet paper = la carta igienica

tomato *noun*
 a tomato = un pomodoro
 tinned tomatoes = i pelati

tomorrow *adverb* ▶ **267**|
 = domani

tongue *noun* ▶ **137**|
 the tongue = la lingua

tonight *adverb*
 (*this evening*) = stasera
 (*during the night*) = stanotte

too *adverb*
• (*also*) = anche
 I'm going too = ci vado anch'io
• (*more than is necessary or desirable*)
 = troppo   ····▶

to

As a preposition

- When **to** is used as a preposition after verbs of movement (**go**, **travel**, etc) it is often translated by **a**; but with countries remember to use **in**.

*I'm going **to** school*	= vado **a** scuola
*can you take me **to** Paris with you?*	= mi porti **a** Parigi?
*we're going **to** Greece*	= andiamo **in** Grecia

  Remember that **a** combines with the definite article **il/la**, etc:

  *are you coming **to the** supermarket?* = vieni **al** supermercato?

  Other translations are sometimes necessary:

  *I have to go **to** the bank* = devo andare **in** banca

- When **to** is used as a preposition after verbs such as **give**, **show**, **speak**, etc, it is usually translated by **a**. Remember that **a** combines with **il/la**, etc:

*I gave some red roses **to** Paola*	= ho dato delle rose rosse **a** Paola
*I explained it **to the** children*	= l'ho spiegato **ai** bambini

- When **to** is used together with a personal pronoun (**me**, **you**, **him**, **her**, **it**, **us**, **them**), Italian uses an indirect object pronoun (**mi**, **ti**, **gli**, **le**, **ci**, **vi**, **loro**). Note that these combine with the verb when it is in the infinitive, imperative, or gerund form:

*I want to speak **to you***	= **ti** voglio parlare
*explain **to me** where you are*	= spiega**mi** dove sei

  ▶ Look in the entries for the personal pronouns for more information and examples.

- When **to** follows a noun or adjective, it is translated in various ways:

*the road **to** Modena*	= la strada **per** Modena
*he was kind **to** me*	= è stato gentile **con** me

  ▶ Look at the entries for the individual nouns and adjectives for more information and examples.

As part of an infinitive

- When **to** is part of the infinitive (**to drive**), its translation will depend on which verb it comes after in Italian. Sometimes it is not translated:

  *I had **to** say no* = ho dovuto dire di no

  Some verbs in Italian require **a** or **di** before the infinitive:

*I'm trying **to** understand*	= sto cercando **di** capire
*did you manage **to** find her?*	= sei riuscito **a** trovarla?

- When **to** means 'in order to', use **per**:

  *he stood up **to** make a speech* = si è alzato in piedi **per** fare un discorso

- When **to** follows an adjective, it is translated in various ways. With **troppo**, use **per**:

*it's difficult **to** understand him*	= è difficile capirlo
*are you ready **to** go?*	= sei pronto **a** partire?
*is she able **to** do it?*	= è capace **di** farlo?
*he's too short **to** reach the switch*	= è troppo basso **per** arrivare all'interruttore

  ▶ Look at the entries for the individual verbs and adjectives for more information and examples.

- When **to do** means 'to be done', use **da**:

  *I have loads of things **to** do* = ho un sacco di cose **da** fare

it's too [big | dear | far] = è troppo [grande | caro | lontano]
too much = troppo/troppa (+ *singular*)
too many = troppi/troppe (+ *plural*)
I ate too much = ho mangiato troppo

tool *noun*
a tool = un attrezzo

tooth *noun* ▶ 137 |
a tooth = un dente
a set of false teeth = una dentiera

toothache *noun* ▶ 193 |
to have a toothache = avere mal di denti

toothbrush *noun*
a toothbrush = uno spazzolino da denti

toothpaste *noun*
toothpaste = il dentifricio

top
1 *noun*
• (*the highest part or level*)
the top of the hill = la cima della collina
the top of the stairs = la cima delle scale
at the top of [the page | the stairs | street]
= in cima [alla pagina | alle scale | alla strada]
she got to the top = è arrivata in cima
• (*a cover, a lid*)
a top (*on a bottle*) = un tappo
(*on a pan*) = un coperchio
(*on a pen*) = un cappuccio
2 *adjective*
the top [shelf | drawer | button] = [la mensola | il cassetto | il pulsante] in alto

torch *noun* (*British English*)
a torch = una torcia

torn *adjective*
= strappato/strappata

tortoise *noun*
a tortoise = una tartaruga

total
1 *noun*
the total = il totale
2 *adjective*
= totale

touch
1 *verb*
= toccare
don't touch my things = non toccare le mie cose
2 *noun*
to get in touch with someone = mettersi in contatto con qualcuno (**!** + *essere*)
let's stay in touch = rimaniamo in contatto

tough *adjective*
• (*not soft, not sensitive*) = duro/dura
• (*rough*) = violento/violenta
a tough area = una zona violenta
• (*difficult*) = difficile

tour
1 *noun*
• (*by a team, a band, a theatre group*)
a tour = una tournée
on tour = in tournée
• (*by tourists, visitors*)
a tour = una visita
to go on a tour of the castle = visitare il castello
2 *verb*
to tour Scotland = visitare la Scozia

tourism *noun*
tourism = il turismo

tourist *noun*
a tourist = un/una turista

tourist office *noun*
a tourist office = un ufficio del turismo

toward(s) *preposition*
• (*when talking about place, time*) = verso
towards the east = verso est
towards evening = verso sera
• (*when talking about attitudes*) = nei confronti di
friendly towards someone = amichevole nei confronti di qualcuno

towel *noun*
a towel = un asciugamano

tower *noun*
a tower = una torre

tower block *noun* (*British English*)
a tower block = un palazzone

town *noun*
a town = una città
to go into town = andare in città (**!** + *essere*)

town hall *noun*
a town hall = un municipio

toy *noun*
a toy = un giocattolo

track *noun*
• (*a path*)
a track = un sentiero
• (*for sports*)
a track = una pista
• (*the rails*)
the track(s) = le rotaie
• (*left by a person, an animal, a car*)
tracks = le tracce

tracksuit *noun*
a tracksuit = una tuta da ginnastica

trade *noun*
• trade = il commercio
• a trade = un mestiere

tradition *noun*
a tradition = una tradizione

traffic *noun*
traffic = il traffico

traffic jam *noun*
a traffic jam = un ingorgo

T

traffic lights *noun*
traffic lights = il semaforo (*singular*)

train
1 *noun*
a train = un treno
the train to Genoa = il treno per Genova
2 *verb*
• (*to teach, to prepare*)
to train employees = formare i dipendenti
to train athletes = allenare gli atleti
• (*to learn a job*)
to train as a doctor = fare pratica come
    medico
she trained as a teacher = ha fatto
    tirocinio come insegnante
• (*for a sporting event*) = allenarsi (**!** +
    essere)

trainer *noun* (*British English*)
a trainer = una scarpa da ginnastica

tramp *noun*
a tramp = un barbone/una barbona

translate *verb*
= tradurre
to translate into English = tradurre in
    inglese

translator *noun* ▶ 281 |
a translator = un traduttore/una
    traduttrice

transport, transportation (*US
English*) *noun*
transport = il trasporto
a means of transport = un mezzo di
    trasporto

trap *noun*
a trap = una trappola

trash *noun* (*US English*)
trash = la spazzatura

trash can *noun* (*US English*)
a trash can = una pattumiera

travel *verb*
= viaggiare
to travel abroad = viaggiare all'estero

travel agency *noun* ▶ 281 |
a travel agency = un'agenzia di viaggi

traveller (*British English*), **traveler**
(*US English*) *noun*
a traveller = un viaggiatore/una
    viaggiatrice

traveller's cheque (*British English*),
traveler's check (*US English*) *noun*
a traveller's cheque = un travellers'
    cheque

tray *noun*
a tray = un vassoio

treat *verb*
• (*to deal with, to behave with*) = trattare
to treat someone badly = trattare male
    qualcuno
• (*to pay for*)

to treat someone to lunch = offrire il
    pranzo a qualcuno

treatment *noun*
treatment = una cura
to receive treatment = essere in cura

tree *noun*
a tree = un albero

tremble *verb*
= tremare

trendy *adjective*
= di moda

trial *noun*
a trial = un processo
to go on trial = essere
    processato/processata

triangle *noun*
a triangle = un triangolo

trick
1 *noun*
• (*a joke*)
a trick = uno scherzo
to play a trick on someone = fare uno
    scherzo a qualcuno
• (*a means of deceiving, a knack*)
a trick = un trucco
• (*to entertain*)
a trick = un gioco di prestigio
2 *verb*
= imbrogliare

trip
1 *noun*
a trip (*abroad*) = un viaggio
(*a day out*) = una gita
to be on a business trip = essere in
    viaggio d'affari
2 *verb*
to trip (over something) = inciampare (in
    qualcosa)
to trip someone (up) = fare lo sgambetto
    a qualcuno

trouble *noun*
• (*difficulties*)
trouble = i guai (*plural*)
to be in trouble = essere nei guai
to get someone into trouble = mettere
    qualcuno nei guai
to make trouble = creare problemi
• (*an effort*)
to go to a lot of trouble = darsi da fare
    (**!** + essere)

trousers *noun*
trousers = i pantaloni

trout *noun*
a trout = una trota

truck *noun*
a truck = un camion

truck driver *noun* ▶ 281 |
a truck driver = un/una camionista

true *adjective*
= vero/vera

····▶

is it true that he's leaving? = è vero che se ne va?
to come true = avverarsi (**!** + *essere*)

trumpet *noun*
  a trumpet = una tromba

trunk *noun*
- (*of a tree*)
  a trunk = un tronco
- (*of an elephant*)
  a trunk = una proboscide
- (*US English*) (*in a car*)
  the trunk = il bagagliaio

trust *verb*
  = fidarsi di (**!** + *essere*)
  to trust a friend = fidarsi di un amico
  I don't trust them = non mi fido di loro

truth *noun*
  the truth = la verità

try
1 *verb*
- (*to attempt*)
  to try [to understand | to come | to forget]
  = cercare [di capire | di venire | di dimenticare]
- (*to test, to experiment*) = provare
  to try (out) a recipe = provare una ricetta
  to try (on) a pair of jeans = provare un paio di jeans
  try phoning him = prova a telefonargli
- (*to taste*) = assaggiare
- (*in court*) = processare
2 *noun*
  to score a try = segnare una meta

T-shirt *noun*
  a T-shirt = una maglietta

tube *noun*
- a tube = un tubo
- (*British English*) (*the underground*)
  the tube = la metropolitana

Tuesday *noun* ▶ 155 |
  Tuesday = martedì (*masculine*)

tuna *noun*
  tuna = il tonno

tunnel *noun*
  a tunnel = un tunnel

turkey *noun*
  a turkey = un tacchino

turn
1 *verb*
- (*to move one's body*) = girarsi (**!** + *essere*)
- (*to change direction*) = girare
  to turn right = girare a destra
  to turn the corner = girare l'angolo
- (*to twist*) = girare
  to turn the handle = girare la manovella
- (*to change*)
  to turn the bedroom into an office
  = trasformare la camera in ufficio

- (*to become*) = trasformarsi (**!** + *essere*)
  to turn into a butterfly = trasformarsi in farfalla
  to turn red = arrossire (**!** + *essere*)
2 *noun*
- (*a bend*)
  a turn = una svolta
- (*in games*)
  a turn = un turno
  whose turn is it? = a chi tocca?
  it's my turn = tocca a me
turn around, turn round
- (*to face the other way*) (*if it's a person*)
  = girarsi (**!** + *essere*)
  (*if it's a car*) = girare
  to turn the table around = girare il tavolo nell'altro senso
- (*to go round and round*) = girare
turn back = tornare indietro (**!** + *essere*)
turn down
- (*to lower*) = abbassare
  to turn down the radio = abbassare la radio
- (*to reject*) = respingere
  to turn someone down = respingere qualcuno
turn off
  to turn off the light = spegnere la luce
  to turn the tap off = chiudere il rubinetto
turn on
  to turn on the TV = accendere la TV
  to turn the tap on = aprire il rubinetto
turn out = rivelarsi (**!** + *essere*)
  it turned out to be easy = si è rivelato facile
  to turn out all right (in the end) = finire bene (**!** + *essere*)
turn over
- (*to roll over*) = rigirarsi (**!** + *essere*)
- **to turn over the page** = voltare pagina
turn up
- (*to show up*) = capitare (**!** + *essere*)
- (*to increase*) = alzare

turtle *noun*
- a (sea) turtle = una tartaruga marina
- (*US English*) (*a tortoise*)
  a turtle = una tartaruga

TV *noun*
  a TV = una TV

twelfth *number*
- (*in a series*) = dodicesimo/dodicesima
- (*in dates*) ▶ 155 |
  the twelfth of July = il dodici luglio

twelve *number* ▶ 122 |, ▶ 146 |
  twelve = dodici
  twelve students = dodici studenti
  I've got twelve (of them) = ne ho dodici

twenty *number* ▶ 122 |, ▶ 146 |
  twenty = venti

twice *adverb*
  = due volte
  it happened twice = è successo due volte
  twice as much time = il doppio del tempo

T

twin *noun*
  a twin = un gemello/una gemella
  a twin sister = una sorella gemella

twist *verb*
- *(to bend)* = piegare
- *(to turn)* = girare
- *(to injure)* ▶ **193**|
  to twist one's ankle = slogarsi la caviglia
  (**!** + *essere*)

two *number* ▶ **122**|, ▶ **146**|
  two = due
  two brothers = due fratelli
  I've got two (of them) = ne ho due

type
1 *noun*
  a type = un tipo
  this type of [person | book | work] = questo tipo di [persona | libro | lavoro]
  he's not my type = non è il mio tipo
2 *verb*
  = battere a macchina

typewriter *noun*
  a typewriter = una macchina da scrivere

typical *adjective*
  = tipico/tipica

typist *noun* ▶ **281**|
  a typist = un dattilografo/una dattilografa

tyre *noun* (*British English*)
  a tyre = una gomma

Uu

ugly *adjective*
  = brutto/brutta

umbrella *noun*
  an umbrella = un ombrello

unbelievable *adjective*
  = incredibile

uncle *noun*
  an uncle = uno zio

uncomfortable *adjective*
- *(awkward)* = a disagio
  to feel uncomfortable = sentirsi a disagio
  (**!** + *essere*)
- *(describing shoes, seats)*
  = scomodo/scomoda
  (*describing heat, conditions*)
  = fastidioso/fastidiosa

unconscious *adjective*
  = privo di sensi/priva di sensi
  to knock someone unconscious = far perdere i sensi a qualcuno

under *preposition*
- under = sotto
  he hid under the bed = si è nascosto sotto il letto
  I found the newspaper under it = sotto ci ho trovato il giornale
- *(less than)*
  to earn under five pounds an hour
  = guadagnare meno di cinque sterline all'ora
  children under five = bambini al di sotto dei cinque anni

underground *noun* (*British English*)
  the underground = la metropolitana

underline *verb*
  = sottolineare

underneath
1 *adverb*
  = sotto
  I want to see what's underneath = voglio vedere cosa c'è sotto
2 *preposition*
  = sotto
  underneath the building = sotto il palazzo

underpants *noun*
  underpants = le mutande

understand *verb*
  = capire
  I can't understand what they're saying
  = non capisco cosa dicono
  to make oneself understood = farsi capire
  (**!** + *essere*)

understanding *adjective*
  = comprensivo/comprensiva

underwater *adverb*
  = sott'acqua

underwear *noun*
  underwear = la biancheria intima

undo *verb*
  = disfare
  to undo a button = sbottonare un bottone

undress *verb*
  = spogliarsi (**!** + *essere*)

uneasy *adjective*
  = inquieto/inquieta

unemployed *adjective*
  = disoccupato/disoccupata

unemployment *noun*
  unemployment = la disoccupazione

unfair *adjective*
  = ingiusto/ingiusta

unfortunately *adverb*
  = sfortunatamente

unfriendly *adjective*
  (*describing a person*) = poco amichevole
  (*describing a place*) = inospitale

ungrateful *adjective*
  = ingrato/ingrata

unhappy *adjective*
* (*sad*) = triste
* (*not satisfied*) = scontento/scontenta

unhealthy *adjective*
(*describing a way of life, food*) = poco salutare
(*describing a person*) = malato/malata
(*describing conditions*)
= malsano/malsana

uniform *noun*
a uniform = una divisa

union *noun*
a union = un sindacato

unique *adjective*
= unico/unica

United Kingdom *noun* ▶ 151|
the United Kingdom = il Regno Unito

United States (of America)
noun ▶ 151|
the United States (of America) = gli Stati Uniti (d'America)

universe *noun*
the universe = l'universo

university *noun*
a university = un'università

unkind *adjective*
unkind = poco gentile

unknown *adjective*
= sconosciuto/sconosciuta

unless *conjunction*
it won't work unless you plug it in = non funziona se non inserisci la spina

unlock *verb*
= aprire

unlucky *adjective*
= sfortunato/sfortunata
you were unlucky = sei stato sfortunato

unpack *verb*
to unpack a suitcase = disfare una valigia
to unpack one's belongings = disfare i bagagli

unsuitable *adjective*
= inadatto/inadatta

untidy *adjective* = disordinato/disordinata

until
1 *preposition*
= fino a
I'm staying until Thursday = resto fino a giovedì
until now = finora
she won't get an answer until next week = non avrà una risposta fino alla prossima settimana
2 *conjunction*
I'll wait until I get back home = aspetterò di arrivare a casa

don't look until it's ready = non guardare fino a quando è pronto
we'll stay until they come = resteremo finché arriveranno

> **!** *Note that, when talking about future time, the future tense is used after* **finché**.

unusual *adjective*
= insolito/insolita
it's unusual to see so few people = è insolito vedere così poche persone

up

> **!** *Often* up *occurs in combinations with verbs, for example:* blow up, give up, own up, *etc. To find the correct translations for this type of verb, look up the separate dictionary entries at* blow, give, own *etc.*

1 *preposition*
the cat's up the tree = il gatto è sull'albero
to go up the street = risalire la strada
she ran up the stairs = ha salito le scale di corsa
the library is up those stairs = la biblioteca è su per quelle scale
2 *adverb* = su
up there = lassù
up in the sky = in alto nel cielo
to go up = salire (**!** + *essere*)
I'm going up to Scotland = vado in Scozia
put the picture a bit further up = metti il quadro un po' più in alto
3 *adjective*
(*out of bed*)
are you up? = sei in piedi?
I was up all night = sono stato sveglio tutta la notte
4 up to
* (*well enough*)
  I don't feel up to it = non me la sento
* (*when talking about who is responsible*)
  it's up to [me | you | them] to decide = sta a [me | te | loro] decidere
* (*until*) = fino a
  up to now = finora
  up to 1996 = fino al 1996

upset
1 *adjective*
to be upset = essere dispiaciuto/dispiaciuta
to get upset = prendersela (**!** + *essere*)
2 *verb*
* (*to make someone unhappy*) (*if it's an event*) = turbare
  (*if it's a person*) = offendere

upside down *adverb*
= al rovescio
you're holding the book upside down = tieni il libro al rovescio

U

upstairs *adverb*
= di sopra
to go upstairs = andare di sopra (**!** +
essere)
to bring the cases upstairs = portare di
sopra le valigie

urgent *adjective*
= urgente

us *pronoun*
• = ci

> **!** *Note that* ci *combines with the
> infinitive, the gerund, and the
> imperative.* Noi *is used for emphasis.*

they know us = ci conoscono
he's seen us = ci ha visto
help us! = aiutaci!
don't help us! = non aiutarci!
don't help US! = non aiutare noi!

• (*to us*) = ci

> **!** *Note that* ci *combines with the
> infinitive, the gerund, and the
> imperative.* A noi *is used for emphasis.*
> Ci *beomes* ce *before* lo/la, li/le, *and*
> ne.

she gave the book to us = ha dato il
libro a noi
write to us! = scrivici!
don't show it to us! = non farcelo vedere!
don't show it to US! = non farlo vedere a
noi!

• (*after a preposition*) = noi
he did it for us = l'ha fatto per noi
stand in front of us! = mettiti davanti a
noi!

• **it's us!** = siamo noi!

USA *noun* ▶ 151|
the USA = gli USA

use
1 *verb*
• (*to make use of*) = usare
I use the car to go to work = uso la
macchina per andare al lavoro
he uses the room as an office = usa la
stanza come ufficio
what is it used for? = a cosa serve?
• (*to consume*) = consumare
it uses a lot of petrol = consuma molta
benzina
• (*to take advantage of*)
to use someone = approfittare di
qualcuno
2 *noun*
• **to make use of a room** = utilizzare una
stanza
• (*when talking about what is useful*)
to be of use to someone = essere utile a
qualcuno
to be no use = non servire a niente (**!** +
essere)
what's the use of complaining? = a che
serve lamentarsi?
use up
to use up the milk = finire il latte

used
1 *verb*

> **!** *Note that the imperfect tense in Italian
> is generally used to translate* used
> to + *verb.*

I used to read a lot = leggevo molto
you used not to smoke = prima non
fumavi
there used to be a castle here = una
volta qui c'era un castello
2 *adjective*
to be used to [children | animals | tourists]
= essere abituato/abituata [ai bambini |
agli animali | ai turisti]
he's not used to living on his own = non
è abituato a vivere da solo
to get used to something = abituarsi a
qualcosa (**!** + essere)

useful *adjective*
= utile

useless *adjective*
• (*not working, having no use*)
= inutilizzabile
• (*having no point or purpose*) = inutile
it's useless complaining = è inutile
lamentarsi
• (*describing a person*) = negato/negata
to be useless at chemistry = essere
negato/negata in chimica
to be useless at tennis = essere
negato/negata per il tennis

usually *adverb*
= di solito

vacant *adjective*
= libero/libera

vacation *noun* (*US English*)
a vacation = una vacanza
to take a vacation = prendere una
vacanza
on vacation = in vacanza

vacuum *verb*
to vacuum a room = passare
l'aspirapolvere in una stanza

vacuum cleaner *noun*
a vacuum cleaner = un aspirapolvere

vague *adjective*
= vago/vaga

vain *adjective*
= vanitoso/vanitosa

valid *adjective* = valido/valida

valley *noun*
a valley = una valle

valuable *adjective*
- (*very useful*) = prezioso/preziosa
- (*worth a lot of money*)
to be valuable = essere di valore

van *noun*
a van = un furgone

vanilla *noun*
vanilla = la vaniglia

various *adjective*
= vario/varia
there are various ways of saying it = si
può dire in diversi modi

vary *verb*
= variare
it varies from town to town = varia da
città a città

vase *noun*
a vase = un vaso

veal *noun*
veal = la vitella

vegetable *noun*
a vegetable = una verdura
vegetables = la verdura (*singular*)

vegetarian *noun*
a vegetarian = un vegetariano/una
vegetariana

vein *noun* ▶ 137 |
a vein = una vena

versus *preposition*
= contro

very
1 *adverb*
very = molto

> ! Note that Italian sometimes uses the
> ending -issimo/-issima to express the
> idea of 'very'.

I don't know him very well = non lo
conosco molto bene
to eat very little = mangiare pochissimo
we like them very much = ci piacciono
moltissimo
for the very first time = per la primissima
volta
they called me the very next day = mi
hanno chiamato proprio il giorno dopo
2 *adjective*
at the very beginning = proprio all'inizio
to stay to the very end = restare sino alla
fine
you are the very person I need = sei
proprio la persona che mi serve

vest *noun*
- (*British English*) (*a piece of underwear*)
a vest = una canottiera
- (*US English*) (*a waistcoat*)
a vest = un gilè

vet *noun* ▶ 281 |
a vet = un veterinario/una veterinaria

victory *noun*
a victory = una vittoria

video
1 *noun* ▶ video cassette, video
recorder
2 *verb*
- (*to record*) = registrare
- (*to film*)
to video a wedding = filmare un
matrimonio

video camera *noun*
a video camera = una videocamera

video cassette *noun*
a video cassette = una videocassetta

video game *noun*
a video game = un videogioco

video recorder *noun*
a video recorder = un videoregistratore

view *noun*
- a view = una veduta
if you want to get a better view, come
here = se vuoi vedere meglio vieni qui
- (*an opinion, an attitude*)
a view = un'opinione
a point of view = un punto di vista

village *noun*
a village = un paese

vinegar *noun*
vinegar = l'aceto

vineyard *noun*
a vineyard = una vigna

violent *adjective*
= violento/violenta

violin *noun*
a violin = un violino

Virgo *noun*
Virgo = Vergine (*feminine*)

visit
1 *verb*
to visit Ferrara = visitare Ferrara
to visit someone (*to call on*) = andare a
trovare qualcuno (! + *essere*)
2 *noun*
a visit (*a call*) = una visita
(*a stay*) = un soggiorno
to pay someone a visit = fare una visita a
qualcuno

visitor *noun*
- (*a guest*)
a visitor = un ospite/un'ospite
to have visitors = avere ospiti
- (*a tourist*)
a visitor = un visitatore/una visitatrice

vocabulary *noun*
vocabulary = il vocabolario

V

voice noun
  a voice = una voce
  to speak in a low voice = parlare a voce
  bassa
  to sing at the top of one's voice = cantare
  a voce alta

volleyball noun ▶ 178 |
  volleyball = la pallavolo

vomit verb
  = vomitare

vote verb
  = votare

Ww

wages noun
  wages = la paga (singular)

waist noun ▶ 137 |
  the waist = la vita

waistcoat noun (British English)
  a waistcoat = un gilè

wait verb
• to wait = aspettare
  to wait for someone = aspettare qualcuno
  I'm waiting to use the phone = sto
  aspettando di poter telefonare
  to wait for someone to leave = aspettare
  che qualcuno se ne vada

  ! Note that the subjunctive is used after
  aspettare che.

  I can't wait to see them = non vedo l'ora
  di vederli
• (in a restaurant)
  to wait on table, to wait table (US
  English) = lavorare come
  cameriere/cameriera

wait up
  I'll wait up for him = resto alzato ad
  aspettarlo

waiter noun ▶ 281 |
  a waiter = un cameriere

waiting room noun
  a waiting room = una sala d'attesa

waitress noun ▶ 281 |
  a waitress = una cameriera

wake verb
  to wake someone = svegliare qualcuno
wake up = svegliarsi (! + essere)

Wales noun ▶ 151 |
  Wales = il Galles

walk
1 verb
  (rather than run) = camminare

  (rather than drive) = andare a piedi (! +
  essere)
  (for pleasure) = passeggiare
  let's walk to the pool = andiamo alla
  piscina a piedi
  to walk the dog = portare a passeggio il
  cane
2 noun
  a walk = una passeggiata
  to go for a walk = andare a fare una
  passeggiata (! + essere)
  it's five minutes' walk from here = sono
  cinque minuti a piedi da qui
walk around = passeggiare
  to walk around town = gironzolare per la
  città
walk away = allontanarsi (! + essere)
walk back = tornare a piedi (! + essere)
  to walk back home = tornare a casa a
  piedi
walk by = passare (! + essere)
walk in = entrare (! + essere)
walk out = uscire (! + essere)
  to walk out of the room = uscire dalla
  stanza
walk round = fare un giro
  to walk round the exhibition = visitare la
  mostra
walk up to = avvicinarsi a (! + essere)

walkman® noun
  a walkman = un walkman®

wall noun
  a wall = un muro

wallet noun
  a wallet = un portafoglio

wallpaper noun
  wallpaper = la carta da parati

wander verb
  to wander around town = gironzolare per
  la città
wander away, wander off = allontanarsi
  (! + essere)

want verb
  to want = volere
  do you want another coffee? = vuoi un
  altro caffè?
  he wants [to go out | to go home | to play]
  = vuole [uscire | andare a casa | giocare]
  she didn't want to stay = non voleva
  restare
  do you want me to come with you?
  = vuoi che venga con te?

  ! Note that the subjunctive is used after
  volere che.

war noun
  a war = una guerra

wardrobe noun
  a wardrobe = un armadio

warm
1 adjective
  = caldo/calda   ····▶

to be warm, to feel warm = avere caldo
I'm very warm = ho molto caldo
it's warm today = oggi fa caldo
2 *verb*
to warm the plates = riscaldare i piatti
to warm one's hands = riscaldarsi le
mani (**!** + *essere*)
warm up
• (*to get warm*) = riscaldarsi (**!** + *essere*)
• (*for a sporting event*) = fare
riscaldamento
• (*to make warm*) = riscaldare

warn *verb*
= avvertire
to warn someone about the risks
= mettere in guardia qualcuno contro i
rischi
I warned him not to take the car = l'avevo
avvertito di non prendere la macchina

wash *verb*
• (*to clean*) = lavare
to wash the car = lavare la macchina
to wash one's face = lavarsi la faccia (**!** +
essere)
• (*to get clean*) = lavarsi (**!** + *essere*)
wash up
• (*British English*) (*to do the dishes*)
= lavare i piatti
• (*US English*) (*to clean oneself*) = lavarsi
(**!** + *essere*)

washbasin (*British English*), **wash-
hand basin** *noun*
a washbasin = un lavandino

washing *noun*
the washing = il bucato
to do the washing = fare il bucato

washing machine *noun*
a washing machine = una lavatrice

washing-up *noun* (*British English*)
to do the washing-up = lavare i piatti

wasp *noun*
a wasp = una vespa

waste
1 *verb*
= sprecare
to waste energy = sprecare energia
to waste time = perdere tempo
2 *noun*
• it's a waste of money = è uno spreco di
soldi
a waste of time = una perdita di tempo
it's a waste of time going there = andarci
è una perdita di tempo
• waste = i rifiuti (*plural*)

watch
1 *verb*
• (*to look at, to observe*) = guardare
to watch television = guardare la
televisione
• (*to pay attention to*)

watch what you're doing = fai attenzione
a ciò che fai
watch you don't fall = fai attenzione a
non cadere
2 *noun*
a watch = un orologio
watch out = fare attenzione

water
1 *noun*
water = l'acqua
drinking water = l'acqua potabile
2 *verb*
= annaffiare

waterfall *noun*
a waterfall = una cascata

water-skiing *noun* ▶ **178**|
water-skiing = lo sci nautico

wave
1 *verb*
• (*to signal with one's hand*) = salutare con
la mano
• to wave flags = sventolare le bandierine
2 *noun*
a wave = un'onda

way
1 *noun*
• (*a means, a method*)
a way = un modo
it's a good way to make friends = è un
buon modo per farsi degli amici
he does it the wrong way = lo fa nel
modo sbagliato
that's not the way to do it = non si fa così
I like the way she dresses = mi piace il
modo in cui si veste
I prefer to do it my way = preferisco farlo
a modo mio
• (*a route, a road*)
a way = una strada
I can't remember the way = non mi
ricordo la strada
we can buy something to eat along the
way = possiamo comprare qualcosa da
mangiare per strada
on the way back = sulla via del ritorno
I met them on the way back from town
= li ho incontrati mentre tornavo dalla
città
on the way to Rimini = andando a Rimini
where's the way out? = dov'è l'uscita?
to make one's way to the stairs
= dirigersi verso le scale (**!** + *essere*)
to lose one's way = smarrirsi (**!** +
essere)
• (*a direction*)
which way are you going? = da che parte
vai?
they went that way = sono andati da
quella parte
come this way = vieni da questa parte
• (*someone's route*)
to be in someone's way = essere
d'intralcio a qualcuno   ⋯➤

W

to be in the way = bloccare il passaggio
get out of the way! = levatevi dai piedi!
- (*when talking about distances*)
it's a long way from here = è lontano da
    qui
- (*what one wants*)
she always wants her own way = vuole
    sempre fare a modo suo
2 by the way = a proposito
what's his name, by the way? = a
    proposito, come si chiama?

we *pronoun*
we = noi
we're coming next week = arriviamo la
    settimana prossima
we do all the work here = qui facciamo
    tutto noi
they work in London but we don't = loro
    lavorano a Londra ma noi no
here we are! = eccoci!

weak *adjective*
- (*having very little power*) = debole
- (*not good or able*) = scarso/scarsa
to be weak at languages = essere scarso
    in lingue
- (*describing tea or coffee*)
    = leggero/leggera

wealthy *adjective*
    = ricco/ricca

wear *verb*
- (*to be dressed in*) = indossare
to be wearing jeans = indossare i jeans
to wear black = vestire di nero
- (*to put on*) = mettersi (**!** + *essere*)
what will you wear? = cosa ti metti?
I've got nothing to wear = non ho niente
    da mettermi
wear out
to wear out = logorarsi (**!** + *essere*)
to wear one's shoes out = consumare le
    scarpe
to wear someone out = stancare qualcuno

weather *noun*
the weather = il tempo
what's the weather like? = che tempo fa?
the weather is [bad | hot] = fa [brutto |
    caldo]
in [cold | warm | wet] **weather** = quando [fa
    freddo | fa caldo | piove]

weather forecast *noun*
the weather forecast = le previsioni del
    tempo
> **!** *Note that* **previsioni** *is plural.*

Web *noun*
the Web = il Web

website *noun*
a website = un sito web

wedding *noun*
a wedding = un matrimonio

Wednesday *noun* ▶ **155**
Wednesday = mercoledì (*masculine*)

week *noun* ▶ **267**
a week = una settimana
in two weeks' time = tra quindici giorni

weekend *noun* ▶ **267**
a weekend = un fine settimana

weigh *verb* ▶ **202**
    = pesare
what do you weigh? = quanto pesi?
to weigh oneself = pesarsi (**!** + *essere*)

weight *noun* ▶ **202**
weight = il peso
to lose weight = dimagrire (**!** + *essere*)

weird *adjective*
    = strano/strana

welcome
1 *verb*
to welcome someone = accogliere
    qualcuno
2 *adjective*
- (*when receiving people*)
welcome to the United States!
    = benvenuti negli Stati Uniti!
- (*when acknowledging thanks*)
'thanks'—'you're welcome'
    = 'grazie'—'prego'

well
1 *adverb*
- well = bene
the interview went well = il colloquio è
    andato bene
the work is well paid = il lavoro è ben
    pagato
- (*other uses*)
we may as well go home = tanto vale
    andare a casa
you may well be right = magari hai
    ragione
2 *adjective*
I feel well = mi sento bene
I'm very well = sto bene
to get well = ristabilirsi (**!** + *essere*)
3 as well = anche
I'm going as well = ci vado anch'io
4 as well as = oltre a

well-known *adjective*
    = noto/nota

Welsh ▶ **199**
1 *adjective*
    = gallese
2 *noun*
- (*the people*)
the Welsh = i gallesi
- (*the language*)
Welsh = il gallese

west
1 *noun*
the west = l'ovest (*masculine*)
in the west of France = nella Francia
    occidentale
2 *adverb*
to go west = andare verso ovest   ⋯▶

to live west of Milan = abitare a ovest di
Milano
3 *adjective*
= ovest (**!** *never changes*)
to work in west London = lavorare nella
zona ovest di Londra
West Indies *noun* ▶ **151** |
the West Indies = le Indie Occidentali
wet
1 *adjective*
• (*damp*) = bagnato/bagnata
your hair is wet = hai i capelli bagnati
to get wet = bagnarsi (**!** + *essere*)
she got her feet wet = si è bagnata i piedi
• (*when talking about weather*)
= piovoso/piovosa
in wet weather = con la pioggia
on a wet day = quando piove
2 *verb*
= bagnare
what
1 *pronoun*
• (*used in questions*) = che
= (che) cosa
what's happening? = che succede?
what's that box? = cos'è quella scatola?
what's this button for? = a cosa serve
questo pulsante?
what's her phone number? = qual è il suo
numero di telefono?
what's the Italian for 'boring'? = come si
dice 'boring' in italiano?
what does he look like? = com'è?
• (*used as a relative pronoun*)
do what you want = fai quello che vuoi
2 *determiner*
do you know what train to take? = sai
quale treno bisogna prendere?
what a great idea! = che idea geniale!
3 *exclamation*
= cosa?
4 what if = e se
what if I don't get there on time? = e se
non arrivo in tempo?
whatever *pronoun*
take whatever you want = prendi quello
che vuoi
wheat *noun*
wheat = il grano
wheel *noun*
a wheel = una ruota
wheelchair *noun*
a wheelchair = una sedia a rotelle
when
1 *adverb*
= quando
when did she leave? = quando è partita?
when is your birthday? = quand'è il tuo
compleanno?
I don't know when the film starts = non
so a che ora comincia il film
! *See the usage note on* **The clock**
▶ **267** | *for further information on time
expressions.*

2 *conjunction*
= quando
I was asleep when the phone rang
= stavo dormendo quando ha squillato
il telefono
when I'm 18 I'll have my own car
= quando compirò 18 anni avrò la
macchina

! *Note that, when talking about future
time, the future tense is used after*
quando.

3 *pronoun*
(*used as a relative pronoun*) = in cui
in the days when there was no TV
= all'epoca in cui non c'era la TV
where
1 *adverb*
= dove
where are you going? = dove vai?
where do they work? = dove lavorano?
do you know where he is? = sai dov'è?
the village where we live = il paese in cui
abitiamo
2 *conjunction*
that's where she fell = è caduta lì
whether *conjunction*
= se
I don't know whether or not to accept
= non so se accettare
which
1 *determiner*
which bus leaves first? = quale autobus
parte per primo?
which one shall I buy? = quale compro?
which shoes do you like? = quali scarpe
ti piacciono?
2 *pronoun*
• (*used in questions*) = quale
which is the best one? = qual è il
migliore?
• (*used in relative clauses*) = che
the letter which I received = la lettera che
ho ricevuto
(*after prepositions*) = cui
the house which I told you about = la
casa di cui ti ho parlato
while *conjunction*
= mentre
**I had a party while my parents were in
Spain** = ho fatto una festa mentre i
miei erano in Spagna
she fell asleep while watching TV = si è
addormentata guardando la TV
whisper *verb*
= bisbigliare
whistle
1 *verb*
= fischiare
2 *noun*
a whistle = un fischietto
white *adjective* ▶ **147** |
= bianco/bianca

W

who *pronoun*
- (*used in questions*) = chi
  who told you? = chi te l'ha detto?
  who did you invite? = chi hai invitato?
  who did he buy the book for? = per chi l'ha comprato, il libro?
- (*used as a relative pronoun*)
  my friend who lives in Rome = il mio amico che abita a Roma
  those who can't come by car = quelli che non possono venire in macchina
  a friend who I see at work = un amico che vedo al lavoro

whole
1 *noun*
  the whole of London = tutta Londra
  the whole of August = tutto agosto
2 *adjective*
  a whole day = un giorno intero
  three whole weeks = tre settimane intere
  I don't want to spend my whole life here = non voglio passare tutta la vita qui

whom *pronoun*
- (*used in questions*) = chi
  whom did you meet? = chi hai incontrato?
- (*used as a relative pronoun*) = che
  the person whom I contacted = la persona che ho contattato
  (*used after prepositions*) = cui
  the person to whom I spoke = la persona con cui ho parlato

whose
1 *pronoun*
- (*used in questions*) = di chi
  whose is the dog? = di chi è il cane?
- (*used as a relative pronoun*) = il/la cui
  the woman whose son was arrested = la madre del ragazzo che hanno arrestato
2 *determiner*
  whose car is that? = di chi è quella macchina?

why
1 *adverb*
- (*used in questions*) = perché
  why did you do that? = perché l'hai fatto?
  why aren't they coming? = perché non vengono?
  why not? = perché no?
- (*when making suggestions*)
  why don't we eat out tonight? = perché non andiamo fuori a cena stasera?
2 *conjunction*
  = perché
  that's why I can't stand him = ecco perché non lo sopporto

wide *adjective* ▶ **202**
- (*in size*) = largo/larga
  a wide road = una strada larga
  the room is ten metres wide = la stanza misura dieci metri di larghezza
- (*in range*)
  a wide range of games = una vasta gamma di giochi

width *noun* ▶ **202**
  width = la larghezza

wife *noun*
  a wife = una moglie

wild *adjective*
- (*describing animals, birds*) = selvatico/selvatica
- (*noisy, out of control*) = sfrenato/sfrenata
  to go wild = scatenarsi (**!** + *essere*)

wildlife *noun*
  wildlife = la fauna

will *verb*

> **!** Note that, when referring to the future, Italian generally uses the future tense of the verb to translate **will** + *verb*.

- (*when talking about the future*)
  it will be sunny tomorrow = domani farà bello
  what will we do? = cosa faremo?
- (*when talking about intentions*)
  I'll wait for you at the airport = ti aspetto all'aeroporto
  we won't stay too long = non restiamo tanto
- (*in invitations and requests*)
  will you have some coffee? = vuoi del caffè?
  will you ask him for me? = glielo chiedi tu da parte mia?
- (*when making assumptions*)
  the film will be finished by now = il film sarà finito ormai
- (*in short questions and answers*)
  you'll come again, won't you? = ritornerai, no?
  that will be cheaper, won't it? = sarà meno caro, vero?
  'he won't be ready'—'yes he will' = 'non sarà pronto'—'e invece sì'

win *verb*
  = vincere

wind *noun*
  a wind = un vento

window *noun*
  a window (*in a house*) = una finestra
  (*in a shop*) = una vetrina
  (*in a car, a bus*) = un finestrino

windsurfing *noun* ▶ **178**
  windsurfing = il windsurf

windy *adjective*
  it's windy = c'è vento

wine *noun*
  wine = il vino

wing *noun*
  a wing = un'ala
  a bird's wings = le ali di un uccello

winter *noun*
  winter = l'inverno
  in winter = d'inverno

Work and jobs

what do you do?   = che lavoro fai?

- In Italian the indefinite article **un/una** is never used when specifying what job someone does:

  *I'm **a** teacher*   = sono insegnante
  *he's **a** taxi-driver*   = fa il tassista
  *I want to be **a** lawyer*   = voglio fare l'avvocato

- However, it may be used when describing what kind of teacher/taxi-driver/lawyer a person is:

  *she's **a** very good teacher* = è **un**'insegnante molto brava

---

wipe *verb*
= pulire
wipe your feet! = pulisciti i piedi!

wise *adjective*
= saggio/saggia

wish
1 *noun*
- **a wish** = un desiderio
  to make a wish = esprimere un desiderio
- (*in greetings*)
  best wishes = tanti auguri
  (*in a letter*) = cordiali saluti
2 *verb*
- (*expressing what one would like*)
  I wish I could help you = vorrei poterti
  aiutare
  she wished she hadn't lied = si è pentita
  di aver detto le bugie
- (*in greetings*) = augurare
  to wish someone a happy birthday
  = augurare buon compleanno a
  qualcuno

with *preposition*
- **with** = con
  with the = col/colla (**!** + *singular*)
  = coi/colle (+ *plural*)

  > **!** *Before masculine nouns beginning
  > with z, ps, gn, or s + another
  > consonant, **collo** is used in the singular
  > and **cogli** in the plural. Before
  > masculine and feminine singular nouns
  > beginning with a vowel, **coll'** is used.
  > Note that these forms are optional: **con**
  > may also be used with **il/la**, etc.*

  to go away with friends = andare via con
  gli amici
  I'm living with my parents = abito con i
  miei genitori
  we're pleased with the house = siamo
  contenti della casa
- (*when describing*)
  a girl with black hair = una ragazza coi
  capelli neri
  his clothes were covered with mud = i
  suoi abiti erano coperti di fango
  **he was walking along with his hands in
  his pockets** = camminva con le mani in
  tasca

without *preposition*
= senza
we got in without paying = siamo entrati
senza pagare

wolf *noun*
a wolf = un lupo

woman *noun*
a woman = una donna

wonder *verb*
- (*to ask oneself*) = domandarsi (**!** +
  essere)
  I wonder [who | what | where] they are = mi
  domando [chi | cosa | dove] siano

  > **!** *Note that the subjunctive is used after
  > **domandarsi**.*

- (*in polite requests*)
  I wonder if you could help me? = mi può
  aiutare?

wonderful *adjective*
= meraviglioso/meravigliosa

wood *noun*
- (*timber*)
  wood = il legno
  made of wood = di legno
- (*a small forest*)
  a wood = un bosco

wool *noun*
wool = la lana

word *noun*
a word = una parola
what's the Italian word for 'break'?
= come si dice 'break' in italiano?
in other words = in altri termini

work
1 *verb*
- (*to have or do a job*) = lavorare
  to work as a doctor = fare il medico
- (*to operate properly, to be effective*)
  = funzionare
  the TV isn't working = la TV non funziona
  the plan didn't work = il piano non ha
  funzionato
- (*to use, to operate*) = usare
  do you know how to work the computer?
  = sai usare il computer?
2 *noun*
- **work** = il lavoro
  I've got work to do = ho del lavoro da
  fare ····➤

to be out of work = essere
disoccupato/disoccupata
it's hard work learning Italian = è faticoso
imparare l'italiano
- (*for building, for repairs*)
work(s) = i lavori
there are road works at the moment = al
momento ci sono dei lavori stradali
- (*by an artist, a musician*)
a work = un'opera

work out
- (*to find*) = trovare
to work out the answer = trovare la
soluzione
- (*to understand*) = capire
- (*with figures*) = calcolare
- (*to go well*) = riuscire (**!** + *essere*)
- (*to take exercise*) = fare ginnastica

work up
to get worked up = arrabbiarsi (**!** +
essere)

worker *noun*
a worker (*in a factory*) = un
operaio/un'operaia
(*in an office, a bank*) = un
impiegato/un'impiegata

world *noun*
the world = il mondo
all over the world = in tutto il mondo
the biggest city in the world = la città più
grande del mondo

World Cup *noun*
the World Cup = i mondiali di calcio

worm *noun*
a worm = un verme

worried *adjective*
= preoccupato/preoccupata
I'm worried about him = sono preoccupato
per lui

worry *verb*
- (*to be worried*) = preoccuparsi (**!** +
essere)
there's nothing to worry about = non c'è
da preoccuparsi
- (*to make someone worried*) = preoccupare
it's worrying me = mi preoccupa

worse *adjective*
= peggiore
this book is worse than the others
= questo libro è peggiore degli altri
she's worse than me at tennis = è peggio
di me a tennis
the weather is going to get worse = il
tempo peggiorerà
he's getting worse = sta peggiorando

worst
1 *adjective*
= peggiore
the worst hotel in town = il peggior
albergo della città

the worst film I've ever seen = il peggior
film che abbia mai visto

! *Note that the subjunctive is used after
the superlative* **il/la peggiore che**.

the worst thing to do is to tell him = la
cosa peggiore da fare è dirglielo
2 *noun*
the worst = il peggio

worth *adjective*
to be worth = valere (**!** + *essere*)
it's worth £100 = vale 100 sterline
it's not worth the trouble = non vale la
pena

would *verb*
- (*when talking about hypothetical
situations*)
if I had more money, I would buy a car
= se avessi più soldi comprerei una
macchina
- (*in reported speech*)
we were sure she would read it
= eravamo sicuri che lo avrebbe letto
- (*when making an assumption*)
she'd be 30, I think = avrà circa
trent'anni, credo
it would have been about midday = sarà
stato verso mezzogiorno
- (*to be prepared to*)
he wouldn't listen to me = non mi ha
voluto ascoltare
- (*when talking about one's wishes*)
I'd like a beer = vorrei una birra
we would like to stay another night
= vorremmo restare un'altra notte
- (*when asking or offering*)
would you turn the TV off? = spegni la
TV, per favore
would you excuse me? = scusate
would you like something to eat? = vuoi
qualcosa da mangiare?

wrap *verb*
= incartare
to wrap (up) a present = incartare un
regalo

wreck
1 *verb*
(*if it's a person*) = rovinare
(*if it's a fire, a bomb*) = distruggere
2 *noun*
a wreck = un rottame

wrist *noun* ▶ **137**❘
the wrist = il polso

write *verb*
= scrivere
to write to someone, to write someone
(*US English*) = scrivere a qualcuno
to write a cheque = fare un assegno
write back = rispondere
write down = annotare

writing *noun*
writing = la scrittura
your writing is good = scrivi bene

wrong *adjective*
• (*not as it should be*)
there's something wrong = c'è qualcosa
  che non va
what's wrong? = cosa c'è che non va?
what's wrong with you? = cos'hai?
• (*not correct*) = sbagliato/sbagliata
I took the wrong key = ho preso la chiave
  sbagliata
to go the wrong way = sbagliare strada
to say the wrong thing = fare una gaffe
to dial the wrong number = sbagliare
  numero
to be wrong (*if it's a person*) = sbagliarsi
  (**!** + *essere*)
• (*not honest, not good*)
it's wrong to steal = non si deve rubare
she hasn't done anything wrong = non
  ha fatto niente di male
there's nothing wrong with trying = non
  c'è niente di male a provare

Xx

X-ray
1 *noun*
an X-ray = una radiografia
to have an X-ray = farsi una radiografia
  (**!** + *essere*)
2 *verb*
= radiografare

Yy

yacht *noun*
a yacht = uno yacht

yard *noun*
• (*when measuring*) ▶ **202**
a yard = una iarda
  ! Note that a **yard** = 0.9144 m.
• (*of a building*)
a yard = un cortile
• (*US English*) (*a garden*)
a yard = un giardino

yawn *verb*
= sbadigliare

year *noun*
• (*when talking about time*) ▶ **267**
a year = un anno
last year = l'anno scorso

two years ago = due anni fa
to work all year round = lavorare tutto
  l'anno
he's lived there for years = ci abita da
  anni
that'll take years! = ci vorranno degli
  anni!
• (*when talking about age*) ▶ **125**
a year = un anno
to be 15 years old, to be 15 years of age
  = avere 15 anni
a four-year old = un bambino/una
  bambina di quattro anni

yell
1 *verb*
= urlare
to yell at someone = urlare a qualcuno
2 *noun*
a yell = un urlo

yellow *adjective* ▶ **147**
= giallo/gialla
to go yellow = ingiallire (**!** + *essere*)

yes *adverb*
yes = sì
'are you coming with us?'—'yes I am'
  = 'vieni con noi?'—'sì'
'they don't know each other'—'yes they
  do' = 'non si conoscono'—'ma sì'
'didn't he tell you?'—'yes he did' = 'non
  te l'ha detto?'—'sì'

yesterday *adverb*
= ieri

yet
1 *adverb*
= ancora
not yet = non ancora
it's not ready yet = non è ancora pronto
have they arrived yet? = sono arrivati?
has she met them yet? = li ha già
  incontrati?
2 *conjunction*
= eppure

yogurt *noun*
yogurt = lo yogurt

you *pronoun*
▶ See the boxed note on **you** for detailed
information and examples.

young
1 *adjective*
= giovane
a young lady = una signorina
young people = i giovani
she is a year younger than me = ha un
  anno meno di me
a younger sister = una sorella minore
to look young = avere un'aria giovane
2 *noun*
the young (*of an animal*) = i piccoli

your *determiner*
▶ See the boxed note on **your** for detailed
information and examples. See also the
usage note on **The human body** ▶ **137**

you

- In English **you** is used to address everybody, whereas Italian has various forms. The usual form for addressing someone you do not know particularly well is **lei**, which is followed by a third person singular verb. Unlike in English, the pronoun can be omitted when it is the subject of the sentence, and the verb ending does the job of showing the subject:

there's a letter for you	= c'è una lettera per **lei**
are you the doctor's wife?	= **lei** è la moglie del dottore?
can you help me?	= mi può aiutare?

  Lei has the forms **la** for the direct object and **le** for the indirect object. **Your** is expressed by **il suo/la sua**, etc:

do I know you?	= **la** conosco?
I'll explain to you how it works	= **le** spiego come funziona
you forgot your umbrella	= ha dimenticato **il suo** ombrello

- The more informal pronoun **tu** is used between friends and family members. It is always used to address children, and young people generally address each other as **tu**. **Tu** is used as the subject of the sentence, but can often be omitted:

do you speak English, Daniela?	= Daniela, **tu** parli inglese?
did you get the keys?	= hai preso le chiavi?

  The direct and indirect object is **ti**, and **te** is used after prepositions. **Your** is expressed by **il tuo/la tua**, etc:

I heard you the first time	= **ti** ho sentito la prima volta
can I come with you?	= posso venire con **te**?
where's your ticket?	= dov'è **il tuo** biglietto?

- **Voi** is used as the plural of **lei** and **tu**. It is used when addressing two or more people. When it is the subject of the sentence it can be omitted.

have you had dinner?	= **voi** avete mangiato?
how are you all?	= come state tutti?
I bought something for you	= ho comprato qualcosa per **voi**

  The direct and indirect object form is **vi**, and **your** is expressed by **il vostro/la vostra**, etc:

I'll wait for you here	= **vi** aspetto qui
I like your house	= mi piace **la vostra** casa

Used impersonally

When **you** means 'one' or 'people in general', Italian often uses a construction with **si** to say the same thing:

you pay at the checkout	= si paga alla cassa
you never know	= non si sa mai

yours *pronoun*
▶ *See also the boxed notes on* **you** *for more information.*
yours (*informal*) = il tuo/la tua (*singular*)
    = i tuoi/le tue (*plural*)
    (*polite*) = il suo/la sua (*singular*)
    = i suoi/le sue (*plural*)
    (*to several people*) = il vostro/la vostra (*singular*)
    = i vostri/le vostre (*plural*)

> **!** *Note that* il/la, *etc is used when comparing things belonging to different people, but not when saying who something belongs to.*

my garden is small but yours is big = il mio giardino è piccolo ma il tuo/suo/vostro è grande
my sister is taller than yours = mia sorella è più alta della tua/sua/vostra
the red car is yours = la macchina rossa è tua/sua/vostra
a friend of yours = un tuo/suo/vostro amico

yourself *pronoun*
• (*when used as a reflexive pronoun*)
    (*informal*) = ti
    (*polite*) = si

> **!** *Note that* ti *and* si *combine with the infinitive and the gerund.* Ti *also combines with the imperative.* Ti *and* si *beome* te *and* se *before* lo/la, li/le, *and* ne.

you'll enjoy yourself = ti divertirai/si divertirà
did you hurt yourself? = ti sei fatto male/si è fatto male?
enjoy yourself! = divertiti!/si diverta!
• (*when used for emphasis*)
    you said it yourself = l'hai detto tu stesso/l'ha detto lei stesso
    did you do it all by yourself? = l'hai fatto tutto da te/l'ha fatto tutto da sé?

yourselves *pronoun*
• (*when used as a reflexive pronoun*) = vi

> **!** *Note that* vi *combines with the infinitive, the gerund, and the imperative.* Vi *beomes* ve *before* lo/la, li/le, *and* ne.

you'll enjoy yourselves = vi divertirete
did you hurt yourselves? = vi siete fatti male?
• (*when used for emphasis*)
    you said it yourselves = l'avete detto voi stessi
    did you do it all by yourselves? = l'avete fatto tutto da voi?

youth *noun*
• (*a young man*)
    a youth = un ragazzo
• (*young people*)
    the youth of today = i ragazzi d'oggi

youth club *noun*
    a youth club = un circolo giovanile

youth hostel *noun*
    a youth hostel = un ostello della gioventù

Zz

---

zebra *noun*
    a zebra = una zebra

zebra crossing *noun* (*British English*)
    a zebra crossing = le strisce pedonali (*plural*)

zero *number*
    zero = zero

zip (*British English*), **zipper** (*US English*) *noun*
    a zip = uno zip
    to undo a zip = aprire uno zip

zip code *noun* (*US English*)
    a zip code = un codice postale

zodiac *noun*
    the zodiac = lo zodiaco

zone *noun*
    a zone = una zona

zoo *noun*
    a zoo = uno zoo

Z

Italian verb tables

Present
(io) guido = *I drive, I am driving*

Perfect
(io) ho guidato = *I have driven, I drove*

Future
(io) guiderò = *I will drive*

Imperfect
(io) guidavo =
I was driving, I used to drive

Past historic
(io) guidai = *I drove*

Present subjunctive
che (io) guidi =
that I (should) drive, that I might drive

Imperative
guida/guidi/guidate! = *drive!*

1 parlare

present	past historic
parlo	parlai
parli	parlasti
parla	parlò
parliamo	parlammo
parlate	parlaste
parlano	parlarono

perfect	present subjunctive
ho parlato	parli
hai parlato	parli
ha parlato	parli
abbiamo parlato	parliamo
avete parlato	parliate
hanno parlato	parlino

future	imperative
parlerò	parla!
parlerai	parli!
parlerà	parlate!
parleremo	
parlerete	
parleranno	

imperfect
parlavo
parlavi
parlava
parlavamo
parlavate
parlavano

2 cominciare

present	past historic
comincio	cominciai
cominci	cominciasti
comincia	cominciò
cominciamo	cominciammo
cominciate	cominciaste
cominciano	cominciarono

perfect	present subjunctive
ho cominciato	cominci
hai cominciato	cominci
ha cominciato	cominci
abbiamo cominciato	cominciamo
avete cominciato	cominciate
hanno cominciato	comincino

future	imperative
comincerò	comincia!
comincerai	cominci!
comincerà	cominciate!
cominceremo	
comincerete	
cominceranno	

imperfect
cominciavo
cominciavi
cominciava
cominciavamo
cominciavate
cominciavano

3 mangiare

present	past historic
mangio	mangiai
mangi	mangiasti
mangia	mangiò
mangiamo	mangiammo
mangiate	mangiaste
mangiano	mangiarono

perfect	present subjunctive
ho mangiato	mangi
hai mangiato	mangi
ha mangiato	mangi
abbiamo mangiato	mangiamo
avete mangiato	mangiate
hanno mangiato	mangino

future	imperative
mangerò	mangia!
mangerai	mangi!
mangerà	mangiate!
mangeremo	
mangerete	
mangeranno	

imperfect
mangiavo
mangiavi
mangiava
mangiavamo
mangiavate
mangiavano

5 legare

present	past historic
lego	legai
leghi	legasti
lega	legò
leghiamo	legammo
legate	legaste
legano	legarono

perfect	present subjunctive
ho legato	leghi
hai legato	leghi
ha legato	leghi
abbiamo legato	leghiamo
avete legato	leghiate
hanno legato	leghino

future	imperative
legherò	lega!
legherai	leghi!
legherà	legate!
legheremo	
legherete	
legheranno	

imperfect
legavo
legavi
legava
legavamo
legavate
legavano

4 giocare

present	past historic
gioco	giocai
giochi	giocasti
gioca	giocò
giochiamo	giocammo
giocate	giocaste
giocano	giocarono

perfect	present subjunctive
ho giocato	giochi
hai giocato	giochi
ha giocato	giochi
abbiamo giocato	giochiamo
avete giocato	giochiate
hanno giocato	giochino

future	imperative
giocherò	gioca!
giocherai	giochi!
giocherà	giocate!
giocheremo	
giocherete	
giocheranno	

imperfect
giocavo
giocavi
giocava
giocavamo
giocavate
giocavano

6 studiare

present	past historic
studio	studiai
studi	studiasti
studia	studiò
studiamo	studiammo
studiate	studiaste
studiano	studiarono

perfect	present subjunctive
ho studiato	studi
hai studiato	studi
ha studiato	studi
abbiamo studiato	studiamo
avete studiato	studiate
hanno studiato	studino

future	imperative
studierò	studia!
studierai	studi!
studierà	studiate!
studieremo	
studierete	
studieranno	

imperfect
studiavo
studiavi
studiava
studiavamo
studiavate
studiavano

7 inviare

present	past historic
invio	inviai
invii	inviasti
invia	inviò
inviamo	inviammo
inviate	inviaste
inviano	inviarono

perfect	present subjunctive
ho inviato	invii
hai inviato	invii
ha inviato	invii
abbiamo inviato	inviamo
avete inviato	inviate
hanno inviato	inviino

future	imperative
invierò	invia!
invierai	invii!
invierà	inviate!
invieremo	
invierete	
invieranno	

imperfect	
inviavo	
inviavi	
inviava	
inviavamo	
inviavate	
inviavano	

9 finire

present	past historic
finisco	finii
finisci	finisti
finisce	finì
finiamo	finimmo
finite	finiste
finiscono	finirono

perfect	present subjunctive
ho finito	finisca
hai finito	finisca
ha finito	finisca
abbiamo finito	finiamo
avete finito	finiate
hanno finito	finiscano

future	imperative
finirò	finisci!
finirai	finisca!
finirà	finite!
finiremo	
finirete	
finiranno	

imperfect	
finivo	
finivi	
finiva	
finivamo	
finivate	
finivano	

8 vendere

present	past historic
vendo	vendei or vendetti
vendi	vendesti
vende	vendé or vendette
vendiamo	vendemmo
vendete	vendeste
vendono	venderono or vendettero

perfect	present subjunctive
ho venduto	venda
hai venduto	venda
ha venduto	venda
abbiamo venduto	vendiamo
avete venduto	vendiate
hanno venduto	vendano

future	imperative
venderò	vendi!
venderai	venda!
venderà	vendete!
venderemo	
venderete	
venderanno	

imperfect	
vendevo	
vendevi	
vendeva	
vendevamo	
vendevate	
vendevano	

10 sentire

present	past historic
sento	sentii
senti	sentisti
sente	sentì
sentiamo	sentimmo
sentite	sentiste
sentono	sentirono

perfect	present subjunctive
ho sentito	senta
hai sentito	senta
ha sentito	senta
abbiamo sentito	sentiamo
avete sentito	sentiate
hanno sentito	sentano

future	imperative
sentirò	senti!
sentirai	senta!
sentirà	sentite!
sentiremo	
sentirete	
sentiranno	

imperfect	
sentivo	
sentivi	
sentiva	
sentivamo	
sentivate	
sentivano	

11 essere

present	past historic
sono	fui
sei	fosti
è	fu
siamo	fummo
siete	foste
sono	furono

perfect	present subjunctive
sono stato/stata	sia
sei stato/stata	sia
è stato/stata	sia
siamo stati/state	siamo
siete stati/state	siate
sono stati/state	siano

future	imperative
sarò	sii!
sarai	sia!
sarà	siate!
saremo	
sarete	
saranno	

imperfect
ero
eri
era
eravamo
eravate
erano

13 andare

present	past historic
vado	andai
vai	andasti
va	andò
andiamo	andammo
andate	andaste
vanno	andarono

perfect	present subjunctive
sono andato/andata	vada
sei andato/andata	vada
è andato/andata	vada
siamo andati/andate	andiamo
siete andati/andate	andiate
sono andati/andate	vadano

future	imperative
andrò	va'! or vai!
andrai	vada!
andrà	andate!
andremo	
andrete	
andranno	

imperfect
andavo
andavi
andava
andavamo
andavate
andavano

12 avere

present	past historic
ho	ebbi
hai	avesti
ha	ebbe
abbiamo	avemmo
avete	aveste
hanno	ebbero

perfect	present subjunctive
ho avuto	abbia
hai avuto	abbia
ha avuto	abbia
abbiamo avuto	abbiamo
avete avuto	abbiate
hanno avuto	abbiano

future	imperative
avrò	abbi!
avrai	abbia!
avrà	abbiate!
avremo	
avrete	
avranno	

imperfect
avevo
avevi
aveva
avevamo
avevate
avevano

14 apparire

present	past historic
appaio	apparvi
appari	apparisti
appare	apparve
appariamo	apparimmo
apparite	appariste
appaiono	apparvero

perfect	present subjunctive
sono apparso/apparsa	appaia
sei apparso/apparsa	appaia
è apparso/apparsa	appaia
siamo apparsi/apparse	appariamo
siete apparsi/apparse	appariate
sono apparsi/apparse	appaiano

future	imperative
apparirò	appari!
apparirai	appaia!
apparirà	apparite!
appariremo	
apparirete	
appariranno	

imperfect
apparivo
apparivi
appariva
apparivamo
apparivate
apparivano

15 aprire

present	past historic
apro	aprii
apri	apristi
apre	aprì
apriamo	aprimmo
aprite	apriste
aprono	aprirono

perfect	present subjunctive
ho aperto	apra
hai aperto	apra
ha aperto	apra
abbiamo aperto	apriamo
avete aperto	apriate
hanno aperto	aprano

future	imperative
aprirò	apri!
aprirai	apra!
aprirà	aprite!
apriremo	
aprirete	
apriranno	

imperfect
aprivo
aprivi
apriva
aprivamo
aprivate
aprivano

16 assistere

present	past historic
assisto	assistei or assistetti
assisti	assistesti
assiste	assisté or assistette
assistiamo	assistemmo
assistete	assisteste
assistono	assisterono or assistettero

perfect	present subjunctive
ho assistito	assista
hai assistito	assista
ha assistito	assista
abbiamo assistito	assistiamo
avete assistito	assistiate
hanno assistito	assistano

future	imperative
assisterò	assisti!
assisterai	assista!
assisterà	assistete!
assisteremo	
assisterete	
assisteranno	

imperfect
assistevo
assistevi
assisteva
assistevamo
assistevate
assistevano

17 assumere

present	past historic
assumo	assunsi
assumi	assumesti
assume	assunse
assumiamo	assumemmo
assumete	assumeste
assumono	assunsero

perfect	present subjunctive
ho assunto	assuma
hai assunto	assuma
ha assunto	assuma
abbiamo assunto	assumiamo
avete assunto	assumiate
hanno assunto	assumano

future	imperative
assumerò	assumi!
assumerai	assuma!
assumerà	assumete!
assumeremo	
assumerete	
assumeranno	

imperfect
assumevo
assumevi
assumeva
assumevamo
assumevate
assumevano

18 bere

present	past historic
bevo	bevvi or bevetti
bevi	bevesti
beve	bevve or bevette
beviamo	bevemmo
bevete	beveste
bevono	bevvero or bevettero

perfect	present subjunctive
ho bevuto	beva
hai bevuto	beva
ha bevuto	beva
abbiamo bevuto	beviamo
avete bevuto	beviate
hanno bevuto	bevano

future	imperative
berrò	bevi!
berrai	beva!
berrà	bevete!
berremo	
berrete	
berranno	

imperfect
bevevo
bevevi
beveva
bevevamo
bevevate
bevevano

19 cadere

present	past historic
cado	caddi
cadi	cadesti
cade	cadde
cadiamo	cademmo
cadete	cadeste
cadono	caddero

perfect	present subjunctive
sono caduto/caduta	cada
sei caduto/caduta	cada
è caduto/caduta	cada
siamo caduti/cadute	cadiamo
siete caduti/cadute	cadiate
sono caduti/cadute	cadano

future	imperative
cadrò	cadi!
cadrai	cada!
cadrà	cadete!
cadremo	
cadrete	
cadranno	

imperfect
cadevo
cadevi
cadeva
cadevamo
cadevate
cadevano

20 chiedere

present	past historic
chiedo	chiesi
chiedi	chiedesti
chiede	chiese
chiediamo	chiedemmo
chiedete	chiedeste
chiedono	chiesero

perfect	present subjunctive
ho chiesto	chieda
hai chiesto	chieda
ha chiesto	chieda
abbiamo chiesto	chiediamo
avete chiesto	chiediate
hanno chiesto	chiedano

future	imperative
chiederò	chiedi!
chiederai	chieda!
chiederà	chiedete!
chiederemo	
chiederete	
chiederanno	

imperfect
chiedevo
chiedevi
chiedeva
chiedevamo
chiedevate
chiedevano

21 chiudere

present	past historic
chiudo	chiusi
chiudi	chiudesti
chiude	chiuse
chiudiamo	chiudemmo
chiudete	chiudeste
chiudono	chiusero

perfect	present subjunctive
ho chiuso	chiuda
hai chiuso	chiuda
ha chiuso	chiuda
abbiamo chiuso	chiudiamo
avete chiuso	chiudiate
hanno chiuso	chiudano

future	imperative
chiuderò	chiudi!
chiuderai	chiuda!
chiuderà	chiudete!
chiuderemo	
chiuderete	
chiuderanno	

imperfect
chiudevo
chiudevi
chiudeva
chiudevamo
chiudevate
chiudevano

22 cogliere

present	past historic
colgo	colsi
cogli	cogliesti
coglie	colse
cogliamo	cogliemmo
cogliete	coglieste
colgono	colsero

perfect	present subjunctive
ho colto	colga
hai colto	colga
ha colto	colga
abbiamo colto	cogliamo
avete colto	cogliate
hanno colto	colgano

future	imperative
coglierò	cogli!
coglierai	colga!
coglierà	cogliete!
coglieremo	
coglierete	
coglieranno	

imperfect
coglievo
coglievi
coglieva
coglievamo
coglievate
coglievano

23 concedere

present	past historic
concedo	concessi
concedi	concedesti
concede	concesse
concediamo	concedemmo
concedete	concedeste
concedono	concessero

perfect	present subjunctive
ho concesso	conceda
hai concesso	conceda
ha concesso	conceda
abbiamo concesso	concediamo
avete concesso	concediate
hanno concesso	concedano

future	imperative
concederò	concedi!
concederai	conceda!
concederà	concedete!
concederemo	
concederete	
concederanno	

imperfect	
concedevo	
concedevi	
concedeva	
concedevamo	
concedevate	
concedevano	

25 conoscere

present	past historic
conosco	conobbi
conosci	conoscesti
conosce	conobbe
conosciamo	conoscemmo
conoscete	conosceste
conoscono	conobbero

perfect	present subjunctive
ho conosciuto	conosca
hai conosciuto	conosca
ha conosciuto	conosca
abbiamo conosciuto	conosciamo
avete conosciuto	conosciate
hanno conosciuto	conoscano

future	imperative
conoscerò	conosci!
conoscerai	conosca!
conoscerà	conoscete!
conosceremo	
conoscerete	
conosceranno	

imperfect	
conoscevo	
conoscevi	
conosceva	
conoscevamo	
conoscevate	
conoscevano	

24 confondere

present	past historic
confondo	confusi
confondi	confondesti
confonde	confuse
confondiamo	confondemmo
confondete	confondeste
confondono	confusero

perfect	present subjunctive
ho confuso	confonda
hai confuso	confonda
ha confuso	confonda
abbiamo confuso	confondiamo
avete confuso	confondiate
hanno confuso	confondano

future	imperative
confonderò	confondi!
confonderai	confonda!
confonderà	confondete!
confonderemo	
confonderete	
confonderanno	

imperfect	
confondevo	
confondevi	
confondeva	
confondevamo	
confondevate	
confondevano	

26 correre

present	past historic
corro	corsi
corri	corresti
corre	corse
corriamo	corremmo
correte	correste
corrono	corsero

perfect	present subjunctive
ho corso	corra
hai corso	corra
ha corso	corra
abbiamo corso	corriamo
avete corso	corriate
hanno corso	corrano

future	imperative
correrò	corri!
correrai	corra!
correrà	correte!
correremo	
correrete	
correranno	

imperfect	
correvo	
correvi	
correva	
correvamo	
correvate	
correvano	

27 crescere

present
cresco
cresci
cresce
cresciamo
crescete
crescono

past historic
crebbi
crescesti
crebbe
crescemmo
cresceste
crebbero

perfect
sono cresciuto/cresciuta
sei cresciuto/cresciuta
è cresciuto/cresciuta
siamo cresciuti/cresciute
siete cresciuti/cresciute
sono cresciuti/cresciute

present subjunctive
cresca
cresca
cresca
cresciamo
cresciate
crescano

future
crescerò
crescerai
crescerà
cresceremo
crescerete
cresceranno

imperative
cresci!
cresca!
crescete!

imperfect
crescevo
crescevi
cresceva
crescevamo
crescevate
crescevano

28 cuocere

present
cuocio
cuoci
cuoce
cuociamo
cuocete
cuociono

past historic
cossi
cuocesti
cosse
cuocemmo
cuoceste
cossero

perfect
ho cotto
hai cotto
ha cotto
abbiamo cotto
avete cotto
hanno cotto

present subjunctive
cuocia
cuocia
cuocia
cuociamo
cuociate
cuociano

future
cuocerò
cuocerai
cuocerà
cuoceremo
cuocerete
cuoceranno

imperative
cuoci!
cuocia!
cuocete!

imperfect
cuocevo
cuocevi
cuoceva
cuocevamo
cuocevate
cuocevano

29 dare

present
do
dai
dà
diamo
date
danno

past historic
diedi *or* detti
desti
diede *or* dette
demmo
deste
diedero *or* dettero

perfect
ho dato
hai dato
ha dato
abbiamo dato
avete dato
hanno dato

present subjunctive
dia
dia
dia
diamo
diate
diano

future
darò
darai
darà
daremo
darete
daranno

imperative
da'! *or* dai!
dia!
date!

imperfect
davo
davi
dava
davamo
davate
davano

30 decidere

present
decido
decidi
decide
decidiamo
decidete
decidono

past historic
decisi
decidesti
decise
decidemmo
decideste
decisero

perfect
ho deciso
hai deciso
ha deciso
abbiamo deciso
avete deciso
hanno deciso

present subjunctive
decida
decida
decida
decidiamo
decidiate
decidano

future
deciderò
deciderai
deciderà
decideremo
deciderete
decideranno

imperative
decidi!
decida!
decidete!

imperfect
decidevo
decidevi
decideva
decidevamo
decidevate
decidevano

31 dire

present	past historic
dico	dissi
dici	dicesti
dice	disse
diciamo	dicemmo
dite	diceste
dicono	dissero

perfect	present subjunctive
ho detto	dica
hai detto	dica
ha detto	dica
abbiamo detto	diciamo
avete detto	diciate
hanno detto	dicano

future	imperative
dirò	di'!
dirai	dica!
dirà	dite!
diremo	
direte	
diranno	

imperfect
dicevo
dicevi
diceva
dicevamo
dicevate
dicevano

33 discutere

present	past historic
discuto	discussi
discuti	discutesti
discute	discusse
discutiamo	discutemmo
discutete	discuteste
discutono	discussero

perfect	present subjunctive
ho discusso	discuta
hai discusso	discuta
ha discusso	discuta
abbiamo discusso	discutiamo
avete discusso	discutiate
hanno discusso	discutano

future	imperative
discuterò	discuti!
discuterai	discuta!
discuterà	discutete!
discuteremo	
discuterete	
discuteranno	

imperfect
discutevo
discutevi
discuteva
discutevamo
discutevate
discutevano

32 dirigere

present	past historic
dirigo	diressi
dirigi	dirigesti
dirige	diresse
dirigiamo	dirigemmo
dirigete	dirigeste
dirigono	diressero

perfect	present subjunctive
ho diretto	diriga
hai diretto	diriga
ha diretto	diriga
abbiamo diretto	dirigiamo
avete diretto	dirigiate
hanno diretto	dirigano

future	imperative
dirigerò	dirigi!
dirigerai	diriga!
dirigerà	dirigete!
dirigeremo	
dirigerete	
dirigeranno	

imperfect
dirigevo
dirigevi
dirigeva
dirigevamo
dirigevate
dirigevano

34 distinguere

present	past historic
distinguo	distinsi
distingui	distinguesti
distingue	distinse
distinguiamo	distinguemmo
distinguete	distingueste
distinguono	distinsero

perfect	present subjunctive
ho distinto	distingua
hai distinto	distingua
ha distinto	distingua
abbiamo distinto	distinguiamo
avete distinto	distinguiate
hanno distinto	distinguano

future	imperative
distinguerò	distingui!
distinguerai	distingua!
distinguerà	distinguete!
distingueremo	
distinguerete	
distingueranno	

imperfect
distinguevo
distinguevi
distingueva
distinguevamo
distinguevate
distinguevano

35 dovere

present	past historic
devo	dovetti
devi	dovesti
deve	dovette
dobbiamo	dovemmo
dovete	doveste
devono	dovettero

perfect	present subjunctive
ho dovuto	deva
hai dovuto	deva
ha dovuto	deva
abbiamo dovuto	dobbiamo
avete dovuto	dobbiate
hanno dovuto	devano

future
dovrò
dovrai
dovrà
dovremo
dovrete
dovranno

imperfect
dovevo
dovevi
doveva
dovevamo
dovevate
dovevano

36 esigere

present	past historic
esigo	esigei or esigetti
esigi	esigesti
esige	esigé or esigette
esigiamo	esigemmo
esigete	esigeste
esigono	esigero or esigettero

perfect	present subjunctive
ho esatto	esiga
hai esatto	esiga
ha esatto	esiga
abbiamo esatto	esigiamo
avete esatto	esigiate
hanno esatto	esigano

future	imperative
esigerò	esigi!
esigerai	esiga!
esigerà	esigete!
esigeremo	
esigerete	
esigeranno	

imperfect
esigevo
esigevi
esigeva
esigevamo
esigevate
esigevano

37 esprimere

present	past historic
esprimo	espressi
esprimi	esprimesti
esprime	espresse
esprimiamo	esprimemmo
esprimete	esprimeste
esprimono	espressero

perfect	present subjunctive
ho espresso	esprima
hai espresso	esprima
ha espresso	esprima
abbiamo espresso	esprimiamo
avete espresso	esprimiate
hanno espresso	esprimano

future	imperative
esprimerò	esprimi!
esprimerai	esprima!
esprimerà	esprimete!
esprimeremo	
esprimerete	
esprimeranno	

imperfect
esprimevo
esprimevi
esprimeva
esprimevamo
esprimevate
esprimevano

38 fare

present	past historic
faccio	feci
fai	facesti
fa	fece
facciamo	facemmo
fate	faceste
fanno	fecero

perfect	present subjunctive
ho fatto	faccia
hai fatto	faccia
ha fatto	faccia
abbiamo fatto	facciamo
avete fatto	facciate
hanno fatto	facciano

future	imperative
farò	fa'! or fai!
farai	faccia!
farà	fate!
faremo	
farete	
faranno	

imperfect
facevo
facevi
faceva
facevamo
facevate
facevano

39 leggere

present	past historic
leggo	lessi
leggi	leggesti
legge	lesse
leggiamo	leggemmo
leggete	leggeste
leggono	lessero

perfect	present subjunctive
ho letto	legga
hai letto	legga
ha letto	legga
abbiamo letto	leggiamo
avete letto	leggiate
hanno letto	leggano

future	imperative
leggerò	leggi!
leggerai	legga!
leggerà	leggete!
leggeremo	
leggerete	
leggeranno	

imperfect	
leggevo	
leggevi	
leggeva	
leggevamo	
leggevate	
leggevano	

40 mettere

present	past historic
metto	misi
metti	mettesti
mette	mise
mettiamo	mettemmo
mettete	metteste
mettono	misero

perfect	present subjunctive
ho messo	metta
hai messo	metta
ha messo	metta
abbiamo messo	mettiamo
avete messo	mettiate
hanno messo	mettano

future	imperative
metterò	metti!
metterai	metta!
metterà	mettete!
metteremo	
metterete	
metteranno	

imperfect	
mettevo	
mettevi	
metteva	
mettevamo	
mettevate	
mettevano	

41 morire

present	past historic
muoio	morii
muori	moristi
muore	morì
moriamo	morimmo
morite	moriste
muoiono	morirono

perfect	present subjunctive
sono morto/morta	muoia
sei morto/morta	muoia
è morto/morta	muoia
siamo morti/morte	moriamo
siete morti/morte	moriate
sono morti/morte	muoiano

future	imperative
morirò	muori!
morirai	muoia!
morirà	morite!
moriremo	
morirete	
moriranno	

imperfect	
morivo	
morivi	
moriva	
morivamo	
morivate	
morivano	

42 muovere

present	past historic
muovo	mossi
muovi	muovesti
muove	mosse
muoviamo	muovemmo
muovete	muoveste
muovono	mossero

perfect	present subjunctive
ho mosso	muova
hai mosso	muova
ha mosso	muova
abbiamo mosso	muoviamo
avete mosso	muoviate
hanno mosso	muovano

future	imperative
muoverò	muovi!
muoverai	muova!
muoverà	muovete!
muoveremo	
muoverete	
muoveranno	

imperfect	
muovevo	
muovevi	
muoveva	
muovevamo	
muovevate	
muovevano	

43 nascere

present	past historic
nasco	nacqui
nasci	nascesti
nasce	nacque
nasciamo	nascemmo
nascete	nasceste
nascono	nacquero

perfect	present subjunctive
sono nato/nata	nasca
sei nato/nata	nasca
è nato/nata	nasca
siamo nati/nate	nasciamo
siete nati/nate	nasciate
sono nati/nate	nascano

future
nascerò
nascerai
nascerà
nasceremo
nascerete
nasceranno

imperfect
nascevo
nascevi
nasceva
nascevamo
nascevate
nascevano

44 parere

present	past historic
pare	parve
paiono	parvero

perfect	present subjunctive
è parso/parsa	paia
sono parsi/parse	paiano

future
parrà
parranno

imperfect
pareva
parevano

45 perdere

present	past historic
perdo	persi
perdi	perdesti
perde	perse
perdiamo	perdemmo
perdete	perdeste
perdono	persero

perfect	present subjunctive
ho perso	perda
hai perso	perda
ha perso	perda
abbiamo perso	perdiamo
avete perso	perdiate
hanno perso	perdano

future	imperative
perderò	perdi!
perderai	perda!
perderà	perdete!
perderemo	
perderete	
perderanno	

imperfect
perdevo
perdevi
perdeva
perdevamo
perdevate
perdevano

46 persuadere

present	past historic
persuado	persuasi
persuadi	persuadesti
persuade	persuase
persuadiamo	persuademmo
persuadete	persuadeste
persuadono	persuasero

perfect	present subjunctive
ho persuaso	persuada
hai persuaso	persuada
ha persuaso	persuada
abbiamo persuaso	persuadiamo
avete persuaso	persuadiate
hanno persuaso	persuadano

future	imperative
persuaderò	persuadi!
persuaderai	persuada!
persuaderà	persuadete!
persuaderemo	
persuaderete	
persuaderanno	

imperfect
persuadevo
persuadevi
persuadeva
persuadevamo
persuadevate
persuadevano

47 piacere

present	past historic
piaccio	piacqui
piaci	piacesti
piace	piacque
piacciamo	piacemmo
piacete	piaceste
piacciono	piacquero

perfect	present subjunctive
sono piaciuto/piaciuta	piaccia
sei piaciuto/piaciuta	piaccia
è piaciuto/piaciuta	piaccia
siamo piaciuti/piaciute	piacciamo
siete piaciuti/piaciute	piacciate
sono piaciuti/piaciute	piacciano

future
piacerò
piacerai
piacerà
piaceremo
piacerete
piaceranno

imperfect
piacevo
piacevi
piaceva
piacevamo
piacevate
piacevano

49 piovere

present	past historic
piove	piovve

perfect	present subjunctive
è piovuto	piova

future
pioverà

imperfect
pioveva

48 piangere

present	past historic
piango	piansi
piangi	piangesti
piange	pianse
piangiamo	piangemmo
piangete	piangeste
piangono	piansero

perfect	present subjunctive
ho pianto	pianga
hai pianto	pianga
ha pianto	pianga
abbiamo pianto	piangiamo
avete pianto	piangiate
hanno pianto	piangano

future	imperative
piangerò	piangi!
piangerai	pianga!
piangerà	piangete!
piangeremo	
piangerete	
piangeranno	

imperfect
piangevo
piangevi
piangeva
piangevamo
piangevate
piangevano

50 porre

present	past historic
pongo	posi
poni	ponesti
pone	pose
poniamo	ponemmo
ponete	poneste
pongono	posero

perfect	present subjunctive
ho posto	ponga
hai posto	ponga
ha posto	ponga
abbiamo posto	poniamo
avete posto	poniate
hanno posto	pongano

future	imperative
porrò	poni!
porrai	ponga!
porrà	ponete!
porremo	
porrete	
porranno	

imperfect
ponevo
ponevi
poneva
ponevamo
ponevate
ponevano

51 possedere

present
possiedo
possiedi
possiede
possediamo
possedete
possiedono

past historic
possedei *or* possedetti
possedesti
possedè *or* possedette
possedemmo
possedeste
possederono *or*
possedettero

perfect
ho posseduto
hai posseduto
ha posseduto
abbiamo posseduto
avete posseduto
hanno posseduto

present subjunctive
possieda
possieda
possieda
possediamo
possediate
possiedano

future
possiederò
possiederai
possiederà
possiederemo
possiederete
possiederanno

imperative
possiedi!
possieda!
possedete!

imperfect
possedevo
possedevi
possedeva
possedevamo
possedevate
possedevano

53 prendere

present
prendo
prendi
prende
prendiamo
prendete
prendono

past historic
presi
prendesti
prese
prendemmo
prendeste
presero

perfect
ho preso
hai preso
ha preso
abbiamo preso
avete preso
hanno preso

present subjunctive
prenda
prenda
prenda
prendiamo
prendiate
prendano

future
prenderò
prenderai
prenderà
prenderemo
prenderete
prenderanno

imperative
prendi!
prenda!
prendete!

imperfect
prendevo
prendevi
prendeva
prendevamo
prendevate
prendevano

52 potere

present
posso
puoi
può
possiamo
potete
possono

past historic
potei
potesti
poté
potemmo
poteste
poterono

perfect
ho potuto
hai potuto
ha potuto
abbiamo potuto
avete potuto
hanno potuto

present subjunctive
possa
possa
possa
possiamo
possiate
possano

future
potrò
potrai
potrà
potremo
potrete
potranno

imperfect
potevo
potevi
poteva
potevamo
potevate
potevano

54 ridurre

present
riduco
riduci
riduce
riduciamo
riducete
riducono

past historic
ridussi
riducesti
ridusse
riducemmo
riduceste
ridussero

perfect
ho ridotto
hai ridotto
ha ridotto
abbiamo ridotto
avete ridotto
hanno ridotto

present subjunctive
riduca
riduca
riduca
riduciamo
riduciate
riducano

future
ridurrò
ridurrai
ridurrà
ridurremo
ridurrete
ridurranno

imperative
riduci!
riduca!
riducete!

imperfect
riducevo
riducevi
riduceva
riducevamo
riducevate
riducevano

55 riempire

present	past historic
riempio	riempii
riempi	riempisti
riempie	riempì
riempiamo	riempimmo
riempite	riempiste
riempiono	riempirono

perfect	present subjunctive
ho riempito	riempia
hai riempito	riempia
ha riempito	riempia
abbiamo riempito	riempiamo
avete riempito	riempiate
hanno riempito	riempiano

future	imperative
riempirò	riempi!
riempirai	riempia!
riempirà	riempite!
riempiremo	
riempirete	
riempiranno	

imperfect
riempivo
riempivi
riempiva
riempivamo
riempivate
riempivano

57 risolvere

present	past historic
risolvo	risolsi
risolvi	risolvesti
risolve	risolse
risolviamo	risolvemmo
risolvete	risolveste
risolvono	risolsero

perfect	present subjunctive
ho risolto	risolva
hai risolto	risolva
ha risolto	risolva
abbiamo risolto	risolviamo
avete risolto	risolviate
hanno risolto	risolvano

future	imperative
risolverò	risolvi!
risolverai	risolva!
risolverà	risolvete!
risolveremo	
risolverete	
risolveranno	

imperfect
risolvevo
risolvevi
risolveva
risolvevamo
risolvevate
risolvevano

56 rimanere

present	past historic
rimango	rimasi
rimani	rimanesti
rimane	rimase
rimaniamo	rimanemmo
rimanete	rimaneste
rimangono	rimasero

perfect	present subjunctive
sono rimasto/rimasta	rimanga
sei rimasto/rimasta	rimanga
è rimasto/rimasta	rimanga
siamo rimasti/rimaste	rimaniamo
siete rimasti/rimaste	rimaniate
sono rimasti/rimaste	rimangano

future	imperative
rimarrò	rimani!
rimarrai	rimanga!
rimarrà	rimanete!
rimarremo	
rimarrete	
rimarranno	

imperfect
rimanevo
rimanevi
rimaneva
rimanevamo
rimanevate
rimanevano

58 rispondere

present	past historic
rispondo	risposi
rispondi	rispondesti
risponde	rispose
rispondiamo	rispondemmo
rispondete	rispondeste
rispondono	risposero

perfect	present subjunctive
ho risposto	risponda
hai risposto	risponda
ha risposto	risponda
abbiamo risposto	rispondiamo
avete risposto	rispondiate
hanno risposto	rispondano

future	imperative
risponderò	rispondi!
risponderai	risponda!
risponderà	rispondete!
risponderemo	
risponderete	
risponderanno	

imperfect
rispondevo
rispondevi
rispondeva
rispondevamo
rispondevate
rispondevano

59 rivolgere

present	past historic
rivolgo	rivolsi
rivolgi	rivolgesti
rivolge	rivolse
rivolgiamo	rivolgemmo
rivolgete	rivolgeste
rivolgono	rivolsero

perfect	present subjunctive
ho rivolto	rivolga
hai rivolto	rivolga
ha rivolto	rivolga
abbiamo rivolto	rivolgiamo
avete rivolto	rivolgiate
hanno rivolto	rivolgano

future	imperative
rivolgerò	rivolgi!
rivolgerai	rivolga!
rivolgerà	rivolgete!
rivolgeremo	
rivolgerete	
rivolgeranno	

imperfect
rivolgevo
rivolgevi
rivolgeva
rivolgevamo
rivolgevate
rivolgevano

61 salire

present	past historic
salgo	salii
sali	salisti
sale	salì
saliamo	salimmo
salite	saliste
salgono	salirono

perfect	present subjunctive
sono salito/salita	salga
sei salito/salita	salga
è salito/salita	salga
siamo saliti/salite	saliamo
siete saliti/salite	saliate
sono saliti/salite	salgano

future	imperative
salirò	sali!
salirai	salga!
salirà	salite!
saliremo	
salirete	
saliranno	

imperfect
salivo
salivi
saliva
salivamo
salivate
salivano

60 rompere

present	past historic
rompo	ruppi
rompi	rompesti
rompe	ruppe
rompiamo	rompemmo
rompete	rompeste
rompono	ruppero

perfect	present subjunctive
ho rotto	rompa
hai rotto	rompa
ha rotto	rompa
abbiamo rotto	rompiamo
avete rotto	rompiate
hanno rotto	rompano

future	imperative
romperò	rompi!
romperai	rompa!
romperà	rompete!
romperemo	
romperete	
romperanno	

imperfect
rompevo
rompevi
rompeva
rompevamo
rompevate
rompevano

62 sapere

present	past historic
so	seppi
sai	sapesti
sa	seppe
sappiamo	sapemmo
sapete	sapeste
sanno	seppero

perfect	present subjunctive
ho saputo	sappia
hai saputo	sappia
ha saputo	sappia
abbiamo saputo	sappiamo
avete saputo	sappiate
hanno saputo	sappiano

future	imperative
saprò	sappi!
saprai	sappia!
saprà	sappiate!
sapremo	
saprete	
sapranno	

imperfect
sapevo
sapevi
sapeva
sapevamo
sapevate
sapevano

63 scendere

present	past historic
scendo	scesi
scendi	scendesti
scende	scese
scendiamo	scendemmo
scendete	scendeste
scendono	scesero

perfect	present subjunctive
sono sceso/scesa	scenda
sei sceso/scesa	scenda
è sceso/scesa	scenda
siamo scesi/scese	scendiamo
siete scesi/scese	scendiate
sono scesi/scese	scendano

future	imperative
scenderò	scendi!
scenderai	scenda!
scenderà	scendete!
scenderemo	
scenderete	
scenderanno	

imperfect	
scendevo	
scendevi	
scendeva	
scendevamo	
scendevate	
scendevano	

65 scrivere

present	past historic
scrivo	scrissi
scrivi	scrivesti
scrive	scrisse
scriviamo	scrivemmo
scrivete	scriveste
scrivono	scrissero

perfect	present subjunctive
ho scritto	scriva
hai scritto	scriva
ha scritto	scriva
abbiamo scritto	scriviamo
avete scritto	scriviate
hanno scritto	scrivano

future	imperative
scriverò	scrivi!
scriverai	scriva!
scriverà	scrivete!
scriveremo	
scriverete	
scriveranno	

imperfect	
scrivevo	
scrivevi	
scriveva	
scrivevamo	
scrivevate	
scrivevano	

64 scorgere

present	past historic
scorgo	scorsi
scorgi	scorgesti
scorge	scorse
scorgiamo	scorgemmo
scorgete	scorgeste
scorgono	scorsero

perfect	present subjunctive
ho scorto	scorga
hai scorto	scorga
ha scorto	scorga
abbiamo scorto	scorgiamo
avete scorto	scorgiate
hanno scorto	scorgano

future	imperative
scorgerò	scorgi!
scorgerai	scorga!
scorgerà	scorgete!
scorgeremo	
scorgerete	
scorgeranno	

imperfect	
scorgevo	
scorgevi	
scorgeva	
scorgevamo	
scorgevate	
scorgevano	

66 scuotere

present	past historic
scuoto	scossi
scuoti	scuotesti
scuote	scosse
scuotiamo	scuotemmo
scuotete	scuoteste
scuotono	scossero

perfect	present subjunctive
ho scosso	scuota
hai scosso	scuota
ha scosso	scuota
abbiamo scosso	scuotiamo
avete scosso	scuotiate
hanno scosso	scuotano

future	imperative
scuoterò	scuoti!
scuoterai	scuota!
scuoterà	scuotete!
scuoteremo	
scuoterete	
scuoteranno	

imperfect	
scuotevo	
scuotevi	
scuoteva	
scuotevamo	
scuotevate	
scuotevano	

67 sedersi

present	past historic
mi siedo	mi sedei or sedetti
ti siedi	ti sedesti
si siede	si sedè or sedette
ci sediamo	ci sedemmo
vi sedete	vi sedeste
si siedono	si sederono or sedettero

perfect	present subjunctive
mi sono seduto/seduta	mi sieda
ti sei seduto/seduta	ti sieda
si è seduto/seduta	si sieda
ci siamo seduti/sedute	ci sediamo
vi siete seduti/sedute	vi sediate
si sono seduti/sedute	si siedano

future	imperative
mi siederò	siediti!
ti siederai	si sieda!
si siederà	sedetevi!
ci siederemo	
vi siederete	
si siederanno	

imperfect	
mi sedevo	
ti sedevi	
si sedeva	
ci sedevamo	
vi sedevate	
si sedevano	

69 spegnere

present	past historic
spengo	spensi
spegni	spegnesti
spegne	spense
spegniamo	spegnemmo
spegnete	spegneste
spengono	spensero

perfect	present subjunctive
ho spento	spenga
hai spento	spenga
ha spento	spenga
abbiamo spento	spegniamo
avete spento	spegniate
hanno spento	spengano

future	imperative
spegnerò	spegni!
spegnerai	spenga!
spegnerà	spegnete!
spegneremo	
spegnerete	
spegneranno	

imperfect	
spegnevo	
spegnevi	
spegneva	
spegnevamo	
spegnevate	
spegnevano	

68 spargere

present	past historic
spargo	sparsi
spargi	spargesti
sparge	sparse
spargiamo	spargemmo
spargete	spargeste
spargono	sparsero

perfect	present subjunctive
ho sparso	sparga
hai sparso	sparga
ha sparso	sparga
abbiamo sparso	spargiamo
avete sparso	spargiate
hanno sparso	spargano

future	imperative
spargerò	spargi!
spargerai	sparga!
spargerà	spargete!
spargeremo	
spargerete	
spargeranno	

imperfect	
spargevo	
spargevi	
spargeva	
spargevamo	
spargevate	
spargevano	

70 stare

present	past historic
sto	stetti
stai	stesti
sta	stette
stiamo	stemmo
state	steste
stanno	stettero

perfect	present subjunctive
sono stato/stata	stia
sei stato/stata	stia
è stato/stata	stia
siamo stati/state	stiamo
siete stati/state	stiate
sono stati/state	stiano

future	imperative
starò	sta'! or stai!
starai	stia!
starà	state!
staremo	
starete	
staranno	

imperfect	
stavo	
stavi	
stava	
stavamo	
stavate	
stavano	

71 stringere

present	past historic
stringo	strinsi
stringi	stringesti
stringe	strinse
stringiamo	stringemmo
stringete	stringeste
stringono	strinsero

perfect	present subjunctive
ho stretto	stringa
hai stretto	stringa
ha stretto	stringa
abbiamo stretto	stringiamo
avete stretto	stringiate
hanno stretto	stringano

future	imperative
stringerò	stringi!
stringerai	stringa!
stringerà	stringete!
stringeremo	
stringerete	
stringeranno	

imperfect	
stringevo	
stringevi	
stringeva	
stringevamo	
stringevate	
stringevano	

73 tenere

present	past historic
tengo	tenni
tieni	tenesti
tiene	tenne
teniamo	tenemmo
tenete	teneste
tengono	tennero

perfect	present subjunctive
ho tenuto	tenga
hai tenuto	tenga
ha tenuto	tenga
abbiamo tenuto	teniamo
avete tenuto	teniate
hanno tenuto	tengano

future	imperative
terrò	tieni!
terrai	tenga!
terrà	tenete!
terremo	
terrete	
terranno	

imperfect	
tenevo	
tenevi	
teneva	
tenevamo	
tenevate	
tenevano	

72 tacere

present	past historic
taccio	tacqui
taci	tacesti
tace	tacque
tacciamo	tacemmo
tacete	taceste
tacciono	tacquero

perfect	present subjunctive
ho taciuto	taccia
hai taciuto	taccia
ha taciuto	taccia
abbiamo taciuto	tacciamo
avete taciuto	tacciate
hanno taciuto	tacciano

future	imperative
tacerò	taci!
tacerai	taccia!
tacerà	tacete!
taceremo	
tacerete	
taceranno	

imperfect	
tacevo	
tacevi	
taceva	
tacevamo	
tacevate	
tacevano	

74 trarre

present	past historic
traggo	trassi
trai	traesti
trae	trasse
traiamo	traemmo
traete	traeste
traggono	trassero

perfect	present subjunctive
ho tratto	tragga
hai tratto	tragga
ha tratto	tragga
abbiamo tratto	traiamo
avete tratto	traiate
hanno tratto	traggano

future	imperative
trarrò	trai!
trarrai	tragga!
trarrà	traete!
trarremo	
trarrete	
trarranno	

imperfect	
traevo	
traevi	
traeva	
traevamo	
traevate	
traevano	

75 uscire

present
esco
esci
esce
usciamo
uscite
escono

past historic
uscii
uscisti
uscì
uscimmo
usciste
uscirono

perfect
sono uscito/uscita
sei uscito/uscita
è uscito/uscita
siamo usciti/uscite
siete usciti/uscite
sono usciti/uscite

present subjunctive
esca
esca
esca
usciamo
usciate
escano

future
uscirò
uscirai
uscirà
usciremo
uscirete
usciranno

imperative
esci!
esca!
uscite!

imperfect
uscivo
uscivi
usciva
uscivamo
uscivate
uscivano

76 valere

present
valgo
vali
vale
valiamo
valete
valgono

past historic
valsi
valesti
valse
valemmo
valeste
valsero

perfect
sono valso/valsa
sei valso/valsa
è valso/valsa
siamo valsi/valse
siete valsi/valse
sono valsi/valse

present subjunctive
valga
valga
valga
valiamo
valiate
valgano

future
varrò
varrai
varrà
varremo
varrete
varranno

imperative
vali!
valga!
valete!

imperfect
valevo
valevi
valeva
valevamo
valevate
valevano

77 vedere

present
vedo
vedi
vede
vediamo
vedete
vedono

past historic
vidi
vedesti
vide
vedemmo
vedeste
videro

perfect
ho visto
hai visto
ha visto
abbiamo visto
avete visto
hanno visto

present subjunctive
veda
veda
veda
vediamo
vediate
vedano

future
vedrò
vedrai
vedrà
vedremo
vedrete
vedranno

imperative
vedi!
veda!
vedete!

imperfect
vedevo
vedevi
vedeva
vedevamo
vedevate
vedevano

78 venire

present
vengo
vieni
viene
veniamo
venite
vengono

past historic
venni
venisti
venne
venimmo
veniste
vennero

perfect
sono venuto/venuta
sei venuto/venuta
è venuto/venuta
siamo venuti/venute
siete venuti/venute
sono venuti/venute

present subjunctive
venga
venga
venga
veniamo
veniate
vengano

future
verrò
verrai
verrà
verremo
verrete
verranno

imperative
vieni!
venga!
venite!

imperfect
venivo
venivi
veniva
venivamo
venivate
venivano

79 vincere

present	past historic
vinco	vinsi
vinci	vincesti
vince	vinse
vinciamo	vincemmo
vincete	vinceste
vincono	vinsero

perfect	present subjunctive
ho vinto	vinca
hai vinto	vinca
ha vinto	vinca
abbiamo vinto	vinciamo
avete vinto	vinciate
hanno vinto	vincano

future	imperative
vincerò	vinci!
vincerai	vinca!
vincerà	vincete!
vinceremo	
vincerete	
vinceranno	

imperfect
vincevo
vincevi
vinceva
vincevamo
vincevate
vincevano

81 volere

present	past historic
voglio	volli
vuoi	volesti
vuole	volle
vogliamo	volemmo
volete	voleste
vogliono	vollero

perfect	present subjunctive
ho voluto	voglia
hai voluto	voglia
ha voluto	voglia
abbiamo voluto	vogliamo
avete voluto	vogliate
hanno voluto	vogliano

future
vorrò
vorrai
vorrà
vorremo
vorrete
vorranno

imperfect
volevo
volevi
voleva
volevamo
volevate
volevano

80 vivere

present	past historic
vivo	vissi
vivi	vivesti
vive	visse
viviamo	vivemmo
vivete	viveste
vivono	vissero

perfect	present subjunctive
sono vissuto/vissuta	viva
sei vissuto/vissuta	viva
è vissuto/vissuta	viva
siamo vissuti/vissute	viviamo
siete vissuti/vissute	viviate
sono vissuti/vissute	vivano

future	imperative
vivrò	vivi!
vivrai	viva!
vivrà	vivete!
vivremo	
vivrete	
vivranno	

imperfect
vivevo
vivevi
viveva
vivevamo
vivevate
vivevano